Jewish Law and American Law

A Comparative Study

Volume 1

Touro College Press

Jewish Law and American Law

A Comparative Study

Samuel J. Levine

Volume 1

New York

2018

Library of Congress Cataloging-in-Publication Data

Names: Levine, Samuel J., author.

Title: Jewish law and American law : a comparative study / Samuel J. Levine.

Description: New York, NY : Touro College Press, 2018. | Includes bibliographical references and index. | Description based on print version record and CIP data provided by publisher; resource not viewed.

Identifiers: LCCN 2017042989 (print) | LCCN 2017043274 (ebook) | ISBN 9781618116567 (e-book) | ISBN 9781618116581 (e-book) | ISBN 9781618116550 (vol. I) | ISBN 9781618116574 (vol. II)

Subjects: LCSH: Law—United States—Jewish influences. | Jews—Legal status, laws, etc.—United States. | Mishpat Ivri. | BISAC: LAW / Essays. | SOCIAL SCIENCE / Jewish Studies.

Classification: LCC KF358 (ebook) | LCC KF358 .L48 2018 (print) | DDC 349.73—dc23

LC record available at https://lccn.loc.gov/2017042989

ISBN (hardback) 9781618116550 (vol. I)
ISBN (hardback) 9781618116574 (vol. II)
ISBN (electronic) 9781618116567 (vol. I)
ISBN (electronic) 9781618116581 (vol. II)

Book design by Kryon Publishing Services (P) Ltd.
www.kryonpublishing.com

Cover design by Ivan Grave

Touro College Press
Michael A. Shmidman and Simcha Fishbane, Editors
27 West 23rd Street
New York, NY 10010, USA
touropress.admin@touro.edu

Academic Studies Press
28 Montfern Avenue
Brighton, MA 02135, USA
press@academicstudiespress.com
www.academicstudiespress.com

Table of Contents

Acknowledgments

The chapters in these volumes were written over the course of fifteen years and originally published as individual articles, with most appearing in law journals across the United States. The chapters are collected here, organized sequentially by topic, with each chapter building on the previous chapter. As such, the volumes can be studied as a single work, while at the same time, each chapter can be read and understood on its own. It should be noted that, although the chapters have been lightly edited for inclusion in this collection, they are not presented chronologically, and there remains some repetition in material among the chapters, as well as occasional variation in writing style and citation form. A list of references to the original articles is provided below.

I would like to briefly express my appreciation to family, friends, teachers, and colleagues, who have offered me advice and encouragement over the years, in connection with these chapters and beyond. Among countless others, Russell Pearce, Thomas Shaffer, Kent Greenawalt, Judge Loretta Preska, and the late Abraham Abramovsky provided thoughtful guidance and support, and in my capacity as Director of the Jewish Law Institute at Touro Law Center, I have had the pleasure of working alongside a terrific staff and faculty, under the leadership of Deans Lawrence Raful, Patricia Salkin, and Harry Ballan. In connection with these volumes, I would also like to thank Michael Shmidman, Editor at Touro College Press, as well as Alessandra Anzani, Senior Editor, and Kira Nemirovsky, Production Editor, at Academic Studies Press.

Second Annual Holocaust Remembrance Lecture at Washington University-Jewish Law From Out of the Depths: Tragic Choices in the Holocaust, 10 **Washington University Global Studies Law Review** 133 (2011)

Applying Jewish Legal Theory in the Context of American Law and Legal Scholarship: A Methodological Analysis, 40 **Seton Hall Law Review** 933 (2010)

Goldman v. Weinberger: Religious Freedom Confronts Military Uniformity, 66 **Air Force Law Review** 205 (2010)

Miranda, Dickerson, and Jewish Legal Theory: The Constitutional Rule in a Comparative Analytical Framework, 69 **Maryland Law Review** 78 (2009)

Of lnkblots and Omnisignificance: Conceptualizing Secondary and Symbolic Functions of the Ninth Amendment in a Comparative Hermeneutic Framework, 2009 **Michigan State Law Review** 277 (2009)

Louis Marshall, Julius Henry Cohen, Benjamin Cardozo, and the New York Emergency Rent Laws of 1920: A Case Study of the Role of Jewish Lawyers and Jewish Law in Early Twentieth Century Public Interest Litigation, 33 **Journal of the Legal Profession** 1 (2008)

Taking Ethical Obligations Seriously: A Look at American Codes of Professional Responsibility Through a Perspective of Jewish Law and Ethics, 57 **Catholic University Law Review** 165 (2007)

Lost in Translation: The Strange Journey of an Anti-Semitic Fabrication, From a Late Nineteenth Century Russian Newspaper to an Irish Legal Journal to a Leading Twentieth Century American Criminal Law Textbook, 29 **Dublin University Law Journal** 260 (2007)

Reflections on Responsibilities in the Public Square, Through a Perspective of Jewish Tradition: A Brief Biblical Survey, 56 **Catholic University Law Review** 1203 (2007)

A Look at American Legal Practice Through a Perspective of Jewish Law, Ethics, and Tradition: A Conceptual Overview 20 **Notre Dame Journal of Law, Ethics and Public Policy** 11 (2006)

Looking Beyond the Mercy/Justice Dichotomy: Reflections on the Complementary Roles of Mercy and Justice in Jewish Law and Tradition, 45 **Journal of Catholic Legal Studies** 455 (2006)

Richard Posner Meets Reb Chaim of Brisk: A Comparative Study in the Founding of lntellectual Legal Movements, 8 **San Diego International Law Journal** 95 (2006)

An Introduction to Self-Incrimination in Jewish Law, With Application to the American Legal System: A Psychological and Philosophical Analysis, 28 **Loyola of Los Angeles International and Comparative Law Review** 257 (2006)

Reflections on the Practice of Law as a Religious Calling, From a Perspective of Jewish Law and Ethics, 32 **Pepperdine Law Review** 411 (2005)

The Yale L. Rosenberg Memorial Lecture: Taking Prosecutorial Ethics Seriously: A Consideration of the Prosecutor's Ethical Obligation to "Seek Justice" in a Comparative Analytical Framework, 41 **Houston Law Review** 1337 (2004)

Taking Ethics Codes Seriously: Broad Ethics Provisions and Unenumerated Ethical Obligations in a Comparative Hermeneutic Framework 77 **Tulane Law Review** 527 (2003)

Professionalism Without Parochialism: Julius Henry Cohen, Rabbi Nachman of Breslov, and the Stories of Two Sons, 71 **Fordham Law Review** 1339 (2003)

Playing God: An Essay on Law, Philosophy, and American Capital Punishment, 31 **New Mexico Law Review** 2 77 (2001)

Teshuva: A Look at Repentance, Forgiveness and Atonement in Jewish Law and Philosophy and American Legal Thought 27 **Fordham Urban Law Journal** 1677 (2000)

An Introduction to Legislation in Jewish Law, With References to the American Legal System, 29 **Seton Hall Law Review** 916 (1999)

Teaching Jewish Law in American Law Schools: An Emerging Development in Law and Religion, 26 **Fordham Urban Law Journal** 1041 (1999)

Halacha and *Aggada*: Translating Robert Cover's *Nomos and Narrative*, **Utah Law Review** 465 (1998)

Unenumerated Constitutional Rights and Unenumerated Biblical Obligations: A Preliminary Study in Comparative Hermeneutics, 15 **Constitutional Commentary** 511 (1998)

Capital Punishment in Jewish Law and its Application to the American Legal System: A Conceptual Overview, 29 **St. Mary's Law Journal** 1037 (1998)

Jewish Legal Theory and American Constitutional Theory: Some Comparisons and Contrasts, 24 **Hastings Constitutional Law Quarterly** 441 (1997)

Introduction

Recent decades have seen the emergence of comparative law, both as an important area of American legal practice and as a significant field of academic study in American law schools and universities. The increasing attention to comparative law may be the result of a number of interrelated factors, such as a growing awareness and acceptance of various forms of multiculturalism, an acknowledgment of the impact of international developments on the practice of law, and a general recognition that the nations of the world, their religions, and their legal systems have become interconnected in new and exciting ways, accompanied by both challenges and corresponding opportunities.

The comparative study of Jewish law and American law stands out as a particularly notable avenue of inquiry, gaining substantial prominence among legal scholars and garnering considerable interest among broader audiences. The Jewish legal system, produced over the course of thousands of years and spanning geographical locations across the world, provides analogues and counter-models for substantive, procedural, and conceptual aspects of American law, including important, unsettled, and controversial issues in American legal thought and practice. Indeed, in light of the wide-ranging scope of Jewish law, addressing every area of human behavior, it may not prove surprising that American legal scholars and, at times, American courts, have turned to Jewish legal thought to help illuminate complex areas of the American legal system.

These volumes contribute to the growing field of comparative Jewish and American law, presenting twenty-six chapters, grouped in eight sections and organized by topic, including an introductory section and seven substantive sections. The first section offers a general introduction to the comparative study of Jewish and American law, considering methodological issues related to the place—and increasing prominence—of Jewish law in both the American law school curriculum and American legal scholarship.

This section also includes chapters that provide a comparative overview of the role of interpretation and legislation in the two legal systems.

Subsequent sections turn to specific areas of substantive and conceptual comparison. Topics in these sections range from complex doctrinal discussions of capital punishment and self-incrimination, to applications of Jewish law in American legal practice, to more conceptual considerations of constitutional theory and the relationship between law and public policy. Still other sections add an interdisciplinary component, looking at legal history and connections between law and narrative.

The chapters in these volumes are characterized by a number of distinct features. For example, the chapters are written, in form and content, in a manner that is intended both to appeal to legal scholars and to be accessible and of interest to a more general audience of educated and intellectually curious readers. In addition, the chapters are faithful to Jewish law on its own terms, while at times applying comparative methods to offer fresh perspectives on complex issues in the Jewish legal system. Finally, through careful comparative analysis, nearly all of the chapters turn to Jewish law to provide insights into substantive and conceptual areas of the American legal system, particularly areas of American law that are complex, controversial, and unsettled.

The Comparative Study of Jewish Law and American Law: An Introduction

CHAPTER 1

Teaching Jewish Law in American Law Schools: An Emerging Development in Law and Religion

INTRODUCTION

In recent years, religion has gained increasing prominence among both the legal profession and the legal academy. Through the emergence of the "religious lawyering movement,"[1] lawyers and legal scholars have demonstrated the potential relevance of religion to many aspects of lawyering. Likewise, legal scholars have incorporated religious thought into their work through books, law journals, and classroom teaching relating to various areas of law and religion.[2]

---

1 The term "religious lawyering movement" was coined by Professor Russell Pearce. See Russell G. Pearce, *Symposium, Foreword: The Religious Lawyering Movement: An Emerging Force in Legal Ethics and Professionalism*, 66 Fordham L. Rev. 1075 (1998). For a history of the movement, see Samuel J. Levine, *Introductory Note: Symposium on Lawyering and Personal Values— Responding to the Problems of Ethical Schizophrenia*, 38 Cath. Law. 145 (1998); Pearce, supra.

2 There are numerous examples of the increased interest in law and religion, in books, law journals and the classroom. The term "law and religion" is a broad one, which may encompass

The aim of this chapter is to discuss one particular aspect of these efforts, the place of Jewish law in the American law school curriculum.[3] Specifically, I will briefly outline three possible models for a course in Jewish law in an American law school and consider some of the advantages and disadvantages of each model. I will then describe the structure I have chosen, in an attempt to synthesize these models, for the seminars in Jewish law that I have taught, over the course of twenty years, at a number of law schools across the United States.[4]

MODEL ONE

In the first model, a Jewish law course serves as a course in comparative law, emphasizing conceptual foundations of the Jewish legal system. Focusing on substantive areas of law that find their parallels in the American legal system, this model analyzes different concepts through comparisons and contrasts to American law. Such an approach has at least two apparent advantages. First, students who may be unfamiliar with Jewish law are likely to have some familiarity with and/or interest in the substantive areas of American law discussed. Indeed, one of the aims of this model is for students to appreciate the way a study of each legal system can illuminate an understanding of the other.

---

many areas, including Free Exercise and Establishment Clause issues. Although such issues are certainly relevant to this chapter, I focus here on the direct or indirect influence of religious concepts on the substance of the law, rather than discussing religion as the subject of constitutional law. Of course, a better understanding of religion on its own terms should ideally inform and improve Free Exercise and Establishment Clause jurisprudence as well.

3 Approximately thirty to forty American law schools include courses in Jewish law as part of the curriculum. See Edward H. Rabin, *Symposium: The Evolution and Impact of Jewish Law, Foreword*, 1 U.C. Davis J. Int'l L. & Pol'y 49, 56 (1995); Jeffrey I. Roth, *Fraud on the Surviving Spouse in Jewish and American Law: A Model Chapter for a Jewish Law Casebook*, 28 Case W. Res. J. Int'l L. 101, 101 n.1 (1996).

4 It should be noted that there may exist numerous models for a course in Jewish law at American law schools, in addition to variations and hybrids of many of these models. Thus, my descriptions here provide somewhat simplified models for the purpose of sparking further and more complex discussion of the issues I have delineated. Moreover, the suitability of any of the models in a particular setting depends on a number of variables, some of which I acknowledge in the text, including the background of the students, the background of the teacher or teachers, the availability of appropriate course materials, and the academic environment and philosophy of the school. Each of these variables finds a wide range of realities in the different law schools throughout the United States that offer courses in Jewish law. For a collection of syllabi from Jewish law courses in American law schools, see https://www.tourolaw.edu/JewishLawInstitute/?pageid=736

Second, this model may be appropriate for the curriculum in many law schools, as it contains a strong comparative law component.[5] One possible disadvantage to this model is that a teacher of such a course would be expected to have a working knowledge of, if not expertise in, both Jewish and American law.

MODEL TWO

A second model envisions Jewish law as a course in international law, to the extent that Jewish law impacts the legal system in the modern State of Israel. This model allows students to see the application of Jewish law within a modern secular nation, thereby providing an apparent contrast to the American ideal of law that separates church and state. In addition, the subject matter in this model, involving matters that affect the civil law of the State of Israel, may focus on issues that have direct analogues in American jurisprudence. Such a course might be a particularly good fit for a law school curriculum, as it deals with both comparative and international law.[6] However, these strengths may actually suggest inherent weaknesses in the model, as a teacher of such a course would have to be competent to teach both Jewish law and specific modern legal systems. Moreover, an emphasis on the modern State of Israel might detract from the study of the system of Jewish law on its own terms.

MODEL THREE

A possible response to these concerns suggests a third model, which examines Jewish law with little, if any, reference to other legal systems. Because the subject matter is restricted to Jewish law, this model may offer the opportunity for students to study the Jewish legal system in a more comprehensive and systematic manner. Likewise, placing the focus of the course on a single legal system allows for a teacher whose knowledge of other legal systems, though potentially helpful, would seem generally unnecessary. Students in such a course, however, must

---

5 The advantages of the comparative study model are reflected in part in the increasing reliance on the Jewish legal system in American law journals. See generally David Hollander, *Legal Scholarship in Jewish Law* (2017).

6 The late Menachem Elon, a former Israeli Supreme Court Justice, was a leading proponent and practitioner of this method, in both his scholarship and the Jewish law courses he taught in various American law schools. See, e.g., Menachem Elon, *The Legal System of Jewish Law*, 17 N.Y.U. J. Int'l L. & Pol. 221, 239-43 (1985).

be prepared to engage in the study of a legal system that may be unfamiliar to them, relying on their own ability to make comparisons and contrasts to areas of American law. In addition, the subject matter of this model may not find as clear a place within a law school curriculum, though it might complement a curriculum offering courses in Islamic law or Canon law.[7]

MODEL FOUR

The syllabi for the seminars in Jewish law that I have taught at American law schools reflect my attempt to synthesize these different models, with the aim of helping students appreciate the relevance of Jewish law to a broad range of legal issues. As most of the students who enroll in these courses have little or no background in Jewish law, we begin with a discussion of the sources and struc-ture of Jewish law, from both a historical and a conceptual perspective. In an effort to make the students more comfortable with this material, I rely primarily on articles in American law journals. While I try to draw parallels to American legal structure and history whenever possible, this part of the course primarily provides an opportunity for a broad understanding of the mechanics of Jewish law through an examination of the Jewish legal system on its own terms.

We continue the introductory stage of the course with a look at interpre-tation and legislation in Jewish law. Through examples of both civil law and ritual law, I seek to demonstrate that these two components of the Jewish legal system share a common analytical framework and are inextricably linked. We thus continue the process of looking at Jewish law on its own terms by rely-ing on the works of scholars of Jewish law, although a number of the examples I select yield obvious comparisons to issues in American law, in both substance and methodology. Likewise, discussions of legal authority lead to comparisons to the structure and function of the American judiciary and legislatures.

After these lessons, students usually feel that they have obtained a working knowledge of the Jewish legal system, sufficient to allow them to undertake explicit comparison of substantive areas of law in the two systems. Therefore, the next stage of the course consists of discussions of criminal law, capital punishment, self-incrimination, confidentiality and abortion in Jewish law and American law. Most students already have a substantial interest in, if not a famil-iarity with, these areas of law. In addition, they often gain a new perspective on American law as a result of examining the contrast cases in Jewish law. In keeping

---

7   Indeed, some law schools offer courses in Jewish law as part of a program in law and religion.

with the comparative component of the course, materials for these subjects are drawn from both American law journals and works of Jewish law.

The final stage of the course looks at the intersection of Jewish law with modern legal systems, particularly the United States and the State of Israel. Focusing on American *get* laws and kosher fraud laws involves American constitutional law, which, in turn, is compared and contrasted with the dynamic of incorporation of Jewish law in certain areas of Israeli law. Moreover, the Israeli model introduces an international component to the course and exemplifies the differences between Jewish law and the law of the modern, secular State of Israel.

My syllabus thus offers but one attempt to synthesize elements of potential models for a course in Jewish law in American law schools, consistent with my goals in teaching the course. The substance and style of Jewish law courses vary widely in schools offering such a course. It is my hope that, as both the legal profession and the legal academy increasingly continue to recognize the importance of religion in the lives and work of lawyers, Jewish law courses and scholarship will be seen as an integral part of the interface of law and religion.

CHAPTER 2

Applying Jewish Legal Theory in the Context of American Law and Legal Scholarship: A Methodological Analysis

INTRODUCTION

In the past few decades, Jewish legal theory has gained increasing prominence as both an area of study in law schools and a field of scholarship among the American legal academy.[1] Dozens of American law schools include courses on Jewish law in the curriculum.[2] Several law schools have established centers dedicated to the study of Jewish law,[3] while other schools include discussions of Jewish law as an important component of centers and programs on law and religion.[4] The prominence of Jewish legal theory in American legal scholarship

---

1   Samuel J. Levine, *Emerging Applications of Jewish Law in American Legal Scholarship: An Introduction*, 23 J.L. & Religion 43, 43 & n.1 (2007).

2   See generally Chapter 1 in this Volume; Sherman L. Cohn, *Yale Rosenberg: The Scholar and the Teacher of Jewish Law*, 39 Hous. L. Rev. 872 (2002); Samuel J. Levine, *Teaching Jewish Law in American Law Schools - Part II: An Annotated Syllabus*, 2 Chi.-Kent J. Int'l & Comp. L. 1 (2002) [hereinafter Levine, *Teaching Jewish Law, Part II*]; Edward H. Rabin, *Symposium: The Evolution and Impact of Jewish Law - Foreword*, 1 U.C. Davis J. Int'l L. & Pol'y 49 (1995); Jeffrey I. Roth, *Fraud on the Surviving Spouse in Jewish and American Law: A Model Chapter for a Jewish Law Casebook*, 28 Case W. Res. J. Int'l. L. 101 (1996); Alan M. Sokobin, *A Program in Comparative Jewish Law*, 33 U. Tol. L. Rev. 795 (2002).

3   These institutes include The Berkeley Institute for Jewish Law and Israel Studies; The DePaul University College of Law Center for Jewish Law & Judaic Studies; The Institute of Jewish Law, Boston University School of Law; The Jewish Law Institute, Touro College Jacob D. Fuchsberg Law Center; The Yeshiva University Center for Jewish Law and Contemporary Civilization, Cardozo School of Law; and The Tikvah Center for Law & Jewish Civilization, New York University.

4   These programs include The Center for the Study of Law and Religion, Emory University School of Law; The Institute on Religion, Law & Lawyer's Work, Fordham University School

has been even more pronounced, giving rise to an extensive body of literature exploring both Jewish law on its own terms and its potential applications to American law.[5]

In light of these developments, this chapter briefly considers the current state of the field of Jewish law and Jewish legal theory within the context of the American legal academy. Specifically, the chapter suggests that it may be instructive to step back and focus on a methodological assessment of these developments, taking into account a number of salient features of the Jewish legal model. These aspects of Jewish law both complicate and enrich the application of Jewish legal perspectives to issues of American law and public policy.

First, the Jewish legal system has developed over the course of thousands of years, functioning within a broad range of societal and geographical settings, amidst benign and, all-too-often, belligerent and oppressive circumstances.[6] This historical experience has resulted in the production of a voluminous library of legal literature, with contributions from virtually every generation and, over time, nearly all parts of the world.[7] Therefore, an attempt to consider the approach of the Jewish legal system to an issue of significance in the American legal system might require an initial effort to grapple with the various primary and secondary sources of Jewish law that address the issue directly and indirectly. Through the course of millennia—and up to this day—scholars

---

of Law; The Herbert and Elinor Nootbaar Institute on Law, Religion, and Ethics, Pepperdine University School of Law; The Notre Dame Law School's Program on Church, State & Society; and the University of San Diego Law School's Institute for Law and Religion..

5   See generally Chapters 1 and 3 in this Volume; Levine, supra note 1; Suzanne Last Stone, *In Pursuit of the Counter-Text: The Turn to the Jewish Legal Model in Contemporary American Legal Theory*, 106 Harv. L. Rev. 813 (1993).

6   See *An Introduction to the History and Sources of Jewish Law*, at xvi (N.S. Hecht et al. eds., 1996); 1 Menachem Elon, *Jewish Law: History, Sources, Principles: Ha-Mishpat Ha-Ivri* 1 (Bernard Auerbach & Melvin J. Sykes trans., The Jewish Publ'n Soc'y 1994) (1988).

7   For helpful introductions to the history, sources, and structure of Jewish law, see *An Introduction to the History and Sources of Jewish Law*, supra note 6; Irving A. Breitowitz, *Between Civil Law and Religious Law: The Plight of the Agunah in American Society* 307-13 (1993); Menachem Elon et al., *Jewish Law (Mishpat Ivri): Cases and Materials* (1999); 1 Elon, supra note 6; David M. Feldman, *Birth Control in Jewish Law: Marital Relations, Contraception, and Abortion as Set Forth in the Classic Texts of Jewish Law* 3-18 (1968); *Jewish Law and Legal Theory* (Martin P. Golding ed., 1993); Aryeh Kaplan, *The Aryeh Kaplan Reader* 211-19 (1985); Aaron Kirschenbaum, *Equity in Jewish Law: Halakhic Perspectives in Law: Formalism and Flexibility in Jewish Civil Law* 289-304 (1991); Nahum Rakover, *A Guide to the Sources of Jewish Law* (1994); Aaron M. Schreiber, *Jewish Law and Decision-Making: A Study Through Time* (1979); Menachem Elon, *The Legal System of Jewish Law*, 17 N.Y.U. J. Int'l L. & Pol. 221 (1985); Steven F. Friedell, *Aaron Kirschenbaum on Equity in Jewish Law*, 1993 BYU L. Rev. 909 (book review).

have explored Jewish law on its own terms, providing instrumental and arguably indispensable studies and insights into ways Jewish law might help illuminate contemporary American legal thought.

Second, the Jewish legal system addresses nearly every aspect of human endeavor, from the seemingly mundane to the profound, from ritual to interpersonal activities, from civil and commercial law to criminal law.[8] The scope of the Jewish legal system not only adds to the volume of legal material that constitutes the corpus of Jewish law but also serves as a reminder of the underlying religious character of the Jewish legal system, premised upon express and implicit theological principles that infuse and affect the function of the law.[9] Although it is possible to debate the extent to which, as both a descriptive and normative matter, religion informs American law,[10] it is not plausible to picture

---

8 See, e.g., Aryeh Kaplan, *The Handbook of Jewish Thought* 78 (1979) ("The . . . commandments . . . penetrate every nook and cranny of a person's existence, hallowing even the lowliest acts and elevating them to a service to God. . . . The multitude of laws . . . sanctify every facet of life, and constantly remind one of [one's] responsibility toward God."); Joseph B. Soloveitchik, *Halakhic Man* 20, 22 (Lawrence Kaplan trans., Jewish Publ'n Soc'y of Am. 1983) (1944) (observing that "there is no phenomenon, entity, or object in this concrete world" beyond the grasp of *halacha*, and noting that "just a few of the multitude of hala[c]hic subjects" include "sociological creations: the state, society, and the relationship of individuals within a communal context"; "laws of business, torts, neighbors, plaintiff and defendant, creditor and debtor, partners, agents, workers, artisans, bailees"; "family life"; "war, the high court, courts and the penalties they impose"; and "psychological problems . . . ."); id. at 93-94 (explaining that *Halacha* (i.e., Jewish law) "does not differentiate between the [person] who stands in [the] house of worship, engaged in ritual activities, and the mortal who must wage the arduous battle of life"; rather it "declares that [a person] stands before God not only in the synagogue but also in the public domain, in [one's] house, while on a journey, while lying down and rising up," and that "the marketplace, the street, the factory, the house, the meeting place, the banquet hall, all constitute the backdrop for the religious life"); Moshe Silberg, *Law and Morals in Jewish Jurisprudence*, 75 Harv. L. Rev. 306, 322 (1961) ("The . . . mode of dress, . . . diet, dwelling, behavior, relation with [others], . . . family affairs, and . . . business affairs were all prefixed and premolded, in a national cloak, in a set of laws that was clear, severe, strict, detailed, that accompanied [an individual] day by day, from cradle to grave."). See also Samuel J. Levine, *The Broad Life of the Jewish Lawyer: Integrating Spirituality, Scholarship and Profession*, 27 Tex. Tech L. Rev. 1199, 1199 (1996) ("The religious individual faces the constant challenge of reconciling religious ideals with the mundane realities of everyday life. Indeed, it is through the performance of ordinary daily activities that a person can truly observe such religious duties as serving G-d and loving one's neighbor.").

9 See, e.g., *Introduction to Jewish Law and Legal Theory*, supra note 7, at xiii, xiii; Menachem Elon, *The Legal System of Jewish Law*, 17 N.Y.U. J. Int'l L. & Pol. 221, 227 (1985).

10 For discussions of the relationship between religion and American law and politics, see Robert Audi, *Religious Commitment and Secular Reason* (2000); Stephen L. Carter, *The Culture of Disbelief: How American Law and Politics Trivialize Religious Devotion* (1993); Kent Greenawalt, *Private Consciences and Public Reasons* (1995); Kent Greenawalt, *Religious*

the American legal system as a consciously religious—let alone Jewish—system of law. Therefore, in addition to challenges that generally confront attempts to apply the laws of foreign legal systems in the context of American law,[11] greater

---

Convictions and Political Choice (1988); Michael J. Perry, *Love and Power: The Role of Religion and Morality in American Politics* (1991); Michael J. Perry, *Morality, Politics, and Law* (1988); Michael J. Perry, *Religion in Politics: Constitutional and Moral Perspectives* (1997); *Religion and Contemporary Liberalism* (Paul J. Weithman ed., 1997); Suzanna Sherry, *Religion and the Public Square: Making Democracy Safe for Religious Minorities*, 47 DePaul L. Rev. 499 (1998); *Symposium, Law and Morality*, 1 Notre Dame J.L. Ethics & Pub. Pol'y 1 (1984); *Symposium, Religion and the Judicial Process: Legal, Ethical, and Empirical Dimensions*, 81 Marq. L. Rev. 177 (1998); *Symposium, Religion in the Public Square*, 42 Wm. & Mary L. Rev. 647 (2001); *Symposium on Religion in the Public Square*, 17 Notre Dame J.L. Ethics & Pub. Pol'y 307 (2003); *Symposium, Religiously Based Morality: Its Proper Place in American Law and Public Policy*, 36 Wake Forest L. Rev. 217 (2001); *Symposium, The Role of Religion in Public Debate in a Liberal Society*, 30 San Diego L. Rev. 849 (1993); Ruti Teitel, *A Critique of Religion as Politics in the Public Sphere*, 78 Cornell L. Rev. 747 (1993).

11   The ongoing debate among prominent justices, judges, and scholars over reliance on foreign authority in American constitutional interpretation provides a poignant illustration of some of the complexities confronting efforts to apply foreign law in the context of the American legal system. See, e.g., *Roper v. Simmons*, 543 U.S. 551, 567, 576-78 (2005); id. at 622-28 (Scalia, J., dissenting); *Lawrence v. Texas*, 539 U.S. 558, 576-77 (2003); id. at 598 (Scalia, J., dissenting); *Atkins v. Virginia*, 536 U.S. 304, 316 n.21 (2002); id. at 324-25 (Rehnquist, C.J., dissenting); Roger P. Alford, *In Search of a Theory for Constitutional Comparativism*, 52 UCLA L. Rev. 639 (2005); Stephen Breyer, Assoc. Justice, U.S. Supreme Court, *Keynote Address at the Ninety-Seventh Annual Meeting of the American Society of International Law* (Apr. 4, 2003), in 97 Am. Soc'y Int'l L. Proc. 265, 265-66 (2003); Steven G. Calabresi, *"A Shining City on a Hill": American Exceptionalism and the Supreme Court's Practice of Relying on Foreign Law*, 86 B.U. L. Rev. 1335 (2006); Frank H. Easterbrook, *Foreign Sources and the American Constitution*, 30 Harv. J.L. & Pub. Pol'y 223 (2006); David Fontana, *Refined Comparativism in Constitutional Law*, 49 UCLA L. Rev. 539 (2001); Ruth Bader Ginsburg, Assoc. Justice, U.S. Supreme Court, *A Decent Respect to the Opinions of Humankind: The Value of a Comparative Perspective in Constitutional Adjudication, Keynote Address at the Ninety-Ninth Annual Meeting of the American Society of International Law* (Apr. 1, 2005), in 99 Am. Soc'y Int'l L. Proc. 351, 355 (2005); Vicki Jackson, *Constitutional Comparisons: Convergence, Resistance, Engagement*, 119 Harv. L. Rev. 109 (2005); Ronald J. Krotoszynski, Jr., *"I'd Like To Teach the World To Sing (In Perfect Harmony)": International Judicial Dialogue and the Muses - Reflections on the Perils and the Promise of International Judicial Dialogue*, 104 Mich. L. Rev. 1321, 1322-25, 1335-36, 1356-58 (2006); John O. McGinnis, *Foreign to Our Constitution*, 100 Nw. U. L. Rev. 303 (2006); Eric A. Posner & Cass R. Sunstein, *The Law of Other States*, 59 Stan. L. Rev. 131 (2006); Richard A. Posner, *Foreword: A Political Court*, 119 Harv. L. Rev. 31 (2005); *Symposium, Global Constitutionalism*, 59 Stan. L. Rev. 1153 (2007); Mark Tushnet, *When Is Knowing Less Better Than Knowing More? Unpacking the Controversy over Supreme Court Reference to Non-U.S. Law*, 90 Minn. L. Rev. 1275 (2006); Melissa A. Waters, *Getting Beyond the Crossfire Phenomenon: A Militant Moderate's Take on the Role of Foreign Authority in Constitutional Interpretation*, 77 Fordham L. Rev. 635 (2008); Melissa A. Waters, *Mediating Norms and Identity: The Role of Transnational Judicial Dialogue in Creating and Enforcing International Law*, 93 Geo. L.J. 487 (2005).

challenges may face any effort to apply concepts from a religious legal system, particularly the Jewish legal system.

These characteristics of Jewish law may suggest the need to employ an effective methodology for applying a given principle from Jewish legal theory to American law and public policy. Specifically, such an analysis may require a methodology that: (a) carefully and accurately depicts the principle, as understood within Jewish legal theory, in a way that is faithful to the Jewish legal system on its own terms; (b) considers carefully the extent to which the principle incorporates theological underpinnings that are particular to the Jewish legal model and, accordingly, may not be suitable in the context of the American legal model; and (c) applies the lessons from the Jewish legal system only to the extent that they make sense within the internal logic of the American legal system, thus remaining faithful to American jurisprudence as well.

This chapter illustrates the promise and potential limitations posed by this methodology through a close look at perhaps the most prominent references to Jewish law in the history of the American legal system: the United States Supreme Court's citations to the rule against self-incrimination in Jewish law.[12] This chapter compares the Court's reliance on Jewish law in

---

12 See *Garrity v. New Jersey*, 385 U.S. 493, 497 n.5 (1967); *Miranda v. Arizona*, 384 U.S. 436, 458 n.27 (1966). For examples of other American cases citing Jewish law in the context of discussions of self-incrimination, see *United States v. Gecas*, 120 F.3d 1419, 1425 (11th Cir. 1997); *United States v. Huss*, 482 F.2d 38, 51 (2d Cir. 1973); *Moses v. Allard*, 779 F. Supp. 857, 870 (E.D. Mich. 1991); *Roberts v. Madigan*, 702 F. Supp. 1505, 1517 n.20 (D. Colo. 1989); In re Agosto, 553 F. Supp. 1298, 1300 (D. Nev. 1983); *State v. McCloskey*, 446 A.2d 1201, 1208 n.4 (N.J. 1982); *People v. Brown*, 86 Misc. 2d 339, 487 n.5 (N.Y. Nassau County Ct. 1975).

For examples of references to the Jewish law of self-incrimination in American legal scholarship, see Leonard W. Levy, *Origins of the Fifth Amendment: The Right Against Self-Incrimination* 433-41 (2d ed., Macmillan Publ'g Co. 1986) (1968); Chapters 7 and 8 in this Volume; Albert W. Alschuler, *A Peculiar Privilege in Historical Perspective*, in R. H. Helmholz et al., *The Privilege Against Self-Incrimination: Its Origins and Development* 181, 279 n.28 (1997); Cheryl G. Bader, *"Forgive Me Victim for I Have Sinned": Why Repentance and the Criminal Justice System Do Not Mix - A Lesson from Jewish Law*, 31 Fordham Urb. L.J. 69, 88 (2003); Isaac Braz, *The Privilege Against Self-Incrimination in Anglo-American Law: The Influence of Jewish Law*, in *Jewish Law and Current Legal Problems* 161 (Nahum Rakover ed., 1984); Debra Ciardiello, *Seeking Refuge in the Fifth Amendment: The Applicability of the Privilege Against Self-Incrimination to Individuals Who Risk Incrimination Outside the United States*, 15 Fordham Int'l L.J. 722, 725 (1992); Suzanne Darrow-Kleinhaus, *The Talmudic Rule Against Self-Incrimination and the American Exclusionary Rule: A Societal Prohibition Versus an Affirmative Individual Right*, 21 N.Y.L. Sch. J. Int'l & Comp. L. 205 (2002); Malvina Halberstam, *The Rationale for Excluding Incriminating Statements: U.S. Law Compared to Ancient Jewish Law*, in *Jewish Law and Current Legal Problems*, supra, at 177; George Horowitz, *The Privilege Against Self-Incrimination - How Did It Originate?*, 31 Temp. L.Q. 121, 125

the landmark 1966 case of *Miranda v. Arizona*,[13] with the Court's reference to Jewish law less than one year later, in *Garrity v. New Jersey*.[14] The chapter argues that, in contrast to *Miranda*, which relies upon a largely mechanical reference to religious principles in Jewish law, *Garrity* employs a more conceptual methodology, exploring the conceptual underpinnings of Jewish law and, accordingly, drawing more insightful lessons to be applied in the context of the American legal system. Building on this distinction, this chapter examines applications of Jewish legal theory in a variety of areas of contemporary American legal scholarship. The chapter concludes that, similar to the Court's approach in *Garrity*, American legal theory draws important insights from Jewish legal theory through scholarship that employs a conceptual methodology for the application of principles in Jewish law.

PART ONE | *MIRANDA V. ARIZONA*: LIMITATIONS OF THE APPLICATION OF JEWISH LEGAL THEORY IN AMERICAN LAW

In the landmark case of *Miranda v. Arizona*, Section II of Chief Justice Earl Warren's majority opinion begins, "We sometimes forget how long it has taken to establish the privilege against self-incrimination, the sources from which it

---

(1958); Simcha Mandelbaum, *The Privilege Against Self-Incrimination in Anglo-American and Jewish Law*, 5 Am. J. Comp. L. 115, 116-18 (1956); Irene Merker Rosenberg & Yale L. Rosenberg, *In the Beginning: The Talmudic Rule Against Self-Incrimination*, 63 N.Y.U. L. Rev. 955 (1988); Aaron M. Schreiber, *The Jurisprudence of Dealing with Unsatisfactory Fundamental Law: A Comparative Glance at the Different Approaches in Medieval Criminal Law, Jewish Law and the United States Supreme Court*, 11 Pace L. Rev. 535, 550 (1991); Daniel J. Seidmann & Alex Stein, *The Right to Silence Helps the Innocent: A Game Theoretic Analysis of the Fifth Amendment Privilege*, 114 Harv. L. Rev. 431, 452 n.70 (2000); Michelle M. Sharoni, *A Journey of Two Countries: A Comparative Study of the Death Penalty in Israel and South Africa*, 24 Hastings Int'l & Comp. L. Rev. 257, 263 (2001); Erica Smith-Klocek, *A Halachic Perspective on the Parent-Child Privilege*, 39 Cath. Law. 105, 109 (1999); Gregory Thomas Stremers, *The Self-Incrimination Clause and the Threat of Foreign Prosecution in Bankruptcy Proceedings: A Comment on Moses v. Allard*, 70 U. Det. Mercy L. Rev. 847, 854-55 (1993); Bernard Susser, *Worthless Confessions: The Torah Approach*, 130 New L.J. 1056 (1980).

For a general survey and analysis of references to Jewish law in American judicial opinions, see Bernard J. Meislin, *Jewish Law in American Tribunals* (1976); Daniel G. Ashburn, *Appealing to a Higher Authority?: Jewish Law in American Judicial Opinions*, 71 U. Det. Mercy L. Rev. 295 (1994); Charles Auerbach, *The Talmud - A Gateway to the Common Law*, 3 W. Res. L. Rev. 5 (1951); Bernard J. Meislin, *Jewish Law in America*, in *The Jewish Law Annual: Jewish Law in Legal History and the Modern World* (Bernard S. Jackson ed., Supp. II 1980); Bernard J. Meislin, *Jewish Law in American Tribunals*, 7 Isr. L. Rev. 349 (1972).

13 384 U.S. 436, 458 n.27.
14 385 U.S. 493, 497 n.5.

came and the fervor with which it was defended."[15] Before launching into a historical survey, starting with the events of the Star Chamber in 1637, the opinion asserts that the "roots" of the privilege against self-incrimination "go back into ancient times."[16] The opinion documents this assertion with a footnote stating, "Thirteenth century commentators found an analogue to the privilege grounded in the Bible."[17] The footnote quotes a translation of a ruling found in Maimonides' Code of Law: "To sum up the matter, the principle that no man is to be declared guilty on his own admission is a divine decree."[18] Finally, the footnote concludes: "See also Lamm, The Fifth Amendment and Its Equivalent in the *Halakhah*, 5 Judaism 53 (Winter 1956)."[19]

Miranda's reliance on Jewish law, in this manner, is notable for a number of reasons. First, *Miranda* presents us with the phenomenon of one of the most influential Chief Justices of the United States starting a crucial section of the majority opinion of one of the most important Fifth Amendment decisions in the history of the United States—and one of the most famous decisions in any area of law—with a reference to Jewish law.

Second, the opinion is careful to describe Jewish law on its own terms, quoting directly from Maimonides to provide an accurate depiction of the law within the Jewish legal system. As the quotation makes clear, Jewish law includes an absolute ban on the admissibility of confessions as evidence against criminal defendants.[20] In further reliance on Maimonides, the opinion accepts the characterization of this rule as ancient, which is consistent with the understanding of the rule within Jewish legal tradition.[21]

Third, in further fidelity to Jewish law on its own terms, rather than citing a law review article or the work of an American lawyer, the footnote cites the work of scholars of Jewish law: the Code of Law of Maimonides, a comprehensive restatement of the entire corpus of Jewish law written by one of the most important medieval scholars of Jewish law and philosophy,[22] and an article by

---

15 384 U.S. at 458.

16 Id.

17 Id. at 458 n.27.

18 Id. (quoting Laws Concerning the Sanhedrin and the Penalties within Their Jurisdiction, in The Code of Maimonides (*Mishneh Torah*), Book 14, The Book of Judges treatise 1, ch. 18, paragraph 6, at 53 (3 Yale Judaica Series, Julian Obermann et al. eds., Abraham M. Hershman trans., 1977) (1949)).

19 Id.

20 Id.

21 See *Miranda*, 384 U.S. at 458 n.27.

22 For a discussion of Maimonides and the *Mishne Torah*, see Isadore Twersky, *Introduction to the Code of Maimonides (Mishneh Torah)* (22 Yale Judaica Series, Leon Nemoy et al. eds., 1980).

Rabbi Norman Lamm, a leading twentieth century scholar of Jewish law and philosophy and later the president of Yeshiva University, written less than a decade before *Miranda* was decided.[23]

Nevertheless, some questions may arise as to the *Miranda* Court's methodology in applying Jewish law. The *Miranda* case famously established the *Miranda* warnings as a means toward preventing coerced confessions.[24] The Court delineated in great detail a number of interrogation methods widely in use at the time, finding that the function—if not the design—of many of these methods was to produce conditions under which a suspect was subjected to both subtle and more blatant forms of psychological coercion.[25] Thus, the confessions obtained through these methods could not be deemed sufficiently voluntary to satisfy the requirements of the Constitution.[26]

In setting forth such a landmark rule, which was to prove in many ways both revolutionary and controversial,[27] the Court looked to offer historical support for its conclusions. The Court's reference to the Star Chamber[28] seems quite apt, both as a representation of the kind of coercion the Court was determined to prevent and as an illustration of the abuses that, as a historical matter, gave rise to the protections incorporated into the Fifth Amendment.

---

23 For a biography of Rabbi Lamm and a bibliography of his scholarship, see www.yutorah.org/rabbi-norman-lamm

24 See *Miranda*, 384 U.S. at 467-79.

25 See id. at 448-56.

26 See id. at 457-58.

27 In addition to the sharp concurring and dissenting opinions offered in response to the *Miranda* Court's majority opinion, see id. at 499 (Clark, J., concurring in part and dissenting in part); id. at 504 (Harlan, J., dissenting); id. at 536 (White, J., dissenting), the decision has prompted ongoing debate among both Supreme Court Justices, see, e.g., *Dickerson v. United States*, 530 U.S. 428 (2000), and scholars, over both the Court's methodology and the outcome of the case. See, e.g., Evan H. Caminker, *Miranda and Some Puzzles of "Prophylactic" Rules*, 70 U. Cin. L. Rev. 1 (2001); Gerald M. Caplan, *Questioning Miranda*, 38 Vand. L. Rev. 1417 (1985); Paul G. Cassell, *All Benefits, No Costs: The Grand Illusion of Miranda's Defenders*, 90 Nw. U. L. Rev. 1084 (1996); Paul G. Cassell & Richard Fowls, *Handcuffing the Cops? A Thirty-Year Perspective on Miranda's Harmful Effects on Law Enforcement*, 50 Stan. L. Rev. 1055 (1998); Joseph D. Grano, *Prophylactic Rules in Criminal Procedure: A Question of Article III Legitimacy*, 80 Nw. U. L. Rev. 100 (1985); Yale Kamisar, *The Warren Court (Was It Really So Defense-Minded?), The Burger Court (Is It Really So Prosecution-Oriented?), and Police Investigatory Practices*, in *The Burger Court: The Counter-Revolution That Wasn't* 62, 82 (Vincent Blasi ed., 1983); Stephen J. Schulhofer, *Miranda's Practical Effect: Substantial Benefits and Vanishingly Small Social Costs*, 90 Nw. U. L. Rev. 500 (1996); Stephen J. Schulhofer, *Reconsidering Miranda*, 54 U. Chi. L. Rev. 435 (1987); David A. Strauss, *The Ubiquity of Prophylactic Rules*, 55 U. Chi. L. Rev. 190 (1988); Symposium, *Miranda After Dickerson: The Future of Confession Law*, 99 Mich. L. Rev. 879 (2001).

28 See *Miranda v. Arizona*, 384 U.S. 436, 458-59 (1966).

In contrast, the reference to—and at least partial reliance on—the rule of criminal confessions in Jewish law, though notable, seems substantively, conceptually, and historically misplaced. Most basically, as the footnote in *Miranda* acknowledges, the Jewish legal system prescribes an absolute ban on the admissibility of a criminal defendant's self-incriminating statements.[29] In stark contrast, pursuant to the rule established in *Miranda*, interrogation of criminal defendants remains among the most important and effective tools of law enforcement, and voluntary criminal confessions remain among the most valuable pieces of prosecutorial evidence. It seems anomalous to rely on a legal system with an outright ban on criminal confessions in support of a rule that fully accepts criminal confessions, as long as they are not the product of coercion.

As a conceptual matter, *Miranda*'s reliance on Jewish law seems ill-suited for application in the American legal system. Notably, in the same section of the Code of Law, Maimonides offers possible rationales for the ban on criminal confessions in Jewish law, rooted in psychological and philosophical insights into the human condition.[30] Strikingly, however, rather than applying these more accessible reasons for the rule, the Supreme Court quoted exclusively from Maimonides' conclusion that, ultimately, the ban on criminal confessions stands as a "divine decree."[31] The theological expression of a rule in Jewish law, premised on divine authority, does not translate to the American legal system.[32] The *Miranda* Court fails to offer an explanation as to why American law should

---

29 See id. at 458 n.27.

30 See Laws Concerning the Sanhedrin and the Penalties within Their Jurisdiction, supra note 18:

> It is possible that [the confessor] was confused in mind when he made the confession. Perhaps he was one of those who are in misery, bitter in soul, who long for death, thrust the sword into their bellies or cast themselves down from the roofs. Perhaps this was the reason that prompted him to confess to a crime he had not committed, in order that he might be put to death.

Id. For more complete discussions of the psychological analysis provided by Maimonides and its potential application to the American legal system, see Norman Lamm, *The 5th Amendment and Its Equivalent in Jewish Law*, Decalogue J., 1, Jan.-Feb. 1967, at 1, 11-12; Chapter 7 in this Volume.

31 See *Miranda*, 384 U.S. at 458 n.27 (quoting Laws Concerning the Sanhedrin and the Penalties within Their Jurisdiction, supra note 18).

32 To use an admittedly overstated analogy, we would not accept an argument that the United States should allow only kosher food because in the Jewish legal system, based on divine decree, only kosher food is permitted.

accord even persuasive authority to a religious rule, and does not identify a rationale for the rule that would prove applicable in the context of the logic of the American legal system.

Finally, to the extent that the Court was merely referencing Jewish law as part of the historical establishment of "*the* privilege against self-incrimination,"[33] there is scant evidence of a direct historical connection between the rules against self-incrimination in the Jewish and American legal systems.[34] Although some have attempted to trace the origins of the Fifth Amendment back to antecedents in Jewish law,[35] the Court does not offer this argument, and in the view of most scholars, any such efforts remain tenuous at best.[36]

In short, *Miranda's* references to Jewish law are certainly significant—and, appropriately, rely on the work of scholars of Jewish law—but the Court's attempt to apply these lessons from Jewish law to the American rule of criminal interrogation remains vulnerable to questions of both relevance and methodology.

PART TWO | *GARRITY V. NEW JERSEY*: AN ALTERNATIVE APPROACH FOR THE APPLICATION OF JEWISH LEGAL THEORY IN AMERICAN LAW

At the same time, a critique of the analysis in *Miranda* need not preclude the application of insights and lessons from Jewish law and legal theory within the context of the American legal system. In fact, less than one year after *Miranda*, the Supreme Court issued another opinion that relied, in part, on the rule against self-incrimination in Jewish law, as well as on a reprinted version of Rabbi Lamm's

---

33 *Miranda*, 384 U.S. at 458 (emphasis added).

34 See, e.g., Aaron Kirschenbaum, *Self-Incrimination in Jewish Law* 19-21 (1970); Levy, supra note 12, at 439-40 (stating that "whether the existence of the right against self-incrimination in Talmudic law in any way influenced the rise of the right in Anglo-American law is an intriguing question" but concluding that "the answer, if based on evidence rather than speculation, must be negative"); Arnold Enker, *Self-Incrimination*, in *Jewish Law and Current Legal Problems*, supra note 12, at 169, 169 ("The thesis of my presentation today will be that exaggerated claims have been and are being made for the sources of self-incrimination in Jewish law, and for the notion that important lessons can be learned from Jewish law with respect to self-incrimination.").

35 See Braz, supra note 12, at 162 (arguing that "Jewish law and Talmudic jurisprudence constitute one of the main streams that converged to form the unique common law doctrine against self-incrimination"); Horowitz, supra note 12, at 125-27 (indicating that the source of the principle against self-incrimination lies in Talmudic law).

36 See sources cited supra note 34.

article.[37] This time, however, the Court applied Jewish legal theory in a manner that is more satisfying and convincing.

In the 1967 case of *Garrity v. New Jersey*, the state conducted an investigation into alleged fixing of traffic tickets by police officers.[38] Prior to being questioned, the officers were told that they had the right to refuse to answer questions on the grounds that the response would incriminate them, but that refusal to answer would subject them to removal from office.[39] The Supreme Court focused on the issue of whether the responses to these questions were admissible as voluntary confessions.[40]

Writing for the majority, Justice Douglas posed the issue in clear and stark terms, stating that "the choice imposed on petitioners was one between self-incrimination or job forfeiture."[41] Relying on prior decisions, the Court emphasized that "coercion that vitiates a confession . . . can be mental as well as physical,"[42] and "subtle pressures may be as telling as coarse and vulgar ones."[43] The Court viewed the relevant question as "whether the accused was deprived of his "free choice to admit, to deny, or to refuse to answer,"[44] and found that "the option to lose their means of livelihood or to pay the penalty of self-incrimination is the antithesis of free choice to speak out or to remain silent."[45] Therefore, the Court concluded, "the statements were infected by the coercion inherent in this scheme of questions and cannot be sustained as voluntary under our prior decisions."[46]

As in *Miranda*, the majority opinion in *Garrity* includes a footnote referencing Jewish law in support of the Court's conclusion.[47] When compared with the footnote in *Miranda*, however, the discussion of Jewish law in *Garrity* is more complete, more conceptual, in some ways more modest in its potential

---

37 See Lamm, supra note 30, at 1.
38 385 U.S. 493, 494 (1967).
39 Id.
40 Id. at 496.
41 Id.
42 Id. (quoting *Blackburn v. Alabama*, 361 U.S. 199, 206 (1960) (internal quotation marks omitted)).
43 Id. at 496 (citing *Haynes v. Washington*, 373 U.S. 503 (1963); *Leyra v. Denno*, 347 U.S. 556 (1954)).
44 Id. (quoting *Lisenba v. California*, 314 U.S. 219, 241 (1941)).
45 Id.
46 Id. at 497-98.
47 Id. at 497 n.5.

application to the American legal system, and, accordingly, more convincing and effective.

The footnote in *Garrity*, which consists entirely of an extensive quotation from sections of Rabbi Lamm's article, opens with the acknowledgment that Jewish law and American law differ substantively—and substantially—with respect to rules of self-incrimination:

> It should be pointed out, at the very outset, that the Halakhah does not distinguish between voluntary and forced confessions . . . . And it is here that one of the basic differences between Constitutional and Talmudic Law arises. According to the Constitution, a man cannot be *compelled* to testify against himself. . . . The Halakhah . . . does not *permit* self-incriminating testimony. It is inadmissible, even if voluntarily offered. Confession . . . is simply not an instrument of the Law. The issue [in Jewish law], then, is not compulsion, but the whole idea of legal confession.[48]

In light of these basic distinctions, in both the scope and the apparent concerns behind the limitations on confessions in Jewish law and American law, respectively, it seems surprising that the *Garrity* Court would derive any lessons from the absolute ban on criminal confessions in the Jewish legal system. If anything, Jewish legal theory, which bans confessions without any consideration of voluntariness, appears completely irrelevant to the Court's analysis in *Garrity*, which turned entirely on the issue of coercion.[49]

The Court's reasoning becomes apparent from the remaining two paragraphs of the footnote. Moving from the substance and scope of the rule against self-incrimination in Jewish law, the Court quotes Rabbi Lamm's analysis of possible rationales underlying the rule. Building on Maimonides' insights into human psychology, Rabbi Lamm explains that, although the rule is a divine decree, "The Halakhah . . . is . . . concerned with protecting the confessant from his own aberrations which manifest themselves, either as completely fabricated confessions, or as exaggerations of the real facts."[50] Drawing on modern psychoanalytic theory, Rabbi Lamm adds that, "while certainly not all, or even most criminal confessions are directly attributable, in whole or in part, to the

---

48   Id. (quoting Lamm, supra note 30, at 10) (emphasis added).
49   See id., 385 U.S. at 496-98.
50   Id. at 497 n.5 (quoting Lamm, supra note 30, at 12).

Death Instinct, the Halakhah is sufficiently concerned with the minority of instances, where such is the case, to disqualify all criminal confessions and to discard confession as a legal instrument."[51]

Finally, the Court quotes Rabbi Lamm's conclusion:

> The Constitutional ruling on self-incrimination concerns only forced confessions, and its restricted character is a result of its historical evolution as a civilized protest against the use of torture in extorting confessions. The Halakhic ruling, however, is much broader and discards confessions in toto, and this because of its psychological insight and its concern for saving man from his own destructive inclinations.[52]

Although the Court does not offer any comments on Rabbi Lamm's remarks, the implications derived from Jewish law are quite clear, adding considerable depth to the Court's analysis. The Court was not addressing the general question of whether the Constitution—or Jewish law—permits the use of self-incrimination to obtain evidence in a criminal case; as the Court observes, the Constitution admits voluntary confessions and Jewish law does not. This substantive distinction, however, was not pertinent to the issue in *Garrity*.

Instead, in an effort to analyze the voluntariness of the police officers' statements, the *Garrity* Court engaged in a complex consideration of various forms of coercion, both blatant and subtle. The footnote referencing Jewish law is offered in support of the Court's assertion that "the statements were infected by the coercion inherent in this scheme of questioning and cannot be sustained as voluntary. . . ."[53] In fact, the footnote signal is placed in the middle of this sentence, modifying the word "coercion."[54]

Accordingly, the Court's decision turned on the recognition that, for the purposes of assessing the voluntariness of a statement, courts must consider both physical and more subtle—but no less real—forms of psychological coercion.[55] This recognition is precisely the insight that Rabbi Lamm, more

---

51 Id. at 497-98 n.5 (quoting Lamm, supra note 30, at 12).
52 Id. (quoting Lamm, supra note 30, at 12).
53 Id. at 497-98 & n.5.
54 See id.
55 Id. at 497-99.

than ten years earlier,[56] and Maimonides, more than 700 years earlier,[57] had derived from the ban on self-incrimination in Jewish law. The Court in *Garrity* applied the conceptual lesson from Jewish law to support its conclusion that American law should likewise take into account more complex and subtle forms of coercion, such as the threat of losing a job, that can impose sufficient psychological pressure as to render involuntary—and therefore, inadmissible—any ensuing confessions.[58]

Thus, the methodology in *Garrity* provides a model preferable to the approach in *Miranda* on a number of grounds. *Garrity* more clearly emphasizes the distinction between the rules of self-incrimination in Jewish law and American law, remaining faithful to each legal system on its own terms. Therefore, *Garrity* makes no attempt at an unlikely substantive or historical reconciliation between the two rules. Instead, *Garrity* draws a conceptual lesson from Jewish law, in a way that accurately conveys the logic of the Jewish legal system, and then applies that lesson to American law, in a way that makes sense within the logic of the American legal system. As a result, the lessons derived from Jewish legal theory contribute depth to the Court's understanding, interpretation, and determination of American law and legal theory.

PART THREE | APPLICATIONS OF JEWISH LEGAL THEORY IN AMERICAN LEGAL SCHOLARSHIP

To be sure, this discussion is not intended to imply a strict dichotomy between substantive and conceptual applications of Jewish law in the American legal system, or to suggest that the reference to Jewish law in *Miranda* is without value. Instead, the contrast between *Miranda* and *Garrity* illustrates the broader methodological point, that effective application of a principle in Jewish law entails the ability to identify, independent of theological justifications, an underlying rationale for the principle that can be evaluated within the internal logic of the American legal system. Indeed, this methodology has been widely employed in American legal scholarship, resulting in a substantial body of literature dedicated to the application of Jewish legal theory to American legal theory.

---

56 See Lamm, supra note 30.
57 See Laws Concerning the Sanhedrin and the Penalties within Their Jurisdiction, supra note 18.
58 *Garrity*, 385 U.S. at 497-99.

Much of this literature has examined substantive areas of law, including, among others, criminal law and procedure,[59] capital punishment,[60]

---

59 See, e.g., 1 Emanuel B. Quint & Neil S. Hecht, *Jewish Jurisprudence: Its Sources and Modern Applications* 34-37, 44-51, 154-72 (1980); 2 Emanuel B. Quint & Neil S. Hecht, *Jewish Jurisprudence: Its Sources and Modern Applications* 2-8 (1986); Chapters 7 and 8 in this Volume; J. David Bleich, *Jewish Law and the State's Authority to Punish Crime*, 12 Cardozo L. Rev. 829 (1991); Moshe A. Bleich & Daniel Pollack, *Search and Seizure in Schools: A Comparison of Historical Jewish Legal Sources and Contemporary United States Law*, 7 Ind. Int'l & Comp. L. Rev. 379 (1997); Arnold N. Enker, *Aspects of Interaction Between the Torah Law, The King's Law, and the Noahide Law in Jewish Criminal Law*, 12 Cardozo L. Rev. 1137 (1991); Arnold N. Enker, *Error Juris in Jewish Criminal Law*, 11 J.L. & Religion 23 (1994); Clifford S. Fishman, *The Mirror of Justice Lecture: "Old Testament Justice,"* 51 Cath. U. L. Rev. 405 (2002); Aaron Kirschenbaum, *M'kohmah shel Ha'ohnishah B'mishpat Ha'ivri Ha'plili Perek B'hashkafah Ha'pinologist shel Chazal v'shel Harishohnim [The Role of Punishment in Jewish Criminal Law: A Chapter in Rabbinic Penological Thought]*, 12 Tel Aviv U. L. Rev. 253 (1987), translated in 9 Jewish L. Ann. 123 (1991); Beth C. Miller, *A Comparison of American and Jewish Legal Views on Rape*, 5 Colum. J. Gender & L. 182 (1996); Martin H. Pritikin, *Punishment, Prisons, and the Bible: Does "Old Testament Justice" Justify Our Retributive Culture?*, 28 Cardozo L. Rev. 715 (2006); Irene Merker Rosenberg & Yale L. Rosenberg, *Advice From Hillel and Shammai on How to Read Cases: Of Specificity, Retroactivity and New Rules*, 42 Am. J. Comp. L. 581 (1994); Irene M. Rosenberg & Yale L. Rosenberg, *"Cain Rose up Against His Brother Abel and Killed Him": Murder or Manslaughter?*, 30 Ga. J. Int'l & Comp. L. 37 (2001); Irene Merker Rosenberg & Yale L. Rosenberg, *Guilt: Henry Friendly Meets the MaHaRaL of Prague*, 90 Mich. L. Rev. 604 (1991); Rosenberg & Rosenberg, supra note 12; Irene Merker Rosenberg et al., *Murder by Gruma: Causation in Homicide Cases Under Jewish Law*, 80 B.U. L. Rev. 1017 (2000); Irene Merker Rosenberg & Yale L. Rosenberg, *"Perhaps What Ye Say Is Based Only on Conjecture": Circumstantial Evidence, Then and Now*, 31 Hous. L. Rev. 1371 (1995); Irene Merker Rosenberg et al., *Return of the Stubborn and Rebellious Son: An Independent Sequel on the Prediction of Future Criminality*, 37 Brandeis L.J. 511 (1999); Aaron M. Schreiber, *The Jurisprudence of Dealing with Unsatisfactory Fundamental Law: A Comparative Glance at the Different Approaches in Medieval Criminal Law, Jewish Law and the United States Supreme Court*, 11 Pace L. Rev. 535 (1991).

60 See, e.g., 1 Quint & Hecht, supra note 59, at 15-18, 34-37, 154-72; Chapters 5 and 6 in this Volume; Chad Baruch, *2000 McElroy Lectures: In the Name of the Father: A Critique of Reliance upon Jewish Law to Support Capital Punishment in the United States*, 78 U. Det. Mercy L. Rev. 41 (2002); Gerald J. Blidstein, *Capital Punishment - The Classic Jewish Discussion*, 14 Judaism 159 (1965); Steven Davidoff, *A Comparative Study of the Jewish and the United States Constitutional Law of Capital Punishment*, 3 ILSA J. Int'l & Comp. L. 93 (1996); Bruce S. Ledewitz & Scott Staples, *Reflections on the Talmudic and American Death Penalty*, 6 U. Fla. J.L. & Pub. Pol'y 33 (1993); Samuel J. Levine, *Capital Punishment and Religious Arguments: An Intermediate Approach*, 9 Wm. & Mary Bill Rts. J. 179 (2000); Irene Merker Rosenberg & Yale L. Rosenberg, *Lone Star Liberal Musings on "Eye for Eye" and the Death Penalty*, 1998 Utah L. Rev. 505; Irene Merker Rosenberg & Yale L. Rosenberg, *Of God's Mercy and the Four Biblical Methods of Capital Punishment: Stoning, Burning, Beheading, and Strangulation*, 78 Tul. L. Rev. 1169 (2004); Daniel A. Rudolph, *Note, The Misguided Reliance in American Jurisprudence on Jewish Law to Support the Moral Legitimacy of Capital Punishment*, 33 Am. Crim. L. Rev. 437 (1996).

torts,[61] property,[62] tax,[63] and commercial law.[64] Drawing upon thousands of years of Jewish legal scholarship, this work relies on sometimes surprising insights from the Jewish legal system to provide fresh ways of looking at American law.

For example, in considering the perennially perplexing issue of capital punishment, American legal scholars have examined the Talmud and other sources of Jewish law only to find a diversity of approaches, including a debate between abolitionists at one end of the spectrum and those advocating the deterrent value of capital punishment at the other end, with still others taking

---

61 See, e.g., 1 Quint & Hecht, supra note 59, at 41-49, 86-122, 126-38, 206-13; 2 Quint & Hecht, supra note 59, at 2-8, 91-144; Steven F. Friedell, *Medical Malpractice in Jewish Law: Some Parallels to External Norms and Practices*, 6 Chi.-Kent J. Int'l & Comp. L. 1 (2006); Steven F. Friedell, *Nobody's Perfect: Proximate Cause in American and Jewish Law*, 25 Hastings Int'l & Comp. L. Rev. 111 (2002); Sheldon Nahmod, *The Duty to Rescue and the Exodus Meta-narrative of Jewish Law*, 16 Ariz. J. Int'l & Comp. L. 751 (1999); Elie Mischel, *Note, "Thou Shalt Not Go About as a Talebearer Among Thy People": Jewish Law and the Private Facts Tort*, 24 Cardozo Arts & Ent. L.J. 811 (2006); Shaya Rochester, *Note, What Would Have Seinfeld Done Had He Lived in a Jewish State? Comparing the Halakhic and Statutory Duties to Aid*, 70 Wash. U. L.Q. 1185 (2001).

62 See, e.g., 1 Quint & Hecht, supra note 59, at 41-45, 64-70, 86-88, 94-98, 104-8, 110-19, 126-32; 2 Quint & Hecht, supra note 59, at 115-32; Michael J. Broyde & Michael Hecht, *The Return of Lost Property According to a Jewish & Common Law: A Comparison*, 12 J.L. & Religion 225 (1995); Joshua A. Klarfeld, *Note, Chazakah: Judaic Law's Non-Adverse Possession*, 52 Clev. St. L. Rev. 623 (2004-2005); Ora R. Sheinson, *Note, Lessons from the Jewish Law of Property Rights for the Modern American Takings Debate*, 26 Colum. J. Envtl. L. 483 (2001).

63 See, e.g., 2 Quint & Hecht, supra note 59, at 137-40; Adam S. Chodorow, *Agricultural Tithing and (Flat) Tax Complexity*, 68 U. Pitt. L. Rev. 267 (2006); Adam S. Chodorow, *Biblical Tax Systems and the Case for Progressive Taxation*, 23 J.L. & Religion 51 (2007-2008); Adam S. Chodorow, *Maaser Kesafim and the Development of Tax Law*, 8 Fla. Tax. Rev. 153 (2007).

64 See, e.g., 1 Quint & Hecht, supra note 59, at 39-41, 84-86; 2 Quint & Hecht, supra note 59, at 8-32, 135-37; Dennis W. Carlton & Avi Weiss, *The Economics of Religion, Jewish Survival, and Jewish Attitudes Toward Competition in Torah Education*, 30 J. Legal Stud. 253 (2001); Aaron Levine, *Aspects of the Lemons Problem as Treated in Jewish Law*, 23 J.L. & Religion 379 (2008); Shahar Lifshitz, *Oppressive-Exploitative Contracts: A Jewish Law Perspective*, 23 J.L. & Religion 425 (2008); James Scheinman, *Jewish Business Ethics*, 1 U.C. Davis J. Int'l L. & Pol'y 63 (1995); Keith Sharfman, *The Law and Economics of Hoarding*, 19 Loy. Consumer L. Rev. 179 (2007); Shayna M. Sigman, *Kosher Without Law: The Role of Nonlegal Sanctions in Overcoming Fraud Within the Kosher Food Industry*, 31 Fla. St. U. L. Rev. 509 (2004); Leon Wildes, *A Modern Restatement of Jewish Civil Law*, 18 Cardozo L. Rev. 2037, 2038 (1997) (book review).

intermediate positions.[65] These debates offer valuable conceptual discussions from a legal system that has addressed for millennia some of the same arguments that arise in contemporary American legal discourse.

Other scholarship applies substantive Jewish law to emerging and cutting-edge issues in American law. Because Jewish law relates to all areas of life and all realms of human activity,[66] it must address questions that arise as a result of technological advances in areas such as bioethics[67] and intellectual property.[68] Indeed, over thousands of years, the Jewish legal system has been continuously confronted with the ongoing challenge of applying the law to newly emerging

---

65 See, e.g., Talmud Bavli, Makkoth 7a.

66 See supra note 8 and accompanying text.

67 See, e.g., Feldman, supra note 7, at 251-94; Darrel W. Amundsen, *The Ninth Circuit Court's Treatment of the History of Suicide by Ancient Jews and Christians in Compassion in Dying v. State of Washington: Historical Naivete or Special Pleading?*, 13 Issues L. & Med. 365 (1998); J. David Bleich, *Abortion in Halakhic Literature*, in Jewish Bioethics 155 (Fred Rosner & J. David Bleich eds., augmented ed. 2000); Michael Broyde, *Cloning People: A Jewish Analysis of the Issues*, 30 Conn. L. Rev. 503 (1998); Michael Broyde, *Genetically Engineering People: A Jewish Law Analysis of Personhood*, 13 St. Thomas L. Rev. 877 (2001); Elliot N. Dorff, *Human Cloning: A Jewish Perspective*, 8 S. Cal. Interdisc. L.J. 117 (1998); Immanuel Jakobovits, *Jewish Views on Abortion*, in Jewish Bioethics, supra, at 139; Daniel Pollack et al., *Anderson v. St. Francis-St. George Hospital: Wrongful Living from an American and Jewish Legal Perspective*, 45 Clev. St. L. Rev. 621 (1997); Chaim Povarsky, *Regulating Advanced Reproductive Technologies: A Comparative Analysis of Jewish and American Law*, 29 U. Tol. L. Rev. 409 (1998); Steven H. Resnicoff, *Jewish Law Perspectives on Suicide and Physician-Assisted Dying*, 13 J.L. & Religion 289 (1999); Steven H. Resnicoff, *Physician Assisted Suicide Under Jewish Law*, 1 DePaul J. Health Care L. 589 (1997); Steven H. Resnicoff, *Supplying Human Body Parts: A Jewish Perspective*, 55 DePaul L. Rev. 851 (2006); Daniel B. Sinclair, *Assisted Reproduction in Jewish Law*, 30 Fordham Urb. L.J. 71 (2002); Daniel Sinclair, *The Obligation to Heal and Patient Autonomy in Jewish Law*, 13 J.L. & Religion 351 (1999); Alan Mayor Sokobin, *Shaken Baby Syndrome: A Comparative Study: Anglo-American Law and Jewish Law - Legal, Moral, and Ethical Issues*, 29 U. Tol. L. Rev. 513 (1998); Marc D. Stern, *"And You Shall Choose Life": Futility and the Religious Duty to Preserve Life*, 25 Seton Hall L. Rev. 997 (1995); Miryam Z. Wahrman, *Fruit of the Womb: Artificial Reproductive Technologies & Jewish Law*, 9 J. Gender Race & Just. 109 (2005); Stephen J. Werber, *Ancient Answers to Modern Questions: Death, Dying, and Organ Transplants - A Jewish Law Perspective*, 11 J.L. & Health 13 (1996).

68 See, e.g., Neil Weinstock Netanel, *From Maimonides to Microsoft: The Jewish Law of Copyright Since the Birth of Print* (2016); Jack Achiezer Guggenheim, *KOA is A.O.K.: The Second Circuit's Recent Kosher Trademark Decision Further Illustrates that the Patent and Trademark Office Must Answer to a Higher Authority*, 22 Colum. J.L. & Arts 203 (1998); Matthew I. Kozinets, *Copyright and Jewish Law: The Dilemma of Change*, 1 U.C. Davis J. Int'l L. & Pol'y 83 (1995); Roberta Rosenthal Kwall, *Inspiration and Innovation: The Intrinsic Dimension of the Artistic Soul*, 81 Notre Dame L. Rev. 1945 (2006); David Nimmer, *Adams and Bits: Of Jewish Kings and Copyrights*, 71 S. Cal. L. Rev. 219 (1998).

realities.[69] Thus, the Jewish legal model and Jewish legal history provide not only substantive responses to specific questions, but also a conceptual framework for the broader and more universal issue of adapting a legal system to inevitable advances in science and technology.

Not surprisingly, Jewish legal theory has also played a central role in emerging areas of American legal scholarship that relate directly to issues of religion. As one particularly poignant example, recent decades have experienced the growth of the religious lawyering movement, comprised of lawyers and scholars exploring the relationship between religion and the practice of law.[70] The movement has succeeded as an intellectual force within the legal academy, in part due to contributions reflecting a variety of religious perspectives—including insights from Jewish legal theory, that address substantive areas of American legal practice, such as criminal advocacy and corporate counseling, as well as conceptual approaches to the roles of the lawyer within

---

69 See, e.g., Aryeh Kaplan, *The Aryeh Kaplan Reader*, supra note 7, at 83-88; Adin Steinsaltz, *The Essential Talmud* 234-38 (Chaya Galai trans., 1976); Chapter 3 in this Volume; Michael Broyde & Howard Jachter, *The Use of Electricity on Shabbat and Yom Tov*, 21 J. Halacha & Contemp. Soc'y 4 (1991); Howard Jachter & Michael Broyde, *Electrically Produced Fire or Light in Positive Commandments*, 25 J. Halacha & Contemp. Soc'y 89 (1993); Arthur Schaffer, *The History of Horseradish as the Bitter Herb on Passover*, 8 Gesher 217 (1981).

70 See, e.g., Thomas E. Baker & Timothy W. Floyd, *A Symposium Precis*, 27 Tex. Tech L. Rev. 911, 911 (1996) (including essays "in the nature of personal narratives" that detail how the author "reconciled [his/her] professional life with [his/her] faith life"); *Colloquium, Can the Ordinary Practice of Law Be a Religious Calling?*, 32 Pepp. L. Rev. 373 (2005); Marie A. Failinger, *Editor's Preface to the AALS Section on Professional Responsibility 2006 Annual Meeting Papers*, 21 J.L. & Religion 265, 265 (2006); Rose Kent, *What's Faith Got to Do With It?*, Fordham Law., Summer 2001, at 10; Howard Lesnick, *Riding the Second Wave of the So-Called Religious Lawyering Movement*, 75 St. John's L. Rev. 283 (2001); Russell G. Pearce & Amelia J. Uelmen, *Religious Lawyering in a Liberal Democracy: A Challenge and an Invitation*, 55 Case W. Res. L. Rev. 127 (2004); *Symposium on Law & Politics as Vocation*, 20 Notre Dame J.L. Ethics & Pub. Pol'y 1 (2006) (discussing religious perspectives of American legal practice and how being an attorney might be a divine calling); *Symposium on Lawyering and Personal Values*, 38 Cath. Law. 145, 149 (1998) (focusing on the personal, religious, and other ethical values of lawyers in the legal profession); *Symposium, Rediscovering the Role of Religion in the Lives of Lawyers and Those They Represent*, 26 Fordham Urb. L.J. 821 (1999); *Symposium, The Relevance of Religion to a Lawyer's Work: An Interfaith Conference*, 66 Fordham L. Rev. 1075 (1998); Robert K. Vischer, *Heretics in the Temple of Law: The Promise and Peril of the Religious Lawyering Movement*, 19 J.L. & Religion 427 (2004); Gerry Whyte, *Integrating Professional Practice and Religious Faith: The Religious Lawyering Movement*, Doctrine & Life, May-June 2005, at 18.

the American adversary system.[71] Notably, some of the most significant lessons are derived though careful analysis of Jewish law on its own terms, including exploration of ways in which the Jewish legal system differs, at times dramatically, from the American legal system. Serving as a contrast case, the Jewish legal model enables American legal scholars to see the American legal system and American legal practice in a new light.

CONCLUSION

Along with the preceding analysis of contributions from Jewish legal theory to the study of various substantive areas of American law, it may be fitting to close this chapter on a conceptual level, noting some of the insights that Jewish

---

71 See, e.g., Michael J. Broyde, *The Pursuit of Justice and Jewish Law: Halakhic Perspectives on the Legal Profession* (1996); Chapters 13, 14, 15, and 16 in this Volume; Chapter 18 in Volume 2; Mordecai Biser, *Can an Observant Jew Practice Law?: A Look at Some Halakhic Problems*, 11 Jewish L. Ann. 101 (1994); Michael J. Broyde, *Practicing Criminal Law: A Jewish Analysis of Being a Prosecutor or Defense Attorney*, 66 Fordham L. Rev. 1141 (1998); Monroe H. Freedman, *Legal Ethics from a Jewish Perspective*, 27 Tex. Tech L. Rev. 1131 (1996); Dov I. Frimer, *The Role of a Lawyer in Jewish Law*, 1 J.L. & Religion 297 (1983); Jerome Hornblass, *The Jewish Lawyer*, 14 Cardozo L. Rev. 1639 (1993); Levine, supra note 8; Samuel J. Levine, *Further Reflections on the Role of Religion in Lawyering and in Life*, 11 Regent U. L. Rev. 31 (1999); Samuel J. Levine, *Introductory Note: Symposium on Lawyering and Personal Values-Responding to the Problems of Ethical Schizophrenia*, 38 Cath. Law. 145 (1998); Sanford Levinson, *Identifying the Jewish Lawyer: Reflections on the Construction of Professional Identity*, 14 Cardozo L. Rev. 1577 (1993); Russell G. Pearce, *Jewish Lawyering in a Multicultural Society: A Midrash on Levinson*, 14 Cardozo L. Rev. 1613 (1993); Russell G. Pearce, *The Jewish Lawyer's Question*, 27 Tex. Tech L. Rev. 1259 (1996); Russell G. Pearce, *Reflections on the American Jewish Lawyer*, 17 J.L. & Religion 179 (2002); Pearce & Uelmen, supra note 70; Russell G. Pearce, *To Save a Life: Why a Rabbi and a Jewish Lawyer Must Disclose a Client Confidence*, 29 Loy. L.A. L. Rev. 1771 (1996); Amy Porter, *Representing the Reprehensible and Identity Conflicts in Legal Representation*, 14 Temp. Pol. & Civ. Rts. L. Rev. 143 (2004); Nancy B. Rapoport, *Living "Top-Down" in a "Bottom-Up" World: Musings on the Relationship Between Jewish Ethics and Legal Ethics*, 78 Neb. L. Rev. 18 (1999); Steven H. Resnicoff, *The Attorney-Client Relationship: A Jewish Law Perspective*, 14 Notre Dame J.L. Ethics & Pub. Pol'y 349 (2000); Steven H. Resnicoff, *A Jewish Look at Lawyering Ethics: A Preliminary Essay*, 15 Touro L. Rev. 73 (1998); Steven H. Resnicoff, *Lying and Lawyering: Contrasting American and Jewish Law*, 77 Notre Dame L. Rev. 937 (2002); Arthur Gross Schaefer & Peter S. Levi, *Resolving the Conflict Between the Ethical Values of Confidentiality and Saving a Life: A Jewish View*, 29 Loy. L.A. L. Rev. 1761 (1996); Daniel B. Sinclair, *Advocacy and Compassion in the Jewish Tradition*, 31 Fordham Urb. L.J. 99 (2003); Abbe Smith & William Montross, *The Calling of Criminal Defense*, 50 Mercer L. Rev. 443 (1999); Marc D. Stern, *The Attorney as Advocate and Adherent: Conflicting Obligations of Zealousness*, 27 Tex. Tech L. Rev. 1363 (1996); Israel Greisman, *Note, The Jewish Criminal Lawyer's Dilemma*, 29 Fordham Urb. L.J. 2419 (2002).

legal theory continues to provide in theoretical areas of American law, such as jurisprudence,[72] legal interpretation,[73] and legal narrative.[74] Indeed, the current turn to Jewish legal theory in American legal scholarship may be attributed in large part to the contributions of Robert Cover,[75] whose groundbreaking work,

---

72 See, e.g., Chapter 23 in Volume 2; Yitzchok Adlerstein, *Lawyers, Faith, and Peacemaking: Jewish Perspectives on Peace*, 7 Pepp. Disp. Resol. L.J. 177 (2007); J. David Bleich, *Was Spinoza a Jewish Philosopher?*, 25 Cardozo L. Rev. 571 (2003); Michael J. Broyde, *A Jewish Law View of the World*, 54 Emory L.J. 79 (2005); Robert A. Baruch Bush, *Mediation and ADR: Insights from the Jewish Tradition*, 28 Fordham Urb. L.J. 1007 (2001); David C. Flatto, *The Historical Origins of Judicial Independence and Their Modern Resonances*, 117 Yale L.J. Pocket Part 8 (2007), http://www.yalelawjournal.org/forum/the-historical-origins-of-judicial-independence-and-their-modern-resonances; Aaron Kirschenbaum, *Modern Times, Ancient Laws - Can the Torah Be Amended? Equity as a Source of Legal Development*, 39 St. Louis U. L.J. 1219 (1995); Norman Lamm & Aaron Kirschenbaum, *Freedom and Constraint in the Jewish Judicial Process*, 1 Cardozo L. Rev. 99 (1979); Donna Litman, *Jewish Law: Deciphering the Code by Global Process and Analogy*, 82 U. Det. Mercy L. Rev. 563 (2005); Timothy D. Lytton, *"Shall Not the Judge of the Earth Deal Justly?": Accountability, Compassion, and Judicial Authority in the Biblical Story of Sodom and Gomorrah*, 18 J.L. & Religion 31 (2002); Chaim Saiman, *Legal Theology: The Turn to Conceptualism in Nineteenth-Century Jewish Law*, 21 J.L. & Religion 39 (2005).

73 See, e.g., Chapters 3 and 9 in this Volume; Burton Caine, *"The Liberal Agenda": Biblical Values and the First Amendment*, 14 Touro L. Rev. 129 (1997); Kent Greenawalt, *The Implications of Protestant Christianity for Legal Interpretation*, 23 J.L. & Religion 131 (2007); Michael Rosensweig, *Eilu ve-Eilu Divrei Elokim Hayyim: Halakhic Pluralism and Theories of Controversy*, in *Rabbinic Authority and Personal Autonomy* 93 (Moshe Sokol ed., 1992); Jeffrey I. Roth, *The Justification for Controversy Under Jewish Law*, 76 Cal. L. Rev. 337 (1988); Chaim Saiman, *Jesus' Legal Theory - A Rabbinic Reading*, 23 J.L. & Religion 97 (2007); Maimon Schwarzschild, *Pluralist Interpretation: From Religion to the First Amendment*, 7 J. Contemp. Legal Issues 447 (1996); David A. Skeel, Jr., *What Were Jesus and the Pharisees Talking About When They Talked About Law?*, 23 J.L. & Religion 141 (2007); *Symposium, Text, Tradition, and Reason in Comparative Perspective*, 28 Cardozo L. Rev. 1 (2006); Emil A. Kleinhaus, *Note, History as Precedent: The Post-Originalist Problem in Constitutional Law*, 110 Yale L.J. 121 (2000); *Note, Looking to Statutory Intertext: Toward the Use of the Rabbinic Biblical Interpretive Stance in American Statutory Interpretation*, 115 Harv. L. Rev. 1456 (2002).

74 See, e.g., Chapter 17 in Volume 2; George Dargo, *Deriving Law from the Biblical Narrative: The Book of Ruth*, 40 New Eng. L. Rev. 351 (2006); Itzhak Englard, *Majority Decision vs. Individual Truth: The Interpretations of the "Oven of Achnai" Aggadah*, Tradition, Spring-Summer 1975, at 137; Daniel J.H. Greenwood, *Akhnai*, 1997 Utah L. Rev. 309; Jennifer Nadler, *Mar Ukba in the Fiery Furnace*, 19 L. & Literature 1 (2007); Suzanne Last Stone, *Justice, Mercy, and Gender in Rabbinic Thought*, 8 Cardozo Stud. L. & Literature 139 (1996); *Symposium, Rethinking Robert Cover's "Nomos and Narrative,"* 17 Yale J.L. & Human. 1 (2005).

75 See Stone, supra note 5, at 819-20.

> The publication of Cover's work was a significant turning point in the growth of this new literature in American law and Judaism.... Robert Cover made it

particularly near the end of his life, explored a number of areas of American jurisprudence through a prism of Jewish law and legal theory.[76]

Though Cover's scholarship stands out in many respects, his reliance on Jewish law is notable, in part, for the attempt to explore Jewish law on its own terms. Indeed, Cover often included his own translations of primary and secondary sources of Jewish law that were unfamiliar to most scholars of American law.[77] As Cover acknowledged, at times these sources highlighted stark differences between the American legal system and the Jewish legal system, in both substance and underlying assumptions.[78] Nevertheless, Cover was able to identify, within Jewish legal theory, theoretical lessons and conceptual insights that add to our understanding of American law and legal thought. Likewise, consistent with the methodology suggested in this chapter, scholars continue to look to sources of Jewish law on its own terms as a model for the application of Jewish legal theory to American law and legal scholarship.

---

respectable to draw on the Jewish tradition in public discourse. Many of the articles citing Jewish sources in the past decade are either direct responses to Cover's work, whether critical or admiring, or attempts to carry forward Cover's intellectual project. Finally, Robert Cover's work cuts across many of the important debates in contemporary American jurisprudence.

Id.; see also Bernard J. Hibbits, *Making Sense of Metaphors: Visuality, Aurality, and the Reconfiguration of American Legal Discourse*, 16 Cardozo L. Rev. 229, 339 (1994) (describing Cover as "the prime mover in the reintroduction of Jewish values to contemporary American legal discourse"); Steven L. Winter, *The Cognitive Dimension of the Agon Between Legal Power and Narrative Meaning*, 87 Mich. L. Rev. 2225, 2225 n.3 (1989) (acknowledging "the liberating effect" of Cover's work on the author's "sense of [his] own past" and stating that Cover's work has shown "how the intellectual abundance of these materials [i.e., Jewish sources] can be a profound source of analytic insight"); Stephen Wizner, *Repairing the World Through Law: A Reflection on Robert Cover's Social Activism*, 8 Cardozo Stud. L. & Literature 1 (1996); Stephen Wizner, *Tributes to Robert M. Cover*, 96 Yale L.J. 1707 (1987).

76 See, e.g., Robert M. Cover, *Bringing the Messiah Through Law: A Case Study*, in NOMOS XXX: Religion, Morality, and the Law (J. Roland Pennock & John W. Chapman eds., 1988); Robert M. Cover, *The Folktales of Justice: Tales of Jurisdiction*, 14 Cap. U. L. Rev. 179 (1985); Robert M. Cover, *Obligation: A Jewish Jurisprudence of the Social Order*, 5 J.L. & Religion 65 (1987) [hereinafter Cover, *Obligation*]; Robert M. Cover, "The Supreme Court, 1982 Term—Foreword: *Nomos* and Narrative," 97 Harv. L. Rev. 4 (1983) [hereinafter Cover, "*Nomos* and Narrative"].

77 See, e.g., Cover, "*Nomos* and Narrative," supra note 76, at 12.

78 See, e.g., Cover, *Obligation*, supra note 76.

CHAPTER 3

An Introduction to Interpretation in Jewish Law, with References to American Legal Theory

INTRODUCTION

In 1993, Suzanne Stone wrote of "a growing body of legal scholarship that is turn-ing... to the Jewish legal tradition to advance debate in contemporary American legal theory."[1] Professor Stone documented "the startling increase of citations to Jewish sources in public American legal discourse" during the decade preceding her article.[2] This trend has continued, as scholars have employed concepts from Jewish law in the analysis of such areas as health law,[3] criminal law,[4] legal ethics,[5]

---

1 Suzanne Last Stone, *In Pursuit of the Counter-Text: The Turn to the Jewish Legal Model in Contemporary American Legal Theory*, 106 Harv. L. Rev. 813, 814 (1993).

2 Id. at 816 (citation omitted).

3 See, e.g., Dena S. Davis, *Method in Jewish Bioethics: An Overview*, 20 J. Contemp. L. 325 (1994); Joshua Fruchter, *Doctors on Trial: A Comparison of American and Jewish Legal Approaches to Medical Malpractice*, 19 Am. J.L. & Med. 453 (1993); Daniel J.H. Greenwood, *Beyond Dworkin's Dominions: Investments, Memberships, the Tree of Life, and the Abortion Question*, 72 Tex. L. Rev. 559 (1994); Marc D. Stern, *"And You Shall Choose Life": Futility and the Religious Duty to Preserve Life*, 25 Seton Hall L. Rev. 997 (1995).

4 See, e.g., Irene Merker Rosenberg & Yale L. Rosenberg, *"Perhaps What Ye Say Is Based Only on Conjecture": Circumstantial Evidence, Then and Now*, 31 Hous. L. Rev. 1371 (1995).

5 See, e.g., Gordon J. Beggs, *Proverbial Practice: Legal Ethics from Old Testament Wisdom*, 30 Wake Forest L. Rev. 831 (1995); Russell G. Pearce, *To Save a Life: Why a Rabbi and a Jewish Lawyer Must Disclose a Client Confidence*, 29 Loy. L.A. L. Rev. 1771 (1996); Arthur Gross Schaefer & Peter S. Levi, *Resolving the Conflict Between the Ethical Values of Confidentiality and Saving a Life: A Jewish View*, 29 Loy. L.A. L. Rev. 1761 (1996).

legal interpretation,[6] and constitutional amendment,[7] among others.

Despite this trend, however, scholars differ in their views toward the value and validity of applying principles of Jewish law to American legal theory. For example, David Dow, who argued that Jewish law can be used to resolve the counter-majoritarian difficulty,[8] writes that "the normative ontology of the systems of Jewish and American law are so nearly identical that the Judaic resolution of certain theoretical difficulties can be wholly transplanted to the American domain."[9] Others appear less optimistic. Steven Friedell, for example, who compared Jewish legal attitudes with feminist jurisprudence,[10] observes that "Jewish law has policies and purposes that are unique and that make the application of Jewish law in a modern legal system difficult."[11] Similarly, Stone notes one of the fundamental differences between the Jewish and American legal systems: "Jewish law is not only a legal system; it is the life work of a religious community. The Constitution, on the other hand, is a political document."[12] Therefore, Stone warns, American theorists "should be cautious not

---

6 See, e.g., Benjamin L. Apt, *Aggadah, Legal Narrative, and the Law*, 73 Or. L. Rev. 943 (1994); Shael Herman, *The "Equity of the Statute" and Ratio Scripta: Legislative Interpretation Among Legislative Agnostics and True Believers*, 69 Tul. L. Rev. 535 (1994); Irene Merker Rosenberg & Yale L. Rosenberg, *Advice from Hillel and Shammai on How to Read Cases: Of Specificity, Retroactivity and New Rules*, 42 Am. J. Comp. L. 581 (1994).

7 See Professor Sanford Levinson's discussion of why the book he edited on constitutional amendment includes a chapter on changes within Jewish law. Sanford Levinson, *Introduction: Imperfection and Amendability, in Responding to Imperfection: The Theory and Practice of Constitutional Amendment* 8 (Sanford Levinson ed., 1995) (discussing the inclusion in the book of Noam J. Zohar, *Midrash: Amendment Through the Molding of Meaning*).

   The last few decades have seen a similar increase in Jewish law courses in American law schools. Professor Jeffrey Roth cited a February 1994 survey that documented 33 courses in Jewish law at 28 American law schools. See Jeffrey I. Roth, *Fraud on the Surviving Spouse in Jewish and American Law: A Model Chapter for a Jewish Law Casebook*, 28 Case W. Res. J. Int'l L. 101, 101 n.1 (1996). In addition, Roth noted the significance of the formation of the American Association of Law Schools Section on Jewish Law. Id. at 101. As a result of the increased interest in Jewish law in American law schools, Roth called for a casebook on Jewish law and proposed a model chapter on the subject of wills.

8 David R. Dow, *Constitutional Midrash: The Rabbis' Solution to Professor Bickel's Problem*, 29 Hous. L. Rev. 543 (1992).

9 Id. at 544.

10 Steven F. Friedell, *The "Different Voice" in Jewish Law: Some Parallels to a Feminist Jurisprudence*, 67 Ind. L.J. 915 (1992).

11 Steven F. Friedell, *Book Review: Aaron Kirschenbaum on Equity in Jewish Law*, 1993 B.Y.U. L. Rev. 909, 919 (1993).

12 Stone, supra note 1, at 894.

to derive too many lessons from the counter-text of Jewish law."[13] Conversely, Stone asserts that "the Jewish legal tradition is being subtly reinterpreted to yield a legal counter-model embodying precisely the qualities many contemporary theorists wish to inject into American law."[14]

This chapter explores some of the ways in which Jewish law may shed light on issues in American legal theory. While acknowledging that there are fundamental differences between a religious legal system and a secular one, the chapter attempts to show that certain conceptual similarities between American law and Jewish law allow for meaningful, yet cautious, comparison of the two systems.

Specifically, this chapter provides a broad historical and analytical overview of interpretation in Jewish law, exploring a number of themes including sources and methods of interpretation, expansion and limitation through interpretation, authority in interpretation, and precedent. As I am mindful of Stone's observations, one of the aims of this chapter is to provide a framework through which to consider the Jewish legal system on its own terms, before applying it to American legal theory.[15] Many of the issues discussed in this chapter find their parallels, to varying degrees, in American legal interpretation. Some of the similarities are addressed expressly, while others are more implicit. This chapter also demonstrates, if only implicitly, some of the difficulties involved in trying to compare a religious legal system with a secular system of law.

The late professor and former Israeli Supreme Court Justice Menachem Elon aptly summarized the "one basic norm and one single supreme value" of Jewish law: "the command of [God] as embodied in the Torah given to Moses at Sinai."[16]

---

13 Id. at 893-94.

14 Id. at 814.

15 This chapter is prompted, in part, by Professor Lawrence Lessig's comment on the inclusion, in a book on constitutional amendment, of Noam Zohar's essay on changes within Jewish law. See supra note 7. In acknowledging the value of Zohar's essay in relation to American legal theory, Lessig laments that "there is no way that lawyers can properly enter the world of Judaic interpretation through a single essay." Lawrence Lessig, *What Drives Derivability: Responses to Responding to Imperfection*, 74 Tex. L. Rev. 839, 842 (1996). It is my hope that this chapter will help contribute to the ability of legal scholars to better understand Jewish legal interpretation.

16 Menachem Elon, *Jewish Law: History, Sources, Principles* 233 (Bernard Auerbach & Melvin J. Sykes trans., Jewish Publication Soc'y 1994); see also Aaron Kirschenbaum, *Equity in Jewish Law: Halakhic Perspectives in Law* 10 (1991) ("The ultimate legal principle (*Grundnorm*) is the rule that the Torah, the Five Books of Moses, is of binding authority for the Jewish legal system. Parallel to this Written Torah is the Oral Tradition, which Jewish theology traces back to Moses from [God]."). According to the medieval scholar Maimonides, two of the thirteen fundamental principles of Judaism are that Moses received both the Written and Oral Torah from God at Sinai and that the Torah has immutable authority. See Maimonides, *Introduction to Perek Chelek*, in *Introductions to Commentary on the Mishna* 107, 144-46 (Mordechai Rabinowitz, ed., 1961).

The term "Torah," in this sense, refers to the entire corpus of revealed law that Moses received at Sinai. Part of the revelation at Sinai consisted of the Written Torah—the Five Books of Moses. Because it is a written text, in order to be understood, the Written Torah must be interpreted. To facilitate its interpretation, God revealed to Moses an Oral Torah as well.[17] Moses was given specific details of some of the laws, obviating the need for human interpretation of the text with respect to those details.[18] Thus, the substance of those details, albeit an interpretation of the text, was part of the revealed Torah. In addition, the Oral Torah included a number of techniques through which the text of the Written Torah is interpreted.[19] Among the most important techniques were the hermeneutic rules, which comprise a system of legal interpretation through a specialized method of literary analysis.

Laws and principles mandated by both the Written and Oral Torah have the authority of being *d'oraita*, a Talmudic adjectival form of the Aramaic translation of "Torah."[20] To describe a law or legal principle as *d'oraita* is roughly equivalent to describing a law or principle in American law as being based in the Constitution. The serious nature of interpretation of the Torah is underscored by the fact that the substantive interpretation itself takes on constitutional authority: *d'oraita*. For example, the Torah states that on the Sabbath, it is forbidden to engage in *melakha*[21]—usually translated as "work."[22] Other than a prohibition against lighting a fire on the Sabbath,[23] the text of the Torah offers

---

17 The Oral Torah was transmitted orally, from generation to generation, through a carefully administered educational system. See Mishna, Avoth 1:1; Maimonides, *Introduction to Mishne Torah* [hereinafter Maimonides, Code of Law]. As a result of persecution and exile, the Oral Torah was ultimately recorded in writing. See Talmud Bavli, Gittin 60a, especially the Tosafoth Rid commentary. See also Asher Weiss, *Minchas Asher, Shemos* 412-23 (2017). The Talmud is the written, authoritative compilation of the oral traditions and interpretations. See Maimonides, *Introduction to the Mishna*, in *Introductions to Commentary on the Mishna*, supra note 16, at 1, 85 [hereinafter, Maimonides, *Introduction to the Mishna*]. It is comprised of the Mishna, which was compiled in the Land of Israel around the year 188 C.E., and the Gemara, which was compiled in Babylonia around the year 589 C.E. See Aryeh Kaplan, *The Handbook of Jewish Thought* 187, 237 (1974). A version of the Gemara was compiled in the Land of Israel as well (Talmud Yerushalmi), but the Babylonian Talmud, or Talmud Bavli, is more complete and more authoritative. See Maimonides, *Introduction to the Mishna*, supra, at 84.
18 See Maimonides, *Introduction to the Mishna*, supra note 17, at 37.
19 See id. at 37-38; Elon, supra note 16, at 318-70.
20 See Nachmanides, *Commentary to Maimonides, Book of Commandments*, especially commentary to Chapter 2.
21 See Exodus 20:10.
22 See, e.g., The Holy Scriptures 173 (Jewish Publication Society 1955).
23 See Exodus 35:3.

no express details of what work is forbidden.[24] Thus, it became necessary for legal authorities to interpret the term *melakha* to determine what actions or activities are forbidden on the Sabbath. Once the authorities determined that writing, for example, is one of the activities prohibited on the Sabbath,[25] the law against writing became *d'oraita*, and it carries the same import as the law against lighting a fire, which is spelled out in the text.

This quality of legal interpretation in Jewish law finds its parallel in American constitutional interpretation. If the Supreme Court, through interpreting the Constitution, determines that there is a substantive right to abortion, then this right is understood to be part of constitutional law. As a result of the Court's interpretation, for most practical purposes there is no qualitative difference between the rights to free speech or the free exercise of religion, which have been part of the text of the Constitution for more than two hundred years, and the more recently articulated right to an abortion. Similarly, an interpretation of the text of the Torah, which expounds on or clarifies the law, extends, beyond the text, the range of laws and principles that are considered *d'oraita*.[26]

PART ONE | SOURCES AND METHODS OF INTERPRETATION

There are three basic sources and methods of legal interpretation in Jewish law:[27]

---

24 There are less explicit descriptions of activities prohibited on the Sabbath, in Exodus 16:29 and Numbers 15:32-36.

25 See Talmud Bavli, Shabbath 73a.

26 If the Supreme Court were to overrule *Roe v. Wade*, 410 U.S. 113 (1973), or if Congress and the States were to pass an amendment to the Constitution contrary to the rights recognized therein, the right to obtain an abortion would lose its constitutional basis. A similar, though more limited, dynamic exists in Jewish law as well. If the Sanhedrin (High Court) interprets the revealed law in a certain way, that interpretation becomes the authoritative definition of what the Torah requires. However, a later Sanhedrin has the authority to interpret the law differently. The later interpretation overrules the earlier one, replacing it as the authoritative definition of the Torah's laws. See infra text accompanying notes 145-87.

In Jewish law, legal interpreters lack the authority to "amend" the Torah. See Deuteronomy 13:1; Maimonides, Code of Law, supra note 17, at Laws of *Yesodei Ha-Torah* 9:1, Laws of *Mamrim* 2:9. In this way, however, they are no different from American judges. The Supreme Court does not amend the Constitution when it interprets its provisions. It is only through the legislative process of amendment that the actual text of the Constitution may be changed. In Jewish law, the courts' role as legislators is distinct from their role as interpreters, and there are broad limitations on their legislative power. See id. at Laws of *Mamrim* 2:9. One basic limitation is that judicial "legislation" may not contradict the substance of the Torah's laws. See id.; Elon, supra note 16, at 478-81; Chapter 4 in this Volume.

27 See generally Maimonides, *Introduction to the Mishna*, supra note 17, at 30-40; Rabbi Zvi Hirsch Chajes, *Introduction to the Talmud*, in *Collected Writings of Rabbi Zvi Hirsch Chajes* 281, 284-91 (1985).

A. Interpretations Revealed to Moses at Sinai

As noted above, certain interpretations were revealed to Moses through the Oral Torah, and therefore need not be derived. In the *Introduction to Commentary on the Mishna*, Maimonides compiled a list of numerous examples where the Talmud concludes that details of textual laws were given as part of the Oral Law to Moses at Sinai.[28] Maimonides divides this list into two categories. One category consists of details that cannot be derived through logical or textual analysis.[29] It is understandable that if there are no means to interpret a vague law, a definition must somehow be supplied. Maimonides notes that in these cases, the Talmud states the details of the law without attempting to explain their derivation.[30]

The other category includes definitions that, although presented to Moses at Sinai, could have been derived as well.[31] In these cases, the Talmud undertakes an analysis to derive the definition based on the text of the Torah.[32] Nevertheless, Maimonides notes, these definitions, recorded in the Talmud over hundreds of years, are never subject to debate or doubt.[33] The aim of the Talmudic exercise is only to show that the laws find support in the written text.

B. Exegetical Interpretation of the Text

There are many different methods of textual hermeneutics employed throughout the Talmud and other works of halakhic interpretation.[34] Most of these methods involve a specialized form of literary analysis. On one level, the logic of these methods is often accessible to us; in fact, some of the methods find their parallels in American constitutional and statutory interpretation. Yet, the ultimate determination of which method to apply under which circumstances is not always apparent, and the conclusions of law are based on an internal logic specific to a unique and lost art.

C. Logic and Observation

A final source of legal interpretation is reasoning that originates in logic and observation rather than in textual analysis. Sometimes this type of reasoning is

---

28 Maimonides, *Introduction to the Mishna*, supra note 17, at 34-36.
29 See id. at 33.
30 See id.
31 See id. at 31-32.
32 See id. at 32-33.
33 See id. at 31.
34 For an extensive discussion of these methods, see Elon, supra note 16, at 318-70. See also Moshe Chaim Luzzatto, *Ma'amar Ha-Ikarim*.

used to determine how to properly interpret the text itself, while at other times it is used to extrapolate a principle from a text or to extend a clearly stated principle to new situations. In addition, logic and observation are occasionally used as a source of law, largely independent of any text.

D. Methods of Interpretation in Practice

To understand how these sources and methods of interpretation are used in practice, it is helpful to look at some specific laws. For example, the Torah contains a *mitzva*,[35] a commandment, to eat the paschal lamb on the first night of Passover.[36] Two of the central verses relating to this *mitzva*, presented in the context of the exodus from Egypt, state in part that "all of the assembled Nation of Israel shall slaughter [the paschal lamb on the fourteenth day of the first month],"[37] and "they will eat the meat [of the paschal lamb] on that night."[38]

Some details of these laws, which cannot be derived from either textual or logical analysis, were revealed to Moses at Sinai.[39] One basic detail not supplied by the text relates to the method through which the meat must be prepared before it is eaten. The Torah commands "slaughter[ing]" the animal, but it does not elaborate on the method of slaughtering. The Talmud concludes that, because the details of ritual slaughtering cannot be deduced through textual or logical analysis, they were therefore revealed to Moses at Sinai, as part of the Oral Torah.[40]

Once the method of preparing the meat is determined, the next question involves how to fulfill the commanded action of eating the meat. The text, however, does not specify the quantity of meat that must be consumed. In fact, there are a number of both positive and negative *mitzvot* in the Torah relating to the consumption of food,[41] but the Torah does not quantify how much food must or must not be eaten in each case. Nor does there seem to be a system of logical and/or textual analysis through which it would be possible to interpret the word "eat." The Talmud concludes that the definition of eating falls within the category of laws revealed to Moses at Sinai through the Oral Torah.[42]

---

35 The plural of *mitzva* is *mitzvot*.
36 See, e.g., Exodus 12:8; Talmud Bavli, Pesachim 99b. In Jewish law and religion, the calendar date begins and ends at night. Thus, the fourteenth day of the first month of the year is the eve of Passover, while that night is the fifteenth of the month, the first night of Passover.
37 Exodus 12:6.
38 Id. at 12:8.
39 See supra notes 16-25 and accompanying text.
40 See Chajes, supra note 27, at 287 (citing generally to Talmud Bavli, Chulin).
41 See, e.g., discussion infra notes 64-82 and accompanying text.
42 See Talmud Bavli, Eruvin 4a-4b. See also Asher Weiss, *Minchas Asher, Devarim* 85-92 (2017).

Another question is when the meat must be eaten. Although the Torah expressly states that the meat must be eaten at "night," it does not define until what time the technical term "night" extends. Nor did the Oral Torah supplement the Written Torah in this case by providing a definition of "night." Therefore, legal authorities relied on textual hermeneutics to arrive at a definition.[43] Rabbi Elazar ben Azaria looked to another context in which the phrase "that night" is found. He noted that just a few verses later, in the same discussion of the exodus, God said to Moses, "I will pass through Egypt on that night."[44] The definition of the phrase "that night" in the second verse can be obtained by examining a third verse, in which God stated that "at midnight, I will pass into the land of Egypt."[45] The third verse supplies details not included in the second verse, indicating that the time period at which "that night" ends is midnight. Rabbi Elazar thus concluded that the paschal lamb may be eaten until midnight.[46]

The majority of the sages disagreed with Rabbi Elazar, based on a different method of hermeneutics. The sages also relied on other verses, but instead of looking to verses that include the term "that night," they looked to verses that relate directly to the commandment of eating the paschal lamb. They observed that the text of the Torah further commanded that the meat be eaten "with haste."[47] The use of the phrase "with haste" in the context of the exodus is understood by the sages to refer to the point in time in which the Nation of Israel was to proceed with haste.[48] The identity of this point in time is derived from yet a third verse. God told Moses that on the night of the exodus, the Nation of Israel should not leave their houses "until morning."[49] The arrival of morning, then, is the time at which they would leave their houses and proceed "with haste" in order to flee Egypt. Thus, the sages interpreted the phrase commanding the consumption of the paschal lamb "with haste" as teaching that it may be eaten until morning.[50]

---

43 See Talmud Bavli, Berachoth 9a; Talmud Bavli, Pesachim 120b.

44 Exodus 12:12.

45 Id. at 11:4.

46 "Midnight" in this context is defined not as 12:00 a.m., but as the mid-point between sunset and sunrise on the first night of Passover. See Maimonides, *Commentary on the Mishna,* Berachoth 9b.

47 Exodus 12:11.

48 See Talmud Bavli, Berachoth 9a; Talmud Bavli, Pesachim 120b.

49 Exodus 12:22.

50 Although the sages held that, in principle, the paschal lamb could be eaten until morning, in practice they held that a person should eat the meat before midnight, to avoid the possibility of violating a commandment. See Talmud Bavli, Berachoth 9a. One of the sources

There are also a number of laws relating to the paschal lamb that are derived through the third method of interpretation, originating in logic and observation, which are then applied in order to understand the text or to derive legal principles. One such interpretation relates to further details of the preparation of the meat from the paschal lamb. To prepare this meat for the *mitzva*, one must comply with the general laws of *kashruth*,[51] which apply to any food that is eaten and which include the command not to eat the blood of an animal.[52] Although it was revealed to Moses to what extent blood must first be removed from an animal before meat may be eaten,[53] there were no guidelines for how to remove the blood. To arrive at such a method, the authorities relied on logic and observation. Based on observation of the physical properties of different objects, the authorities determined a method of "salting" the meat to draw out the blood.[54]

Finally, through logic and observation, the Talmud relies on an analysis of a verse relating to the paschal lamb to extrapolate a general legal principle. The Torah commands "all of the Children of Israel" to slaughter the paschal lamb on the eve of Passover.[55] The Talmud notes that, in practice, not every individual slaughtered a lamb on that day;[56] indeed, given the various regulations regarding sacrifices, this would have been physically impossible. Every individual did eat from a paschal lamb that night, however, with most eating from animals slaughtered by a much smaller number of individuals.[57] The Talmud, therefore, looked for a legal principle to reconcile the commandment, that each individual slaughter a lamb, with the practice that most individuals did not perform this action themselves. The Talmud concluded that through the principle of agency, the majority of individuals could appoint those who actually performed the act of slaughtering to be their agents.[58] Thus, the Talmud employed logic and observation, recognizing the impossibility of interpreting the law to

---

of authority for rabbinic legislation is Leviticus 18:30, which is understood as requiring legal authorities to insure adherence to the laws by instituting preventive safeguards. See Talmud Bavli, Yevamoth 21a; Chapter 4 in this Volume. In the case of the paschal lamb, the Torah not only mandates eating meat, but adds a prohibition against leaving over the meat until morning. See Exodus 12:10. Thus, to guard against violation of this prohibition, the sages advised that the meat be eaten before midnight, far in advance of the morning hour.

51   *Kashruth* is the noun form of the adjective kosher.
52   See, e.g., Leviticus 3:17.
53   See Chajes, supra note 27, at 284.
54   See id. at 313.
55   Exodus 12:6.
56   See Talmud Bavli, Kiddushin 41b.
57   See id.
58   See id.

require each individual to slaughter a lamb personally, as a basis for interpreting the text to extrapolate the legal principle of agency.

PART TWO | INTERPRETATIVE EXPANSION AND LIMITATION

A. *Mitzvot*

As a general rule, in considering interpretation in Jewish law, it may be useful to divide the legal segments of the Torah into two categories. The first category is the *mitzvot*, which mandate or prohibit certain activities. While it is often necessary to determine the precise scope of each of the *mitzvot*, the activities are largely well defined; if the text of the Torah does not provide a working definition, the Oral Law ordinarily provides the necessary details.[59] Thus, authorities who interpret the Torah have a limited role as well as limited discretion in defining these activities. Although a certain level of interpretation will be necessary to apply these laws to new circumstances or to interpret vague terms that are not explained by the Oral Law, the revealed and hermeneutically derived laws present a broad and clear understanding of what activities are mandated or prohibited.

Along with the fact that the basic details of *mitzvot* often do not require interpretation, interpretive authorities have narrow discretion to limit the application of these laws. To be sure, in a sense, any interpretation may, upon application, function as a limitation. However, the license to interpret and perhaps limit the *mitzvot* extends only to questions of applying the *mitzvot* to new circumstances or interpreting vague terms. There is no license, for example, to conclude, based on a consideration of what may appear to be the rationale behind a commandment, that a clearly expressed and defined commandment should not apply under unusual circumstances or to particular individuals.

These concepts may be understood through an examination of one of the *mitzvot*. In a number of places, the Torah mandates eating *matzo* on Passover.[60] In fact, the *matzo* is to be eaten on the first night of Passover, together with the paschal lamb.[61] To allow for the proper observance of this commandment, many questions of interpretation had to be answered.

---

59 See supra notes 17-19 and accompanying text.
60 See, e.g., Exodus 12:8, 15, 18, 20; Leviticus 23:6; Deuteronomy 16:3, 8.
61 See Exodus 12:8.

The most basic question involves the definition of *matzo*. Although there would not seem to be a system of logical or textual analysis through which to interpret the word "*matzo*," it appears that there was no question, at the time of the commandment, as to what food qualified as *matzo*. Perhaps, for example, at the time and place of the commandment, *matzo* referred to a clearly identifiable food. In comparison, a criminal statute referencing cocaine does not have to provide a technical definition of cocaine.[62] In any event, in the absence of a widely recognized definition, Moses would presumably have been instructed, with sufficient detail, that *matzo* was a baked mixture of grain and water that did not leaven. Implicit in this basic information would have been a definition of the leavening process as well. Thus, with regard to these details, there was neither a need for nor the possibility of interpretation.

With the subject matter of the commandment somewhat clearly defined, the next set of questions might involve the nature of the commanded action. These questions, as well as the answers, are the same as those related to the commanded action of eating from the paschal lamb. First, the Torah did not articulate what quantity of *matzo* must be consumed in order to fulfill the requirements of the commandment; it simply stated that all individuals must "eat" *matzo* on Passover. The quantity of *matzo* to be eaten, like all of the Torah's laws involving quantities and measurements,[63] was revealed to Moses at Sinai, and is the quantity applicable to most *mitzvot* that involve eating—including the *mitzva* to eat the paschal lamb.

In addition, the Torah did not state until what time the *matzo* may be consumed. The answer to this question was not clear from the text and was not revealed to Moses at Sinai; therefore, it had to be derived through textual exegesis. In fact, the analysis is identical to the one relating to the proper time frame for eating from the paschal lamb, because the Torah commands that the paschal lamb be eaten together with the *matzo*.[64] As a result, the time frame is the same for both foods, and the same dispute in the Talmud concerning the

---

62 Similarly, in Professor Kent Greenawalt's hypothetical, when Georgia, the head of the household, tells Kent, the housekeeper, to buy "soupmeat," the range of choice for soupmeat "may have been narrowed by past understandings or in some other way. If . . . Georgia and Kent have established together that a certain kind of meat is what they will use for soupmeat in the household, then Georgia's reference to soupmeat may be taken to refer . . . to the precise kind of meat involved." Kent Greenawalt, *From the Bottom Up*, 82 Cornell L. Rev. 994 (1997); see also *Transcript of Proceedings, Northwestern University/Washington University Law and Linguistics Conference*, 73 Wash. U. L.Q. 800, 940-52 (1995).

63 See Talmud Bavli, Eruvin 4a-4b.

64 See Exodus 12:8.

time frame for eating the meat from the paschal lamb arose with regard to eating the *matzo*.[65]

The revealed Written and Oral Torah, along with textual exegesis, thus provide the details necessary to fulfill the commandment to eat *matzo* on the first night of Passover. Yet, even when the details of a *mitzva* are resolved, it seems inevitable that circumstances will arise that are not explicitly covered by the revealed law. It will then be necessary to interpret the *mitzva* to determine whether the parameters of the *mitzva* extend to the unaddressed circumstances.

One category of new circumstances relating to a *mitzva* involves destruction or unavailability of the subject matter of the *mitzva*. The Torah commands eating the paschal lamb together with *matzo*, as well as with *marror*—a bitter herb.[66] With the destruction of the Temple in Jerusalem, it became impossible, for a number of reasons, to prepare the paschal lamb. Thus, with regard to the commandment to eat the paschal lamb, under present circumstances, the subject matter of the *mitzva* no longer exists. As it is currently impossible to eat the paschal lamb, the *mitzva* cannot technically be observed.

A more difficult question for legal authorities after the destruction of the Temple related to whether the Torah's commandments to eat *matzo* and to eat *marror* remained intact. The answer was once again the subject of a dispute in the Talmud. The crux of the dispute was based on textual interpretation. Rava observed that, in addition to the verse that commands eating *matzo* and *marror* together with the paschal lamb, another verse in the Torah commands eating *matzo* on the first night of Passover,[67] without mention of either the paschal lamb or *marror*.[68] In interpreting the Torah, there is a strong presumption against superfluity.[69] Thus, the additional verse's commandment to eat the *matzo* must indicate an additional law. Rava concluded that the second verse establishes an independent obligation to eat the *matzo*, even in the absence of the paschal lamb.[70] In contrast, Rava held, because the command to eat the *marror* is found only in conjunction with the paschal lamb, when the paschal lamb cannot be eaten, there is no independent obligation to eat the *marror*.[71]

---

65 See supra text accompanying notes 43-50.

66 See Exodus 12:8.

67 See id. at 12:18.

68 See Talmud Bavli, Pesachim 120a.

69 See, e.g., id. See also Chapter 11 in this Volume.

70 See Talmud Bavli, Pesachim 120a.

71 See id. Although the Torah's command to eat the *marror* is dependent on the paschal lamb, in the absence of the paschal lamb there is still a rabbinically mandated requirement to eat *marror* on the first night of Passover. Rabbinic legislative authority extends not only to enacting laws to protect against the violation of *mitzvot* but also to enacting affirmative laws.

Rav Acha bar Yaakov, however, focused on the first verse, and concluded that the obligation to eat *matzo* is also dependent on eating the paschal lamb.[72] With regard to the other verse noted by Rava, Rav Acha agreed that the verse cannot be superfluous, but he interpreted the verse to teach a different law relating to eating *matzo*.[73] Rava, in turn, held that the law that Rav Acha deduced from the second verse can be derived from the logical extension of yet another verse.[74] In Rava's view, then, the second verse regarding the *matzo* remained apparently superfluous, and thus had to teach an otherwise unknown law: the obligation to eat *matzo* even without the paschal lamb.[75]

Another new circumstance could involve a somewhat reversed situation, in which an object is discovered that had not been known to exist but apparently may be suitable as the subject matter of a *mitzva*. In the case of *matzo*, one such circumstance involves the type of grain acceptable in the ingredients of *matzo*. The revealed law enumerated certain grains suitable for *matzo*,[76] but did not address all grains—and, indeed, could not have meaningfully discussed those grains not identifiable in the part of the world where the Torah was given. Thus, the Talmud records that the legal authorities considered whether certain unenumerated grains could be used for *matzo*.[77] Faced with the need to interpret the law, the authorities noted that a grain could be used for *matzo* only if it could potentially undergo the chemical reaction of leavening.[78] They then performed an experiment on the grains in question, and through a comparison to the grains that were known to be suitable, observed whether the unaddressed grains could undergo the same chemical reaction.[79] If so, those grains were determined to be suitable for *matzo*.[80]

A similar question arose in post-Talmudic times with regard to *marror*. The Talmud lists a number of vegetables suitable to fulfill the commandment to eat *marror* on the first night of Passover.[81] The list consists of a number of

---

See Maimonides, Code of Law, supra note 17; Elon, supra note 16, at 481-83; Chapter 4 in this Volume.

72 See Talmud Bavli, Pesachim 120a.

73 See id.

74 See id.

75 Outside of the Land of Israel, a rabbinically mandated Seder is conducted on the second night of Passover as well, at which the *matzo* and *marror* again must be eaten.

76 See Talmud Bavli, Pesachim 35a; Talmud Yerushalmi, Chalah 1:1.

77 See id.

78 The Talmud derives this rule from Deuteronomy 16:3.

79 See Talmud Bavli, Pesachim 35a; Talmud Yerushalmi, Chalah 1:1.

80 See id.

81 Although the Torah's commandment to eat *marror* is currently no longer in effect due to the destruction of the Temple and the resulting situation wherein the *marror* can no longer be

leafy vegetables, all of which were common in the Middle East in the times of the Talmud. In later centuries, however, Jews were dispersed to many parts of the world, including areas with colder climates that were not conducive to growing those leafy vegetables. In a sense, it would seem that the inability to obtain the vegetables listed in the Talmud presents a situation of destruction of the subject matter of the *mitzva*. However, some legal authorities suggested that it would be proper to use an available bitter vegetable, even if it was not one of those listed in the Talmud. For example, in the colder climates, the practice of using an available bitter vegetable, horseradish, developed to fulfill the commandment to eat *marror*.[82]

A similar category of unaddressed circumstances necessitating legal interpretation includes circumstances that were not in existence at the time that the Torah was given. Such circumstances usually arise through scientific discovery, and they have been particularly common in the past century. One issue that has presented legal authorities with many questions is the application of electricity to the laws of the Torah.

The question of electricity is particularly relevant to the laws of the Sabbath. As noted above, a number of activities, which fall under the category of *melakha*, are prohibited on the Sabbath. The Written Torah appears to list explicitly only one such activity, lighting a fire,[83] but through a combination of the revealed Oral Torah and textual interpretation, legal authorities arrived at a total of thirty-nine categories of *melakha*, all of which include subcategories as

---

eaten together with the paschal lamb, the question of which vegetables can be used for *marror* continues to have practical ramifications. Rabbinic legislation mandates eating *marror* on the first night of Passover, even in the absence of the paschal lamb. See supra note 71.

82 See generally Arthur Schaffer, *The History of Horseradish as the Bitter Herb on Passover*, 8 Gesher 217 (1981). Professor Schaffer also cites conflicting opinions holding that, even in the absence of the leafy vegetables, horseradish may not be substituted. The inability to obtain one of the vegetables listed in the Talmud has some similarities to Greenawalt's example of a housekeeper who, due to certain factors, chooses to buy chicken instead of following instructions to buy soupmeat. See generally Greenawalt, supra note 62. While in the case of *marror* it was impossible to use the proper vegetable, Greenawalt's discussions still seem relevant, including issues of "changed circumstances," "radically changed circumstances," "carrying out" a directive, and a directive's "losing force." Id.

In this understanding, even if the *mitzva* to eat *marror* is considered technically to "lose force" in the absence of the proper vegetable, it is clearly only a temporary loss of force, until the proper vegetable is available. See id. Similarly, while the Torah's commandments to eat from the paschal lamb along with the *marror* have temporarily lost force in the absence of the Temple, when the Temple is rebuilt it will again be possible to fulfill these commandments.

83 See Exodus 35:3.

well.[84] These categories and subcategories are considered *d'oraita* laws, and are part of the Torah's definition of *melakha*.[85]

Twentieth century legal authorities were required to interpret the many categories of *melakha* to determine whether various uses of electricity are permitted on the Sabbath.[86] Some prohibited the active use of electricity based on the finding that causing the flow of an electric current is sufficiently similar to lighting a fire.[87] Others held that completing an electrical circuit falls under the category of "building" a vessel or of "completing" a vessel so that it can serve its function.[88]

Turning on an electric light is even more likely to fall directly under one of the categories of *melakha*. For example, the close analogy of a glowing filament to a burning fire strongly implicates the prohibition against burning a fire. Alternatively, the Talmud extends another *melakha*—cooking—to apply to non-food objects, when the objects are softened as a result of heat.[89] Turning on an electric light may thus involve "cooking" the filament.[90]

Questions about the status of electricity in Jewish law relate to *matzo* as well. In addition to the requirements for *matzo* listed above, the Talmud delineates a number of conditions that must be met for *matzo* to be suitable for the *mitzva* to eat *matzo* on the first night of Passover. One such condition is that the person who bakes the *matzo* must intend, when preparing the *matzo*, that the *matzo* be eaten in fulfillment of the commandment.[91] When it became technologically possible to bake *matzos* with machines rather than by hand, legal authorities had to determine whether the intention requirement could be satisfied through a machine. Some argued that because a machine cannot have intent, the *matzos* baked by machine are not suitable for the *mitzva*.[92] Others

---

84 See Talmud Bavli, Shabbath 73a.

85 See supra text accompanying notes 20-21.

86 See generally Michael J. Broyde & Howard Jachter, *The Use of Electricity on Shabbat and Yom Tov*, 21 J. Halacha & Contemp. Soc'y 4 (1991).

87 See id. at 12.

88 See id. at 12-13.

89 See id. at 13.

90 It should be noted that beyond the Torah's categories of *melakha*, there are a number of rabbinically mandated prohibitions on the Sabbath, instituted by rabbis in their role as legislators. Although the discussion here relates specifically to interpretation of laws in the Torah, a number of rabbinically mandated laws may also be interpreted to prohibit the active use of electricity on the Sabbath. See id.

91 See Talmud Bavli, Pesachim 38b.

92 See Hershel Schachter, *Ma'ase U'grama B'halakha*, 1 Beit Yosef Shaul 70 (1985).

argued that the intention requirement is satisfied if the individual who pushes the button to start the machine has the proper intent.[93]

The example of the commandment to eat *matzo* on Passover thus offers insight into the nature of interpreting *mitzvot*. While many of the basic details of the *mitzvot* were revealed through the Written and Oral Torah and thus were not subject to interpretation, other details were not included in the revealed law. When certain details of a law are not clear, there is a definite need for interpretation. In addition, when circumstances arise that were not addressed by the details given with the law, the only way to apply the law in a meaningful way is through interpretation. This interpretation has the power either to extend or to limit the parameters of the law vis-à-vis the new circumstances.

There are, however, extensive checks on the extent to which legal interpretation can place limitations on the scope of a commandment. The Talmud records a dispute concerning whether interpreters may limit the applicability of a *mitzva* based on a consideration of the apparent rationale underlying the *mitzva*.[94] Rabbi Shimon held that it is proper to determine the reason for a particular commandment and then to determine whether this reason applies under a given set of circumstances; if the reason does not apply, then the commandment does not apply.[95] Rabbi Yehuda, however, whose opinion is followed, held that a *mitzva* must always be observed, even if the apparent reason for the *mitzva* does not seem relevant under the circumstances.[96]

Thus, the Talmud concludes that, absent express support in the Written or Oral Torah, legal authorities may not find *mitzvot* inapplicable merely because of unusual circumstances. If the law on its face is concrete, to the extent that it covers a set of circumstances, there is no room for interpretation. Authorities are precluded from suggesting that, because the rationale that appears to be the basis of a commandment does not apply to a given individual or social setting, then the commandment itself does not apply.

The Talmud records the dispute between Rabbi Shimon and Rabbi Yehuda with respect to a number of commandments. For example, the Torah commands that if a creditor takes an item of clothing as security from a poor person who possesses only one set of clothes for day and night, respectively, then the creditor must go to the debtor's house and return the clothing each

---

93 See id.

94 Talmud Bavli, Sanhedrin 21a. See Hershel Schachter, *Eretz Hatzevi* 135 (1992); Asher Weiss, *Minchas Asher, Bamidbar* 285-96 (2017) [hereinafter, Weiss, *Minchas Asher, Bamidbar*]; Asher Weiss, *Minchas Asher, Devarim* 274 (2017); Weiss, supra note 16, at 409.

95 See id.

96 See id.

time it is to be worn.[97] The Torah also states that a creditor may never take the clothing of a widow as security.[98] Rabbi Shimon held that the rationale for the second law was based on the first law.[99] He deduced that the reason the Torah prohibited taking a widow's clothes as security is that, if the widow is poor, the creditor will have to go daily to the widow's house, holding her clothes in his hands. Rabbi Shimon concluded that the Torah prohibited such conduct to prevent the appearance of impropriety.[100] Accordingly, Rabbi Shimon reasoned, if a given widow is not poor, and therefore the rationale he found for the commandment does not apply, then the commandment itself does not apply, and the creditor may take a piece of the widow's clothing as security.[101]

Rabbi Yehuda, however, held that the applicability of a *mitzva* does not depend on the reason for the *mitzva*.[102] The Torah's words are clear on their face: it is prohibited to take the clothing of a widow as security for a loan.[103] When the words of a commandment are clear, the commandment is applied as stated, even under unusual circumstances. Unlike electricity, which raised new questions of interpretation regarding the Sabbath and *matzo*, there already existed widows, clothing, and loans at the time that the Torah was given. Perhaps the law prohibiting taking a widow's garment appears particularly logical if the widow is poor. Perhaps it was also unusual at the time the Torah was given for a widow to possess more than a single garment for either day or night. Even if these propositions are correct, however, the *mitzvot*, when stated clearly and unequivocally, are not dependent on circumstances such as these.[104]

Nor is the applicability of definitely stated *mitzvot* dependent on individual psychological factors. For example, the Torah states that eating the *matzo* is to be a reminder of the haste with which the Nation of Israel fled Egypt;[105] because the people had to hurry, there was no time to allow the bread to leaven,

---

97 See Deuteronomy 24:13.

98 See id. at 24:17.

99 See Talmud Bavli, Bava Metzia 115a.

100 See id.

101 See id.

102 See id.

103 See Deuteronomy 24:17

104 The attempt to discover a rationale for *mitzvot* is generally considered a noble pursuit. For example, Maimonides writes that it is proper to contemplate the *mitzvot* and, if possible, to suggest reasons for them. See Maimonides, Code of Law, supra note 17, at Laws of *Temurah* 4:13. Nevertheless, Maimonides stresses that if an individual is unable to discover a rationale for a particular *mitzva*, he or she should recognize that there is still a divine rationale for it. See id. at Laws of *Me'ilah* 8:8.

105 See Deuteronomy 16:3.

resulting in the unleavened *matzo*. Yet, one may suggest additional reasons for the commandment to eat *matzo* on Passover. Indeed, a central part of the Passover Seder is the explanation for why *matzo* is eaten. Some of these reasons focus on eating *matzo*—symbolic of the bread of the poor—to evoke feelings of the hardships suffered in slavery in Egypt. It is possible, however, that an individual would feel, on a personal level, that eating *matzo* does not contribute to the commemoration of slavery. To the contrary, an individual may enjoy the taste of the *matzo*. Such an individual is nevertheless required to eat *matzo* on Passover, because the obligation to perform the *mitzva* is not dependent on the apparent rationale for the *mitzva*.[106]

Thus, it can be stated, as a general rule, that interpretation cannot restrict the scope of a *mitzva* to fewer circumstances than are implied by the plain meaning of the *mitzva*. At most, if the *mitzva* is not clear or if a new circumstance arises, rabbinic authorities may logically decide not to extend the *mitzva* beyond the scope of its plain meaning. There is, however, an exception to the rule that the application of a clearly stated *mitzva* is not dependent on the relevance of its rationale to a given set of circumstances. The Talmud states that if the Torah itself expressly declares the reason for a *mitzva* as part of the text of the *mitzva*, then the application of that *mitzva* is regulated by the relevance of the reason.[107] For example, the Torah commands a king not to obtain

---

106 A similar analysis applies to *marror*. As noted above, it is preferable to use for *marror* the vegetables listed in the Talmud. See supra text accompanying notes 81-82. One of these vegetables is romaine lettuce, which has a bitter root. Some individuals, faced with the choice of eating romaine lettuce or horseradish, may feel that the best way to fulfill the *mitzva* of eating bitter herbs is to eat the food which is more bitter, the horseradish. Although these individuals correctly note that the rationale for the *mitzva* to eat bitter herbs on Passover is to recall the bitterness of slavery in Egypt, the text of the commandment does not indicate that it is preferable to eat a more bitter food. Therefore, the Talmud's authoritative list of preferable foods should arguably be followed over a food that may seem to better match the rationale of the *mitzva*.

In a sense, questions about the relationship between a *mitzva's* rationale and its performance relate to issues of the spirit of the law and the letter of the law. Jewish belief certainly recognizes the importance of the spirit of the law. See Samuel J. Levine, *The Law and the "Spirit of the Law" in Legal Ethics*, 2015 J. Prof. Law. 1, 30-31 n.123 (2015). Thus, even in the absence of an express textual requirement or prohibition, certain activities may be required or prohibited. See, e.g., 2 Nachmanides, *Commentary on the Torah* 115-16, 376 (Chaim Chavel ed., 1960) (commenting on Leviticus 19:2 and Deuteronomy 6:18). The principle expressed by Rabbi Yehuda seems to be that, ordinarily, the spirit of the law may not supplant the letter of the law, to relieve a person from an obligation or prohibition.

107 See Talmud Bavli, Sanhedrin 21a; Yosef Engel, *Sefer Lekach Tov*, ch. 8 n.14; Schachter, supra note 94, at 135; Weiss, *Minchas Asher, Bamidbar*, supra note 42, at 285-96.

"too many" horses.[108] While the phrase "too many" must be interpreted, whatever the definition, the command on its face clearly prohibits, categorically, the
acquisition of too many horses. In the text of the command, however, the Torah
supplies the rationale for this commandment; it continues, "lest he return the
nation back to the Land of Egypt, to obtain horses."[109] The Talmud notes that
in discussing most *mitzvot*, the Torah does not provide a reason; in the rare case
that a reason is given, that reason qualifies the law.[110] Thus, the command stating that "a king should not obtain too many horses lest he return the nation to
Egypt" is understood to mean that a king should not obtain too many horses if
he will thereby return the nation back to Egypt. If it is clear that he will not lead
the nation back to Egypt, then this commandment does not limit how many
horses he may obtain.[111]

Nevertheless, there is a caveat. In theory, under these limited circumstances, the Talmud does license restricting the scope of certain *mitzvot* to
fewer situations than implied by the plain meaning of the *mitzvot*. In practice,
however, the Talmud does not seem to recommend that a person be so confi-
dent that the rationale that the Torah gives for a *mitzva* truly does not apply.[112]
In fact, the Talmud notes that the wise King Solomon felt that he was not in

---

108 Deuteronomy 17:16.
109 Id.
110 See Talmud Bavli, Sanhedrin 21a.
111 Interestingly, the rules about when *mitzvot* may or may not be limited through interpreta-
     tion may parallel Judge Easterbrook's rule of when a statute should or should not be
     interpreted. Judge Easterbrook wrote that

     > [U]nless the statute plainly hands courts the power to create and revise a form
     > of common law, the domain of the statute should be restricted to cases antic-
     > ipated by its framers and expressly resolved in the text. Unless the party rely-
     > ing on the statute could establish either express resolution or creation of the
     > common law power of revision, the court would hold the matter in question
     > outside the statute's domain. The statute would become irrelevant, the parties
     > (and court) remitted to whatever other sources of law might be applicable.

     Frank A. Easterbrook, *Statutes' Domains*, 50 U. Chi. L. Rev. 533, 544 (1983). The cases
     Easterbrook considers to be within the domain of a statute may parallel those cases in
     which *mitzvot* are applied as stated, with no possibility of restricting the scope of the *mitzva*
     based on interpretation. The cases that he considers to be outside the statute's domain may
     parallel the new or unaddressed circumstances, which require interpretation of the *mitzvot*,
     though in these scenarios Easterbrook opts for non-application. Finally, Easterbrook's
     discussion of a statute's handing the court the power to revise the common law may parallel
     the cases in which the reasons for the *mitzvot* are expressly incorporated into the *mitzvot*,
     allowing for restrictive interpretation.
112 See Talmud Bavli, Sanhedrin 21a.

danger of returning to Egypt if he obtained too many horses.[113] As the Bible records, however, Solomon obtained many horses and, as a result, returned to Egypt.[114] The case of Solomon illustrates the danger that a person may erroneously believe that the rationale behind a *mitzva* does not apply, and may then unjustifiably conclude that the *mitzva* does not apply.[115]

B. Principles

The other category of laws found in the Torah consists of legal rules that typically do not command actions that a person must or must not undertake, but instead prescribe various legal principles for the way society should function. Generally, these laws relate to monetary/commercial or "civil" matters,[116] while *mitzvot* usually refer to ritual or technically "religious" matters. It should be remembered, however, that although Jewish law differentiates between monetary and ritual law, it is less than accurate to use the term "religious law" exclusively for ritual law. As implied by the very phrase "Jewish law," as well as by the fact that the Torah contains both monetary and ritual laws, these two areas of law together comprise the law of the Jewish religion. Moreover, many areas of "civil law," such as marriage, incorporate religious ritual—often *mitzvot*—as well as monetary principles.[117]

On the whole, however, most of what we would categorize as monetary matters can often be analyzed and interpreted with little reference to ritual law. Compared with *mitzvot*, these matters usually require considerably broader

---

113 See id.

114 See 1 Kings 10:29. To use Greenawalt's terms, at best it may be said that Solomon "innocently" or "justifiably" failed to comply with the commandment, as he may have reasonably believed, based on the express rationale for the commandment, that the commandment was inapplicable to him. Greenawalt, supra note 62. However, with regard to most commandments, for which the Torah does not reveal the rationale, failure to comply based on a presumed rationale is never justified. Nor would such behavior be considered a "mistaken" failure to comply; it would simply be a case of disobedience. See id.

115 Indeed, the Talmud cites the case of Solomon to explain why the Torah did not reveal the rationale behind most of the *mitzvot*. See Talmud Bavli, Sanhedrin 21a. The Talmud observes that Solomon, one of the wisest and most righteous of individuals, nonetheless erred in believing that the rationale of the *mitzva* did not apply to him. See id. The Talmud reasons that, had the Torah given the rationale for other commandments, it would have led others to commit similar errors. See id.; see also Maimonides, *Book of Commandments*, negative commandment 365.

116 The term "monetary law" is a rough translation of the Hebrew term *dinei mammon*, which refers to a broad range of civil laws, including commercial law, contract law, and other laws implemented for social welfare.

117 See infra notes 138-41 and accompanying text.

interpretation and allow for considerably more discretion on the part of interpreters. This increased interpretation and discretion result from both the form and the substantive nature of the monetary laws.

In terms of form, these laws are often expressed as general legal principles, without much specific elaboration in the revealed Oral Law. The principles, therefore, must be interpreted to establish concrete rules for society. To be sure, within the category of *mitzvot* as well, although certain concrete details are revealed in both the Written and Oral Law, some details are left to interpretation. For example, the revealed law was specific in stating that *matzo* is an unleavened, baked mixture of grain and water, and in setting the quantity of *matzo* that must be eaten on the first night of Passover.[118] Yet, the revealed law was general enough to be open to interpretation with regard to the time limit for eating the *matzo* and questions related to new circumstances.[119] Thus, with regard to the form of the law, it seems that the central difference between monetary laws and *mitzvot* is the level of generality. Because monetary laws are more general, they require more interpretation.

It is possible that this difference in form is itself an expression of the difference in substantive nature between *mitzvot* and monetary law. *Mitzvot* involve ritualistic activities that reflect an often unarticulated and sometimes undiscernible divine will. Therefore, while some interpretation is possible, through textual analysis or application of the internal logic of *mitzvot*, there are limits to the understanding attainable through any method of rational human interpretation. In contrast, while the monetary legal principles in the Torah also express divine will, they are readily comprehensible through human logic. Given general monetary principles, humans can employ a meaningful and broad form of rational interpretation to construct a legal system that applies those principles.

This difference in substantive nature may likewise account for the difference in discretion available to interpreters in the two areas. With regard to *mitzvot*, when the Torah does not reveal the divine rationale for a *mitzva*, interpreters do not have the discretion to restrict the scope of the *mitzva* based on the apparent rationale.[120] When considering monetary principles, however, interpreters deal with a divine system whose rationale is readily attainable through human logic and, thus, subject by its nature to broad and extensive rational interpretation. Because the system is inherently rational, it may be

---

118 See supra notes 60-63 and accompanying text.
119 See supra notes 64-80 and accompanying text.
120 See supra text accompanying notes 94-115.

interpreted, applied, and restricted through an exploration of the rationale underlying the principles. If interpreters find that the rationale behind a particular principle does not apply in a given case, they have the discretion to decide that the principle itself does not apply.[121]

Here again, it is helpful to look at some specific laws to illustrate how monetary principles are interpreted. The Torah's system of tort law discusses not only liability for damages caused directly by a person's actions, but also liability for damages caused by a person's property.[122] The framework for the laws of the latter category is based largely on a few verses in Exodus that list four general tort scenarios: (1) a person digs a pit in which another person's animal falls and dies;[123] (2) one person's ox gores another's ox, killing it;[124] (3) a person sends an animal to graze in someone else's field; and (4) a fire consumes someone's

---

121 In discussing levels of abstraction in law, Bernard Jackson has written that

> Ronald Dworkin . . . attributes to "legal principles" the role of guidance only; unlike rules, they do not dictate the outcome of problems to which they apply. Interestingly, the strict distinction proposed by Dworkin between "principles" and "rules," and with it the strict distinction between the roles of guidance and determination, has been heavily attacked in jurisprudential literature, on the grounds that they are matters of degree rather than quality.

Bernard S. Jackson, *Modern Research in Jewish Law: Some Theoretical Issues,* in *Modern Research in Jewish Law* 136, 153 (Bernard S. Jackson ed., 1980) (citations omitted).

In Jewish law, monetary laws generally provide guidance, while ritual laws generally dictate outcomes. In a sense, however, this distinction is largely one of degree, as even ritual laws often require further interpretation. Yet, on a fundamental level, the distinction is one of quality, as ritual law is not only more specific and concrete, but leaves relatively little room for judicial discretion. As the sixteenth century scholar Rabbi Judah Loew of Prague (Maharal) put it:

> The monetary laws and . . . the ritual laws are distinct from one another . . . [and] with regard to the monetary laws, it is necessary to understand the [logical] source of the law . . . which depends on a logical understanding of the basis of the law . . . a logic that is not written in the Torah. Those monetary laws which are written in the Torah are only the basic rules of law, but not every dealing between individuals is written in the Torah.

Maharal, *Derekh Hachayim* 21. See also Shimon Shkop, *Sha'arei Yosher* 5:1.

Greenawalt's analysis of "abstract and specific purposes" of directives also appears to be relevant to this discussion. Greenawalt, supra note 62.

122 See Exodus 21:28-36, 22:4-5.

123 See id. at 21:33.

124 See id. at 21:35.

field.[125] The Torah also lists the various forms of compensation appropriate in each of these cases. These scenarios, which are clearly broad examples rather than a comprehensive list, require much interpretation.

Any student of the law will recognize that there are numerous issues that must be resolved to arrive at even a basic framework for adjudicating cases covered by these principles. The Talmud engages in interpretation of many of the conceptual principles that can be gleaned from these examples, and through a combination of textual hermeneutics and logical analysis arrives at certain concrete laws. A look at even a few of these issues reveals certain parallels to issues common in American tort law. The Talmud's discussion of damages caused by an animal addresses, for example, such issues as the duty of care imposed on owners of specific animals and how far the duty extends.[126] The Talmud expands the scenario of digging of a pit to include scenarios involving people who place various obstacles in a public place.[127] Regarding the fire scenario, the Talmud discusses questions of causation.[128] In addition, the Talmud contains an extensive analysis of systems of compensation for each kind of tort.[129] Finally, in the real world, there is an endless variety of complex fact patterns in which the general legal principles must be applied; the Talmud is filled with discussions of many such cases.[130]

Because the Talmudic discussions are intended to apply the principles found in the text of the Torah, there are certain constraints on the discretion available to interpreters. Specifically, both the legal analysis and the conclusions of law must fit broadly within the framework set by the text. Yet, within this framework there is much room for human logic to decide such concrete issues as what standard of care should be required with respect to specific animals. Conclusions in such matters are possible only through identifying the conceptual principles underlying the textual laws and applying them to the myriad of scenarios not present in the text. In contrast to *mitzvot*, which are often interpreted without the need to examine conceptual bases underlying the rituals, tort law can be applied only through consideration of the conceptual principles behind the generally stated rules.

Another example of the Torah's monetary laws is the law of bailments. The Torah provides general principles for bailments, listing different categories of

---

125 See id. at 22:6.
126 See generally Talmud Bavli, Bava Kama, chs. 1-6.
127 See id. at ch. 3.
128 See, e.g., id. at 22a-24a.
129 See generally Talmud Bavli, Bava Kama.
130 See generally id.

bailments and the corresponding duties of care required. The first scenario listed in the Torah involves a bailee who is liable if the goods are lost or destroyed as a result of the bailee's "negligence," but not if the goods are "stolen." The Talmud interprets this scenario as referring to a gratuitous bailee. In the Torah's second scenario, the bailee is liable for stolen goods as well, but not in a case of duress. This scenario, according to the Talmud, refers to a bailment for hire or a rental agreement. In the final scenario, the Torah states that a person who borrows an object is liable even in the case of duress.[131]

Again, the Talmud engages in extensive interpretation in order to apply these general principles to more concrete situations. There are many basic variables that arise within each of the Torah's scenarios, such as the nature and quantity of the goods. The text contains terms, such as "negligence" and "duress," whose definitions will depend in part on these variables. Arriving at definitions may involve a degree of textual analysis, but will depend largely on rational conceptions of fairness and justice.[132]

Moreover, unlike the *mitzvot*—which are definite and permanent reflections of divine will and logic, not subject to human modification—the Torah's monetary laws are essentially guidelines, such that, in addition to being defined, in large part, on the basis of human logic, they also can be modified by human choice. Ritual areas are considered to be in God's province; *mitzvot* are statements of what actions and activities must or must not be performed. While many of the *mitzvot* relate to the way a person treats others, the duty to perform the *mitzvot* is ultimately a duty to God. Therefore, it is outside human discretion to relieve a person of such a duty. Monetary issues, in contrast, are subject to human convention. Therefore, the Talmud states, individuals have broad discretion over monetary matters.[133]

---

131 See Exodus 22:6-14; see also Talmud Bavli, Bava Metzia chs. 3, 7, 8.

132 In addition, the definition of "negligence" or "duress" is largely measured by the prevailing standard of care, which may vary according to time and place. Thus, interpretation of these principles usually follows Cardozo's prescription:

> [W]e look to custom . . . for the tests and standards that are to determine how established rules shall be applied. . . . The master in the discharge of his duty to protect the servant against harm must exercise the degree of care that is commonly exercised in like circumstances by men of ordinary prudence. The triers of the facts in determining whether that standard has been attained, must consult the habits of life, the everyday beliefs and practices, of the men and women about them.

Benjamin N. Cardozo, *The Nature of the Judicial Process* 60, 63 (1921).

133 See, e.g., Talmud Bavli, Bava Metzia 84a. The difference between ritual and monetary obligation is roughly similar to the difference between criminal and civil liability. A guilty

For example, a creditor has the discretion to forgive a debt, even if that debt is mandated by the Torah.[134] Similarly, if a person sustains damages to self or to property because of a pit that has been dug in a public place, the Torah states that the person who dug the pit is liable;[135] yet, the victim has the discretion to forgive the debt.[136] Likewise, individuals have discretion to place conditions on activities relating to monetary matters. In the case of the gratuitous bailment, according to the Torah's guidelines, the bailee is liable if the goods are lost or destroyed as a result of the bailee's negligence, but not if the goods are stolen. The bailee and bailor have discretion, however, to contractually agree that the bailee will be liable if the goods are stolen as well.[137]

In contrast, in ritual areas, individuals do not have the same discretion in relation to the performance of the dictates of the Torah. For example, the Torah's prescription for divorce proceedings includes the requirement that a husband give his wife a *get*, or writ of divorce.[138] As a ritual matter, the wife may not marry again until she has received a *get*; her duty not to remarry without obtaining a *get* is owed not to her husband, but to God. Therefore, the husband does not have control over the ritualistic mechanics of a *get*. The husband may

---

criminal defendant has committed a crime against the People of the State. Therefore, it is the People of the State, and not the individual victim of the crime, who prosecute the criminal defendant. While the victim may often be in a position to prevent criminal prosecution by refusing to testify, the ultimate decision of whether to prosecute a defendant is in the discretion of the prosecutor, as the representative of the People. The victim may not "forgive" the crime; it was committed against the People as a whole, not against the victim on a personal level. Similarly, ritual obligations, though they may manifest themselves in actions conducted toward other people, are ultimately obligations toward G-d.

By contrast, a victim of a tort may forgive civil obligation. The State has an interest in the satisfaction of civil liability, and failure to pay the damage award may result in criminal prosecution by the State, but if the plaintiff forgives the liability, the State has no grounds to prosecute. In Jewish law, if a defendant fails to fulfill a monetary obligation, the defendant thereby violates ritual prohibitions, such as those against stealing or withholding wages. If the plaintiff forgives the obligation, however, there are no grounds for a violation of ritual law.

Similarly, adjudication of questions of monetary law will often determine whether there is a violation of ritual law. As the twentieth century scholar Rabbi Shimon Shkop observed, "The law against stealing prohibits taking something that, according to monetary law, belongs to someone else; the law against withholding a worker's wages refers to that which must be paid according to monetary law." Shkop, supra note 121, at 5:1.

134 See, e.g., Maimonides, Code of Law, supra note 17, at Laws of Sales 5:11.

135 See Exodus 21:33-34.

136 See, e.g., Maimonides, Code of Law, supra note 17, at Laws of Sales 5:11.

137 See Talmud Bavli, Bava Metzia 84a.

138 See Deuteronomy 24:1.

not "forgive" the requirement of a *get* by allowing his wife to remarry without obtaining a *get* from him.

Similarly, a condition may not be placed on the ritual characteristics of a *get*. Therefore, a husband could not give his wife a *get* with the stipulation that she may not marry a particular man. Even if she were to agree to such a stipulation, the *get* would not be valid. This is because the ritual law defines a *get* as permitting a woman to marry whomever she wants;[139] it is not within the province of a particular husband and wife to change the ritual function of a *get*. In the same way, a person does not have discretion to decide to eat a smaller quantity of *matzo* than the amount required by the Torah.

It should be noted, however, that ritual areas sometimes have monetary characteristics as well, which may be subject to conditions. In the case of the *get*, for example, the mechanics of conveying the physical *get* are based on monetary principles. Although a husband may be compelled under certain circumstances to give his wife a *get*, ritual law does not dictate the details of the monetary aspect of the conveyance of a *get*. Therefore, a husband may place certain conditions on the conveyance of the *get*. In fact, the Talmud records that in the time of King David, before going to battle, husbands would present their wives with a *get*, subject to their not returning from battle within a stated period of time.[140] This would prevent the possibility of a wife becoming an *agunah*, a woman prohibited from remarrying because she does not know if her husband is still alive.[141]

---

139 See Talmud Bavli, Gittin 81a-81b. Cf. Asher Weiss, *Minchas Asher, Vayikra* 22 (2017).

140 See Talmud Bavli, Kethuboth 9b.

141 The distinction between monetary and ritual law is important in applying the Talmudic rule *dina de-malkhuta dina*—the law of the land is the law. Under Jewish law, the secular law of a valid government is binding, to the extent that it relates to monetary law. The law of the land does not have authority, however, to contradict ritual law. See Elon, supra note 16, at 132-37; Rabbi Hershel Schachter, *"Dina de-malkhuta Dina": Secular Law as a Religious Obligation*, 1 J. Halacha & Contemp. Soc'y 103 (1981).

The rule that a secular law has the authority to regulate only monetary issues complicates the drafting of *get* laws, which are designed to insure that a husband will grant a *get* to his wife if the couple undergoes a civil divorce. Under Jewish law, without obtaining a *get*, the woman may not remarry. See Deuteronomy 24:1-2; Talmud Bavli, Kiddushin 2a. Statutes must be drafted carefully to affect only the monetary aspects of the conveyance of a *get*, not the ritual laws involved. Similar restrictions apply to prenuptial agreements, through which a future husband agrees to certain terms to insure that, in the event of divorce, he will provide his future wife with a *get*. As noted above, a husband and wife may agree to conditions on the monetary aspects relating to the conveyance of the *get*, but not to conditions affecting the ritual validity of the *get*. For a discussion of the legal and religious issues relating to *get* laws, see generally Irving A. Breitowitz, *Between Civil and Religious Law: The*

Finally, monetary laws are considered to be with in the province of humans to such an extent that they are often developed independent of any text. Instead, legal authorities may rely entirely on human custom and convention,[142] establishing the laws largely on the basis of observing business practices and human nature. The details of how best to form a legal structure to manage these human practices are totally within the discretion of human authorities, subject only to the Torah's general commands for justice and fairness.[143]

PART THREE | AUTHORITY IN INTERPRETATION

In one sense, Jewish law does not recognize the inherent authority of a particular individual or body to interpret the law. Because the source of Jewish law is the Torah, which represents the revealed will of God, legal interpretation is a discipline aimed at discovering God's will in issues and cases for which the Torah has not provided comprehensive details. Even in monetary matters, and even in those areas of monetary law based largely on human custom and behavior, the goal of an interpreter is to arrive at a result that would best achieve divine justice, in accordance with divine will. This element of religious morality, so central to Jewish law, may suggest that there should not be a notion of interpretive authority in Jewish law. As Joseph Raz has written, "[m]orality is not based on authority."[144]

As indicated by its very title, however, Jewish law is not simply a "religiously based system[ ] of moral theorizing."[145] Jewish law consists of a detailed legal

---

Plight of the Agunah in American Society (1993), and Irving A. Breitowitz, *The Plight of the Agunah: A Study in Halacha, Contract, and the First Amendment*, 51 Md. L. Rev. 312 (1992).

142 See Chajes, supra note 27, at 312-13; Shkop, supra note 121, at 5:1; Weiss, supra note 42, at 186-88.

143 Cf. Cardozo, supra note 132, at 62-63 ("General standards of right and duty are established. Custom must determine whether there has been adherence or departure. . . . Innumerable . . . are the cases where the course of dealing to be followed is defined by the customs, or, more properly speaking, the usages of a particular trade or market or profession.") (citation omitted).

As a nineteenth century scholar noted, the Torah allows judges to interpret most laws of monetary litigation according to their own judgment, subject only to a single general rule that "you shall judge your fellow with justice." Israel Lifschitz, *Commentary to Bava Bathra*, in *Tifereth Yisrael* 10:8 (citing Leviticus 19:15).

144 Joseph Raz, *Why Interpret?*, 9 Ratio Juris 349 (1996).

145 Charles Fried, *The Artificial Reason of the Law or: What Lawyers Know*, 60 Tex. L. Rev. 35, 58 (1981). As Fried characterized it,

the closest moral philosophy has come to the forms and methods peculiar to law has been some religiously based systems of moral theorizing, such as

system, regulating both public and private life, to a far greater extent than would be acceptable in American law. In short, Jewish law presents at least guidelines for virtually every aspect of societal and personal behavior. As a practical matter, then, there is a definite need for an authoritative interpretation of the law to determine how society should function.

The tension between Jewish law's emphasis on the search for "Truth," or God's will, and the need to adapt the theoretical law to the practical needs of a functioning society, expresses itself in some of the principles relating to authority in Jewish law. The tension, in fact, is grounded in the interpretation of the following passage in the Torah: "[W]hen there is a matter of law that you are unable to decide . . . you will go up to the place that God will choose. And you will approach the . . . judge who will be in those days and you will inquire, and [he] will tell you the law. And you will act according to that which [he] tell[s] you."[146] Based on the presumption against superfluity, the Talmud asks why the Torah adds the phrase "who will be in those days" in reference to the judge who is to be approached. Indeed, the Talmud asks rhetorically whether it would be possible for a person living in a certain generation to approach any judge other than one who lives in "those days." As the Talmud explains, the verses teach that a person should recognize that the judges of each generation are entrusted with the responsibility and authority to interpret and apply the law.[147] Thus, even if the courts in a certain generation do not appear to be of the same caliber as those of another generation, each court must rely on its own interpretation of the law.[148] Accordingly, because legal conclusions must be based on an understanding of truth, a court need not accept another court's interpretation as inherently authoritative.

Maimonides codified this principle in his Code of Law. He wrote that if one court arrives at a legal ruling based on a certain line of reasoning, a later court has the discretion to adjudicate the same issue differently, based on its

---

the Talmudic or Thomistic. . . . Where they assume the function of public judgment with public—sometimes even coercive—consequences . . . they begin to display the very characteristics that I ascribe to law. Indeed, they become just specialized systems of law.

Id. Though Judge Fried ultimately recognizes a Talmudic "system of law," it seems odd that he appears reluctant to do so, stating only that the Talmudic system sometimes "begin[s] to display the . . . characteristics" of law.

146 Deuteronomy 17:8-10.

147 See Talmud Bavli, Rosh ha-Shana 25b.

148 See id., especially the Tosafoth commentary.

own reasoning.[149] As a source, Maimonides cited the biblical phrase "to the judge who will be in those days" and commented that "you are required to approach only the court in your day."[150]

Yet, while granting a court discretion to disagree with the ruling of an earlier court, the Torah also limits the discretion of an individual judge to disagree with the court's ruling. The Torah states that the court's ruling is authoritative: "according to the teaching which they instruct you and according to the law which they tell you, you will act; do not veer from that which they tell you, to the right or to the left."[151] In fact, the Torah prohibits rulings that contradict the court's ruling.[152] The Talmud explains that this law was required to maintain unity in the nation.[153]

Maimonides codified these laws as well, in a discussion of the judicial structure and the method of adjudicating questions of interpretation in Jewish law.[154] In its ideal state, the judiciary of the Jewish legal system consists of a hierarchy of courts, which includes lower courts, higher courts, and the High Court, the Sanhedrin.[155] The difference in judicial function is based primarily on jurisdiction.[156] Unlike the American judicial system, ordinarily there is no formal process to appeal a lower court decision to a higher court.[157] Instead, certain matters are in the exclusive jurisdiction of the lower courts, while other matters are in the jurisdiction of the higher courts.[158]

The Sanhedrin, in this system, had a unique status. In addition to having original jurisdiction over issues carrying a certain level of importance, the Sanhedrin was the final arbiter of all questions of law.[159] When a question arose that could not be answered by a lower court, the question was then referred to a higher court.[160] If the higher court could not arrive at a decision—"a matter of law that you are unable to decide"—then the question was presented to the Sanhedrin for a decision.[161] The decision reached by the majority of the

---

149 See Maimonides, Code of Law, supra note 17, at Laws of *Mamrim* 2:1 (quoting Deuteronomy 17:8-10).
150 Id.
151 Deuteronomy 17:11.
152 See id. at 17:12.
153 See Talmud Bavli, Sanhedrin 88b.
154 See Maimonides, Code of Law, supra note 17, at Laws of *Sanhedrin* chs. 1, 5.
155 See id.
156 See id.
157 See id. at 6:1-5.
158 See Maimonides, Code of Law, supra note 17, at Laws of *Sanhedrin* chs. 1, 5.
159 See id. at Laws of *Mamrim* 1:1.
160 See id. at 1:4.
161 Id.; see also Deuteronomy 17:8.

Sanhedrin was binding on the entire nation. Thus, as a practical matter, the Sanhedrin was the ultimate authority of legal interpretation.[162]

Another medieval scholar, Nachmanides, elaborated on the Talmud's rationale for the principle that the Sanhedrin's ruling is not subject to dispute.[163] Nachmanides explained that, in giving courts the authority to interpret the Written Torah, God knew that there would be disagreements.[164] Indeed, Nachmanides noted an intrinsic difference between legal reasoning and the logic employed in the exact sciences, such as engineering.[165] While it is possible, in the field of engineering, to prove demonstrably, with mathematical precision, that a particular theory is correct, legal reasoning often involves issues that can be resolved logically in more than one way. The role of a legal interpreter is to examine the evidence motivating each of the possible conclusions, and to determine which conclusion appears most accurate.[166]

---

162 See Maimonides, Code of Law, supra note 17, at Laws of *Mamrim* 1:1.

163 See Nachmanides, *Introduction to Commentary on Rif.*

164 See id.

165 See id.

166 See id. Cardozo similarly recognized that certain cases lend themselves to more than one viable interpretation, and that in these cases a judge must balance different considerations to arrive at a conclusion:

> It is with these cases that I have chiefly concerned myself in all that I have said to you. In a sense it is true of many of them that they may be decided either way. By that I mean that reasons plausible and fairly persuasive might be found for one conclusion as for another. Here come into play that balancing of judgment, that testing and sorting of considerations of analogy and logic and utility and fairness.

Cardozo, supra note 132, at 165-66. Professor Owen Fiss has similarly noted that interpretation is not an exact science: "[T]he meaning of a text does not reside in the text, as an object might reside in physical space or as an element might be said to be present in a chemical compound, ready to be extracted if only one knows the correct process." Owen M. Fiss, *Objectivity and Interpretation*, 34 Stan. L. Rev. 739, 744 (1982).

The imprecise nature of legal decision-making necessitates what Cardozo called "the serious business of a judge." Cardozo, supra note 132, at 21. Cardozo criticized those judges whose "notion of their duty is to match the colors of the case at hand against the colors of many sample cases spread out upon their desk," id. at 20, and wrote that, according to such a view, "[t]he man who had the best card index of cases would also be the wisest judge," id. at 21. According to Cardozo, judges must decide cases "when the colors do not match, when the references in the index fail, when there is no decisive precedent." Id.

A contemporary scholar of Jewish law, who is also a professor of American law, has updated Cardozo's observation in applying it to Jewish law. Rabbi J. David Bleich writes that effective decision-making in Jewish law "lies precisely in the ability to make judgment calls in evaluating citations, precedents, arguments, etc. It is not sufficient . . . to have a full command of

The possibility of numerous logical conclusions can be problematic. While in theory, proponents of each of these conclusions have a logical claim to a correct interpretation, in practice, there must be one rule of law for society to follow. If all logical conclusions are accepted as valid rulings, Nachmanides wrote, there will no longer be a single "Torah" for the nation to follow; instead, it will be replaced by "many Torahs."[167] To prevent this possibility, and to provide for a unified rule of law, God commanded that when there is indecision about an issue, the High Court functions as the ultimate and unifying decisor.[168]

The tension between legal interpreters' search for the truth and the need for a practical method of establishing the law is expressed perhaps most dramatically in a narrative in the Talmud that, for centuries, has received the attention of scholars of Jewish law, and, more recently, has been examined by a number of contemporary American legal scholars.[169] The Talmud refers to a dispute between Rabbi Eliezer and the majority of sages, during the course of which Rabbi Eliezer summoned a number of miraculous events as proof of his position, culminating in a heavenly voice declaring that his view was correct.[170] The sages responded by noting that, the heavenly voice notwithstanding, the

---

relevant sources. If so, in theory at least, the decisor par excellence would be a computer rather than a person." 4 J. David Bleich, *Contemporary Halakhic Problems* at ix (1995).

167 See 2 Nachmanides, supra note 106, at 423 (commenting on Deuteronomy 17:11).

168 See id.; cf. Fiss, supra note 166, at 747 ("[A] hierarchy of authority for resolving disputes that could potentially divide or destroy an interpretive community is one of the distinctive features of legal interpretation.").

In the poetic language of Robert Cover,

> It is the problem of the multiplicity of meaning . . . that leads at once to the imperial virtues and the imperial mode of world maintenance. . . . Let loose, unfettered, the worlds created would be unstable and sectarian in their social organization, dissociative and incoherent in their discourse, wary and violent in their interactions. The sober imperial mode of world maintenance holds the mirror of critical objectivity to meaning, [and] imposes the discipline of institutional justice upon norms . . . .

Robert M. Cover, "The Supreme Court, 1982 Term—Foreword: *Nomos* and Narrative," 97 Harv. L. Rev. 4, 16 (1983). Cover identified similar arguments in The Federalist for a national supreme court. See id. at 41.

169 Stone has referred to this narrative as "possibly the most frequently cited talmudic passage in modern literature." Stone, supra note 1, at 855. Stone's article focuses on Robert Cover's use of sources from Jewish law in many of his later pieces, including "*Nomos* and Narrative," which cites the aforementioned narrative in a footnote. See Cover, supra note 168, at 23 n.66.

170 See Talmud Bavli, Bava Metzia 59b.

Torah instructs that in adjudicating a matter, the majority view is followed.[171] The law is "not in heaven," but instead was given to humans to determine.[172] Therefore, the law was interpreted according to the view of the majority of sages, against the view of Rabbi Eliezer.

This narrative has been analyzed in numerous ways, but on a basic level, the narrative serves as an illustration of the tension between searching for truth and following conventions of decision-making. If the heavenly voice is viewed as reflecting the divine "opinion" regarding the dispute, then Rabbi Eliezer was the one who seems to have accurately interpreted the divine will. Indeed, as Rabbenu Nissim Gerondi (Ran), a medieval legal authority, explained, the sages acknowledged that Rabbi Eliezer's opinion was "closer to the truth."[173] Yet, they followed the majority opinion.[174] As Ran further explained, "the determination of the law was entrusted to the sages of each generation," regardless of whether their determination is consistent with the "truth."[175]

---

171 See id. (analyzing Exodus 23:2).

172 Id.; see also Deuteronomy 30:12. Fiss has used similar imagery, stating that "to search for the brooding omnipresence in the sky [...] is to create a false issue." Fiss, supra note 166, at 746 (citation omitted). Fiss attributes this imagery to Justice Holmes, who wrote that "[t]he common law is, not a brooding omnipresence in the sky, but the articulate voice of some sovereign." *Southern Pacific Co. v. Jensen*, 244 U.S. 205, 222 (1916) (Holmes, J., dissenting), quoted in Fiss, supra note 166, at 746 n.15.

173 Ran, *Derashot* 112 (Leon A. Feldman ed., 1973).

174 See id. (citing Talmud Bavli, Bava Metzia, 59b).

175 Id. The process of arriving at an authoritative conclusion in Jewish law thus depends on what is termed, in contemporary American legal scholarship, an "interpretive community." See Stanley Fish, *Is There a Text in This Class?* (1980); Fiss, supra note 166. To a certain degree, then, Fiss's observations that "[j]udicial interpretations are binding, whether or not they are correct," id. at 755, and that "[a]n interpretation is binding even if [it is] mistaken," id. at 758, are applicable to Jewish law. Yet, it appears more accurate to say that in Jewish law, there may exist more than one correct "truth." See generally Michael Rosensweig, *Eilu ve-Eilu Divrei Elokim Hayyim: Halakhic Pluralism and Theories of Controversy*, in *Rabbinic Authority and Personal Autonomy* 93 (Moshe Sokol ed., 1992).

Fiss made his observations in the context of depicting legal reasoning as a system of "bounded objectivity" rather than of "nihilism." Fiss, supra note 166, at 745-46. In a similar vein, Rabbi Rosensweig has written that

[P]luralism is not a blank check. There are objective limitations to a sincere interpretation of sources.... [M]ost ... debates [in Jewish law] revolve around details and the application of principles, not the principles themselves.... R. Moshe Feinstein in the introduction to his [*Responsa*] cautions about the need for *yirat shamayim* (fear of [G-d], i.e., piety) and intellectual rigor to insure valid conclusions.

Rosensweig, supra, at 120.

This narrative need not suggest, however, that the majority opinion was in some sense "false." As Nachmanides noted, legal reasoning can result in more than one logically viable solution.[176] This principle is illustrated by another Talmudic passage, which recognizes the possibility of a rejected, yet viable, legal opinion. The Talmud records a number of disputes between two schools, the School of Hillel and the School of Shamai. The Talmud follows the opinions of the School of Hillel, which represented the majority view, yet the Talmud states that "these and these are both the words of the Living God."[177] Thus, according to the Talmud, when there is a dispute in Jewish legal interpretation between two logical points of view, both opinions may be authentic reflections of divine will.[178]

Rabbi Feinstein's focus on piety as a component of legal decision-making reflects a common theme in Jewish law, dating back to the Talmud. Rabbi Feinstein emphasized the level of care central to the exercise of legal interpretation, based in the recognition that such decisions are religiously binding on others, thereby representing an articulation of divine will. Although American law does not contain this aspect of divinity, interpretation of American law is similarly binding. Thus, Fiss has suggested that "the authoritative quality of legal interpretation . . . creates a strong critical environment; it provides unusually strong incentives to criticize and defend the correctness of the interpretation. Something practical and important turns on judicial interpretations. They are binding." Fiss, supra note 166, at 757.

176 See supra text accompanying notes 163-66.

177 Talmud Bavli, Eruvin 13b. This concept is somewhat similar to Cover's view, regarding *Bob Jones University v. United States*, 461 U.S. 574 (1983), that "within the domain of constitutional meaning, the understanding of the Mennonites assumes a status equal (or superior) to that accorded to the understanding of the Justices of the Supreme Court." Cover, supra note 168, at 28.

178 Cover similarly wrote of "a multiplicity of coherent systems" and of "interpretive efforts or traditions, each of which is independently defensible, or even 'right.'" Cover, supra note 168, at 17 n.45.

In Jewish law, there is an important difference, in practice, between a view that is viable and "true" but rejected, and one that is inherently "false." Although the interpretation of the Sanhedrin is binding on all judges, as a result of persecution and exile there has not always been a functioning Sanhedrin, even in Talmudic times. When there is no Sanhedrin, the majority interpretation is followed by most of the Nation, but those who are qualified to offer their own opinion on the matter may follow that opinion. Thus, the Talmud states that despite the majority's rejection of their views, in matters that were not determined by a Sanhedrin, both the School of Shamai and Rabbi Eliezer—as well as those who fell under their jurisdiction—followed their own views. See Elchanan Wasserman, *Kuntrus Divre Soferim*, in 2 *Kobetz Shiurim* 112 (Elazar Wasserman ed., 4th ed. 1989).

In this sense, it may be said, using Cover's terms, that Jewish law "acknowledge[s] the nomic integrity of each of the communities that have generated principles and precepts. . . . [E]ach 'community of interpretation' that has achieved 'law' has its own *nomos*." Cover, supra note 168, at 42.

Additionally, even when an opinion is rejected by a Sanhedrin, it still may have future value if it is a viable interpretation. As noted above, a later Sanhedrin has the authority to

Similarly, the opinion of the sages who disagreed with Rabbi Eliezer was a viable legal position, and thus an authentic expression of divine will, which was followed because it was held by the majority. The fact that Rabbi Eliezer's opinion was "closer to the truth" does not invalidate the sages' opinion. In deciding an unclear law, human interpreters may strive to attain the view closest to the truth, but may not rely on heavenly assistance. Instead, they must follow the dictates of human logic.[179] If more than one view appears logical, although they are both potentially viable solutions, to attain a unified legal system, legal authorities follow the Torah's instruction to accept the majority view.[180]

PART FOUR | PRECEDENT

A final issue related to Jewish legal interpretation involves the question of precedent in Jewish law. In those areas of law that rely on definitive revelation rather than human interpretation,[181] the "interpretation" of the Torah has immutable

---

disagree with the interpretation of an earlier Sanhedrin. See supra note 26. Thus, a later Sanhedrin may endorse as correct an interpretation that had previously been rejected.

Cf. Gerald Graff, *"Keep off the Grass," "Drop Dead," and Other Indeterminacies: A Response to Sanford Levinson*, 60 Tex. L. Rev. 405, 410 (1982) ("[T]he practice of interpretation doesn't depend on interpreters' possessing godlike powers to arrive at an 'ultimately provable right answer' that closes the books on further argument about the meaning of a text. Therefore the lack of such godlike power doesn't entail indeterminacy.").

179 Elaborating on Ran's analysis above, the eighteenth century scholar Rabbi Aryeh Leb Heller wrote that the Torah is properly interpreted according to human logic, and that an interpretation is considered "true" if determined to be so through human reasoning. Aryeh Leb Heller, *Introduction to Ketzot Hachoshen*.

180 In fact, some medieval legal authorities such as Ritva have explained that as part of the revelation to Moses, God provided for the existence of different, yet viable, interpretations. See Ritva, *Commentary to the Talmud*, Eruvin 13b. As noted above, together with the Written Law, certain details of laws were revealed orally to Moses at Sinai, while other laws were left open to interpretation. See supra notes 17-19 and accompanying text. Ritva suggested that Moses was told that many of these laws have more than one viable interpretation, and that each generation must interpret these laws for itself, according to its own reasoning. See Ritva, supra, at Eruvin 13b; see also Talmud Yerushalmi, Sanhedrin 4:2.

Alternatively, it is possible to understand the Talmudic narrative as suggesting that, on a level of divine logic, Rabbi Eliezer's opinion was indeed "true" and the opinion of the sages was "false." This appears to be the view of Ran and Rabbi Feinstein, who write that, at times, a binding decision may be in conflict with a transcendental "truth." Nevertheless, human logic is followed, as it produces a "practical truth," regardless of any theoretical or divine "truth." The analysis in note 178, supra, applies in this conceptual framework as well, as there may be more than one correct "practical truth," even if there is a single transcendental "truth."

181 See supra text accompanying notes 27-58.

divine authority. In instances of actual interpretation of the law, however, just as the search for truth ideally does not respect a specific interpreter as inherently authoritative, there should be no reliance on precedent in an effort to arrive at the truth. Moreover, there would not seem to be a practical need to accept precedent, even to the extent that society must accept one particular interpretive view out of many viable opinions. Indeed, Maimonides allows—and requires—each generation to interpret the law through its own reasoning.[182]

Authorities in Jewish law observed, however, that in the Talmud, legal authorities who lived after the compilation of the Mishna did not dispute the rulings of those who lived before them.[183] According to the principle articulated by Maimonides, the later authorities should have had discretion to offer their own views on matters of legal interpretation. Apparently, although perhaps not strictly bound by precedent, the later authorities nevertheless accepted as binding upon themselves the decisions of the earlier authorities. Similarly, when the Talmud was compiled, later authorities accepted as binding the legal decisions found in it.[184] In practice, then, the laws of the Mishna and the Talmud gained the immutable authority that had previously applied only to the revealed law.

There are a number of possible motivations for this commitment to precedent on the part of later authorities. For example, these authorities may have adopted the position that the preceding generations were more likely to accurately interpret the Torah. Such a view may have been based in the practical recognition that those closer in time to the revelation at Sinai are likely to have a better understanding of the meaning of the law. A more mystical or religious-based version of this argument posits that, since the revelation, there has been a gradual diminishing of the spiritual nature of humanity; as earlier generations are spiritually superior, so is their interpretation of religious law.

Alternatively, just as the need arises for Restatements in American law to unify the common law, there may have been a sense, at certain point in time,

---

182 See Zerah Warhaftig, *Precedent in Jewish Law*, 6-7 Shenaton Ha-Mishpat Ha-Ivri 105 (1979-80).

183 See Joseph Karo, *Kesef Mishna*, on Maimonides, Laws of *Mamrim* 2:1.

184 See id.; Hershel Schachter, *Ginas Egoz* 157-58 (2007); Hershel Schachter, *B'Ikvei ha-Tzon* 243-44 (1997); Joseph B. Soloveitchik, *Two Types of Tradition*, in 1 *Sheurim L'Zekher Abba Mori Z"L* 241-61 (2002); Yitzchak Zeev ha-Levi Soloveitchik, *Chidushei Maran Ri'z ha-Levi al ha-Torah* 116-17 (2003) (commenting on Ruth 4:6); Wasserman, 1 *Kobetz Shiurim*, supra note 178, at 335-36; Elchanan Wasserman, *Kobetz He'aroth* 115 (Elazar Wasserman ed., 2003); Weiss, supra note 42, at 180-82. Some have suggested additional points in history at which it appears that legal authorities accepted, as strongly persuasive precedent, the opinions of those who preceded them. See Kaplan, supra note 17, at 237-41.

that the developing law should be uniformly codified. While a Restatement does not have the authority of the Mishna or the Talmud, it is significant that each of these redactions of Jewish law reflected hundreds of years of legal development. Perhaps at some point in the future of American legal history, there will be a similar call for a binding codification of interpreted law.

CONCLUSION

The Jewish legal system has evolved over thousands of years, developing in a variety of settings, ranging from Mount Sinai to the Land of Israel in the period of the Temples to contemporary countries around the world. Many laws were clearly defined at the revelation at Sinai, or required a limited amount of interpretation and are now largely unchanging. Other laws depend, to varying degrees, on the customs of society, and thus are continuously reinterpreted, as fundamental principles are applied to changing situations. Finally, even those laws that appear to be well-defined often require interpretation in order to be applied, due to unanticipated scenarios involving new technology or the unavailability of materials ordinarily essential for fulfillment of the law.

There is currently no Sanhedrin to decide questions of Jewish law. Nor is it always clear which interpretive position represents the majority view. As a result, contemporary authorities in Jewish law possess a wide range of autonomy.[185] Rabbi Moshe Feinstein, who was generally regarded as the preeminent authority on Jewish law in the latter half of the twentieth century, stated unequivocally that a legal decisor is not only permitted, but required, to interpret the law independently.[186] Citing the Talmud, he noted that "a judge must rely on his own judgment" and is prohibited from accepting a ruling that he considers to be incorrect.[187]

With this increased autonomy comes increased responsibility. When a new question arises, contemporary authorities cannot rely on a high court to decide the issue. Moreover, emerging technology increasingly presents legal authorities with issues for which there is no clear precedent. The role of the interpreter of Jewish law is to apply the laws and methods that have come before, to decide new issues in an effort to conform as closely as possible to the will of God.

---

185 See Maimonides, Code of Law, supra note 17, at Laws of *Mamrim* 1:4-5.
186 See Moshe Feinstein, *Igroth Moshe*, III Yore Deah 88 (citing Talmud Bavli, Bava Bathra 130b).
187 Id.

CHAPTER 4

An Introduction to Legislation in Jewish Law, with References to the American Legal System

INTRODUCTION

The separation of powers among different branches of government stands as one of the fundamental institutions of the American legal system. The Constitution vests in Congress "[a]ll legislative Powers,"[1] in the President "[t]he executive Power,"[2] and in federal courts "[t]he judicial Power."[3] Thus, for example, in the landmark 1997 case, *Boerne v. Flores*,[4] the United States Supreme Court affirmed the vital nature of the separation of powers by striking down, as a violation of this doctrine, the Religious Freedom Restoration Act.[5]

Nevertheless, it would be inaccurate to suggest that courts do not serve a legislative function. In addition to the central role courts play in the legislative process, through interpreting statutes and through the power of judicial review,[6] it is not uncommon for judges to legislate from the bench.[7]

---

1 U.S. Const. art. I, § 1.
2 U.S. Const. art. II, § 1, cl. 1.
3 U.S. Const. art. III, § 1.
4 521 U.S. 507 (1997).
5 The Religious Freedom Restoration Act, 42 U.S.C. § 2000bb (1993), was enacted by Congress in response the Supreme Court's decision in *Employment Division v. Smith*, 494 U.S. 872 (1990).
6 See *Marbury v. Madison*, 5 U.S. (1 Cranch) 137, 177 (1803).
7 See, e.g., Benjamin N. Cardozo, *The Nature of the Judicial Process* 113 (1921) ("If you ask me how [the judge] is to know when one interest outweighs another, I can only answer that he must get his knowledge just as the legislator gets it, from experience and study and reflection; in brief, from life itself."). Judge Richard Posner has written that Cardozo thus

Indeed, it is somewhat ironic that the same Court term that produced the *Boerne* decision, emphasizing the exclusive power of the courts to adjudicate the law, saw the emergence of what *New York Times* reporter Linda Greenhouse called "a striking amount of . . . judicial legislating."[8] In fact, according to Greenhouse, even those who publicly decry judicial legislating have come to view it as part of a "tacitly understood and widely accepted reality."[9]

This chapter examines the roles of legislative and judicial bodies, in the context of a discussion of broader principles of legislation in the Jewish legal system.[10] Indeed, the Jewish legal system provides a particularly illuminating contrast to the American legal system, in part because in Jewish law, the same authority—the Sanhedrin, or High Court—serves in both a legislative and judicial capacity. Interestingly, though, as a result of the express license for the same authority in Jewish law to serve two separate functions, the two functions are rather clearly delineated, each bounded by specific rules and regulations. Thus, an analysis of the legislative function of the Sanhedrin may shed light on an analysis of the proper legislative function of American courts.

Part one of the chapter describes the different categories of legislation in Jewish law, exploring the distinction between divine legislation, found in the Torah, and rabbinic legislation, enacted by human authorities. Part two discusses the sources for and scope of rabbinic legislative authority. Part three of the chapter examines the issue of interpreting legislation over time, when circumstances may have changed since the enactment of the legislation. The chapter concludes with the hope that this project, building on the increased interest in Jewish law among American legal scholars, will further demonstrate the relevance of Jewish law to the study of American law.

"appears to license uncanalized judicial discretion." Richard A. Posner, *Cardozo: A Study in Reputation* 29-30 (1990).

8 Linda Greenhouse, *Sure Justices Legislate: They Have To*, N.Y. Times, July 5, 1998, § 4, at 1.

9 Id.

10 In recent years, American legal scholars have increasingly looked to the Jewish legal model as an alternative legal system that considers many issues present in American law. See, e.g., Chapter 3 in this Volume; Suzanne Last Stone, *In Pursuit of the Counter-Text: The Turn to the Jewish Legal Model in Contemporary American Legal Theory*, 106 Harv. L. Rev. 813, 817-19 nn.14-28 (1993).

PART ONE | CATEGORIES OF LEGISLATION

A. The Torah

Professor Menachem Elon aptly described the "one basic norm and one single supreme value" in Jewish law: "the command of God as embodied in the Torah given to Moses at Sinai."[11] In his Code of Law, the medieval scholar Maimonides explains that the commandments in the Torah are eternally binding and not subject to abrogation.[12] Indeed, in his discussion of thirteen fundamental principles of Judaism, Maimonides repeatedly emphasizes the immutable authority of the laws in the Five Books of Moses.[13] Therefore, in categorizing legislation in Jewish law, Professor Elon has observed that the Torah is "the supreme legislation of the Jewish legal system. It is the written 'constitution' of Jewish law, having its ultimate source in divine revelation.... [A]ll legislation promulgated after the revelation of the supreme legislation has been subordinate."[14]

Though divine in origin, the Torah requires human interpretation to be understood and applied as a legal text. To facilitate such interpretation, God revealed to Moses at Sinai, together with the Written Torah, an Oral Torah,[15] consisting of revealed interpretations of certain laws as well as hermeneutic rules to be used by legal authorities to derive further interpretations.[16] Both the written text of the Torah and the interpretations carry the authority of supreme legislation, incorporated in the term *d'oraita*, a Talmudic adjective form of the

---

11 Menachem Elon, *Jewish Law: History, Sources, Principles* 233 (Bernard Auerbach & Melvin J. Sykes trans., 1994) [hereinafter Elon, *Jewish Law*]. A number of works in English provide a general introduction to the history, structure, and methodology of the Jewish legal system. See generally, e.g., Chapter 3 in this Volume; Irving A. Breitowitz, *Between Civil Law and Religious Law: The Plight of the Agunah in American Society* 307-13 (1993); Elon, *Jewish Law*, supra, at 228-39, 281-399; Menachem Elon, *The Legal System of Jewish Law*, 17 N.Y.U. J. Int'l L. & Pol. 221 (1985); David M. Feldman, *Birth Control in Jewish Law: Marital Relations, Contraception and Abortion* 3-18 (1968); Aaron Kirschenbaum, *Equity in Jewish Law: Halakhic Perspectives in Law: Formalism and Flexibility in Jewish Civil Law* 289-304 (1991); Nahum Rakover, *A Guide to the Sources of Jewish Law* (1994).

12 See Maimonides, Mishne Torah [hereinafter, Maimonides, Code of Law], Laws of *Yesodei Ha-Torah* 9:1 (citing Leviticus 23:14; Deuteronomy 13:1, 29:28, 30:12); Laws of *Mamrim* 2:9.

13 See Maimonides, *Introduction to Perek Chelek*, in *Introductions to Commentary on the Mishna* 107, 139-47 (Mordechai Rabinowitz, ed., 1961) [hereinafter Maimonides, *Perek Chelek*].

14 Elon, *Jewish Law*, supra note 11, at 479, 481.

15 See Chapter 3 in this Volume.

16 For a discussion of different sources and methods of interpretation in Jewish law, see id.

Aramaic translation of "Torah."[17] Unlike the revealed text and interpretations, however, laws derived through human interpretation are subject to dispute and reversal by later legal authorities.[18] In fact, one of the principal functions of the Sanhedrin in each generation was to serve as the ultimate arbiter of the law through its own interpretation of the Torah.[19]

B. Rabbinic Legislation

Although the laws in the Torah can be described as "legislation," because those laws are divinely mandated and therefore not subject to legislative modification, an analysis of legislative principles in Jewish law might instead focus on rabbinic legislation.[20] Aside from its adjudicatory function, the Sanhedrin served in a legislative capacity. Legislation enacted by the Sanhedrin, subordinate to the legislation in the Torah, is termed *d'rabbanan*, from the Aramaic for "rabbinic."[21]

---

17 See Nachmanides, *Commentary to Maimonides, Book of Commandments*, commentary to Chapter 2.

18 See Maimonides, Code of Law, supra note 12, Laws of *Mamrim* 2:1; Chapter 3 in this Volume.

19 See Maimonides, Code of Law, supra note 12, Laws of *Mamrim* 1:1-1:2, 2:1. Thus, as I have suggested elsewhere, interpretation of the Torah parallels interpretation of the United States Constitution by the Supreme Court, which has the authority and duty to determine the meaning of the Constitution. See Chapter 3 in this Volume.

20 See Elon, *Jewish Law*, supra note 11, at 480-81, noting that

> [t]he substance of the supreme legislation is fixed, perpetual, and beyond change . . . . Thus, when we speak of legislation as one of the legal sources of Jewish law (i.e., a source recognized in the Jewish legal system itself as an instrument for continued [legal] creativity and development), we refer, of course, to legislation by [legal] authorities and other competent legislators. Although such legislation is subordinate legislation, we refer to it, for convenience and brevity, simply as "legislation."

Id. In a roughly similar manner, the United States Constitution was enacted through a legislative act, but retains the status of supreme legislation, binding on and setting boundaries for all subordinate legislation. Of course, the Constitution differs from the Torah in that it is subject to amendment, though the process of constitutional amendment presents its own practical and theoretical issues. See generally, *Responding to Imperfection: The Theory and Practice of Constitutional Amendment* (Sanford Levinson ed., 1995).

21 Historically, there existed a functioning Sanhedrin from the time of Moses through the fourth century C.E. See Aryeh Kaplan, *The Handbook of Jewish Thought* 209 (1979). After the Sanhedrin was disbanded, there remained, for many centuries, central legal authorities that continued to adjudicate the law and enact legislation, though these courts did not have the status of a Sanhedrin. See id. at 236-38. In later times, in the absence of a central authority, local courts adjudicated and enacted local laws. See Elon, *Jewish Law*, supra note 11, at 486-89, 666-75. For the purposes of analyzing legal and conceptual issues in legislation in

Like the laws of the Torah, which consist of both positive commandments and negative commandments, rabbinic legislation can also take both positive and negative form. In addition, although all negative legislation in a sense serves to safeguard adherence to the laws in the Torah, conceptually, negative rabbinic legislation can be further divided into subcategories of legislation, relating to both the purpose and the parameters of the legislation.

1. Positive Legislation

As Maimonides explains in his introduction to the Mishna,[22] one category of rabbinic legislation is *takanot*, or positive legislation, which includes both laws implemented for a clearly religious or ritual purpose and laws implemented to improve the nature of interpersonal dealings.[23] Because these laws were enacted by the same legal authorities who functioned as arbiters of the laws of the Torah, these authorities were careful to distinguish rabbinic legislation from divine legislation or from interpretations of divine legislation.[24] The most poignant illustration of these distinctions may be the variety of functions that Moses served after the revelation at Sinai. In listing some examples of positive legislation, Maimonides includes legislation enacted by Moses.[25] Thus, Moses played at least three different and distinct roles in the legal system. First, he transmitted the revealed Written and Oral Torah. Second, he served as a judge and an interpreter of those areas of the law that required interpretation. Finally, he served as a legislator of rabbinic law. Although Moses was unique in the first of these roles,[26] his functioning as both a judge and a legislator provides an analogue for the dual function of the Sanhedrin.

Perhaps the most widely known example of positive rabbinic legislation is the obligation to light the menorah on Chanuka. This legislation was enacted

---

Jewish law, this chapter focuses on the Sanhedrin, which functioned in the full capacity of a central, authoritative adjudicatory and legislative body.

22 The Mishna, which was compiled in the Land of Israel around the year 188 C.E., documented and codified the Oral Torah. The Mishna serves as the basis for the further development of the Oral Law in the Gemara, which was redacted in Babylonia around the year 589 C.E. Together, the Mishna and the Gemara comprise the Talmud. See Chapter 3 in this Volume.

23 See Maimonides, *Introduction to the Mishna*, in *Introductions to Commentary on the Mishna* 41-42 (Mordechai Rabinowitz, ed., 1961) [hereinafter Maimonides, *Introduction to the Mishna*].

24 See infra part two, section B.1.

25 See Maimonides, *Introduction to the Mishna*, supra note 23, at 41.

26 See Maimonides, *Perek Chelek*, supra note 13, at 140-46 (describing the unique nature and status of Moses' prophecy).

to commemorate the miraculous events of the Nation of Israel's military victory over the Syrian-Greeks and the subsequent burning of a small amount of oil in the Temple menorah that lasted for eight days.[27] Although the practice of lighting the menorah in the Temple had been divinely mandated,[28] there was no such obligation incumbent upon individuals prior to the events of Chanuka. As these events occurred more than one thousand years after the revelation at Sinai, it was the legal authorities living at the time of the miracles who enacted rabbinic legislation requiring individuals to light the menorah on Chanuka.

2. Negative Legislation

a. Meat and Milk

The other category of rabbinic legislation that Maimonides lists is *gezeirot*, negative legislation.[29] This legislation was enacted in order to safeguard many of the laws of the Torah by adding a protective "fence" around those laws.[30] For example, in three separate places, the Torah prohibits cooking the kid of a goat in its mother's milk.[31] Through expansive interpretation of these verses, the Talmud understands this prohibition to include not only cooking meat and milk together, but also eating and deriving benefit from meat and milk that are cooked together.[32] At the same time, the Talmud employs hermeneutic principles to limit the prohibition to the meat of certain animals that are similar to goats, excluding other meat such as poultry.[33] Yet, the Talmud adds that rabbinic legislation was enacted prohibiting eating any meat together with milk.[34] This legislation was based on the concern that people would not distinguish between different kinds of meat, and therefore, if permitted to eat poultry and milk together, would believe that they were likewise permitted to eat all meats together with milk.[35] Thus, to protect against a violation of the laws in the

---

27 See Maimonides, Code of Law, supra note 12, Laws of *Chanuka*, 3:1-3:2.
28 See Numbers 8:1-4.
29 See Maimonides, *Introduction to the Mishna*, supra note 23, at 40-41.
30 See id.; see also infra part two, section A.
31 See Exodus 23:19, 34:26; Deuteronomy 14:21.
32 See Talmud Bavli, Chulin 115b.
33 See id. at 113a. For a discussion of the hermeneutic principles, see Elon, *Jewish Law*, supra note 11, at 281-399; Bernard Rosensweig, *The Hermeneutic Principles and Their Application*, 13 Tradition 49 (Summer 1972).
34 See Talmud Bavli, Chulin 103a-104b, 113a.
35 See Maimonides, Code of Law, supra note 12, Laws of Dietary Restrictions 9:4; Maimonides, *Introduction to the Mishna*, supra note 23, at 40.

Torah, the legal authorities enacted broader subordinate legislation that would help insure adherence to supreme legislation.

b. The Sabbath

A particularly illuminating example of negative rabbinic legislation is found in the various forms of legislation enacted in connection with the Sabbath. The Torah prohibits engaging in *melakha*[36]on the Sabbath.[37] Interpreting the term *melakha*, the Talmud delineates numerous activities that are prohibited on the Sabbath.[38] These prohibitions have the status of supreme legislation because they are the product of authoritative judicial interpretation of the Torah.

In addition to interpreting the biblical prohibitions, legal authorities enacted negative rabbinic legislation prohibiting other activities in order to safeguard the observance of the Sabbath.[39] According to Maimonides, some of these activities were prohibited because they are similar to activities that are biblically prohibited, while others, though not inherently similar to biblical prohibitions, were prohibited out of a concern that such conduct might nevertheless lead to the violation of biblical prohibitions.[40] Finally, Maimonides lists a third category of rabbinic legislation intended to preserve the unique qualities of the Sabbath by prohibiting conduct not conducive to the spiritual nature of the day.[41]

The laws involving the institution of *mukza* illustrate some of the concerns that serve as a basis for these categories. The Talmud relates that among the activities that were rabbinically prohibited on the Sabbath was the moving of objects that had no purpose on the Sabbath. The Talmud describes a structure of rabbinic legislation that classified various objects as *mukza*, or set aside from use on the Sabbath, either because they had no intrinsic purpose on the Sabbath or because they were designated not to be used on that day.[42] These objects generally could not be moved on the Sabbath, although the legislation

---

36 This term is often translated as "work," see, e.g., The Holy Scriptures 173 (Jewish Publication Society 1955), but denotes a broad range of physically creative activity prohibited on the Sabbath.

37 See, e.g., Exodus 20:10.

38 See Talmud Bavli, Shabbath 73a.

39 See Maimonides, Code of Law, supra note 12, Laws of the Sabbath, chs. 21-28.

40 See id. at 28:1.

41 See id. at 24:1 (citing Talmud Bavli, Shabbath 113a-b, 150a).

42 See Talmud Bavli, Shabbath; Maimonides, Code of Law, supra note 12, Laws of the Sabbath 24:12-26:23.

incorporated exceptions that permitted certain types of objects to be moved when a need arose on the Sabbath. For example, writing is among the activities biblically prohibited on the Sabbath;[43] therefore, it is rabbinically prohibited to move a pen, which has the primary function of being used for a biblically prohibited activity, and thus generally serves no purpose on the Sabbath. However, because a pen may function as an intrinsically useful object for purposes other than writing, it can be moved if a permitted use for it arises on the Sabbath.[44]

A number of reasons are provided by the Talmud and by Maimonides for the legislation establishing the institution of *mukza*, corresponding to some of the general rationales Maimonides offers for rabbinic legislation relating to the Sabbath. The Talmud states that the rabbinic prohibition against moving objects that are *mukza* was enacted as a safeguard against violation of the biblical law prohibiting carrying objects between private and public domains on the Sabbath. By limiting the class of objects permitted to be moved, to include only those necessary on the Sabbath, the legislation aimed to decrease the possibility that objects would be improperly carried from a private domain to a public domain.[45] Maimonides suggests that the laws of *mukza* serve to safeguard many other biblical prohibitions as well. For example, preventing the moving of objects that have a primary use for activities prohibited on the Sabbath will help deter the performance of those activities.[46] Finally, Maimonides adds a third reason for the laws of *mukza*, explaining that refraining from moving objects that are ordinarily associated with weekday activities will highlight the unique spiritual nature of the Sabbath.[47]

Contemporary scholars of Jewish law have likewise distinguished between categories of rabbinic legislation relating to the Sabbath and have noted the legal significance of such classifications. An illustration of the legal ramifications that emerge from these classifications involves the case of a minor illness on the Sabbath. With the exception of murder, idolatry, and certain forms of illicit sexual relations, all of the laws in the Torah may and must be violated

---

43   See Talmud Bavli, Shabbath 73a.
44   See id. at 124a-b; Maimonides, Code of Law, supra note 12, Laws of the Sabbath 25:3.
45   See Talmud Bavli, Shabbath 123a-24b; Ra'avad, *Commentary to Maimonides, Mishne Torah, Laws of the Sabbath* 24:12. The parameters of the biblical prohibition are complex, and were supplemented by various forms of rabbinic legislation. See Maimonides, Code of Law, supra note 12, at 12:8-19:26.
46   See Maimonides, Code of Law, supra note 12, at 24:13.
47   See id. at 24:12-13.

when necessary to save a life.[48] Thus, if necessary, the laws of the Sabbath are suspended in the face of a life-threatening illness.[49]

However, when there is a minor illness that poses no possible threat to human life, biblical prohibitions remain intact, and only some forms of rabbinic legislation are suspended. Rabbi Hershel Schachter has observed that the instances of suspended rabbinic legislation, delineated by the Talmud and later legal authorities, fall under the category of laws enacted specifically out of the concern that permitting these activities might lead to the violation of biblical laws. In contrast, rabbinic legislation that was enacted because of an activity's intrinsic similarity to a biblical prohibition remains in effect when there is a minor illness.[50]

---

48 See id., Laws of *Yesodei Ha-Torah* 5:1-2.

49 See id., Laws of the Sabbath 2:1. Indeed, Maimonides describes at length the imperative to violate the Sabbath even when there is only a possibility of danger to human life. See id. at ch. 2. See also Talmud Bavli, Yoma 85a-b; 2 Aryeh Kaplan, *The Handbook of Jewish Thought* 38-49 (Abraham Sutton ed., 1992); Hershel Schachter, *B'Ikvei Hatzoan* 14-18 (1997); Joseph B. Soloveitchik, *Halakhic Man* 34-35 (Lawrence Kaplan trans., 1983); Yitzchak Zeev ha-Levi Soloveitchik, *Chidushei Maran Ri'z ha-Levi* 12-13 (1998). Cf. Samuel J. Levine, *Taking Ethical Discretion Seriously: Ethical Deliberation as Ethical Obligation*, 37 Ind. L. Rev. 21, 57 n.151 (2003) ("[N]early every obligation in Jewish law is suspended to save a life.").

50 See Hershel Schachter, *Eretz Hatzevi* 50-51 (1992). Rabbi Schachter dedicates a chapter of this book to illustrations of many other legal ramifications that emerge from the distinction between these categories of legislation. See id. at 50-61; see also infra note 69. Rabbi Schachter also observes that, in addition to legislation relating to the Sabbath, the distinction has numerous other applications in Jewish law. See Schachter, supra, at 51-52, 60.

Another contemporary scholar, Rabbi Yitzchak Adler, has observed similar distinctions in Jewish law. Rabbi Adler identifies "secondary legal rules which are intended to enlarge the scope of the base law beyond its original parameters." See Yitzchak Adler, *Lomdus: A Substructural Analysis* 1 (English section) (1989). Rabbi Adler refers to such a secondary rule as an "expansionary vehicle" and distinguishes between "extensions of the parent statute" and expansions which "may be perceived as newly created, independent and external such that the secondary prohibitions and obligations are not actual extensions of the base law." Id. at 1-2. According to Rabbi Adler, "extensions" will share the characteristics and properties of the base law more closely than will "creations." See id.

Rabbi Adler applies this framework to many areas of Jewish law, including rabbinic legislation relating to the Sabbath, mirroring the observations of Rabbi Schachter. In Rabbi Adler's terminology, rabbinic legislation enacted as a "creation" is suspended in the case of a minor illness, while legislation enacted as an "extension" remains intact, more closely approximating the base law of biblical prohibitions that are suspended only when a life is in danger. See id. at 11-12 (Hebrew section).

In a sense, it would seem that rabbinic legislation, subordinate to the base laws of the Torah, is a prime example of such "expansions." Indeed, Rabbi Adler applies his framework to a number of areas of rabbinic legislation. See id. at 10-14. It is interesting, then, that Rabbi Adler also applies his analysis to biblical laws. Although the laws within the Torah cannot be distinguished as "supreme" or "subordinate," conceptually some of the laws can be understood as expansions of other laws. See id. at 1-10.

PART TWO | SCOPE OF RABBINIC LEGISLATION: LICENSE AND LIMITATIONS

Because the Written Torah and its definitive interpretations serve as supreme and constitutional legislation in Jewish law, rabbinic license to enact additional subordinate legislation must find its authority in these sources. Moreover, the scope of rabbinic authority in enacting legislation is subject to limitations, based in the Torah, which serve as a checking device on the discretion of rabbinic legislators.

A. Sources of Authority

In its discussion of the rabbinic command to light the menorah on Chanuka, the Talmud notes that, similar to the observance of biblical commandments, the act of lighting the menorah is preceded by the recitation of a blessing acknowledging God's command.[51] The text of the blessing includes the statement that God "commanded us to kindle the Chanuka lights."[52]

The Talmud suggests two possible biblical sources to support the notion that lighting the menorah, though rabbinically legislated, is, in another sense, divinely mandated. One source, which Maimonides cites in his Code of Law, is the biblical prescription of rabbinic judicial authority, stating that:

> When there is a matter of law that you are unable to decide . . . you shall
> go up to the place that God will choose. And you shall approach the . . .
> judge[s] who will be in those days and you shall inquire, and they will you
> tell you the law. And you shall act according to that which they will tell you
> . . . and you will observe all that which they will teach you. According to
> [that] which they will tell you, you shall act; do not veer from that which
> they tell you, to the right or to the left.[53]

The Talmud understands this passage, carrying the warning not to veer from the judge's teachings, to authorize not only rabbinic adjudication, but rabbinic legislation as well.[54] Thus, as Maimonides explains, although lighting the

---

51 See Talmud Bavli, Shabbath 21b.

52 Id.

53 Deuteronomy 17:8-11.

54 See also Maimonides, Code of Law, supra note 12, Introduction. Some scholars suggest that this verse also explains why the enactment of positive rabbinic legislation, such as lighting

menorah is, in fact, an example of subordinate rabbinic legislation, the blessing recited before lighting the menorah acknowledges the divine command to observe rabbinic legislation.[55]

Similarly, the Talmud identifies a biblical source for the authority of negative rabbinic legislation, such as the protective measures implemented to prevent violation of the biblical laws of the Sabbath or the biblical prohibition against eating meat and milk together. The Talmud interprets the biblical verse "You shall keep My charge"[56] as a mandate for legal authorities to enact safeguards to biblical prohibitions.[57]

B. Limitations on Legislative Authority

1. "You shall not add"

The Torah commands, "every matter which I command to you, you shall take care to observe it; you shall not add to it and you shall not take away from it."[58] Although this verse apparently places broad limitations on subordinate rabbinic legislation, the precise parameters of the verse are subject to interpretation, as developed in both the revealed and derived Oral Torah.[59] As a threshold matter, it seems clear that the verse cannot preclude all forms of subordinate legislation, in light of other verses in the Torah that license both positive and negative rabbinic legislation.[60] Maimonides explains that the verse specifically

---

the Chanuka menorah, does not violate the biblical prohibition against adding to the divine law. See Schachter, supra note 49, at 110; see also infra part two, section B.1.

55 See Maimonides, Code of Law, supra note 12, Laws of Blessings 11:3. The same principle is supported by the Talmud's second source for the authority of rabbinic legislation, the biblical verse "[a]sk your father and he will inform you, your elders and they will tell you." Deuteronomy 32:7.

56 Leviticus 18:30. Although this verse is often translated using the disparate terms "keep" and "charge," in the original Hebrew, both words are derived from the same root denoting "guard" or "protect," thus implying a mandate for the enactment of additional safeguards.

57 See Talmud Bavli, Yevamoth 21a; see also Maimonides, Code of Law, supra note 12, Introduction; Maimonides, *Introduction to the Mishna*, supra note 23, at 40.

58 Deuteronomy 13:1.

59 See supra part one, section A. In a sense, the necessity to interpret the parameters of the broad and seemingly categorical command "you shall not add to it" parallels the need to interpret broad and seemingly categorical dictates in the United States Constitution, such as "Congress shall make no law . . ." U.S. Const. amend. I.

60 See supra part two, section A. Similarly, the interpretation of any segment of a statutory code must integrate an understanding of the structure of the entire statutory scheme. Again, the United States Constitution presents a particularly useful parallel, as each section of the

prohibits adding to the Torah per se, in the sense of enacting subordinate laws in a manner that suggests supreme authority.[61] For example, to protect against the violation of the biblical prohibition on eating certain forms of meat cooked with milk, legal authorities are authorized to prohibit eating poultry and milk together as well, as long as they proclaim that the legislation is a rabbinic decree designed to safeguard the biblical law.[62] They are precluded, however, from bolstering such legislation by stating that poultry is included in the biblical category of meat, and thereby part of the biblical prohibition.[63]

Moreover, the command not to add to the Torah places additional checks on rabbinic legislative discretion, while further emphasizing the distinction between biblical and rabbinic legislation. The Talmud relates the rule that rabbinic legislation was enacted only if there existed a substantial need for such legislation.[64] A number of scholars have posited that this rule is derived from the prohibition against adding to the Torah. These scholars explain that the prohibition requires tempering the broad rabbinic legislative authority by limiting it to situations of significant necessity. Legislation in the absence of such need is considered an improper and, accordingly, prohibited addition to the laws of the Torah.[65]

Scholars likewise apply the same principal to explain the Talmudic rule restricting legislation enacted to safeguard against violation of a previously established rabbinic prohibition.[66] These scholars suggest that the requirement of a substantial need for the enactment of rabbinic legislation precludes such legislation in the absence of a concern for violation of biblical law. The possibility

---

Constitution, often containing broad language, must be interpreted in conjunction with both the text and interpretations of other sections. See generally, e.g., Charles L. Black, Jr., *Structure and Relationship in Constitutional Law* (1969).

61 See Maimonides, Code of Law, supra note 12, Laws of *Mamrim* 2:9. According to the Talmud, the verse in Deuteronomy 13:1 also prohibits additions to the mode of performance of specific biblical commandments, such as observing an eighth day to a holiday that lasts seven days, in a manner that suggests biblical authority. See Talmud Bavli, Rosh ha-Shana 28b; Schachter, supra note 49, at 111-12 & 111 n.3.

62 See supra part one, section B.2.a.

63 See Maimonides, Code of Law, supra note 12, Laws of *Mamrim* 2:9; see also 2 Nachmanides, *Commentary on the Torah* 360-61 (Chaim Chavel ed., 1960) (commenting on Deuteronomy 4:2). Likewise, in enacting positive legislation, such as the lighting of the menorah on Chanuka, rabbinic authorities were required to describe the legislation as rabbinic in origin and were prohibited from stating that it was a biblical law. See Maimonides, supra.

64 See, e.g., Talmud Bavli, Eruvin 63b; Schachter, supra note 50, at 135.

65 See Schachter, supra note 50, at 135.

66 See Talmud Bavli, Shabbath 11a.

that a rabbinic prohibition may be violated does not qualify as sufficiently substantial to allow for further rabbinic legislation.[67]

Nevertheless, it is important to distinguish the scenario of rabbinic legislation enacted to prevent violation of previously enacted rabbinic law from a scenario in which two separate rabbinic prohibitions act in concert. For example, scholars of Jewish law addressed the question of whether poultry and milk products that have not been cooked together may be eaten together. The biblical prohibition against eating meat and milk products together applies only to food cooked together, and does not include poultry.[68] However, to safeguard against eating meat and milk products that were cooked together, rabbinic legislation was enacted prohibiting eating meat and milk products that were not cooked together as well. In addition, as noted above, to safeguard against eating milk products together with those kinds of meat included in the biblical prohibition, rabbinic legislation was enacted extending the category of meat products to include poultry. Thus, any prohibition involving poultry and milk that were not cooked together would rely on two rabbinic enactments. Still, scholars explain, the prohibition against eating poultry and milk that were not cooked together remains intact, because it is premised on two separate rabbinic prohibitions, enacted as a result of two independent concerns, acting in concert with one another. Such a dynamic does not constitute a rabbinic prohibition enacted for the purpose of safeguarding a previously enacted rabbinic prohibition.[69]

---

67 See Schachter, supra note 49, at 48; Schachter, supra note 50, at 58-59.

68 See supra part one, section B.2.a.

69 See Schachter, supra note 49, at 48. Thus, according to most views, separate rabbinic prohibitions can work in concert on the condition that one prohibition was not enacted to safeguard against violation of the other. Notably, though, some scholars have attributed to one Talmudic authority the view that, under certain circumstances, independent rabbinic prohibitions cannot be enforced together. This approach is particularly relevant in relation to negative rabbinic legislation involving observance of the Sabbath, as such legislation can be divided into different categories. See supra part one, section B.2. b. & note 50.

Scholars suggest that, according to one opinion in the Talmud, see Talmud Bavli, Shabbath 11a-11b, rabbinic prohibitions can work in concert only if at least one of the prohibitions falls under the category of laws enacted as independent rabbinic prohibitions due to a similarity to a biblical prohibition. Under this view, if both prohibitions fall under the category of laws enacted not because of an intrinsic similarity to a biblical prohibition, but out of a concern that permitting certain activities might lead to the violation of biblical laws, then the two prohibitions, even if separate and independent of each other, cannot be enforced together. See Schachter, supra note 50, at 58-59.

2. "You shall not take away"

Like the command "you shall not add"[70] to the Torah, the biblical decree "you shall not take away"[71] appears to place broad restrictions on the scope and authority of subordinate rabbinic legislation. Moreover, the implication of the verse, prohibiting abrogation of biblical commandments, is consistent with a number of other verses in the Torah that declare the immutability of biblical commandments.[72] Nevertheless, even this principle is subject to limited exceptions that exemplify the extent of the discretion available to rabbinic legislators.

The Talmud states that, when necessary, the Sanhedrin has the authority to enact legislation mandating the passive violation of a positive biblical commandment.[73] For example, the Torah commands that on the holiday of Rosh Hashana, it is incumbent on individuals to hear the sound of the *shofar*, typically a ram's horn.[74] Depending on the calendar of a specific year, Rosh Hashana may fall on different days of the week, including the Sabbath. Under biblical law, the obligation to sound the *shofar* on Rosh Hashana applies on both weekdays and the Sabbath.[75]

However, rabbinic authorities were concerned about the possibility that the obligation to hear the sound of the *shofar* might lead to violation of the Sabbath. Specifically, as the Talmud explains, individuals in possession of a *shofar* but not adept at sounding the *shofar* might come to carry the *shofar* to someone else, who would sound the *shofar* for them.[76] Carrying the *shofar* between public and private domains would constitute a violation of the Sabbath.[77] Therefore, to protect against the active violation of the Sabbath, for years that Rosh Hashana fell on the Sabbath, legal authorities enacted rabbinic legislation mandating passive violation of the positive commandment to sound the *shofar*.[78]

Scholars have suggested a biblical source for the rabbinic authority, delineated in the Talmud, to enact legislation involving the passive violation of a biblical commandment. In the principal passage authorizing rabbinic adjudication and legislation, the Torah states, "do not veer from that which they tell

---

70 Deuteronomy 13:1.
71 Id.
72 See supra note 12.
73 See Talmud Bavli, Yevamoth 89b-90b.
74 See Leviticus 23:24, 25:9; Numbers 29:1.
75 See Talmud Bavli, Rosh ha-Shana 29b.
76 See id.
77 See supra text accompanying note 45.
78 See supra text accompanying note 45.

you, to the right or to the left."[79] Rabbinic exegesis understands this verse to require adherence to the teachings of legal authorities, "even if it appears they are telling you that your left is your right and your right is your left."[80] Thus, the verse authorizes a ruling that seems to contradict that which is clearly correct. According to some scholars, the verse serves as the source of authority for rabbinic legislation which, in a sense, might seem incorrect, or anomalous, because it prevents observance of a biblical law.[81]

Moreover, despite the Talmud's conclusion that rabbinic legislation may not require the active violation of a biblical commandment,[82] under exceptional circumstances the Talmud extends the command to heed the words of rabbinic authorities to include the temporary suspension of a negative biblical commandment.[83] The Talmud cites the biblical example of Elijah, who, to stem the rampant practice of idolatry and return the nation to the proper path, offered a sacrifice on an altar at Mount Carmel, despite a prohibition against bringing a sacrifice outside the Temple in Jerusalem.[84] The medieval legal scholar Ra'avad explains that the source of authority for the temporary suspension of a negative biblical commandment is the verse in Psalms stating that when "it is a time to work for God, suspend your Torah."[85]

Based on Talmudic sources such as the legal exegesis of the episode of Elijah on Mount Carmel, Maimonides confirms the rabbinic authority to temporarily suspend a biblical law, when necessary to restore the nation's religious faith and observance.[86] Maimonides explains the logic behind such authority through an analogy to the work of a doctor. He writes that, as a doctor may

---

79   See supra part two, section A.

80   See Sifri, *Shoftim* 154.

81   See Schachter, supra note 50, at 133 (citing Elchanan Wasserman, *Kuntrus Divrei Soferim* 108-9 (Eliezer Wasserman ed., 4th ed. 1989)). See also Rabbi Moshe Chaim Luzzatto, *Ma'amar Ha-Ikarim*; Asher Weiss, *Minchas Asher, Shemos* 213-14 (2017).

  Scholars of Jewish law have identified two possible ways of conceptualizing the legal effect of rabbinic legislation that requires passive violation of a positive biblical commandment. See Adler, supra note 50, at 151 (Hebrew section). In the terminology of Rabbi Yitzchak Adler, the rabbinic legislation can be seen as resulting in the "temporary abolition" of the biblical law, or, alternatively, as placing the biblical law "in abeyance." See id. at 44 (English section). These different conceptualizations can help explain the nature of rabbinic authority to enact such legislation. See id. at 151 (Hebrew section). In addition, Rabbi Adler applies this framework to a number of other areas of Jewish law. See id. at 150-64 (Hebrew section).

82   See Talmud Bavli, Yevamoth 89b-90b.

83   See id. at 90b.

84   See id.; Rashi, *Commentary on the Talmud* (citing 1 Kings 18).

85   Ra'avad, supra note 45, Laws of *Mamrim* 2:9 (citing Psalms 119:126).

86   See Maimonides, Code of Law, supra note 12, Laws of *Mamrim* 2:4.

amputate an arm or a leg so that an entire organism may live, similarly, in rare occasions, a court may permit the temporary violation of some commandments in order to safeguard communal observance of the law as a whole.[87]

3. Communal Role in Legislation

The Talmud states that rabbinic legislation is legally binding only if is determined that the majority of the nation will be able to abide by the legislation.[88] Therefore, Maimonides explains, if the court enacts legislation with the erroneous belief that most of the nation can abide by the legislation, but later finds this not to be the case, the legislation is invalid and, thus, may not be enforced.[89]

PART THREE | LEGISLATION OVER TIME: CHANGED CIRCUMSTANCES

Statutory interpretation plays a central role in American legal practice and scholarship.[90] One of the vexing questions in statutory interpretation involves the proper way to approach a statute over time, particularly when, as a result of changes in circumstances, the rationale for a statute is apparently no longer applicable.[91] Again, it may be helpful to look at the contrast case of the Jewish legal system, which includes a complex framework for considering the application of legislation when the reason for the legislation no longer applies.

A. Biblical Legislation

Because of the immutable authority of the laws in the Torah,[92] biblical legislation is generally not subject to abrogation or modification. Thus, the Talmud concludes that the commandments in the Torah remain in force even if the

---

87 See id. Similarly, the Talmud describes rabbinic authority to enact laws of criminal justice contrary to those delineated in the Torah, when the "needs of the hour" so demand. See Talmud Bavli, Sanhedrin 27a, 46a; Maimonides, Code of Law, supra note 12, Laws of *Sanhedrin* 24:4-10.

88 See Talmud Bavli, Avoda Zara 36b-37a.

89 See Maimonides, Code of Law, supra note 12, Laws of *Mamrim* 2:6. Moreover, according to Maimonides, if, after enacting legislation, a court erroneously believes that the majority of the nation has abided by the law, a later court that identifies this error may nullify the law. See id. at 2:7. For an analysis of these scenarios, see generally Joseph B. Soloveitchik, *Shnei Sugei Mesoret*, in *Sheurim L'zekher Abba Mori* (1983).

90 For a list of some of the scholarship on statutory interpretation, see Richard A. Posner, *Legislation and its Interpretation: A Primer*, 68 Neb. L. Rev. 431, 451-53 (1989).

91 See, e.g., Ronald Dworkin, *Law's Empire* 348-50 (1986).

92 See supra part one, section A.

apparent rationale for a commandment no longer applies.[93] However, in the rare event that the Torah expressly provides the reason for a particular commandment, the Talmud concludes that the force of the commandment is dependent on the applicability of its rationale.[94] Nevertheless, it should be noted that, in practice, the Talmud appears to discourage reliance on even this limited license for restricting the scope of a commandment, due to the abiding concern that an individual may be mistaken in believing that the rationale does not apply in a given situation.[95]

B. Rabbinic Legislation

1. General Principles

Unlike the laws of the Torah, rabbinic legislation can be modified by later legal authorities, subject to a complex set of rules regulating such discretion.[96] For example, the Talmud states that a Sanhedrin generally cannot abrogate the legislation of an earlier Sanhedrin, unless the later Sanhedrin is "greater in wisdom and in number."[97] According to Maimonides, the limitations of this rule govern even when, as a result of changing circumstances, the reason for the

---

93   See Talmud Bavli, Sanhedrin 21a. For a description of the Talmudic dispute, see Chapter 3 in this Volume.

94   See Talmud Bavli, Sanhedrin 21a; Chapter 3 in this Volume. Compare Frank A. Easterbrook, *Statutes' Domains*, 50 U. Chi. L. Rev. 533, 544 (1983), with Chapter 3 in this Volume.

95   See Chapter 3 in this Volume.

96   In this regard, it is important to distinguish the court's legislative function from its judicial or interpretive function. In contrast to the strict regulations on a later court's legislative authority, later courts have broad interpretive discretion. As Maimonides explains, if one court arrives at a legal ruling based on a particular line of reasoning, a later court has the authority—and obligation—to adjudicate the same issue according to its own reasoning, even if the outcome is different. Maimonides, Code of Law, supra note 12, Laws of *Mamrim* 2:1.

Nevertheless, if a particular interpretation is codified through legislative action, that interpretation takes on the status of legislation, and as such, ordinarily may not be subject to modification by later courts serving in an adjudicative capacity. See infra notes 97-100 and accompanying text. This dynamic is again similar to the relationship between courts and legislatures in the American legal system. Although courts have the authority to interpret statutes, if the legislature enacts legislation codifying a particular interpretation of a statute, courts interpreting the statute are then bound by the legislative action.

For a broader discussion of this principle in Jewish law, and its relationship to issues of legal authority and precedent, see generally Chapter 3 in this Volume; Joseph Karo, *Kesef Mishna* on Maimonides, Code of Law, supra note 12, Laws of *Mamrim* 2:1; Schachter, supra note 50; Soloveitchik, supra note 89; Elchanan Wasserman, supra note 81.

97   E.g., Talmud Bavli, Eduyoth 1:5. Legal scholars have provided a variety of interpretations for the definition of "wisdom" and "number" in this context. See Kaplan, supra note 21, at

initial legislation no longer applies.[98] Moreover, Maimonides holds that even this modest license to abrogate rabbinic legislation applies only in the context of positive legislation; negative rabbinic legislation, enacted to safeguard biblical laws, can never be abrogated by later authorities.[99]

Ra'avad, however, limits the Talmudic rule, requiring that the later court be greater than the legislating court, to situations in which the reason for the legislation still applies. Therefore, he holds, although rabbinic legislation remains in force even if the reason for a particular law no longer applies, in such a situation, a later court has the authority to repeal the legislation even if the later court is not greater than the legislating court.[100]

2. Suspension of Rabbinic Legislation Without Further Legislative Action: Fringes on Four-Cornered Linen Garments

Notwithstanding the dispute regarding the criteria and mechanics generally necessary for a later court to abrogate rabbinic legislation, scholars have suggested that in certain scenarios, rabbinic legislation loses force even without further official legislative action.[101] Rabbi Hershel Schachter has identified a number of laws that seem to fall under this category, apparently patterned after the limited rule that the applicability of biblical laws can be subject to the reasons for the laws that are expressly presented in the Torah.[102] At the same time, these scenarios serve as a further illustration of limitations on rabbinic legislative authority.

For example, the Torah commands the placing of fringes on four-cornered garments.[103] As the Talmud documents, the proper fulfillment of the commandment requires that some of the fringes be of a particular color and of wool material.[104] The Talmud also notes that the requirement to affix wool fringes to all four-cornered garments, including those of linen, is an exception to the general biblical prohibition against wearing a garment composed of a mixture of wool and linen materials.[105] Nevertheless, despite the propriety of placing wool fringes on a linen garment, as an exception to the general rule, Talmudic

---

224-25 & nn.90-91; Samuel J. Levine, *Breadth and Boundary: The Powers of Beit Din*, Hamevaser, December 1990, at 4.

98 See Maimonides, Code of Law, supra note 12, Laws of *Mamrim* 2:2.

99 See id. at 2:3.

100 See Ra'avad, supra note 45, Laws of *Mamrim* 2:2.

101 See Kaplan, supra note 21, at 229 & nn.128-32.

102 See supra part three, section A; Schachter, supra note 50, at 135-40.

103 See Numbers 15:37-40.

104 See Talmud Bavli, Menachoth 40a.

105 See id.

authorities were concerned that such a practice might, at times, lead to the violation of the biblical prohibition.[106] To prevent such a violation, these authorities
enacted rabbinic legislation prohibiting placing fringes on linen garments.[107]

According to a number of scholars, however, just as rabbinic legislation must
generally be formulated in a manner that does not to appear to suggest biblical
legislation,[108] so too, rabbinic legislation that suspends a biblical law must be formulated in a way that is not an outright contradiction of biblical law.[109] Instead,
Rabbi Schachter explains, the formulation of such legislation must clearly demonstrate the law's status as subordinate legislation, enacted for the express purpose
of preventing the violation of a particular biblical law.[110] Thus, the Talmudic
legislators were required to state, as part of the legislation prohibiting fringes on
linen garments, that the purpose of the legislation was to protect against the biblical violation of wearing a garment composed of wool and linen.[111]

In later times, though, as a result of persecution and dispersion of the Jewish
nation, the identity of the proper color for the fringes was lost. As a result, the
commandment continued to be fulfilled, but without the requirement that some
fringes be composed of the unique color and of wool material.[112] As wool was no
longer required for the fringes, linen became a suitable replacement, and there was
no longer a viable concern that placing fringes on four-cornered garments made of
linen might lead to a violation of the biblical prohibition against wearing a garment
composed of wool and linen. Thus, Rabbi Schachter explains, parallel to biblical
laws, because the express reason for the rabbinic legislation no longer applied, the
legislation itself likewise no longer applied.[113] In this way, Rabbi Schachter explains a
medieval legal authority's suspension of the Talmudic legislation prohibiting placing
fringes on linen garments, without the need for further official legislative action.[114]

CONCLUSION

The turn to Jewish law as a contrast case in contemporary American legal
scholarship has offered American legal scholars an opportunity to reexamine
concepts important to American law, through the prism of a legal system that

---

106 See id.
107 See id. See also Weiss, supra note 81.
108 See supra part two, section B.1.
109 See Schachter, supra note 50, at 135.
110 See id.
111 See id.
112 See id. at 137. See generally Responsum of Rosh 2:8; Levine, supra note 97.
113 Schachter, supra note 50, at 137.
114 See id.; see also Levine, supra note 97, at 4, 10.

shares many conceptual similarities, yet is based in fundamentally different assumptions. Law review pages continue to reflect the growing interest in the Jewish legal system as an alternative model that may shed light on complex and controversial issues in American law.[115]

This study of legislation in Jewish law represents an attempt to build on the increased interest in Jewish law among American legal scholars. Looking at the doctrine of the separation of powers, a legal concept that remains central to American jurisprudence, this chapter observes many comparisons and contrasts in the way the two systems approach this doctrine. At the same time, the chapter explores a number of both conceptual and substantive areas of Jewish law, through a variety of sources in Jewish legal thought. In particular, the chapter introduces the work of contemporary scholars of Jewish law, in an effort to demonstrate the importance of recognizing emerging scholarship when engaging in studies of comparative law, and in the hope that this approach will spark similar modes of scholarship in the future.

---

115 See supra note 10.

Capital Punishment

CHAPTER 5

Capital Punishment in Jewish Law and Its Application to the American Legal System: A Conceptual Overview

INTRODUCTION

In recent years, a growing body of scholarship has developed in the United States that applies concepts in Jewish law to unsettled, controversial, and challenging areas of American legal thought.[1] While some scholars endorse the application of Jewish legal theory to American law,[2] others are more

---

1 See Chapter 3 in this Volume (citing sources that apply Jewish law to American legal theory); Suzanne Last Stone, *In Pursuit of the Counter-Text: The Turn to the Jewish Model in Contemporary American Legal Theory*, 106 Harv. L. Rev. 813, 814 (1993) (discussing the use of Jewish law in American legal scholarship).

2 See David R. Dow, *Constitutional Midrash: The Rabbis' Solution to Professor Bickel's Problem*, 29 Hous. L. Rev. 543, 544 (1992) (stating that "the normative ontology of the systems of Jewish and American law are so nearly identical that the Judaic resolution of certain theoretical difficulties can be wholly transplanted to the American domain"); Irene Merker Rosenberg & Yale L. Rosenberg, *Guilt: Henry Friendly Meets the MaHaRaL of Prague*, 90 Mich. L. Rev. 604, 614-15 (1991). In this article, Irene and Yale Rosenberg note:

> [T]o be sure, Jewish law may be considered irrelevant to American constitutional analysis, separated as the two systems are not only by millennia, but

cautious.[3] One area of Jewish legal thought that has found prominence in both American court opinions[4] and American legal scholarship[5] involves the approach to capital punishment in Jewish law.

> by religious, cultural, social, and economic differences . . . . That American law does not accept an omniscient and omnipotent God . . . does not, however, preclude comparison of the two legal systems. This country is in many ways religiously oriented, and, in any event, moral and ethical beliefs . . . surely pervade our society . . . . Furthermore, the differences between Jewish and American law should not obscure their similarities . . . . Indeed, Jewish law is a fundamental building block of Western civilization. Consciously or not, the United States has adopted basic concepts of Jewish criminal procedure . . . . Moreover, the Supreme Court itself has referred to Jewish law in support of some of its most important rulings.

3 See, e.g., Steven F. Friedell, *Aaron Kirschenbaum on Equity in Jewish Law,* 1993 BYU L. Rev. 909, 919 (book review) (observing that "Jewish law has policies and purposes that are unique and that make the application of Jewish law in a modern legal system difficult"); Suzanne Last Stone, *In Pursuit of the Counter-Text: The Turn to the Jewish Model in Contemporary American Legal Theory,* 106 Harv. L. Rev. 813, 893-94 (1993) (warning that American theorists "should be cautious not to derive too many lessons from the counter-text of Jewish law," because "Jewish law is not only a legal system; it is the life work of a religious community. The Constitution, on the other hand, is a political document.").

Despite the inherent differences between a religious legal system and a secular one, conceptual similarities between American law and Jewish law allow for a meaningful comparison of the two systems. This chapter focuses on the conceptual similarities between American and Jewish legal approaches to the death penalty, and emphasizes the limitations on such comparisons due to the lack of parallels between religious bases of Jewish law and the American legal system. As Bruce S. Ledewitz and Scott Staples have explained,

> simply incorporating Talmudic practice in the American legal system would not be coherent or possible. Nor would it make sense to grant normative supremacy to the Talmud, per se. The two systems are different; the two societies are different.
>
> So, why compare them? The Talmud is a legal system that aspired to reflect God's purpose in the world. If such a system could confidently put men and women to death, then perhaps so can we. If, on the other hand, the rabbis of the Talmud agonized over execution, limited its reach, and sought to excuse where possible, perhaps we need to imitate their voices.

Bruce S. Ledewitz & Scott Staples, *Reflections on the Talmudic and American Death Penalty,* 6 U. Fla. J.L. & Pub. Pol'y 33, 37-38 (1993).

4 See Daniel A. Rudolph, *Note, The Misguided Reliance in American Jurisprudence on Jewish Law to Support the Moral Legitimacy of Capital Punishment,* 33 Am. Crim. L. Rev. 437, 439-41 nn.11-21 (1996) (discussing American court opinions which employed Jewish law).

5 See generally Steven Davidoff, *A Comparative Study of the Jewish and the United States Constitutional Law of Capital Punishment,* 3 ILSA J. Int'l & Comp. L. 93 (1996); Bruce S. Ledewitz & Scott Staples, *Reflections on the Talmudic and American Death Penalty,* 6 U. Fla. J. L. & Pub. Pol'y 33 (1993); Daniel A. Rudolph, Note, *The Misguided Reliance in American Jurisprudence on Jewish Law to Support the Moral Legitimacy of Capital Punishment,*

This chapter aims to explore the issue of the death penalty in Jewish law as it relates to the question of the death penalty in American law, through a discussion that rejects simplistic conclusions and instead confronts the complexities of the Jewish legal system. It is not uncommon to find both proponents and opponents of the death penalty attempting to support their respective positions through citations to sources in Jewish law. Such attempts, however, often fail to consider the full range of Jewish legal scholarship, relying only on a few sources that appear, superficially, to favor one position over the other.[6] Thus, this chapter looks to present a broad and balanced overview of Jewish law with respect to legal and historical attitudes towards the death penalty. More specifically, this chapter focuses on the conceptual underpinnings behind pertinent areas of Jewish law, considering the potential relevance and effect of those conceptualizations on American legal thought.

Part one of this chapter discusses the United States appellate court case of *Hayes v. Lockhart*,[7] which references the death penalty in Jewish law. This case illustrates some of the methods employed by American judges, scholars, and advocates who seek to support their positions on the death penalty through reliance on Jewish law. Part two takes a close look at the death penalty in the Written Torah, which is often cited by those favoring capital punishment. Part three examines the complex position taken by the Oral Torah towards the death penalty as reflected in the Talmud and other rabbinic sources.

---

33 Am. Crim. L. Rev. 437 (1996); Aaron M. Schreiber, *The Jurisprudence of Dealing with Unsatisfactory Fundamental Law: A Comparative Glance at the Different Approaches in Medieval Criminal Law, Jewish Law and the United States Supreme Court*, 11 Pace L. Rev. 535 (1991); Kenneth Shuster, *Halacha As a Model for American Penal Practice: A Comparison of Halachic and American Punishment Methods*, 19 Nova L. Rev. 965 (1995).

    In a 1997 debate at Georgetown University Law Center entitled "The Modern View of Capital Punishment," the moderator, Professor Samuel Dash, started the discussion with references to the Torah and the Talmud, and observed that "[t]he debate we are going to hear today on the death penalty began many years ago, actually in biblical times . . . and that debate is still here today." Alex Kozinski et al., *The Modern View of Capital Punishment*, 34 Am. Crim. L. Rev. 1353-54 (1997).

6 A number of works written in English provide helpful and stimulating discussions of Jewish law as it relates to capital punishment. See generally Basil F. Herring, *Jewish Ethics and Halakhah for Our Time: Sources and Commentary* 149-73 (1984); Emanuel B. Quint & Neil S. Hecht, 1 *Jewish Jurisprudence: Its Sources and Modern Applications* 154-63 (1980); Adin Steinsaltz, *The Essential Talmud* 163-74 (Chaya Galai ed., 1976); Gerald J. Blidstein, *Capital Punishment—The Classic Jewish Discussion*, 14 Judaism 159 (1965); Aaron Kirschenbaum, *The Role of Punishment in Jewish Criminal Law: A Chapter in Rabbinic Penological Thought*, 9 Jewish L. Ann. 123 (1991); Moshe Sokol, *Some Tensions in the Jewish Attitude Toward the Taking of Human Life: A Philosophical Analysis of Justified Homicide in Jewish Legal and Aggadic Literature*, 7 Jewish L. Ann. 97 (1988). See also Chapter 6 in this Volume.

7 852 F.2d 339 (8th Cir. 1988).

This chapter concludes that meaningful application of Jewish law to the contemporary death penalty debate is impossible without an accurate and complete analysis and understanding of Jewish law in its proper context.

PART ONE | *HAYES V. LOCKHART*—A CASE IN POINT

The 1988 case of *Hayes v. Lockhart*[8] offers one example of the injection of Jewish law into the American death penalty debate, and illustrates some of the ways both sides rely on Jewish law to support their respective position. At the same time, this case arguably illustrates a failure of both sides to appreciate fully the complexity of the Jewish legal system with respect to capital punishment.

In *Hayes*, the United States Court of Appeals for the Eighth Circuit considered the habeas petition of a defendant who had been convicted of capital felony murder and sentenced to death. During his rebuttal argument at the penalty phase of the trial, the prosecutor referred to a biblical verse stating, "he that strikes a man and he dies shall surely be put to death."[9] Although the majority did not "condone the prosecutor's remarks," it found that the defense counsel's failure to object to the remarks did not constitute ineffective assistance of counsel.[10]

In a dissenting opinion, Judge Bright described the case as involving "a prosecutor's overzealous and unprincipled pursuit of the death penalty and defense counsel's passive response."[11] Judge Bright characterized the prosecutor's "selective quoting" from the Bible as "not only incendiary, but also misleading."[12] Judge Bright also asserted that "[i]n fact, the Old Testament does not advocate the death penalty. Rather, ancient Jewish law abhors the death penalty and sets forth such a multitude of procedural barriers as to render execution, in the words of Gerald Blidstein, 'a virtual impossibility.'"[13]

The prosecutor's reliance on the biblical verse to support the implementation of the death penalty in the United States was indeed problematic and misplaced. As Judge Bright correctly noted, the prosecutor's citation to the biblical text, without further reference to its foundation in Jewish law, resulted

---

8 Id.

9 Id. at 356 (Bright, J., dissenting) (quoting the prosecutor's reference to biblical passages). The prosecutor appears to have been referring to Exodus 21:12.

10 See id. at 346.

11 Id. at 353.

12 Id. at 356.

13 Id. at 356 n.8 (quoting Gerald J. Blidstein, *Capital Punishment—The Classic Jewish Discussion*, 14 Judaism 159, 165 (1965)).

in an incomplete and inaccurate interpretation. Thus, Judge Bright's emphasis on the need to consult the work of Jewish legal scholars is instructive, but his brief discussion of the issue is incomplete. The Talmud clearly details the painstaking procedural safeguards that were required to be observed before the death penalty could be carried out.[14] Nevertheless, it is evident from biblical, Talmudic, and post-Talmudic sources that capital punishment was, at times, an actual element of the authority of both the judiciary and the king.[15]

Perhaps more problematic than the failure of both the prosecution and the appellate judges in *Hayes* to fully investigate the role of the death penalty in Jewish law was the judges' apparently unquestioned presumption that the resolution of the religious issue should influence their approach to capital punishment in the United States. Although it is not unusual for courts to turn to other legal systems, including the Bible, for guidance in addressing unsettled areas of law— particularly those with profound moral implications,[16] it remains problematic to rely so directly on an entirely different legal and religious system to help resolve a question of American jurisprudence.

A deeper problem lies in the apparent attitudes of both the prosecution and Judge Bright in *Hayes*. There seems to be a troubling lack of sophistication in the apparent supposition that a simple historical determination of the frequency of implementation of the death penalty in the Jewish legal system should determine how Jewish law would prescribe the use of the death penalty in the American legal system. Such a supposition ignores the fact that Jewish laws are premised on diverse underlying conceptual foundations, some of which may be applicable to American law and others which are rooted in religious principles foreign to American jurisprudential thought. Thus, parts two and three of this chapter examine these conceptual foundations more closely, in an attempt to arrive at a more nuanced application of the approach to capital punishment in Jewish law.

---

14 See infra part two.

15 See infra notes 47-49, 62-64 and accompanying text. In fact, Professor Blidstein finds in the Talmud "expressions of opposition" to a "virtual abolition of the death penalty." Gerald J. Blidstein, *Capital Punishment—The Classic Jewish Discussion*, 14 Judaism 159, 165 (1965). Blidstein further notes that "[i]n practice," post-Talmudic legal authorities "found the abolition of capital punishment . . . impossible to maintain." Id. at 170 n.23.

16 See, e.g., *Bowers v. Hardwick*, 478 U.S. 186, 192 (1986) (noting references to common law and early colonial law); *Roe v. Wade*, 410 U.S. 113, 160 & n.57 (1973) (observing that Stoic and Jewish faiths believe life begins at birth); *Miranda v. Arizona*, 384 U.S. 436, 458 n.27 (1966) (commenting on influence of Bible in development of analogue to right against self-incrimination).

PART TWO | CAPITAL PUNISHMENT IN THE WRITTEN TORAH

The fundamental source of all Jewish law is the Written Torah—the Five Books of Moses. As the prosecutor in *Hayes* observed, the Torah does prescribe the death penalty for murder. In fact, those seeking a legal text that incorporates capital punishment as part of a legal system can readily look to the text of the Torah for support, because it contains numerous references to the death penalty. In his Code of Law, Moses Maimonides, the medieval legal authority, documented a total of thirty-six such offenses subject to the death penalty in the Torah.[17]

Yet, despite the availability of the death penalty for a variety of crimes enumerated in the Torah, reliance on the text of the Torah to support the implementation of the death penalty in the United States is tenuous at best. First, the very fact that the Torah prescribes the death penalty for many offenses other than murder represents a fundamental difference between the law of the Torah and American law. Serving as a basic religious document as well as a legal document, the Torah consists not only of civil law but also of ritual law, in addition to historical narrative that pervades and unites the text. The religious nature of the Torah is dramatically illustrated in the many offenses deemed punishable by death, including for example, various forms of idolatry and violation of the Sabbath. In fact, the majority of capital offenses listed in the Torah relate to purely religious matters, with relatively few involving actions that would be considered criminal in the United States.[18] Thus, the religious objectives of the legal system manifested in the Written Torah make it an unlikely model for American jurisprudence in this regard.

Indeed, one of the central functions of capital punishment in the biblical justice system was to provide a means for the offender to atone for the capital offense.[19] The concepts of repentance and atonement are central to Jewish

---

17 3 *The Code of Moses Maimonides (Mishneh Torah),* Book 14, The Book of Judges, Laws Concerning the Sanhedrin and the Penalties within Their Jurisdiction 15:13, at 44 (Julian Obermann et al. eds. & Abraham M. Hershman trans., 1949).

18 See Leviticus 20:1-27; Numbers 15:32-36.

19 As Basil F. Herring has stated, "the evil is removed not only from the people of Israel but from the sinner in addition." Basil F. Herring, *Jewish Ethics and Halakhah for Our Time: Sources and Commentary* 157 n.7 (1984). Herring quotes a contemporary scholar who writes that, "Notwithstanding the high regard for man, the cherished value of every unique individual, and the great love that we have for every individual made in the image of God, even those condemned to death . . . nonetheless an evil man cannot be permitted to remain alive, for by his death he gains atonement, even as he is removed from life." Id. (quoting B. Rabinowitz-Teomim, *Mishpetei Nefashot be'Din ha-Sanhedrin u-ve'Din ha-Malkhut, ha-Torah ve'ha-Medinah* 48-50 (1952)). See also Kenneth Shuster, *Halacha As a Model for American*

religious thought and practice.[20] Even those who commit the most grievous sins have the opportunity and obligation to repent from those sins.[21] Those who commit capital offenses thus receive the harshest of punishments, in part because only such a harsh punishment is considered sufficient to merit complete spiritual atonement.[22] In contrast, the various rationales that have been offered to support the use of the death penalty in the American criminal justice system do not include the grounds of repentance. Applying the notion of repentance in the context of American capital punishment would presumably be regarded as an unacceptable incorporation of a purely religious basis for criminal penalty.[23] Any such theory would likely be discredited as a violation of the Establishment Clause, or, more generally, as an improper appeal to religious concepts that have no place in American legal doctrine.[24]

Penal Practice: A Comparison of Halachic and American Punishment Methods, 19 Nova L. Rev. 965, 974 n.60 (1995) (discussing the role of Halachic punishment in the expiation of sin).

20 See 3 The Code of Moses Maimonides (Mishneh Torah), Book 1, The Book of Knowledge, Laws of Repentance (Moses Hyamson trans., 1981); Joseph D. Soloveitchik, On Repentance (1984). See also Chapter 26 in Volume 2.

21 See 3 The Code of Moses Maimonides (Mishneh Torah), Book 1, The Book of Knowledge, Laws of Repentance 1:1, at 81b-82a (Moses Hyamson trans., 1981).

22 Indeed, after a conviction on a capital offense, the process of capital punishment includes a mandatory confession as part of the process of repentance and atonement. See 3 The Code of Moses Maimonides (Mishneh Torah), Book 14, The Book of Judges, Laws Concerning the Sanhedrin and Penalties within Their Jurisdiction 13:1, at 36 (Moses Hyamson trans., 1981).

23 See Bruce S. Ledewitz & Scott Staples, Reflections on the Talmudic and American Death Penalty, 6 U. Fla. J.L. & Pub. Pol'y 33, 37 (1993) (citations omitted). As Ledewitz and Staples explain,

> the American death penalty differs from that of the Talmud in that it is part of a secular criminal justice system.... the death penalty shows that at least in some contexts, a culture either has a religious perspective or it does not. An important part of the Talmudic death penalty—some say its overriding purpose—was to attain atonement for the condemned through a trial.... The Talmudic death penalty is unfathomable apart from atonement and ritual. The American death penalty does not have and cannot have, given the assumptions of our constitutional order, any focus on ritual and atonement. It would probably be reversible error for a jury even to consider that by condemning a defendant to death, they might be guaranteeing to him "a portion in the world to come."

But see Stephen P. Garvey, Punishment as Atonement, 46 UCLA L. Rev. 1801 (1999).

24 A number of courts have rejected references to religious and biblical sources in relation to the death penalty. See Bruce S. Ledewitz & Scott Staples, Reflections on the Talmudic and American Death Penalty, 6 U. Fla. J.L. & Pub. Pol'y 33, 37 n.22 (1993) (citing cases in which references to religion are rejected); Daniel A. Rudolph, Note, The Misguided Reliance in American Jurisprudence on Jewish Law to Support the Moral Legitimacy of Capital Punishment, 33 Am. Crim. L. Rev. 437, 438-39 (1996).

Second, and perhaps more fundamentally, reliance on the text of the Torah to support the death penalty in American law assumes that the text of the Torah is a complete depiction of the Jewish legal system. Such an assumption overlooks another basic premise of Jewish legal and religious thought, that as a written text, the Torah must be contextually interpreted in order to be understood and applied within a living society. Under Jewish legal theory, in conjunction with the Written Torah, God gave to Moses at Mount Sinai an Oral Torah equal in authority to the Written Torah. The Oral Torah was orally transmitted from generation to generation and ultimately compiled as the Talmud. Thus, it is nearly impossible—as well as inaccurate—to envision the Jewish legal system based solely on the Written Torah.[25] The law of capital punishment is a prime example of the need to consider both the Oral and Written Torahs, as the Written Torah provides broad principles, while the Oral Torah provides most of the legal details that determine the practical application of the law.

PART THREE | CAPITAL PUNISHMENT IN THE ORAL TORAH

As Judge Bright accurately observed in *Hayes v. Lockhart*,[26] "selective quoting" from the text of the Torah to suggest that the ancient Jewish law supports the use of the death penalty is "misleading."[27] Judge Bright further noted that a failure to refer to the Oral Torah ignores the "multitude of procedural barriers" set forth in the Oral Law that render the imposition of the death penalty a rare event.[28] Such

---

For discussions of the place of religion in public spheres, including law and politics, see generally Stephen L. Carter, *The Culture of Disbelief: How American Law and Politics Trivialize Religion* (1993); Kent Greenawalt, *Private Consciences and Public Reasons* (1995); Kent Greenawalt, *Religious Convictions and Political Choice* (1988); Michael J. Perry, *A Review of Religion in Politics: Constitutional and Moral Perspectives* (1997); Frederick Schauer, *May Officials Think Religiously?*, 27 Wm. & Mary L. Rev. 1075 (1986); Ruti Teitel, *A Critique of Religion As Politics in the Public Sphere*, 78 Cornell L. Rev. 747 (1993).

25 For discussions of the history, structure, and methodology of the Jewish legal system, including the relationship between the Written Torah and the Oral Torah, see generally Irving A. Breitowitz, *Between Civil Law and Religious Law: The Plight of The Agunah in American Society* 307-13 (1993); Menachem Elon, *Jewish Law: History, Sources, Principles* 228-39, 281-399 (Bernard Auerbach & Melvyn J. Sykes trans., 1994); David M. Feldman, *Birth Control in Jewish Law: Marital Relations, Contraception and Abortion* 3-18 (1968); Aaron Kirschenbaum, *Equity in Jewish Law: Halakhic Perspectives in Law* 289-304 (1991); Chapter 3 in this Volume; Menachem Elon, *The Legal System of Jewish Law*, 17 N.Y.U. J. Int'l L. & Pol. 221 (1985).

26 852 F.2d 339 (8th Cir. 1988).

27 Id. at 356 (Bright, J. dissenting).

28 Id. at 356-57 n.8.

safeguards were implemented throughout the Jewish criminal justice process, during the apprehension of the individual, the introduction of evidence at trial, the deliberations, the rendering of a verdict, and post-verdict proceedings.[29]

The Talmud describes, at considerable length, the various safeguards to be carried out. Among the most noteworthy safeguards, and perhaps those which most contribute to the infrequency of actual judicial imposition of the death penalty, are: (1) in the process of the apprehension, there must be at least two witnesses who observe the defendant while observing each other;[30] (2) the defendant must be told in advance of the nature of the offense and its punishment; (3) the defendant must immediately declare an intention to commit the offense anyway; and (4) the defendant must immediately carry it out.[31] Throughout the introduction of evidence, each of the witnesses is rigorously cross-examined, while being repeatedly reminded of the grave nature of the proceeding and the dearness of the human life at stake.[32] During the deliberations, any feasible argument for acquittal must be considered by the court, even if the argument was developed by students, who are not allowed to present arguments for conviction.[33] If a guilty verdict is found to be erroneous, the ruling is reversed, while an erroneous acquittal cannot be reversed.[34] After a guilty verdict is returned, messengers are dispatched to announce the verdict and call on anyone who can provide exculpatory information; the court then reconvenes to consider any exculpatory information, including claims made by the defendant.[35] These and numerous other safeguards produced a criminal justice system in which the death penalty was implemented somewhat infrequently—certainly not with the frequency that might be suggested by reading the Written Torah alone.

---

29 See Donald L. Beschle, *What's Guilt (or Deterrence) Got to Do with It? The Death Penalty, Ritual, and Mimetic Violence,* 38 Wm. & Mary L. Rev. 487, 508 (1997) (stating that "[t]he procedural demands necessary to sustain a capital sentence [in ancient Israel] were increased to a level that would [have] put the Warren Court to shame," and citing observers who "have noted that this same phenomenon has become manifest in contemporary Israel," including "the recent remarkable restraint of Israeli appellate courts in freeing John Demanjanjuk, accused of atrocities during World War II").

30 See 3 *The Code of Moses Maimonides (Mishneh Torah),* Book 14, The Book of Judges, Laws Concerning Evidence 4:1, at 89 (Julian Obermann et al. eds. & Abraham M. Hershman trans., 1949).

31 See 3 *The Code of Moses Maimonides (Mishneh Torah),* Book 14, The Book of Judges, Laws Concerning the Sanhedrin and Penalties within Their Jurisdiction 12:1-2, at 34 (Julian Obermann et al. eds. & Abraham M. Hershman trans., 1949).

32 See id. 12:3, at 34-36.

33 See id. 10:8, at 30.

34 See id. 10:9, at 30-31.

35 See id. 13:1, at 36-37.

Perhaps the most dramatic—and the most famous—expression of the reluctance of ancient Jewish legal authorities to implement the death penalty is found in a Talmudic dialogue between several rabbis that transpired shortly after the destruction of the Temple in Jerusalem, a time when courts no longer had the authority to adjudicate capital cases.

Without attributing the initial statement to any particular individual, the Talmud first asserts that a court that implements the death penalty once in seven years is a violent court.[36] The Talmudic discussion continues with the opinions of authorities who found even rare use of capital punishment to be far too frequent. One such authority, Rabbi Elazar ben Azaria, insists that a court that imposes the death penalty even one time in seventy years is a violent court.[37] The Talmud further documents the views of Rabbi Tarfon and Rabbi Akiva, who declare that, had they been members of a court with the authority to adjudicate capital cases, there would never have been an execution.[38] Neither Rabbi Tarfon nor Rabbi Akiva explains the precise reason for this absolute opposition to capital punishment; however, the approach appears to be abolitionist in spirit. The discussion concludes with a retort by Rabbi Simeon ben Gamliel that a total abolition of the death penalty would increase the number of murderers.[39] This response seemingly posits that the death penalty serves in some way as a deterrent to murder and that the abolitionist approach would impede this deterrent effect; the result would be an increase in murders.

Despite the obvious parallels to the current debate over the death penalty, meaningful application of the views presented in the Talmud requires further analysis of the rationale underlying the various positions, including careful consideration of their religious bases. The abolitionist views of Rabbi Tarfon and Rabbi Akiva, in particular, demand careful examination, because they are sometimes cited in contemporary American legal scholarship to support the abolitionist approach. Indeed, Judge Bright's reference to the "virtual impossibility" of an execution in ancient Jewish law[40] seems to draw directly on the views of Rabbi Tarfon and Rabbi Akiva.

---

36 See 4 The Babylonian Talmud, Seder Nezikin, Tractate Makkoth 7a, at 35-36 (I. Epstein ed. & H.M. Lazarus trans., 1935).

37 See id.

38 See id.

39 See id.

40 See supra notes 10-12 and accompanying text.

Scholars have suggested a number of theories to explain the abolitionist positions of Rabbi Tarfon and Rabbi Akiva.[41] One theory is that Rabbi Tarfon and Rabbi Akiva were concerned with the abiding possibility of human error, despite the numerous and elaborate safeguards that were implemented as standard procedure in capital cases.[42] Similar concerns resonate throughout the abolitionist movement in the United States.

Other scholars suggest that these rabbis were opposed to capital punishment not only because of the practical uncertainties involved, but because they were opposed to execution in principle, even when the defendant was unquestionably guilty.[43] According to this theory, the rabbis felt an overriding concern for the sanctity of human life that outweighed any justification for implementing the death penalty. Such an approach has likewise been adopted by modern abolitionists, who value human life so highly as to preclude the killing of anyone, even proven murderers. Yet, while the ethical basis for protecting human life need not be rooted in religion, Rabbi Tarfon and Rabbi Akiva likely argued from a decidedly religious perspective, which again raises the question of the propriety of utilizing their opinions to decide legal issues in the United States.[44]

Moreover, the views of Rabbi Tarfon and Rabbi Akiva do not comprise the whole of Jewish law; rather, their opinions are two among many, and did not represent the opinions of the majority of mainstream Jewish legal authorities. Thus, Judge Bright's statement regarding the "virtual impossibility" of an execution in ancient Jewish law reflects a minority opinion.[45] In fact, Professor

---

41 For a philosophical approach to the debate, that attributes absolutist positions to Rabbi Tarfon and Rabbi Akiva and a consequentialist position to Rabbi Simeon ben Gamliel, see Moshe Sokol, *Some Tensions in the Jewish Attitude Toward the Taking of Human Life: A Philosophical Analysis of Justified Homicide in Jewish Legal and Aggadic Literature*, 7 Jewish L. Ann. 97, 102-5 (1988).

42 See Basil F. Herring, *Jewish Ethics and Halakhah for Our Time: Sources and Commentary* 156 (1984). For references to similar concerns in contemporary American legal scholarship, see Kenneth Shuster, *Halacha as a Model for American Penal Practice: A Comparison of Halachic and American Punishment Methods*, 19 Nova L. Rev. 965, 975 n.68 (1995).

43 See Basil F. Herring, *Jewish Ethics and Halakhah for Our Time: Sources and Commentary* 156 (1984); Gerald J. Blidstein, *Capital Punishment—The Classic Jewish Discussion*, 14 Judaism 159, 164 (1965).

44 In addition, some medieval Jewish legal authorities interpreted the abolitionist views of Rabbi Tarfon and Rabbi Akiva as referring only to periods of proliferation in murders; according to these authorities, under ordinary conditions these Rabbis would not support an abolitionist approach. See Basil F. Herring, *Jewish Ethics and Halakhah for Our Time: Sources and Commentary* 156 (1984).

45 In addition to enumeration of authorities who openly dispute the views of Rabbi Tarfon and Rabbi Akiva, a Talmudic discussion of these different opinions suggests that a majority of

Blidstein, whose article Judge Bright cited, deemed Rabbi Akiva to be "the final expositor of a muted tradition."[46] Blidstein further observed that Rabbi Simeon ben Gamliel, who contested the views of Rabbi Tarfon and Rabbi Akiva, "was probably not alone in protesting this virtual abolition of the death penalty. His is merely the clearest voice."[47]

The view of Rabbi Simeon ben Gamliel appears to find support in other rabbinic statements, which dispute whatever overriding concerns motivated Rabbi Tarfon and Rabbi Akiva. For example, the rabbis of the Talmud comment on the biblical verse which instructs that in executing a murderer, "do not pity him."[48] According to the rabbis, this verse was a response to those who would oppose the execution of a murderer on the grounds that, because the victim is already dead, the taking of another life serves no purpose.[49] As Blidstein explains, "[h]owever generous the motive, the perversion of justice is evil, its motivation misguided. The Rabbis feared that true love of humanity could only be undermined by indiscriminate recourse to 'mercy,' which, as Rabbi Simeon ben Gamliel pointed out, would deny an innocent society the concern shown the criminal."[50]

Similarly, those opinions that decried the use of the death penalty even one time in seven years or in seventy years would not necessarily support opposition to the death penalty in the United States. It is evident that rabbis who made such statements, despite registering their disapproval of the common use of the death penalty, were not outright abolitionists. At best, incorporating such views into American jurisprudence might suggest that the current number of executions in the country as a whole—and in the state of Texas in particular—should decrease considerably, to prevent the development of "violent courts" in the United States.

Even this modest hypothesis, however, remains an inconclusive inference from the statements of the rabbis. Although their views appear to focus on the mere number of executions, the rabbis' primary concerns might have

---

rabbis disagreed with the approach of Rabbis Tarfon and Akiva. See 4 The Babylonian Talmud, Seder Nezikin, Tractate Makkoth 7a, at 35-37 (I. Epstein ed. & H.M. Lazarus trans., 1935).

46 Gerald J. Blidstein, *Capital Punishment—The Classic Jewish Discussion*, 14 Judaism 159, 165 (1965).

47 Id.

48 Deuteronomy 19:13.

49 See Midrash Tannaim (commenting on Deuteronomy 19:13) (cited in Basil F. Herring, *Jewish Ethics and Halakhah For Our Time: Sources and Commentary* 152 (1984)).

50 Gerald J. Blidstein, Capital Punishment—The Classic Jewish Discussion, 14 Judaism 159, 167 (1965).

been based specifically on the number of executions relative to the general population. Consider that the Jewish population in the Land of Israel at that time was probably no larger than a few million;[51] thus, the rabbis' statements criticized the execution of one out of a few million individuals every seven or seventy years. A proportionate analysis in the United States, a nation of more than three hundred million people, would result in the condemnation of the execution of approximately one hundred people every seven or seventy years. Although this analysis still supports a modification in the current pace of executions, the resulting criticism of the current system is somewhat muted. Another relevant consideration is that the rabbis issued their opinions in the context of a society that was probably not plagued by the level of violence currently experienced in United States.[52] Had they been theorizing in a more violent society, the rabbis may have approved of larger number of executions.

Conversely, however, the high degree of violence that has permeated the United States may ultimately provide the most convincing argument that Jewish law would not support this nation's implementation of the death penalty. The Talmud indicates that forty years prior to the destruction of the Second Temple in Jerusalem, the Sanhedrin—the High Court—moved from its location near the Temple in order to negate its own authority to adjudicate capital cases.[53] According to the Talmud, upon the proliferation of capital offenses, the court recognized that it could no longer judge these cases properly and subsequently decided not to render any more death sentences.[54] Despite the mainstream acceptance of capital punishment, the rabbis evidently concluded that if capital offenses are committed to such an extent that courts lose their ability to

---

51 See 13 *Encyclopedia Judaica* 871-72 (1971) (estimating the Jewish population in the Land of Israel "shortly before the fall of Jerusalem" in 70 C.E. at "not more than 2,350,000-2,500,000" and noting that after the fall of Jerusalem, "[u]nquestionably the total number of Jews rapidly declined").

52 Professors Ledewitz and Staples suggest that "[t]he differences between Israel in the period of time before the redaction of the Talmud and America today are obviously great . . . . The most significant difference between ancient Israel and modern America is the level of violence." See Bruce S. Ledewitz & Scott Staples, *Reflections on the Talmudic and American Death Penalty*, 6 U. Fla. J.L. & Pub. Pol'y 33, 36 (1993).

53 See 4 The Babylonian Talmud, Seder Nezikin, Tractate Abodah Zarah 8b, at 42 (I. Epstein ed. & A. Cohen trans., 1935).

54 The precise rationale for the Sanhedrin's actions remains nebulous. See id.; Aaron Kirschenbaum, *The Role of Punishment in Jewish Criminal Law: A Chapter in Rabbinic Penological Thought*, 9 Jewish L. Ann. 123, 141 (1991); Bruce S. Ledewitz & Scott Staples, *Reflections on the Talmudic and American Death Penalty*, 6 U. Fla. J.L. & Pub. Pol'y 33, 36 (1993).

properly adjudicate such cases, then the death penalty should be suspended.[55] It follows from this view that the proliferation of murders in the United States mandates at least a temporary cessation of capital punishment.[56]

Finally, two additional factors might complicate any attempt to oppose the death penalty by reference to Jewish law. Both factors involve fundamental components of the Jewish legal system that do not have parallels in American law. The first factor relates to the uniquely religious considerations that often underlie principles in the Jewish criminal justice system.[57] Specifically, the willingness of Jewish legal authorities to limit the use of the death penalty was based, at least in part, on an abiding trust in God as the ultimate arbiter of justice. The Talmud relates the belief that even when the High Court ceased to adjudicate capital cases, the Heavenly Court continued to mete out the death penalty through a variety of seemingly natural or accidental events.[58] In contrast, the United States criminal justice system is premised on the principle that the nation's courts are the final forums of justice,[59] and thus fundamentally inconsistent with the religious aspects of Jewish law that allow for the limitation or abolishment of capital punishment.

The second factor complicating the use of Jewish law to oppose the death penalty is that Jewish law provides for extrajudicial imposition of capital

---

55 Basil F. Herring has cited the view that "when the crime rate increases, indicating that the deterrent function of the death penalty is irrelevant, there is even more reason to oppose its implementation." Basil F. Herring, *Jewish Ethics and Halakhah for Our Time: Sources and Commentary* 161 (1984).

56 Professors Ledewitz and Staples reason that "[i]f we are to have a death penalty at all, with over 20,000 homicides a year, it must be a massively widespread penalty compared to that of Israel." Bruce S. Ledewitz & Scott Staples, *Reflections on the Talmudic and American Death Penalty*, 6 U. Fla. J.L. & Pub. Pol'y 33, 36 (1993). They conclude that "[t]he Rabbis of the Talmud could not have accepted the routinization of the death penalty necessitated by such large numbers." Id.

57 See notes 20-26 and accompanying text.

58 See 3 The Babylonian Talmud, Seder Nezikin, Tractate Sanhedrin 37b, at 235-36 (I. Epstein ed. & Jacob Shachter trans., 1935); see also Aaron Kirschenbaum, *The Role of Punishment in Jewish Criminal Law: A Chapter in Rabbinic Penological Thought*, 9 Jewish L. Ann. 123, 138-41 (1991).

59 See Irene Merker Rosenberg & Yale M. Rosenberg, *Guilt: Henry Friendly Meets the MaHaRaL of Prague*, 90 Mich. L. Rev. 604, 614-15 (1991) (contrasting the American criminal justice system's approach to guilt with the Jewish legal system's underlying assumption that "in any case of acquittal of the factually guilty, God will ultimately assess culpability correctly and completely and punish accordingly"). Despite this contrast, the authors cite a number of similarities between the two systems and endorse "meaningful comparison of the Jewish and American views on factual and legal guilt." Id. at 616; see also supra note 3.

punishment.[60] For example, the Talmud instructs that if the "needs of the hour" so demand, a court may issue a capital sentence without invoking the ordinary evidentiary and procedural safeguards. The Talmud also permits, under extraordinary circumstances, the imposition of the death penalty for offenses that are not otherwise considered capital offenses.[61] In addition, if a murderer is not subject to the death penalty through the usual judicial process, the king has the prerogative to execute the murderer based on "societal need" and "the needs of the hour."[62]

The very fact that Jewish law authorizes multiple avenues for imposing capital punishment weakens modern attempts to rely on Jewish law to oppose the death penalty.[63] The extrajudicial imposition of capital punishment is, by definition, extraordinary, even within the Jewish legal system, and has no parallel in American law. Moreover, the existence of extrajudicial alternatives to the judicial imposition of capital punishment may have provided a measure of assurance to authorities who limited the judicial enforcement of the death penalty.[64] If so, it is perhaps less certain that the positions taken by these authorities provide support for modern opponents of capital punishment in the United States, where there are no extrajudicial means for imposing capital punishment.

---

60 See Aaron M. Schreiber, *The Jurisprudence of Dealing with Unsatisfactory Fundamental Law: A Comparative Glance at the Different Approaches in Medieval Criminal Law, Jewish Law and the United States Supreme Court*, 11 Pace L. Rev. 535, 545-51 (1991).

61 See 3 The Babylonian Talmud, Seder Nezikin, Tractate Sanhedrin 46a, at 303, 72a, at 488-89 (I. Epstein ed. & H. Freedman & Jacob Shachter trans., 1935). For discussions of the court's exigency jurisdiction, see Basil F. Herring, *Jewish Ethics and Halakhah for Our Time: Sources and Commentary* 158-59 (1984); Emanuel B. Quint & Neil S. Hecht, 1 *Jewish Jurisprudence: Its Sources and Modern Applications* 139-213 (1980); Aaron Kirschenbaum, *The Role of Punishment in Jewish Criminal Law: A Chapter in Rabbinic Penological Thought*, 9 Jewish L. Ann. 123, 132-35 (1991).

62 See Maimonides, Code of Law (*Mishneh Torah*), Book 14, The Book of Judges, Laws of Mamrim 2:4 (Julian Obermann et al. eds. & Abraham M. Hershman trans., 1949); see generally J. David Bleich, *Jewish Law and the State's Authority to Punish Crime*, 12 Cardozo L. Rev. 829 (1991); Arnold N. Enker, *Aspects of Interaction Between the Torah Law, the King's Law, and the Noahide Law in Jewish Criminal Law*, 12 Cardozo L. Rev. 1137 (1991).

63 See Aaron M. Schreiber, *The Jurisprudence of Dealing with Unsatisfactory Fundamental Law: A Comparative Glance at the Different Approaches in Medieval Criminal Law, Jewish Law and the United States Supreme Court*, 11 Pace L. Rev. 535, 545-51 (1991).

64 See Aaron Kirschenbaum, *The Role of Punishment in Jewish Criminal Law: A Chapter in Rabbinic Penological Thought*, 9 Jewish L. Ann. 123, 141 (1991) (asserting "[o]nly the exigency jurisdiction of the courts . . . remained to cope with the proliferation of murderers, plunderers and men of violence").

CONCLUSION

Any student of the law who studies the Jewish legal system and the American legal system will observe many parallels, in both substance and methodology. As a result of these parallels, and various similarities in the moral beliefs found in Jewish tradition and American society, some legal scholars look to Jewish law to help resolve complex issues in American law, particularly those with deep moral implications.

Inasmuch as the death penalty persists as one of the most complex and controversial moral questions in American legal thought, it is not surprising that courts and legal scholars have turned to Jewish law for guidance. Unfortunately, however, references to Jewish law in the area of the death penalty are often incomplete and inaccurate. A prudent application of Jewish law to the modern death penalty requires a complete analysis of the Jewish legal system in its proper context. In particular, one must acknowledge, appreciate, and understand the interaction between fundamental legal and religious principles that are central to Jewish law in order to make meaningful and illuminating comparisons and contrasts between the Jewish and American legal systems.

CHAPTER 6

Playing God: An Essay on Law, Philosophy, and American Capital Punishment

INTRODUCTION

As Professor Stephen Garvey has aptly described the process, the penalty phase in a capital case begins when a defendant has "pass[ed] the critical threshold of death-eligibility," a determination of which is subject to a number of constitutional limitations.[1] At that point, Garvey writes, the defendant "enters the individualized death-selection phase," in which the capital sentencer decides whether the defendant, already found to be eligible for the death penalty, should in fact receive this sentence.[2] In stark contrast to the death-eligibility stage, Garvey identifies in the death-selection stage a "laissez-faire character."[3] Specifically, he notes, consistent with the "individualization principle [that] governs this second stage," in deciding whether to impose the death penalty, a capital sentencer may consider almost any relevant mitigating or aggravating factor.[4]

On one level, the sheer quantity and range of factors that may be explored in the penalty stage of a capital case illustrate the broad responsibility and discretion entrusted to a capital sentencer. On a deeper—and perhaps more significant—level, however, the nature of a number of these factors reveals an anomalous and

---

1 See Stephen P. Garvey, *"As the Gentle Rain from Heaven": Mercy in Capital Sentencing*, 81 Cornell L. Rev. 989, 1009-11 & nn.74-81 (1996) (detailing constitutional limitations on categories of crimes that can lead to imposition of the death penalty).

2 Id. at 1011.

3 See id.

4 See id. (citing *Zant v. Stephens*, 462 U.S. 862, 877 (1983); *Lockett v. Ohio*, 438 U.S. 586, 604 (1978)). Indeed, Garvey cites the view that at this stage the sentencer is subject to "no substantive limitation at all." See id. (quoting Carol S. Steiker & Jordan M. Steiker, *Let God Sort Them Out? Refining the Individualization Requirement in Capital Sentencing*, 102 Yale L.J. 835, 853 (1992) (Review Essay)).

somewhat disturbing aspect of the capital sentencer's function in the American legal system. At least three of these factors, in particular, implicate difficult philosophical and psychological issues that appear to require that a capital sentencer answer challenging questions often viewed as insoluble through human reasoning.

In part through a comparison to principles of Jewish law and philosophy,[5] this chapter aims to show that many of the questions that the American capital sentencer is expected to answer can be resolved only on the basis of divine knowledge. Part one of the chapter discusses the unfair expectation that a capital sentencer will be able to resolve age-old questions of free will and moral luck, and their relationship to criminal culpability. Part two identifies another troubling aspect of the capital sentencer's decision: determination of a defendant's moral worth, ostensibly through an examination of every aspect of the defendant's life. Finally, part three critiques the assumption that the capital sentencer can predict with substantial accuracy the future dangerousness of a defendant. Thus, the chapter argues that the American capital sentencer is asked to "play God"—an expectation that, by its very nature, carries with it a daunting and unreasonable responsibility.[6]

PART ONE | CULPABILITY, FREE WILL, AND MORAL LUCK

According to the Supreme Court, and in the view of many scholars, one of the primary factors a capital sentencer should consider in deciding whether to impose the death penalty is the level of the defendant's culpability. As Professor Garvey has put it, "[t]he more culpable a capital defendant is for his conduct,

---

5   Consistent with my approach elsewhere, rather than mechanically applying substantive conclusions in Jewish law regarding the place of capital punishment in the Jewish legal system, this chapter instead "focuses on the conceptual underpinnings behind pertinent Jewish law [and philosophy], considering the potential relevance and effect of those conceptualizations on American legal thought." See Chapter 5 in this Volume. See also Samuel J. Levine, *Capital Punishment and Religious Arguments: An Intermediate Approach*, 9 Wm. & Mary Bill Rts. J. 179 (2000).

6   For examples of commentators who have viewed the implementation of the death penalty as an exercise in "playing God" in a different sense, see, e.g., Eugene B. Block, *When Men Play God: The Fallacy of Capital Punishment* (1983); Steven Brill, *An Innocent Man on Death Row*, Am. Law., Dec. 1983, at 1 ("Having read the trial record and having found new evidence, I am convinced that he is innocent and that the Knapp case should remind us that a legal system—even our best of all legal systems—is too plain mortal to play God with life and death."), cited in Hugo Adam Bedau & Michael L. Radelet, *Miscarriages of Justice in Potentially Capital Cases*, 40 Stan. L. Rev. 21, 30 n.40 (1987); Judith A. Hagley, *The Lawyer's Bookshelf*, N.Y.L.J., Jan. 5, 1996, at 2 ("Given human fallibility, should jurors be handed the death penalty and asked to play God?").

the more deserving he is of death."[7] Consistent with this understanding of the concept of culpability and its relationship to capital punishment, the Supreme Court has authorized a capital sentencer to take into account broad indicia of culpability or a lack thereof. The factors to be considered include "any aspect of a defendant's character and any of the circumstances of the offense that the defendant proffers as a basis for a sentence less than death."[8] In support of the Court's approach, Professor Louis Bilionis has explained that "[t]he Constitution permits only morally appropriate impositions of the death penalty; it requires in every case that the capital sentencer reliably determine that death is indeed the morally appropriate penalty."[9] In a number of cases, the Court has, in fact, expressly emphasized the need for an approach to capital punishment that fully incorporates principles of culpability and morality.[10]

The underlying rationale for this emphasis on culpability is the fundamental recognition that "death is different."[11] According to Professor Bilionis,

---

7 Garvey, supra note 1, at 1022. Garvey incorporates a definition of culpability as "the factors of intent, motive and circumstance that determine the extent to which the offender should be held accountable for an act." See id. at 1022 n.130 (quoting Andrew von Hirsch & Nils Jarenborg, *Gauging Criminal Harm: A Living Standard Analysis*, 11 Oxford J. Legal Studies 1, 1 (1990)).

8 *Lockett v. Ohio*, 438 U.S. 586, 604 (1978) (plurality opinion).

9 Louis D. Bilionis, *Moral Appropriateness, Capital Punishment, and the Lockett Doctrine*, 82 J. Crim. L. & Criminology 283, 288 (1991). See also Stephen P. Garvey, *Death-Innocence and the Law of Habeas Corpus*, 56 Alb. L. Rev. 225, 233 (1992) ("[T]o do justice to a particular [capital] defendant requires that the punishment reflect his particular moral guilt. Every morally relevant feature of the offender and the offense is to be accounted for and weighed in the death-selection decision."); Laura S. Underkuffler, *Agentic and Conscientic Decisions in Law: Death and Other Cases*, 74 Notre Dame L. Rev. 1713, 1724 (1999) ("Focus on the defendant 'as a "uniquely individual human being'" in deciding whether he should live or die is deeply rooted in another principle: that the selection of an individual for death is based upon the 'moral culpability' of that person.") (quoting *Booth v. Maryland*, 482 U.S. 496, 504 (1987) (internal citations omitted)). Cf. Carol Steiker & Jordan Steiker, *Defending Categorical Exemptions to the Death Penalty: Reflections on the ABA's Resolutions Concerning the Execution of Juveniles and Persons with Mental Retardation*, 61 Law & Contemp. Probs. 89, 102 (1998) ("[T]he requirement of individualized sentencing derives from a commitment to individual moral culpability [...] as the central inquiry in a constitutional scheme of capital punishment."); Steiker & Steiker, supra note 4, at 844-58.

10 William J. Bowers & Benjamin D. Steiner, *Death by Default: An Empirical Demonstration of False and Forced Choices in Capital Sentencing*, 77 Tex. L. Rev. 605, 625 & nn.95-101 (1999) (citing cases); Phyllis L. Crocker, *Concepts of Culpability and Deathworthiness: Differentiating between Guilt and Punishment in Death Penalty Cases*, 66 Fordham L. Rev. 21, 36 n.65 (1997) (citing cases); Underkuffler, supra note 9, at 1724-25 (citing cases).

11 See, e.g., *Harmelin v. Michigan*, 501 U.S. 957, 995 (1991) ("Our cases creating and clarifying the 'individualized capital sentencing doctrine' have repeatedly suggested that there is no comparable requirement outside the capital context, because of the qualitative difference between death and all other penalties."). See also *Harris v. Alabama*, 513 U.S. 504, 516 n.1

"[t]he eighth amendment requires a uniquely high degree of confidence in the moral appropriates of any death sentence imposed, for the death sentence—unlike any other judgment rendered in our criminal or civil courts—calls for an incomparably severe and uniquely irrevocable action."[12] In the language of Justice Stevens, the death penalty represents "an expression of the community's outrage—its sense that an individual has lost his moral entitlement to live."[13] Thus, "capital punishment rests on not a legal but an ethical judgment—an assessment of the [defendant's] 'moral guilt.'"[14]

As the Court "has not developed any well-defined theory of moral culpability"[15] and has—properly, according to some[16]—declined to delineate

---

(1995) (Stevens, J., dissenting) (citing Supreme Court cases confirming that "death is a fundamentally different kind of penalty"); *Simmons v. South Carolina*, 512 U.S. 154, 185 (1994) (identifying "death-is-different" jurisprudence); *Spaziano v. Florida*, 468 U.S. 447, 468 (1984) (Stevens, J., concurring in part and dissenting in part).

> [E]very member of this Court has written or joined at least one opinion endorsing the proposition that because of its severity and irrevocability, the death penalty is qualitatively different from any other punishment, and hence must be accompanied by unique safeguards to ensure that it is a justified response to a given offense.

Id.; *Woodson v. North Carolina*, 428 U.S. 280, 303-4 (1976) ("[D]eath is a punishment different from all other sanctions in kind rather than degree.") (citations omitted). For scholarly treatment of the "death is different" doctrine, see, e.g., Hugo Adam Budau, *Death Is Different: Studies in the Morality, Law, and Politics of Capital Punishment* (1987); Sherry F. Colb, *The Qualitative Dimension of Fourth Amendment "Reasonableness"*, 98 Colum. L. Rev. 1642, 1674 (1998) ("The Supreme Court [...] has rested an entire jurisprudence of capital punishment on the premise that state killing is *sui generis* and that noncapital precedents sometimes provide insufficient protection when applied in the capital context. The Court has declared by way of justification that 'death is different.'"); Garvey, supra note 9, at 233 ("Death is different, and doctrinally its distinctness is expressed by this attention to moral detail. Nothing of moral relevance must be disregarded or overlooked."); *Note, The Rhetoric of Difference and the Legitimacy of Capital Punishment*, 114 Harv. L. Rev. 1599 (2001); Underkuffler, supra note 9, at 1729 (citing Supreme Court cases that describe uniqueness of death penalty and stating that "[a]s a result of this uniqueness, it is particularly critical that the correct decision in each case be made, and correctness requires that all factors, circumstances, and aspects of the case be heard and weighed, without hindrance, by the sentencer."). But see Carol S. Steiker & Jordan M. Steiker, *Sober Second Thoughts: Reflection on Two Decades of Constitutional Regulation of Capital Punishment*, 109 Harv. L. Rev. 355, 397 (1995) (finding that "[t]he Court echoed the 'death is different' principle in a number of [...] cases, but close examination of the Court's decisions over the past twenty years reveals that the procedural safeguards in death cases are not as different as one might suspect.").

12 See Bilionis, supra note 9, at 318.
13 *Spaziano*, 468 U.S. at 469 (Stevens, J., concurring in part and dissenting in part).
14 Id. at 481.
15 Garvey, supra note 1, at 1023.
16 See Bilionis, supra note 9, at 302 (suggesting virtues of Court's approach).

specific kinds of mitigating evidence, scholars, courts, and legislatures have suggested numerous categories of evidence that may be considered as both aggravating and mitigating factors to determine the moral culpability of a capital defendant.[17] Notably, a number of the categories appear to implicate considerations and decisions that, in various systems of moral and legal philosophy—including Jewish law—are thought to require powers of knowledge and judgment outside the range of human capability.

A. Free Will Theories

Garvey sets forth two categories of mitigation that rest on an evaluation of the degree to which the criminal act was a product of the defendant's free will: "will" or "choice" theory and "character-will" theory.[18] As Garvey observes, both of these theories "forge a link between the offender's act and his free will"; under both theories, "the measure of deserved punishment depends on the choices the defendant has made."[19]

The first theory "holds an offender responsible for his act if and only if it was the product of his free will."[20] Although this principle applies to criminal law more generally,[21] Garvey explains its unique significance in capital cases. Unlike the general rule, which "shield[s] an offender from criminal liability only where his will has been almost completely overborne" due to conditions such as insanity, duress, and involuntary intoxication, a "defect in the [capital] defendant's will," though "less than total," serves to mitigate the severity of the punishment.[22]

The second theory, which Garvey calls the "character-will" theory, "locates responsibility not so much in the defendant's free will, but in his character."[23] Having determined the nature of a defendant's character, he explains, the capital sentencer must decide whether the criminal act was "out of character."[24] If so—similar to will theory—the facts or circumstances, if any, that caused the defendant to act in this way may be mitigating factors.[25] Alternatively, if the criminal act is consistent with the defendant's malevolent character, the

---

17 See, e.g., id. at 302-5 & nn.60-82; Phyllis L. Crocker, *Childhood Abuse and Adult Murder: Implications for the Death Penalty*, 77 N.C. L. Rev. 1143, 1153 n.36 (1999).

18 See Garvey, supra note 1, at 1023.

19 Id. at 1026.

20 Id. at 1023.

21 See, e.g., H.L.A. Hart, *Punishment and Responsibility* 152 (1968).

22 See Garvey, supra note 1, at 1023.

23 Id. at 1024.

24 See id.

25 See id.

question becomes "whether the defendant's character is the product of events beyond his control."[26] Ultimately, Garvey observes, both theories "ground culpability in some conception of free will."[27]

Questions regarding free will and its relationship to criminal law take many forms and are not restricted to the context of capital punishment.[28] In other types of criminal cases, though, notwithstanding the "millennia-old moral, religious, and philosophical debate over free will,"[29] the American criminal justice system generally presumes that a defendant has acted voluntarily.[30] As one court put it, "an individual determined to be 'sane' within the traditional constructs of the criminal law is held accountable for his actions, regardless of his particular disabilities, weaknesses, poverty, religious beliefs, social deprivation or educational background."[31]

Though different courts[32] and theorists have offered a wide range of rationales for this presumption, they generally recognize that, ultimately, "the problem [of free will and determinism] remains, and is likely to remain for the

---

26 Id. at 1025.

27 See id. Cf. Kent Greenawalt, *Punishment*, 74 J. Crim. L. & Criminology 343, 348 (1983) (stating that "acceptance of free will [...] is certainly the undergirding for the ordinary sense of morality").

28 For a long list of works discussing issues of free will, see Sherman J. Clark, *The Courage of Our Convictions*, 97 Mich. L. Rev. 2381, 2402 n. 39 (1999).

29 Id. at 2402.

30 Professor Kent Greenawalt explains the centrality of this presumption in the retributive theory of punishment:

> If all of our acts are consequences of preceding causes over which we ultimately have no control, causes that were set in motion before we were born-if, in other words, philosophical determinism is true-then the thief or murderer is, in the last analysis, more a victim of misfortune than a villain on the cosmic stage. Although he may be evil in some sense and able to control his actions, his character has been formed by forces outside himself, and that ultimately determines the choices he makes. [...] Unless one wishes to take the paradoxical position [...] that people are guilty for qualities and acts they cannot help, the simple retributive theory is incompatible with determinism. It requires some notion of free will that attributes to humans responsibility for doing wrong in a way that is not attributed to other animals.

Greenawalt, supra note 27, at 343.

31 *Johnson v. State*, 439 A.2d 542, 551 (Md. 1982). See also *Steward Mach. Co. v. Davis*, 301 U.S. 548, 590 (1936) ("[T]he law has been guided by a robust common sense which assumes the freedom of the will as a working hypothesis in the solution of its problems.").

32 See e.g., *Stewart v. Gramley*, 74 F.3d 132 (7th Cir. 1996); *State ex rel. D.D.H. v. Dostert*, 269 S.E.2d 401 (W. Va. 1980); *United States v. Brawner*, 471 F.2d 969 (D.C. Cir. 1972); *Blocker v. United States*, 288 F.2d 853 (D.C. Cir. 1961); *Cole v. State*, 128 A.2d 437 (Md. 1957); *State v. Macias*, 131 P.2d 810 (Ariz. 1942); *Orme v. Rogers*, 260 P. 199 (Ariz. 1927).

foreseeable future, unresolved."[33] Nevertheless, as a convention, "[t]he law treats man's conduct as autonomous and self-willed, not because it is, but because it is desirable to proceed as if it were,"[34] thereby avoiding "determinism's constant threat to undermine liberal accounts of moral desert."[35]

---

33 Clark, supra note 28, at 2402-3. See also Meir Dan-Cohen, *Responsibility and the Boundaries of the Self*, 105 Harv. L. Rev. 959, 960 n.1 (1992) (stating "the free will problem is far from solved") (citing Thomas Nagel, *The View from Nowhere* 110-37 (1986)).

34 Herbert L. Packer, *The Limits of the Criminal Sanction* 74-75 (1968). See also Craig Haney, *Psychological Secrecy and the Death Penalty: Observations on "The Mere Extinguishment of Life"*, 16 Stud. in Law, Politics & Soc'y 3, 29 (1997) ("In general, our criminal law embraces the fiction of free, unencumbered choice to facilitate the creation of a more easily managed system of responsibility.").

   In a classic article, Judge David Bazelon observed that "[a]lthough it has been asserted repeatedly that only a free choice to do wrong will be punished, in practice the law presumes, almost irrefutably, that proscribed behavior is the product of a 'free agent confronted with a choice between doing right and wrong and choosing freely to do wrong.'" See David L. Bazelon, *The Morality of the Criminal Law*, 49 S. Cal. L. Rev. 385, 387 (1976) (quoting Roscoe Pound, *Introduction to F. Sayre, Cases on Criminal Law* at xxxvii (1927)).

   For normative critiques of this position, see, e.g., Michael S. Moore, *Causation and the Excuses*, 73 Cal. L. Rev. 1091, 1122 (1985) (arguing that "the law demands more than that we pretend people are free and thus hold them responsible as if they were. A just legal system requires people to be truly responsible."); R. George Wright, *The Progressive Logic of Criminal Responsibility and the Circumstances of the Most Deprived*, 43 Cath. U. L. Rev. 459, 495 (1994) ("There should be a natural uneasiness with the deployment of any admitted legal fiction for the sake of utility.").

   Indeed, Judge Bazelon viewed the presumption of free will as an illustration of "the conflict between certain moral pretenses and practices." See Bazelon, supra, at 389. Cf. David Luban, *What's Pragmatic about Legal Pragmatism?*, 18 Cardozo L. Rev. 43, 55 (1996).

   > The philosophical problem [. . .] is that once you admit one deterministic excuse, it becomes hard to exclude others. [. . .] However, no judge [. . .] has ever argued that because all behavior is caused no one should ever be convicted of a crime. [. . .] Instead, the legal system draws philosophically arbitrary lines that reflect little more than legislative and judicial hunches about who is responsible and who is not. This strategy [. . .] combines compatibilism (the view that determinism is compatible with responsibility) with conventionalism (the view that there is no such thing as responsibility apart from social conventions for ascribing it).

   Id.

35 Peter Aranella, *Convicting the Morally Blameless: Reassessing the Relationship Between Legal and Moral Accountability*, 39 UCLA L. Rev. 1511, 1611 (1992); See also Jody Armour, *Just Deserts: Narrative, Perspective, Choice, and Blame*, 57 U. Pitt. L. Rev. 525, 538 (1996).

   > [D]eterminist doctrines like duress severely threaten the coherence and cogency of the intentionalist assumptions of ordinary criminal law discourse. Once we admit that decisions to break the law are sometimes blameless because

The penalty phase of a capital case, which includes free will considerations, stands out as a significant exception to these general principles.[36] This exception is an expression of the emphasis on moral culpability as a justification for imposing the most severe and irreversible of sentences.[37] Regardless of the reason for the exception, however, it appears that the requirement that a capital sentencer arrive at a definitive moral judgment of the defendant, through a precise estimation of the extent to which the defendant acted out of free will, imposes upon the sentencer a burden beyond the capabilities of human beings.[38] Such a decision requires qualities of knowledge and wisdom available only to an omniscient God. As Professor Kent Greenawalt has written, "[o]ne human can rarely

---

> those decisions are determined by preceding factors, and once we acknowledge that in some cases we must inquire into the roots of bad intentions and choices to evaluate blameworthiness, we actually begin to wonder why we do not inquire into the roots of decisions to break the law in all criminal cases.

Id. See also Bazelon, supra note 34, at 389 (quoting Oliver Wendell Holmes, *The Common Law* 45 (1881)).

> [I]f punishment "stood on the moral grounds which are proposed for it, the first thing to be considered would be those limitations in the capacity of choosing rightly which arise from abnormal instincts, want of education, lack of intelligence, and all other defects which are most marked in the criminal classes."

Id.

36 See Haney, supra note 34, at 30 ("Because of the unusually broad scope of capital penalty phases [...] they offer the potential to both contextualize the nature of choice and convey a richer and more compelling account of the causes of violent crime.").

37 As one federal judge has put it,

> one area where a deterministic view of behavior would make a heavy impact is the death penalty. Society may be able to confine some individuals because they are a danger to society even if due to their genetic wiring their antisocial actions are not morally culpable. However, imposition of the death penalty is predicated on the moral culpability of the defendant.

Gilbert S. Merritt, *From the Scopes Trial to the Human Genome Project: Where Is Biology Taking the Law?*, 67 U. Cin. L. Rev. 365, 375 (1999). At least one scholar rejects the notion that the qualitative difference between death and other punishments serves as an adequate basis to explain "the courts' inconsistency in this regard." See Wright, supra note 34, at 492. Instead, he suggests, "it may be simply that we are more reluctant to tolerate judicial hypocrisy and illogic in condemning a defendant to death." Id.

38 In addition, as one empirical study found, "experts' explanations of human behavior that run contrary to notions of free will are hard to sell to the jury." See Scott E. Sundby, *The Jury as Critic: An Empirical Look at How Capital Juries Perceive Expert and Lay Testimony*, 83 Va. L. Rev. 1109, 1139 (1997).

judge with confidence the moral guilt of others."[39] This inability of humans to calculate, with precision, the moral guilt of others is of particular concern when an erroneous evaluation may result in an improper execution.[40]

B. Victim Impact Evidence—Acceptance of Moral Luck

In most death penalty states, another factor that a capital sentencer may consider during the penalty phase is evidence of the impact of the crime on the victim or on the victim's family.[41] Though the view of the Supreme Court has changed over time with respect to victim impact evidence, under *Payne v. Tennessee*, current legal doctrine allows for the introduction of such evidence in the penalty phase of a capital case.[42] Based on the premise that "victim impact

---

39 Greenawalt, supra note 27, at 348. Cf. Haney, supra note 34, at 29 (describing the "complicated questions of causality and blameworthiness that capital jurors must work through in choosing between life and death"); Steiker & Steiker, supra note 11, at 433 (arguing that the Supreme Court has "create[d] a false aura of rationality, even science, around the necessarily moral task of deciding life or death"); Robert Weisberg, *Deregulating Death*, 1983 Sup. Ct. Rev. 305, 353 (describing the "inscrutability of the death judgment" and terming it "an existential moment of moral perception, neither right nor wrong"); id. at 393 (describing the "inevitably unsystematic, irreducibly personal moral elements of the choice to administer the death penalty").

40 In the Court's language, "[b]ecause the death penalty is unique 'in both its severity and its finality,' we have recognized an acute need for reliability in capital sentencing proceedings." *Monge v. California*, 524 U.S. 721, 732 (1998) (quoting *Gardner v. Florida*, 430 U.S. 349, 357 (1977)). For other expressions of the unique nature of the death penalty, see id. (citing cases); sources cited supra note 11 (supporting proposition that "death is different").

41 See Garvey, supra note 1, at 1018 & n.108 (citing *State v. Muhammad*, 678 A.2d 164, 177-78 (N.J. 1996)); Wayne A. Logan, *Through the Past Darkly: A Survey of the Uses and Abuses of Victim Impact Evidence in Capital Trials*, 41 Ariz. L. Rev. 143, 150 (1999) ("Today, at least thirty-two of the thirty-eight death penalty states, as well as the federal government, permit victim impact evidence in capital trials, on the basis of either judicial or legislative authority.").

42 See *Payne v. Tennessee*, 501 U.S. 808 (1991) (overruling *South Carolina v. Gathers*, 490 U.S. 805 (1989) & *Booth v. Maryland*, 482 U.S. 496 (1987)); Stephen P. Garvey, *The Emotional Economy of Capital Sentencing*, 75 N.Y.U. L. Rev. 26, 48 (2000).

> In 1987, the Supreme Court decided *Booth v. Maryland*, holding that victim impact evidence has nothing to do with a capital defendant's moral culpability and thus had no business being introduced into a capital trial. Four years later, the Court decided *Payne v. Tennessee*, changing its mind and holding that a state could fairly conclude that a capital defendant's culpability does depend on the details of the victim's life and the impact of her death on the members of her family.

Id.

evidence is evidence of harm the defendant could not have reasonably foreseen," Garvey argues that, in permitting victim impact as a factor in capital sentencing, the Court has concluded that "moral blameworthiness can depend upon unforeseen and unforeseeable harm."[43] The Court's conclusion is controversial because, as Garvey explains, the Court's approach implicates the complex and perhaps insoluble philosophical question of "moral luck."[44]

As Thomas Nagel explains, the concept of moral luck describes an underlying assumption in some systems, including the American legal system, through which "a significant aspect of what someone does depends on factors beyond his control, yet we continue to treat him in that respect as an object of moral judgement."[45] Applying this concept to victim impact evidence, Garvey notes that distinguishing between capital defendants based on unforeseeable

---

43 Garvey, supra note 1, at 1019.

44 See id. at 1020. For a compilation of sources discussing issues of moral luck, see Alan Strudler & Eric W. Orts, *Moral Principles in the Law of Insider Trading*, 78 Tex. L. Rev. 375, 417 n.179 (1999).

45 Thomas Nagel, *Moral Luck*, in Thomas Nagel, *Mortal Questions* 26 (Cambridge University Press 1979). In fact, Nagel delineates four categories of moral luck: (1) "constitutive luck," which refers to "the kind of person you are" by virtue of "inclinations, capacity, and temperament"; (2) "luck in one's circumstances," which includes "the kinds of problems and situations one faces"; (3) "luck in how one is determined by antecedent circumstances"; and (4) "luck in the way one's actions and projects turn out." See id. at 28.
   Cf. Stephen J. Morse, *Brain and Blame*, 84 Geo. L.J. 527, 536-37 (1996).

> All human action is, in part, the product of but-for causes over which agents have no control and which they are powerless to change, including their genetic endowments and the nature and context of their childrearing. If people had different genes, different parents, and different cultures, they would be different. Moreover, situational determinants over which agents have no control are but-for causes of much behavior. A victim in the wrong place at the wrong time is as much a but-for cause of the mugging as the mugger's genetics and experiences. If no victim were available, no mugging occurs, whatever the would-be mugger's intentions. Such considerations are treated by philosophers under the rubric, "moral luck." Our characters, and our opportunities are in large measure the product of luck, and if luck excused, no one would be responsible.

Id.; Stephen J. Morse, *Crazy Reasons*, 10 J. Contemp. Legal Issues 189, 208 (1999).
   Thus, according to both Nagel and Morse, the concept of moral luck has considerable relevance to discussions of the death penalty, beyond its implications regarding the inclusion of victim impact evidence in capital sentencing. More generally, moral luck raises profound questions about many of the fundamental concepts of moral culpability involved in the administration of the death penalty, including issues of free will. See supra part one, section A.

harm allows the severity of sentence to be dependent on "a matter of luck."[46] Therefore, he finds that the Court's acceptance of victim impact evidence "rejects th[e] immunity-from-luck principle," which stands for the proposition that "[a]s much as possible, punishment should be immune from luck's vagaries."[47] Critics of the Court's approach have argued that permitting victim impact evidence in capital sentencing thus punishes defendants for factors for which they are not culpable. For example, in dissenting from the Court's approach in *Payne*, Justice Stevens wrote that "defendants will be sentenced arbitrarily to death on the basis of evidence that would not ordinarily be admissible because it is irrelevant to the defendants' moral culpability."[48]

---

46 See Garvey, supra note 1, at 1020.

47 Id. See also Basil A. Umari, *Note, Is Tort Law Indifferent to Moral Luck?*, 78 Tex. L. Rev. 467, 469 (1999) ("Moral luck conflicts with our basic intuition that a person's moral culpability should not depend on events beyond that person's control."). But see David D. Friedman, *Should the Characteristics of Victims and Criminals Count?: Payne v. Tennessee and Two Views of Efficient Punishment*, 34 B.C. L. Rev. 731, 765 (1993) (finding that "punishment does, and [...] to most people it seems that punishment should, depend on factors unrelated to how wicked the crime shows the perpetrator to have been").

48 *Payne v. Tennessee*, 501 U.S. 808, 866 (1991) (Stevens, J., dissenting). See also Jeffrey L. Kirchmeier, *Aggravating and Mitigating Factors: The Paradox of Today's Arbitrary and Mandatory Capital Punishment Scheme*, 6 Wm. & Mary Bill Rts. J. 345, 385 (1998) ("The murderer [...] often does not know the specific information about the victim, so such specific information is not relevant to the defendant's culpability."); *Note, The Supreme Court: 1990 Term, Leading Cases*, 105 Harv. L. Rev. 177, 177 (1991) (criticizing the Court in *Payne* for "eviscerat[ing] the fundamental principle that capital sentencing should focus solely on the individual culpability of the defendant"); id. at 181 (arguing that the Court "in no way demonstrated how the unforeseeable harm the defendant caused [...] illuminates his personal blameworthiness" and that "[t]hus, without explicitly disavowing the underlying premise of its previous capital sentencing jurisprudence, the Court unmistakably moved toward abandoning the notion that individual culpability alone should guide these decisions").

Cf. Kenneth W. Simons, *When is Strict Criminal Liability Just?*, 87 J. Crim. L. & Criminology 1075, 1110 (1997).

> In its classic exposition, at least, the principle of moral luck asserts that equally culpable individuals can deserve different punishments in light of the difference they actually make in the world. It is a principle of responsibility for actual harm. But that principle does not justify a form of constructive culpability, in which the difference an offender actually makes in the world is the trigger for conclusively treating an individual as if he possessed a higher level of culpability than he actually possessed.

Id. As Garvey has noted, there is a difference of opinions among scholars regarding whether "only intended harm is relevant to deserved punishment" or "actual harm is also relevant." See Garvey, supra note 1, at 1021 & nn.124-25 (collecting sources).

The Court has responded to this criticism by noting other areas of American criminal law that incorporate into sentencing schemes differences in outcome that are beyond defendants' control, such as the distinction between an attempted crime and a completed one.[49] Judge Richard Posner has offered a similar depiction of the criminal law's acceptance of moral luck. Judge Posner noted that "in a system of morality in which only intentions and behaviors, but not consequences, count, there is no moral distinction between dangerous conduct that causes harm and otherwise identical dangerous conduct that does not. The only difference is luck, not usually considered a moral attribute."[50] By contrast, in describing the American legal system, Judge Posner explained that "'moral luck,' as philosophers refer to distinctions in culpability that are based on consequences rather than intentions, is, rightly or wrongly, a pervasive characteristic of moral thought in our society, at least the moral thought that informs the criminal law."[51]

Such justifications, however, offer only descriptions of American criminal law, not normative arguments for allowing the determination of a capital sentence based on circumstances beyond the control of a defendant. Indeed, Judge Posner seems unwilling to decide, on a normative level, whether the law's acceptance of moral luck in criminal sentencing is "right or wrong."[52] Perhaps, as some have suggested, it can be reasoned that "since fortuity pervades every aspect of our lives, the law must blind itself to fortuity, otherwise the whole legal enterprise is in danger of collapse."[53]

---

49 See *Payne*, 501 U.S. at 819-20.
50 *United States v. Martinez*, 16 F.3d 202, 205-6 (7th Cir. 1994).
51 Id. at 206.
52 See id.
53 See Umari, supra note 47, at 470 n.18 (describing this view, as well as a similar view that "because chance limits our control over the consequences of our actions, it tends to undermine our responsibility-based legal system and therefore must be ignored to some extent for our legal system to survive"). See also Friedman, supra note 47, at 763-64.

> On the face of it, the moral argument against basing punishment on actual consequences seems to apply to all crimes and punishments, not merely murder and execution. If punishment ought to be a function of how blameworthy the criminal is, then punishment should never be affected by factors that the criminal did not know about or could not control. That sounds persuasive, but it does not describe how our legal system actually works. Indeed, it probably does not describe how any legal system actually works. [. . .] In a wide range of civil and criminal cases, the sanction visited upon an offender depends in part on things that have little or nothing to do with how bad a person he is.

Id.; Craig A. Stern, *Crime, Moral Luck, and The Sermon on the Mount,* 48 Cath. U. L. Rev. 801, 839 n.111 (1999) ("Michael S. Moore has demonstrated that a consistent application

Yet, like the similar argument for the presumption of free will in the law, such an approach falls short with respect to capital punishment. If we are to take seriously the Court's insistence that a sentence of death must be morally justified based on the defendant's culpability,[54] pragmatic acceptance of moral luck, though perhaps useful in other areas of criminal law, should not play a role in capital sentencing.[55] As Justice Stevens forcefully and eloquently declared in his dissent in *Payne*, "[t]he notion that the inability to produce an ideal system of justice somehow justifies a rule that completely divorces some capital sentence determinations from moral culpability is incomprehensible to me."[56]

Like the question of free will and determinism, moral luck, in the words of Thomas Nagel, is a "problem about moral responsibility to which we possess no satisfactory solution."[57] Indeed, the problem of moral luck is so vexing because it involves wisdom beyond that available to humans, judgments possible only on a divine level. Nevertheless, the Court's decision in *Payne* permits victim impact to affect the sentence of a capital defendant. Thus, once again, the Court's approach requires that a capital sentencer decide the fate of a defendant's life by considering factors implicating deep and insoluble moral and philosophical questions.

C. Jewish Law and Philosophy on Free Will, Luck, and Moral Culpability

Like other moral and legal philosophers, scholars of Jewish law and philosophy have long recognized and addressed complex questions regarding free will and luck and their relationship to moral culpability.[58] Following in this tradition, a

---

of the doctrine that moral luck is to be eliminated from moral judgments would remove all human responsibility. One's character, one's health, one's opportunity to act, one's ability to choose, all depend, at least in part, upon luck."). But see Eric Lotke, *Reflection and the Limits of Liability: Necessary Blindness in the Legal System*, 54 Ohio St. L.J. 1425, 1433 (1993) (identifying and rejecting view that "[a]s a practical matter, people must be held legally liable— even if they are not responsible in a deep moral sense").

54 See sources cited supra note 10.

55 Cf. Arnold H. Loewy, *Culpability, Dangerousness, and Harm: Balancing the Factors on Which Our Criminal Law is Predicated*, 66 N.C. L. Rev. 283, 288 (1988) ("To the extent that culpability ought to be the sole criterion in assessing criminality [...] harm should be irrelevant to criminality.").

56 *Payne v. Tennessee*, 501 U.S. 808, 866 (1991) (Stevens, J., dissenting).

57 Nagel, supra note 45, at 25. See also Garvey, supra note 1, at 1021 ("The problem of moral luck defies easy solution. [...] Insofar as victim impact evidence raises the problem of moral luck, no simple solution exists.").

58 See, e.g., discussions in 1 Eliyahu Dessler, *Michtav M'Eliyahu* 111-20, 278-83 (Aryeh Carmell & Alter Halpern eds., 1954); 4 Eliyahu Dessler, *Michtav M'Eliyahu* 93-120, 321-23 (Aryeh Carmell ed., 1983); 5 Eliyahu Dessler, *Michtav M'Eliyahu* 351-58, 500 (editor's

leading contemporary American scholar of Jewish law and philosophy, Rabbi Joseph Soloveitchik, offered an analysis that captures the emphasis in Jewish thought on God's unique ability to engage in true moral judgment of human beings.

At the outset, Rabbi Soloveitchik notes the fundamental principle in Jewish thought that human beings have free will.[59] Nevertheless, he recognizes that "[e]ven as we emphasize man's free will, we are also aware that so much of what happens in life is not of man's making."[60] Indeed, Rabbi Soloveitchik enumerates a long list of forces and factors, outside of the realm of an individual's free will, that may affect the course of a person's actions. He observes, for example, that a person

> does not choose the family into which he is born and reared nor the society whose values will have such an impact upon him. He makes choices, yet major aspects of his life seem governed by capricious, chance events and circumstances beyond his control. He is a vulnerable creature whose serenity may suddenly be jarred by overpowering temptations, peculiar turns of events, unexpected political coups, an economic collapse, a terminal illness, or traumatic shocks.[61]

After elaborating on the "[i]rrational events [. . .] the instability, uncertainty and vulnerability which characterize human life [. . .] the sudden turns of fortune, lurking dangers, the fickleness of life,"[62] Rabbi Soloveitchik explains the legal relevance of these realities. Significantly, though he acknowledges that forces beyond a person's control may suggest a lower level of culpability for wrongdoing, Rabbi Soloveitchik does not recommend that these forces be considered within the context of human administration of justice. Rather, he emphasizes that these factors play a role in divine justice, as only God can truly adjudicate moral culpability.

---

note) (Aryeh Carmell ed., 1997); 1 Aryeh Kaplan, *The Handbook of Jewish Thought* ch. 3 (Maznaim Publishing 1979).

59 See Abraham R. Besdin, *Reflections of the Rav: Lessons in Jewish Thought* 40 (Ahva Co-op Press 1979) (adapted from lectures of Rabbi Joseph B. Soloveitchik); see also Kaplan, supra note 58, at ch. 3 (describing this principle and citing sources); Yitzchok Hutner, *Pachad Yitzchok: Purim* 79-81 (6th ed., 1998).

60 Besdin, supra note 59, at 41. See also Joseph B. Soloveitchik, *Family Redeemed: Essays on Family Relationships* 168-71 (David Shatz & Joel B. Wolowelsky eds., 2000) (discussing the "inner contradiction of the idea of free will").

61 See Besdin, supra note 59, at 41.

62 Id. at 45.

Specifically, he explains, on the plane of true moral culpability, it must be recognized that "[o]ne individual may be saintly because he was reared in noble surroundings; another succumbs to evil because his home background lacked moral instruction and inspiration. [T]he difference in their environments has affected their personalities."[63] Thus, in judging individuals, Rabbi Soloveitchik asks, "[s]hould all sinners, then, be deemed equally guilty? Is not much of man's waywardness due to his susceptibility to external pressures? He finds himself almost overwhelmed by situations not of his own making, and by chance circumstances which propel him in various directions."[64]

---

63 Id. at 45-46.

64 Id. at 46. For similar expressions of concern by American legal scholars in the context of the actions of capital defendants, see William S. Geimer, *Law and Reality in the Capital Penalty Trial*, 18 N.Y.U. Rev. L. & Soc. Change 273, 295 (1990-91).

> Capital defendants are rarely, if ever, solely accountable for their crimes, and certainly their accountability never reaches the point where society can justifiably require them to forfeit their lives. Precisely because capital defendants did not spring full blown onto the earth at the moment of their crimes [...] they cannot justly be killed as punishment.

Id.; Gary Goodpaster, *The Trial for Life: Effective Assistance of Counsel in Death Penalty Cases*, 58 N.Y.U. L. Rev. 299, 335-36 (1983).

> [T]he defense must attempt to show that the defendant's capital crimes are humanly understandable in light of his past history and the unique circumstances affecting his formative development, that he is not solely responsible for what he is. Many child abusers, for example, were abused as children. The knowledge that a particular abuser suffered abuse as a child does not, of course, excuse the conduct, yet it makes the crime, inconceivable to many people, more understandable and evokes at least partial forgiveness. Counsel's demonstration that upbringing and other formative influences may have distorted the defendant's personality or led to his criminal behavior may spark in the sentencer the perspective or compassion conducive to mercy.

Id.; Craig Haney, *The Social Context of Capital Murder: Social Histories and the Logic of Mitigation*, 35 Santa Clara L. Rev. 547, 560-61 (1995).

> Social histories [...] are not excuses, they are explanations. An explanation does not necessarily dictate an outcome ... [b]ut no jury can render justice in the absence of an explanation. In each case, the goal is to place the defendant's life in a larger social context and, in the final analysis, to reach conclusions about how someone who has had certain life experiences, been treated in particular ways, and experienced certain kinds of psychologically-important events has been shaped and influenced by them.

Id.; Andrea D. Lyon, *Defending the Death Penalty Case: What Makes Death Different?*, 42 Mercer L. Rev. 695, 703 (1991) (arguing that "mitigation begins with the onset of the

These considerations, according to Rabbi Soloveitchik, form the basis for the fundamental principle of *teshuva*, as "God forgives man's sinfulness precisely because He acknowledges human vulnerability to changing fortunes, pressing circumstances, and the intrusion of the unexpected."[65] Indeed, "[i]t is because of this [vulnerability] that man can stand before the Heavenly Bar of Justice, hoping for compassion and forgiveness."[66] Thus, "[d]espite his free will and his accountability for his deeds, man enters his plea before the Almighty, claiming that he is not the author and designer of the worldly pressures that were too powerful for him. These subverting temptations were thrust upon him by [the] circumstances."[67] Ultimately, "the basis for a penitent's claim to forgiveness [is] that his moral directions were [. . .] influenced by forces beyond his control, that his sinning was not entirely a free and voluntary choice."[68] Nevertheless, this claim of reduced culpability is not brought before a human court of justice. Rabbi Soloveitchik emphasizes that "[o]nly the Almighty can evaluate the extent

---

[defendant's] life" because "[m]any [defendants'] problems start with things like fetal alcohol syndrome, head trauma at birth, or their mother's drug addiction during pregnancy").

65 Besdin, supra note 59, at 45. For further discussions of the fundamental principle of *teshuva*, see, e.g., 2 Aryeh Kaplan, *The Handbook of Jewish Thought* ch. 15 (Abraham Sutton ed., 1992); Chapter 26 in Volume 2; Pinchas D. Peli, *Soloveitchik on Repentance* (1984); Adin Steinsaltz, *Teshuva* (Michael Swirsky ed. & trans., 1996). Cf. *Symposium: The Role of Forgiveness in the Law*, 27 Fordham Urb. L.J. 1351 (2000); Dennis M. Cariello, *Forgiveness and the Criminal Law: Forgiveness Through Medicinal Punishment*, 27 Fordham Urb. L.J. 1607 (2000); Stephen P. Garvey, *Punishment as Atonement*, 46 UCLA L. Rev. 1801 (1999); David M. Lerman, *Forgiveness in the Criminal Justice System: If It Belongs, Then Why Is It So Hard to Find?*, 27 Fordham Urb. L.J. 1663 (2000).

66 Besdin, supra note 59, at 46. Rabbi Soloveitchik's focus on divine mercy is evoked in Garvey's description of mercy in capital sentencing. See Garvey, supra note 1. Indeed, the title of Garvey's article is quoted from Shakespeare, who refers to mercy as "the gentle rain from heaven" and as "an attribute to God himself." See id. at 989 n.1 (quoting William Shakespeare, *The Merchant of Venice*, act 4, sc. 1).

67 Besdin, supra note 59, at 46.

68 Id. Cf. Soloveitchik, supra note 60, at 169-70.

No matter how free a man is if seen under the aspect of the original scheme of creation, in the course of time and history he gradually becomes the slave of circumstances, an obedient servant of his milieu. He loses his courage and forfeits the heroic capability of defying everything and everybody. Temptation is too strong, sin fascinates, unredeemed vulgar beauty attracts with an irresistible force. . . . In other words, we deal here with an antinomy . . . the thesis says: man is an adult, free and independent. The antitheses states: man is a child, weak and helpless.

Id.

of human culpability in situations which are not entirely of man's making," as "[o]nly God knows to what extent a man was a free agent in making his decisions."[69]

It is instructive, then, to appreciate the similarities and differences between the approach of Rabbi Soloveitchik and that of the Supreme Court with respect to limitations on free will and their place in the administration of justice. While both acknowledge that human beings are subject to overwhelming forces that affect their free will and thus reduce their culpability, Rabbi Soloveitchik insists that only God possesses the wisdom to judge all of the circumstances that impact on an individual's moral guilt; the Court, in contrast, places on the capital sentencer the humanly impossible burden of determining the precise level of a defendant's moral culpability.[70]

Likewise, with respect to the problem of moral luck, Rabbi Soloveitchik again emphasizes the unique nature of divine justice, explaining that "[e]vents which we label as accidents belong to a higher Divine order into which man has not been initiated . . . not decrees of fate, but rather reasons beyond our comprehension operate in such instances."[71] Like issues of free will, humans cannot fully understand how to incorporate apparent luck into a system of

---

69 Besdin, supra note 59, at 46.

70 Cf. Cesare Beccaria, *Of Crimes and Punishments*, in Allesandro Manzoni, *The Column of Infamy* 64-65 (Kenelm Foster & Jane Grigson trans., 1964) ("[W]hat insect will dare take the place of divine justice? The gravity of sin depends upon the inscrutable wickedness of the heart. No finite being can know it without revelation. How then can it furnish a standard for the punishment of crimes?"), cited in Michael S. Moore, *The Independent Moral Significance of Wrongdoing*, 1994 J. Contemp. Legal Issues 237, 252 n.56 (1994); Jeffrie G. Murphy, *Does Kant Have a Theory of Punishment?*, 87 Colum. L. Rev. 509, 516-17 (1987) (proposing "a reasonably consistent [. . .] philosophical account of state punishment [that] emerges" from Kant's writings):

> Moral iniquity is a function of inner dispositions and acts of will rather than external actions. Not only should the state not be concerned with such inner matters, it is in fact impossible—for both metaphysical and epistemological reasons—for the state to base rational policy on such inner concerns. . . . Persons who advocate retributivist goals for punishment reveal serious character defects-specifically a hardness of heart and a lack of proper moral humility. Many of those who are law-abiding are so only through luck—e.g., accident of temperament or freedom from temptation—and self-knowledge on such matters should make one cautious about setting the goal that others get exactly what they deserve. This is an attempt to play God, and human beings should avoid such attempts. From the point of view of God, who alone can see into the inner heart, the infliction of just punishment is a categorical imperative; but from the human point of view it is merely hypothetical.

71 Besdin, supra note 59, at 48.

justice based on moral culpability. "To God," however, "there are no accidents, though they often appear so to us."[72]

Indeed, the overwhelming presence of apparent luck in human endeavors often confounds philosophical and theological attempts to understand the nature of divine justice.[73] The problem of why the wicked sometimes prosper and why the righteous suffer has perplexed philosophers and troubled Jewish religious thinkers since ancient times. Though these questions figure most prominently in the book of Job,[74] numerous biblical passages express the bewilderment of wise and prophetic individuals who long to discern the justice underlying these situations.[75] In fact, the Talmud interprets Moses' request that God "inform me please of Your ways"[76] as a plea to understand divine justice.[77]

Despite attempts throughout the ages to begin to answer these questions,[78] in the words of one contemporary scholar of Jewish law, in the end, "God's justice is hidden . . . . Though we can begin to understand some general rules regarding God's justice, the details are far beyond human understanding and everything ultimately is in the hands of God alone. We must only realize that all is just."[79] It is in recognition of "God's absolute knowledge" that "none can question His judgment."[80] As Rabbi Soloveitchik put it, "[e]ssentially this is God's answer to Job, who sought to reconcile his painful plight with his faith in God's justice. There is no deterministic fate; all operates on a transcendental plane which is beyond the grasp of man's finite mind."[81]

Again, the contrast to capital sentencing in the American legal system is striking. If a punishment is from God, human beings can acknowledge their inability to understand, but their willingness ultimately to respect divine justice administered by an omniscient God. In a human justice system, however, allowing a capital sentencer to consider victim impact evidence asks the sentencer to act with divine wisdom. The judge or jury is expected to determine

---

72 Id.

73 Cf. Lloyd L. Weinreb, *Law as Order*, 91 Harv. L. Rev. 909, 949 (1978) ("Job, we are inclined to believe, was the victim not only of misfortune but—were it not for deference to divine majesty—also of injustice.").

74 See, e.g., Job 12:6.

75 See, e.g., Jeremiah 12:1; Malachi 3:15; Psalms 73:2-3, 12-14; Ecclesiastes 8:14.

76 Exodus 33:13.

77 See Talmud Bavli, Berachoth 7a; 4 Dessler, supra note 58, at 100-101.

78 For a compilation of many of these answers, see 2 Kaplan, supra note 65, at ch. 20.

79 Id. at 20:53 (citations omitted).

80 Id.

81 Besdin, supra note 59, at 48.

a just punishment by incorporating into its calculus factors beyond the control of the defendant. The capital sentencer is thus authorized to disregard the problem of moral luck, and is advised to ignore the apparent injustice that may result. As if in possession of divine knowledge, the capital sentencer thereby functions as an arbiter of the role of luck in human behavior and punishment.[82]

PART TWO | CHARACTER EVIDENCE

Another factor that the Supreme Court has deemed relevant in determining the sentence of a capital defendant is "character evidence."[83] According to Garvey, this factor relates to "the content of the defendant's character itself."[84] Thus, he explains, "[t]he character theory requires a jury to make a direct assessment of the defendant's moral worth."[85] In other words, this factor "is concerned,

---

82 Cf. Friedman, supra note 47, at 766-67 (citing the argument that "punishment according to outcome [. . .] is the best that human beings can do, and God will take care of correcting the inevitable errors in both directions" and adding that,

> [f]or those of us who are concerned with providing justice without divine assistance, however, the prudential argument still leaves a moral problem. Even if it is prudent to use selective punishment to provide selective deterrence, is it just to punish differently offenders who may be equally wicked, merely because one had the good luck to miss the intended target or to choose a less attractive victim?);

Stern, supra note 53, at 829-30 (distinguishing between the "perspective of God's government," which reflects the notion that "[a]s a matter of absolute morality, both [a murderer and an attempted murderer] may deserve the same punishment," and "the perspective of human government," which is based on "our limited knowledge").

83 See Garvey, supra note 1, at 1026 n.145 (citing Supreme Court cases enumerating various elements relating to a capital defendant's character). See also Scott W. Howe, *Resolving the Conflict in Capital Cases: A Desert-Oriented Theory of Regulation*, 26 Ga. L. Rev. 323, 351 n.111 (1992) (citing cases).

84 See Garvey, supra note 1, at 1026.

85 See id. See also Howe, supra note 83, at 351 ("[E]vidence about the offender's background and character [. . .] need not bear on his volitional capacity at the time of the capital offense. [T]he sentencing inquiry must extend to an evaluation of what we might call the offender's general 'moral merit' or 'general deserts'"); Steiker & Steiker, supra note 4, at 847:

> [C]onsideration of good character evidence can be retrospective and nonutilitarian. Evidence of positive character traits and past good works may reveal a defendant's "general desert" and contribute to a moral assessment of the defendant's entire life that includes, but is not limited to, the defendant's culpability for the crime. A jurisdiction might regard such a general assessment particularly appropriate where the sentencing decision could result in execution.

as some might put it, with the state of the defendant's 'soul.'"[86] Garvey's use of such terms as "moral worth" and "soul" reflects the extent to which this factor places upon a capital sentencer the obligation to "play God." As difficult, and arguably impossible, as it may be for humans to judge the moral culpability of a single act, the task is that much more unreasonable when it requires a moral judgment of the essence of another human being, taking into account everything that makes up the person's inner nature.[87]

It may be argued that despite the difficulty inherent in judging moral character, consideration of "general moral merit ha[s] typically influenced sentencing judgments about the appropriate level of punishment."[88] As one scholar observed, "the argument of character [...] bring[s] into the sentencing process all of that soft data upon which sentencing judges have relied for the last hundred years—the defendant's religion, his past employment, his relations with his spouse, his childhood history, whether he loves animals, and so forth."[89]

Such an argument, like those regarding the place of free will and moral luck in the general criminal law, fails to sufficiently acknowledge the fundamental difference between the death penalty and other punishments. The fact that the law generally allows sentencing decisions to be based, in part, on a rough estimation of a defendant's moral worth does not imply that such a precarious and necessarily imprecise enterprise should play a role in the decision of whether to impose a capital sentence, a decision that leaves no room for error.

Here too, a look at Jewish law and philosophy helps illustrate the extent to which judgment of an individual's inner character is possible only on the basis

---

Id. Additionally,

> consideration of good character evidence can be forward-looking and consequentialist. Evidence of a defendant's special talents or close family ties may suggest the defendant's capacity to make continuing contributions to society. And evidence of a defendant's religious devotion and remorse for the crime may reflect a defendant's commitment to observe legal norms in the future. A jurisdiction guided by utilitarian considerations would undoubtedly regard these types of good character evidence as indispensable components of individualized sentencing.

Id.

86 Garvey, supra note 1, at 1026. See also Howe, supra note 83, at 351 ("In effect the sentencer may determine what punishment the offender deserves by judging his 'soul.'").

87 Cf. Howe, supra note 83, at 351 ("The sentencer may evaluate the offender's deserts based on all of his life works.").

88 Id. at 352.

89 Richard G. Singer, *Just Deserts: Sentencing Based on Equality and Desert* 70 (1979), cited in Howe, supra note 83, at 352 n.115.

of a degree of wisdom and knowledge that lies beyond human capabilities.[90] Complementing his thoughts on the mysteries of free will, luck, and culpability, Rabbi Soloveitchik offers valuable insights in describing the impossibility that one person will truly understand the essence of another human being.

In the eloquent words of Rabbi Soloveitchik, "[M]an has an inner world.... Man's ontological essence, that is, the essence of his being, is not to be equated with his conduct or routine activities. There is a *homo absconditus*, a 'hidden man' whom no one knows . . . a mystery which no one can unravel . . . . The uniqueness of man-persona expresses itself in the *mysterium magnum* which no one except God can penetrate."[91] Indeed, it is striking that the very kind of judgment expected of a capital sentencer is that which, in Jewish thought, is reserved for God, Who decides who will live and who will die based on divine examination and evaluation of individual merit.[92] Although the precise nature of this divine judgment is, by definition, beyond human comprehension, it is clear from the Talmud and other sources of Jewish law that only God has the ability to determine an individual's true moral worth.

In describing the process through which God judges an individual, Maimonides, the great medieval legal codifier and philosopher, writes that God balances a person's merits against that person's wrongdoings.[93] Significantly, Maimonides posits that God's calculus does not involve a mere tallying of the number of good deeds against the number of sins.[94] Rather, he explains, an accurate measurement of an individual's moral worth requires a careful weighing of different actions, good and bad, in accordance with their moral gravity.[95]

---

90 Cf. Edward M. Wise, *The Concept of Desert*, 33 Wayne L. Rev. 1343, 1358 (1987).

> [Q]uestions of pure moral entitlement are impossibly difficult to decide. They ultimately require summing up the sole of a person's character and actions in a single overall assessment. There is no rational way for human judges to do this, to tote up and balance off all of a person's moral excellences and failings. Thus a secular court has no practical use for the total picture of his virtues and vices pertinent to the ideal moral appraisal of an offender's conduct. Desert in an earthly forum never corresponds exactly to pure moral desert. It must inevitably be a rough estimate of the ideal.

Id.

91 Soloveitchik, supra note 60, at 21.
92 See Maimonides, *Mishne Torah* [Code of Law], Laws of *Teshuva* 3:2-3.
93 See id. at 2:2.
94 See id.
95 See id.

Therefore, Maimonides emphasizes, only God possesses the knowledge and wisdom necessary to make such a precise, complex, and vital determination.[96]

Thus, the expectation that a human capital sentencer can estimate, with any measure of precision, the level of a defendant's moral character is highly problematic on at least two grounds. First, "[a]s a practical matter, a system for proportioning sentences to desert cannot be taken to require limitless inquiry into an offender's character."[97] Only God can inquire into and evaluate every aspect of a person's character. Second, and more profoundly, as Maimonides and Rabbi Soloveitchik demonstrate, it is unrealistic, and therefore unfair—both to the sentencer and to the defendant—to expect any person to have the ability to assign an ultimate moral weight to different aspects of a defendant's character, and to then balance these factors in a way that arrives at a fair and just decision of life or death.[98]

PART THREE | FUTURE DANGEROUSNESS

Finally, perhaps more than any other factor relevant to the determination of a capital sentence, a consideration of a defendant's "future dangerousness" requires that a human capital sentencer "play God" by predicting future events.[99] Nevertheless, in *Jurek v. Texas*,[100] the Supreme Court upheld the practice of incorporating predictions of future dangerousness into a death penalty sentencing scheme. In addition, in *Barefoot v. Estelle*,[101] the Court held that the

---

96 See id.; Yitzchok Hutner, *Pachad Yitzchok: Rosh Hashana* 136-38 (4th ed., 1997). Cf. Greenawalt, supra note 27, at 348 ("[A] penalty supposed to redress a moral imbalance should perhaps depend upon an offender's overall moral record and how good and bad fortunes of his life compare with that record; yet making such an evaluation with any accuracy is even more beyond human capacities than judging the moral guilt attaching to a particular act.").

97 Wise, supra note 90, at 1358.

98 Cf. Friedman, supra note 47, at 769 (citing position that "reject[s] punishment by moral desert not because it is inappropriate but because it is inappropriate to human courts and should therefore be left to divine justice"); Greenawalt, supra note 27, at 349 ("Even if one believes that a just God would strike some such balance [in punishment], he may think that restoring the moral order is not an appropriate human purpose, limited as the state should be in its capacities to learn about events and to dispose of people's lives.").

99 Cf. Bruce Vincent, *Prosecutors Shun Death Penalty Expert: Dr. Death's Demise?*, Leg. Times, Jan. 1, 1996, at 4 ("[Dr. Grigson] testified [...] in capital cases approximately 150 times for the state and eight times for the defense. [M]any of Grigson's peers think the doctor is playing God. Psychiatry is an inexact science where predicting a patient's future behavior is a goal, not a skill, one doctor says.").

100 428 U.S. 262 (1976).

101 463 U.S. 880 (1983).

prosecution may present a psychiatrist's testimony regarding a capital defendant's propensity for committing future crimes.

The Court's willingness to allow a capital sentencer to rely on such a speculative consideration has drawn widespread criticism, beginning with Justice Blackmun's dissenting opinion in *Barefoot*. Citing an amicus brief filed by the American Psychiatric Association, Justice Blackmun noted that "[t]he unreliability of psychiatric predications of long-term future dangerousness is by now an established fact within the profession," and that "[t]he APA's best estimate is that two out of three predictions of long-term future violence made by psychiatrists are wrong."[102] Justice Blackmun's concerns have been shared by judges, legal commentators, and mental health professionals, among others.[103]

---

102 Id. at 920 (Blackmun, J. dissenting).
103 For examples of legal scholars who have criticized the Court's approach and have compiled numerous sources in support of this criticism, see, e.g., Bowers & Steiner, supra note 10, at 667 & n.240 ("Judging a person's likely future dangerousness is far from foolproof; indeed, those who have examined such assessments find that they are often unreliable because they are subject especially to 'false positives' or predictions of dangerousness that do not materialize."); Garvey, supra note 1, at 1031 & n.167 ("Unfortunately, our power to predict future dangerousness seems on a par with our power to predict next month's weather. Study after study shows that long-term predictions of future dangerousness are more often wrong than right"); Steven G. Gey, *Justice Scalia's Death Penalty*, 20 Fla. St. L. Rev. 67, 118 & n. 216 (1992) (observing that "[n]o jury has the power to ascertain with 100 percent certainty the future actions of the defendant" and referring to "the dubious scientific or predictive value of future dangerousness evidence"); Lynne N. Henderson, *The Wrongs of Victim's Rights*, 37 Stan. L. Rev. 937, 973 n.183 (1985) ("Despite the Supreme Court's recent acceptance of the notion that psychiatrists can predict future dangerousness for the purposes of imposing the death penalty, the ability of anyone to predict future dangerousness with much accuracy is questionable"); Kirchmeier, supra note 48, at 370-72 & nn. 177-84 ("The use of the 'future danger' aggravating factor as a tool for determining who receives the death penalty is highly suspect"); Douglas Mossman, *The Psychiatrist and Execution Competency: Fording Murky Ethical Waters*, 43 Case W. Res. L. Rev. 1, 3-4 & n.10 (1992) (stating that the Court's approach "has been roundly criticized in both medical and legal literature"); Irene Merker Rosenberg, Yale L. Rosenberg & Bentzion S. Turin, *Return of the Stubborn and Rebellious Son: An Independent Sequel on the Prediction of Future Criminality*, 37 Brandeis L.J. 511, 519-21 & nn. 43-48 (1998-99) (stating that "[a]lthough measures for predicting and preventing future crime are very much in vogue, a substantial body of literature suggests that prophecy of this sort is a very speculative business" and criticizing the Supreme Court for "a lack of appreciation of the inherent difficulty of the task and the consequences of using inadequate methodologies to identify the dangerous predator").

But see Albert W. Alschuler, *Preventive Pretrial Detention and the Failure of Interest-Balancing Approaches to Due Process*, 85 Mich. L. Rev. 510, 539 (1986) (characterizing Justice Blackmun's dissent as "inaccurate or misleading in six significant respects" and stating that "[c]ontrary to the 'nearly universal' view of academic and professional communities, the

Despite these objections, however, the Court once again defended a questionable and troubling position on capital sentencing through a comparison to other decisions that are made in the administration of criminal justice. The majority in *Barefoot* responded to the criticisms Justice Blackmun highlighted by quoting at length from Justice Stevens' plurality opinion in *Jurek*: "It is, of course, not easy to predict future behavior. The fact that such determination is difficult, however, does not mean that it cannot be done. Indeed, prediction of future criminal conduct is an essential element in many of the decisions rendered throughout our criminal justice system."[104] Specifically, the Court pointed to such actions as the setting of bail, judicial determination of a sentence, and the decision of parole authorities.[105] Relying on these examples, the Court concluded that a capital sentencer's role in predicting future dangerousness is "no different from the task performed countless times each day throughout the American system of criminal justice."[106]

Thus, the Court's approach again accepted an inherently imprecise determination by a capital sentencer based on the legal system's acceptance of a similar determination in other situations, betraying a continued unwillingness to acknowledge the fundamental difference between death and other sentences. In rejecting the Court's approach, Justice Blackmun retorted that "[i]n the present state of psychiatric knowledge, this is too much for me. One may accept this in a routine lawsuit for money damages, but when a person's life is at stake [...] a requirement of greater reliability should prevail."[107]

Likewise, many scholars have been disturbed by the Court's seemingly callous attitude toward the profound implications of its approach in the context of taking the life of another human being. In a sharply worded critique, Professor Paul Gianelli commented on the Court's rationale that "[n]either petitioner nor the [APA] suggests that psychiatrists are always wrong with respect to future dangerousness, only most of the time."[108] Gianelli found that "[g]iven the context, such a standard—'not always wrong'—shocks the

---

available evidence does not support the claim that predictions of future criminality are inherently or even usually inaccurate").

104 *Barefoot*, 463 U.S. at 897 (quoting *Jurek*, 428 U.S. 274-75 (Stevens, J.)).
105 See id.
106 Id. (quoting *Jurek*, 428 U.S. at 276 (Stevens, J.)).
107 *Barefoot*, 463 U.S. at 916 (Blackmun, J., dissenting).
108 Id. at 901.

conscience,"[109] adding that "[o]ne suspects that the Justices would not choose a neurosurgeon on such a basis, nor even a podiatrist."[110]

Moreover, Professor Serena Stier has argued that the tradition of American criminal justice adjudication precludes the use of predictions of future dangerousness for capital sentencing.[111] Stier posits that "[w]hen it comes to applying the death sentence on the basis of such unreliable predictions of future dangerousness [. . .] we certainly need to have a thorough and thoughtful normative discussion about the rightness of what we are doing."[112] Noting that "[a]ny criminal justice system is likely to make some errors," Stier adds that "American criminal jurisprudence has traditionally taken the view [. . .] that when error occurs, it is better to let the guilty go free than to punish the innocent."[113] Therefore, she concludes, "[i]t seems to be contrary to this tradition to put the costs of error in capital punishment cases on the heads of those who must die for our mistakes."[114]

In the Jewish legal system, courts abide by a nearly universal rule that an individual cannot be punished based on a prediction of future dangerousness.[115] In fact, this rule applies not only to human courts but to God as well;

---

109 Paul C. Giannelli, *"Junk Science": The Criminal Cases*, 84 J. Crim. L. & Criminology 105, 114 (1993).

110 Id. Cf. Rosenberg, et al., supra note 103, at 581-82:

> Although conceivably one might be willing to accept a gaping margin of error in false positives with respect to certain forms of state intervention, such as short-term civil commitment or denial of bail, should we be willing to tolerate it for life sentences of recidivists or with respect to the death penalty?;

Id. at 583 ("[O]ur predictive ability is one for three-not bad for a batting average but somewhat more problematic for imprisonment and execution.").

111 See Serena Stier, *Hybrids and Dangerousness*, 82 Nw. U. L. Rev. 52, 61 (1987).

112 Id.

113 Id.

114 Id. Cf. Rosenberg, et al., supra note 103, at 520-21 (referring to the Court's "lack of appreciation of the inherent difficulty of the task and the consequences of using inadequate methodologies to identify the dangerous predator" and arguing that

> in our constitutional system, primacy presumably should be given to individual liberty, and if mistakes in predicting future criminality are to be made-as they surely will be-they should be on the freedom side of the ledger, particularly when dealing with gross deprivations, such as long-term incarceration and capital punishment.)

115 See Rashi, *Commentary on the Torah* 79 (Chaim Chavel ed., 1986) (commenting on Genesis 21:17). See generally Rosenberg, et al., supra note 103.

116 See 1 Kaplan, supra note 58, at 2:47; 2 Kaplan, supra note 65, at 20:8-20:9 (citing Job 11:11); id. at 21:28. God's knowledge of the future raises a number of profound philosophical questions, including a potential paradox between this foreknowledge and the principles of free will and divine justice. See Avoth 3:15; Sa'adiah Gaon, *Emunoth V'Deoth* 158-59

notwithstanding the utterly unparalleled ability God possesses to know future events—including future wrongdoings—with certainty, God imposes divine justice only on the basis of actions that have already been committed.[116]

The one apparent exception, the case of the "stubborn and rebellious son," proves the general rule, demonstrating the extent to which future dangerousness is excluded from consideration in Jewish criminal law adjudication. This unique case involves a son who is sentenced to death after engaging in a number of wrongful activities, specifically enumerated in the Torah, that evince a particularly definite propensity for future sins of a much greater magnitude.[117] The Talmud states that, although none of these activities are themselves capital crimes, the sentence corresponds to future crimes that the son would ultimately have committed.[118] Thus, in this one scenario, Jewish law apparently sanctions the imposition of capital punishment due to the defendant's future dangerousness. Nevertheless, if anything, this exceptional case proves the rule that such predictions generally play no part in the administration of justice in Jewish law. In fact, upon close examination, this case may present yet a further argument against using human predictions of future harm as a justification for the death penalty.

First, although the Talmud describes the punishment in this case as a means to prevent future harm, this determination of future dangerousness is not the result of an unavoidably uncertain human prediction. Here, the Torah, which is the word of God, mandates that an individual who engages in such activities is subject to the death penalty.[119] Thus, the punishment is proper only because, in this exceptional case, as a result of God's unique knowledge of the future, the prediction of future crimes—unlike those of psychiatrists or other humans—is infallible. The human court, therefore, does not engage in a prediction of future harm, but instead merely adjudicates the case in

---

(Yoseph Kapach trans., 1993); Maimonides, supra note 92, Laws of *Teshuva* 5:5; Ra'avad, *Commentary in Maimonides*, supra; 1 Kaplan, supra note 58, at ch. 3.

117 See Deuteronomy 21:18-21; Talmud Bavli, Sanhedrin, ch.8; Maimonides, supra note 92, Laws of *Mamrim*, ch. 7.

118 See Talmud Bavli, Sanhedrin 71b.

119 See Deuteronomy 21:21.

120 See Maharal, *Gur Aryeh* (commenting on Rashi, supra note 115); Chaim Shmulevitz, *Sichoth Mussar* 87 (1983).

Cf. Bruce S. Ledewitz & Scott Staples, 6 U. Fla. J.L. & Pub. Pol'y 33, 42 (1993).

The American death penalty debate is beset by the justice issue. American opponents of the death penalty do not, by and large, agree that murderers-or

accordance with the procedure delineated through divine revelation.[120] Second, in any event, as the Talmud notes, this case is *sui generis* in the extent to which human administration of justice is based on future events.[121] Finally, the Talmud articulates numerous procedural safeguards that protected the defendant in this case to such a degree that, according to one opinion in the Talmud, there never was and never will be an actual case of an execution of a stubborn and rebellious son.[122]

Ultimately, then, the case of the stubborn and rebellious son demonstrates the degree to which Jewish law and philosophy preclude the imposition of punishment pursuant to an inevitably speculative human prediction that the defendant will engage in future wrongdoing.[123] Even God—Who knows, rather than predicts, the future—rarely, if ever, administers a punishment based on future dangerousness. Thus, the Supreme Court's willingness to allow a fallible capital sentencer to impose the most severe and irreversible of penalties on this basis creates a genuinely anomalous situation: the Court appears to authorize human beings to "play God" with disturbing impunity, entitling them, as it were, to undertake actions beyond those taken by God.[124]

CONCLUSION

By virtually all accounts, capital punishment is fundamentally different from all other forms of punishment in the American legal system.[125] As a result of

---

other wrongdoers-deserve to die. Nor is there a consensus in America about the standards of morality that would allow the death penalty question to be resolved. Proponents of the death penalty may have convinced a majority of voters that murderers deserve to die, but they cannot demonstrate this proposition by reasoning from generally accepted premises. The rabbis did not have this problem. The proper punishments for crime were set forth in God's Word.

Id.

121 See Talmud Bavli, Sanhedrin 71b. See also 2 Nachmanides, *Commentary on the Torah* 445-46 (Chaim Chavel ed., 1960) (commenting on Deuteronomy 21:18).

122 See Talmud Bavli, Sanhedrin 71b. See also Chapter 11 in this Volume.

123 See generally Rosenberg, et al., supra note 103.

124 Cf. id. at 583-84.

[I]f we cannot achieve God's omniscience, that is if we cannot achieve perfection, we should at least be less imperfect. And if one for three is the best that we can do given our present state of knowledge, perhaps it may be time for a time out in the prediction game.

Id.

125 See supra note 11.

the profound difference, "many would say that the severity of death, and the inevitability of decision-makers' human errors, should preclude the sentence of death altogether."[126] Although it has repeatedly acknowledged the unique nature of the death penalty and the corresponding need for unique substantive and procedural safeguards in capital cases,[127] the Supreme Court has sanctioned a wide variety of capital sentencing schemes. One particularly striking element of the Court's jurisprudence has been a willingness to allow a capital sentencer to make determinations that require divine wisdom and knowledge.

Professor Jefferson Powell has offered a cogent warning in describing the limitations of human justice: "Our power is limited by our limited and narrow and fallen vision, as well as other external limitations to our abilities. We are called on to seek human justice to approximate divine justice, but were we tempted to think that we can close the gap altogether we would be starting out on a path that will mislead us."[128] In formulating an approach to capital punishment that expects the human capital sentencer to "play God," the Supreme Court appears to have taken several steps down this dangerous path.

---

126 Underkuffler, supra note 9, at 1729.

127 See supra note 11.

128 Maura Ryan, *Conversation: On Powell's Theology*, 72 Notre Dame L. Rev. 41, 69 (1996) (quoting Powell). Cf. Harold J. Berman, *The Origins of Historical Jurisprudence: Coke, Selden, Hale*, 103 Yale L.J. 1651, 1706 n.147 (1994) (quoting Maija Jansson, *Matthew Hale on Judges and Judging*, 9 J. Leg. Hist. 201, 207-8 (1988)) (internal quotation omitted) ("[T]he hand of divine justice in the way of His providence may reach in after time a guilty person, or of evidence to convict him, he may hereafter repent and amend; but the loss of the life of an innocent is irrecoverable in this world."); Bruce Ledewitz, *Could the Death Penalty Be a Cruel Punishment?*, 3 Widener J. Pub. L. 121, 155 (1993) ("[W]ithout God, the full range of human experience must be accounted for here, in this world. No ultimate, transcendent justice is possible in a secular universe. The death penalty fails to be just without God."); Irene Merker Rosenberg & Yale L. Rosenberg, *Guilt: Henry Friendly Meets the MaHaRaL of Prague*, 90 Mich. L. Rev. 604, 624-25 (1991) ("[I]n our imperfect world there is only one kind of ascertainable guilt, and that is legal guilt. The search for more is nothing less than arrogance.").

Self-Incrimination

CHAPTER 7

An Introduction to Self-Incrimination in Jewish Law, with Application to the American Legal System: A Psychological and Philosophical Analysis

INTRODUCTION

L aw serves a central role in Jewish faith and tradition. Indeed, Jewish law comprises a legal system that has developed over thousands of years, exploring and regulating every form of human endeavor and experience.[1] Thus, it

---

1 See, e.g., Aryeh Kaplan, *The Handbook of Jewish Thought* 78 (1979) (stating that the commandments "penetrate every nook and cranny of a person's existence, hallowing even the lowliest acts and elevating them to a service to God" and that "the multitude of laws governing even such mundane acts as eating, drinking, dressing and business, sanctify every facet of life, and constantly remind one of [one's] responsibilities toward God"). See also Moshe Silberg, *Law and Morals in Jewish Jurisprudence*, 75 Harv. L. Rev. 306, 322 (1961) ("The ... mode of dress, ... diet, dwelling, behavior, relation with [others], ... family affairs, and ... business affairs were all prefixed and premolded, in a national cloak, in a set of laws that was clear, severe, strict, detailed, that accompanied [an individual] day by day, from cradle to grave."). See infra notes 10-13 and accompanying text.

may be unsurprising that American courts and legal scholars have increasingly turned to Jewish legal tradition for insights into various issues confronting the American legal system.[2] Jewish law has provided an alternative model and, at times, a contrast case that some have found particularly helpful in illuminating complex, controversial, and unsettled areas of American law.[3]

In light of these developments, this chapter aims to consider the efficacy of drawing on Jewish law to facilitate a more thoughtful analysis of issues in American law, with a specific focus on the issue of self-incrimination. The chapter begins with a brief description of the function of Jewish law within Jewish faith and tradition. Employing a psychological and philosophical framework, the chapter then explores the issue of self-incrimination in Jewish law, both on its own terms and through an analysis of its potential relevance to difficult questions regarding the use of criminal confessions in the United States.[4] The chapter concludes with

---

2 See, e.g., Chapters 2 and 3 in this Volume; Daniel G. Ashburn, *Appealing to a Higher Authority?: Jewish Law in American Judicial Opinions*, 71 U. Det. Mercy L. Rev. 295, 298-99, 301, 303, 307, 310-13 (1994); Chad Baruch & Karsten Lokken, *Research of Jewish Law Issues: A Basic Guide and Bibliography for Students and Practitioners*, 77 U. Det. Mercy L. Rev. 303-4 (2000); Samuel J. Levine, *Teaching Jewish Law in American Law Schools-Part II: An Annotated Syllabus*, 2 Chi.-Kent J. Int'l & Comp. L. 1 (2002); Suzanne Last Stone, *In Pursuit of the Counter-Text: The Turn to the Jewish Legal Model in Contemporary American Legal Theory*, 106 Harv. L. Rev. 813, 814 (1993).

3 See supra note 2.

4 An examination of self-incrimination may be particularly instructive, as it involves an area of law in which American courts and scholars alike have relied upon the Jewish legal system to analyze and interpret American legal principles. A substantial body of American case law and scholarship has referred to the Jewish law of self-incrimination.

   The list of such cases includes: *Garrity v. State of New Jersey*, 385 U.S. 493, 497-98 n.5 (1967); *Miranda v. Arizona*, 384 U.S. 436, 458 n.27 (1966); *In re Agosto*, 553 F. Supp. 1298, 1300 (D. Nev. 1983); *Moses v. Allard*, 779 F. Supp. 857, 870 (E.D. Mich. 1991); *People v. Brown*, 86 Misc. 2d 339, 487 n.5 (Nassau County Ct. 1975); *Roberts v. Madigan*, 702 F. Supp. 1505, 1517 n.20 (D. Colo. 1989); *State v. McCloskey*, 446 A.2d. 1201, 1208 n.4 (N.J. 1982); *U.S. v. Gecas*, 120 F.3d 1419, 1425 (11th Cir. 1997); *U.S. v. Huss*, 482 F.2d. 38, 51 (2d Cir. 1973).

   The list of scholarship includes: Leonard W. Levy, *Origins of the Fifth Amendment: The Right Against Self-Incrimination* 433-441 (1968); Albert W. Alschuler, *A Peculiar Privilege in Historical Perspective: The Right to Remain Silent*, in *The Privilege Against Self-Incrimination: Its Origins and Development* 181, 279 n.28 (1997); Isaac Braz, *The Privilege Against Self-Incrimination in Anglo-American Law: The Influence of Jewish Law*, in *Jewish Law and Current Legal Problems* 161-168 (Nahum Rakover ed., 1984); Malvina Halberstam, *The Rationale for Excluding Incriminating Statements: U.S. Law Compared to Ancient Jewish Law*, in *Jewish Law and Current Legal Problems*, supra, at 177; Chapters 2 and 8 in this Volume; George Horowitz, *The Privilege Against Self-Incrimination—How Did It Originate?*, 31 Temple L.Q. 121, 125 (1958); Samuel J. Levine, *Rethinking Self-Incrimination, Voluntariness, and Coercion, through the Perspective of Jewish Law and Legal Theory*, 12 J.L. Society 72 (2010-2011); Simcha Mandelbaum, *The Privilege Against*

the cautious proposition that the American law of self-incrimination may benefit from incorporating some of the insights offered by Jewish legal thought.

PART ONE | A BRIEF LOOK AT THE ROLE OF LAW IN JEWISH FAITH AND TRADITION

It would seem difficult to overstate the importance of Jewish law, or *halacha*, in Jewish faith and tradition, particularly for those who appreciate the Torah as divinely authored and immutable. Describing *halacha* as "central" or "essential" does not

---

Self-Incrimination in Anglo-American and Jewish Law, 5 Am. J. Comp. L. 115 (1956); Irene Merker Rosenberg & Yale L. Rosenberg, *In the Beginning: The Talmudic Rule Against Self-Incrimination,* 63 N.Y.U. L. Rev. 955 (1988); Bernard Susser, *Worthless Confessions: The Torah Approach,* 130 New L.J. 1056 (1980); Cheryl G. Bader, *"Forgive me Victim for I Have Sinned": Why Repentance and the Criminal Justice System Do Not Mix—A Lesson From Jewish Law,* 31 Fordham Urb. L.J. 69 (2003); Suzanne Darrow-Kleinhaus, *The Talmudic Rule Against Self-Incrimination and the American Exclusionary Rule: A Societal Prohibition Versus an Affirmative Individual Right,* 21 N.Y. L. Sch. J. Int'l & Comp. L. 205 (2002); Michelle M. Sharoni, *A Journey of Two Countries: A Comparative Study of the Death Penalty in Israel and South Africa,* 24 Hastings Int'l & Comp. L. Rev. 257, 263 (2001); Daniel J. Seidmann & Alex Stein, *The Right to Silence Helps the Innocent: A Game Theoretic Analysis of the Fifth Amendment Privilege,* 114 Harv. L. Rev. 431, 452 n.70 (2000); Erica Smith-Klocek, *Note, A Halachic Perspective on the Parent-Child Privilege,* 39 Cath. Law. 105, 109 (1999); Gregory Thomas Stremers, *The Self-Incrimination Clause and the Threat of Foreign Prosecution in Bankruptcy Proceedings: A Comment on Moses v. Allard,* 70 U. Det. Mercy L. Rev. 847, 854-55 (1993); Debra Ciardiello, *Seeking Refuge in the Fifth Amendment: The Applicability of the Privilege Against Self-Incrimination to Individuals Who Risk Incrimination Outside the United States,* 15 Fordham Int'l L.J. 722, 725 (1992); Aaron M. Schreiber, *The Jurisprudence of Dealing with Unsatisfactory Fundamental Law: A Comparative Glance at the Different Approaches in Medieval Criminal Law, Jewish Law and the United States Supreme Court,* 11 Pace L. Rev. 535, 550 (1991).

Although some of these references to Jewish law are fairly brief and tangential, others demonstrate the significance that has been accorded to Jewish law in considerations of the American rule of self-incrimination. For example, in *Miranda v. Arizona,* the landmark United States Supreme Court case defining the contours of the constitutional privilege against self-incrimination, Chief Justice Warren's majority opinion cited a reference to Jewish law. *Miranda,* 384 U.S. 436, at 458 n.27 (1966). Moreover, Leonard Levy closes his groundbreaking historical study of the origins of the privilege with an Appendix entitled "Talmudic Law," stating that "[n]o description of the origins of the right against self-incrimination would be complete without acknowledgment of the existence of the right in ancient Jewish law." See Levy, supra 4, at 433-41. Finally, in his introduction to Professor Aaron Kirschenbaum's exhaustive study of self-incrimination in Jewish law, Arthur J. Goldberg, a former justice of the United States Supreme Court, writes that "[w]e have something to learn from this ancient tradition, particularly now, when our constitutional privilege against self-incrimination, embodied in the Fifth Amendment, is under attack." Arthur J. Goldberg, *Introduction,* in Aaron Kirschenbaum, *Self-Incrimination in Jewish Law* viii-ix (1970).

capture the extent of the significance that Jewish thought attaches to the letter and the spirit of the law. The Torah and Midrashic exegesis dramatically depict the revelation at Sinai and the giving of the law as both the formative moment for the Nation of Israel and the basis of the Nation's ongoing relationship with God.[5]

Moreover, study of the law is viewed as a powerful means of connecting with God on both intellectual and spiritual levels. As the *halacha* is of divine origin, it serves as a primary source for understanding God's will, God's ways, and God's wisdom.[6] Indeed, God's law provides a unique avenue for relating to the reality of God's world.[7] The Talmud states strikingly that, since the

---

5   See, e.g., Abraham R. Besdin, 1 *Reflections of the Rav: Lessons in Jewish Thought, adapted from Lectures of Rabbi Joseph B. Soloveitchik* 89-98 (2d Rev. ed. 1993); Kaplan, supra note 1, at 53-58; Eliyahu Kitov, 2 *The Book of Our Heritage* 265-69 (Nathan Bulman trans., 1978) (originally published in Hebrew as *Sefer Ha-Toda'ah* (1976)). See also Rabbi Aharon Lichtenstein, 2 *Leaves of Faith: The World of Jewish Learning* 227 (2004):

> It was . . . at Sinai . . . that [the Nation of Israel] attained mature national fruition; and it was there that two new related elements, henceforth cardinal Jewish values, entered the picture. The first was Torah, the content of revelation proper, whose study and perpetuation then became a central Jewish concern. The second was Israel, a covenantal community forged by axiological commitment no less than by historical destiny. . . .

6   See Rabbi Hershel Schachter, *Eretz Hatzevi: Be'urei Sugyot* 1-2 (1992); Rabbi Hershel Schachter, *Ginas Egoz* 2-3 (2007). It may be instructive to quote at length the words of Rabbi Aharon Lichtenstein:

> [The study of the law offers] insight, as direct and profound as [a human] is privileged to attain, into the revealed will of [the] Creator . . . an opportunity to get (*salve reverentia*) a first-hand knowledge of the divine will, to deepen and broaden our minute understanding of God's infinite reason. In its essence, the Torah—particularly the Hala[c]ha—constitutes an immanent expression of God's transcendent rational will. By studying its texts, analyzing its principles, and developing its ideas, we are able to approach, however haltingly, that unattainable goal toward which [Moses] strove so desperately . . . "Let me know Thy ways."

Aharon Lichtenstein, 1 *Leaves of Faith: The World of Jewish Learning* 91 (2003) (quoting Exodus 33:13).

7   As Rabbi Joseph Soloveitchik describes in extensive detail:

> [T]he essence of the Hala[c]ha[], which was received from God, consists in creating an ideal world and recognizing the relationship between that ideal world and our concrete environment in all its visible manifestations and underlying structures. There is no phenomenon, entity or object in this concrete world which the a priori Hala[c]ha[] does not approach with its ideal standard.

Rabbi Joseph B. Soloveitchik, *Halakhic Man* 19-20 (Lawrence Kaplan trans., 1983) (originally published in Hebrew as *Ish ha-halakhah*, in 1 Talpiot 3-4 (1944)).

destruction of the Temple in Jerusalem, God's "place" in the world is found in the *halacha* and its application.[8] Thus, exploring the law in pursuit of the Divine comprises an inherently profound and spiritually transformative experience.[9]

In addition to the cognitive and spiritual significance of the law, as the Hebrew term implies, *halacha* offers a way of life—a path for all of life's endeavors and activities.[10] The substance of *halacha* extends far beyond the "rituals" of Jewish "religious" practice. In the words of Rabbi Joseph B. Soloveitchik, a leading contemporary scholar of Jewish law, "[t]here is no phenomenon, entity, or object in this concrete world" beyond the grasp of *halacha*.[11] For example, he

---

8 See The Babylonian Talmud, Berachoth 8a. See also Rabbi Yitzchak Hutner, *Pachad Yitzchak: Chanuka* 63-75 (1998).

9 Again in the words of Rabbi Lichtenstein:

> Torah study, when properly pursued, affects our total spiritual personality. Partly because it does afford us a better insight into inscrutable divine wisdom, and partly because it engages the mind—and with it the whole [person]— in pursuit of religious knowledge, it transmutes our innermost being. The knowledge we can acquire of God's will increases our conscious, and subconscious, awareness of [God]; the very act of weighing [God's] words or of analyzing [God's] laws draws us imperceptibly nearer to [God] and to them .... Torah study leaves an indelible imprint upon our total personality and, in the process, transforms it.... Torah study becomes the premier agent in effecting a gradual spiritual regeneration. Paradoxically, through a constant reciprocal process, it both sustains piety and is sustained by it. Keener study leads to greater piety, and more fervent devotion leads to profounder knowledge.

> Lichtenstein, supra note 6, at 91-92. Cf. Rabbi Chaim of Volozhin, *Nefesh Hachaim*, Section 4; Soloveitchik, supra note 7, at 87 ("The cognition of the Torah—this is the holiest and most exalted type of service .... The study of the Torah is not a means to another end, but is the end point of all desires. It is the most fundamental principle of all.").

10 See Lichtenstein, supra note 5, at 341-42 (describing the "concept of normative existence, of a life governed by divinely ordained law and organized as an all-embracing religious discipline" and stating that through the *halacha* a person's "whole life is permeated by an awareness of [one's] relation to God"; that "[i]n every sphere of endeavor—be it social or economic, physical or intellectual—conscious choice and religious response are operative"; and that "the Halacha, through its numerous laws concerning various areas, directs ... the sanctification of [self] and ... environment[,] suffus[ing] ... life with spiritual significance, and integrat[ing] ... activity into a divinely ordered whole"). See also Chapter 17 in Volume 2:

> [T]he Hebrew term *halacha*, though implying a legal order and often used to denote "Jewish religious law," suggests a broader range of ideas than those included in legal rules. A more literal translation of *halacha* would evoke a "path" of life; to inhabit the *halacha* is, by definition, to live in it. Thus, the *halacha* truly provides a "world-view" through which all of the world and life's experiences are perceived. Moreover, as a path of life, *halacha* incorporates those aspects of normative life that complement the legal precepts, the *aggada*.

11 Soloveitchik, supra note 7, at 20.

notes, "just a few of the multitude of hala[c]hic subjects" include: "sociological creations: the state, society, and the relationship of individuals within a communal context"; "laws of business, torts, neighbors, plaintiff and defendant, creditor and debtor, partners, agents, workers, artisans, bailees"; "[f]amily life"; "[w]ar, the high court, courts and penalties they impose"; and "psychological problems."[12] Thus, the foundational and authoritative texts of Jewish law—from the Torah and the Talmud to commentaries, codifications, and responsa—contain prescriptions for ethical conduct and moral behavior in both public and private, and through both worship and more worldly activities.[13]

Moreover, lending even further depth to *halacha*, the law has developed over the course of thousands of years in numerous and disparate societal and geographical settings, under both benign and, all too often, belligerent and oppressive circumstances. Consequently, the law has continuously confronted countless varieties of previously unaddressed issues demanding consideration and normative resolution.[14] Through a careful combination of fidelity to the past and, when necessary, innovation and creativity, legal authorities have responded to these challenges by applying settled and known legal principles to resolve the questions accompanying new and unanticipated circumstances.[15]

Acknowledging the range and depth of the Jewish legal system, contemporary American courts and scholars have turned to Jewish law for insights into numerous substantive and theoretical issues. American judicial opinions and law review articles have relied upon substantive parallels in the two legal systems in areas such as criminal law and procedure, family law, torts, property,

---

12 Id. at 22. See also Chapter 14 in this Volume (citing sources for the proposition that "[s]cholars of Jewish law identify 613 commandments enumerated in the Torah, covering nearly every area of human activity"; that "[i]n addition, many of these commandments can further be divided into component parts, resulting in a substantially larger number of enumerated obligations"; and that "there exist other imperatives that, although for methodological reasons are not tallied as commandments, nonetheless present yet additional enumerated obligations"); Chapters 9 and 14 in this Volume (citing sources for the derivation and identification of additional biblical obligations, beyond those enumerated in the Torah).

13 See Chapter 12 in this Volume; Samuel J. Levine, *The Broad Life of the Jewish Lawyer: Integrating Spirituality, Scholarship, and Profession*, 27 Tex. Tech L. Rev. 1199, 1199 (1996).

14 See, e.g., Michael Broyde & Howard Jachter, *Electrically Produced Fire or Light in Positive Commandments*, 25 J. Halacha & Contemp. Soc'y 89 (1993); Michael Broyde & Howard Jachter, *The Use of Electricity on Shabbat and Yom Tov*, 21 J. Halacha & Contemp. Soc'y 4 (1991); Arthur Schaffer, *The History of Horseradish as a Bitter Herb on Passover*, 8 Gesher 217 (1981); Adin Steinsaltz, *The Essential Talmud* 234-38 (Chaya Galai trans., 1976).

15 See Rabbi Hershel Schachter, *B'Ikvei Hatzoan* 1-3 (1997). See also Chapters 3 and 4 in this volume (discussing modification of Rabbinic interpretation and legislation as a result of changed circumstances).

evidence, ethics, commercial law, and health law.[16] Somewhat more ambitiously, and perhaps even more effectively, some scholars have looked at the conceptual underpinnings of various aspects of Jewish law and Jewish legal theory to illuminate not only substantive issues in American law but also some of the more complex and theoretical issues prevalent in American legal scholarship.[17]

Of course, the two legal systems are premised upon fundamentally different assumptions: one is based self-consciously in religion, and the other requires a more generally accessible rationale for legal decisions. Thus, Jewish law and American law sometimes produce radically different responses to similar legal questions. Nevertheless, the two systems share significant conceptual similarities, allowing for careful and productive analytical comparison.[18]

To illustrate the possible application of *halacha* in the analysis of the American legal system, it may be instructive to examine a specific issue of significance in American law through the lens of Jewish law. American courts and scholars face important challenges in the context of the issue of self-incrimination, while the Jewish legal system has addressed the issue since ancient times. In fact, it is not uncommon for both American courts and American legal scholars to refer to and rely on the treatment of self-incrimination in Jewish law.[19] Therefore, a discussion about self-incrimination may serve as a particularly helpful model for a broader understanding of the role of law in Jewish faith and tradition, as well as a consideration of conceptual comparisons between the Jewish legal system and the American legal system.

PART TWO | SELF-INCRIMINATION IN JEWISH LAW: A PSYCHOLOGICAL AND PHILOSOPHICAL ANALYSIS

The rule concerning self-incrimination in Jewish law may be summarized quite succinctly: an individual may not be punished on the basis of self-incriminatory

---

16 See supra note 2.

17 See id.

18 For differing views on the efficacy of such comparative analysis, see Chapter 5 in this Volume (contrasting examples of scholarship endorsing such application, e.g., David R. Dow, *Constitutional Midrash: The Rabbis' Solution to Professor Bickel's Problem*, 29 Hous. L. Rev. 543, 544 (1992); Irene Merker Rosenberg & Yale L. Rosenberg, *Guilt: Henry Friendly Meets the MaHaRaL of Prague*, 90 Mich. L. Rev. 604, 614-15 (1991), with examples of scholarship expressing a more cautious approach, e.g., Steven F. Friedell, *Book Review: Aaron Kirschenbaum on Equity in Jewish Law*, 1993 BYU L. Rev. 909, 919 (1993); Stone, supra note 2, at 893-94). See also infra note 64.

19 See sources cited supra note 4.

statements.[20] Although the precise nature of the rule has been the subject of detailed discussion and debate, from Talmudic times to the present,[21] there is universal agreement among authorities of Jewish law accepting a general rule precluding criminal confessions.[22] Moreover, this rule operates categorically, independent of attempts to ascribe or ascertain a divine rationale for the rule.[23]

Indeed, as Jewish law is understood to reflect God's divine will and wisdom, it is not uncommon for legal authorities and philosophers of Jewish law to consider the law on two different planes. On a practical level, for *halacha* to function, a systematic application of the law requires the derivation and delineation of the substance of the law and its interpretation under various circumstances and conditions. Though neither superficial nor overly formalistic, this level of understanding often addresses primarily the mechanics of the law, without necessitating an investigation into the divine rationale behind the law. As some have put it, this enterprise emphasizes the "what" rather than the "why."[24] In the area of ritual law, in particular, legal interpretation and application, though often complex, generally focus on defining the law and its parameters, rather than on attempting to identify the divine wisdom reflected in the ritual commandment.[25] Likewise, legal authorities interpret and apply the substance

---

20 See, e.g., The Babylonian Talmud, Sanhedrin 9b; Maimonides, Laws of *Sanhedrin* 18:6, in *Mishne Torah* (Abraham M. Hershman trans., Yale Univ. Press 1949). See also Maimonides, Laws of *Eduth* 12:2, in *Mishne Torah*, supra.

21 For works in English analyzing Talmudic and post-Talmudic sources addressing the issue of self-incrimination, see Kirschenbaum, supra note 4, at 34-92; Arnold Enker, *Self-Incrimination in Jewish Law—A Review Essay*, 4 Diné Israel cvii (1973) (reviewing Kirschenbaum, supra); Rosenberg & Rosenberg, supra note 4, at 984-1041.

22 Professor Kirschenbaum identified Rabbi Solomon ben Simeon Duran [Rashbash], an Algerian fifteenth century rabbi, as "to the best of my knowledge, the only Jewish authority who disagrees with the general interpretation of the rabbinic law against criminal confessions." Kirschenbaum, supra note 4, at 68. After carefully analyzing the position set forth by Rashbash, Kirschenbaum responds dismissively, concluding that Rashbash "is not only alone in his opinion on self-incrimination. His proof-texts are not convincing, and the weight of the traditional evidence is in direct opposition to him. No later authority takes up his position, and no later decision follows his line of reasoning." Id. at 72.

23 See Maimonides, Laws of *Sanhedrin* 18:6, in Mishne *Torah*, supra note 20.

24 See Lichtenstein, supra note 6, at 194. See also Abraham R. Besdin, 2 *Reflections of the Rav: Man of Faith in the Modern World, adapted from Lectures of Rabbi Joseph B. Soloveitchik* 91-99 (1989); Joseph B. Soloveitchik, *The Halakhic Mind: An Essay on Jewish Tradition and Modern Thought* 94 (1986).

25 See Chapter 3 in this Volume; Schachter, supra note 6, at 135.

of the rule against self-incrimination largely independent of any reasoning that may be offered as a logical basis for the rule.[26]

On a more theoretical level, however, philosophers of Jewish law often look beyond the mechanics of the law and attempt to glean the divine wisdom present in legal rules.[27] Indeed, Maimonides, one of the most influential medieval legal authorities and philosophers, dedicates a substantial portion of *Moreh Hanevuchim*, his philosophical magnum opus, to uncovering divine reasoning for ostensibly arational biblical laws.[28] Such an endeavor requires not only a healthy dose of ambition, sufficient to motivate pursuit of the divine rationale behind the law, but also an appropriate measure of humility, allowing for the acknowledgment that, ultimately, God's reasoning remains unknowable to humans.[29] In the context of the rule against self-incrimination,

---

26 Cf. Rosenberg & Rosenberg, supra note 4, at 1027 n.256 (stating that "[a]t the risk of oversimplification, the traditional view is that Jewish law embodies an absolute prohibition against the use of confessions in criminal and quasi-criminal cases because God has so decreed" but adding that "[f]aith does not, however, preclude intellectual grappling with such issues").

27 See Besdin, supra note 24, at 91-92 ("[O]ne may distinguish between motivations, explanations, and interpretations. Ascribing Divine motivations is a hopeless exercise; explaining how the ritual achieves its purpose is a futile enterprise. But offering a subjective interpretation which will strengthen its spiritual meaning for the worshipper is not only permissible, but should even be encouraged."); see also id. at 98 ("Accepting [commandments] . . . with pious obedience is meritorious, but ascribing an interpretive meaning, heightens the spiritual experience . . . engaging us both intellectually and emotionally in the worship of God").

See also Besdin, supra note 5, at 91-99; Yitzchak Heinemann, *Ta'amei Ha-Mitzvot Besafrut Yisrael* (1954); David Novak, *Natural Law in Judaism* 62-91 (1998); Soloveitchik, supra note 24, at 91-99. See generally Samuel J. Levine, *Ours to Reason Why: The Quest for Ta'amei HaMitzvot*, Hamevaser 7 (May 1990).

28 See Maimonides, *Moreh Hanevuchim [Guide of the Perplexed]*, Section 3 (Univ. of Chicago Press 1963); Soloveitchik, supra note 24, at 91-92 (declaring that "[o]ne of the most perplexing problems" in Jewish philosophy "is that of the rationalization for the commandments" and observing that "[t]wenty-five chapters of the Guide [for the Perplexed] are devoted exclusively to the solution of this problem"). See also Besdin, supra note 24, at 101 (citing the writings of Maimonides in the *Mishne Torah* in support of the proposition that "even as we perform rituals in accordance with God's will, whose reasons are inscrutable, we may ascribe interpretations in order to give meaning to our spiritual experience").

29 As I have written elsewhere, "[t]he attempt to discover a rationale for [commandments] is generally considered a noble pursuit. For example, Maimonides writes that it is proper to contemplate the [commandments] and if possible to suggest reasons for them." See Chapter 3 in this Volume (quoting Maimonides, supra note 20, Laws of *Temurah* 4:13). "Nevertheless, Maimonides stresses that if an individual is unable to discover a rationale for a particular [commandment], he or she should recognize that there is still a Divine rationale for it." Id. (quoting Maimonides, supra note 20, Laws of *Me'ilah* 8:8).

attempts to identify a divine rationale have produced a variety of penetrating insights into the law.[30]

In the *Mishne Torah*, Maimonides' monumental codification of the entire corpus of Jewish law, the discussion of self-incrimination is comprised of a two-tiered analysis.[31] Maimonides first introduces the rule against self-incrimination as a "scriptural decree."[32] In an apparent reference to biblical verses,[33] he writes that capital or corporal punishment may be implemented based only upon the testimony of two witnesses.[34] Although divine decree is, by definition, binding and authoritative without need for further justification, Maimonides nevertheless suggests a rationale for the law.[35] According to Maimonides, confessions may not serve as the basis for punishment because of a concern that perhaps the defendant confessed out of a "confused mind" in the matter.[36] Maimonides describes a form of extreme depression that results in suicidal tendencies; he explains that an individual suffering from such a condition may falsely confess to a capital offense for the purpose of being executed.[37] Maimonides then concludes his discussion with a reminder that, regardless of any rationale identified and articulated by humans, the exclusion of self-incrimination remains a divine decree.[38]

---

30 See Haim H. Cohn, *Privilege Against Self-Incrimination: Israel*, 51 J. Crim. L. Criminology & Police Sci. 175, 177-78 (1960); Rosenberg & Rosenberg, supra note 4, at 1027-41.

31 For works in English discussing the analysis presented by Maimonides, see Kirschenbaum, supra note 4, at 62-68; Rosenberg & Rosenberg, supra note 4, at 1032-41.

32 See Maimonides, supra note 20, Laws of *Sanhedrin* 18:6. For a discussion of the implications of the term "scriptural decree" in this context, see Rosenberg & Rosenberg, supra note 4, at 1033-34 n.284.

33 See, e.g., Numbers 35:30; Deuteronomy 17:6; Deuteronomy 19:15. For works in English analyzing biblical sources for the prohibition against self-incrimination, see Kirschenbaum, supra note 4, at 25-33; Rosenberg & Rosenberg, supra note 4, at 974-84.

34 See Maimonides, supra note 20, Laws of *Sanhedrin* 18:6.

35 See supra notes 25-29 and accompanying text.

36 See Maimonides, supra note 20, Laws of *Sanhedrin* 18:6.

37 See id. A number of scholars of Jewish law have offered alternative psychological explanations for the ban on self-incrimination, identifying ulterior motives that may induce a false confession. Professor Kirschenbaum has cited the following suggestions:

> [An individual] may have been present at certain business transactions or ritual ceremonies, and now, summoned to testify . . . "confesses" to a sin which disqualifies [the individual from testifying as a witness] and thereby "escapes." A confession to having committed a minor violation may furnish . . . an alibi for a major crime . . . perpetrated. Ulterior motives may vary: from a desire to save a beloved friend from punishment to an attempt to obtain warm shelter and food in winter—the possibilities are limitless.

Kirschenbaum, supra note 4, at 64-65.

38 See Maimonides, supra note 20, Laws of *Sanhedrin* 18:6.

Throughout his many works of law and philosophy, Maimonides developed groundbreaking frameworks for the analysis of nearly every area of Jewish thought.[39] His discussion of self-incrimination has provided fertile ground for later commentators, perhaps most significant among them Rabbi David ben Zimra [Radbaz], who lived several centuries after Maimonides and authored an important commentary on the *Mishne Torah*.[40] Like Maimonides, Radbaz states that the rule against self-incrimination is a divine decree; therefore, its inherent wisdom is beyond question.[41] Nevertheless, again like Maimonides, Radbaz engages in an attempt to understand the divine logic underlying the rule.[42]

Expounding upon, or perhaps adding to, the rationale that Maimonides proposes, Radbaz emphasizes a distinction between two kinds of confessions: criminal confessions, which potentially result in capital or corporal punishment and are excluded from evidence, and concessions to monetary obligations, which are admissible as evidence and bind the defendant to satisfy the obligation.[43] Radbaz explains that in Jewish thought, human beings have legal authority over their physical possessions, including both the autonomy to give their possessions to others and, consequently, the authority to admit to and thereby obligate themselves in a monetary debt.[44] In contrast, Jewish thought views both human life and the human body as sacred, to the extent that humans do

---

39 See Isadore Twersky, *Introduction to the Code of Maimonides (Mishneh Torah)* 1 (1980). Professor Twersky observed that

> [Maimonides'] reputation needs no inflation or exaggeration, for his stature is nearly sui generis and his commanding influence has been almost universally recognized . . . . He wrote epoch-making works in the central areas of halaka and religious philosophy—an achievement that is unquestionably, almost overpoweringly, characterized by monumentality, using the term very literally. His works, representing an unprecedented conjunction of halakic authority and philosophic prestige, were extensively studied, meticulously annotated, frequently translated, and intensively interpreted. Their influence, direct as well as indirect, reflected through many works in various genres by a host of authors, was global.

40 For works in English analyzing the position of Radbaz, see Kirschenbaum, supra note 4, at 72-77; Rosenberg & Rosenberg, supra note 4, at 1036-41.

41 See Radbaz, *Commentary*, in Maimonides, *Mishne Torah*, Laws of *Sanhedrin* 18:6, supra note 20.

42 See id. See also supra notes 25-29 and accompanying text.

43 See Radbaz, supra note 41.

44 See id.

not have legal autonomy to commit suicide or even harm their own bodies.[45] Therefore, because human life remains within God's province, human beings may not offer a legally valid confession resulting in their lives being taken or in another form of corporal punishment.[46]

As divine law is deemed eternally and universally binding on all segments of the Jewish nation, in any time or place, it is not uncommon for legal philosophers to seek philosophical or psychological lessons in the law that are particularly suitable to the societal context in which they live. Thus, for example, Rabbi Norman Lamm, later president of Yeshiva University, authored an influential 1956 article providing a decidedly modern understanding of the theories of Maimonides and Radbaz.[47] Observing that Maimonides premised his analysis on psychological considerations of suicidal tendencies, Rabbi Lamm asserts that Maimonides "anticipated by some seven hundred years, albeit in rudimentary fashion, a major achievement of psychoanalysis," namely, Freud's theory of "Death Wish" or "Death Instinct."[48] In Freud's view, Rabbi Lamm explains, at a basic level the Death Wish "reveals itself generally as destructiveness, in its many varied forms, and, in extreme cases, in homicide."[49] However, "because of a variety of reasons, the Death Wish, originally felt toward others, is usually frustrated and as a result is redirected toward the self."[50] Thus, "[a]t times . . . this Death Wish when it reaches its ultimate expression and is redirected towards the self, appears as suicide."[51]

---

45 See id. (quoting Ezekiel 18:4).

46 See id. Other scholars have offered alternative explanations for the different rules regarding criminal confessions and monetary admissions. "[B]y an admission, an obligation was created which had only to be enforced by the court; whereas the conviction of a criminal offence was not in the nature of the enforcement by the court of an obligation voluntarily undertaken by a party but of a creation by the court of the party's liability." Cohn, supra note 30, at 178 (quoting Mordechai Epstein, Levush Mordechai (19th Century)). For further discussion of differences in the nature of criminal and monetary obligations, see Kirschenbaum, supra note 4, at 78-81; Schachter, supra note 15, at 266-68; Schachter, supra note 6, at 276; Asher Weiss, *Minchas Asher, Shemos* 279-85 (2017).

47 Norman Lamm, *The Fifth Amendment and Its Equivalent in the Halakhah,* 5 Judaism 53, 56 (1956).

48 Id. (citing Sigmund Freud, *New Introductory Lectures on Psychoanalysis* 147 (W. W. Norton & Co. 1965); Sigmund Freud, *Beyond the Pleasure Principle* (W. W. Norton & Co. 1961); Sigmund Freud, *Mourning and Melancholia,* in IV *Collected Papers* 156 (Hogarth Press, London 1925)).

49 Id.

50 Id.

51 Id.

Moreover, Rabbi Lamm finds a further analogue to modern psychoanalytical theory, in the exclusion of self-incrimination in Jewish law in cases involving forms of corporal punishment other than capital punishment. Turning to the work of Karl Menninger, Rabbi Lamm notes that because the Death Instinct is usually only partially neutralized by the Life Instinct, the emerging tension produces not suicide, but "a variety of forms of partial or chronic self-destruction," including "self-injury and self-mutilation."[52] Thus, Rabbi Lamm concludes, "[w]hile certainly not all, or even most criminal confessions are directly attributable, in whole or in part, to the Death Instinct, the Hala[c]ha is sufficiently concerned with the minority of instances, where such is the case, to disqualify all criminal confessions and to discard confession as a legal instrument."[53]

PART THREE | APPLICATION TO THE AMERICAN LEGAL SYSTEM

In light of the foregoing overview of the nature of *halacha* in general and the rule in Jewish law regarding self-incrimination in particular, it may be instructive to explore possible applications to the American legal system. One perspective for analyzing this question might operate from within Jewish legal theory, accepting the inherent authority of Jewish law to prescribe rules for the proper administration of justice in contemporary American society. Such an approach would involve a consideration of the Noachide laws, which, under Jewish thought, comprise a legal system applicable to all of humanity.[54]

Although the overwhelming majority of material comprising the corpus of Jewish law addresses the legal obligations of the Jewish nation, the substance of the Noachide laws has occupied a prominent position in Jewish legal discussion from ancient times through the present.[55] These discussions have resulted in

---

52 Id. at 57 (citing Karl Menninger, *Man Against Himself* 82 (1938)).

53 Id. at 59.

54 Under Jewish legal theory, God commanded all of humanity, through Adam, to observe a universal legal system comprised of six basic laws. See Kaplan, supra note 1, at 40. A seventh law was commanded to all of humanity through Noah, accounting for the appellation of the Noachide laws. See id. God then began to command additional laws, to Abraham, Isaac, Jacob, and their descendants, culminating in the Revelation at Mount Sinai, at which the Nation of Israel received, through Moses, all of the commandments that constitute the Jewish legal system. See id. at 45-62.

55 See, e.g., The Babylonian Talmud, Sanhedrin 56a-59b; Maimonides, supra note 20, Laws of Kings, chs. 9-10; Rabbi Zvi Hirsch Chajes, 1 *Kol Sifrei Maharitz Chayos (Collected Works)* 58-63 (1958); Yitzchak Hutner, *Pachad Yitzchak: Shavuoth* 31-34 (1999). Moreover, a

a fairly extensive body of law detailing various rules and regulations governing a parallel legal system that differs in significant respects from the legal system applicable to the Jewish nation. Not surprisingly, however, as it remained largely academic throughout most of Jewish history, the legal literature dealing with Noachide law is not nearly as developed or comprehensive as that relating to the law that was actually practiced among the Jewish nation. In fact, in contrast to the lengthy and wide-ranging discussions of the issue of self-incrimination within the Jewish legal system, the voluminous library of Jewish legal theory is largely bereft of any analysis of the admissibility of confessions under Noachide law.

The most prominent source to present a decisive position on this issue appears to be the medieval work *Sefer Ha-Chinuch*, which declares that Noachide law does not preclude the use of confessions as a basis for criminal punishment.[56] In the absence of a more definitive legal authority, however, a number of scholars have attempted to draw inferences from a variety of additional legal sources,[57] while other scholars have relied on further analysis of pertinent legal principles. For example, some discussions have centered on placing confessions in the context of the distinct rules of evidence that govern the Noachide legal system.[58] At least one scholar has proposed, through a rather complex line of reasoning, alternative resolutions of the issue corresponding to the differing rationales offered by Maimonides and Radbaz[59] for the ban on self-incrimination in proceedings operating under the Jewish legal system.[60] Perhaps ironically, then, although the various explanations offered for the preclusion of confessions in Jewish law seem to have little, if any, effect

---

number of contemporary law professors have produced English works dedicated to discussions of Noachide law. See, e.g., J. David Bleich, *Capital Punishment in the Noachide Code*, in 2 *Contemporary Halakhic Problems* 341-67 (1983); Arnold N. Enker, *Aspects of Interaction Between the Torah Law, the King's Law, and the Noahide Law in Jewish Criminal Law*, 12 Cardozo L. Rev. 1137 (1991); Nahum Rakover, *Jewish Law and the Noahide Obligation to Preserve Social Order*, 12 Cardozo L. Rev. 1073 (1991); Suzanne L. Stone, *Sinaitic and Noahide Law: Legal Pluralism in Jewish Law*, 12 Cardozo L. Rev. 1157 (1991).

56 See *Sefer Ha-Chinuch* 81, 273 (Chaim Dov Chavel ed., 1986). For an analysis of this position, see Kirschenbaum, supra note 4, at 97-98. For a discussion of the authorship of the *Sefer Ha-Chinuch*, see Chaim Dov Chavel, *Editor's Introduction*, in *Sefer Ha-Chinuch*, supra, at 5-7.

57 See Bleich, supra note 55, at 347-48 & nn.6-7 (citing efforts to draw inferences from such authoritative sources as the biblical book of Samuel and the Jerusalem Talmud); Kirschenbaum, supra note 4, at 96-99 & 179 nn.8-16.

58 See Kirschenbaum, supra note 4, at 97-98, 179 nn.13-15.

59 See supra notes 31-46 and accompanying text.

60 See Yechiel Ya'akov Weinberg, 2 *Seridei Esh* 252 (1962), cited in Bleich, supra note 55, at 348 n.6. See also Hershel Schachter, *MiPninei HaRav* 225 (2001).

on the application of the rule within the Jewish legal system,[61] they would have significant practical ramifications for determining the Noachide law of criminal procedure.[62] Ultimately, however, discussions of the issue of self-incrimination in Noachide law remain largely inconclusive.[63]

A different mode of analysis for considering the application of the Jewish law of self-incrimination to the American legal system might address the issue from within the perspective of American law. Under such an approach, it would seem, the substance and reasoning of Jewish law are relevant only to the extent that they are meaningful within the internal logic of American legal discourse. Consequently, this analysis would discount any suggestion that the American legal system should directly adopt the rule of self-incrimination found in the Jewish legal system, or any notion of the authority of Jewish law to prescribe binding rules of evidence for the American legal system. Instead, a conceptual approach to the application of Jewish law might motivate the rethinking and possible modification of the American law of confessions based on insights and lessons that arise out of an analysis of the Jewish law regarding self-incrimination.[64]

---

61 See supra notes 20-26 and accompanying text.

62 Professor Kirschenbaum suggested that the alternative explanations of Maimonides and Radbaz may have practical legal ramifications in the Jewish legal system as well, in relation to the issue of disqualification of witnesses. See Kirschenbaum, supra note 4, at 75-77. However, as Kirschenbaum emphasized, according to either explanation, "under no circumstances can [one] be punished, capitally or corporally, on the basis of [one's] own statements." Id. at 77.

63 See Bleich, supra note 55, at 348 (describing "conflicting views with regard to the acceptance of a confession by Noachide courts").

64 A conceptual approach to the role of Jewish law, as a form of comparative law for the analysis of American law, is consistent with the approach I have advocated elsewhere. See Chapter 3 in this Volume (stating that "conceptual similarities between American law and Jewish law allow for meaningful yet cautious comparison of the two systems"); Chapter 5 in this Volume (focusing on "the conceptual underpinnings behind pertinent Jewish law, considering the potential relevance and effect of those conceptualizations on American legal thought"); Samuel J. Levine, *Capital Punishment and Religious Arguments: An Intermediate Approach*, 9 Wm. & Mary Bill Rts. J. 179, 190 (2000) (describing "the possibility and utility of looking to religious thought, not as binding legal authority, but as a comparative law model deserving attention in the consideration of American legal issues"); Samuel J. Levine, *Law, Ethics, and Religion in the Public Square: Principles of Restraint and Withdrawal*, 83 Marq. L. Rev. 773, 780 (2000) (calling for "a consideration of the conceptual foundations underlying the approach [to a legal issue] in Jewish law, with the aim of identifying and applying those that are suitable to the American legal [system]").

   See also Rosenberg & Rosenberg, supra note 4, at 1041-42 (internal citations omitted):

   Comparative law is tricky. The danger (or absurdity) of trying to stuff a whale into a molted snakeskin is obvious. There is nonetheless an irresistible

Significantly, numerous courts and scholars alike have turned to Jewish law to help frame the American law of self-incrimination, without advocating that the American legal system incorporate an outright ban on criminal confessions.[65] Writing for the United States Supreme Court in *Miranda v. Arizona*,[66] the landmark case defining the contours of the constitutional privilege against self-incrimination, Chief Justice Earl Warren quoted the view of Maimonides and referred to Rabbi Lamm's article.[67] Less than one year later, addressing concerns over coercion in the context of self-incrimination, Justice William Douglas included in the Court's majority opinion an extensive quotation from Rabbi Lamm's article.[68] Likewise, a number of other courts and several scholars have found in the Jewish legal system an illuminating antecedent for English and American laws providing protections against self-incrimination.[69] Although some have questioned the evidence of any direct historical connection between Jewish law and American law in this area,[70] such objections should not preclude careful, yet valuable, conceptual comparison.

---

temptation to try to derive at least some insights from a legal system two thousand years old, that was quite advanced and sophisticated not only for its time, but for ours, and that some claim to be the source of the self-incrimination clause of the fifth amendment.

Both cultures faced head on the question of the appropriate stance for government with respect to inculpatory statements in criminal cases. On the surface, the United States and ancient Israel appear to have made dissimilar choices. Yet the two approaches are not unrelated, and their touch points can perhaps assist in analysis of contemporary law.

Cf. Randy Lee, *A Look at God, Feminism, and Tort Law*, 75 Marq. L. Rev. 369 (1992); Steven D. Smith, *Legal Discourse and the De Facto Disestablishment*, 81 Marq. L. Rev. 203 (1998).

65 See sources cited supra note 4.

66 *Miranda v. Arizona*, 384 U.S. 436 (1966).

67 Id. at 458 & n.27 (citing Maimonides, supra note 20, Laws of *Sanhedrin* 18:6; Lamm, supra note 47). Chief Justice Warren observed that the "roots [of the privilege against self-incrimination] go back into ancient times," and, quoting Maimonides, stated that "[t]hirteenth century commentators found an analogue to the privilege grounded in the Bible." Id. See Chapter 2 in this Volume.

68 See *Garrity v. State of New Jersey*, 385 U.S. 493, 497 n.5 (1967) (quoting Lamm, supra note 47). See Chapter 2 in this Volume.

69 See supra note 4.

70 See, e.g., Arnold Enker, *Self-Incrimination*, in *Jewish Law and Current Legal Problems*, supra note 4, at 169 (stating that "[t]he thesis of my presentation today will be that exaggerated claims have been and are being made for the sources of self-incrimination in Jewish law, and for the notion that important lessons can be learned from Jewish law with respect to self-incrimination"); Kirschenbaum, supra note 4, at 19-21; Levy, supra note 4, at 439-40 (stating that "[w]hether the existence of the right against self-incrimination in Talmudic law in any way influenced the rise of the right in Anglo-American law is an intriguing question" but

In fact, applying the reasoning behind the categorical exclusion of criminal confessions in Jewish law does not imply mechanical imposition of a similar ban in American law.[71] As many scholars have noted, an outright preclusion of self-incrimination would appear highly impractical in contemporary American society, as well as contrary to the internal logic and experience of the American legal system.[72] Nevertheless, a thoughtful consideration of self-incrimination in Jewish law may lead to a rethinking of the treatment of confessions in American law, to include a more subtle and nuanced definition and application of the basic concept of voluntariness. In light of the seemingly perennial problem of wrongfully obtained, and even false, confessions in the United States,[73] it may

---

concluding that "the answer, if based on evidence rather than speculation, must be negative"). But see Braz, supra note 4, at 162 (arguing that "Jewish law and Talmudic jurisprudence constitute one of the main streams that converged to form the unique common law doctrine against self-incrimination"); Horowitz, supra note 4. See also Rosenberg & Rosenberg, supra note 4, at 1042 n.310.

71 Moreover, although the ban on self-incrimination represents the general normative standard prescribed by the Jewish legal system, in practice, the system provided a license for deviation from this standard under exigent circumstances. See Enker, supra note 21, at cxxiii; Enker, supra note 69, at 1141-47; Halberstam, supra note 4, at 187; Kirschenbaum, supra note 4, at 82-92, 135-36; Rosenberg & Rosenberg, supra note 4, at 1018-27. These deviations would seemingly have to be acknowledged and addressed as part of an attempt to incorporate lessons from Jewish law into the American law of self-incrimination. Indeed, at least one scholar finds the existence of such deviations so significant as to preclude any relevance of the Jewish law of self-incrimination to contemporary American law. See Enker, supra note 21, at cxxiii. Arguably, though, the conceptual approach to the application of Jewish law to American law appears largely immune to such objections, as the analysis relies not upon the practical implementation of the rule in Jewish law, but instead upon its conceptual articulation and its theoretical and philosophical underpinnings.

72 See, e.g., Enker, supra note 21, at cxxii (concluding that "the Jewish Law treating confessions is not particularly relevant to the [contemporary] confessions debate, primarily because the procedural and evidentiary premises of the Jewish legal system which developed these rules are so radically different from our own that the legal issues posed are equally different"); Kirschenbaum, supra note 4, at 134-37 (stating that, for the rules of self-incrimination in Jewish law to "be used intelligently" in contemporary consideration of the issue, "certain factors must be mentioned and dealt with," including: "whether the fact that the Jewish ancients lived a rather uncomplicated life in smaller, relatively homogeneous groupings—both geographically and sociologically— allowed for features in their judicial system that may strike us as starry-eyed and impractical"; and "that the Rabbis believed sincerely that [humans] could not and [were] not commanded to solve all problems of law-enforcement" as "Divine Justice and Divine Retribution were realities in the world-view of the Rabbis," and thus "the liberal judicial procedure and heavy protection of the rights of the accused in Jewish law were coupled with a deep religious confidence that the criminal will eventually receive . . . just deserts and that justice will triumph"); Rosenberg & Rosenberg, supra note 4, at 1042-46. See also Chapter 2 in this Volume.

73 See, e.g., Steven A. Drizin & Richard A. Leo, *The Problem of False Confessions in the Post-DNA World*, 82 N. C. L. Rev. 891, 901-7 (2004) (citing Hugo Adam Bedau & Michael L. Radelet,

be wise to incorporate some of the philosophical and psychological insights that scholars of Jewish law have offered into the nature of, and possible motivations behind, an admission of criminal conduct.[74]

Miscarriages of Justice in Potentially Capital Cases, 40 Stan. L. Rev. 21, 47, 49, 57 (1987); Edward Connor et al., *Convicted by Juries, Exonerated by Science: Case Studies in the Use of DNA Evidence to Establish Innocence After Trial* 15-17 (1996); *https://www.innocenceproject. org/cases/*; Barry Scheck, Peter Neufeld & Jim Dwyer, *Actual Innocence* (2000)).

74 In fact, on the basis of an examination of Jewish law, a number of American legal scholars have proposed and justified modifications to the American law of self-incrimination. See, e.g., Goldberg, supra note 4, at viii-ix (describing ways in which "[w]e have something to learn from this ancient tradition"); Halberstam, supra note 4, at 186–87 (suggesting that "perhaps, as the [American] privilege [against self-incrimination] approaches the absolute[,] ... [i]t must be justified, if at all, only morally, as in ancient Jewish law"); Rosenberg & Rosenberg, supra note 4, at 1042-46:

> The rock bottom teaching of the Talmud is that a unitary, per se exclusionary rule with respect to confessions is the preferred way to deal with this issue. In this country, we have no single, absolute rule; instead, various provision give piecemeal protection. . . .
>
> . . . *Miranda*'s method is more tenuous because the very people responsible for obtaining evidence of crimes are also made responsible for assuring voluntariness. When judicial inroads and excisions are added to that inherent systemic weakness—inroads and excisions that tend to make the means as relative as the ultimate standard—there is a corresponding increase in the possibility of abusive police methods. The danger of a relative rule with respect to confessions is that one's starting point is already at, or near, the cusp, and any relaxation enhances the risk that resulting confessions will fall into the realm of involuntariness and perhaps unreliability.
>
> *Miranda* is the bright line in American law, our functional equivalent of the Talmudic no-confessions rule. . . . *Miranda*'s irrebuttable presumption was an attempt to confine the vagaries of relativity, and every modification of it resonates ominously. The more *Miranda* is devitalized, the greater and more reasonable the doubts as to voluntariness of confession in this country. This once bright line has become enshrouded with restrictive interpretations that form part of the rule and impede its essential purpose.

75 Drizin & Leo, supra note 73, at 919. See id. at 910-11 (stating that "[s]ocial scientists and legal scholars have amply documented that contemporary methods of psychological interrogation can, and sometimes do, lead innocent individuals to confess falsely to serious felony crimes") (citing Gisli Gudjonsson, *The Psychology of Interrogations and Confessions* 205-58 (2003); Saul Kassin, *The Psychology of Confession Evidence*, 52 Am. Psychol. 221, 224-25 (1997); Richard A. Leo & Richard J. Ofshe, *The Consequences of False Confessions: Deprivations of Liberty and Miscarriages of Justice in the Age of Psychological Interrogations*, 88 J. Crim. L. & Criminology 429, 440-49 (1988); Richard J. Ofshe & Richard A. Leo, *The Decision to Confess Falsely: Rational Choice and Irrational Action*, 74 Den. L. Rev. 979, 981-1001 (1997) [hereinafter Ofshe & Leo, *Decision to Confess Falsely*]; Richard A. Leo &

Indeed, a leading contemporary study of false confessions in the American legal system describes two substantial factors contributing to the phenomenon of "interrogation-induced false confession."[75] The study identifies the primary factor as a complex process of "psychological manipulation" and "psychological coercion."[76] Additionally, according to the study, "some individuals—particularly juveniles and the mentally retarded—are more vulnerable to the pressures of interrogation and are therefore less likely to possess or to be able to muster the psychological resources of perspective necessary to withstand accusatorial police questioning."[77] These discussions of the role of psychological confusion as a cause of false confessions, with special attention to the impact on individuals with particular psychological vulnerabilities, echo—and, thus, may offer a trenchant illustration of the potentially illuminating application of—the psychological insights Maimonides and others offered in their analysis of the ban on confessions in Jewish law.[78]

CONCLUSION

The issue of self-incrimination has confronted Anglo-American scholars and jurists for centuries,[79] resulting in the adoption of the Fifth Amendment right against self-incrimination as a central tenet of American constitutional law.[80] In the words that conclude a leading historical study of the subject, "[a]bove all,

---

Richard J. Ofshe, *The Social Psychology of Police Interrogations: The Theory and Classification of True and False Confessions*, 16 Stud. L. Pol. & Soc'y 189, 191-94 (1997)). See generally id. at 907-23 (2004).

76   Drizin & Leo, supra note 73, at 914. See id. at 918 (characterizing "[m]odern psychological interrogation [as] a gradual yet cumulative process [in which] each technique builds on the next as the investigator seeks to emphasize the overriding strength of the State's case and the futility of the suspect's denials" and concluding that "[i]ntended for the guilty, modern interrogation techniques are psychologically powerful enough to elicit confessions from the innocent"). See generally id. at 914-19. See also Ofshe & Leo, *Decision to Confess Falsely*, supra note 75, passim.

77   Drizin & Leo, supra note 72, at 919 (citing Morgan Cloud et al., *Words Without Meaning: The Constitution, Confessions, and Mentally Retarded Suspects*, 69 U. Chi. L. Rev. 495, 499-516 (2002); James W. Ellis & Ruth A. Luckasson, *Mentally Retarded Criminal Defendants*, 53 Geo. Wash. L. Rev. 414, 445-52 (1985); Paul Hourihan, *Earl Washington's Confession: Mental Retardation and the Law of Confessions*, 81 Va. L. Rev. 1471, 1491-94 (1995), Gudjonsson, supra note 75, at 285 (recommending the use of broad, general questions to avoid suggestibility and acquiescence)).

78   See supra notes 31-53 and accompanying text.

79   See Helmholz, supra note 4, at 279 n.28; Levy, supra note 4.

80   See Levy, supra note 4, at 405-32.

the Fifth Amendment reflected [the framers'] judgment that in a free society, based on respect for the individual, the determination of guilt or innocence by just procedures, in which the accused made no unwilling contribution to his conviction, was more important than punishing the guilty."[81]

If this right is to continue to be taken seriously, the American legal system should acknowledge and work to protect against the variety of ways in which a seemingly voluntary confession may, in fact, be less than willful, or even the product of coercion, however subtle.[82] Conceptual consideration of the approach to self-incrimination in Jewish law may help facilitate such a reassessment of American law. As one scholar put it, "[w]hile there is no room in the contemporary system of proof for the absolute exclusion of confessions and guilty pleas, an increased sensitivity to their limitations as proof and the introduction of a requirement that the judge ascertain what other evidence exists to be weighed with the confession before entering the conviction would be a warranted lesson to learn from the Jewish Law."[83]

---

81 See id. at 432.

82 See supra notes 75-77 and accompanying text. Cf. Drizin & Leo, supra note 75, at 910 (finding that "[a]s psychological methods of interrogation have evolved over the years, they have become increasingly sophisticated, relying on more subtle forms of manipulation, deception, and coercion"); id. at 918 (concluding that "[t]he primary psychological cause of most false confessions is . . . the investigator's use of improper, coercive interrogation techniques"); Rosenberg & Rosenberg, supra note 4, at 1043-44 ("Inability to choose freely whether to assist the prosecution in securing one's own conviction—no matter how reliable or ostensibly imperative that assistance may be—is by any other name coercion."); Stephen J. Schulhofer, *Miranda's Practical Effect: Substantial Benefits and Vanishingly Small Social Costs*, 90 Nw. L. Rev. 500 (1996):

> [W]hatever one may think of *Miranda*, it is clear—and uncontroversial— that pressure need not rise to the level of overbearing physical or psychological coercion, in the due process sense, before it is sufficiently compelling to violate the Fifth Amendment . . . [A] formalistic showing of compulsion by legal process or official punishment cannot be essential. . . . Indeed, as the *Miranda* Court noted . . . the "interrogation environment is created for no purpose other than to subjugate the individual to the will of his examiner." As a result, the typical custodial police interrogation, even if not brutally coercive in the due process sense, will readily (perhaps almost invariably) violate the Fifth Amendment bar on the use of compelling pressure, at least in the absence of safeguards sufficient to dispel that pressure.

Id. at 551-53 (quoting *Miranda v. Arizona*, 384 U.S. 436, 457 (1966)).

83 See Enker, supra note 21, at cxxiv.

CHAPTER 8

Miranda, Dickerson, and Jewish Legal Theory: The Constitutional Rule in a Comparative Analytical Framework

INTRODUCTION

This chapter briefly explores *Dickerson v. United States,*[1] the important 2000 decision in which a divided United States Supreme Court held that the standard established in *Miranda v. Arizona*[2] continues to govern the admissibility of confessions, notwithstanding a federal statute enacted subsequent to *Miranda* that provided an alternative standard.[3] Rather than focusing on substantive issues of the Fifth Amendment and self-incrimination,[4] this chapter addresses broader theoretical implications of the approaches adopted by the majority and dissenting opinions in *Dickerson*. The majority of the Court concluded that *Miranda* set forth a "constitutional rule," and therefore could not be superseded by a legislative act of Congress.[5] The dissent argued that in establishing such a "rule," which is prophylactic in nature and subject to exceptions

---

1   530 U.S. 428 (2000).
2   384 U.S. 436 (1966).
3   See 18 U.S.C. § 3501 (establishing that the admissibility of a confession depends upon whether the confession was "voluntarily given"), invalidated by *Dickerson v. United States*, 530 U.S. 428 (2000).
4   For a substantive discussion of self-incrimination in Jewish law and American law, see Chapters 2 and 7 in this Volume; Samuel J. Levine, *Rethinking Self-Incrimination, Voluntariness, and Coercion, through the Perspective of Jewish Law and Legal Theory*, 12 J.L. Society 72 (2010-2011).
5   *Dickerson*, 530 U.S. at 444.

and modifications, the Court impermissibly took on the role of a legislature rather than the role of interpreter of the Constitution.[6]

Drawing a parallel to the interpretation of the Torah in Jewish legal theory,[7] this chapter proposes a comparative framework for analyzing the division between the majority and dissent over the concept and status of a "constitutional rule." This chapter finds a similar debate among medieval legal authorities over the status of a rule in the Jewish legal system that appears to function in a manner ordinarily reserved for legislation.[8] Some authorities categorize the rule as rabbinic legislation, while others understand the rule as a biblical law, derived through biblical interpretation, with quasi-legislative characteristics.[9] Taking the conceptual comparison a step further,

---

6 Id. at 450-61 (Scalia, J., dissenting).

7 This framework relies, in part, on my work elsewhere. See, e.g., Chapter 9 in this Volume (exploring a similarity in biblical and constitutional interpretation, through which unenumerated rights and principles emerge by reference to enumerated rights and principles); Chapter 10 in this Volume (developing a conceptual framework by which to apply the notion of "rules and standards" in Jewish law to address contemporary constitutional issues); Chapter 11 in this Volume (looking to the case of the "stubborn and rebellious son" in Deuteronomy 21:18-21, which prescribes a capital penalty for an unlikely offense, as a means by which to understand the apparent superfluity of the Ninth Amendment). This framework also builds upon the work of a number of legal scholars. See, e.g., Robert M. Cover, "The Supreme Court, 1982 Term—Foreword: *Nomos* and Narrative," 97 Harv. L. Rev. 4 (1983) (developing a normative conception of the legal world by reference to biblical text); David R. Dow, *Constitutional Midrash: The Rabbis' Solution to Professor Bickel's Problem*, 29 Hous. L. Rev. 543 (1992) (drawing parallels between biblical and constitutional interpretation while highlighting common interpretive principles and the analogous roles of judge and rabbi); Ronald R. Garet, *Comparative Normative Hermeneutics: Scripture, Literature, Constitution*, 58 S. Cal. L. Rev. 35 (1985) (discussing, at length, common hermeneutic principles applied in biblical, literary, and legal scholarship); Thomas C. Grey, *The Constitution as Scripture*, 37 Stan. L. Rev. 1 (1984) (analogizing the conflict between "textualists" and "supplementers" in constitutional interpretation to the conflict between Protestant and Catholic biblical interpretation); Gregory A. Kalscheur, *Christian Scripture and American Scripture: An Instructive Analogy?*, 21 J.L. & Religion 101 (2005-2006) (reviewing Jaroslav Pelikan, *Interpreting the Bible and the Constitution* (2004)); Sanford Levinson, *"The Constitution" in American Civil Religion*, 1979 Sup. Ct. Rev. 123 (identifying similarities between conflicts over constitutional interpretation and conflicts over scriptural interpretations between the Catholic and Protestant churches); Michael J. Perry, *The Authority of Text, Tradition, and Reason: A Theory of Constitutional "Interpretation,"* 58 S. Cal. L. Rev. 551, 557-64 (1985) (analogizing certain forms of constitutional interpretation to the interpretation of sacred texts by religious communities); see generally Sanford Levinson, *Constitutional Faith* (1988) (exploring the effects of sanctifying the Constitution by placing it at the center of American political life).

8 See infra part two, section B.

9 See infra part two, section B.

this chapter considers ways in which Jewish legal theory might elucidate the nature of the "constitutional rule" delineated in *Miranda*.[10]

PART ONE | *MIRANDA, DICKERSON,* AND THE "CONSTITUTIONAL RULE"

A. *Miranda*

In the landmark 1966 case, *Miranda v. Arizona,*[11] the United States Supreme Court considered the applicability of the Fifth Amendment privilege against self-incrimination[12] in the context of custodial police interrogation. The Court declared unequivocally that "there can be no doubt that the Fifth Amendment privilege is available outside of criminal court proceedings and serves to protect persons in all settings in which their freedom of action is curtailed in any significant way from being compelled to incriminate themselves."[13] Moreover, the Court emphasized that "without proper safeguards the process of in-custody interrogation . . . contains inherently compelling pressures which work to undermine the individual's will to resist and to compel him to speak where he would not otherwise do so freely."[14] The Court held that "[i]n order to combat these pressures and to permit a full opportunity to exercise the privilege against self-incrimination, the accused must be adequately and effectively apprised of his rights and the exercise of those rights must be fully honored."[15]

Strikingly, in contrast to the Court's forceful affirmation of the applicability of Fifth Amendment rights during police interrogation, the Court was unwilling to conclude that "the Constitution necessarily requires adherence to any particular solution" as a means of protecting those rights.[16] Instead, the Court encouraged Congress and the States to "exercise . . . their creative rule-making capacities" to formulate effective methods of protecting the rights of individuals interrogated by the police.[17] Nevertheless, the Court also prescribed its own set of safeguards, thus establishing the procedures that would constitute

---

10 See infra part two, sections B–C.
11 384 U.S. 436 (1966).
12 See U.S. Const. amend. V ("No person shall be . . . compelled in any criminal case to be a witness against himself. . . .").
13 *Miranda,* 384 U.S. at 467.
14 Id.
15 Id.
16 Id.
17 Id.

the *Miranda* warnings.[18] Notably, notwithstanding the Court's insistence that the Constitution does not require a particular solution, the Court stated that "unless we are shown other procedures which are at least as effective in apprising accused persons of their right of silence and in assuring a continuous opportunity to exercise it, the [*Miranda* warnings] must be observed."[19]

The majority opinion in *Miranda* faced considerable criticism on a number of grounds, including the argument that the Court's methodology was "not constitutional interpretation . . . but legislation from the bench."[20] Even defenders of *Miranda* acknowledged that the opinion "does not even look like an ordinary opinion," but instead "reads more like a legislative committee report with an accompanying statute."[21] Among other unusual characteristics of the opinion, critics of *Miranda* pointed to the apparently "prophylactic" nature of the *Miranda* requirements[22] as more akin to legislation than judicial interpretation of the Constitution. Indeed, the language and logic employed in a number of subsequent United States Supreme Court decisions reinforce the impression that *Miranda* established "prophylactic standards," beyond the protections provided by the Constitution,[23] and thus "sweeps more broadly than the Fifth Amendment itself."[24] Likewise, the process through which the Court

---

18 See id. at 479. The Court explained:

> [An individual in police custody] must be warned prior to any questioning that he has the right to remain silent, that anything he says can be used against him in a court of law, that he has the right to the presence of an attorney, and that if he cannot afford an attorney one will be appointed for him prior to any questioning if he so desires. . . . [U]nless and until such warnings and waiver [of those rights] are demonstrated by the prosecution at trial, no evidence obtained as a result of interrogation can be used against him.

Id.

19 Id. at 467.

20 Mitchell N. Berman, *Constitutional Decision Rules*, 90 Va. L. Rev. 1, 19 & n.57 (2004) (citing Justice Harlan's *Miranda* dissent as well as a number of "especially prominent assaults" leveled on *Miranda* by legal scholars).

21 David A. Strauss, *The Ubiquity of Prophylactic Rules*, 55 U. Chi. L. Rev. 190, 190 (1988); see also Richard H. Fallon, Jr., *Judicial Legitimacy and the Unwritten Constitution: A Comment on Miranda and Dickerson*, 45 N.Y.L. Sch. L. Rev. 119, 122 (2000-2001) ("Even on the surface, *Miranda*'s insistence on detailed warnings looks legislative.").

22 See, e.g., Joseph D. Grano, *Prophylactic Rules in Criminal Procedure: A Question of Article III Legitimacy*, 80 Nw. U. L. Rev. 100, 106-11 (1985) (explaining how the *Miranda* holding is prophylactic).

23 E.g., *Michigan v. Tucker*, 417 U.S. 433, 445-46 (1974).

24 *Oregon v. Elstad*, 470 U.S. 298, 306 (1985); see also Richard H.W. Maloy, *Can a Rule Be Prophylactic and Yet Constitutional?*, 27 Wm. Mitchell L. Rev. 2465, 2471-74 (2001) (noting

has since adopted various exceptions to *Miranda* arguably resembles legislative modification rather than constitutional interpretation.[25]

In addition to the criticisms leveled against *Miranda* by Justices and scholars alike, a federal statute[26] enacted just two years after the *Miranda* decision presented a more direct challenge, by providing an alternative standard for the admissibility of statements obtained through custodial interrogation. In place of the *Miranda* requirements, the statute proposed that the admissibility of a confession should turn on the issue of "voluntariness," which is to be determined through "consideration [of] all the circumstances surrounding the giving of the confession."[27] On one level, the statute may have simply represented Congress's attempt to comply with the Court's suggestion that legislatures develop effective procedures to protect suspects' Fifth Amendment rights during police interrogation.[28] More significantly, however, the statutory response to *Miranda* would ultimately compel the Court to carefully reexamine the precise nature of the *Miranda* requirements and their relationship to the Constitution.[29]

B. *Dickerson*

In 2000, more than three decades after the enactment of the federal statute, the United States Supreme Court decided *Dickerson v. United States*,[30] thus finally addressing the competing standards for the admissibility of custodial confessions. The majority opinion presented the issue in stark and ostensibly clear

---

that five members of the seven Justice majority in *Dickerson* had authored opinions indicating that *Miranda* was not a "constitutional" decision).

25 See *Dickerson v. United States*, 530 U.S. 428, 455 (2000) (Scalia, J., dissenting).
   As Justice Scalia explained:

> [I]f confessions procured in violation of *Miranda* are confessions "compelled" in violation of the Constitution, the post-*Miranda* decisions I have discussed [that did not require suppression of such confessions] do not make sense. The only reasoned basis for their outcome was that a violation of *Miranda* is *not* a violation of the Constitution.

   Id. (emphasis in original).

26 See 18 U.S.C. § 3501 (establishing that a confession shall be admissible in evidence if "voluntarily given"), invalidated by *Dickerson v. United States*, 530 U.S. 428 (2000).

27 Id.

28 See supra text accompanying note 17.

29 See infra part one, section B.

30 530 U.S. 428 (2000).

terms. As a threshold matter, notwithstanding the Court's "supervisory author-ity ... to prescribe rules of evidence and procedure" in federal courts, "Congress retains the ultimate authority to modify or set aside any judicially created rules of evidence and procedure that are not required by the Constitution."[31] Conversely, however, "Congress may not legislatively supersede [the Court's] decisions interpreting and applying the Constitution."[32] Therefore, the case turned on the basic question: "whether the *Miranda* Court announced a consti-tutional rule or merely exercised its supervisory authority to regulate evidence in the absence of congressional direction."[33]

As the Court acknowledged in *Dickerson*, however, this seemingly straightfor-ward articulation of the question belied the complex and somewhat elusive nature of its answer. After all, in decisions subsequent to *Miranda*, the United States Supreme Court had carved out "several exceptions" to *Miranda*'s requirements and had "repeatedly referred to the *Miranda* warnings as 'prophylactic' and 'not themselves rights protected by the Constitution.'"[34] As the Court conceded, the language in some of these cases supported the conclusion of the Court of Appeals in *Dickerson* that "the protections announced in *Miranda* are not constitutionally required."[35]

Nevertheless, the Supreme Court rejected this approach, instead charac-terizing *Miranda* as a "constitutional decision."[36] The Court emphasized that the *Miranda* opinion "is replete with statements indicating that the [*Miranda*] majority thought it was announcing a constitutional rule."[37] As for subsequent United States Supreme Court decisions modifying *Miranda*, the Court explained that "[t]hese decisions illustrate the principle—not that *Miranda* is not a constitutional rule—but that no constitutional rule is immutable."[38] In this light, "the sort of modifications represented by these cases are as much a normal part of constitutional law as the original decision."[39]

In a stinging dissent, Justice Scalia questioned the notion that *Miranda* set forth a "constitutional rule." In a careful reading of the majority opinion, Justice Scalia observed that the Court's depiction of *Miranda* was limited to

---

31 Id. at 437.

32 Id.

33 Id.

34 Id. at 437-38 (internal citations omitted); see id. at 438 n.2 (citing cases).

35 Id. at 438 (citing *United States v. Dickerson*, 166 F.3d 667, 687-90 (4th Cir. 1999), rev'd, 530 U.S. 428 (2000)).

36 Id.

37 Id. 439.

38 Id. at 441.

39 Id.

characterizing the case as "'a constitutional decision'" that is "'constitutionally based'" and that has "'constitutional underpinnings.'"[40] Significantly, he noted, the court did not directly state that "'custodial interrogation that is not preceded by *Miranda* warnings or their equivalent violates the Constitution of the United States.'"[41]

In addition, Justice Scalia found the prophylactic aspects of *Miranda* and the later modifications of *Miranda* inconsistent with the notion that *Miranda* delineated constitutional protections.[42] Instead, he insisted, these cases demonstrate that "a violation of *Miranda* is not a violation of the Constitution."[43] Quoting approvingly from a dissenting opinion in the 1969 case *North Carolina v. Pearce*,[44] Justice Scalia wrote that "Justice Black surely had the right idea when he derided [the *Pearce* majority's similarly prophylactic rule] as 'pure legislation if there ever was legislation.'"[45] Justice Scalia took this critique even further in *Dickerson*, arguing that "*Pearce's* ruling pales as a legislative achievement when compared to the detailed code promulgated in *Miranda*."[46] In short, Justice Scalia rejected the majority's conception of *Miranda* as judicial interpretation of the Constitution.

Justice Scalia's dissatisfaction with the majority opinion in *Dickerson* was shared by a wide range of scholars, including many who supported the outcome of the case.[47] In turn, scholars have offered a variety of responses to

---

40 Id. at 446 (Scalia, J., dissenting) (quoting id. at 438, 440 & n.5 (majority opinion)).

41 Id.

42 Id. at 450-54.

43 Id. at 455 (emphasis in original).

44 395 U.S. 711 (1969).

45 *Dickerson*, 530 U.S. at 460 (quoting *Pearce*, 395 U.S. at 741 (Black, J., dissenting)).

46 Id.

47 See, e.g., Berman, supra note 20, at 26 & n.94 (stating that "[u]nfortunately, the majority did not engage Justice Scalia's attack" and noting that "[t]his is a wholly unoriginal observation, one frequently expressed by those who applaud, as well as by those who decry, the outcome in *Dickerson*" and citing sources); Evan H. Caminker, *Miranda and Some Puzzles of "Prophylactic" Rules*, 70 U. Cin. L. Rev. 1, 5 (2001) (referring to *Dickerson's* "lack of intellectual coherence, or at least candor" and stating that in the majority opinion, Chief Justice Rehnquist "certainly made little effort to square the decision with the Court's (and his) repeated disparagement of *Miranda* as articulating merely a prophylactic rule not required by the Fifth Amendment"); Fallon, supra note 21, at 126 ("Frustratingly, the Court in *Dickerson* never faced up to the challenge posed by the dissent. . . .").

Paul Cassell, whose scholarship and legal arguments were instrumental throughout the course of the *Dickerson* litigation, recalled his immediate reaction to the decision: "Where's the rest of the opinion?" Paul G. Cassell, *The Paths Not Taken: The Supreme Court's Failures in Dickerson*, 99 Mich. L. Rev. 898, 898 (2001).

the Court's ruling, providing both theories to justify the majority's decision and further grounds for criticism.[48]

The next section of this chapter aims to provide a conceptual framework for understanding the division between the majority and dissenting opinions in *Dickerson*. Turning to Jewish legal theory, this section draws a parallel to a dispute in the Jewish legal system regarding the status of laws that, similar to *Miranda* warnings, operate in a manner that resembles legislation, but that, according to some authorities, are derived through a form of judicial decision-making rather than a legislative process.

PART TWO | THE JEWISH LEGAL MODEL

A. The Torah, Biblical Interpretation, and Rabbinic Legislation: A Brief Introduction

In Jewish legal theory, the Torah, consisting of the Five Books of Moses, serves as the foundational source of the legal system and carries the authority of supreme law.[49] In the words of a leading contemporary scholar, the Torah is the "written 'constitution' of Jewish law."[50] Somewhat parallel to principles of American constitutional doctrine, biblical authority extends not only to laws that are delineated in the text of the Torah, but also to those derived from the text through methods of interpretation.[51] Laws that are based in the biblical text and its interpretation thus have the status of *d'oraita*, a Talmudic term drawing upon the Aramaic translation of "Torah."[52] An additional category of laws, enacted by legal authorities through a legislative process, has the subordinate status of *d'rabbanan*, Aramaic for "rabbinic."[53]

---

48 See, e.g., *Symposium, Miranda After Dickerson: The Future of Confession Law*, 99 Mich. L. Rev. 879 (2001) (including eleven articles discussing the status of *Miranda* following the *Dickerson* decision); Berman, supra note 20 (suggesting how the *Dickerson* majority could have responded to the complex doctrine announced by the *Miranda* court); Caminker, supra note 47 (using both *Miranda* and *Dickerson* as a means of defending the legitimacy of prophylactic doctrinal rules); Fallon, supra note 21 (arguing that the *Dickerson* opinion is a legitimate one).

49 See Chapter 4 in this Volume (citing 2 Menacham Elon, *Jewish Law: History, Sources, Principles* 479, 481 (Bernard Auerbach & Melvin J. Sykes trans., 1994)).

50 2 Menachem Elon, *Jewish Law: History, Sources, Principles* 479 (Bernard Auerbach & Melvin J. Sykes trans., 1994).

51 See Chapters 3 and 4 in this Volume.

52 See Chapter 4 in this Volume.

53 See id.

A helpful illustration of the different categories of laws may be found in the Torah's instruction not to engage in *melacha* on the Sabbath.[54] Although *melacha* is sometimes translated as "work," a more accurate legal definition of this term denotes a variety of ritually prohibited activities.[55] Specifically, in addition to the enumeration in the Torah of certain examples of *melacha*,[56] the Talmud, through textual exegesis, delineates thirty-nine principal activities that constitute *melacha*.[57] Because these laws are derived through interpretation of the biblical text, the prohibition on these activities as *melacha* has the status of *d'oraita* laws.[58] Supplementing and safeguarding these forms of biblically prohibited *melacha*, legal authorities enacted additional rabbinic legislation, prohibiting various other activities as well, which have the status of *d'rabbanan* laws.[59]

The relative status of laws that are *d'oraita* and *d'rabbanan*, respectively, is expressed in functional differences, premised largely on fundamental distinctions in the purposes of the laws.[60] Under Jewish legal theory, biblical laws are of divine origin and command, and thus are inherently justified as a manifestation of divine will.[61] Rabbinic legislation, in contrast, serves the express prophylactic purpose of safeguarding compliance with biblical laws.[62] Accordingly, in the context of *melacha* on the Sabbath, rabbinic legislation functions primarily as a means of protecting against violation of biblically prohibited activities.[63]

---

54 See, e.g., Exodus 20:10; Exodus 35:2; Leviticus 23:3; Deuteronomy 5:14.

55 See, e.g., Chapters 3 and 4 in this Volume (explaining that *melacha*, variously transliterated as *melakha*, denotes a broad range of activity categorized ritually as "work"). See also Aryeh Kaplan, *Sabbath: Day of Eternity*, in II *The Aryeh Kaplan Anthology* 107, 128 (1998) ("[T]he prohibition is not against actual labor as much as against ritual work.").

56 See Exodus 16:29 ("'let no man leave his place'"); Exodus 35:3 ("kindle no fire"); Numbers 15:32-36 ("gathering wood").

57 See Talmud Bavli, Shabbath, passim. Most of the literature on Jewish law is written in Hebrew. For helpful depictions of *melacha* written in English, see, for example, Kaplan, supra note 55, at 133-44; Baruch Chait, *The 39 Avoth Melacha of Shabbath* (1992) (illustrated book with scholarly commentary).

58 See supra text accompanying note 52.

59 E.g., Kaplan, supra note 55, at 132; Chapter 4 in this Volume.

60 See Chapter 4 in this Volume (explaining limitations on rabbinic legislative authority); see also Chait, supra note 57, at 13.

61 See Chapter 3 of this Volume (describing the general rule that rabbinical authorities may not place limitations upon the applicability of a commandment on the basis of the commandment's ostensible rationale).

62 See Chapter 4 of this Volume ("[T]he Talmud identifies a biblical source for the authority of negative rabbinic legislation, such as the protective measures implemented to prevent violation of the biblical laws of the Sabbath . . . ."). For a discussion of positive rabbinic legislation, which mandates—rather than prohibits—certain activities, see id..

63 For a more detailed and nuanced discussion of different functions and sub-categories of rabbinic legislation related to the Sabbath, see id.

In addition to the laws of the Sabbath, the Torah also proscribes *melacha* on a number of holidays that take place at various times throughout the year.[64] Although, in comparison with the laws of the Sabbath, the range of activities prohibited on these holidays is somewhat more limited, and violations are not quite as consequential,[65] most of these laws are derived from the text and interpretation of the Torah, and thus likewise have the status of *d'oraita*.

B. *Melacha* on *Chol Ha-Moed*: A Comparative Conceptual Framework

A more complex question surrounds the status of the prohibition of *melacha* on *chol ha-moed*,[66] the relatively less sacred days that comprise the intermediate portion of lengthier holiday periods.[67] Noting that *melacha* is permitted on *chol ha-moed* under a variety of circumstances, including when necessary to prevent substantial monetary loss or in deference to other important needs of the day,[68] a number of medieval legal authorities argued that such exceptions to a legal rule are characteristic of legislative enactment rather than textual interpretation. Therefore, they concluded, unlike the laws of the Sabbath and other holidays, the prohibition of *melacha* on *chol ha-moed* has the status of *d'rabbanan* law rather than *d'oraita* law.[69] Moreover, based on a Talmudic statement that "they prohibited" *melacha* on *chol ha-moed* to encourage activities more consistent with the spirit of the holiday, such as the study of the Torah,[70] these authorities inferred that the prohibition was derived through prophylactic rabbinic legislation, to protect the sanctity of the day, and not through biblical interpretation.[71]

---

64 See, e.g., Leviticus 23:4-44 (listing sacred days on which *melacha* is prohibited); Numbers 28:16-31, 29:1-39 (same).

65 See generally Talmud Bavli, Beitza (delineating the contours of the prohibition of *melacha* on holidays).

66 Discussions of this issue, originating in the Talmud, have produced a substantial body of literature. See, e.g., Yosef Babad, *Minchas Chinuch* (commenting on *Sefer Ha-Chinuch*, Commandment 323); Aryeh Loeb ben Asher, *Turei Even* (commenting on Talmud Bavli, Chagiga 18a); Joseph B. Soloveitchik, *Shiurei ha-Gri'd al Inyanei Tefillin, Ketivat Sta'm v'Tzizit* 75-77 (Menachem Kahn ed., 2004). For a brief discussion in English, see Dovid Zucker & Moshe Francis, *Chol HaMoed* 5-10 (1981).

67 See Leviticus 23:4-8, 33-38 (discussing Passover and Sukkot).

68 Zucker & Francis, supra note 66, at 6.

69 See, e.g., Tosafoth (commenting on Talmud Bavli, Chagiga 18a); Rabbenu Asher, *Introduction to Talmud Bavli, Moed Katan*.

70 Talmud Yerushalmi, Moed Katan 2:3.

71 See, e.g., Tosafoth (commenting on Talmud Bavli, Chagiga 18a); Rabbenu Asher, *Introduction to Talmud Bavli, Moed Katan*.

This analysis seems to correlate with Justice Scalia's arguments in *Dickerson*. Justice Scalia similarly cited exceptions to *Miranda* requirements as indicating that *Miranda* operated as a form of legislation and not as constitutional law.[72] Likewise, as Justice Scalia emphasized, and as the majority in *Dickerson* conceded, several United States Supreme Court decisions point to the prophylactic role that *Miranda* warnings play in safeguarding a suspect's Fifth Amendment rights.[73] In Justice Scalia's view, references to a prophylactic purpose demonstrate that *Miranda* embodied legislative decision-making rather than constitutional interpretation.[74]

In contrast to these approaches, however, other medieval authorities of Jewish law adopted an alternative position.[75] Citing the Talmud's apparent reliance on methods of biblical exegesis to derive the prohibition of *melacha* on *chol ha-moed*,[76] these authorities concluded that the prohibition is based on the text of the Torah, and therefore has the status of *d'oraita* law.[77] As to characteristics of the prohibition that resemble rabbinic legislation, including the broad range of exceptions to the rule and the ostensibly prophylactic purpose of the law, they turned to another Talmudic statement: *"lo m'saran ha'katuv ella l'chachamim"*—the Torah granted to rabbinic decision-makers the authority to determine the precise contours of the law.[78] Thus, these commentators explained, the prohibition of *melacha* on *chol ha-moed* represents an instance in which a law has the status of *d'oraita*, but the details of the law are subject to methods of decision-making more commonly associated with rabbinic legislation.

---

72 See supra text accompanying notes 42-46. It should be noted, however, that Justice Scalia's analysis was aimed at demonstrating that *Miranda* was an illegitimate exercise of legislative authority by the Court, which, in the American legal system, is charged with interpreting the law. In the Jewish legal system, the high court had the authority both to interpret the biblical text and to legislate. See generally Chapters 3 and 4 in this Volume. Thus, the debate among medieval legal authorities revolved around which of these two legitimate functions the rabbinic decision-makers exercised in instituting the prohibition of *melacha* on *chol ha-moed*.

73 See supra text accompanying notes 34-35, 42-43.

74 See supra text accompanying notes 42-46.

75 See Rashi, *Commentary on the Talmud* (commenting on Talmud Bavli, Moed Katan 11b); Rambam, *Mishne Torah,* Laws of *Yom Tov* 7:1.

76 See Talmud Bavli, Chagiga 18a (citing biblical verses to support the prohibition of *melacha* on *chol ha-moed*).

77 Legal authorities advocating the opposing view understand this exegesis as a largely homiletic reading of the biblical text, offered in connection with rabbinic legislation, rather than as an exercise of deriving laws through biblical interpretation. See, e.g., Tosafoth (commenting on Talmud Bavli, Chagiga 18a); Rabbenu Asher, *Introduction to Talmud Bavli, Moed Katan.* See also Moshe Chaim Luzzatto, Ma'amar Ha-Ikarim.

78 Talmud Bavli, Chagiga 18a; see also id. (commentary of Zevi Hirsch Chajes); Asher Weiss, *Minchas Asher, Devarim* 89-91, 183-89 (2017).

Perhaps a similar analytical framework would provide a response to Justice Scalia's objections in *Dickerson*. Under this framework, the *Miranda* requirements are based in the Fifth Amendment, but they are instituted through an unusual form of constitutional adjudication—a "constitutional rule"—which is derived through a process that more closely resembles judicial legislation. Accordingly, the law includes exceptions and prophylactic purposes, characteristics that are more commonly reserved for legislative enactments.[79]

C. Further Theoretical Applications of Jewish Law to *Miranda* and *Dickerson*

In addition to providing a conceptual framework for responding to Justice Scalia's arguments, the analogue to the prohibition of *melacha* on *chol ha-moed* may help further elucidate the majority position in *Dickerson*. Scholars of Jewish law have employed a close reading of the biblical text to explain the view that the prohibition of *melacha* on *chol ha-moed* is *d'oraita* law, albeit with legislative characteristics.[80] Specifically, unlike the biblical prohibitions of *melacha* on the Sabbath and more sacred holidays, which are stated expressly,[81] the prohibition of *melacha* on *chol ha-moed* is drawn from the Torah's command that these days be observed as "holy."[82] Thus, under the terms of the biblical text, refraining from *melacha* on *chol ha-moed* serves a primarily prophylactic function of safeguarding the sanctity of *chol ha-moed* by distinguishing it from an ordinary weekday.[83] Accordingly, in contrast to the contours of the prohibition of *melacha* on the Sabbath and other holidays, which are derived through standard forms of biblical interpretation, the precise details of the prohibition on *chol ha-moed* are subject to quasi-legislative determinations of rabbinic decision-makers, aimed at promoting the underlying prophylactic purpose of the biblical law.[84]

---

79 It should be noted that some leading scholars reject the notion that prophylactic rules are either unusual or illegitimate in constitutional adjudication. See, e.g., Caminker, supra note 47, at 25-28 (finding *Miranda*'s "prophylactic" rule to be indistinguishable from "run-of-the-mill" judicial doctrine applied to First Amendment, equal protection, and interstate commerce questions); Strauss, supra note 21, at 195-207 (arguing that prophylactic rules are not "of questionable legitimacy," but rather "are a central and necessary feature of constitutional law"). Likewise, some suggest that it may not be unusual for biblical laws to have prophylactic characteristics. See, e.g., Yosef Engel, *Sefer Lekach Tov* 167-80; Asher Weiss, *Minchas Asher, Shemos* 408-9 (2017). See also Yitzchak Adler, *Lomdus: A Substructural Analysis* 1-10 (1989).

80 See Soloveitchik, supra note 66, at 75-76.

81 See supra notes 54 and 64 and accompanying text.

82 Leviticus 23:37. This reading of the biblical text represents one view in the Talmud. See Talmud Bavli, Chagiga 18a ("'Holy' implies the prohibition of *melacha*.").

83 See Soloveitchik, supra note 66, at 75-76.

84 See id.

A similar analysis may shed light on the majority opinion in *Dickerson.* The Fifth Amendment states: "No person shall be . . . compelled in any criminal case to be a witness against himself . . . ."[85] Although the constitutional text refers specifically to testimonial settings, without mention of police interrogation, the *Miranda* opinion emphasized the Court's understanding that Fifth Amendment protections against compelled self-incrimination extend beyond the courtroom.[86] Accordingly, the majority in *Dickerson* may have concluded that, in place of standard methods of constitutional analysis, the *Miranda* court found it necessary to employ a prophylactic interpretive approach, to protect against the compulsion inherent in the interrogation process. In short, under this analysis, similar to the prohibition of *melacha* on *chol ha-moed, Miranda* warnings operate as a constitutionally required rule that functions to safeguard Fifth Amendment rights.[87] Therefore, the details of the rule are likewise established through quasi-legislative determinations of the Court.

Finally, comparisons to the prohibition of *melacha* on *chol ha-moed* may have procedural ramifications as well. Under Jewish legal theory, courts generally have the authority to interpret the law on the basis of their own reasoning, rather than deferring to prior interpretations.[88] When functioning in a legislative capacity, however, courts are far more limited in their ability to abrogate previous legislation.[89] In the context of biblical laws that are delineated

---

85 U.S. Const. amend. V.

86 See supra text accompanying notes 13-15.

87 Cf. Berman, supra note 20, at 154 (distinguishing between "judge-interpreted constitutional meaning and constitutional decision rules" and conceptualizing *Miranda* as a "constitutional decision rule . . . adopted to *optimally* enforce constitutional meaning," and therefore arguing that *Miranda* is not an instance of illegitimate prophylactic rule-making, because "it does not *overenforce* constitutional meaning as measured against the appropriate baseline") (emphasis in original).

88 See Chapter 3 in this Volume; Joseph Karo, *Kesef Mishna,* on Maimonides, Laws of *Mamrim* 2:1; Hershel Schachter, *B'Ikvei ha-Tzon* 243-44 (1997) [hereinafter Schachter, *B'Ikvei ha-Tzoan*]; Hershel Schachter, *Ginas Egoz* 157-58 (2007) [hereinafter Schachter, *Ginas Egoz*]; Joseph B. Soloveitchik, *Two Types of Tradition,* in 1 *Sheurim L'Zekher Abba Mori Z"L* 241-61 (2002) [hereinafter Soloveitchik, *Sheurim L'Zekher Abba Mori Z"L*]; Yitzchak Zeev ha-Levi Soloveitchik, *Chidushei Maran Ri'z ha-Levi al ha-Torah* 116-17 (2003) (commenting on Ruth 4:6); Elchanan Wasserman, 1 *Kobetz Shiurim* 335-36 (Elazar Wasserman ed., 4th ed. 1989); Elchanan Wasserman, *Kobetz He'aroth* 115 (Elazar Wasserman ed., 2003); Weiss, supra note 78, at 180-82. It should be noted, however, that in the course of Jewish history, legal authorities have often found it necessary to defer to the interpretations of earlier authorities. See Chapter 3 in this Volume.

89 See Chapter 4 in this Volume (describing the complex rules restricting the power of a later court to modify earlier rabbinic legislation); see also Schachter, *B'Ikvei ha-Tzoan,* supra note 88, at 243-44; Soloveitchik, *Sheurim L'Zekher Abba Mori Z"L,* supra note 88, at 241-61.

through quasi-legislative rabbinic determinations, some scholars have suggested that the interpretive authority of later courts would be subject to the more extensive constraints that ordinarily govern legislative action.[90]

Applying these principles to *Dickerson* may offer support for the majority's adherence to the validity of *Miranda*. The majority declared that, notwithstanding the merits of arguments questioning the Court's holding and reasoning in *Miranda*, "the principles of stare decisis weigh heavily against overruling it."[91] In response, Justice Scalia quoted from yet another United States Supreme Court case: "'Where . . . changes have removed or weakened the conceptual underpinnings from the prior decision, . . . or where the later law has rendered the decision irreconcilable with competing legal doctrines or policies, . . . the Court has not hesitated to overrule an earlier decision.'"[92] As per Justice Scalia's analysis, to the extent that it represented constitutional adjudication, *Miranda*'s reasoning was no longer viable. Thus, he argued, stare decisis should not preclude overruling *Miranda*, through the standard process of constitutional interpretation.[93]

Perhaps the majority's abiding reliance on stare decisis to uphold *Miranda* can be premised on an alternative conception of *Miranda*, as an instance in which the United States Supreme Court has engaged in a quasi-legislative form of constitutional decision-making. In this perspective, parallel to the status of biblical laws derived by courts through quasi-legislation—and contrary to Justice Scalia's analysis—*Miranda* warnings represent a constitutional law that is not susceptible to abrogation through the ordinary process of constitutional interpretation. Instead, the United States Supreme Court would be more limited in its authority to overrule *Miranda*, perhaps requiring a more formal quasi-legislative decision expressly overturning its earlier holding.[94] Accordingly, the majority in *Dickerson* may have concluded that, short of such a decision by the Court, *Miranda* maintains its status as a constitutional rule.

---

90 See Schachter, *Ginas Egoz*, supra note 88, at 7.

91 *Dickerson v. United States*, 530 U.S. 428, 443 (2000).

92 Id. at 462-63 (Scalia, J., dissenting) (quoting *Patterson v. McLean Credit Union*, 491 U.S. 164, 173 (1989)). Moreover, Justice Scalia added, this quotation referred to overruling "statutory cases," while "the standard for constitutional decisions is somewhat more lenient." Id. at 462.

93 For an elaboration on Justice Scalia's argument, see Berman, supra note 20, at 27-28 n.101.

94 Cf. id. at 28 n.101 ("[E]ven were the majority to concede that *Miranda* is most fairly read as conceiving of itself as engaged in constitutional interpretation, it is not at all obvious why it should not frankly construe *Miranda* as announcing a prophylactic rule and then afford it stare decisis deference on *that* rationale.") (emphasis in original).

Constitutional Theory

CHAPTER 9

Unenumerated Constitutional Rights and Unenumerated Biblical Obligations: A Preliminary Study in Comparative Hermeneutics

INTRODUCTION

In 1986, Robert Cover wrote of an "explosion of legal scholarship placing interpretation at the crux of the enterprise of law."[1] As examples of this phenomenon, Cover cited the works of such influential scholars as Ronald Dworkin[2] and James Boyd White,[3] as well as law review symposia,[4] which, Cover noted, focused on "interpretation" or "hermeneutics."[5] As part of the continuing emphasis on hermeneutics in constitutional interpretation, a body

---

1   Robert M. Cover, *Violence and the Word*, 95 Yale L.J. 1601, 1601-2 n.2 (1986).
2   See Ronald Dworkin, *Law's Empire* (Belknap Press, 1986).
3   See James Boyd White, *Heracles' Bow* (U. of Wisconsin Press, 1985); James Boyd White, *When Words Lose Their Meaning* (U. of Chicago Press, 1984).
4   See *Interpretation Symposium*, 58 S. Cal. L. Rev. 1 (1985); *Symposium, Law and Literature*, 60 Tex. L. Rev. 373 (1982).
5   Cover, 95 Yale L.J. at 1602 n.2 (cited in note 1).

of literature has emerged comparing constitutional textual analysis to biblical hermeneutics.[6] This scholarship has been premised on the recognition that, like the Constitution, the Bible functions as an authoritative legal text that must be interpreted in order to serve as the foundation for a living community.

This chapter looks at a basic hermeneutic device common to both biblical and constitutional interpretation: the identification of unenumerated principles through reference to textually enumerated principles. The chapter observes that, in addition to the numerous obligations listed and detailed in the Torah, legal authorities have interpreted the Torah to mandate many other obligations, not enumerated in the text. The chapter suggests that a similar methodology has been applied to the United States Constitution, to derive rights beyond those enumerated in the text. The chapter thus examines ways in which American judges and constitutional scholars have relied on methods of textual analysis that find analogues in the interpretation of the Torah by Jewish legal authorities.

PART ONE | SUBSTANTIVE DUE PROCESS AND "YOU SHALL BE HOLY"

Despite its function as the guarantor of individual rights against infringement by the government, the United States Constitution, including the Bill of Rights, is surprisingly limited in its enumeration of substantive rights.[7] Nevertheless,

---

6   See, e.g., Jim Chen, *Book Review*, 11 Const. Comm. 599 (1994-95) (reviewing H. Jefferson Powell, *The Moral Tradition of American Constitutionalism: A Theological Interpretation*); Robert M. Cover, "The Supreme Court, 1982 Term—Foreword: *Nomos* and Narrative," 97 Harv. L. Rev. 4 (1983); David R. Dow, *Constitutional Midrash: The Rabbis' Solution to Professor Bickel's Problem*, 29 Houston L. Rev. 543 (1992); Edward M. Gaffney, Jr., *Politics Without Brackets on Religious Convictions: Michael Perry and Bruce Ackerman on Neutrality*, 64 Tulane L. Rev. 1143, 1166 n.102 (1990); Thomas C. Grey, *The Constitution as Scripture*, 37 Stan. L. Rev. 1 (1984); Morton J. Horwitz, *The Supreme Court, 1992 Term—Foreword: The Constitution of Change: Legal Fundamentality Without Fundamentalism*, 107 Harv. L. Rev. 30, 48-51 & 50 n.90 (1993); *Interpretation Symposium* (cited in note 4); Sanford Levinson, *Constitutional Faith* (Princeton U. Press, 1988); Lawrence B. Solum, *Originalism as Transformative Politics*, 63 Tulane L. Rev. 1599 (1989); Steven D. Smith, *Idolatry in Constitutional Interpretation*, 79 Va. L. Rev. 583 (1993). See also Chapters 3, 8, 10, and 11 in this Volume and Chapter 17 in Volume 2.

7   In fact, as Professor Charles Black observed, "[i]f one ... looks over th[e] canvas of textually expressed guarantees of human rights against actions of the States, one has to be impressed with their entire inadequacy, by a very wide margin, as a corpus of human-rights substantive protections that could possibly characterize any society generally as a free society by law." Charles L. Black, Jr., *"One Nation Indivisible": Unnamed Human Rights in the States*, 65 St. John's L. Rev. 17, 21 (1991).

the United States Supreme Court has consistently held that the Constitution protects a number of rights beyond those listed in the text. To support these conclusions, the Court has engaged in a variety of interpretive techniques that, to a significant extent, parallel various methods of biblical interpretation.

In the 1923 case of *Meyer v. Nebraska*,[8] the Supreme Court was faced with a challenge to a Nebraska state law that prohibited the teaching of "any language other than the English language" prior to high school.[9] Though the text of the Constitution does not explicitly protect the right to education, the Court found that such a right is guaranteed by the Constitution, and held that the Nebraska statute violated the individual's right to pursue and select a reasonable and beneficial means of education.

In recognizing this unnamed right, the Court relied on an interpretation of the Fourteenth Amendment, which guarantees that "[n]o State shall . . . deprive any person of life, liberty, or property, without due process of law."[10] Focusing on the ambiguity of the word "liberty," the Court understood the Fourteenth Amendment to protect a broad range of rights, including

> [w]ithout doubt . . . not merely freedom from bodily restraint but also the right of the individual to contract, to engage in any of the common occupations of life, to acquire useful knowledge, to marry, establish a home and bring up children, to worship God according to the dictates of his own conscience, and generally to enjoy those privileges long recognized at common law as essential to the orderly pursuit of happiness by free men.[11]

Turning to education, the Court stated that "[t]he American people have always regarded education and acquisition of knowledge as matters of supreme importance which should be diligently promoted."[12] Therefore, the Court concluded that the teacher's "right thus to teach and the right of parents to engage him so to instruct their children . . . are within the liberty of the Amendment."[13] The Nebraska law violated the Constitution because it "attempted materially to interfere with the calling of modern language teachers, with the opportuni-

---

8   262 U.S. 390 (1923).
9   Id. at 397.
10   U.S. Const., Amend. XIV, § 1.
11   *Meyer*, 262 U.S. at 399.
12   Id. at 400.
13   Id.

ties of pupils to acquire knowledge, and with the power of parents to control the education of their own."[14]

Two years later, in *Pierce v. Society of Sisters*,[15] a Catholic parochial school and a private military academy challenged an Oregon statute requiring children between the ages of eight and sixteen to attend public school. Relying on *Meyer*, the Court found it "entirely plain" that the statute "unreasonably interferes with the liberty of parents and guardians to direct the upbringing and education of children under their control."[16] Elaborating on the concept of liberty, the Court declared that

> [t]he fundamental theory of liberty upon which all governments in this Union repose excludes any general power of the State to standardize its children by forcing them to accept instruction from public school teachers only. ... [T]hose who nurture him and direct his destiny have the right, coupled with the high duty, to recognize and prepare him for additional obligations.[17]

The Court's approach in these two cases reflects a willingness to look beyond those rights enumerated in the text of the Constitution, by suggesting that additional rights are encompassed under the Fourteenth Amendment's broad guarantee of "liberty." According to the Court, the term "liberty" clearly includes a wide range of activities and privileges—such as education—that, although absent from the constitutional text, are apparently so basic to the idea of freedom as to make their enumeration unnecessary. Although at times, the Court's reliance on "substantive due process" has prompted criticism,[18] the abiding influence of *Meyer* and *Pierce* is evident in the Court's further articulation of unenumerated rights.

In the 1977 case *Moore v. City of East Cleveland*,[19] for example, the Court declared unconstitutional a housing ordinance that prohibited a woman from living in her home with her two grandsons. In his plurality opinion, Justice Powell noted that "[a] host of cases, tracing their lineage to *Meyer* ... and *Pierce* ... have

---

14 Id. at 401.

15 268 U.S. 510 (1925).

16 Id. at 534-35.

17 Id. at 535.

18 Even those justices who have relied on substantive due process have acknowledged that "[s]ubstantive due process has at times been a treacherous field for this Court." *Moore v. City of East Cleveland*, 431 U.S. 494, 502 (1977) (Powell, J.).

19 431 U.S. 494 (1977).

consistently acknowledged a 'private realm of family life which the state cannot enter.'"[20] Indeed, applying the concept of substantive due process, the opinion further observed that "[t]his Court has long recognized that freedom of personal choice in matters of marriage and family life is one of the liberties protected by the Due Process Clause of the Fourteenth Amendment."[21] Within this area of liberty, the opinion included the right of a grandmother to live with her grandchildren.

As Justice Powell conceded, the right he articulated was not only absent from the text of the Constitution, but had not been identified in prior case law. In response to the criticism of the dissenters in the case, however, Justice Powell insisted that "unless we close our eyes to the basic reasons why certain rights associated with the family have been accorded shelter under the Fourteenth Amendment's Due Process Clause, we cannot avoid applying the force and rationale of these precedents to the family choice involved in this case."[22] Justice Powell quoted extensively from an earlier opinion of Justice Harlan, which explained that

> the full scope of the liberty guaranteed by the Due Process Clause cannot be found in or limited by the precise terms of the specific guarantees elsewhere provided in the Constitution. This "liberty" is not a series of isolated points pricked out in terms of the taking of property; the freedom of speech, press, and religion; the right to keep and bear arms; the freedom from unreasonable searches and seizures; and so on. It is a rational continuum which, broadly speaking, includes a freedom from all substantial arbitrary impositions and purposeless restraints.[23]

Thus, Justice Powell relied on Justice Harlan's eloquent declaration, that a proper understanding of the guarantees of liberty requires looking beyond the specific rights enumerated in the Constitution, to uncover the underlying principles those rights represent. According to Justice Powell, these principles mandate protecting "the sanctity of the family precisely because the institution of the family is deeply rooted in this Nation's history and tradition."[24] He concluded that "[t]he tradition of... grandparents sharing a household along with

---

20 Id. at 499 (Powell, J.) (quoting *Prince v. Massachusetts*, 321 U.S. 158, 166 (1944)).

21 Id. (quoting *Cleveland Board of Education v. LaFleur*, 414 U.S. 632, 639-40 (1974)).

22 Id. at 501 (Powell, J.).

23 Id. at 502 (Powell, J.) (quoting *Poe v. Ullman*, 367 U.S. 497, 542-43 (1961) (Harlan, J., dissenting)).

24 Id. at 503 (Powell, J.).

parents and children has roots equally venerable and equally deserving of constitutional recognition."[25]

This expansive approach to interpreting the term "liberty" parallels Jewish legal interpretation of the Torah, the primary source of Jewish law and religious obligations. The Torah enumerates a large number of commandments—obligations and prohibitions—incumbent upon both individuals and the community as a whole. In fact, according the Talmud, the Torah contains 613 commandments, many of which may in turn be analyzed to include more than a single obligation or prohibition. Yet, despite the large number of enumerated commandments, which provide a somewhat comprehensive guide to religious life, the text of the Torah, like the Constitution, does not detail every area of human behavior.[26]

Thus, just as the Constitution is interpreted to protect rights that are not listed explicitly, the biblical text is interpreted to impose unenumerated religious obligations. Parallel to the Supreme Court's understanding of the concept of "liberty," found in the Fourteenth Amendment's Due Process Clause, as a broad directive to guarantee unnamed rights, some Jewish legal authorities have understood the command "you shall be holy"[27] as broadly mandating adherence to unenumerated obligations and prohibitions.

In his commentary on the Torah, Nachmanides, one of the most influential of medieval Jewish legal scholars, explains the function of this command as a basis for unnamed obligations. Citing Talmudic sources that interpret the concept of "holiness" as requiring separation from improper activities, Nachmanides observes that the Torah enumerates many, but not all, forms of behavior that fall within this category.[28]

Indeed, like the Constitution, which enumerates certain rights but does not mention explicitly the areas of "liberty" relating to education and family life, the Torah does not detail all aspects of "holiness." Instead, in addition to listing a number of obligations included within the concept of "holiness," the Torah commands a general obligation to "be holy." Jewish legal authorities viewed the broad principle of "holiness" as an extension of those obligations

---

25 Id. at 504 (Powell, J.).

26 Among others, Robert Cover explored the substantive difference between the American legal system's emphasis on rights and the Jewish legal system's emphasis on obligations. See Robert M. Cover, *Obligation: A Jewish Jurisprudence of the Social Order*, 5 J.L. & Rel. 65 (1987). This chapter focuses on the similarity in interpretive methodologies in the two systems rather than on the substantive interpretations themselves.

27 Leviticus 19:2.

28 See 2 Nachmanides, *Commentary on the Torah* 115-16 (Chaim Chavel, ed., Mossad Harav Kook, 1960) (commenting on Leviticus 19:2).

found in the text, analogous to the function of the broad constitutional term "liberty" in relation to those rights found in the text of the Constitution.

Through an analysis parallel to that later employed by the Court in *Meyer* and *Pierce*, and by Justice Powell in *Moore*, the rabbinic authorities looked to the religious tradition to define the scope of activity implicit in the command to "be holy." For example, the Torah contains various dietary laws, listing foods that are not kosher and describing the manner in which kosher food must be prepared. As Nachmanides notes, however, the Torah does not enumerate all religious obligations relating to the consumption of food, such as prohibitions against gluttony and drunkenness.[29] Accordingly, Jewish legal authorities relied on biblical stories, describing the sinful behavior that resulted from the drunkenness of Noah and Lot, as indications that drunkenness is inconsistent with holiness. Applying this method more generally, rabbinic authorities concluded that the command to "be holy" required abstention from various activities, beyond those explicitly prohibited in the Torah, that contradict the concept of holiness, including various improper modes of eating, speech, dress, and sexual activity.[30]

PART TWO | PRIVACY, PENUMBRAS, AND "YOU SHALL DO THE JUST AND THE GOOD"

Another area in which the Supreme Court has identified constitutionally protected rights beyond those enumerated in the text is the sphere of privacy. Though the Court's general approach in this area has been similar to its approach in identifying liberty rights, in this case the Court has employed a somewhat different methodology. The Court's approach to privacy again finds parallels in Jewish religious interpretation, here to rabbinic exegesis of the command in Deuteronomy to "do the just and the good," which likewise appears to differ in subtle ways from the method of interpreting the command to "be holy."

The concept of a right to privacy in American law is an old one. For example, constitutional amendments protecting the rights of criminal defendants demonstrate a fundamental appreciation for an individual's privacy rights, reflected in Supreme Court decisions in the criminal procedure context. However, it was

---

29 See id.

30 See also Maimonides, *Mishne Torah*, Laws of *De'oth* 3:2, 5:1-13 (Mossad Harav Kook, 1990); Nachmanides, 2 *Commentary* at 151-52 (cited in note 28) (commenting on Leviticus 23:24); Asher Weiss, *Minchas Asher, Devarim* 190 (2017).

not until the 1965 case of *Griswold v. Connecticut*[31] that the Court recognized a general constitutional protection of the individual's right to privacy.

In *Griswold*, the Court struck down as unconstitutional a state statute prohibiting the use of contraceptives. Although the Constitution obviously does not enumerate a right to use a contraceptive, or even a general right to privacy, the Court held that the rights enumerated in the Constitution should not be read as narrow or exclusive declarations of those rights that are to be protected. Instead, the Court stated, "specific guarantees in the Bill of Rights have penumbras, formed by emanations from those guarantees that help give them life and substance."[32]

In order to connect the concept of a "penumbra" to some of its earlier decisions, the Court focused on the "penumbra" emanating from the Free Speech Clause of the First Amendment. The Court cited cases that it understood as recognizing that "the First Amendment has a penumbra where privacy is protected from governmental intrusion."[33] For example, although the First Amendment does not enumerate a "freedom of association," in a 1958 case the Court had identified the "freedom to associate and privacy in one's associations" as a "peripheral First Amendment right.[34] The Court in *Griswold* explained that "while [association] is not expressly included in the First Amendment its existence is necessary in making the express guarantees fully meaningful."[35]

Moreover, the Court found, other aspects of the unenumerated right to privacy emanated from other enumerated rights. According to the Court, "[v]arious guarantees create zones of privacy."[36] As a further example, the Third Amendment's protection against the quartering of soldiers in a house during peacetime without the owner's consent represents "another facet of that privacy."[37]

Similarly, the Court had previously observed that the Fourth and Fifth Amendments' protections of criminal defendants' rights recognized the "sanctity of a man's home and the privacies of life."[38] In fact, the Court had stated that the Fourth Amendment's prohibition against unreasonable searches and seizures created a "right to privacy, no less important than any other right carefully and particularly reserved to the people."[39] Likewise, the Court in *Griswold* found that

---

31 381 U.S. 479 (1965).
32 Id. at 484.
33 Id. at 483.
34 Id. (citing *NAACP v. Alabama*, 357 U.S. 449, 462 (1958)).
35 Id.
36 Id. at 484.
37 Id.
38 Id. (quoting *Boyd v. United States*, 116 U.S. 616, 630 (1886)).
39 Id. at 485 (quoting *Mapp v. Ohio*, 367 U.S. 643, 656 (1961)).

the Fifth Amendment's protection against self-incrimination "enables the citizen to create a zone of privacy which government may not force him to surrender to his detriment."[40] Finally, the Court pointed to the Ninth Amendment's explicit statement that "[t]he enumeration in the Constitution, of certain rights, shall not be construed to deny or disparage others retained by the people."[41]

Turning to the Connecticut statute that prohibited the use of contraceptives, the Court described the case as "concern[ing] a relationship lying within the zone of privacy created by several fundamental constitutional guarantees."[42] Declaring a respect for "the sacred precincts of marital bedrooms" the Court concluded that "[t]he very idea" of allowing the police to search such areas for contraceptives "is repulsive to the notions of privacy surrounding the marriage relationship."[43]

The Court's reliance on the concept of "penumbras" in *Griswold* and subsequent cases was controversial. A number of Justices in *Griswold* either concurred in the decision but relied on other modes of analysis, or dissented outright. In his dissenting opinion, Justice Stewart, joined by Justice Black, asked rhetorically, "[w]hat provision of the Constitution . . . does make the state law invalid? The Court says it is the right of privacy 'created by several fundamental constitutional guarantees.' With all deference, I can find no such general right of privacy in the Bill of Rights, in any other part of the Constitution, or in any case ever before decided by this Court."[44]

The Court's extension of its holding in *Griswold* to other contexts engendered more controversy. In 1972, in *Eisenstadt v. Baird*,[45] the Court struck down a Massachusetts statute prohibiting distribution of contraceptives to single persons, stating that, "[i]f the right of privacy means anything, it is the right of the *individual*, married or single, to be free from unwarranted governmental intrusion into matters so fundamentally affecting a person as the decision whether to bear or beget a child."[46] Chief Justice Burger's dissent—though it did not challenge the authority of *Griswold*—referred to *Griswold*'s "tenuous moorings to the text of the Constitution."[47] Additionally, the Chief Justice

---

40 Id. at 484.
41 U.S. Const., Amend. IX.
42 *Griswold*, 381 U.S. at 485.
43 Id. at 485-86.
44 Id. at 530 (Stewart, J., dissenting).
45 405 U.S. 438 (1971).
46 Id. at 453.
47 Id. at 472 (Burger, C.J., dissenting).

criticized the majority in *Eisenstadt* for "pass[ing] beyond the penumbras of the specific guarantees into the uncircumscribed area of personal predilections."[48]

Notwithstanding such criticisms, however, the majority of the Court prevailed, identifying unenumerated rights through an extension of the principles embodied in those rights enumerated in the constitutional text. The Court determined that an analysis of several amendments pointed clearly to the underlying principle of a general, more encompassing right of privacy. Similarly, in Jewish thought, in addition to those obligations enumerated in the text or implied through the command to "be holy," many obligations are subsumed under the general concept of doing "the just and the good."[49]

Both the enumerated commands generally associated with "holiness" —such as eating kosher food, as well as those imperatives cited by Nachmanides and other legal authorities as examples of "holiness" and "separation"—such as refraining from drunkenness, are largely limited to one category of obligation in Jewish thought, involving the relationship between a human being and God. The other major category of obligation, though also reflecting on an individual's relationship to God, involves those commandments directed primarily toward interpersonal relationships. Although the Torah enumerates many commandments within this category, these commands are likewise not a comprehensive list of obligations. Rather, rabbinic authorities found many unenumerated obligations mandated by the general obligation to "do the just and the good."

Like his explication of the command to "be holy," Nachmanides' discussion of the command to "do the just and the good" is instructive. Nachmanides again explains the reasoning behind the rabbinic interpretations, through which Jewish legal authorities derived principles of interpersonal obligation beyond those enumerated in the text. Looking at the context of the command, Nachmanides notes that the previous verse commands observance of the laws "which [God] has commanded you."[50] Thus, the verse that immediately follows, describing a more general obligation to do the "just and the good," apparently refers to obligations beyond those which God has expressly commanded.[51] As Nachmanides further explains, the second verse is necessary because it would

---

48 Id. (Burger, C.J., dissenting).

49 Deuteronomy 6:18.

50 Nachmanides, 2 *Commentary* at 376 (cited in note 28) (commenting on Deuteronomy 6:18) (citing Deuteronomy 6:17)).

51 Id.

be impossible for the Torah to prescribe the proper mode of behavior for every situation that arises in the course of interpersonal dealings.[52]

Instead, according to Nachmanides, the Torah enumerates numerous obligations and prohibitions that are fundamental to the way humans should treat each other, including, among many others, respecting elders, preventing harm to others, and not seeking revenge.[53] Yet, like those rights enumerated in the Constitution, these commandments all have their own penumbras, formed by emanations creating a zone of the just and the good, analogous to a "zone of privacy." Thus, parallel to the court in *Griswold* and *Eisenstadt*, rabbinic authorities inferred, from the nature of the enumerated laws, a number of unenumerated interpersonal obligations falling within the zone of the just and the good—such as according neighbors the right of first refusal on land, dressing and speaking in a respectful manner, and behaving courteously in litigious settings.[54]

It should be noted that, although the phrase "the just and the good" appears in the text of the Torah, the methodology for its interpretation is closer to the constitutional interpretation of "privacy" than to that of "liberty." Unlike the interpretation of the term "liberty"—and, indeed, unlike the interpretation of the phrase "be holy"—religious authorities did not point to historical definitions or traditions that would help elucidate the meaning of the words "just" and "good." Rather, using a technique more similar to the Court's approach to the broad concept of privacy, as emanating from specific guarantees, religious authorities looked to the underlying principles of "just and good" behavior, as emanating from enumerated interpersonal obligations, then applied those principles to situations that were not addressed in the text. Thus, just as the Court derived constitutional rights based on the broad and unenumerated concept of privacy, Jewish legal authorities derived a range of "just" and "good" behavior, not found in the biblical text, but nevertheless required by the Torah.

PART THREE | THE NINTH AMENDMENT AND "LOVE YOUR NEIGHBOR AS YOURSELF"

Perhaps the broadest potential source of unenumerated constitutional rights is the Ninth Amendment, which states, "The enumeration in the Constitution, of certain rights, shall not be construed to deny or disparage others retained

---

52 See id.
53 See id. (citing Leviticus 19:16, 18, 22).
54 Id. See also Weiss, supra note 30, at 73-74, 190.

by the people."[55] Though in practice, the derivation of unenumerated rights based on the Ninth Amendment has been controversial, on its face the Amendment clearly appears, as Justice Goldberg put it, to "show [...] a belief of the Constitution's authors that fundamental rights exist that are not expressly enumerated in the first eight amendments and an intent that the list of rights included there not be deemed exhaustive."[56]

Although the court in *Griswold* referred to the Ninth Amendment as one source of penumbras contributing to the zone of privacy, the majority relied primarily on other parts of the Constitution to derive a right of privacy protecting the use of contraceptives. Justice Goldberg, however, in his concurring opinion, "emphasize[d] the relevance of th[e Ninth] Amendment to the Court's holding."[57] Focusing on both the language and the history of the Ninth Amendment, Justice Goldberg concluded that "the Framers of the Constitution believed that there are additional fundamental rights, protected from governmental infringement, which exist alongside those fundamental rights specifically mentioned in the first eight constitutional amendments."[58] Indeed, Justice Goldberg argued that, to refuse to recognize the right of privacy in marriage because it is not mentioned explicitly in the first eight amendments, "is to ignore the Ninth Amendment and give it no effect whatsoever," and, in fact "would violate the Ninth Amendment."[59]

Despite the vitality of Justice Goldberg's arguments, however, his views did not prevail in *Griswold*, and appear to have had little influence on the Court's later decisions. Nevertheless, a number of constitutional scholars have advanced theories relying on the Ninth Amendment to derive unenumerated rights. One of the most prominent and influential scholars in this endeavor was Charles Black, whose declared aim was "the rational development of an open-edged corpus juris of human-rights constitutional law."[60] Through arguments similar to Justice Goldberg's, Professor Black insists that

> preponderance of reason leaves us with the conclusion, about as well-supported as any we can reach in law, that the Ninth Amendment declares

---

55 U. S. Const, Amend. IX.

56 *Griswold v. Connecticut*, 381 U.S. 479, 492 (1964) (Goldberg, J., concurring).

57 Id. at 487 (Goldberg, J., concurring).

58 Id. at 488 (Goldberg, J., concurring).

59 Id. at 491 (Goldberg, J., concurring).

60 Charles L. Black, Jr., *On Reading and Using the Ninth Amendment*, in *Power and Policy in Quest of Law: Essays in Honor of Eugene Victor Rostow* 187, 197 n* (M. McDougal & W.M. Reisman, eds., Martinos Nijhoff, 1985). See also Samuel J. Levine, *Reflections on the Constitutional Scholarship of Charles Black: A Look Back and A Look Forward*, 28 Seton Hall L. Rev. 142, 144 (1997).

as a matter of law—of constitutional law, overriding other law—that some other rights are "retained by the people," and that these shall be treated as *on an equal footing* with rights enumerated.[61]

Black rejects the attitude of those who find application of the Ninth Amendment unworkable because "[w]e are not told what [the unenumerated rights] are" and thus claim that "no action is possible, because you haven't been told exactly how to act."[62] Instead, Black prescribes "tak[ing] the Ninth Amendment as a command to use any rational methods available to the art of law, and with these in hand to set out to discover what it is you are to protect."[63] In particular, Black envisions a constitutional imperative that would require "a radical redirection of theory and practice toward wiping out poverty."[64]

To arrive at his view of a "constitutional justice of livelihood," Black suggests that the Ninth Amendment "command[s] us to use the methods available within our legal system in an ongoing search for 'unenumerated' rights."[65] As a means for identifying those rights, Black looks to the Declaration of Independence. Turning specifically to poverty and its effect on "Life, Liberty, and the pursuit of Happiness," Black writes hauntingly that

> many people do die, quickly sometimes, sometimes more slowly, of poverty; poverty may be the leading cause of death. Liberty is very often made into a mocking simulacrum by poverty. But I would lay strongest stress on the phrase, "the pursuit of happiness." ... The possession of a decent material basis for life is an indispensable condition, to almost all people and at almost all times, to this "pursuit." The lack of this basis—the thing we call "poverty"—is overwhelmingly, in the whole human world, the commonest, the grimmest, the stubbornest obstacle we know to the pursuit of happiness. I have suggested that poverty may be the leading cause of death; it is pretty certain that it is the leading cause, at least among material causes, of despair in life .... [T]he right to the pursuit of happiness is going to be, for all but a small minority of those in poverty, the palest grinning ghost of a right.[66]

---

61 Black, supra note 60, at 188.
62 Id. at 188-89.
63 Id. at 189.
64 Charles L. Black, Jr., *On Worrying About the Constitution*, 55 U. Colo. L. Rev. 469, 471 (1984).
65 Charles L. Black. Jr., *Further Reflections on the Constitutional Justice of Livelihood*, 86 Colum. L. Rev. 1103, 1104 (1986).
66 Id. at 1105-6.

Black also responds to those who would oppose his arguments in favor of a constitutional justice of livelihood by asking "How much?" or "Where do you draw the line?" Focusing on the evils of poverty, Black writes powerfully that

> [w]hen we are faced with these difficulties of "how much," it is often help-
> ful to step back and think small, and to ask not, "What is the whole extent
> of what we are bound to do?" but rather, "What is the clearest thing we
> ought to do first?" When we descend to that level, one reasonable answer
> occurs. Somebody's count [in 1985] is that a million and a half people in
> the State of New York are undernourished; somebody else's count is that
> 13% of the American people live in poverty, which pretty much always
> implies hunger more or less serious. This hunger is disproportionately
> high among children; about half our black children under six lived in pov-
> erty in 1984. Some helpless old people eat dog food when they can get
> it . . . . Now you can bog down in a discussion about the exact perime-
> ter of "decent livelihood," or you can cease for a moment from that com-
> monly diversionary tactic and note that, wherever the penumbra may be,
> malnourished people are not enjoying a decent livelihood.[67]

While Black's eloquent testimony about poverty may render academic any questions about where to draw the line in guaranteeing a justice of livelihood, his critics raise a valid concern for the need to identify limits to the obligations that are implied by the Ninth Amendment. Even an open-ended corpus of human rights must acknowledge that not all imagined rights can be guaranteed by the Constitution. There must be some lines drawn and limitations recognized in what can be expected and required of society. Nevertheless, these considerations do not invalidate Black's call for an acceptance of the Ninth Amendment as a general command to discover and protect unenumerated human rights. In fact, a possible parallel to his approach may be found in the biblical command to "Love your neighbor as yourself."

Together with enumerated commandments addressing interpersonal relationships and the broad commandment to do the "just" and the "good," the Torah contains another broad commandment governing interpersonal conduct, "Love your neighbor as yourself."[68] Parallel to the Ninth Amendment in Professor Black's system, this commandment is understood by Jewish religious authorities to clearly indicate that, in addition to the interpersonal obligations enumerated in

---

67 Id. at 1114-15 (footnotes omitted).
68 Leviticus 19:18.

the biblical text, there are other obligations incumbent on an individual to comply with loving one's neighbor as one's self. Moreover, just as Black emphasized that he considered his interpretation of the Ninth Amendment to be grounded in a basic analysis of American constitutional law, the Talmudic sage Rabbi Akiva emphasized the significance of the command to "love your neighbor" in Jewish law, referring to it as "a fundamental principle in the Torah."[69]

Perhaps the most striking similarity between the commandment to "love your neighbor" and the Ninth Amendment is the broad language used in both phrases. It is the broad reference to "other [rights] retained by the people"[70] that leads Black to consider the Ninth Amendment to be the basis for "the rational development of an open-edged corpus juris of human-rights constitutional law."[71] Toward that end, Black declares a duty to search for and discover unenumerated human rights that the Constitution protects.

Likewise, the broad language of the phrase "love your neighbor as yourself" implies an obligation to identify unenumerated obligations that would express loving one's neighbor as one's self, and then to treat others as one would wish to be treated. Indeed, in his Code of Law, Maimonides cites Talmudic sources listing examples of conduct required by the command, including speaking words of praise for others and being concerned for the monetary welfare of others, just as one would seek one's own honor and be concerned for one's own financial well-being.[72] Emphasizing the importance of these principles, Maimonides quotes the Talmudic statement that "one who gains honor through disgracing another has no place in the World to Come."[73]

Despite the broad obligation to love one's neighbor as one's self, though, the commandment has one more element in common with the Ninth Amendment. Although the Ninth Amendment, according to Black and others, mandates the identification of a wide range of human rights not enumerated in the constitutional text, there are limits on what rights society will recognize and protect. Likewise, there are limits to the conduct mandated as part of loving one's neighbor as one's self. For example, as Nachmanides notes in his biblical commentary, the Talmud concludes that preserving one's own life generally takes

---

69 See Rashi, *Commentary on the Torah* (commenting on Leviticus 19:18) (quoting Torath Kohanim).

70 U.S. Const., Amend. IX.

71 Black, *On Reading and Using the Ninth Amendment* (cited in note 60).

72 See Maimonides, Laws of *De'oth* at 6:3 (cited in note 30). See also Weiss, supra note 30, at 189-90.

73 Id.

precedence over preserving the life of another.[74] Indeed, on a more general level, Nachmanides suggests that the Torah's commandment to love others as one's self should be understood more in the nature of an aspiration than an actual requirement, because he finds it psychologically unfeasible that the Torah would obligate individuals truly to love others to the same degree as they love themselves.[75] Thus, a final similarity between the Ninth Amendment and loving one's neighbor appears to be that, although there are limits to the scope of each principle, an honest evaluation of human nature suggests that the more relevant question in each case is usually not going to be "how much?" but rather "where do we start?"

CONCLUSION

In 1987, Professor William Wagner wrote of the "apparent crisis that has emerged in the Nation's understanding of civil rights law" which prompted the Columbus School of Law, Catholic University, to conduct a symposium addressing the relationship between religion and human rights.[76] The symposium produced a variety of illuminating papers and discussions identifying a religious basis for human rights. At the same time, however, Professor Wagner acknowledged that the symposium was founded upon certain presuppositions, two of which, in particular, are not shared by all legal theorists. One presupposition, "that the law's meaning and validity requires grounding in an extra-legal source," apparently contradicts positivist viewpoints.[77] The symposium's "further presupposi[tion] that religion can serve, if only in some attenuated sense, as such a source of meaning and validity," contradicts the view that "religion is in principle not suited to this role, e.g., the position that religion is a private preference unrelated to the public meaning of civil rights."[78]

To the extent that these two presuppositions remain controversial among legal theorists, despite its significance, the symposium was inevitably limited in the influence it was able to exert on legal discourse. One aim of this chapter is to carry forward the pursuit of advancing the discussion of human rights through

---

74 Nachmanides, *Commentary on the Torah* at 119 (cited in note 28) (commenting on Leviticus 19:17).

75 See id. See also Yitzchak Hutner, *Pachad Yitzchak: Shavuoth* 134-37 (1999); Asher Weiss, *Minchas Asher, Vayikra* 276-78 (2017).

76 See William Joseph Wagner, *Reflections on the Symposium: An Ordered Inquiry Into the Relation of Civil Rights Law and Religion*, 5 J.L. & Rel. 5 (1987).

77 Id. at 9.

78 Id.

an examination of religious texts, while avoiding the controversial elements of the approach propounded at the symposium. Toward that end, the chapter looks to a religious text, the Torah, not as a substantive source of human rights law, but instead as a model of an authoritative legal text that must be interpreted to serve as a foundation for a living community. In so doing, the chapter builds on the work of several prominent American legal scholars who have compared constitutional textual analysis to biblical hermeneutics. Thus, while the approach offered in this chapter may raise questions of its own, the emphasis on textual analysis, rather than on substantive law, adds a new dimension to the discussion of the relationship between religion and human rights, through a method that may prove to be more acceptable among legal theorists.

CHAPTER 10

Rules and Standards in Jewish Law and American Constitutional Law

INTRODUCTION

An important issue of debate that can be traced through American legal history relates to how much flexibility and discretion should be employed in interpreting the Constitution. A similar debate is found in Jewish legal history with respect to interpreting legal principles. The debate in American legal thought has taken various forms, as has the terminology theorists have used to describe the debate.[1] For the purposes of this chapter, terminology distinguishing between a jurisprudence based on rules and a jurisprudence based on standards is particularly useful. In fact, a number of American legal scholars—perhaps most prominently, Kathleen Sullivan— have employed such terminology in analyzing contemporary Supreme Court jurisprudence.[2] Moreover, this terminology is readily adaptable to Jewish law, and indeed, a contemporary scholar of Jewish law has used similar terminology to trace different approaches to the proper level of flexibility and discretion in interpreting Jewish legal principles.[3]

PART ONE | PHARISEES, SADDUCEES, CATHOLICS, AND PROTESTANTS

A number of scholars comparing the Jewish legal system with the American legal system have considered the similarities between biblical interpretation in

---

1 See, e.g., Marc Kelman, *A Guide to Critical Legal Studies* 303-4 nn.1-3 (1987); Pierre Schlag, *Rules and Standards*, 33 UCLA L. Rev. 379, 382 n.16 (1985); various works cited in Kathleen M. Sullivan, *The Supreme Court, 1991 Term: Foreword: The Justices of Rules and Standards*, 106 Harv. L. Rev. 22, 57-58 nn.230-31 (1992).

2 See generally Sullivan, supra note 1.

3 See Yitzchak Adler, *Lomdus: A Substructural Analysis* 21-24 (1989).

Jewish law and American constitutional interpretation.[4] These scholars have noted that a basic issue in both legal systems is the question of how to interpret an authoritative text. Some scholars have further tried to demonstrate that issues arising in American law sometimes find their analogues in biblical textual interpretation.[5] Despite the apparent parallels, however, a careful look at the two systems reveals the problems that may arise in drawing too close an analogy with regard to literal and expansive textual interpretation.

Professor Sanford Levinson has been a leading proponent of comparing biblical textual interpretation with constitutional textual interpretation. In his convincing depiction of the Constitution as a "sacred object" in "American Civil Religion," Levinson compares competing views of constitutional interpretation with different strains of biblical interpretation.[6] He develops the thesis that the different approaches to constitutional interpretation parallel the different approaches in Christianity to interpretation of Scriptures.[7] Levinson posits that those who favor an interpretation more faithful to the text of the Constitution are similar to the Protestant reformers, who emphasized the centrality of scriptural text alone as the basis of their religious behavior and belief.[8] Conversely, constitutional interpreters favoring a more flexible understanding of the text reflect an attitude closer to that of Catholics, who read the Scriptures with an emphasis on the oral tradition taught by the Church.[9]

Levinson traces back to 1798 the dichotomy between "protestant" and "catholic" constitutional interpretation.[10] In *Calder v. Bull*,[11] Justice Chase stated that the Court could find a particular act of Congress unconstitutional even though there was no express restraint on such an act in the text of the Constitution (a "catholic" result).[12] Justice Iredell, however, stated that the

---

4 See generally Sanford Levinson, *Constitutional Faith* (1988); Robert M. Cover, "The Supreme Court, 1982 Term—Foreword: Nomos and Narrative," 97 Harv. L. Rev. 4 (1983); David R. Dow, *Constitutional Midrash: The Rabbis' Solution to Professor Bickel's Problem*, 29 Hous. L. Rev. 543 (1992); Thomas C. Grey, *The Constitution as Scripture*, 37 Stan. L. Rev. 1 (1984); *Interpretation Symposium*, 58 S. Cal. L. Rev. 1 (1985).

5 See id.

6 Levinson, supra note 4, at 18-53.

7 See id.

8 See id.

9 See id.

10 Id. at 35-36.

11 3 U.S. (3 Dall.) 386 (1798).

12 See id. at 387-89.

Court could not place such a limitation on legislative power absent textual constitutional support (a "protestant" result).[13]

Levinson finds this dichotomy in modern jurisprudential attitudes as well.[14] He contrasts Justice Black's "protestant" approach in *Griswold v. Connecticut*,[15] with Justice Harlan's "catholicism" in *Poe v. Ullman*.[16] Justice Black argued that Connecticut's prohibition on contraceptives for married couples did not violate the Constitution because there was no provision in the Constitution granting a right to privacy that would invalidate the legislation.[17] Justice Harlan's view of tradition allowed for a reading of the Constitution that recognized rights beyond those expressly stated in the text.[18]

In support of Levinson's thesis, Professor Thomas Grey extended to religions other than Christianity the phenomenon of "catholic" and "protestant" attitudes toward an authoritative text.[19] For example, according to Grey, orthodox Sunni Islam believes that the Koran should be supplemented by oral tradition.[20] Certain Islamic modernizers, however, are skeptical of the authenticity of the oral tradition and stress the authority of the writings.[21]

Grey also applies Levinson's theory to Judaism and Jewish law, arguing that the views of the Sadducees and Pharisees paralleled those of the Protestants and Catholics, respectively.[22] In Grey's description of the ancient debate, the Pharisees transmitted an oral tradition to supplement the Written Torah, while the Sadducees considered only the written law as binding.[23] Levinson, in turn, cites Grey approvingly, and notes a revival of this debate in Judaism, when the ninth century Karaite community rebelled against Rabbinic Judaism's reliance on the Oral Torah.[24] Levinson concludes that the differences between Karaite Judaism and Rabbinic Judaism, like those between Protestantism and Roman

---

13 See id. at 399 (Iredell, J. concurring).

14 See Levinson, supra note 4, at 31-35.

15 381 U.S. 479, 507 (1965) (Black, J., dissenting).

16 367 U.S. 497, 522 (1961) (Harlan, J., dissenting).

17 See *Griswold*, 381 U.S. at 508.

18 See *Poe*, 367 U.S. at 496.

19 Grey, supra note 1, at 6-7. Grey commented on Sanford Levinson, *The Constitution in American Civil Religion*, 1979 Sup. Ct. Rev. 123, which Levinson later developed as part of Constitutional Faith.

20 See Grey, supra note 1, at 7.

21 See id.

22 See id. at 6-7.

23 See id. at 7.

24 See Levinson, supra note 4, at 25.

Catholicism, can serve as a basis of comparison for his analysis of "protestant" and "catholic" interpretations of the Constitution.[25]

Levinson and Grey have thus identified a broadly similar tension within different religions, including the American "Civil Religion," regarding the manner in which an authoritative text may be interpreted. Yet, a careful study of these tensions within Jewish law suggests that parallels to constitutional textual interpretation are less than precise.

First, the portrayal of Sadducean practice rooted in the biblical text and Pharisaic practice relying more heavily on tradition appears inaccurate. In his work on the controversy between the Pharisees and the Sadducees, Professor Louis Finkelstein analyzed some of the recorded debates between the two sects.[26] Finkelstein concluded that, in fact, of the two competing interpretations, that of the Pharisees was more often closer to the literal biblical text.[27] For example, in considering a point of dispute relating to the Temple service on Yom Kippur, Finkelstein noted that the Pharisees' interpretation was consistent with the plain meaning of the biblical verses.[28] The Sadducees, however, "violated the written word" and "were guided in their interpretation of the law solely by the actual custom."[29] In this area, then, the Sadducees resemble constitutional "catholics" rather than constitutional "protestants."[30]

Second, and more fundamentally, the nature of these controversies within Jewish legal history would not seem likely to provide a helpful model for the dichotomy in American legal tradition described by Levinson and Grey. As Finkelstein wrote of the Pharisees and Sadducees, "[n]either sect determined its views by such artificial and spurious principles as 'literal' and 'liberal' interpretation of Scripture."[31] Moreover, unlike the ongoing debate that Levinson identifies in American constitutional interpretation,[32] any dispute in Jewish history regarding the supremacy of oral interpretation proved to be short-lived.

---

25 See id.

26 See Louis Finkelstein, *The Pharisees* 101 (1962).

27 See id.

28 See id. at 119, 654-57.

29 Id. at 120.

30 Similarly, in a dispute relating to the calendar, which Finkelstein called "the most bitter and the most prominent" of the controversies, the Sadducees again rejected the literal interpretation of the Biblical text. Id. at 647-48.

31 Id. at 101.

32 See Levinson, supra note 4, at 36.

There remains no substantial segment of the Jewish people that follows the text over the oral tradition. Thus, Finkelstein's conclusions, together with the realities of Jewish legal history, belie too close an analogy to literal and expansive constitutional textual interpretation.

PART TWO | RULES AND STANDARDS—A BASIC FRAMEWORK

A more accurate description of the tension in Jewish law relating to discretion in legal interpretation might focus on the broader issue of interpretation of legal principles, rather than on the literary and exegetical interpretation of the Bible as an authoritative text. Such an alternative analysis might also allow for a more useful comparison to American legal theory. Indeed, Kathleen Sullivan's formulation of the question of judicial discretion in interpreting the Constitution is an apt description of questions of flexibility in interpretation in Jewish law as well. Sullivan wrote that "[b]ecause virtually nobody really believes the no-judicial-legislation argument in its strongest and most naive form, the real question is not whether the Court should exercise discretion in constitutional interpretation, but rather how much."[33]

Similarly, virtually no authorities in Jewish law have really believed the argument, in its most naive form, that the biblical text should not be interpreted. After all, the Bible is full of laws that are impossible to implement without meaningful interpretation of biblical passages. For example,[34] the Bible prohibits the performance of *melakha* on the Sabbath. The legal term *melakha*, usually translated in English as "work," is nearly as ambiguous in the ancient Hebrew form of the word as in the English translation. Other than an express prohibition against lighting a fire on the Sabbath, the Bible offers few, if any, details of what work is forbidden. The only means of deriving a definition of the term *melakha* is, therefore, through oral tradition and exegetical principles of interpretation.

Because it is clear that the Bible cannot be understood and applied without interpretation, a basic question in Jewish law, as in constitutional law, revolves around how much discretion is available to interpretive authorities. Although constitutional disputes sometimes involve the interpretation of a particular word in the text of the Constitution, Sullivan has observed that "the constitutional interpretation debate converges with pervasive jurisprudential debates over the relative merits of the choice of legal form, because in these debates the

---

33 Sullivan, supra note 1, at 56-57.
34 See Chapter 3 in this Volume.

amount of judicial discretion has been thought to depend on the form in which legal directives are addressed to judges."[35] Similarly, in Jewish law, disputes in legal interpretation occasionally focus on the interpretation of the biblical text. Yet, regardless of how closely the questions relate to biblical interpretation, the underlying and conceptual basis of the disputes often depends on more fundamental questions of how to understand the form and interpretation of legal directives.

Indeed, Sullivan shows how splits between Justices in the 1991 Supreme Court term can be analyzed in the context of "rules and standards."[36] In addition to being an effective way to understand contemporary American legal theory,[37] the distinction between rules and standards is particularly helpful in discussing questions in Jewish law regarding flexibility in interpreting legal principles. A discussion of Jewish law in such a context may, in turn, help illuminate related issues in American legal thought.

In discussing different methods of interpreting legal directives, Sullivan delineates two categories of judges: those who consider laws to be "rules," and those who interpret laws as "standards."[38] Basic to Sullivan's framework is the notion that "[r]ules, once formulated, afford decisionmakers less discretion than do standards."[39] Before discussing the relative merits of interpreting legal directives either as rules or as standards, Sullivan first sets down functional definitions for the different categories.[40] When a legal directive operates as a rule, according to Sullivan, it minimizes the decision-maker's discretion by requiring a specific decision when certain facts are present in a case.[41] Although a rule is an expression of a background principle or policy, once formulated, the rule operates independently.[42] Thus, the rule, as formulated, is applied to the operative facts, even when such an application, under the circumstances, would contradict the principle or policy underlying the rule.[43] A standard, on the other hand, relates the decision directly to the background principle or policy underlying the legal directive.[44] Thus, when treating a legal directive as a standard,

---

35   Sullivan, supra note 1, at 56-57.
36   Id. at 57.
37   See id.
38   See id.
39   Id.
40   See id.
41   See id.
42   See id.
43   See id.
44   See id.

a decision-maker has more discretion, "tak[ing] into account all relevant factors or the totality of the circumstances."[45]

A contemporary scholar of Jewish law, Rabbi Yitzchak Adler, has articulated a similar dichotomy to categorize different ways of interpreting legal directives in the Jewish legal system.[46] One view, parallel to Sullivan's description of "rules," is that legal directives must be applied as formulated. This position holds that, although certain conceptual constructs may have formed the foundation for the legal directive, there is no license to reinterpret the directive in light of its conceptual basis.[47]

The competing view, which parallels Sullivan's description of "standards," is that the conceptual ideas that form the basis of legal directives are a part of the law, to be applied together with the stated directives. Under this view, while it is true that legal directives are usually expressed in definite form, this is largely for the sake of convenience and simplicity. In applying the directive, it is necessary to interpret it not in terms of its simplistic formulation, but through understanding the more complex policies behind the law.[48]

The rules/standards dichotomy may be particularly useful in tracing some of the continuing conflicts in constitutional interpretation, along the lines identified by Levinson. For example, Pierre Schlag has equated constitutional "textualists" with those who favor viewing legal directives as rules.[49] Conversely, Schlag argues, a decision-maker who interprets the Constitution with more flexibility, and who is sensitive to considerations other than the text of the Constitution, sees a legal directive as a standard, to be applied in light

---

45 Id.

46 See Adler, supra note 3, at 21-24. I am mindful of Suzanne Stone's observation that "[t]he Jewish legal tradition is being subtly reinterpreted to yield a legal counter-model embodying precisely the qualities many contemporary theorists wish to inject into American law." Suzanne Last Stone, *In Pursuit of the Counter-Text: The Turn to the Jewish Legal Model in Contemporary American Legal Theory*, 106 Harv. L. Rev. 813, 814 (1993). Specifically, while my use of the terminology of rules and standards is based on the works of contemporary American legal theorists, my application of the principles reflected in this terminology to describe Jewish law is based on the works of Rabbi Adler, a contemporary Jewish scholar, who analyzes the Jewish legal system on its own terms. Therefore, although I express the hope that interpretation in the Jewish legal tradition can shed light on views of interpreting the Constitution, my discussion of the Jewish tradition is based on Jewish legal scholarship rather than on a reinterpretation of the Jewish tradition to match any desired view of American legal theory.

47 See Adler, supra note 3, at 21-22.

48 See id. at 22. Interpreting directives as standards involves applying legal principles conceptually, which differs from restricting the application of *mitzvot* based on their rationale. See Chapter 3 in this Volume.

49 Schlag, supra note 1, at 390-91.

of the values represented by the directive.[50] If Schlag's equations are accurate, through the rules/standards dichotomy, Jewish law can serve as an analogue both to Sullivan's analysis of American law and, broadly, to Levinson's catholic/protestant dichotomy.[51]

PART THREE | RULES AND STANDARDS IN AMERICAN CONSTITUTIONAL LAW

While Levinson referred to Justice Black's "protestant" approach to the Constitution,[52] Justice Black can likewise be pictured as a justice who favors absolute rules. Justice Black's words in *Rochin v. California*[53] reflect the rule-based approach: "faithful adherence to the specific guarantees in the Bill of Rights insures a more permanent protection of individual liberty than that which can be afforded by the nebulous standards stated by the majority."[54] In writing the majority opinion and formulating what Justice Black called "nebulous standards," Justice Frankfurter stated, "in dealing . . . with human rights, the absence of formal exactitude, or want of fixity of meaning, is not an unusual or even regrettable attribute of constitutional provisions."[55] Thus, Justice Frankfurter's view provided a standard-based contrast to Justice Black, parallel to the "catholic" contrast provided by Justice Harlan in Levinson's framework.[56]

---

50 See id. at 392-93.

51 See supra text accompanying notes 26-32.

52 The rules/standards dichotomy can be traced back as far as Levinson's catholic/protestant dichotomy, to *Calder v. Bull*, 3 U.S. (3 Dall.) 386 (1798). See supra text accompanying notes 10-13. Justice Chase, whom Levinson described as a "catholic" interpreter of the Constitution, employed a standard-based view, looking to the reasons that motivated the constitutional clause under consideration. See *Calder*, 3 U.S. at 388-89. Justice Iredell, a "protestant" in Levinson's framework, responded with a rule-based approach, looking for "fixed standards" and delineating "but two lights, in which the subject can be viewed: If the Legislature pursue the authority delegated to them, their acts are valid. If they transgress the boundaries of that authority, their acts are invalid." Id. at 399 (Iredell, J., concurring).

53 342 U.S. 165 (1952).

54 Id. at 175 (1952) (Black, J., concurring); see also Sullivan, supra note 1, at 26 n.19 (classifying Justices Black and Frankfurter's views in *Rochin* as consistent with their favoring rules and standards, respectively).

55 *Rochin*, 342 U.S. at 169.

56 Levinson similarly writes of Justice Frankfurter's nontextualist view, which recognized the "unwritten Constitution." See Levinson, supra note 4, at 33-34.

Furthermore, Levinson's analysis of the views of Justices Black and Harlan, in *Griswold* and *Poe* respectively,[57] is consistent with an understanding of their differing views in terms of rules and standards. Elaborating on his dissenting opinion in *Griswold*, Justice Black later wrote that he could not grant protection to married couples to use contraceptives, absent a "specific provision" granting such a right.[58] Justice Black argued in *Griswold* that if the law granting certain rights does not address a specific set of facts, the rule should not be interpreted to apply to those facts.[59] In *Poe*, Justice Harlan rejected such a rule-based juris-prudence, declaring that "due process has not been reduced to any formula; its content cannot be determined by reference to any code."[60] Instead of relying on a rule or formula, Justice Harlan based his interpretation of the Fourteenth Amendment on "the balance . . . built upon postulates of respect for the liberty of the individual . . . between the liberty and the demands of organized soci-ety."[61] Thus, he understood and applied the Due Process Clause in light of the principles of respect for individual liberties upon which it was based.[62]

The debate between those who favor a jurisprudence of rules and those who view legal directives as standards has continued. For example, in *Immigration and Naturalization Service v. Chadha*,[63] the Court held that granting veto power to one house of Congress was a violation of the presentment and bicameralism clauses.[64] Chief Justice Burger's majority opinion focused on the constitutional text, holding that the clauses of the Constitution are precise rules, not to be considered "empty formalities."[65] Justice White dissented, criticizing Chief Justice Burger's approach as grouping together all legislative vetoes, rather than properly considering the standards represented by the constitutional clauses

---

57 See supra text accompanying notes 15-18.

58 Hugo Black, *A Constitutional Faith* 9 (1968).

59 See *Griswold*, 381 U.S. 479, 507 (1965) (Black, J., dissenting); see also Black, supra note 58, at 9.

60 367 U.S. 497, 542 (1961) (Harlan, J., dissenting).

61 Id.

62 Schlag offers a similar description of the differing views of Justices Holmes and Cardozo regarding the obligation of a driver who approaches an unguarded railroad crossing. See Schlag, supra note 1, at 379. In *Baltimore & Ohio Railroad Co. v. Goodman*, 275 U.S. 66, 70 (1927), Justice Holmes posited a rule that the driver must stop and look, while in *Pokora v. Wabash Railway Co.*, 292 U.S. 98, 104-6 (1934), Justice Cardozo relied on a standard, hold-ing that the driver must act with reasonable caution.

63 462 U.S. 919 (1983).

64 See id.; see also Schlag, supra note 1, at 393 (identifying the rules/standards dichotomy in *Chadha*).

65 *Chadha*, 462 U.S. at 958 n.23.

and applying them to the different circumstances, which vary with the "form or subject" of each veto.[66]

Sullivan has shown that the rules/standards dichotomy can be used to explain many other debates among Supreme Court Justices.[67] In *Michael H. v. Gerald D.*,[68] for example, Justice Scalia, a strict "protestant" in the interpretation of the constitutional text, used a rule-based view to formulate the legal principle at issue in the case.[69] Justice Scalia stated the issue as whether the Due Process Clause had been interpreted as "relating to the rights of an adulterous natural father."[70] Justice Brennan's dissent offered a broader standard, which described "parenthood" as the "interest" being protected.[71] In their concurring opinion, Justices O'Connor and Kennedy also rejected Justice Scalia's strict adherence to a rule-based mode of legal interpretation, quoting Justice Harlan's dissenting opinion in *Poe* and echoing Justice White's criticism of Chief Justice Burger's opinion in *Chadha*.[72] They argued that Justice Scalia's approach did not pay sufficient attention to particular circumstances, but instead "foreclose[d] the unanticipated by the prior imposition of a single mode of... analysis."[73]

Sullivan's discussion of the rules/standards dichotomy in the 1991 Supreme Court term is perhaps most significant in her analysis of the different views expressed in the complex and controversial case of *Planned Parenthood v. Casey*.[74] In their plurality opinion joined by Justice Souter, Justices O'Connor and Kennedy again quoted Justice Harlan in *Poe*, and echoed both Justice White's thoughts in *Chadha* as well as their own opinion in *Michael H.*[75]

---

66 Id. at 974 (White, J., dissenting).

67 See Sullivan, supra note 1, at 77-79.

68 491 U.S. 110 (1989).

69 See Antonin Scalia, *The Rule of Law as a Law of Rules*, 56 U. Chi. L. Rev. 1175, 1184 (1989) ("[I]t is perhaps easier for me than it is for some judges to develop general rules, because I am more inclined to adhere closely to the plain meaning of a text."); see also George Kannar, *The Constitutional Catechism of Antonin Scalia*, 99 Yale L.J. 1297, 1299 (1990); Eric J. Segall, *Justice Scalia, Critical Legal Studies, and the Rule of Law*, 62 Geo. Wash. L. Rev. 991, 993 (1994) ("[Justice Scalia's] well-known preferences for textualism, originalism, and traditionalism derive in large part from, but are also secondary to, his passion for strict legal rules that he believes will provide greater certainty and uniformity to the law.").

70 *Michael H.*, 491 U.S. at 127 n.6.

71 Id. at 139 (Brennan, J., dissenting).

72 See id. at 132 (O'Connor, J., concurring).

73 Id.

74 505 U.S. 833 (1992).

75 See id. at 843-901 (plurality opinion).

They wrote that liberty is interpreted by judges through "reasoned judgment" and is "not susceptible of expression as a simple rule."[76] Justice Scalia again attacked this balancing, standard-based approach, calling it "nothing but philosophical predilection and moral intuition."[77]

Sullivan aptly summarizes the standard-based plurality opinion: "*Casey* simply abandoned a rule that *all* regulatory burdens on adult abortions are coercive no matter how great or how small in favor of a standard that takes into account the quantity of impact on pregnant women."[78] In contrast, Sullivan notes, Justice Scalia relied on a rule-based view, arguing in part that the Court would strike down "'a state law requiring purchasers of religious books to endure a 24-hour waiting period, or to pay a nominal additional tax of 1 [cent].'"[79] Justice Scalia thus ignored the plurality's quantitative analysis of the actual effect of the law, rejecting its careful consideration of the impact of a law in favor of a rule.[80]

In many landmark decisions issued subsequent to the publication of Sullivan's article, the Justices continued to split along the lines of rules and standards. For example, in interpreting the Establishment Clause in *Board of Education of Kiryas Joel Village School District v. Grumet,*[81] Justice O'Connor continued to emphasize the need for balancing the effects of laws, writing that "[e]xperience proves that the Establishment Clause . . . cannot easily be reduced to a single test."[82] She repeated this statement in *Rosenberger v. Rector and Visitors of the University of Virginia,*[83] rejecting "categorical answers" to Establishment Clause questions.[84]

The dissenting opinion in *Rosenberger* adopted the rigid logic of a rule-based attitude. The dissent cited the view that "[a]lthough Establishment Clause jurisprudence is characterized by few absolutes, the Clause does absolutely prohibit government-financed . . . indoctrination into the beliefs of a particular religious faith."[85] Having stated a precise rule, the dissent asked a

---

76 Id. at 849.
77 Id. at 1000 (Scalia, J., concurring in part and dissenting in part).
78 Sullivan, supra note 1, at 34.
79 Id. at 34 n.69 (citing *Casey*, 505 U.S. at 988 (Scalia, J., concurring in part and dissenting in part)).
80 See id.
81 512 U.S. 687 (1994).
82 Id. (O'Connor, J., concurring in part and concurring in the judgment).
83 515 U.S. 819 (1995).
84 Id. (O'Connor, J., concurring).
85 Id. (Souter, J., dissenting) (quoting *School Dist. of Grand Rapids v. Ball*, 473 U.S. 373, 385 (1985)).

question that epitomizes the rule-based approach: "Why does this Court not apply this clear law to these clear facts . . . ?"[86]

PART FOUR | RULES AND STANDARDS IN JEWISH LAW

The corpus of Jewish law comprises a complex legal system, encompassing both civil (monetary or commercial) and religious (ritual) legal principles. For a number of reasons, it is not always easy or even productive to attempt to classify specific laws as either "civil" or "religious." First, on a theological level, the entire Jewish legal system is considered to be religious in nature. Even those laws that involve civil principles are reflections of divine will regarding the manner in which society should function. Second, analytically, many laws governing civil matters also involve religious duties and obligations, complicating any classification of these laws into a single category.[87] Third, all laws, including those which involve purely civil or religious matters, share a common methodological framework. Legal principles such as conditions and agency, for example, are as relevant to religious acts and obligations as they are to civil issues of property or contract law.

At the same time, these characteristics of Jewish law may facilitate a structural and conceptual analysis of the Jewish legal system. Because civil and religious law share much common ground, it is possible to apply many of the same legal principles, in a similar manner, to both settings. For example, to address a question regarding the application of conditions to contract law, Jewish law may look to the way conditions operate in relation to a certain religious obligation. Thus, the Jewish legal system can be viewed, through a variety of analytical methods, as a unified system, with principles that can be applied uniformly to understand and classify different laws.

One method that can be used to analyze the Jewish legal system parallels Sullivan's method of analyzing constitutional law, which divides interpretation of legal directives into rule-based interpretation and standard-based interpretation. A number of legal directives in Jewish law have been open to different interpretations by legal authorities. The different interpretations can often be understood in terms of whether the interpreting authority viewed a particular directive as a "rule," which is to be applied as formulated without further

---

86 Id.

87 In Rabbi Adler's terminology, this phenomenon presents a category of "dual classification." Adler, supra note 3, at 18-20; see also Chapter 3 in this Volume.

consideration of the conceptual framework that motivated the law, or as a "standard," a simplified formulation of more complex principles that govern the application of the law.

Rabbi Adler has explored the dichotomy between rule-based legal interpretation and standard-based interpretation in Jewish law by classifying legal directives into three categories: (1) general laws; (2) laws of equivalence; and (3) laws of quantification.[88] An example of each of these types of law, and the conceptual analysis applicable to each, should help illustrate some of the parallels and differences between Jewish legal interpretation and American legal interpretation.

A. General Laws[89]

The Talmud states the following law: when agency may not be employed for a given activity, conditions may not be placed on the performance of that activity.[90] The application of this law to the case of the nazarite[91] illustrates the two ways of viewing a legal directive. Although a nazarite may not appoint an agent to observe the prohibitions required under the nazarite oath, it is clear from the Talmud that the nazarite may place certain conditions on the oath.[92] Thus, at first glance, the laws relating to the nazarite seem to contradict the principle that when an agent cannot be appointed, conditions may not be applied. In resolving the apparent contradiction, medieval authorities took one of two basic approaches, evidently relying on either rule-based interpretation or standard-based interpretation.

---

88 See Adler, supra note 3, at 21-30. The application of Sullivan's terms, "rules" and "standards," to Jewish law is my own; Rabbi Adler does not use these terms. Rather, Rabbi Adler refers to what I call "legal directives" or "laws" as "rules." He then delineates two possible ways of interpreting these "rules": applying them either precisely as stated or through uncovering the conceptual bases for the rules.

 To avoid the obvious confusion that would result in using Sullivan's terminology together with that of Rabbi Adler, I have chosen to use uniform terminology for both legal systems. I have chosen to use Sullivan's terminology because of its common use in contemporary American legal scholarship. As noted above, and as the present analysis should make clear, Sullivan's terminology is adaptable to the Jewish legal system and consistent with the scholarship described by Rabbi Adler.

89 Rabbi Adler discusses general laws in the English section of his book, supra note 3, at 22-24, and more extensively in the Hebrew section, id. at 77-85.

90 See Talmud Bavli, Kethuboth 74a.

91 The Bible states that a man or woman who takes the nazarite oath may not drink wine, come in contact with dead bodies, or take a shave or haircut. See Numbers 6:3-6.

92 See Talmud Bavli, Nazir 11a, the Tosafoth commentary.

Some authorities viewed the Talmudic principle as a rule, to be applied precisely as stated.[93] These authorities accepted the law as formulated, holding that in any case in which a person may not appoint an agent to perform a particular activity, the person may not place conditions on the performance of the activity.[94] According to this reasoning, if a person may not appoint an agent for the performance of the nazarite obligations, that person should be precluded from placing conditions on the performance of those obligations. These authorities noted, however, that although agency is inapplicable to the observance of the prohibitions incumbent on a nazarite, a nazarite may appoint an agent to bring the sacrifice required at the end of the nazarite period.[95] Due to this limited power of agency, the nazarite's ability to place certain conditions on the observance of other nazarite obligations does not violate the Talmudic principle.

Others suggested a different approach, based on a consideration of the conceptual basis of the law that precludes conditions when agency does not apply.[96] These authorities viewed the Talmudic principle as a general expression of the relationship between agency and conditions in Jewish law.[97] The common ground of these two legal functions is that the authority either to appoint an agent to perform an activity or to place conditions on the performance of an activity indicates a certain level of control over that activity. The Talmudic principle is then understood as teaching, generally, that if a person does not have the authority to appoint an agent to perform a given activity, then the person likewise does not possess the requisite level of control over that activity to impose conditions on its performance. According to these authorities, however, the Talmudic law should be applied not as stating a definite rule, but only as reflecting the standard by which authority and control are generally measured and related.[98] By viewing the legal directive as a standard, these authorities allow for exceptions to the law when the rationale underlying the law does not apply.[99] One such case is the nazarite.

An individual has broad control over the observance of the nazarite laws. After all, a person has the autonomy to choose voluntarily whether and when to take the nazarite oath. Using a standard-based interpretation of the Talmudic

---

93 See Adler, supra note 3, at 22-24 (English section), 77-78 (Hebrew section).
94 See id.
95 See id.; see also Numbers 6:14-21.
96 See Adler, supra note 3, at 22-24 (English section), 77 (Hebrew section).
97 See id.
98 See id.
99 See id.

principle, we can understand that such control similarly enables a person to place conditions on the oath. Although a nazarite may not appoint an agent to observe the prohibitions, this limitation does not indicate a lack of control over the activities. Rather, it is technically impossible to appoint an agent in the context of the nazarite oath, because the oath imposes personal modes of behavior on the individual that simply cannot be performed by an agent.[100] Therefore, according to these authorities, the Talmudic principle should not be applied to the nazarite as stated; instead, the case of the nazarite represents an exception.[101] Once the Talmudic law is viewed as an expression of the conceptual framework relating to individual control over an activity, its application to the nazarite allows for the imposition of conditions even though agency cannot apply.

The example of the nazarite laws offers a look at the way Jewish legal directives can be viewed through the rules/standards dichotomy. The laws regarding the nazarite have been debated by classical authorities in Jewish law in a way that parallels Sullivan's analysis of constitutional interpretation. In addition, the application of the laws of agency and conditions to the nazarite helps illustrate the conceptual consistency within the Jewish legal system. The case of the nazarite, who takes it upon himself or herself to refrain from certain activities, may be seen as paradigmatic of religious or ritual areas of Jewish law. Yet, the case of the nazarite also involves the legal principles of agency and conditions, which are an important part of Jewish civil law, and, indeed, central to many areas of American law. The conceptual analysis relating to agency and conditions is identical in both Jewish religious law and Jewish civil law and, therefore, could theoretically be adaptable to secular legal systems as well.

B. Laws of Equivalence[102]

The Talmud draws the following legal equivalence in the context of monetary adjudication: an admission is equivalent to the testimony of one hundred witnesses.[103] Although Jewish law ordinarily requires the testimony of two

---

100 See supra note 91. For example, if a nazarite drinks wine, the nazarite obviously violates the prohibition on this activity, even if an "agent" refrains from drinking wine. Thus, nazarite requirements differ fundamentally from obligations which can be performed by an agent on behalf of the principal.

101 See Adler, supra note 3, at 22-24 (English section), 77 (Hebrew section).

102 Rabbi Adler discusses laws of equivalence in the English section of his book, id. at 24-27, and in the Hebrew section, id. at 86-93.

103 See, e.g., Talmud Bavli, Bava Metzia 3b.

witnesses for the adjudication of a monetary obligation, while excluding the testimony of a party to a case, an individual's admission to an obligation is accepted as dispositive.[104] The Talmud thus recognizes a certain equivalence between an individual's admission and the testimony of two witnesses.[105] Yet, Jewish legal authorities have debated the interpretation of this law.

Some authorities have interpreted the Talmud's statement of equivalence as a rule, to be applied precisely as formulated, indicating that an admission has an effect identical to that of the testimony of witnesses.[106] Others have understood the law as a general expression of the fact that a confession shares certain legal properties with the testimony of two witnesses, not as a statement of absolute equivalence between an admission and the testimony of witnesses.[107]

One of the legal ramifications of the debate involves the question of when an obligation vests if it is realized through a confession. Legal authorities split over the two possible answers to this question. One view is that an admission works retroactively, and therefore the obligation vests from the time that, according to the admission, the obligation originated.[108] The other view is that the obligation vests only from the time that the admission itself occurs.[109] These two views seem to diverge along the lines of the rules/standards dichotomy.

If the Talmudic statement equating an admission with the testimony of witnesses is interpreted as a precise rule, then the equivalence is to be taken literally. The rule-based view would hold that, although on one level there are clear differences between an admission and the testimony of witnesses, in terms of legal effect they share identical properties. According to a rule-based reading of the Talmud's formulation of the law, an admission, like two witnesses, is a form of sufficient testimony, constituting a unique situation in which a party to a case is permitted to testify because the testimony is against financial self-interest. Therefore, just as an obligation realized through the testimony of witnesses vests retroactively from the time that, according to the testimony, the obligation arose, an admission has the same retroactive effect.

---

104 See id.
105 For the purposes of a monetary obligation, two witnesses are thus as effective as one hundred witnesses. The language of the Talmud, equating an admission to one hundred witnesses, is an emphatic way of teaching that an admission is clearly sufficient.
106 See Adler, supra note 3, at 88-90.
107 See id. See also Asher Weiss, *Minchas Asher, Shemos* 279-85 (2017).
108 See *Beith Shemuel*, Even Ha'ezer 38:31.
109 See *Chelkat Mechokek*, Even Ha'ezer 38:22.

According to a standard-based interpretation, however, this law is a general statement of equivalence, articulating the legal similarities between an admission and the testimony of witnesses vis-à-vis the level of proof required to adjudicate a monetary obligation. The Talmud does state that, like the testimony of witnesses, an admission is sufficient to impose a monetary obligation.[110] Yet, authorities applying a standard-based approach may view this law through a conceptual interpretation, allowing for flexibility in considering the precise nature of the equivalence between an admission and witnesses. These authorities would hold that the testimony of a party to a case is never admissible, even against that party's monetary interests.[111] Rather, the legal effect of an admission stems from its status as the granting of a gift on the part of the admitting party. Clearly, the benefactor's obligation for a gift can vest only from the time of the granting of the gift. Therefore, these authorities hold, an obligation realized through an admission does not vest retroactively.

C. Laws of Quantification[112]

Many areas of the Jewish legal system involve specific measurements or quantities. For example, the Torah prohibits eating or drinking on Yom Kippur and mandates a strict punishment for an individual who violates this prohibition.[113] The Talmud, in turn, quantifies the amount of food that must be consumed to warrant such a harsh punishment.[114]

The Talmud also states that the prohibition against eating or drinking on Yom Kippur is not violated through the consumption of foods or objects that

---

110 See Talmud Bavli, Bava Metzia 3b.

111 See Adler, supra note 3, at 88-90.

112 Rabbi Adler discusses laws of quantification in the English section of his book, id. at 28-30, and in the Hebrew section, id. at 94-100.

113 See Leviticus 23:29.

114 See Talmud Bavli, Yoma 73b. For eating, the quantity is *kotheveth hagasah*, roughly between one and two ounces, while for drinking, the quantity is *melo lugmav*, the amount of liquid that would fill one cheek. See Maimonides, Code of Law, Laws of *Yom Kippur* 2:1. While the precise quantity of *melo lugmav* varies according to the individual, it is generally around 1.5 fluid ounces. Consumption of these quantities subjects the individual to the harsh biblical punishment. The Talmud also records a prohibition against the consumption of any amount of food or drink on Yom Kippur, though consumption of a smaller quantity violates a lesser prohibition, and thus does not incur the same harsh punishment. See Talmud Bavli, Yoma 73b. There is a dispute in the Talmud whether the lesser prohibition is of biblical or rabbinic origin. The prevailing opinion is that the prohibition is of biblical origin. See Maimonides, supra, Laws of *Yom Kippur* 2:3.

are spoiled or inedible, such as pure vinegar; in legal terms, consumption of these objects is not considered "eating" or "drinking," since it does not conform to the ordinary manner of eating or drinking.[115] Yet, the Talmudic law, stating that drinking pure vinegar does not violate the prohibition against drinking on Yom Kippur, is open to interpretation. The application of the law may again depend on the rules/standards dichotomy in interpreting legal directives.

The question arose among medieval legal authorities as to whether it is permissible to drink a quantity of pure vinegar substantially larger than the quantity of consumption ordinarily prohibited on Yom Kippur.[116] Rabbenu Yerucham wrote that the exemption for eating or drinking spoiled or inedible objects applies only when small quantities are consumed.[117] Drinking a large quantity of vinegar, however, violates the prohibition against drinking.[118] Maimonides is of the opposite opinion, holding that regardless of how much vinegar is drunk, there is no violation of the biblical prohibition.[119]

This dispute can be understood in terms of the rules/standards dichotomy. Maimonides views the Talmudic laws for eating and drinking on Yom Kippur as formal rules. One rule is that a person may not drink a certain quantity on Yom Kippur.[120] Another rule, generally applicable in Jewish law, is that consuming a spoiled or inedible object does not qualify as eating or drinking.[121] When these rules are applied formally, as stated, they produce the logical conclusion that regardless of how large a quantity of vinegar one actually drinks on Yom Kippur, there is no violation of the prohibition. The prohibition, as formulated, prohibits only consumption that fits the legal definition of eating or drinking. Therefore, the exemption, as formulated, excludes the consumption of pure vinegar from the legal category of drinking.

Rabbenu Yerucham, however, interprets the two laws as reflections of the standard of behavior that the Torah and the Talmud mandate on Yom Kippur. The Torah states that on Yom Kippur, as part of the process of repentance, a

---

115 See Talmud Bavli, Yoma 81a-81b.

116 See Joseph Karo, *Beith Yosef: Laws of Yom Kippur* 612.

117 See id.

118 See id.

119 See id.; see also Maimonides, Code of Law, Laws of *Yom Kippur* 2:5 (holding that a person who drinks even a large quantity of pure vinegar on Yom Kippur does not violate the biblical prohibition). It should be noted that Maimonides holds that there is still a rabbinic prohibition against drinking large quantities of vinegar on Yom Kippur. See id.

120 See Leviticus 23:29.

121 See Maimonides, Code of Law, Laws of *Yom Kippur* 2:5.

person must experience a certain degree of affliction.[122] The Talmud explains that fasting on Yom Kippur is the primary way to observe this obligation.[123] Rabbenu Yerucham therefore interprets the laws of fasting in the context of the broader standards of affliction required on Yom Kippur.[124] Thus, he understands the Talmudic law, exempting vinegar from the prohibition on drinking, to be based on the principle that, generally, drinking vinegar or consuming other inedible foods will not ameliorate the experience of affliction resulting from fasting.[125] However, if one drinks a sufficiently large quantity of vinegar, the satiety resulting from the sheer amount of liquid consumed will, in fact, ameliorate the affliction from fasting.[126] Therefore, consumption of such a quantity is prohibited on Yom Kippur.

To an extent, the application of the rules/standards dichotomy to laws of quantification in the Jewish legal system resembles the rules/standards debate in *Planned Parenthood v. Casey*.[127] As Sullivan explained, the standard-based plurality opinion in *Casey* considered regulations on abortions in the context of the impact that the regulations would have on pregnant women.[128] Similarly, Rabbenu Yerucham views the laws regarding fasting on Yom Kippur, including the exemption for drinking pure vinegar, in the context of the effect that drinking vinegar would have on the fulfillment of the biblical imperative to afflict one's self on Yom Kippur.[129]

In contrast, Justice Scalia's rule-based opinion in *Casey* discussed a hypothetical case in which a state law imposed minor restrictions on the purchase of religious books, and concluded that the laws would clearly be unconstitutional, regardless of the actual nature of their effect on religious practice.[130] Similarly, Maimonides held that the laws of Yom Kippur, when viewed as strict rules, yield the conclusion that drinking even a large quantity of vinegar does not violate the prohibition against drinking because it simply does not conform to the legal definition of drinking.[131] Interpretation of the laws as rules leaves no room for consideration of whether

---

122 See Leviticus 23:27.
123 See Talmud Bavli, Yoma 74b.
124 See Adler, supra note 3, at 29-30 (English section), 98 (Hebrew section).
125 See id.
126 See id.
127 505 U.S. 833 (1992).
128 See Sullivan, supra note 1, at 34.
129 See Adler, supra note 3, at 29-30 (English section), 98 (Hebrew section) (citing and explaining Rabbenu Yerucham).
130 See 505 U.S. at 988 (Scalia, J., concurring in part and dissenting in part).
131 See Adler, supra note 3, at 29-30 (English section), 98 (Hebrew section) (citing and explaining Maimonides).

drinking a large quantity of vinegar is conceptually inconsistent with the fulfillment of the biblical command requiring affliction on Yom Kippur.

PART FIVE | REASONS FOR RULES OR STANDARDS

Contemporary American legal theorists have identified arguments for and against each of the positions in the rules/standards debate. Duncan Kennedy was one of the first scholars to offer a systematic analysis of the relative pros and cons for rules or standards.[132] Schlag relied heavily on Kennedy's work, and dedicated much of his response to dissecting Kennedy's propositions.[133]

This chapter aims not to evaluate the relative merits of the various arguments, but rather to consider the application of these arguments to the rules/standards dichotomy that exists within Jewish law. Sullivan's more recent analysis of the arguments for rules or standards, which draws from many earlier sources and presents the arguments and counter-arguments in a clear and considered manner, provides a helpful framework for this discussion.

Sullivan has identified four central categories of argument that can be offered to support each side of the rules/standards debate. One argument in favor of rules is that they produce "fairness as formal equality," preventing arbitrary decisions by "requir[ing] decisionmakers to act consistently [in] treating like cases alike."[134] Another reason to employ rules is based on their "utility," affording both private actors and judges certainty and predictability.[135] Third, Sullivan identifies advocates of the rule of law who argue that rules promote "liberty" by setting in advance the extent of governmental authority.[136] Finally, rules are seen by some as important for "democracy" because they "allocate roles or power among competing decisionmakers."[137]

Sullivan suggests that arguments for standards can be placed in the same four general categories, viewed from the opposite perspective.[138] In contrast to "fairness as formal equality," standards offer "fairness as substantive justice";

132　See Duncan Kennedy, *Form and Substance in Private Law Adjudication*, 89 Harv. L. Rev. 1685, 1687-1701 (1976).

133　See Schlag, supra note 1, at 383-430; see also John P. Goebel, *Rules and Standards: A Critique of Two Critical Theorists*, 31 Duq. L. Rev. 51 (1992) (concluding that Schlag's argument fails to replace Kennedy's convincing position); Kelman, supra note 1, at 40-63.

134　Sullivan, supra note 1, at 62.

135　See id. at 62-63.

136　See id. at 63-64.

137　Id. at 64.

138　See id. at 66.

standards enable decision-makers to explore among cases relevant similarities and differences that would not be discovered through the strict application of rules.[139] Similarly, standards may be better suited for "utility," increasing productivity because they "allow decisionmakers to adapt [the law] to changing circumstances."[140] In contrast to the value of "liberty," some scholars argue that standards contribute to the value of "equality" by serving "redistributive purposes."[141] Finally, in response to the claim that rules promote "democracy," it is arguable that, in reality, rules favor "judicial abdication of responsibility," while standards promote "deliberation" by forcing decision-makers to "face up to [their] choices."[142]

A number of the arguments for rules or standards are relevant to the Jewish legal system, in a similar—if not identical—manner. The fact that other arguments do not apply to Jewish law may help illustrate some of the basic differences between the Jewish and American legal systems, as well as some of the limitations on their comparison.

The first two categories of argument seem readily applicable to Jewish law. As in American law, arguments for a rule-based approach in Jewish law can include the claim that rules help produce "fairness as formal equality," by resulting in a uniformity of decision in cases that share broadly similar facts. Similarly, rules offer "utility" and are economical[143] because they are relatively simple to apply[144] and do not require the difficult analysis sometimes necessary for the application of standards.[145]

The corresponding arguments in favor of standards are likewise applicable in the context of Jewish law. In a standard-based approach, there is an emphasis on the important and relevant details of each individual case.[146] The result is "fairness in substantive justice," as each case is considered on its specific facts. The "utility" of standards in Jewish law is also apparent. Standards give the decision-maker the opportunity to engage in "flexibility and a degree of interpretive license" when the situation so demands.[147]

---

139 Id.
140 Id.
141 Id. at 67.
142 Id.
143 See Adler, supra note 3, at 21.
144 See id. at 24.
145 See id. at 30.
146 See Sullivan, supra note 1, at 66.
147 Adler, supra note 3, at 30.

Yet, it is difficult—and probably unproductive—to try to apply to Jewish law the other two categories of argument that Sullivan identifies for rules or standards. Concepts of both "liberty" and "equality" have their place in the Jewish legal system, but their definition in Jewish law would likely differ substantially from the way they are understood in American legal and political thought.[148] Arguments based on notions of "democracy," particularly those based specifically on the American system of government, are even less likely to apply to the Jewish legal system.

Many of these difficulties relate to the fact that the Jewish "legal system" consists of more than civil law. Equally important to the system is the corpus of religious law, and a central characteristic of the system as a whole is the religious element present in all areas of Jewish law.[149] Indeed, without recognizing the religious basis of the entire Jewish legal system, it is impossible to understand the fundamental source and authority of the civil law.

As a result of religious principles, Jewish law imposes many duties and obligations on the individual that are inconsistent with Western definitions of "liberty" and autonomy.[150] Similarly, questions of "equality" within the Jewish legal system often involve religious issues concerning the individual's place and role in the world, depending on each individual's unique relationship to God. Many of these religious considerations, which can define an individual's role in society, run counter to basic assumptions underlying the American notion of "equality."[151]

The difficulties that would arise in applying to the Jewish legal system the goals of "democracy" noted by Sullivan are symptomatic of more general

---

148 See Sol Roth, *Halakhah and Politics: The Jewish Idea of the State* 97 (1988). For a general discussion of the different concepts of "liberty" found in Western and Jewish thought, see id. at 93-103.

149 See supra text accompanying note 87.

150 As Rabbi Sol Roth has written, "Judaism's ... characterization of its conception of freedom is a direct consequence of its supreme concern with duties or obligations." Roth, supra note 335, at 97; see also id. at 93-103.

Robert Cover writes of the difference between the Jewish legal system and the American legal system in terms of an approach to civil rights. Cover writes that unlike the American system, the Jewish legal system places on individuals an obligation not only to recognize the rights of others, but to realize those rights. Robert M. Cover, *Obligation: A Jewish Jurisprudence of the Social Order*, 5 J.L. & Religion 65 (1989).

It should be noted that some scholars identify a similar affirmative duty on Congress to protect constitutional human rights. See, e.g., Charles L. Black, Jr., *Further Reflections on the Constitutional Justice of Livelihood*, 86 Colum. L. Rev. 1103, 1107 (1986).

For a discussion of human rights in Jewish law, see Roth, supra note 148, at 117-26.

151 See Roth, supra note 148, at 52-55.

obstacles that arise in attempts to classify Jewish law in terms of modern political theory. One obstacle results from the unique structure of the American political/legal system. The arguments relating rules and standards to issues of "democracy" focus on the role of the judiciary as one of the three branches of government. Understanding the precise place of judges within a Jewish political system requires a complex analysis, but it is clear that these judges play a much different role from that of their counterparts in the American system.

Apart from the unique nature of the American political structure, a more fundamental obstacle complicates attempts to classify "the Jewish legal system" within the categories of Western democratic thought. The basic source for all Jewish thought, relating to religious, legal, or political matters, is a single religious guide, the Torah. In fact, even a delineation of these different elements of the social structure is challenging, as the Torah does not seem to distinguish between religious, legal, and political arenas. Instead, it prescribes a complex and comprehensive system of the interrelated and intertwined areas of religious, legal, and political life that together form Jewish society. A classification of this system within Western democratic political theory does not easily emerge.[152]

Thus, the first two classes of argument described by Sullivan in favor of rules or standards are readily applicable to Jewish law, while there does not appear to be a systematic way of applying the other two types of arguments in the context of the Jewish legal system. These distinctions may, in turn, result from the fundamental differences that exist in the nature of Sullivan's arguments.

The first two arguments, which invoke conceptual properties of law, discuss the pros and cons of rules or standards largely in terms of the relationships of the judge and the individual to the law.[153] Such an analysis is relevant to both Jewish law and American law, because the two systems share a sufficiently similar conceptual basis. Regardless of their specific roles within the larger socio-political structures, judges and individuals in both legal systems will form their relationships to the law in part based on whether laws are conceptually viewed as rules or as standards.

---

152 While the society described by Jewish law may be consistent with some of the "fundamental principles of democracy, namely representative government and rule by majority . . . ," Roth, *supra* note 148, at 141, many aspects of Jewish law are inconsistent with Western democratic ideals. Indeed, within the vast amount of scholarship in Jewish law, there have not been many attempts to categorize the Jewish legal system as complying with a particular political system. See *id.* at 1 (finding that "while Jewish social philosophy [is] an area of philosophic activity that has been largely neglected in the course of the history of Jewish thought . . . [p]olitical philosophy elicited even less interest").

153 See Sullivan, *supra* note 1, at 62-63, 66.

The other two arguments discussed by Sullivan involve the place of the judge and the individual within society.[154] Applying these arguments to Jewish law would require comparisons between the Jewish and American legal systems that go beyond considerations of legal concepts, to include considerations of larger socio-political issues. Such comparisons would prove particularly difficult, if not unsuccessful, in large part due to the religious nature of the Jewish socio-political structure. Indeed, while the Jewish and American legal systems may be well suited for conceptual comparisons, it appears that attempts at larger socio-political comparisons would fail to account for the uniquely religious nature of Jewish law.[155]

PART SIX | PROBLEMS WITH RULES AND STANDARDS IN AMERICAN CONSTITUTIONAL LAW

Attempts to categorize constitutional interpreters as "rule-based" or "standard-based" raise a number of problems. On a practical level, some may argue that the very practice of assigning to judges such labels is flawed, because each individual judge does not always follow a single interpretive approach. Even those judges who, in most cases, fit into one category of decision-makers, occasionally issue decisions that place them in the other category. This inevitable inconsistency on the part of almost all judges complicates, and perhaps even calls into question, the validity of attempts to classify them.

On a more philosophical level, the classification of decision-makers into these two categories may be troubling because it seems to eliminate a certain degree of both autonomy and analytical thinking in legal interpretation. If an individual's legal views all stem from the choice of which approach to utilize— rule-based or standard-based—then the individual's autonomy is limited by one initial decision. After the choice has been made to follow one approach, the applicable legal directive will often be interpreted mechanically, with no need or possibility for further analysis based on the facts of a specific case. Similarly, if an individual decides that all laws should be interpreted through the same approach, rather than based on a consideration of a law's specific characteristics, there is less need and opportunity for careful and productive legal reasoning.[156]

---

154 See id. at 62-67.

155 See Chapter 3 in this Volume.

156 Indeed, Schlag has suggested that "[t]he arguments we make for or against rules or standards tend to be pretty much the same regardless of the specific issue involved.... The ... substantive context in which the arguments arise hardly seems to influence their basic character. The arguments are drearily predictable, almost routine...." Schlag, supra note 1, at 380.

Sullivan does not ignore the fact that "[n]o Justice is perfectly consistent on the rules/standards choice."[157] Indeed, Sullivan cites many examples of such inconsistencies, some of which are found within the same 1991 Court term. For example, she writes that although she has categorized Justices O'Connor, Kennedy, and Souter as favoring standards, the latter two Justices sometimes favor rules.[158] In one case,[159] Sullivan notes, Justice Kennedy "[went] flat out for [the] bright-line rul[e]" in "advocat[ing] an approach to resolving content censorship claims that was even more categorical than the strict scrutiny rule: namely, per se invalidation."[160]

Justice Souter also showed an occasional acceptance of rules over standards. Perhaps the most obvious example of this phenomenon is *Rosenberger v. Rector and Visitors of the University of Virginia*,[161] in which Justice Souter wrote the dissenting opinion. Justice O'Connor advocated a standard-based approach in her concurring opinion, warning against categorical answers and simple tests in construing the Establishment Clause.[162] In direct contrast, Justice Souter interpreted the Establishment Clause in absolute terms and asked, with seeming incredulity, why the Court was unwilling to apply the clear law to the clear facts.[163]

Sullivan uncovered inconsistencies in the approaches of many other Justices. She observes, for example, that although Justice Stevens "most consistently advocates standard-like approaches,"[164] in his opinion for the majority in *Quill Corp. v. North Dakota ex rel. Heitkamp*,[165] he reaffirms a bright-line holding.[166] In *Quill Corp.*, Justice Stevens acknowledged that "bright-line tests . . . appear[ ] artificial at [the] edges," but favored the test because of "the benefits of a clear rule."[167]

---

157 Sullivan, supra note 1, at 103 n.529.

158 See id. at 92 n.482.

159 *Simon & Schuster, Inc. v. Members of the N.Y. State Crime Victims Bd.*, 502 U.S. 105, 124-28 (1991).

160 Sullivan, supra note 1, at 92 n.482 (discussing Justice Kennedy's concurring opinion in *Simon & Schuster*).

161 515 U.S. 819 (1995).

162 See id. (O'Connor, J. concurring) (quoting *Board of Educ. of Kiryas Joel Village School Dist. v. Grumet*, 512 U.S. 687, 720 (1994) (O'Connor, J., concurring in part and concurring in judgment)).

163 See id. (Souter, J., dissenting).

164 Sullivan, supra note 1, at 113 n.567.

165 504 U.S. 298 (1992).

166 See Sullivan, supra note 1, at 123.

167 Id.

Sullivan also identified inconsistencies in the approaches of Justices White, Blackmun, Scalia, and Thomas.[168] In fact, in *Forsyth County v. Nationalist Movement*,[169] the Justices of rules and standards reversed their roles in reviewing a county ordinance permitting a government administrator to vary the fee for assembling and parading.[170] The majority, consisting of Justices who ordinarily favor standards, (Blackmun, Stevens, O'Connor, Kennedy, and Souter), adopted a bright-line test, holding that "[a] tax based on the content of speech does not become more constitutional because it is a small tax."[171] Conversely, the typically rules-favoring Justices (Rehnquist, White, Scalia, and Thomas) would allow for an adjustable permit fee scheme at the discretion of the county administrator.[172]

Despite these occasional inconsistencies, Sullivan does identify at least general trends within the views of the different Justices. Having demonstrated these trends, Sullivan searches further for reasons underlying the Justices' choices of which approach to adopt in the rules/standards dichotomy. Sullivan engages in an extensive analysis of two "perspectives" of why a particular Justice chooses one approach over the other. The first perspective, which she describes as "tempting," offers a "political explanation."[173] Sullivan acknowledges that rules often correspond to extreme ideological poles, while standards are more conducive to intermediate positions.[174] Yet, she rejects the notion that rules or standards are inherently more similar to either conservative or liberal political views.[175] Instead, Sullivan prefers a second perspective, which she terms the "jurisprudential perspective."[176] According to this theory, "[all judges] aim at maintaining judicial legitimacy," but they disagree as to which approach better serves this goal.[177] Sullivan develops, through an examination of rules and standards, two differing conceptions of the judicial role, as reflected in attitudes towards "history, knowledge and power."[178]

Regardless of which perspective best describes why a decision-maker favors rules or standards, the entire exercise of seeking to explain a judge's

---

168 See id. at 113 n.567.
169 505 U.S. 123 (1992).
170 See Sullivan, supra note 1, at 51.
171 *Forsyth County*, 505 U.S. at 136.
172 See id. at 141 (Rehnquist, C.J., dissenting).
173 Sullivan, supra note 1, at 96.
174 See id.
175 See id.
176 Id.
177 Id. at 112.
178 Id. at 112-21.

choice results in a somewhat unsettling conclusion. If we accept the theory that individual judges choose one approach over the other based on general perspectives of law, then we largely reject the judge's role as an impartial arbiter whose decisions are based on the specific facts of each case. A judge need only decide the broader question of rules against standards; once this decision is made, the decision in an individual case is often already determined. There may be little need for—or even possibility of—careful analysis of the facts and legal issues involved in a particular case.[179]

PART SEVEN | A POTENTIAL SOLUTION FROM JEWISH LAW

Perhaps a potential solution to the different problems that arise from categorizing decision-makers as rule-based judges and standard-based judges can be found in the way the categories of rules and standards apply to Jewish law. Rabbi Adler's statement, at the conclusion of his analysis of rules and standards in the context of laws of quantification, is instructive:

> It should be noted that one is not restricted to accepting one or the other of these two views relative to all cases. Rather, these theories define two ways of viewing any prescribed quantity measure, and in each particular case an independent decision will have to be made as to the nature of the quantitative measurement.[180]

The rules/standards dichotomy appears to apply conceptually to Jewish law in a manner that parallels its application to American law. Yet, as this quotation suggests, in Jewish law, individual decision-makers do not necessarily view all laws through the same approach, based on a set perspective of the role of the judge. Rather, because the choice of rules or standards describes a method of interpreting laws, Jewish decision-makers who apply the rules/ standards dichotomy tend to focus on the nature of the individual law. Instead of assuming that a decision-maker must choose, in advance, between rules and

---

179 Schlag has put this observation in stark and sarcastic terms, suggesting the possibility that "much of legal discourse (including the very fanciest law-talk) might be nothing more than the unilluminating invocation of 'canned' pro and con arguments about rules and standards." Schlag, supra note 1, at 380. A troubling corollary to this discovery is that, if individual judges are generally consistent in their choice of rules or standards, we can frequently—if not usually—predict the outcome of a case, without looking to the specific facts of the case.

180 Adler, supra note 3, at 30.

standards, scholars of Jewish law have recognized that individual laws may possess certain properties that make them more likely to be understood by particular decision-makers in terms of either rules or standards.[181]

Employing such an approach, these scholars have not been troubled by the problems that American legal scholars have encountered in analyzing the rules/standards dichotomy. When the focus is on the law, rather than on the individual decision-maker's perspective, there is no reason to expect a decision-maker to choose consistently one side of the rules/standards option. Instead, it is to be expected that the same authority will interpret some laws as rules and other laws as standards, depending on the authority's understanding of the nature of each individual law.

Moreover, the decision-maker's choice of placing laws into categories is far from predetermined. To the contrary, the decision-maker who has not made a general choice between rules and standards will have to examine each law carefully to determine its category. This decision may depend, in part, on the specific facts of the case in which the law is to be applied. Thus, in each case, the decision-maker both retains autonomy and is required to engage in extensive legal analysis, considering both the unique nature of each legal directive and, at least to some extent, the specific facts of the case.

Notably, in discussing the views of individual Supreme Court Justices, Sullivan appears to allude to an approach based more on individual laws and cases than on general and predetermined considerations. Having recognized the reality that "[n]o Justice is entirely consistent," Sullivan explains that "[m]uch depends on the nature of the constitutional claim at issue."[182] Indeed, she cites many examples of inconsistencies in the approaches of a number of Justices.[183] These examples seem to indicate that, at times, Justices pay closer attention to the specific laws and facts of cases than to concerns related to rules or standards. Ultimately, however, Sullivan categorizes the Justices in terms of whether, for the most part, they favor rules or standards.[184]

There may be reasons the approach to rules and standards in Jewish law cannot be applied to the American legal system. Perhaps as descriptive matter, American decision-makers have, in fact, generally favored either rules or standards, without considering the individual laws before deciding which method to apply. Indeed, Sullivan and others have made convincing arguments that

---

181 See id.
182 Sullivan, supra note 1, at 113 n.567.
183 See supra text accompanying notes 68-80.
184 See Sullivan, supra note 1, at 122.

many debates throughout American legal history can be understood through the lens of the rules/standards dichotomy.

Nevertheless, this depiction of past American constitutional jurisprudence need not preclude the possibility of applying to American law an approach to rules and standards more similar to that found in Jewish law. First, as a matter of historical reality, many Justices have been far from consistent in their choices of rules or standards. Indeed, as Sullivan pointed out, in the 1991 term alone there were many notable exceptions to the rules and standards analysis. One of the advantages of the approach used in Jewish law is that these inconsistencies do not pose a problem, as there is no need to view the Justices in terms of general views and troubling exceptions.

Second, even if the American rules/standards approach proves to be a moderately accurate descriptive device for American jurisprudential debates, perhaps the problems presented by this approach should motivate consideration of a different approach. The fact that one theory offers an accurate description of a given set of facts does not disqualify other theories, particularly theories that may be appealing in other ways.

At the very least, even if the current rules/standards approach developed by Sullivan and others is the most accurate way to describe past jurisprudential attitudes, it would seem possible that the problems present in the current approach might lead us to look to a different method for both judges and scholars to follow in the future. Such a method could maintain the structure of rules and standards, yet avoid some of the troubling results stemming from the current emphasis on the decision-makers' choice of uniformly applying one of the options. The approach in Jewish law might provide a basis for such a method.

CONCLUSION

Perhaps there is a fundamental reason that the approach to the rules/standards dichotomy in Jewish law is not likely to offer a plausible alternative for American law, related to Sullivan's explanation for the choice of either rules or standards in the American legal system. It is notable that, in her general analysis of reasons for rules or standards, Sullivan offers four possible arguments for rules, and four parallel arguments for standards.[185] Two of these arguments, which are somewhat universal to systems of laws and judges, are applicable in the context

---

185 See id. at 62-67.

of both the Jewish legal system and the American legal system. The other two arguments, which are unique to Western thought and American political structure, are unlikely to have particular relevance to Jewish law.[186]

Significantly, in analyzing the specific issue of why American judges choose either rules or standards, Sullivan offers only two perspectives, both of which relate uniquely to the American political system. One perspective is explicitly political, to such an extent that Sullivan called it "the political perspective." Decisions in Jewish law regarding rules and standards are not based on politically liberal or conservative philosophy.[187] The other perspective, which Sullivan finds more convincing, relates to judges' aims of maintaining judicial legitimacy.[188] Sullivan's description of the judge's role, in connection with "history, knowledge, and power," also applies specifically to the American political system, without parallels in the Jewish legal system's treatment of rules and standards.

As a descriptive matter, Sullivan's identification of these two approaches to the rules/standards dichotomy—both based in judicial considerations of the American political structure—would seem to preclude any attempt to apply a different approach, such as the one in Jewish law.[189] As a normative matter, however, it can perhaps be suggested that if American judges were to place less emphasis on their role in the American political system, they might be able to apply the Jewish legal approach to rules and standards. The result could be judges and scholars who pay less attention to political and ideological concerns, and more attention to the nature of the individual laws being interpreted and the specific facts of the cases being decided.

---

186 See supra text accompanying notes 148-53.

187 See Sullivan, supra note 1, at 96-112.

188 See id. at 112-21.

189 Indeed, Segall begins his article discussing Justice Scalia and rules with a quotation from Mark Tushnet, stating that "law is politics, all the way down." Mark Tushnet, Critical Legal Studies: A Political History, 100 Yale L.J. 1515, 1526 (1991), quoted in Segall, supra note 69, at 992.

CHAPTER 11

Of Inkblots and Omnisignificance: Conceptualizing Secondary and Symbolic Functions of the Ninth Amendment in a Comparative Hermeneutic Framework

INTRODUCTION

In recent decades, a substantial body of American legal scholarship has been dedicated to comparisons and contrasts between the Bible and the United States Constitution.[1] This scholarship is based, in part, on the premise that

---

1 For examples of groundbreaking work in this area, see Robert M. Cover, "The Supreme Court, 1982 Term—Foreword: *Nomos* and Narrative," 97 Harv. L. Rev. 4 (1983); Ronald R. Garet, *Comparative Normative Hermeneutics: Scripture, Literature, Constitution*, 58 S. Cal. L. Rev. 35 (1985); Thomas C. Grey, *The Constitution as Scripture*, 37 Stan. L. Rev. 1 (1984); Sanford Levinson, *"The Constitution" in American Civil Religion*, 1979 Sup. Ct. Rev.123 (1979); Michael J. Perry, *The Authority of Text, Tradition, and Reason: A Theory of Constitutional "Interpretation,"* 58 S. Cal L. Rev. 551 (1985). See generally Sanford Levinson, *Constitutional Faith* (1988). For more recent scholarship, see, e.g., Jaroslav Pelikan, *Interpreting the Bible and the Constitution* (2004); Chapters 3, 8, 9, and 10 in this Volume; Jack M. Balkin, *Idolatry and Faith: The Jurisprudence of Sanford Levinson*, 38 Tulsa L. Rev. 553, 571-77 (2003); David R. Dow, *Constitutional Midrash: The Rabbis' Solution to Professor Bickel's Problem*, 29 Hous. L. Rev. 543 (1992); Gregory A. Kalscheur, S.J., *Christian Scripture and American Scripture: An Instructive Analogy?*, 21 J.L. & Religion 101 (2005-2006); Francis J. Mootz III, *Belief and Interpretation: Meditations on Pelikan's "Interpreting the Bible and the Constitution,"* 21 J.L. & Religion 385 (2005-2006); Michael

these documents serve similar roles as foundational texts that delineate the supreme doctrine for their respective societies. Moreover, some scholars have found parallels in methods of biblical hermeneutics—including Jewish legal interpretation of the Torah—and American constitutional interpretation.

This chapter focuses on a particular exegetical approach common to the interpretation of the Torah and the United States Constitution: a presumption against superfluity. This presumption accords to the text a considerable degree of omnisignificance,[2] requiring that interpreters pay careful attention to every textual phrase and nuance in an effort to find its legal meaning and implications. In light of this presumption, it might be expected that normative interpretation of both the Torah and the Constitution would preclude a methodology that allows sections of the text to remain bereft of concrete legal application.

In fact, however, both the Torah and the United States Constitution contain sections that, notwithstanding a textual appearance of actual implementation, have been interpreted by at least some legal authorities as not susceptible to practical application. Specifically, in the case of the United States Constitution, the Ninth Amendment appears on its face to serve as a basis for the identification of constitutional rights not enumerated elsewhere in the Constitution. In practice, though, the Ninth Amendment has not served such a function; its harshest critics have characterized the Amendment as the functional equivalent of an inkblot, while the United States Supreme Court, though not as dismissive in tone, has resisted arguments that would rely on the Ninth Amendment as a source for the derivation of unenumerated constitutional rights.[3]

Sink, *Restoring our Ancient Constitutional Faith*, 75 U. Colo. L. Rev. 921 (2004); Steven D. Smith, *Believing Like a Lawyer*, 40 B.C. L. Rev. 1041, 1065-69 (1999); Steven D. Smith, *What Doth It Profit? Pelikan's Parallels*, 90 Minn. L. Rev. 727, 743-44 (2006); *Symposium: Scriptural Interpretation and Constitutional Interpretation*, 2009 Mich. St. L. Rev. 273 (2009).

2 Professor Yaakov Elman, a contemporary biblical scholar, has credited James Kugel with coining the term "omnisignificance" to capture

> the basic assumption underlying all of "rabbinic exegesis" that the slightest details of the biblical text have a meaning that is both comprehensible and significant. Nothing in the Bible ought to be explained as the product of chance, or, for that matter, as an emphatic or rhetorical form, or anything similar, nor ought its reasons to be assigned to the realm of Divine unknowables. Every detail is put there to reach something new and important, and it is capable of being discovered by careful analysis.

Yaakov Elman, *"It is No Empty Thing": Nahmanides and the Search for Omnisignificance*, 4 Torah U-Madda J. 1, 1 (1993) (quoting James Kugel, *The Idea of Biblical Poetry: Parallelism and Its History* 103-4 (1981)).

3 See infra part one.

In an effort to reconceptualize the function of the Ninth Amendment in American constitutional interpretation, this chapter looks to the analogue of the biblical account of the "stubborn and rebellious son," one of three legal scenarios in the Torah that, in the views of some Talmudic authorities, will never occur. According to Jewish legal scholars and philosophers, these sections of the Torah nevertheless carry considerable legal significance, albeit of secondary or symbolic value. Indeed, although these scenarios may never occur, lessons derived from them have both pedagogical and practical implications for understanding and interpreting the laws of the Torah.[4] Likewise, perhaps the Ninth Amendment should be viewed neither as a primary source for the derivation of unenumerated constitutional rights nor as an inkblot. Instead, the Ninth Amendment may serve a secondary role, providing both practical and symbolic lessons for understanding and interpreting the United States Constitution.[5]

PART ONE | THE NINTH AMENDMENT: AN INITIAL LOOK

Over the course of more than two hundred years, the United States Constitution has been the subject of detailed textual analysis. Since *Marbury v. Madison*,[6] the United States Supreme Court has operated under a presumption against superfluity, engaging in an interpretive framework that accords legal significance to every constitutional provision. Moreover, in interpreting constitutional amendments, the Court has employed an interpretive methodology that requires a remarkably close and expansive reading of the constitutional text, through which, at times, a single word can serve as the textual basis for an entire realm of rights jurisprudence. For example, in a number of leading cases addressing some of the most vital and controversial areas of American law, the United States Supreme Court has relied on an expansive interpretation of the range of rights protected under the word "liberty."[7]

In contrast, however, under current Supreme Court jurisprudence, an entire amendment to the Constitution has little, if any, direct practical application.[8]

---

4 See infra part two.

5 See infra part three.

6 5 U.S. (1 Cranch) 137, 174 (1803) ("It cannot be presumed that any clause in the constitution is intended to be without effect; and therefore such a construction is inadmissible, unless the words require it.").

7 See, e.g., *Lawrence v. Texas*, 539 U.S. 558, 577-78 (2003); *Planned Parenthood of Se. Pa. v. Casey*, 505 U.S. 833, 851 (1992).

8 See Daniel A. Farber, *Retained by the People: The "Silent" Ninth Amendment and the Constitutional Rights Americans Don't Know They Have* 1 (2007) ("The Ninth Amendment

The Ninth Amendment states, "The enumeration in the Constitution, of certain rights, shall not be construed to deny or disparage others retained by the people."[9] In the confirmation hearings considering Judge Robert Bork's unsuccessful nomination to the Supreme Court, Judge Bork famously—or notoriously—deemed the Ninth Amendment to have the functional equivalent of an inkblot that covers up the text. Because we are unable to know the substance of a text that is covered by an inkblot, we are unable to interpret and apply that text. Likewise, Judge Bork reasoned, courts cannot apply the Ninth Amendment as grounds for deriving constitutional rights, because courts simply have no means of uncovering the substance of the retained rights referenced in the Amendment.[10]

Of course, Judge Bork's statement was highly unpopular, contributing to the failure of his nomination.[11] Moreover, as a matter of normative constitutional principle, Judge Bork's approach remains the subject of considerable criticism. In contrast to his theory, scholars,[12] lower court judges,[13] and some United States Supreme Court Justices[14] have offered a variety of interpretive frameworks for understanding the Ninth Amendment as a basis for the derivation and identification of specific rights retained by the people. Nevertheless, as a descriptive matter, Judge Bork may have accurately—if inelegantly—captured the dominant approach employed by the United States Supreme Court, which continues to resist interpretive methodologies that would recognize the Ninth Amendment as a primary source for the enumeration of constitutional rights.[15]

---

is a constitutional orphan, forgotten by most and reviled by some. . . .").

9 U.S. CONST. amend. IX.

10 See *Nomination of Robert H. Bork to be Associate Justice of the Supreme Court of the United States: Hearings Before the S. Comm. on the Judiciary*, 110th Cong. 224 (1989) (statement of Judge Robert H. Bork). Cf. *Troxel v. Granville*, 530 U.S. 57, 91 (2000) (Scalia, J., dissenting) (stating that "the Constitution's refusal to 'deny or disparage' other rights is far removed from affirming any one of them, and even further removed from authorizing judges to identify what they might be, and to enforce the judges' list against laws duly enacted by the people").

11 See Sanford Levinson, *Constitutional Rhetoric and the Ninth Amendment*, 64 Chi.-Kent L. Rev. 131, 135 (1988).

12 See, e.g., Randy E. Barnett, *Restoring the Lost Constitution: The Presumption of Liberty* (2004); Farber, supra note 8; Charles L. Black, Jr., On Reading and Using the Ninth Amendment, in *Power and Policy in Quest of Law: Essays in Honor of Eugene Victor Rostow* 187 (Myres S. McDougal & W. Michael Reisman eds., 1985).

13 See, e.g., *Roe v. Wade*, 314 F. Supp. 1217 (N.D. Tex. 1970), aff'd in part, rev'd in part, 410 U.S. 113 (1973).

14 See, e.g., *Griswold v. Connecticut*, 381 U.S. 479, 486-99 (1964) (Goldberg, J., concurring).

15 Cf. Barnett, supra note 12, at 234-35 (stating that Bork's view was "sadly, well within the

PART TWO | THE TORAH AND OMNISIGNIFICANCE

If the United States Constitution can be characterized as largely omnisignificant, based on the presumption against superfluity, the Torah has been understood by legal expositors as *embodying* omnisignificance. In Jewish legal exegesis, each phrase in the Torah and each word in the Torah—indeed, even the form of the letters that comprise the words—serves as a potential source of meaningful legal interpretation.[16] Nevertheless, the Talmud cites the views of various legal authorities who conclude that as many as three legal scenarios detailed in the text of the Torah have never occurred and never will occur.[17]

Of course, consistent with the style of Talmudic analysis and argumentation, these views are not left unchallenged. Instead, the Talmud poses the obvious question: if these legal scenarios will never occur, why are they included in the Torah? The Talmud responds with a somewhat cryptic answer: "*Darosh v'kabel s'char*"—"study [these sections] and receive reward."[18] Although this answer is itself open to a variety of interpretations, the message seems clear: even if these sections of the Torah are not implemented, important lessons are to be derived from these texts.

---

mainstream of legal thought" and that "to this day courts have rarely been willing to rely upon [the Ninth Amendment] when assessing the constitutionality of statutes"); Kurt T. Lash, *Three Myths of the Ninth Amendment*, 56 Drake L. Rev. 875, 875 (2008) (stating that courts are "reluctant to rely on the Ninth Amendment at all" and that "the modern Supreme Court has studiously avoided the Ninth Amendment despite being prodded by parties before the court to rely on it"); Mark C. Niles, *Ninth Amendment Adjudication: An Alternative to Substantive Due Process Analysis of Personal Autonomy Rights*, 48 UCLA L. Rev. 85, 89-90 (2000) ("[N]o Supreme Court decision, and few federal appellate decisions, have relied on the Ninth Amendment for support. Indeed, federal courts that have discussed the Ninth Amendment have almost exclusively held that it does not confer any substantive rights.").

16 See supra note 2; Talmud Bavli, Menachoth 29b; Joseph B. Soloveitchik, *Halakhic Man* 100 (Lawrence Kaplan trans., 1983) (originally published in Hebrew as *Ish ha-halakhah*, in 1 Talpiot 3-4 (1944)) ("Our Torah does not contain even one superfluous word or phrase. Each letter alludes to basic principles of Torah law, each word to 'well-fastened,' authoritative, everlasting [laws]. From the beginning to end it is replete with statutes and judgments, commandments and laws."). See also Rabbi Aryeh Kaplan, *The Handbook of Jewish Thought* 143 (1979) ("[E]ven the most seemingly trivial passages and variations in the Torah can teach many lessons to the person who is willing to explore its depths."); Adin Steinsaltz, *In the Beginning: Discourses on Chasidic Thought* 45 (Yehudah Hanegbi ed. and trans., 1995) ("[T]he Written Torah needs endless amplification, study, and clarification. There are infinite layers of meaning, depthless beauty, and new modes of experientially living that which was revealed.").

17 See Talmud Bavli, Sanhedrin 71a.

18 Id.

To consider the implications of the Talmud's answer more fully, it may be helpful to focus on one of these three exceptional scenarios: the case of the *ben sorer u'moreh*—the "stubborn and rebellious son."[19] The case of the stubborn and rebellious son is described in Deuteronomy 21:18–21, and is expounded in detail in the Talmud and later sources. Briefly, within three months after reaching the age of thirteen, a male child defies his parents, steals from them, eats a certain quantity of meat, and drinks a certain quantity of wine; as a result, the son is subject to capital punishment.[20] As the Talmud observes, the son's conduct does not inherently warrant such a harsh penalty. Instead, according to the Talmud, the Torah prescribes this punishment as a reflection of the divine determination that, under these exceptional circumstances, the son's conduct will inevitably deteriorate until, ultimately, he will develop into a violent criminal. The son is executed while still relatively "innocent," rather than being allowed to continue along the path that will unavoidably result in his commission of a capital crime.[21]

In addition to the decidedly anomalous—indeed, *sui generis*—nature of the punishment,[22] under Talmudic jurisprudence, a number of highly unusual conditions must be met to satisfy the elements of the son's offense. For example, the Torah states that, as part of the adjudicative process, the son's parents must declare to the court that "our son does not listen to our voice."[23] Engaging in a characteristically close reading of this verse, the Talmud observes that, although the parents are depicted as speaking in the first-person plural, their statement refers to their singular "voice." Applying a hermeneutic of omnisignificance to the biblical grammar, the Talmud interprets this verse to require that the parents' voices share the same physical properties, thereby comprising a single voice.[24] In turn, the delineation of such an unlikely condition gives rise to the position that this case will never occur.[25] Somewhat paradoxically, further application of

---

19 See Deuteronomy 21:18-21. The other two exceptional scenarios are those depicted in Leviticus 14:33-53 and Deuteronomy 13:12-18.

20 See Talmud Bavli, Sanhedrin 68b-71a.

21 See id. at 71b-72a. See also Maimonides, *Commentary on the Mishna*, Sanhedrin 71b; Chaim Shmulevitz, *Sichoth Mussar* 87-88 (1980).

22 See Chapter 6 in this Volume.

23 Deuteronomy 21:20.

24 See Talmud Bavli, Sanhedrin 71a. Notably, in the original Hebrew, the distinction between the words denoting "our voice" and "our voices" is dependent on the presence or absence of one letter; thus, the Talmud's careful analysis of this word serves as an instructive illustration of the principle of omnisignificance.

25 See id.

the principle of omnisignificance then leads to the Talmud's conclusion that the study of the biblical scenario will nevertheless prove rewarding.[26]

Scholars of Jewish law and philosophy have offered numerous theories in an effort to elucidate the Talmud's conclusion. Rabbi Samson Raphael Hirsch, a leading nineteenth century biblical and legal scholar, suggests that the scenario of the stubborn and rebellious son presents a variety of salient insights about raising children.[27] For example, drawing upon the Talmud's analysis of the case, Rabbi Hirsch explains that, in addition to the legal rule that the parents' voices must be physically identical, on a secondary level, the Torah provides a symbolic illustration of the importance of parental equality, harmony, and accord.[28] If the parents are not clear, consistent, and unified in the way they educate and raise their child—"speaking in the same voice"—the son will not be punished for his conduct because the fault may lie with them rather than being an indication that he is an irredeemably culpable individual.[29] Thus, according to Rabbi Hirsch, the procedural requirement that the parents of the stubborn and rebellious son literally speak with the same voice carries a symbolic—perhaps more universal—message for other parents as well.

---

26 See id.

27 See VII Samson Raphael Hirsch, *Collected Writings* 333-48 (Feldheim 1996).

28 See id. at 347:

> The son should not be more impressed by one parent than by the other; he must be equally impressed by both. In a case where the parents are not alike, even in such supposedly superficial traits as physical appearance, and hence do not leave the same impression upon the senses, the court of justice has grounds to suspect that even this difference between the parents may have had an adverse effect on the education of the child.
>
> From this word of our Sages we infer (*darosh v'kabel s'char*) a basic prerequisite that may well be the most important factor of all in the raising of a child. In order for their endeavors to succeed, the child's father and mother must be equals, completely in agreement, of one heart and mind with regard to the education of their child and their influence upon him.

Id.

29 See id. at 347-48:

> But the damage is infinitely greater if the child's father and mother differ from one another not merely in their educational methods but on the fundamental rules and principles by which the child is to be raised. If the child sees that his parents cannot agree on what is permitted and what is forbidden then the child will often make his own decision. He will listen neither to his father nor to his mother but will turn inside himself to disobey both his parents.

Id.

Other legal scholars, such as the author of the influential medieval work *Sefer Ha-Chinuch*, explain the scenario of the stubborn and rebellious son as a cautionary tale, dramatically highlighting some of the potentially deleterious results of drunken and gluttonous behavior.[30] Accordingly, the Torah presents the paradigmatic—if unlikely—case of an individual who, upon reaching the age of maturity and legal responsibility (the age of thirteen, or *bar-mitzva*), engages in a particularly egregious pattern of disrespectful overindulgence.[31] More broadly, this section of the Torah has practical—if secondary—legal application as well, implying a general warning against less severe forms of such dangerous and excessive behavior.[32]

Finally, in addition to identifying legal and pedagogical lessons, scholars derive more general principles from the very presence in the Torah of cases that are not to be implemented. On one level, the Torah serves as a source of normative guidance for both the individual and the community, to be applied to all facets of the human condition.[33] However, as indicated by the inclusion of cases such as the stubborn and rebellious son, the Torah functions as a source of profound philosophical, theological, and mystical principles as well.[34] In this perspective, the case of the stubborn and rebellious son proves highly significant precisely because it defies implementation, thereby shedding light on the rest of the laws in the Torah, which likewise are understood to contain additional levels of meaning beyond their practical application.[35]

---

30 See *Sefer Ha-Chinuch* 333 (Chaim Dov Chavel ed., 1986).

31 See id.

32 See id. (explicating Leviticus 19:26). See also Isaac Abravanel, *Commentary on the Torah* (explicating Deuteronomy 21:18). Indeed, this warning is consistent with other biblical narratives and exhortations against such forms of excess. See Chapters 9 and 14 in this Volume. For a discussion of another example of the secondary— but practical—relevance of the laws of the stubborn and rebellious son, in the context of the commandment delineated in Leviticus 23:15-16, see Shlomo Yosef Zevin, *Hamoadim B'Halacha* 295 n.34 (1955).

33 See, e.g., Chapter 16 in this Volume ("[T]he substance of Jewish law comprises a comprehensive set of obligations, in principle addressing every area of human endeavor. Thus, the Jewish legal system regulates activities both public and private, both interpersonal and ritual, both individual and communal, thereby extending the notion of religious observance and ethical obligation to all realms of life.").

34 See Kaplan, supra note 16, at 143 ("The Torah can be understood according to its simple meaning, or according to more complex exegesis. Besides this, many allusions and mysteries can be found when one probes beneath its surface."); Soloveitchik, supra note 16, at 100 ("The mystics discern in our Torah divine mysteries, esoteric teachings, the secrets of creation; the halakhic sages discern in it basic halakhot, practical principles, laws, directives, and statutes.").

35 See Hershel Schachter, *Ginath Egoz* 3 (2007). For other views of the pedagogical value of the case of the stubborn and rebellious son, see, for example, 3 Eliyahu Dessler, *Michtav*

PART THREE | RECONCEPTUALIZING THE NINTH AMENDMENT

In light of this brief survey of approaches to the function of the case of the stubborn and rebellious son, perhaps the Ninth Amendment can be conceptualized through a similar framework. Of course, the comparison between these legal provisions may be seen as inapposite on a number of grounds, ranging from general distinctions between religious and secular legal texts to more specific differences between the roles of these particular provisions within their respective legal systems. In addition, as a threshold matter, those scholars who reject Judge Bork's position outright, who instead contend that the Ninth Amendment should provide a textual basis for the identification of individual constitutional rights,[36] may likewise reject similarities between the Ninth Amendment and the stubborn and rebellious son.[37]

Alternatively, however, given the range of scholarship that has documented parallels between the Bible and the Constitution,[38] coupled with the Supreme Court's resistance to implementing the Ninth Amendment,[39] the exegesis of the case of the stubborn and rebellious son may prove instructive. Indeed, not unlike the case of the stubborn and rebellious son, consistent with notions of omnisignificance that underlie presumptions against superfluity in the constitutional text,[40] the Ninth Amendment may serve secondary and symbolic functions as well.

M'Eliyahu 297-98 (Aryeh Carmell & Chaim Friedlander eds., 1964); Irene Merker Rosenberg, Yale L. Rosenberg & Bentzion S. Turin, *Return of the Stubborn and Rebellious Son: An Independent Sequel on the Prediction of Future Criminality,* 37 Brandeis L.J. 511 (1998-1999); Chapter 6 in this Volume. Cf. Aaron Kirschenbaum, *The Role of Punishment in Jewish Criminal Law: A Chapter in Rabbinic Penological Thought,* 9 Jewish L. Ann. 123 (1991).

36 See supra note 12.

37 To be sure, the opinion that the case of the stubborn and rebellious son will never occur is likewise not universally accepted. Indeed, other Talmudic authorities contend that the case has concrete application, see Talmud Bavli, Sanhedrin 71a, thus suggesting a further parallel to the Ninth Amendment, which is likewise the subject of conflicting views regarding its practical applicability.

38 See supra note 1.

39 See supra note 15 and accompanying text.

40 Cf. Randy E. Barnett, *The Ninth Amendment: It Means What it Says,* 85 Tex L. Rev. 1, 80 (2006) ("When Robert Bork compared the Ninth Amendment to an inkblot, he violated John Marshall's famous dictum that '[i]t cannot be presumed that any clause in the constitution is intended to be without effect; and therefore such a construction is inadmissible, unless the words require it.'"); Calvin R. Massey, *Federalism and Fundamental Rights: The Ninth Amendment,* 38 Hastings L.J. 305, 316-17 (1987) ("Construing the [N]inth [A]mendment as a mere declaration of a constitutional truism, devoid of enforceable content, renders its substance nugatory and assigns to its framers an intention to engage in a purely moot exercise. This view is at odds with the contextual historical evidence and the

For example, Kurt Lash has proposed a theory sympathetic to Judge Bork's skepticism toward deriving unenumerated constitutional rights on the basis of the Ninth Amendment.[41] In fact, Lash cites recently uncovered historical evidence in support of the argument that the Ninth Amendment is unrelated to the identification of unnamed individual liberties.[42] At the same time, however, Lash does not conclude that the Ninth Amendment remains bereft of legal significance. Instead, he proposes a "federalist" reading of the Ninth Amendment as a counterpoint to the Tenth Amendment. In Lash's theory, the Tenth Amendment posits a doctrine of enumerated federal powers that reserves other powers to the states; in turn, the Ninth Amendment emphasizes the existence of powers reserved to the states, thereby mandating a narrow construction of enumerated federal powers.[43] Under this framework, rather than articulating substantive legal doctrine, the Ninth Amendment serves a secondary function, conceptually similar to the case of the stubborn and rebellious son, indicating how to interpret other legal provisions.[44]

Although Lash's theory remains the subject of lively scholarly debate,[45] the notion that the Ninth Amendment serves a secondary interpretive function may be reflected in other approaches as well, perhaps most prominently in prevailing United States Supreme Court jurisprudence. While lower court judges and individual Supreme Court Justices have relied on the Ninth Amendment as a primary source of unenumerated individual rights,[46] the Supreme Court has resisted arguments adopting such an approach.[47] Instead, the Ninth

---

specific, articulated concerns of its framers, and violates the premise of *Marbury v. Madison* that the Constitution contains judicially discoverable and enforceable principles.").

41 See Kurt T. Lash, *Of Inkblots and Originalism: Historical Ambiguity and the Case of the Ninth Amendment*, 31 Harv. J.L. & Pub. Pol'y 467 (2008).

42 See Kurt T. Lash, *The Lost Original Meaning of the Ninth Amendment*, 83 Tex. L. Rev. 331 (2004); Kurt T. Lash, *The Lost Jurisprudence of the Ninth Amendment*, 83 Tex. L. Rev. 597 (2005).

43 See Kurt T. Lash, *A Textual-Historical Theory of the Ninth Amendment*, 60 Stan. L. Rev. 895 (2008); Kurt T. Lash, *The Inescapable Federalism of the Ninth Amendment*, 93 Iowa L. Rev. 801 (2008).

44 Cf. Michael Stokes Paulsen, *Does the Constitution Prescribe Rules for its Own Interpretation?*, 103 Nw. U. L. Rev. 857, 884 (2009) (referring to "the obvious textual fact that the Ninth Amendment is a rule of construction, not a substantive rule").

45 See, e.g., Randy E. Barnett, *Kurt Lash's Majoritarian Difficulty: A Response to a Textual-Historical Theory of the Ninth Amendment*, 60 Stan L. Rev. 937 (2008); Randy E. Barnett, *The Golden Mean Between Kurt & Dan: A Moderate Reading of the Ninth Amendment*, 56 Drake L. Rev. 897 (2008); Daniel A. Farber, *Constitutional Cadenzas*, 56 Drake L. Rev. 833 (2008).

46 See, e.g., *Griswold v. Connecticut*, 381 U.S. 479, 486-99 (1965) (Goldberg, J., concurring); *Roe v. Wade*, 314 F. Supp. 1217 (N.D. Tex. 1970), aff'd in part, rev'd in part, 410 U.S. 113 (1973).

47 See supra note 15 and accompanying text.

Amendment has been referenced in support of the Court's reliance on expansive interpretation of other constitutional provisions to derive unnamed individual liberties.[48] Thus, again not unlike the function of the scenario of the stubborn and rebellious son, the Ninth Amendment may shed light on the meaning of other sections of the Constitution, providing secondary grounds for interpreting enumerated rights to infer and identify unenumerated rights as well.

Finally, perhaps the Ninth Amendment should be understood as functioning on a theoretical or symbolic level, outside of the realm of practical application. In yet another similarity to the case of the stubborn and rebellious son, the Ninth Amendment may serve as a more general expression of the nature of the Constitution as the foundational text of the American legal system. Under such an approach, the Ninth Amendment may be understood to capture the Constitution's emphasis on rights and liberties—whether individual or collective—basic to the American legal system. Thus, through a symbolic reading, the Ninth Amendment might serve an important expressive function that frames our understanding of American law and society.[49]

CONCLUSION

As Rabbi Joseph Soloveitchik observed, Jewish legal tradition "sees the entire Torah as consisting of basic laws and [legal] principles," such that "[e]ven the Scriptural narratives serve the purpose of determining everlasting law."[50] Accordingly, in the context of biblical hermeneutics, principles of omnisignificance are applied to narrative portions of the text as well. Scholars of Jewish law "discern[ ] in every divine pledge man's obligation to bring about its fulfillment, in every promise a specific norm, in every eschatological vision an everlasting commandment . . . . The conversations of the servants,

---

48 See Niles, supra note 15, at 89 ("[A] few Supreme Court justices have mentioned the [Ninth Amendment]—usually to provide a kind of indirect thematic support for the assertion of an unenumerated right identified in another provision of the Constitution. . . ."); id. at 89 nn.11 & 12 (citing Supreme Court cases in which the Ninth Amendment is discussed).

49 For discussions of expressive theories of law, see, for example, Richard H. McAdams, *The Expressive Powers of Law: Theories and Limits* (2015); Matthew D. Adler, *Expressive Theories of Law: A Skeptical Overview*, 148 U. Pa. L. Rev. 1363 (2000); Patricia Funk, *Is There an Expressive Function of Law? An Empirical Analysis of Voting Laws with Symbolic Fines*, 9 Am L. & Econ. Rev. 135 (2007); Alex Geisinger, *A Belief Change Theory of Expressive Law*, 88 Iowa L. Rev. 35 (2002); Richard H. McAdams, *A Focal Point Theory of Expressive Law*, 86 Va. L. Rev. 1649 (2000); Alan Strudler, *The Power of Expressive Theories of Law*, 60 Md. L. Rev. 492 (2001).

50 Soloveitchik, supra note 16, at 99.

the trials of the fathers, the fate of the tribes, all teach the sons Torah and commandments."[51] Indeed, Rabbi Soloveitchik's observation expands upon a central theme in the Jewish hermeneutic tradition, exploring the complementary functions of the *halacha* and the *aggada*—the legal and narrative sections of the Torah and other legal texts.[52]

Relying in part on the complementary functions of *halacha* and *aggada* in Jewish legal theory, Robert Cover developed a similar approach to the relationship of law and narrative in the American legal system.[53] As Cover put it, "[n]o set of legal institutions or prescriptions exists apart from the narratives that locate it and give it meaning. . . . Once understood in the context of the narratives that give it meaning, law becomes not merely a system of rules to be observed, but a world in which we live."[54]

Ultimately, perhaps the Ninth Amendment functions in a manner similar to the role of biblical narrative in Jewish legal tradition. Notwithstanding differences in both form and substance, biblical narrative is no less significant than the legal sections of the Torah, teaching normative lessons that lend further meaning to the legal rules and precepts. Likewise, in both form and function, the Ninth Amendment seems to differ from the rest of the constitutional text.[55] Nevertheless, far from being superfluous, the Ninth Amendment may be understood to serve a variety of significant functions, lending deeper meaning to our understanding of the Constitution as embodying principles central not only to a system of rules, but to the society in which we live.

---

51 Id. at 100. See also Kaplan, supra note 16, at 143 ("Even the seemingly simple narratives in the Torah contain many secret meanings and lessons."). Cf. Steven L. Winter, *The Cognitive Dimension of the Agon Between Legal Power and Narrative Meaning*, 87 Mich. L. Rev. 2225, 2267 (1989) ("The entire Jewish tradition of interpretive storytelling, is a tradition of lawmaking.").

52 Soloveitchik, supra note 16, at 99-105. See generally Chapter 17 in Volume 2.

53 See Cover, supra note 1. Indeed, as I have suggested elsewhere, "Cover's very conception of *nomos* and narrative appears influenced by, if not a direct application of, the parallel notions of *halacha* and *aggada* in Jewish legal thought." See Chapter 17 in Volume 2.

54 Cover, supra note 1, at 4-5.

55 Cf. Paulsen, supra note 44; John Choon Yoo, *Our Declaratory Ninth Amendment*, 42 Emory L.J. 967, 967-68 (1993) ("Unlike other provisions of the Bill of Rights, the Ninth neither acts solely as a limitation on the federal government nor creates new rights through positive enactment. A declaratory vision of the Ninth Amendment is a dynamic one. . . .").

Legal Practice

CHAPTER 12

Reflections on the Practice of Law as a Religious Calling from a Perspective of Jewish Law and Ethics

INTRODUCTION | LIFE AS A RELIGIOUS CALLING

In thinking about the practice of law as a religious calling, it might be helpful to first consider the broader issue of the general relevance of religion to various areas of life, including work. From a perspective of Jewish law and ethics, moral conduct comprises an imperative at home and at the workplace, no less than at the house of worship.[1] Starting with the biblical text and spanning thousands of years of legal interpretation and philosophy, Jewish religious thought has addressed not only the apparently sacred, but also the seemingly mundane aspects of human behavior. Indeed, the range of *halacha*, Jewish legal

---

1 As Rabbi Joseph Soloveitchik has explained, Jewish thought "does not differentiate between the [person] who stands in [the] house of worship, engaged in ritual activities, and the mortal who must wage the arduous battle of life." Rabbi Joseph B. Soloveitchik, *Halakhic Man* 93 (Lawrence Kaplan trans., 1983) (originally published in Hebrew as *Ish ha-halakhah*, in 1 Talpiot 3-4 (1944)). Instead, Jewish law "declares that [a person] stands before God not only in the synagogue but also in the public domain, in [one's] house, while on a journey, while lying down and rising up." Id. In short, "[t]he marketplace, the street, the factory, the house, the meeting place, the banquet hall, all constitute the backdrop for the religious life." Id. at 94.

and ethical thought, encompasses all facets of the human experience, emphasizing the importance of an ethically unified life and demonstrating that every area of life has moral significance.[2]

The biblical verse that may best articulate this concept commands, "[i]n all your ways acknowledge [God]."[3] As noted in the Talmud and elaborated upon in many of the foundational works of Jewish ethical literature, this concise formulation powerfully captures a basic ethos of Jewish thought.[4] Maimonides

---

2 It may be instructive to quote at length from the eloquent words of a leading contemporary scholar of Jewish law and ethics:

> On the one hand, there may be a dualistic conception that would set up a rigid barrier between [religious and secular life], a conception that conceives of [a person's] purely natural life as intrinsically corrupt, that sees the religious as established not upon the secular but despite it. . . . On the other hand, we have a unified conception that stems from a deep-seated belief that life is basically one, that the secular and religious aspects of human experience are in fundamental harmony. . . . I think that the attitude of [the] Torah is clearly aligned with the latter view. . . . Our whole *Weltanschauung*, from eschatology to ethics, is firmly grounded upon the profound conviction that the physical, the natural, the secular, is not to be destroyed but to be sanctified. The Hala[c]ha stresses not rejection but inclusion, not segregation but transmutation. . . . The Torah is neither world-accepting nor world-rejecting. It is world-redeeming.

See 1 Rabbi Aharon Lichtenstein, *Leaves of Faith: The World of Jewish Learning* 103 (2003) [hereinafter Lichtenstein, *Leaves of Faith*].

Cf. Samuel J. Levine, *Introductory Note: Symposium on Lawyering and Personal Values - Responding to the Problems of Ethical Schizophrenia*, 38 Cath. Law. 145 (1998); Thomas L. Shaffer, *On Living One Way in Town and Another Way at Home*, 31 Val. U. L. Rev. 879 (1997).

3 Proverbs 3:6. A literal translation of the quoted phrase might read "in all your ways know Him." I have chosen the term "acknowledge," however, because, as is often true of translations, this substitution for literalism may, in fact, present a more accurate and meaningful connotation of the original as articulated in modern English. See generally Aryeh Kaplan, *Translator's Introduction to Rabbi Aryeh Kaplan, The Living Torah: The Five Books of Moses* v-vii (1981) (describing the perils of a literal translation of the Torah). See also 2 The Holy Scriptures 1763 (Jewish Publication Society of America 1955) (using the term "acknowledge" in translating this verse).

Nevertheless, there is clear significance to the use of the biblical term for "knowledge" in the original Hebrew verse, connoting a close form of intimate connection, which is applied here to an individual's relationship with God. See, e.g., Genesis 4:1; see also Yitzchak Hutner, *Pachad Yitzchak*, Purim 77-78 (1998); Iggeres Ha-Kodesh, in 2 *Kisvei Ramban* 334 (Chaim Dov Chavel ed., 1994); Rabbi Joseph B. Soloveitchik, *Family Redeemed: Essays on Family Relationships* 94-95 (David Shatz & Joel B. Wolowelsky eds., 2000). Finally, the last word in the quoted phrase is actually the pronoun "him," to which the antecedent is clearly "God." See Proverbs 3:6.

For an analysis of some of the more technical legal applications of this verse, in the context of both Jewish law and American legal practice, see Chapter 15 in this Volume.

4 See Talmud Bavli, Berachoth 63a.

understands this verse to teach that all of one's activities, pursued with proper motivation, may—and should—be performed in service to God.[5] Likewise, a classic ethical tract delineating an aspirational path toward "holiness" concludes with a citation to this verse, in support of the proposition that each individual has a unique means of achieving piety, corresponding to the unique circumstances and experiences encountered in one's life.[6]

Indeed, Rabbi Joseph Soloveitchik has explained that "[t]he idea of holiness according to the hala[c]hic world view does not signify a transcendent realm completely separate and removed from reality."[7] Rather, "[h]oliness, according to the outlook of Hala[c]ha, denotes the appearance of a mysterious transcendence in the midst of our concrete world . . . appear[ing] in our actual, very real lives."[8] Thus, "[t]ranscendence becomes embodied in [a person's]

---

5   See Maimonides, *Mishne Torah*, Laws of *De'oth* 3:2-3; Maimonides, *Shemona Perakim*, ch. 5. See also Rabbi Yosef Karo, *Shulchan Aruch* 231; *Address by Rabbi Aharon Lichtenstein*, in *By His Light: Character and Values in the Service of God* 30-32 (Rabbi Reuven Ziegler ed., 2003) [hereinafter Lichtenstein, *By His Light*]. See generally Chapter 18 in Volume 2; Samuel J. Levine, *The Broad Life of the Jewish Lawyer: Integrating Spirituality, Scholarship and Profession*, 27 Tex. Tech L. Rev. 1199 (1996) [hereinafter Levine, *Broad Life*].

  For further explication of this verse in support of the proposition that, when conducted with the proper intention, seemingly optional and mundane activities may be infused with holiness, see Rabbi Yitzchak Hutner, *Pachad Yitzchak, Pesach* 123-26 (1999); Rabbi Aryeh Kaplan, *The Light Beyond: Adventures in Hassidic Thought* 2 (1981); Lichtenstein, *By His Light*, supra, at ch. 2; Rabbi Aharon Lichtenstein, 2 *Leaves of Faith: The World of Jewish Learning* 327-29 (2004); Rabbi Menachem Mendel Schneerson, 23 *Igroth-Kodesh* 450 (1994).

  In fact, Nachmanides understands the command to "be holy" as referring specifically to activities not otherwise regulated under enumerated biblical commands. See 3 Ramban (Nachmanides), *Commentary on the Torah* 282 (Charles B. Chavel trans., 1971) (explicating Leviticus 19:2). See also Rabbi Yosef Engel, *Sefer Lekach Tov*, ch. 8, 165-66; Rabbi Mordechai Yoseph of Izhbitz, *Mei Ha-Shiloach* (explicating Numbers 30:3). See generally Chapters 9 and 14 in this Volume.

6   See Rabbi Moshe Chaim Luzzatto, *Mesillat Yesharim* 336-39 (Shraga Silverstein trans., 1966). The notion that each individual has a unique role and potential is captured in the statement of the Chassidic master Rebbe Zusia, who declared shortly before his death: "When I shall face the celestial tribunal, I shall not be asked why I was not Abraham, Jacob or Moses. I shall be asked why I was not Zusia." Elie Wiesel, *Souls on Fire: Portraits and Legends of Hasidic Masters* 120 (Marion Wiesel trans., 1972). See also Rabbi Hershel Schachter, *Nefesh Harav* 63-68 (1994); Rabbi Joseph B. Soloveitchik, *Yemei Zikaron* 9-27 (Moshe Krone ed., 1996).

7   Soloveitchik, supra note 1, at 45.

8   Id. at 46. For further discussion in Jewish thought of the concept of holiness as manifested specifically when spirituality and morality are applied to the physical aspects of human behavior, see Rabbi Chaim Yaakov Goldvicht, *Arba'a Ma'amrim B'Aggada* 21-31 (1984); Rabbenu Bachya ben Asher, *Kad Ha-kemach*, in *Kisvei Rabbenu Bachya* 350-54 (Chaim Dov Chavel ed., 1995). See also Schachter, supra note 6, at 285-86; Rabbi Mordechai I. Willig, *Am Mordechai on Tractate Berakhot* 13-14 (1992); Rabbenu Bachya ben Asher, *Shulchan Shel Arba*, in *Kisvei Rabbenu Bachya*, supra at 453.

deeds, deeds that are shaped by the lawful physical order of which [humans are] a part."[9] In short, "[t]he true sanctuary is the sphere of our daily, mundane activities, for it is there that the realization of the Hala[c]ha takes place."[10]

PART ONE | WORK AS A RELIGIOUS CALLING

Of all of life's activities, a person's work demands an arguably disproportionate amount of time and energy. Regardless of the particular form it takes, nearly every job occupies a substantial portion of an individual's most productive hours. In addition, depending on the nature of a job, a person may be required to expend considerable physical and/or psychic energy in order to perform an often mundane set of responsibilities. Thus, it would seem that a person's work may present a significant challenge to—and, accordingly, the subject of one's work may likewise be central to a discussion of—the goal of imbuing daily activities with moral and spiritual meaning.

In Jewish legal and ethical tradition, responses to this challenge are based in various conceptions and applications of the moral and spiritual potential latent in the performance of occupational tasks. For example, some jobs, perhaps exemplified in the figure of the biblical shepherd,[11] may allow for thoughtful contemplation and concentration on profound matters, largely unrelated to the often mundane nature of the work. In addition, Jewish law and ethics emphasize the moral and religious significance of fulfilling professional obligations owed to a customer or an employer.[12]

These two approaches are expressed in differing explanations of the biblical narrative stating that "Enoch walked with God."[13] A Midrashic interpretation of this verse posits that Enoch was a shoemaker, who worshipped God with every stitch.[14] This description seems to suggest that, while physically involved

---

9 Soloveitchik, supra note 1, at 45.

10 Id. at 94-95.

11 See, e.g., Malbim, *Commentary on Psalms* (explicating Psalms 23:1 and describing David's days as a shepherd as a uniquely spiritual time in David's life).

12 A biblical model for this virtue may be found in Jacob's description of his meticulous and selfless service in behalf of Laban. See Genesis 31:6, 38-40. See also Maimonides, *Mishne Torah*, Laws of *Sechiruth* 13:7; Lichtenstein, *By His Light*, supra note 5, at 41. Cf. Lichtenstein, supra at 42 (stating that "[i]t is entirely conceivable that a person may be more spiritually engaged in a less inherently spiritual activity, than a person who is engaged in an inherently spiritual activity but performs it in a very lackadaisical manner").

13 Genesis 5:22.

14 See Chapter 18 in Volume 2 (citing 1 Eliyahu Dessler, *Michtav M'Eliyahu* 34 (Aryeh Carmell & Alter Halpern eds., 1954)).

in the mundane work of shoemaking, Enoch directed his attention toward overtly spiritual pursuits, such as prayer.[15] However, some commentators were concerned that under this depiction, Enoch's thoughts might have distracted him and detracted from his work, thereby leading to a violation of his ethical duty to focus all of his energies on the task for which he was employed.[16] Instead, others explained the Midrash as teaching that Enoch worshipped and served God in the measure of honesty and integrity with which he performed his job.[17] Through the virtue of such conduct, Enoch merited the biblical praise of walking with God.[18]

On another level, many jobs may provide an avenue for the service of God through the opportunities they present to help others and to contribute to society. Thus, Rabbi Yitzchak Hutner responded with encouragement to a student who expressed concern that his choice of a secular profession was inappropriate, potentially leading him to live a "double life."[19] Citing the example of a doctor, Rabbi Hutner explained that, through his work, the student was instead engaging in a "broad life," incorporating professional activities consistent with his religious values.[20]

PART TWO | THE PRACTICE OF LAW AS A RELIGIOUS CALLING

In addition to general issues that confront many other occupations as well, lawyers may be presented with unique challenges to and, perhaps, corresponding opportunities for, aspirations of spiritual and religious expression and growth. In considering the relevance of religion to the work of lawyers, it may

---

15 A similar lesson is expressed in a famous Chassidic tale:

> A teamster in Berdichov was saying his morning prayers, and at the same time, was greasing the wheels of his wagon. He was indeed an interesting sight, praying with his grease-covered hands, and townspeople snickered, "Look at this ignoramus. He doesn't know better than to grease his wagon wheels while he is praying." The great Rabbi Levi Yitchok then came along and said, "Master of the universe, look at Your servant, the teamster. Even while he is greasing his wagon wheels he is still praising Your great and holy Name."

Kaplan, supra note 5, at 5.
16 See Chapter 18 in Volume 2.
17 See id. (citing Dessler, supra note 14, at 34-35).
18 See id.; see also Dessler, supra note 14, at 34-35.
19 Levine, *Broad Life*, supra note 5, at 1204 (citing Yitzchak Hutner, *Pachad Yitchak, Letters*, No. 94 (1991)).
20 Id.

be helpful to employ a framework that is familiar in legal thought, looking at what might be termed "substantive" and "procedural" areas of legal practice.

"Substantive" issues might include the clients a lawyer chooses to represent and the goals or causes a lawyer chooses to advocate. Although similar questions undoubtedly apply to many professions, they may be of distinct significance in the practice of law because lawyers may be—or at least may be perceived as—particularly prominent and influential members of society.[21] Moreover, although scholars have debated and offered numerous characterizations of the precise nature of the attorney-client relationship,[22] it may often be necessary for lawyers to become—or, again, lawyers may be perceived as—closely associated with the clients and causes they represent.[23]

Challenges and opportunities for the expression and fulfillment of spiritual and moral values may arise in a variety of areas of legal practice, including representation of low-income clients, vindicating clients' civil rights, family law, and even corporate law.[24] In addition, opposing lawyers in the same arena may encounter respective avenues for religious and ethical growth. Thus, in the area of criminal law, the prosecutor may find that the obligation to serve justice[25] is consistent with concepts in Jewish law and tradition emphasizing the importance of the human role in bringing justice to God's world.[26] At the same time, however, the criminal defense attorney may embrace the role of counseling, comforting, and guiding those who are in many ways often among the most

---

21 See, e.g., Charles W. Wolfram, *Modern Legal Ethics*, ch. 1 (1986).

22 See, e.g., Monroe H. Freedman & Abbe Smith, *Understanding Lawyers' Ethics* 7-9, 56-62 (2d ed. 2002); Thomas L. Shaffer & Robert F. Cochran, Jr., *Lawyers, Clients, and Moral Responsibility* (1994); Wolfram, supra note 21, at 76-78; Edward A. Dauer & Arthur Allen Leff, *Correspondence: The Lawyer as Friend*, 86 Yale L.J. 573 (1977); Charles Fried, *The Lawyer as Friend: The Moral Foundations of the Lawyer-Client Relation*, 85 Yale L.J. 1060 (1976).

23 Indeed, a perception that a lawyer's representation of a client or a cause reflects the lawyer's personal approval was the apparent impetus behind the somewhat anomalous Model Rule stating: "A lawyer's representation of a client . . . does not constitute an endorsement of the client's political, economic, social or moral views or activities." Model Rules of Prof'l Conduct R. 1.2 (b) (1983) [hereinafter Model Rules].

24 Of course, this list is representative rather than comprehensive. A more complete list would extend to many other areas of legal practice that provide a potential means for spiritual growth.

25 See Model Code of Prof'l Responsibility EC 7-13 ("The responsibility of a public prosecutor differs from that of the usual advocate; his duty is to seek justice, not merely to convict.") [hereinafter Model Code]. See also Model Rules, supra note 23, R. 3.8, Comment [1] ("A prosecutor has the responsibility of a minister of justice and not simply that of an advocate."). See generally Chapter 15 in this Volume.

26 See Levine, *Broad Life*, supra note 5, at 1206-10.

vulnerable in society, consistent with religious imperatives to assist the needy and the downtrodden.[27]

"Procedural" aspects of legal practice may likewise present challenges to and, perhaps, opportunities for spiritual expression and growth, relating to the manner in which lawyers conduct their professional obligations. The work of lawyers may often encourage—or even require—behavior that, in other contexts, might be considered less than ideal, if not downright improper. Indeed, a brief look at just a few of the tactics central to a lawyer's work demonstrates the potentially detrimental impact the practice of law may have on an individual's spiritual, moral, and ethical character.

The most fundamental element of the advocate's professional responsibility may be the obligation to argue on behalf of a client—behavior that may have the potential to lead a lawyer to develop an overly contentious personality, which may also extend to other areas of the lawyer's life.[28] Moreover, it is not uncommon for a lawyer to advocate an argument that, although not frivolous, does not comport with the lawyer's own assessment of the issue, thus requiring that the lawyer sacrifice intellectual honesty in favor of supporting the client's position.[29] Likewise, commercial and transactional lawyers, among others, may find themselves involved in a difficult bargaining process that calls

---

27   There are countless enumerations and expositions of these imperatives in sources of Jewish law and ethics, from the Torah to contemporary works. Moreover, the criminal defense attorney might point to Elie Wiesel's characterization of the approach espoused by the Chassidic master Rabbi Nachman of Breslov: "Miscreants need redemption more than saints." Wiesel, supra note 6, at 189. See id. (explaining, according to Rabbi Nachman, that "[t]o pull [others] out of the mud, [a righteous person] must set foot into that mud"; that "[t]o bring back lost souls, [a righteous person] must leave the comfort of [. . .] home and seek them wherever they might be"; and that "[a] Messiah who would seek to save only the Just, would not be the Messiah"). For further discussion of the thought and works of Rabbi Nachman of Breslov, see Chapter 18 in Volume 2.

  For perspectives of contemporary American legal ethics scholars applying many of these concepts to their work as criminal defense attorneys, see, Monroe H. Freedman, *Legal Ethics from a Jewish Perspective*, 27 Tex. Tech. L. Rev. 1131 (1996); Abbe Smith & William Montross, *The Calling of Criminal Defense*, 50 Mercer L. Rev. 443, 451-52 (1999).

28   Although Jewish thought acknowledges the necessity of argument as an element of the process of legal dispute, the Talmud suggests that, when conducted with a proper attitude and an aspiration toward resolution, the process of argument has the potential to bring individuals closer rather than perpetuating personal contentiousness. See Talmud Bavli, Kiddushin 30b; see also Lichtenstein, *Leaves of Faith*, supra note 2, at 14, 90-91.

29   See, e.g., Marvin E. Frankel, *Partisan Justice* (1980); David Luban, *The Adversary System Excuse*, in *The Good Lawyer: Lawyers' Roles and Lawyers' Ethics* (David Luban ed., 1983).

for tough and unpleasant, if not morally questionable, negotiation tactics.[30] In the courtroom, upon cross-examination, lawyers may have to treat opposing witnesses in a way that, at the very least, may be considered hostile, and may result in insult and embarrassment to the witness and to others.[31] Indeed, the prevailing basic norm of lawyering, providing a zealous representation of a client's interests, though open to some degree of interpretation, undeniably elevates the interests of the client as paramount, obligating the lawyer, as a general matter, to disregard any potential detriment to others.[32]

Attempts to confront these challenges, and possibly transform them into opportunities for spirituality, may prove even more difficult than responding to challenges arising out of substantive aspects of the practice of law. The very nature of these procedural questions, relating largely to internal issues of character, seems to defy general prescription. Perhaps resolution of these matters requires even greater attention to individual circumstances and conditions. Ultimately, then, it may be particularly appropriate for the lawyer's religious and personal values to provide moral and ethical guidance in these areas.

CONCLUSION

Numerous scholars have documented a growing ethical, psychic, and spiritual crisis in the legal profession, resulting in the emergence of various responses

---

30 See, e.g., Alvin B. Rubin, *A Causerie on Lawyers' Ethics in Negotiation*, 35 La. L. Rev. 577 (1975); Gerald B. Wetlaufer, *The Ethics of Lying in Negotiations*, 75 Iowa L. Rev. 1219 (1990).

31 See, e.g., Stephen Gillers, *Regulation of Lawyers: Problems of Law and Ethics* 465-69 (6th ed. 2002) (describing the debate over the tactics of Max Steuer's cross-examination of truthful witnesses in the criminal trial connected with the Triangle Shirtwaist Company fire).

32 See Model Code, supra note 27, Canon 7 ("A lawyer should represent a client zealously within the bounds of the law."); Model Rules, supra note 25, R. 1.3, Comment [1] ("A lawyer should also act with commitment and dedication to the interests of the client and with zeal in advocacy upon the client's behalf."). See also Freedman & Smith, supra note 24, at 79-125; Fred C. Zacharias, *Reconciling Professionalism and Client Interests*, 36 Wm. & Mary L. Rev. 1303, 1340 (1995):

> When the codes authorize lawyers to choose between emphasizing partisanship and important third party or societal interests, lawyers' natural [personal and economic] incentives encourage them to select partisanship. Lawyers who make that choice can readily justify their conduct as mandated by the code by claiming adherence to the code provisions that call for zeal.

Id. But see William H. Simon, *The Practice of Justice: A Theory of Lawyers' Ethics* (1998). See generally Samuel J. Levine, *Taking Ethical Discretion Seriously: Ethical Deliberation as Ethical Obligation*, 37 Ind. L. Rev. 21 (2003).

and movements.[33] One of the most promising initiatives in this area, the "religious lawyering movement," examines the relevance of religion to the practice of law, in the interest of demonstrating that religion may serve to provide lawyers a valuable source of moral and ethical values.[34] In recent years, through the development of conferences, symposia, and law school institutes, the movement has gained considerable prominence and many adherents.[35] As explored briefly in this chapter, Jewish legal and ethical thought has much to offer lawyers and scholars involved in this increasingly significant area of legal ethics.[36]

---

33 See, e.g., Samuel J. Levine, *Faith in Legal Professionalism: Believers and Heretics*, 61 Md. L. Rev. 217 (2002); Russell G. Pearce, *The Professionalism Paradigm Shift: Why Discarding Professional Ideology Will Improve the Conduct and Reputation of the Bar*, 70 N.Y.U. L. Rev. 1229 (1995).

34 See, e.g., Russell G. Pearce, *Foreword: The Religious Lawyering Movement: An Emerging Force in Legal Ethics and Professionalism*, 66 Fordham L. Rev. 1075 (1998).

35 See generally Russell G. Pearce & Amelia J. Uelman, *Religious Lawyering in a Liberal Democracy: A Challenge and an Invitation*, 55 Case W. Res. L. Rev. 127 (2004). See, e.g., *Symposium, Can the Ordinary Practice of Law Be A Religious Calling?*, 32 Pepp. L. Rev. 373 (2005); *Symposium, Faith and the Law*, 27 Tex. Tech L. Rev. 911 (1996); *Symposium, Lawyering and Personal Values*, 38 Cath. Law. 145 (1998); *Symposium, Rediscovering the Role of Religion in the Lives of Lawyers and Those They Represent*, 26 Fordham Urb. L.J. 821 (1999); *Symposium, The Relevance of Religion to a Lawyer's Work: An Interfaith Conference*, 66 Fordham L. Rev. 1075 (1998); Rose Kent, *What's Faith Got to Do With It?*, 6 Fordham Law. 11 (2001) (describing Fordham University School of Law's Institute on Religion, Law & Lawyer's Work).

36 See also Chapter 13 in this Volume.

A Look at American Legal Practice through a Perspective of Jewish Law, Ethics, and Tradition: A Conceptual Overview

INTRODUCTION

A discussion of American legal practice through a perspective of Jewish law, ethics, and tradition may be considered under at least two distinct, but interrelated, approaches. A historical approach might focus on the role of lawyers within the Jewish legal system. However, as part one of this chapter briefly explains, because Jewish courts classically operated under an inquisitorial system of justice, relatively few primary sources of Jewish law include material directly addressing the role or work of lawyers. Accordingly, references to lawyers in Jewish law and tradition may remain of little relevance to the practice of law in the contemporary United States, as any normative conclusions derived from these sources likely depend upon underlying assumptions inapplicable to the American adversary legal system.

Instead, as part two of the chapter suggests, an alternative approach might look more generally at areas of Jewish law and ethics that—although perhaps not always directly related to the substance of legal practice—may, in fact, offer a more accurate indication of the attitudes of Jewish tradition toward the work of American lawyers. Toward that end, part two presents a three-tiered conceptual framework suitable for an analysis of the implications, for Jewish law and ethics, of a wide range of human activities—including various aspects of the practice of law. Finally, the chapter concludes with the suggestion that Jewish legal and ethical teachings may present a model for a consideration of the broader potential of religious traditions and other value systems to inform the work and ethics of lawyers.

PART ONE | ABSENCE OF THE LAWYER IN THE TRADITIONAL JEWISH LEGAL SYSTEM

As a historical matter, primary sources of Jewish law and tradition, which include extensive discussions of nearly every aspect of life and law,[1] remain largely bereft of material relating to the role of lawyers. The absence of this material reflects the nature of the Jewish legal system, which classically functioned under an inquisitorial model of court proceedings, rather than employing the kind of adversarial model central to the American legal system.[2] Thus, in place of the expectation that lawyers will formulate, advocate, and challenge legal claims and strategies, the Jewish legal system relied upon the parties to state their claims and upon judges to insure fairness, through active judicial participation in all stages of the trial, including the questioning of parties and witnesses.[3]

Not surprisingly, therefore, the Talmud instructs against engaging in the practice of *orkhe ha-dayanim*, apparently referencing the conduct of lawyers, who provide strategic assistance to their clients.[4] Although on its face, the Talmudic principle seems to present a negative impression of the work of lawyers, the admonition likely addresses judges, who had to take great care not to allow their inquisitorial role to border upon perceived or actual favoritism toward one of the parties.[5] To the extent that the Talmud's instruction to judges incorporates an implicit critique of the practices of lawyers, such criticism is arguably directed at either outright dishonesty or forms of advocacy intended to subvert the proper role of the judges.[6] Thus, in light of the systemic

---

1 See, e.g., 1 Aryeh Kaplan, *The Handbook of Jewish Thought* 78 (1979) (noting "the multitude of laws governing even such mundane acts as eating, drinking, dressing and business . . .").

2 See, e.g., Michael J. Broyde, *The Pursuit of Justice and Jewish Law: Halakhic Perspectives on the Legal Profession* 11-12 (1996); Dov I. Frimer, *The Role of the Lawyer in Jewish Law*, 1 J. L. & Religion 297, 297-301 (1983).

3 Broyde, supra note 2, at 11-12; Frimer, supra note 2, at 297-301. See also Asher Weiss, *Minchas Asher, Devarim* 19-23 (2017).

4 Talmud, Avoth 1:8.

5 See Broyde, supra note 2, at 12-14; Basil F. Herring, *Jewish Ethics and Halakhah for Our Time: Sources and Commentary* 99, 117 n.1 (1984). See also Maimonides, *Mishneh Torah*, Laws of Sanhedrin 21:11; Bachya ben Asher, *Commentary on the Torah* 239 (Chaim Dov Chavel ed., 1991) (explicating Leviticus 23:2).

6 See Broyde, supra note 2, at 21-22. But see Mordecai Biser, *Can an Observant Jew Practice Law? A Look at Some Halakhic Problems*, 11 Jewish L. Ann. 101, 131-32 (1994) (arguing

differences between the Jewish legal model and the American legal model, looking to the historical record of the role of lawyers within the Jewish legal system
likely proves tenuous, at best, for the purposes of ascertaining attitudes in Jewish
law and tradition toward the work of contemporary American lawyers.[7]

PART TWO | A CONCEPTUAL FRAMEWORK

In the apparent absence of a direct analogue in Jewish legal tradition corresponding to the American practice of law, a more helpful mode of analysis
might instead consider attitudes in Jewish law and ethics toward conduct
typical of American lawyers. As scholars of Jewish thought have emphasized,
Jewish law aims to elevate all realms of human endeavor, prescribing ethical
conduct in every area of life.[8] In the words of Rabbi Joseph Soloveitchik,

---

that those engaged in the conduct of *orkhe ha-dayanim* are "criticized not only for seeking
to pervert the [Jewish legal] inquisitorial system by introducing elements of advocacy, but
because engaging in legal legerdemain is itself regarded as unethical.").

Over time, there has developed within courts of Jewish law a form of legal representation, though the parameters of legal advocacy remain limited, so as not to interfere with the
traditional judicial function. See, e.g., Broyde, supra note 2, at 19-23; Frimer, supra note 2, at
301-2; Herring, supra note 5, at 116-17.

7 Notably, although the Jewish legal system relies upon an inquisitorial model rather than an
adversarial model, Jewish tradition adopts the general proposition that, when conducted
with pure motives, an adversarial process will prove valuable in achieving a proper resolution of a legal issue. See, e.g., Talmud, Avoth 5:20; Talmud Bavli, Kiddushin 30b. Indeed, to
some extent the Jewish legal system incorporates an adversarial dynamic, illustrated in one
of the methods of composing a Jewish court of three judges: each party first selects a judge
to serve on the court, and together, the two judges then select a third judge. Although judges
are prohibited from favoring either party, the process is intended to insure that the position of each party will be fully and adequately presented and considered. See Broyde, supra
note 2, at 13-14; Frimer, supra note 2, at 299.

Conversely, there have long existed discussions and debates among American legal
scholars regarding the ethics and effectiveness of a system premised upon advocacy and
adversary justice. For extensive consideration of these issues, see, for example, Monroe
H. Freedman & Abbe Smith, *Understanding Lawyers' Ethics* 13-43 (3d ed. 2004); Stephen
Gillers, *Regulation of Lawyers: Problems of Law and Ethics* 315-31 (7th ed. 2005); Charles W.
Wolfram, *Modern Legal Ethics* 563-92 (1986).

8 See, e.g., Kaplan, supra note 1, at 78 (stating that the commandments "penetrate every nook
and cranny of a person's existence, hallowing even the lowliest acts and elevating them to
a service to God . . . [,] sanctify every facet of life, and constantly remind one of [one's]
responsibilities toward God."). See also Chapter 12 in this Volume; Samuel J. Levine, *The
Broad Life of the Jewish Lawyer: Integrating Spirituality, Scholarship and Profession*, 27 Tex.
Tech L. Rev. 1199 (1996) [hereinafter Levine, *Broad Life*].

"[t]he true sanctuary is the sphere of our daily, mundane activities, for it is there that the realization of [Jewish law] takes place."[9]

Thus, an analysis of the work of lawyers through a perspective of Jewish tradition would require conceptual consideration of the ethics of specific aspects of legal practice, rather than viewing the practice of law as a parochial form of activity, subject only to its own unique rules of morality and, consequently, immune from others.[10] Indeed, a number of American legal ethics scholars have similarly aimed to dispel the notion that the status of legal practice as a "profession" entitles lawyers to inherent claims of virtue and morality. Instead, these scholars have emphasized, the practice of law, like other areas of human endeavor, has the potential for virtue or for vice, depending on the manner in which it is performed.[11]

---

9 Joseph B. Soloveitchik, *Halakhic Man* 94-95 (Lawrence Kaplan trans., 1983) (originally published in Hebrew as *Ish ha-halakhah*, in 1 Talpiot 3-4 (1944)); see also Chaim Yaakov Goldvicht, *Arba'a Ma'amrim B'Aggada* 21-31 (1984); Bachya ben Asher, *Kad Ha-kemach*, in *Kisvei Rabbenu Bachya* 350-54 (Chaim Dov Chavel ed., 1995).

10 On some level, then, an assessment of the attitude of Jewish law and tradition toward the practice of law might resemble Judge Easterbrook's famous approach to the law of property in cyberspace. See Frank H. Easterbrook, *Cyberspace and the Law of the Horse*, 1996 U. Chi. Legal F. 207. Judge Easterbrook posited that "the best way to learn the law applicable to specialized endeavors is to study general rules." Id. at 207. Thus, he argued, in assessing the law of "Property in Cyberspace," the most effective approach would be to "[d]evelop a sound law of intellectual property, then *apply* it to computer networks." Id. at 208 (emphasis in original). See also Frank H. Easterbrook, *Intellectual Property is Still Property*, 13 Harv. J.L. & Pub. Pol'y 108 (1990). Likewise, the most helpful approach to the question of legal practice in Jewish law and tradition might entail the identification of general laws regarding proper and ethical conduct, which are then applied to conduct involved in the practice of law.

11 See, e.g., Robert F. Cochran, Jr., *Professionalism in the Postmodern Age: Its Death, Attempts at Resuscitation, and Alternate Sources of Virtue*, 14 Notre Dame J.L. Ethics & Pub. Pol'y 305 (2000); David Luban, *Asking the Right Questions*, 72 Temple L. Rev. 839 (1999); Russell G. Pearce, *Law Day 2050: Post-Professionalism, Moral Leadership, and the Law-as-Business Paradigm*, 27 Fla. St. U. L. Rev. 9 (1999); Russell G. Pearce, *The Professionalism Paradigm Shift: Why Discarding Professional Ideology Will Improve the Conduct and Reputation of the Bar*, 70 N.Y.U. L. Rev. 1229 (1995) [hereinafter Pearce, *The Professional Paradigm Shift*]; Patrick J. Schiltz, *On Being a Happy, Healthy, and Ethical Member of an Unhappy, Unhealthy, and Unethical Profession*, 52 Vand. L. Rev. 871 (1999); Thomas L. Shaffer, *Inaugural Howard Lichtenstein Lecture in Legal Ethics: Lawyer Professionalism as a Moral Argument*, 26 Gonz. L. Rev. 393 (1990-1991); Thomas L. Shaffer, *The Lost Lawyer: Failing Ideals of the Legal Profession*, 41 Loy. L. Rev. 387 (1995) (book review); Richard Wasserstrom, *Lawyers as Professionals: Some Moral Issues*, 5 Hum. Rts. Q. 1 (1975). See also Chapter 18 in Volume 2; Samuel J. Levine, *Faith in Legal Professionalism: Believers and Heretics*, 61 Md. L. Rev. 217 (2002) [hereinafter Levine, *Faith in Legal Professionalism*]; Samuel J. Levine, *Rediscovering Julius Henry Cohen and the Origins of the Business/Profession Dichotomy: A Study in the Discourse of Early Twentieth Century Legal Professionalism*, 47 Am. J. Legal Hist. 1 (2005).

Accordingly, an effective conceptual analogue within Jewish tradition for a consideration of American legal practice may be found in a more general three-tiered approach, which is similarly helpful in an analysis of the decidedly mundane—and ostensibly unrelated—activity of eating.[12] On one level, Jewish law includes technical legal precepts, in the form of both positive and negative commandments, regarding what food may[13]—and, at times, should[14]—be eaten, the way food should be prepared,[15] and rituals surrounding a meal.[16] More broadly, Jewish law and ethics address the manner in which individuals are instructed to use their resources, including, for example, their willingness to share their food with those who are needy.[17] Finally, Jewish thought teaches the possibility of elevating the act of eating, through the incorporation into a meal of otherwise incidental virtuous conduct, as a result of which participants may be considered, as it were, to be eating at the "table of God."[18] In turn, this analytical framework may be applied to evaluate the practice of law, in terms of technical aspects of legal practice—both substantive and tactical, broader considerations related to legal practice—including utilization of resources and abilities, and conduct incidental to the practice of law.

A. Technical Aspects of Legal Practice

Various technical aspects of the practice of law have potentially significant implications in the context of Jewish law and ethics, raising complex challenges to observance of a number of religious obligations. Concerns over these challenges have led some commentators to conclude that engaging in many areas of American legal practice may entail the express violation of Jewish law.[19]

---

12 See Hershel Schachter, *Eretz Hatzevi: Be'urei Sugyot* 286 (1992). See also Mordechai I. Willig, *Am Mordechai on Tractate Berakhot* 13-14 (1992); Bachya ben Asher, *Shulchan Shel Arba*, in *Kisvei Rabbenu Bachya*, supra note 9, at 453.

13 See, e.g., Maimonides, supra note 5, Laws of Forbidden Foods.

14 See, e.g., id., Laws of Chametz and Matzo, ch. 6.

15 See, e.g., id., Laws of *Shechita*.

16 See, e.g., id., Laws of Blessings.

17 See Schachter, supra note 12, at 286 (citing Talmud Bavli, Berachoth 55a; Maimonides, supra note 5, Laws of *Yom Tov* 6:18).

18 Talmud, Avoth 3:3.

19 See Biser, supra note 6, passim; see also Israel Greisman, *The Jewish Criminal Lawyer's Dilemma*, 29 Fordham Urb. L.J. 2413, 2419 (2002); Steven H. Resnicoff, *A Jewish Look at Lawyering Ethics—A Preliminary Essay*, 15 Touro L. Rev. 73 (1998). But see Broyde, supra note 2, passim; Michael J. Broyde, *On the Practice of Law According to Halacha*, 20 J. Halacha and Contemp. Soc'y 5 (1990); Michael J. Broyde, *Practicing Criminal Law: A Jewish Law Analysis of Being a Prosecutor or Defense Attorney*, 66 Fordham L. Rev. 1141 (1998).

Perhaps the most common concern relates to the Talmudic directive prohibiting Jewish parties from litigating a dispute in a non-rabbinic court.[20] By extension, a Jewish lawyer who represents a party in such litigation may violate a secondary prohibition against assisting others in committing a wrongdoing.[21] Although both of these prohibitions are subject to a number of exceptions and qualifications,[22] there remains a plausible argument that, in adherence to these principles of Jewish law, an attorney practicing in the United States may be obligated, at times, to decline clients, or potentially even to decline positions of employment.[23]

Similarly, a variety of business transactions have the potential of violating biblical and rabbinic prohibitions, including, for example, restrictions on charging or paying interest.[24] Although various methods have been developed for structuring transactions to comply with these restrictions,[25] in practice, the details of these methods are notoriously complex and their requirements are often challenging.[26] To the extent that a given transaction fails to comply with these requirements, and thus violates prohibitions on interest, a lawyer who facilitates the transaction may thereby violate the secondary prohibition against enabling wrongdoing.[27] In addition, the lawyer may concomitantly violate the primary substantive prohibition, which restricts not only paying or collecting interest, but also actively participating in a transaction involving interest.[28]

---

20 See Talmud Bavli, Gittin 88b; see also Broyde, supra note 2, at 41-48, 67-72; Biser, supra note 6, at 103-7; Simcha Krauss, *Litigation in Secular Courts*, 2 J. Halacha & Contemp. Soc'y 35 (1982).

21 See Leviticus 19:14. See also Biser, supra note 6, at 108-12; Steven H. Resnicoff, *Helping a Client Violate Jewish Law: A Jewish Lawyer's Dilemma*, in Jewish Law Association Studies X 191 (H.G. Sprecher ed., 2000). According to at least one commentator, the lawyer in such circumstances violates the primary prohibition against litigating in non-rabbinic courts. See Menasheh Klein, *Mishne Halakhot* cited in Broyde, supra note 2, at 50. For a response to this position, see Broyde, supra note 2, at 50-52.

22 See Broyde, supra note 2, at 53-66; see also Biser, supra note 6, at 112; Resnicoff, supra note 19, at 88-92.

23 See Biser, supra note 6, at 112-16; Dov Bressler, *Arbitration and the Courts in Jewish Law*, 9 J. Halacha & Contemp. Soc'y 105, 109-10 (1985); Resnicoff, supra note 19, at 83-96. But see Broyde, supra note 2, at 53-66.

24 See Meir Tamari, *With All Your Possessions: Jewish Ethics and Economic Life* 159-208 (1987); see also Broyde, supra note 2, at 115-22.

25 See Tamari, supra note 24, at 183-90; see also Aaron Levine, *Economics and Jewish Law: Halakhic Perspectives* 185-213 (1987).

26 See Biser, supra note 6, at 121-22.

27 See id. at 120-21. But see Broyde, supra note 2, at 53-66, 115-22.

28 See Biser, supra note 6, at 121. But see Broyde, supra note 2, at 121 (concluding that contemporary lawyers generally do not violate the primary substantive prohibition even when facilitating a transaction involving interest).

The work of a criminal lawyer represents yet another area in which commentators have evaluated potential conflicts between professional responsibilities of the practice of law and religious obligations under Jewish law. In analyzing the work of a prosecutor, some have noted Talmudic sources critical of those who assisted the Romans in apprehending Jewish defendants.[29] However, a number of scholars have found the Talmudic discussion inapplicable in the context of the American legal system, emphasizing fundamental distinctions between the conditions in contemporary American law and society and those within societies governed by Roman and other oppressive and tyrannical governments.[30] Therefore, consistent with the principle in Jewish law respecting the inherent authority of a just legal system,[31] many have concluded that, under most circumstances, there is no prohibition against assisting the American government in appropriate prosecution of Jewish criminal defendants.[32]

Attitudes under Jewish law toward the practice of criminal defense may depend on the implications and application of yet another Talmudic passage. The Talmud recounts an episode in which a rabbi was approached by individuals who were rumored to have committed a homicide and were attempting to remain in hiding.[33] After some deliberation, the rabbi decided neither to assist the suspects nor to expose them to their pursuers, but instead instructed them to hide by themselves.[34] Although a number of aspects of both the facts of the case and the rabbi's response are open to interpretation,[35] some commentators understand the rabbi's decision not to assist the apparent fugitives as consistent with the biblical command to "eradicate evil from your midst."[36] Based on this explanation, some authorities of Jewish law have found that the work of a

---

29 See Talmud Bavli, Bava Metzia 83b-84a. Over the years, codes of Jewish law have often prohibited facilitating the arrest and prosecution of Jewish criminal defendants outside of the Jewish legal system. See Biser, supra note 6, at 125 (citing sources); Michael J. Broyde, *Informing on Others for Violating American Law: A Jewish Law View*, 43 J. Halacha & Contemp. Soc'y 5, 5-14 (2002).

30 See Biser, supra note 6, at 126-27.

31 See J. David Bleich, *Jewish Law and the State's Authority to Punish Crime*, 12 Cardozo L. Rev. 829 (1991); Aaron Kirschenbaum & Jon Trafimow, *The Sovereign Power of the State: A Proposed Theory of Accommodation in Jewish Law*, 12 Cardozo L. Rev. 925 (1991); Aaron Rakefet-Rothkoff, *Dina D'Malkhuta Dina—The Law of the Land in Halakhic Perspective*, 13 Tradition 5 (1972); Hershel Schachter, *"Dina De'malchusa Dina": Secular Law as a Religious Obligation*, 1 J. Halacha & Contemp. Soc'y 103 (1981).

32 See Broyde, supra note 2, at 83-88; Biser, supra note 6, at 126-27; Broyde supra note 29 passim; Schachter, supra note 31, at 117-19.

33 See Talmud Bavli, Niddah 61a.

34 See id.

35 See Broyde, supra note 2, at 91-94; Schachter, supra note 31, at 120-21.

36 Deuteronomy 19:19. See Schachter, supra note 31, at 121.

criminal defense attorney, typically requiring representation and active assistance of defendants who have—in fact—committed crimes,[37] would likely violate the command.[38] Again, however, in the view of others scholars, this analysis would not pertain to the American criminal justice system, which sanctions—and mandates—the function of the criminal defense attorney, not as a means of subverting justice, but as integral to insuring the fairness of the process through which guilty criminals are prosecuted, and potentially convicted and punished.[39]

In addition to substantive challenges the practice of law may pose to various areas of Jewish religious observance, a number of tactics often expected of lawyers likewise seem to conflict with aspects of Jewish law and ethics. For example, the lawyer's duty to advocate the position of the client includes advancing arguments that, although not frivolous, may not comport with the lawyer's own factual or legal assessment.[40] Commercial and transactional lawyers, among others, may find themselves involved in a difficult bargaining process that calls for tough and aggressive, if not morally questionable, negotiation tactics.[41] In the courtroom, lawyers may have to resort to unpleasant—even insulting or embarrassing—treatment of opposing witnesses.[42] Perhaps most significantly, the prevailing basic norm of lawyering requires zealous representation of a client's interests, broadly understood to include disregarding any consequences the lawyer's actions may have on others.[43]

---

37 See, e.g., Alan M. Dershowitz, *The Best Defense* xiv (1982) (stating that "the vast majority of criminal defendants are [factually] guilty of the crimes with which they are charged.").

38 See Biser, supra note 6, at 128; Schachter, supra note 31, at 121-22.

39 See Broyde, supra note 2, at 94-96. In the words of Lon Fuller, our criminal justice system "aims at keeping sound and wholesome the procedures by which society visits its condemnation on an erring member." Lon L. Fuller, *The Adversary System*, in *Talks on American Law* 35 (Harold J. Berman ed., 1961).

40 Indeed, a criminal defense attorney and, according to some, an attorney in a civil case, may—arguably should—cross-examine a truthful adversarial witness in a manner designed to discredit the witness in the eyes of the jury, and may rely on truthful evidence to persuade the jury of an inference the lawyer knows is false. See Chapter 15 in this Volume.

41 See, e.g., Geoffrey M. Peters, *The Use of Lies in Negotiation*, 48 Ohio St. L.J. 1 (1987); Alvin Rubin, *A Causerie on Lawyers' Ethics in Negotiation*, 35 La. L. Rev. 577 (1975); Gerald Wetlaufer, *The Ethics of Lying in Negotiations*, 75 Iowa L. Rev. 1219 (1990). See also Broyde, supra note 2, at 123-25; Steven H. Resnicoff, *Lying and Lawyering: Contrasting American and Jewish Law*, 77 Notre Dame L. Rev. 937 (2002); Thomas L. Shaffer, *On Lying for Clients*, 71 Notre Dame L. Rev. 195 (1996).

42 See, e.g., Gillers, supra note 7, at 367-71 (describing the debate over the tactics of Max Steuer's cross-examination of truthful witnesses in the criminal trial connected with the Triangle Shirtwaist Company fire).

43 See Model Code of Prof'l Responsibility Canon 7 (1980) ("A lawyer should represent a client zealously within the bounds of the law."); Model Rules of Prof'l Conduct R. 1.3 cmt (2002) ("A lawyer should act with commitment and dedication to the interests of the client

In short, the practice of law in the American adversary system of justice may entail tactics that involve elements of intellectual dishonesty, decidedly hostile behavior toward others, and a general disregard for the interests of anyone but the client. Such tactics seem not only in potential conflict with substantive aspects of Jewish law, but also, on some level, fundamentally incompatible with basic Jewish ethical tenets and teachings.[44] Indeed, concerns over the nature of these and other adversarial tactics have motivated efforts among leading American ethics scholars to reassess, rethink, and even reformulate the ethical obligations of American lawyers.[45]

Thus, even a brief survey of substantive and tactical aspects of legal practice demonstrates a number of areas of potential conflict between the lawyer's professional obligations and the requirements of Jewish law. As presented here, these issues are intended to illustrate some of the considerations involved in analyzing the American practice of law under Jewish legal tradition. Resolution of these issues requires a thorough and accurate understanding of the complexities of Jewish law, American law, and American legal practice, all on their own terms, coupled with the ability to then determine the relationship between them.

B. Broader Aspects of Legal Practice: Utilization of Resources and Abilities

Beyond technical aspects, both substantive and tactical, of the practice of law, a consideration of legal practice through a perspective of Jewish tradition might

---

and with zeal in advocacy upon the client's behalf."). See also Freedman & Smith, supra note 7, at 71-127.

44 See Biser, supra note 6, at 129-35; Greisman, supra note 19, at 2420-26; Resnicoff, supra note 19, at 96-104. See also Rabbi Menachem Mendel Blachman, *The Sacrifice of Intellectual Honesty*, https://www.kby.org/english/torat-yavneh/view.asp?id=4055

45 See, e.g., William H. Simon, *The Practice of Justice: A Theory of Lawyers' Ethics* (1998); David Luban, *The Adversary System Excuse*, in *The Good Lawyer: Lawyers' Roles and Lawyers' Ethics* 83 (David Luban ed., 1983); Heidi Li Feldman, *Codes and Virtues: Can Good Lawyers Be Good Ethical Deliberators?*, 69 S. Cal. L. Rev. 885 (1996); Robert W. Gordon, *Corporate Law Practice as a Public Calling*, 49 Md. L. Rev. 255 (1990); Russell G. Pearce, *Model Rule 1.0: Lawyers are Morally Accountable*, 70 Fordham L. Rev. 1805 (2002); Gerald J. Postema, *Moral Responsibility in Professional Ethics*, 55 N.Y.U. L. Rev. 63 (1980); Murray L. Schwartz, *The Professionalism and Accountability of Lawyers*, 66 Calif. L. Rev. 669 (1978); Thomas L. Shaffer, *The Unique, Novel, and Unsound Adversary Ethic*, 41 Vand. L. Rev. 697 (1988); Serena Stier, *Legal Ethics: The Integrity Thesis*, 52 Ohio St. L. J. 551 (1991); Maura Strassberg, *Taking Ethics Seriously: Beyond Positivist Jurisprudence in Legal Ethics*, 80 Iowa L. Rev. 901 (1995); W. Bradley Wendel, *Public Values and Professional Responsibility*, 75 Notre Dame L. Rev. 1 (1999); Fred C. Zacharias & Bruce A. Green, *Reconceptualizing Advocacy Ethics*, 74 Geo. Wash. L. Rev. 1 (2005); Fred C. Zacharias, *Reconciling Professionalism and Client Interest*, 36 Wm. & Mary L. Rev. 1303 (1995). See generally Samuel J. Levine, *Taking Ethical Discretion Seriously: Ethical Deliberation as Ethical Obligation*, 37 Ind. L. Rev. 21 (2003).

look to the manner in which lawyers utilize their resources and abilities. Drawing upon the example of sanctifying the physical and mundane by providing food for those in need[46] in accordance with the imperative of charity,[47] lawyers may likewise find virtue in providing legal assistance to those for whom it might otherwise remain unavailable, in the form of pro bono representation.[48] Moreover, in spite of the aversion toward professional advocacy in the Jewish legal system,[49] the biblical verse, "[o]pen your mouth for those who are mute . . . open your mouth, judge righteously, and plead the cause of those who are poor and needy,"[50] indicates that Jewish law mandates adequate presentation of the claims of parties unable to represent themselves.[51] Thus, to the extent that Jewish thought would generally approve of the practice of law within the American adversary system of justice,[52] it would seem that protecting the rights of the needy may qualify as a particularly appropriate form of advocacy.[53]

On a broader level, Jewish tradition emphasizes the duty, incumbent upon both individuals and society, to insure justice, with special care for those who are downtrodden and disadvantaged.[54] The Jewish nation originated in the

---

46 See supra note 17 and accompanying text.

47 See, e.g., Maimonides, supra note 5, Laws of *Matanoth Ani'im*, ch. 10; Tamari, supra note 24, at 248-62. See also Joseph B. Soloveitchik, *Yemei Zicharon* 43-45 (1996).

48 See, e.g., Steven Lubet & Cathryn Stewart, *A "Public Assets" Theory of Lawyers' Pro Bono Obligations*, 145 U. Pa. L. Rev. 1245 (1997); Deborah L. Rhode, *Cultures of Commitment: Pro Bono for Lawyers and Law Students*, 67 Fordham L. Rev. 2415 (1999).

49 See supra notes 2-6 and accompanying text.

50 Proverbs 31:8-9. See also Yechiel Hillel Altschuller, *Metzudath Dovid* (commenting on Proverbs 31:8-9).

51 See Joseph Karo, *Kesef Mishne* (commenting on Maimonides, supra note 5, Laws of *Sanhedrin* 21:11); Joseph Karo, *Shulchan Aruch Choshen Mishpat* 17:9; Maimonides, supra note 5, Laws of *Sanhedrin* 21:11.See also Talmud Yerushalmi, Sanhedrin 3:8, cited in Herring, supra note 5, at 96; Broyde, supra note 2, at 13, 21-22; Herring, supra note 5, at 102-6; Rabbi Shlomo ben Adret, *Teshuvoth ha-Rashba* 2:393, cited in Broyde, supra note 2, at 21.

52 See supra part two, section A.

53 See Deborah L. Rhode, *Access to Justice* (2004); *2004 Symposium Transcript: Access to Justice: Does it Exist in Civil Cases?*, 17 Geo. J. Legal Ethics 455 (2004); *Conference on the Delivery of Legal Services to Low-Income Persons: Professional and Ethical Issues*, 67 Fordham L. Rev. 1713 (1999); *Colloquium, Deborah L. Rhode's Access to Justice*, 73 Fordham L. Rev. 841 (2004); Deborah L. Rhode, *Access to Justice*, 69 Fordham L. Rev. 1785 (2001); Deborah L. Rhode, *Access to Justice: Connecting Principles to Practice*, 17 Geo. J. Legal Ethics 369 (2004).

54 See Soloveitchik, supra note 9, at 91 (describing the attributes of the leader who "takes up [a] stand in the midst of the concrete world, [with] feet planted firmly on the ground of reality, and [. . .] looks about and sees, listens and hears, and publicly protests against the oppression of the helpless, the defrauding of the poor, and the plight of the orphan"); see also id. (quoting the renowned scholar and communal leader, Rabbi Chaim of Brisk, stating that the "function of a rabbi" is primarily "[t]o redress the grievances of those who are abandoned and alone, to protect the dignity of the poor, and to save the oppressed from the hands

figure of Abraham, whose arguments in behalf of the people of Sodom and Gomorrah stand as a model of advocating for justice.[55] Likewise, the imperative of striving to achieve social justice and fairness, with an eye toward mercy and compassion for those less fortunate, pervades sources of Jewish law and ethics, in the form of legal precepts, dramatic narrative, and hortatory exhortation.[56] Thus, it is not uncommon for American lawyers working for social justice to see themselves as following the powerful teachings, if not the religious traditions, of the biblical prophets.[57] Indeed, in light of the measure of power and influence lawyers often attain, in both public and private arenas, the practice of law may carry a corresponding obligation to counsel disenfranchised clients[58]and to work to protect their rights and interests.[59]

---

of [the] oppressor," more so than to provide "ritual decisions" or "political leadership"); Tamari, supra note 25, at 242-77.

55 See Genesis 18:20-33.See also Rabbi Nafatali Tzvi Berlin, *Ha'emek Davar, Introduction to Commentary on Genesis* (Yeshivat Volojine ed. 1999); 2 Eliyahu Dessler, *Michtav M'Eliyahu* 181-82 (Aryeh Carmell & Chaim Friedlander eds., 1963).

56 See, e.g., Chapter 17 in Volume 2. See also Maimonides, supra note 5, Laws of *Yom Tov* 6:18, Laws of *Megillah* 2:17; Tamari, supra note 24, at 242-77.

57 See Jerold S. Auerbach, *Rabbis and Lawyers: The Journey from Torah to Constitution*, passim (1990); Thomas L. Shaffer, *The Biblical Prophets as Lawyers for the Poor*, 31 Fordham Urb. L.J. 15 (2003); Thomas L. Shaffer, *Lawyers and the Biblical Prophets*, 17 Notre Dame J.L. Ethics & Pub. Pol'y 521 (2003); Thomas L. Shaffer, *Lawyers as Prophets*, 15 St. Thomas L. Rev. 469 (2003). See also Ronald R. Garet, *Judges as Prophets: A Coverian Interpretation*, 72 S. Cal. L. Rev. 385 (1999).

58 See, e.g., Freedman & Smith, supra note 7, at 6-9, 49-55; Thomas L. Shaffer & Robert F. Cochran, Jr., *Lawyers, Clients, and Moral Responsibility* (1994); Wolfram, supra note 7, at 76-78; Edward Dauer & Arthur Leff, *Correspondence, The Lawyer as Friend*, 86 Yale L.J. 573 (1977); Charles Fried, *The Lawyer as Friend: The Moral Foundations of the Lawyer-Client Relation*, 85 Yale L.J. 1060 (1976).

59 For perspectives of contemporary American legal ethics scholars applying many of these concepts to the work of Jewish lawyers advocating social justice, see, e.g., Monroe H. Freedman, *Legal Ethics from a Jewish Perspective*, 27 Tex. Tech L. Rev. 1131 (1996); Samuel J. Levine & Russell G. Pearce, *Rethinking the Legal Reform Agenda: Will Raising the Standards for Bar Admission Promote or Undermine Democracy, Human Rights, and Rule of Law?*, 77 Fordham L. Rev. 1635, 1658-59 & nn.86-87 (2009); Sanford Levinson, *Identifying the Jewish Lawyer: Reflections on the Construction of Professional Identity*, 14 Cardozo L. Rev. 1577, 1578-79 (1993); Russell G. Pearce, *Jewish Lawyering in a Multicultural Society: A Midrash on Levinson*, 14 Cardozo L. Rev. 1613, 1635-36 (1993); Russell G. Pearce, *The Jewish Lawyer's Question*, 27 Tex. Tech L. Rev. 1259 (1996); Nancy B. Rapoport, *Living "Top-Down" in a "Bottom-Up" World: Musings on the Relationship Between Jewish Ethics and Legal Ethics*, 78 Neb. L. Rev. 18 (1999); Abbe Smith & William Montross, *The Calling of Criminal Defense*, 50 Mercer L. Rev. 443, 451 (1999). See also Chapter 12 in this Volume; Levine, *Broad Life*, supra note 8; Amy Porter, *Representing the Reprehensible and Identity Conflicts in Legal Representation*, 14 Temp. Pol. & Civ. Rts. L. Rev. 143 (2004). Cf. *Conference, Lawyers, Religious Faith, and Social Justice: Our Responsibility to "the Orphan, the Widow, the Alien" and "the Least of These,"* Pepperdine

C. Conduct Incidental to the Practice of Law

Finally, Jewish tradition mandates, more generally, appropriate modes of conduct in the course of all of life's daily activities. Thus, for example, in addition to observing dietary laws and sharing food with those in need, the mundane act of taking part in a meal can be transformed into a noble pursuit. For example, by infusing their meal with spiritual study, participants are considered to be eating at the "table of God."[60] More broadly, building on the biblical verse that commands "in all of your ways acknowledge [God],"[61] Jewish thought has emphasized that all of life's endeavors, viewed and carried out in proper perspective, have the potential to be performed in a way that constitutes serving God.[62]

Among various occupations, the practice of law may present some of the most formidable challenges to and, conversely, some of the most promising opportunities for acknowledging God in all of one's ways.[63] Legal practice increasingly demands a disproportionate degree of the lawyer's time and energy, dominating both the intellect and the emotions, amidst an often pressured and combative atmosphere. Under such circumstances, the lawyer may find it difficult to maintain an appropriate level of respectful behavior toward others, including clients, coworkers, and professional adversaries. Of course, by nature, legal representation and advocacy usually require a measure of argumentation and confrontation.[64] Nevertheless, to the extent that common courtesies and basic morals sometimes seem trivial or quaint in such an atmosphere,[65] Jewish law and ethics may provide lawyers a particularly

---

University School of Law (Feb. 4-5, 2005); Thomas L. Shaffer, *On Being a Christian and a Lawyer* 35-104 (1981); Thomas L. Shaffer, *Should a Christian Lawyer Serve the Guilty?*, 23 Ga. L. Rev. 1021 (1989).

60 Talmud, Avoth 3:3.

61 Proverbs 3:6.

62 See Chapter 12 in this Volume.

63 For more general applications of the principle of serving God through proper conduct in the workplace, see Rabbi Reuven Ziegler, *By His Light: Character and Values in the Service of God, Based on Addresses by Rabbi Aharon Lichtenstein* 1-74 (2003); Chapter 12 in this Volume; Yitzchok A. Breitowitz, *The Spiritual Challenges of the Workplace*, 62 Jewish Action 18 (2002); David Hojda, *Personal and Financial Integrity and Halachah*, 66 Jewish Action 32 (2005) (reviewing several books relevant to these issues). See also Howard Gardner et al., *Good Work: When Excellence and Ethics Meet* (2001).

64 For different views on the appropriate degree of confrontational behavior in practicing law, compare, e.g., *Final Report of the Committee on Civility of the Seventh Federal Judicial Circuit*, 143 F.R.D. 441 (1992), with Amy R. Mashburn, *Professionalism as Class Ideology: Civility Codes and Bar Hierarchy*, 28 Val. U. L. Rev. 657 (1994). See also Freedman & Smith, supra note 8, at 123-27.

65 See, e.g., Robert S. Caine, *Letter, A Lawyer's View of Being a Litigant*, N.Y.L.J., May 16, 1994, at 2, cited in Gillers, supra note 7, at 68:

valuable perspective, serving as a reminder of the imperative to serve God and incorporate morality in all of life's activities.

CONCLUSION

As Rabbi Soloveitchik has eloquently explained, Jewish thought "does not differentiate between the [person] who stands in [the] house of worship, engaged in ritual activities, and the mortal who must wage the arduous battle of life."[66] Jewish tradition "rejects such a personality split, such a spiritual schizophrenia,"[67] instead "declar[ing] that [a person] stands before God not only in the synagogue but also in the public domain, in [one's] house, while on a journey, while lying down and rising up."[68] In short, "[t]he marketplace, the street, the factory, the house, the meeting place, the banquet hall, all constitute the backdrop for the religious life."[69] Thus, Jewish law and ethics inform all facets of human behavior, from overtly religious settings, to the workplace, to leisurely activities.[70] In some ways, from a perspective of Jewish tradition, the

---

> As a litigant, you're often subjected to indignities and lack of consideration by lawyers and judges.
>
> . . .
>
> There's something wrong with us lawyers—and judges, too—when we can't realize the harm we're doing to our clients and to the public, the heartache and frustration and pain we cause to others because we fail to attend civilly and promptly to the needs of others for communication.

Id. See also Steven G. Gey, *A Tribute to Steve Goldstein: Introduction: It Just Isn't Fair*, 22 Fla. St. U. L. Rev. 799, 800 (1995) ("We lawyers are many fine things, but we are usually not very good at impersonating human beings. We are often a cold and competitive lot, and our time is far too precious to squander it on the common decencies of ordinary human interaction."); Thomas L. Shaffer, *Towering Figures, Enigmas, and Responsive Communities in American Legal Ethics*, 51 Me. L. Rev. 229, 239 (1999) (advising graduating law students "not to forget the morals they brought to law school, not to let law professors dissuade them from what they had learned from their mothers and their towns, from their religious formation and from their friends and teachers in college"). For a similar critique of doctors, see Barron H. Lerner, *Practicing Medicine Without a Swagger*, N.Y. Times, Aug. 23, 2005, at F6 (describing "some physicians [who] became vain and arrogant, making extraordinary demands and openly misbehaving," including "certain surgeons who ran operating rooms like fiefs, screaming at staff members and even throwing surgical instruments to signify their discontent").

66 Soloveitchik, supra note 9, at 93.

67 Id.

68 Id.

69 Id. at 94.

70 Indeed, the imperative to behave properly applies as much on a basketball court as in a court of law. Thus, consistent with the three-tiered conceptual framework that illustrates

American practice of law constitutes yet another area of activity, to be analyzed and sanctified in accordance with its intrinsic challenges to, and opportunities for, religious observance and spirituality.

Notably, in recent years there has developed the wide perception of a crisis within legal practice,[71] representative of the kind of "deep fissure in one's

---

different ways legal practice may accord with Jewish law and ethics, various aspects of engaging in sports may provide both challenges to, and opportunities for, serving God.

For example, on a technical level, in adherence to Jewish religious observance, an individual may not participate in sports activities on the Sabbath or a Holy Day. See, e.g., Ira Berkow, *When Basketball is a Matter of Faith: A Budding Star Balances His Game and His Religion*, N.Y. Times, Aug. 25, 2000, at D1 (describing student who accepted offer to play on basketball team at a Division I college, emphasizing that he would not play on the Sabbath); Murray Chass, *On Yom Kippur, Green Opts to Miss at Least One Game*, N.Y. Times, Sept. 23, 2004 (describing baseball player Shawn Green's decision not to play on Yom Kippur during the 1994 pennant race); Levinson, supra note 59, at 1579-81 (describing Sandy Koufax's decision not to pitch on Yom Kippur, including the first game of the 1965 World Series, and Hank Greenberg's decision not to play on Yom Kippur during the 1934 pennant race); Alan Schwarz, *In the Spirit of Koufax*, N.Y. Times, Sept. 9, 2001 (describing Shawn Green's decision not to play on Yom Kippur during the 1991 pennant race).

On a broader level, athletes might dedicate some of the money and fame they have earned for the benefit of noble causes, such as assisting those in need.

Finally, perhaps most instructive for a consideration of the practice of law, athletes may demonstrate moral character in the way they conduct themselves in the midst of competitive play. See Berkow, supra, at D4 (quoting student's observation that "Torah and basketball go hand in hand for me. Torah makes me a better basketball player because it emphasizes good character, integrity and responsibility. You have to be on time, respect others and work hard."); Ziegler, supra note 63, at 42-43:

> [T]he world of sports is, in a certain sense, trivial; mature adults are running around trying to put a ball through a hole. Nevertheless, moral qualities can and do come into play: cooperation, team [ ] play, an attempt to get the maximum out of yourself, etc. The inherent effort of the person . . . or the loneliness of the long-distance runner in . . . isolation, are very significant moral elements. . . . [T]here is no question that within the essentially trivial world of sports, real moral greatness and real moral degradation can be seen. If you see someone on the basketball court who wants only to shoot and score, and defense means nothing to [the player], this is not simply disturbing to another basketball player, but is morally repugnant.

71 See Mary Ann Glendon, *A Nation Under Lawyers: How the Crisis in the Legal Profession is Transforming American Society* (1994); Anthony T. Kronman, *The Lost Lawyer: Failing Ideals of the Legal Profession* (1993); Sol M. Linowitz with Martin Mayer, *The Betrayed Profession: Lawyering at the End of the Twentieth Century* (1994); see also sources cited supra note 11.

psychic identity" described by Rabbi Soloveitchik.[72] Numerous theories have been offered to identify both causes and symptoms of dispirit and discontent among lawyers,[73] prompting the establishment of various movements and proposals in response.[74] One of the most promising responses has resulted in the emergence of a religious lawyering movement,[75] dedicated to examining and demonstrating the relevance of religious values to the practice of law.[76] Ultimately, then, from a perspective of American legal practice, Jewish legal and ethical teachings may present a model for the way religious traditions and other value systems can help inform understanding of—and possibly help improve attitudes toward—the work of American lawyers.[77]

---

72 Soloveitchik, supra note 9, at 93. See also Samuel J. Levine, *Introductory Note: Symposium on Lawyering and Personal Values: Responding to the Problems of Ethical Schizophrenia*, 38 Cath. Law. 145 (1998); Thomas L. Shaffer, *On Living One Way in Town and Another Way at Home*, 31 Val. U. L. Rev. 879 (1997).

73 See supra note 71.

74 See, e.g., Freedman & Smith, supra note 7, at 122-27; Gillers, supra note 7, at 9-13; Rob Atkinson, *A Dissenter's Commentary on the Professionalism Crusade*, 74 Tex. L. Rev. 259 (1995); Levine, *Faith in Legal Professionalism*, supra note 11; Pearce, *The Professional Paradigm Shift*, supra note 11.

75 See, e.g., Howard Lesnick, *Riding the Second Wave of the So-Called Religious Lawyering Movement*, 75 St. John's L. Rev. 283 (2001); Russell G. Pearce, *Foreword: The Religious Lawyering Movement: An Emerging Force in Legal Ethics and Professionalism*, 66 Fordham L. Rev. 1075 (1998); Russell G. Pearce & Amelia J. Uelmen, *William A. Brahms Lecture on Law and Religion: Religious Lawyering in a Liberal Democracy: A Challenge and an Invitation*, 55 Case W. Res. L. Rev. 127 (2004); Robert K. Vischer, *Heretics in the Temple of Law: The Promise and Peril of the Religious Lawyering Movement*, 19 J. L. & Religion 427 (2003-4).

76 See, e.g., Robert F. Cochran, Jr., *Introduction: Can the Ordinary Practice of Law be a Religious Calling?*, 32 Pepp. L. Rev. 373 (2005); Rose Kent, *What's Faith Got to Do With It?*, 6 Fordham Law. 11 (Summer 2001) (describing Fordham University School of Law's Institute on Religion, Law & Lawyer's Work); *Symposium, Faith and the Law*, 27 Tex. Tech L. Rev. 925 (1996); *Symposium, Lawyering and Personal Values*, 38 Cath. Law. 145 (1998); *Symposium, Rediscovering the Role of Religion in the Lives of Lawyers and Those They Represent*, 26 Fordham Urb. L.J. 821 (1999); *Symposium, The Relevance of Religion to a Lawyer's Work: An Interfaith Conference*, 66 Fordham L. Rev. 1075 (1998).

77 Cf. Gardner et al., supra note 63, at 248:

> You—like the rest of us—will find it very difficult to stay on course unless you feel loyal to an enduring tradition. Sometimes your loyalty or trust may be based on religious faith . . . . Without strong foundations in traditions that give meaning to the future, it is hard to keep up professional values under the pressure of countervailing forces. And so, as often as needed, unclutter your mind: Revisit those codes, documents, and exemplars that are integral to your domain—whether they are as ancient as the words of Moses, Hammurabi, or Hippocrates, or as recent as the mission statement of your favorite organization.

CHAPTER 14

Taking Ethics Codes Seriously: Broad Ethics Provisions and Unenumerated Ethical Obligations in a Comparative Hermeneutic Framework

INTRODUCTION

In an influential 1991 law review article, Professor Geoffrey Hazard described the "legalization" of the rules governing the legal profession.[1] As Professor Hazard observed, ethics codes have evolved from the status of "fraternal norms issuing from an autonomous professional society" to become "a body of judicially enforced regulations."[2] In Hazard's words, ethics rules have developed into "a code of public law enforced by formal adjudicative disciplinary process."[3] Building on Hazard's work, Professor Fred Zacharias noted that "[o]ver time, the professional codes governing lawyer behavior have become statutory in form."[4]

Yet, pointing to the presence of broad ethics provisions, leading scholars have questioned the extent to which ethics codes can accurately be conceptualized as a form of legislation. In his landmark *Modern Legal Ethics*, Professor Charles Wolfram faulted both the Model Code of Professional

---

1 Geoffrey C. Hazard, Jr., *The Future of Legal Ethics*, 100 Yale L.J. 1239, 1241-42 (1991).

2 Id. at 1249.

3 Id. at 1241. Cf. Charles W. Wolfram, *Modern Legal Ethics* 67 (1986) (stating that "the enforcement of the provisions of lawyer codes in lawyer discipline and other proceedings demonstrates clearly that the codes are legal prescriptions in every conventional sense").

4 Fred C. Zacharias, *Specificity in Professional Responsibility Codes: Theory, Practice, and the Paradigm of Prosecutorial Ethics*, 69 Notre Dame L. Rev. 223, 223 (1993).

Responsibility and the Model Rules of Professional Conduct for "contain[ing] vague provisions."[5] As Professor Richard Painter put it, although "[ethics] codes have migrated away from broad standards and toward clearly defined rules[,] ... many standards still prevail."[6]

Responding to these critiques, this chapter aims to take seriously both the legislative form of ethics codes and their interpretation. Toward that aim, the chapter looks to interpretive methodologies employed in American constitutional law and Jewish law to provide both descriptive and normative models for the analysis of ethics codes. Specifically, the chapter focuses on the hermeneutic practice, applicable to all three of the legislative systems examined, of deriving unenumerated laws through the interpretation of broad provisions.

Part one of the chapter documents the increasingly legislative form of ethics regulations, resulting, first, in the promulgation of the Model Code and, later, in the appearance of the Model Rules. At the same time, this part addresses the criticism that Professor Wolfram and other scholars have leveled against broad ethics provisions, focusing, in particular, on three provisions that have been the target of this criticism: (1) DR 1-102(A)(6) of the Model Code, which prohibits conduct that adversely reflects on the lawyer's fitness to practice law; (2) DR 1-102(A)(5) of the Model Code, which was later adopted as Model Rule 8.4(d), which prohibits conduct that is prejudicial to the administration of justice; and (3) Canon 9 of the Model Code, which instructs lawyers to avoid even the appearance of impropriety.

In response to the critics, part two of the chapter introduces a comparative framework to examine the necessity and function of broad principles within the legislative structure of ethics codes, the United States Constitution, and the Torah. Part three then presents three related, yet conceptually distinct, interpretive methodologies that have been employed to derive unenumerated constitutional rights and unenumerated biblical obligations. Finally, this part proceeds to apply these methodologies to the three broad ethics provisions noted above, presenting both a descriptive and normative framework for interpreting broad ethics provisions to derive and identify unenumerated ethical obligations. The chapter concludes with a call for scholars and courts that have criticized these broad ethics provisions to reexamine their approach and consider the viability of adopting the interpretive methods presented.

---

5 Wolfram, supra note 3, at 87.
6 Richard W. Painter, *Rules Lawyers Play By*, 76 N.Y.U. L. Rev. 665, 668 (2001).

PART ONE | ETHICS CODES AS LEGISLATION

Numerous scholars have documented the evolution of ethics rules in the twentieth century,[7] "transforming legal ethics into positive law."[8] The transformation began slowly, as the American Bar Association's (ABA) first attempt to establish authoritative guidelines for legal ethics, the 1908 Canons of Professional Ethics, "did not embody . . . enforceable rules."[9] Instead, the Canons consisted of wording "too vague and general to afford guidance"[10] or to serve as "a basis for discipline."[11]

---

7   See, e.g., Wolfram, supra note 3, at 53-63; Mary C. Daly, *The Dichotomy Between Standards and Rules: A New Way of Understanding the Differences in Perceptions of Lawyer Codes of Conduct by U.S. and Foreign Lawyers,* 32 Vand. J. Transnat'l L. 1117, 1124-34 (1999); Bruce A. Green, *Doe v. Grievance Committee: On the Interpretation of Ethical Rules,* 55 Brook. L. Rev. 485, 531-32 (1989); Hazard, supra note 1, at 1249-60; Painter, supra note 6, at 668-69; Tanina Rostain, *Ethics Lost: Limitations of Current Approaches to Lawyer Regulation,* 71 S. Cal. L. Rev. 1273, 1279-80, 1288-99 (1988); Murray L. Schwartz, *The Death and Regeneration of Ethics,* 1980 Am. B. Found. Res. J. 953, 954-55; Maura Strassberg, *Taking Ethics Seriously: Beyond Positivist Jurisprudence in Legal Ethics,* 80 Iowa L. Rev. 901, 905-10 (1995); Charles W. Wolfram, *Toward a History of the Legalization of American Legal Ethics—I: Origins,* 8 U. Chi. L. Sch. Roundtable 469 (2001); Charles W. Wolfram, *Toward a History of the Legalization of American Legal Ethics—II: The Modern Era,* 15 Geo. J. Legal Ethics 205 (2002); Zacharias, supra note 4, at 225-27 & nn.7-10.

    Professor Daly's article considers the issue of specificity in ethics provisions within the broader conceptual framework of the rules/standards dichotomy. In the context of this chapter, the application of this framework to ethics codes is significant because it may point to another similarity in hermeneutic methodologies applied to legal ethics, constitutional law, and Jewish law. The place of the rules/standards dichotomy in constitutional interpretation has been clearly established. See Daly, supra, at 1118 n.1 (citing David L. Faigman, *Constitutional Adventures in Wonderland: Exploring the Debate Between Rules and Standards Through the Looking Glass of the First Amendment,* 44 Hastings L.J. 829 (1993); Antonin Scalia, *The Rule of Law as a Law of Rules,* 56 U. Chi. L. Rev. 1175 (1989); Kathleen M. Sullivan, *The Supreme Court 1991 Term, Foreword: The Justices of Rules and Standards,* 106 Harv. L. Rev. 22 (1992)). Likewise, the rules/standards dichotomy has been applied in the context of Jewish legal theory. See, e.g., Chapter 10 in this Volume; Irene Merker Rosenberg et al., *Murder by Gruma: Causation in Homicide Cases Under Jewish Law,* 80 B.U. L. Rev. 1017, 1038-39 (2000).

    For an analysis of the role that the evolution of ethics rules has played in the "steady growth in the regulation of the legal market . . . from an unregulated market to the high level of regulation we observe today," see Benjamin Hoorn Barton, *Why Do We Regulate Lawyers?: An Economic Analysis of the Justifications for Entry and Conduct Regulation,* 33 Ariz. St. L.J. 429, 430 (2001).

8   Strassberg, supra note 7, at 905; see also Roger C. Cramton & Lisa K. Udell, *State Ethics Rules and Federal Prosecutors: The Controversies over the Anti-Contact and Subpoena Rules,* 53 U. Pitt. L. Rev. 291, 300 (1992) ("Since about 1930, with accelerating speed since 1970, ethical codes have developed into law.").

9   Strassberg, supra note 7, at 908.

10 Wolfram, supra note 3, at 55.

11 Strassberg, supra note 7, at 908.

Decades later, the ABA embarked upon an effort to produce a set of ethics rules that would be "capable of enforcement" and would "facilitate more effective disciplinary action."[12] These efforts produced the 1969 Model Code of Professional Responsibility.[13] Significantly, in contrast to the general nature of the Canons, the Model Code includes "blackletter law"[14] in the form of specific Disciplinary Rules that the Code describes as "mandatory in character" and "stat[ing] the minimum level of conduct below which no lawyer can fall without being subject to disciplinary action."[15] Hazard thus refers to the Model Code as the "crucial step" in the legalization of ethics regulation, having "first embraced legally binding norms."[16]

Moreover, as Professor Mary Daly noted, the Code uses "language equally suitable for a criminal statute"[17] in declaring that "[w]ithin the framework of a fair trial, the Disciplinary Rules should be uniformly applied to all lawyers, regardless of the nature of their professional activities."[18] Indeed, Hazard writes that the Disciplinary Rules "functioned as a statute defining the legal contours of a vocation whose practitioners were connected primarily by having been licensed to practice law."[19] In short, as Professor Maura Strassberg declared, through the inclusion of the Disciplinary Rules, the Model Code "essentially completed the articulation of legal ethics as positive law."[20]

Despite its widespread influence and its adoption by nearly every state,[21] the Model Code was also widely criticized, on a number of grounds.[22] The ABA then responded with yet another set of ethical standards, the 1983 Model Rules of Professional Conduct. The statutory character of the Model Rules was already evident in its drafting process, which Hazard has termed "quasi-legislative"

---

12 Id. (quoting Walter P. Armstrong, *A Century of Legal Ethics*, 64 A.B.A. J. 1063, 1069 (1978)).

13 Wolfram, supra note 3, at 56. Although the Model Code was originally called simply the "Code of Professional Responsibility," in 1978, pursuant to a settlement of Justice Department antitrust charges, the name was changed to its current form. See Wolfram, supra note 3, at 57.

14 See Hazard, supra note 1, at 1251.

15 Model Code of Prof'l Responsibility preliminary statement (1981).

16 Hazard, supra note 1, at 1251.

17 Daly, supra note 7, at 1129. Cf. Schwartz, supra note 7, at 957 ("Analogous to a criminal code, the Disciplinary Rules define minimum acceptable behavior.").

18 Model Code of Prof'l Responsibility preliminary statement (footnote omitted).

19 Hazard, supra note 1, at 1251.

20 Strassberg, supra note 7, at 909.

21 See Wolfram, supra note 3, at 56.

22 See id. at 60. Professor Wolfram observed that "[i]ts critics started from different and sometimes conflicting positions." Id. See also Daly, supra note 7, at 1130-32; Strassberg, supra note 7, at 909.

because of the extent to which it "mirrored that of public lawmaking."[23] Professor Strassberg suggests that the very title of the Model Rules reflects the renunciation of "any intention at articulating ethics,"[24] in favor of "a code of positive law," thereby "remak[ing] the concept of legal ethics."[25] Describing the structure of the Model Rules, Robert Kutak, chair of the ABA commission that drafted the Rules, explained that the "format of black-letter rules accompanied by explanatory comments . . . replicates the familiar, time-tested approach of the American Law Institute's restatements of the law and modern model legislation."[26] Perhaps most significantly, focusing on the "normative rhetoric"[27] of the Model Rules, Hazard similarly observes that "the Rules were rendered in statutory language" and "thus implied that the normative definition of the profession could be expressed only using the medium of legally binding rules."[28]

Along with their legislative form, ethics regulations have evolved to acquire the status of legal authority similar to that of legislation. As Hazard explains, the ABA recognized that it required the "aid of the courts," which possess the authority to enforce such sanctions as disbarment and suspension, as well as

---

23 Hazard, supra note 1, at 1253. Hazard cites Professor Ted Schneyer's description of the adoption of the Model Rules as "the most sustained and democratic debate about professional ethics in the history of the American bar." Id. at 1252 n.64 (quoting Ted Schneyer, *Professionalism as Bar Politics: The Making of the Model Rules of Professional Conduct*, 14 Law & Soc. Inquiry 677, 678 (1989)).

24 Strassberg, supra note 7, at 909. Cf. Daly, supra note 7, at 1125 (stating that the transformation of ethics regulations in the twentieth century is "poignantly captured by the metamorphosis of their titles—from Canons to Code to Rules"). In fact, Professor Schwartz suggested that the relationship between various forms of professional standards and their titles dates back to the nineteenth century. See Schwartz, supra note 7, at 954-55 (citing David Hoffman, *Fifty Resolutions in Regard to Professional Deportment*, in The Canons of Professional and Judicial Ethics & Hoffman's 50 Resolutions (C.E.H. ed., 1959) (1836); George Sharswood, *A Compend of Lectures on the Aims and Duties of the Profession of the Law* (1854)).

25 Strassberg, supra note 7, at 909-10. Cf. Daly, supra note 7, at 1133 (concluding that "[t]he purpose of the Model Rules was to command the conduct of lawyers, not to recommend the consideration of vague and imprecise values in ethical decisionmaking").

26 Robert J. Kutak, *Evaluating the Proposed Model Rules of Professional Conduct*, 1980 Am. B. Found. Res. J. 1016, 1016-17. Cf. Geoffrey C. Hazard, Jr., *Legal Ethics: Legal Rules and Professional Aspirations*, 30 Clev. St. L. Rev. 571, 574 (1981) (stating that unlike the Model Code, the "Model Rules are cast in the familiar and much more reliable form of the restatements . . . provid[ing] a black letter rule and an explanatory comment" because "[t]he practicing lawyer needs and is entitled to legal rules").

27 Hazard, supra note 1, at 1253.

28 Id. at 1254. Cf. Daly, supra note 7, at 1132 (noting that "[t]he overwhelming majority of the Model Rules . . . are cast in the imperative[,] . . . even those that employ permissive language are more detailed and precise than provisions in the 1908 Canons and Model Code").

the authority to "transform[ ] the norms of professional conduct into binding legal rules."[29] As a result, the Model Code, in Hazard's words, was not only "written like a statute" but also "propounded to the states as model legislation" and "adopted by the states as legislation."[30] Likewise, in a draft of his Foreword to The Restatement of the Law Governing Lawyers, referring to ethics codes, Hazard reminded readers to "ke[ep] constantly in mind that these regulations are rules of law and not merely admonitions of the legal profession to its members. . . . [T]he Code and the Rules, as adopted in various states, are a form of legislation with attendant authoritative significance."[31] In sum, as a matter of both form and authority, it is generally recognized that "when a state supreme

---

29 Hazard, supra note 1, at 1250-51. Cf. Green, supra note 7, at 532-33 (emphasizing that "[n]either the adoption of the Code by the ABA nor its endorsement by the Connecticut Bar Association made it enforceable against an attorney who was practicing in Connecticut," but rather that "[t]he Code took legal effect in Connecticut when, in accordance with the state bar's recommendation, the judges of the superior court approved the Code").

30 Geoffrey C. Hazard, Jr., *The Legal and Ethical Position of the Code of Professional Ethics*, in 5 *Social Responsibility: Journalism, Law, Medicine* 5, 6 (Louis Hodges ed., 1979).

   Conversely, describing the drafting of the Model Rules and addressing concerns about "expansions" of provisions found in the Model Code, Kutak emphasized the extent to which the Rules conformed to decisions of the courts, insisting that "[m]any of the expansions . . . merely restate rules developed in cases." Kutak, supra note 26, at 1022; see id. at 1021-23. Cf. Gary A. Munneke & Anthony E. Davis, *The Standard of Care in Legal Malpractice: Do the Model Rules of Professional Conduct Define It?*, 22 J. Legal Prof. 33, 42-44 (1998) (concluding that "approaches to the drafting of the Model Rules produced a document reflecting standards closer to those of civil law than the standards articulated in the Code" because, unlike the Model Code, the Model Rules "are firmly rooted in positive law," "conform to court-made rules of law," and "recognize the role of customary usage in setting standards of behavior for lawyers"). Compare Geoffrey C. Hazard, Jr., *How Far May a Lawyer Go in Assisting a Client in Legally Wrongful Conduct?*, 35 U. Miami L. Rev. 669, 677-81 (1981), with Monroe H. Freedman, *Are the Model Rules Unconstitutional?*, 35 U. Miami L. Rev. 685, 689, 692 (1981) (finding it "significant that Professor Hazard, in discussing the general law relevant to legal ethics, chose to refer to the laws of tort and agency with citation to the Restatement of Agency, but made no reference to constitutional law and no citation to the Bill of Rights" and asserting that "the current revision of the Model Rules, referred to as the final draft, cites none of the foremost constitutional authorities on point to support its position that a lawyer has an obligation to reveal his client's perjury" (footnote omitted)).

31 Restatement (Third) of the Law Governing Lawyers foreword (Tentative Draft No. 8, 1997). Professor Schwartz offered a similar analysis:

   The Model Rules in their present form represent the culmination of a historical process that began a century and a half ago: the shift from articulating professional standards, suffused with ideas of morality and ethics, and enforced if at all by informal sanctions and peer pressure, to enacting comprehensive and explicit legislation attended by formally imposed sanctions for breach.

Schwartz, supra note 7, at 953-54.

court issues an order officially adopting a set of rules of professional conduct, it is establishing legally binding standards of conduct just as a state legislature does when it passes a law proscribing bank robbery."[32]

---

32 Lawrence K. Hellman, *When "Ethics Rules" Don't Mean What They Say: The Implications of Strained ABA Ethics Opinions*, 10 Geo. J. Legal Ethics 317, 321 (1997). Cf. Wolfram, supra note 3, at 67 (finding that "the enforcement of the provisions of lawyer codes in lawyer discipline and other proceedings demonstrates clearly that the codes are legal prescriptions in every conventional sense"); Susan P. Koniak, *The Law Between the Bar and the State*, 70 N.C. L. Rev. 1389, 1411 (1992) (emphasizing that "the state treats ethics rules as 'law' only to the extent that they are (and in the form in which they are) adopted by the state"); L. Ray Patterson, *The Function of a Code of Legal Ethics*, 35 U. Miami L. Rev. 695, 722 (1981) (noting "the fact that the profession only proposes, and the court disposes, since the rules do not become effective until a court adopts them"); Robert Rubinson, *Attorney Fact-Finding, Ethical Decision-Making and the Methodology of Law*, 45 St. Louis U. L.J. 1185, 1188 (2001) (observing that "the primacy of rules as the preeminent object of inquiry in ethics discourse is rarely in question"). The Alaska Supreme Court stated:

> The Bar Association . . . contends that this appeal is not the appropriate vehicle for modifying [Alaska] Rule [of Professional Conduct] 1.8(e) on policy grounds. Instead, it argues that "there is an established procedure for promulgation and adoption of these rules which should not be ignored simply because both parties do not like the present rule." We agree.

In re Matter of K.A.H., 967 P.2d 91, 96-97 (Alaska 1998).
    But see Stephen E. Kalish, *How to Encourage Lawyers to Be Ethical: Do Not Use the Ethics Codes as a Basis for Regular Law Decisions*, 13 Geo. J. Legal Ethics 649, 668 (2000) (stating that "ethics codes are not statutes or administrative regulations"); id. at 656 (noting that although "judicial adoption may politically legitimize the written ethics codes[,] . . . it is the lawyer-drafters who articulate the rules, and it is the ABA that recommends them."). Strassberg pointed out the lack of democratic approval inherent in ethics codes:

> Statutory law's coercive legitimacy stems from its creation by a democratically elected legislature; this legitimacy cannot be transferred to nondemocratic judicial "legislation." In many states, the rules of legal ethics imposed upon the bar are not the product of a democratically elected legislature, but are imposed by the highest court of the state exercising its supervisory powers over lawyers. Although the ABA, which drafted the Model Code and Model Rules, required approval by its House of Delegates before either the Model Code or Model Rules were officially promulgated, and the House voted on all amendments to these models, nonetheless, the models are hardly the sacred products of democracy. This is particularly true since neither the general public nor non-ABA lawyers have a representative voice in the creation of these rules.

Strassberg, supra note 7, at 935-36 (footnotes omitted). In a concurring opinion, Judge Gurfein wrote:

> First, I think a court need not treat the Canons of Professional Responsibility as it would a statute that we have no right to amend. We should not abdicate our constitutional function of regulating the Bar to that extent. When we agree that the Code applies in an equitable manner to a matter before us, we

Nevertheless, many scholars have expressed reservations about the extent to which ethics regulations, which include a number of broad provisions, may be properly conceptualized as having attained a legislative form. Perhaps one of the most powerful and prominent voices expressing such criticism is that of Professor Wolfram. Despite documenting court decisions generally rejecting arguments that broad ethics provisions are void for vagueness, Wolfram asserts conclusively that "if anything is clear, it is that many provisions of the lawyer codes are plainly imprecise."[33]

Wolfram's favorite target is probably Canon 9 of the Model Code,[34] which mandates, in its title, that "A Lawyer Should Avoid Even the Appearance of Professional Impropriety."[35] According to Wolfram, "[i]f carefully analyzed, the appearances standard in any of its incarnations quickly loses much strength."[36] On a practical level, he argues that the standard lacks a workable methodology, because courts will have difficulty ascertaining the identity of "the observers to whom the relevant appearances present themselves," and because "the judge's task of guessing at what those groups might hold in their minds will be extremely speculative."[37] In addition, on a normative level, he questions whether "adverse public reaction [is] generally a basis for [public] decision[s]," particularly in the realm of attorney conduct.[38] Thus, although he acknowledged in his 1986 hornbook that a number of courts relied on the appearances standard, Wolfram concluded in characteristically blunt language that "[i]t stretches the matter to refer to a doctrinal content to the appearances notion. It appears in opinions more in an incantational, intuitive way, and its use is hardly ever defended. Abandoning it would deprive courts of no useful analytical tool and would fittingly narrow courts' range of u[n]bridled discretion in passing on disqualification motions."[39]

---

should not hesitate to enforce it with vigor. When we find an area of uncertainty, however, we must use our judicial process to make our own decision in the interests of justice to all concerned.

J.P. Foley & Co. v. Vanderbilt, 523 F.2d 1357, 1359-60 (2d Cir. 1975) (Gurfein, J., concurring).

33 See Wolfram, supra note 3, at 86-87.

34 See id. at 319-23.

35 Model Code of Prof'l Responsibility Canon 9 (1981).

36 Wolfram, supra note 3, at 320.

37 Id.

38 Id. at 320-21.

39 Id. at 320 n.38; see also id. at 460-61 (referring to the "Alluring 'Appearances' Rationale" as "a vapid concept sometimes employed independently, and thus quite erroneously, to disqualify a former government lawyer and sometimes as a much less direct and meaningful locution that only obscures a sounder reason" and as creating a "fog" that "has done more to retard thinking

In a 1997 article, Wolfram continued his strongly-worded attack on the appearance of impropriety standard, referring to it as an "antiquated . . . concept, which has been discarded almost everywhere."[40] Despite professing to "forego the opportunity to flail, yet again, the mostly dead dog of appearance of impropriety," Wolfram adds that "it is clear that it plays only a minor, if irritating and potentially distorting, role in modern conflicts opinions."[41]

Though somewhat less caustic in his criticism of other ethics provisions he finds improperly vague, Wolfram attacks them as well, because, he asserts, "[u]nnecessary breadth is to be regretted in professional rules that can be used to deprive a person of his or her means of livelihood through sanctions that are universally regarded as stigmatizing."[42] He argues that such provisions "create several difficulties," including potentially "be[ing] applied corruptly or for reasons of impermissible bias" and "substantially dilut[ing] the procedural protections that otherwise narrow the area within which agencies could act arbitrarily or mistakenly."[43]

Among the provisions he cites, two of the broadest rules are DR 1-102(A) (5) of the Model Code, later adopted as Model Rule 8.4(d), prohibiting "conduct that is prejudicial to the administration of justice," and DR 1-102(A)(6) of the Model Code, not adopted by the Model Rules, prohibiting "any other conduct that adversely reflects on [the lawyer's] fitness to practice law."[44] Wolfram does not hide his strong disapproval of these two rules, quoting the view that, together with Canon 9, they comprise "garbage cans of the Code . . . into which anything can be tossed."[45] Other scholars have concurred with Wolfram's contention that, notwithstanding the increased specificity found in

---

on problems of conflicts of former government lawyers than any other concept" (footnotes omitted)); id. at 461 n.73 (describing the standard as "virtually empty of intellectual content").

40 Charles W. Wolfram, *Former-Client Conflicts*, 10 Geo. J. Legal Ethics 677, 686 (1997).

41 Id. at 686-87. Wolfram further notes that "[a]lmost every scholarly analysis of the 'appearance' standard has disapproved of its use as an independent basis for finding conflict." Id. at 686-87 n.35; see also Wolfram, supra note 3, at 322 (stating that "[a]cademic commentators have denounced" the standard); Stephen Gillers, *Regulation of Lawyers: Problems of Law and Ethics* 358-59 (6th ed. 2002) (characterizing the standard as unpredictable).

42 Wolfram, supra note 3, at 87.

43 Id.

44 Model Code of Prof'l Responsibility DR 1-102 (1981).

45 Wolfram, supra note 3, at 87 n.50 (quoting John F. Sutton, *Commentary on the Texas Code of Professional Responsibility*, in *Texas Lawyers' Professional Ethics* 6-2, 6-5 n.37 (1979)). Though again not to the same degree as Canon 9, these provisions have also been subjected, since their inception, to negative academic treatment. See Leonard E. Gross, *The Public Hates Lawyers: Why Should We Care?*, 29 Seton Hall L. Rev. 1405, 1455 n.245 (1999).

the Model Code and, to a greater extent, in the Model Rules, lawyer regulations continue to lack the level of specificity appropriate for legislation.[46]

---

46 See, e.g., Painter, supra note 6, at 669 (arguing that "default rules should be used more extensively in professional responsibility codes" and that "[c]learly-defined default rules could, in some cases, replace the broad standards, permissive rules, or aspirational rules that now govern many controversial topics"); Theodore J. Schneyer, *The Model Rules and Problems of Code Interpretation and Enforcement*, 1980 Am. B. Found. Res. J. 939, 940 (finding that "on some subjects that were dealt with in the [Disciplinary Rules], but in terms so general as to require heroic interpretive effort, the Model Rules are not appreciably more specific— better written and with fewer internal inconsistencies, but not more specific"); Serena Stier, *Legal Ethics: The Integrity Thesis*, 52 Ohio St. L.J. 551, 593 (1991) (describing "the substantial indeterminacies left in the structure of professional ethics by both the Rules and the Code"); id. at 596 n.179 (stating that "[e]ven mandatory standards may leave room for judgment calls"); David B. Wilkins, *Legal Realism for Lawyers*, 104 Harv. L. Rev. 468, 480 (1990) (describing the Model Code as "rife with vague and ambiguous terms," but finding that, while the Model Rules' "self-conscious[ ] attempt to bring more determinacy to the field of professional responsibility by adopting a rule-like structure . . . has eliminated some of the more pervasive ambiguities, vagueness and open-endedness remain").

    Some of these criticisms identify aspects of ethics codes that are, in fact, broader in nature than most forms of legislation. Others, however, invoke aspects of ethics codes that appear to be more reflective of the inherent nature of legal rules that, at times, unavoidably require interpretation of somewhat vague and ambiguous concepts—such as "reasonableness." See, e.g., Painter, supra, at 668 n.19 (citing Model Rules of Prof'l Conduct R. 1.1, 1.3, 1.4(a) (1983)) (stating that "[t]he 'reasonableness' standard is used to define required levels of competence, diligence, and communication with clients[,] . . . but with little guidance as to what conduct is and is not reasonable"); id. at 668 & n.20 (citing Model Rules of Prof'l Conduct R. 1.5(a)) (stating that "when the subject matter of a rule is particularly controversial, the rule has tended to remain a standard that is so broad that it is unenforceable" and criticizing the Rule for "stating that [a] lawyer's fee must be reasonable, and listing eight factors to be considered in determining reasonableness, without discussion of which factors are most important"); Wilkins, supra, at 481 (criticizing the Model Rules because, "[a]s under the Model Code, the meaning of 'reasonable' or 'diligent' performance continues to be susceptible to multiple and conflicting interpretations").

    As Professor Zacharias noted, similar "[e]xamples of flexible standards include the reasonableness standards in common law tort rules and the Uniform Commercial Code." Zacharias, supra note 4, at 237 n.43 (citing several broad U.C.C. provisions and justifications for the use of such flexible rules). In fact, some of the justifications Zacharias cites for broad provisions in the U.C.C., such as the explanation that they are "intended to enable courts to develop law embodied in the Code in the light of unforeseen and new circumstances and practices" appear to apply to broad ethics provisions as well. Id. at 237 n.44 (citing U.C.C. §1-102 cmt. 1 (1989)); see infra notes 48-54 and accompanying text; see also Koniak, supra note 32, at 1390 ("The law of lawyering is not inherently more amorphous, contradictory or obtuse than other law.").

    Nevertheless, Zacharias concluded that "professional codes must be evaluated differently than ordinary legislation and administrative schemes—even those that include legal 'standards' as flexible as the standards in the codes." Zacharias, supra note 4, at 237.

PART TWO | THE NECESSITY AND FUNCTION OF BROAD RULES IN ETHICS CODES, CONSTITUTIONAL LAW, AND JEWISH LAW

Defenders of broad rules in ethics codes have emphasized the necessity and utility of general rules in regulating the ethical conduct of lawyers. In fact, a number of courts have upheld, interpreted, applied, and offered justifications for the kinds of broad ethics provisions that some scholars have repeatedly viewed as unworkable and impermissibly vague.[47] In a 1991 case, the New York Court of Appeals quoted a mid-nineteenth-century United States Supreme Court opinion acknowledging that "it is difficult, if not impossible, to enumerate and define, with legal precision, every offense for which an attorney or counselor ought to be removed."[48] Therefore, according to the New York court, it

---

47 See Gillers, supra note 41, at 359 (stating that "one must . . . caution against dismissing the 'appearance [of impropriety]' test altogether," in part because "some courts . . . may for a time continue to rely on the 'appearance of impropriety' in disqualifying a lawyer"); Wolfram, supra note 3, at 86 & n.48 (observing that "most attacks upon Code provisions charging that they are void for vagueness in violation of the due process clause have been unavailing"); Fred C. Zacharias, *Who Can Best Regulate the Ethics of Federal Prosecutors, or, Who Should Regulate the Regulators?: Response to Little*, 65 Fordham L. Rev. 429, 453-54 (1996) (noting "the frequency with which courts cite the 'appearance of impropriety' in their decisions on lawyer disqualification, even though that rationale for ethics regulation increasingly has been downplayed in scholarship and bar-generated codes" (footnotes omitted)).

48 *In re Holtzman*, 577 N.E.2d 30, 33 (N.Y. 1991) (quoting *Ex parte Secombe*, 60 U.S. (19 How.) 9, 14 (1856)); see also *In re Rinella*, 677 N.E.2d 909, 917 (Ill. 1997) (Freeman, J., concurring in part and dissenting in part) ("As a practical matter, there could never be a set of rules which contemplates every aspect of the many encounters between an attorney and a client."); *In re Illuzzi*, 632 A.2d 346, 349-50 (Vt. 1993) (referring to the "impossibility of enumerating every act that might constitute a violation of professional standards"); *Pantry Pride, Inc. v. Finley, Kumble, Wagner, Heine, Underberg & Casey*, 697 F.2d 524, 530 (3d Cir. 1982) (stating that "[t]he appearance of impropriety standard is necessarily vague"); *In re Hinds*, 449 A.2d 483, 498 (N.J. 1982) (noting that "[a]ttorney disciplinary rules have long been framed in general, rather sweeping language"); *Comm. on Prof'l Ethics v. Durham*, 279 N.W.2d 280, 284 (Iowa 1979) (stating that "guidelines setting standards for members of the bar need not and cannot meet the standard of clarity required of rules of conduct for laymen due to the training and specialized nature of the body being regulated"). The court also stated that

> standards relating to the conduct of attorneys may also be distinguished in that it would be virtually impossible to develop a set of rules to specifically cover all professional activity which could merit discipline, thus necessitating broader standards. The bar must be concerned about the professional activities of its members, and the manner in which these activities reflect upon the integrity of the profession as a whole.

Id.

follows that "[b]road standards governing professional conduct are permissible

---

> Likewise, a number of scholars—among them critics of the broad nature of certain ethics provisions—have acknowledged the utility of broad rules. See, e.g., Heidi Li Feldman, *Codes and Virtues: Can Good Lawyers Be Good Ethical Deliberators?*, 69 S. Cal. L. Rev. 885, 899 (1996) ("Instances of inconclusiveness arise in all areas of the law, including those governed by relatively specific fine-grained rules and regulations. The only way to eliminate inconclusiveness entirely would be to devise a rule to cover every particular case of ethical difficulty—an impossible task, because the cases are infinite."); Kutak, supra note 26, at 1019 ("[I]t is conceivable that a code could prescribe conduct with the minute detail of the Internal Revenue Code, but such specificity would be burdensome and inhibiting and might have an equally adverse impact on enforcement and compliance."); Painter, supra note 6, at 689 (suggesting that in some areas of ethics codes, "a standard is used because a defined rule's prohibitions might sweep too broadly"). Painter went on to state:
>
> > Sometimes the bar prefers that an immutable rule be a standard rather than a defined rule if there is substantial disagreement over what the rule should be. Because immutable rules are inflexible ex ante (they cannot be contracted around), rulemakers who disagree on basic principles underlying a rule are not likely to select an immutable rule that is so well defined that it is also inflexible ex post (preventing an adjudicator from tailoring the rule to adjust for circumstances).
>
> Id. at 690; see also Strassberg, supra note 7, at 902 (observing that "in legal ethics, cases must arise which will not fit within an existing rule"); Wilkins, supra note 46, at 500 ("Formulating more precise rules could reduce the level of indeterminacy in the system. But this clarity comes at a price. By their very nature, rigid rules are either over- or underinclusive (or both) relative to their intended purposes" (footnotes omitted)). Zacharias offered the following analysis:
>
> > By making the elements of [a code provision] unambiguous, drafters run the risk of defining the misconduct so narrowly that it becomes inapplicable to most situations sought to be covered. . . . For example, adding a state of mind element (e.g., intent) or a reasonableness element to the confidentiality rules might eliminate those situations in which lawyers gossip irresponsibly about their clients or use confidential information, without authority, for the clients' benefit. If the amended rule is deemed to cover those situations, enforcers must deal with the fact that extrinsic proof of intent and reasonableness generally are not available.
>
> Zacharias, supra note 4, at 253 n.93; id. at 255 (noting that "a highly specific provision that merely restates, or duplicates, extra-code standards may influence behavior less than a general rule that lawyers might interpret as applying more broadly"); id. at 277 n.162 (citing H.L.A. Hart, *The Concept of Law* 123-32 (1961)) (noting Hart's "preference for generality in lawmaking when legislating in new areas of law, because this generality enables the law to evolve more easily (usually judicially) over time[,] . . . [while] [b]y contrast, highly specific laws tend to remain fixed," and concluding that "[t]he same analysis applies with respect to judicial adoption of specific professional code provisions [that] tend to control courts and limit their ability to adjust as unforeseen cases arise"). See generally Russell W. Damtoft, *Note, Lawyer Disciplinary Standards: Broad vs. Narrow Proscriptions*, 65 Iowa L. Rev. 1386 (1980). Damtoft states:
>
> > Narrow rules of conduct, it is argued, cannot be drawn to encompass every variety of unethical behavior. Therefore, some broad standards must be

and indeed often necessary."[49]

In fact, the Preamble to the 1908 Canons of Professional Ethics contained a similar assertion that

> [n]o code or set of rules can be framed, which will particularize all the duties of the lawyer in the varying phases of litigation or in all the relations of professional life. The following canons of ethics are adopted by the American Bar Association as a general guide, yet the enumeration of particular duties should not be construed as a denial of the existence of others equally imperative, though not specifically mentioned.[50]

The Preamble is instructive not only because it appears to serve as an analogue to the rationale that contemporary courts have offered for the inclusion of broad provisions in ethics codes. Perhaps more importantly, through its striking similarity to principles of constitutional interpretation, the Preamble may have

---

> combined with narrow rules to ensure that attorneys are disciplined for unforeseen types of misconduct. This position is reflected in the several broad disciplinary rules included in the ABA [Model] Code. A related danger is that attorneys inevitably will use the narrowness of some rules to create loopholes for marginal behavior, loopholes that are closed by broad standards.

> Id. at 1399 (footnotes omitted). The two broad Model Code provisions cited to support this analysis are DR 1-102(A)(5) and DR 1-102 (A)(6). Id.

49 *Holtzman*, 577 N.E.2d at 33; see also *In re Rinella*, 677 N.E.2d 909, 914 (Ill. 1997) (stating that "the standards of professional conduct enunciated by this court are not a manual designed to instruct attorneys what to do in every conceivable situation"). The court quoted the preamble to the Illinois Rules of Professional Conduct:

> No set of prohibitions, however, can adequately articulate the positive values or goals sought to be advanced by those prohibitions. This preamble therefore seeks to articulate those values . . . . Lawyers seeking to conform their conduct to the requirements of these rules should look to the values described in this preamble for guidance in interpreting the difficult issues which may arise under the rules.

> Id. at 914 (quoting Ill. Rules of Prof'l Conduct preamble at 470); Santa Clara County Counsel Attorneys Ass'n v. Woodside, 28 Cal. Rptr. 2d 617, 629 (1994) ("Although the question of an attorney's suit against a present client is not explicitly covered in the Rules of Professional Conduct, or by any statute . . . [i]t is clear that the duties to which an attorney in this state are subject are not exhaustively delineated by the Rules of Professional Conduct."); *In re N.P.*, 361 N.W.2d 386, 395 (Minn. 1985) (quoting *In re Gillard*, 271 N.W.2d 785, 809 n.7 (Minn. 1978)) ("We ourselves have, in the comparable situation of applying a legislative standard of judicial conduct, similarly recognized that 'necessarily broad standards of professional conduct' are constitutionally permissible.").

50 Canons of Professional Ethics preface (1908).

profound ramifications for the interpretation and application of contemporary ethics codes.

In addition to, and premised upon, its observation of the inherently and inevitably incomplete nature of ethics codes, the Preamble prescribes adherence to unenumerated ethical obligations as well as to those enumerated. Thus, the Preamble anticipated an approach to unenumerated constitutional rights that would be invoked decades later by Justice Goldberg in his explanation of the function of the Ninth Amendment in the United States Constitution.[51] According to Justice Goldberg, the Ninth Amendment "was proffered to quiet expressed fears that a bill of specifically enumerated rights could not be sufficiently broad to cover all essential rights and that the specific mention of certain rights would be interpreted as a denial that others were protected."[52]

Moreover, the language of the Preamble appears closely modeled after the Ninth Amendment, which states: "The enumeration in the Constitution, of certain rights, shall not be construed to deny or disparage others retained by the

---

51 U.S. Const. amend. IX ("The enumeration in the Constitution, of certain rights, shall not be construed to deny or disparage others retained by the people.").

52 *Griswold v. Connecticut*, 381 U.S. 479, 488-89 (1965) (Goldberg, J., concurring). See Randy E. Barnett, *Reconceiving the Ninth Amendment*, 74 Cornell L. Rev. 1, 10 (1988) (reprinting an excerpt from a speech in which then-Representative James Madison voiced concern that "by enumerating particular exceptions to the grant of power, it would disparage those rights which were not placed in that enumeration; and it might follow by implication, that those rights which were not singled out . . . were consequently insecure" (quoting 1 The Debates and Proceedings in the Congress of the United States 456 (J. Gales & W. Seaton eds., 1834))). In *Moore v. City of East Cleveland*, Justice Powell stated:

> [T]he full scope of the liberty guaranteed by the Due Process Clause cannot be found in or limited by the precise terms of the specific guarantees elsewhere provided in the Constitution. This "liberty" is not a series of isolated points pricked out in terms of the taking of property; the freedom of speech, press, and religion; the right to keep and bear arms; the freedom from unreasonable searches and seizures; and so on. It is a rational continuum which, broadly speaking, includes a freedom from all substantial arbitrary impositions and purposeless restraints. . . .

431 U.S. 494, 502 (1977) (Powell, J., concurring) (quoting *Poe v. Ullman*, 367 U.S. 497, 543 (1961) (Harlan, J., dissenting)).

As I have observed in Chapter 9 in this Volume, the justices adopting this approach acknowledged that "a proper understanding of the guarantees of liberty requires looking beyond the specific rights enumerated in the Constitution, to uncover the underlying principles those rights represent."

Likewise, consistent with the Preamble to the Canons, a number of courts have adopted the position that a proper understanding of the obligations and responsibilities mandated by ethics codes requires looking beyond the specific obligations enumerated in the codes, by interpreting and applying broad ethics provisions to uncover the underlying principles those obligations represent.

people."[53] The similarity, in both form and substance, of the Preamble and the Ninth Amendment is indicative of a more significant similarity in the interpretive methodologies courts have employed in the interpretation of ethics codes and constitutional interpretation, deriving and identifying unenumerated ethical obligations and unenumerated constitutional rights through the interpretation and application of broad provisions.[54]

Extending these concepts beyond the American legal system, the Jewish legal system provides a third set of legal rules consisting, in part, of broad provisions that are interpreted as a basis for deriving unenumerated laws. Many centuries ago, offering justifications similar to those offered in contemporary times for the inclusion of broad provisions in ethics codes and in the Constitution, Nachmanides[55] explained that, notwithstanding the numerous and wideranging positive and negative commandments delineated in the Torah,[56]

---

53 U.S. Const., amend. IX.

54 Likewise, the Preamble's insistence that the unenumerated obligations are "equally imperative" as those obligations enumerated in the Canons presents a further parallel to the way some scholars have understood the Ninth Amendment. See, e.g., Charles L. Black, Jr., *On Reading and Using the Ninth Amendment*, in *Power and Policy in Quest of Law: Essays in Honor of Eugene Victor Rostow* 187 (Myers S. McDougal Cougar & W. Michael Reisman eds., 1988). Black asserted that the Ninth Amendment requires equal treatment of all rights:

> [P]reponderance of reason leaves us with the conclusion, about as well-supported as any we can reach in law, that the Ninth Amendment declares as a matter of law-of constitutional law, overriding other law-that some other rights are "retained by the people," and that these shall be treated as *on an equal footing* with rights enumerated.

Id. at 188.

55 Nachmanides (1195-c.1270), also known by the acronym Ramban (Rabbi Moshe ben Nachman), was a leading medieval Jewish legal scholar, philosopher, and biblical commentator. See Charles B. Chavel, *Ramban, His Life and Teachings* (1960); Charles B. Chavel, *Preface to 1 Moses Ben Nachman, Ramban (Nachmanides), Commentary on the Torah* (Charles B. Chavel, trans., 1971) [hereinafter Nachmanides].

56 See Chapter 4 in this Volume. Scholars of Jewish law identify 613 commandments enumerated in the Torah, covering nearly every area of human activity. See Maimonides, *Sefer Ha-Mitzvoth* (Soncino 1940); *Sefer Hahinnuch: The Book of Mitzvah Education* (Charles Wengrov trans., 1985); see also Chapter 18 in Volume 2; Samuel J. Levine, *The Broad Life of the Jewish Lawyer: Integrating Spirituality, Scholarship and Profession*, 27 Tex. Tech L. Rev. 1199, 1199 (1996) (describing the interaction of the legal profession and a "set of religious laws and principles [that] govern[ ] every area of life"). Cf. Joseph B. Soloveitchik, *Halakhic Man* 33 (Lawrence Kaplan trans., 1983) (originally published in Hebrew as *Ish ha-halakhah*, in 1 Talpiot 3-4 (1944)) ("The task of the religious individual is bound up with the performance of commandments, and this performance is confined to this world, to physical, concrete reality, to clamorous, tumultuous life, pulsating with exuberance and strength."); Moshe Silberg, *Law and Morals in Jewish Jurisprudence*, 75 Harv. L. Rev. 306, 309 (1961) ("[U]nlike the overwhelming majority of other legal systems, Jewish law does not confine itself to relations between man

it would be impossible to mention in the Torah all aspects of man's conduct with his neighbors and friends, and all his various transactions, and the ordinances of all societies and countries. But since [God] mentioned many of them . . . [God] reverted to state in a general way that, in all matters, one should do what is good and right . . . . Thus, [a person must seek to refine his behavior] in every form of activity . . . .[57]

Expressing a concern strikingly similar to that which Justice Goldberg later cited to explain the importance of the Ninth Amendment in the constitutional framework, Nachmanides notes the potential danger that an individual might claim adherence to those obligations enumerated in the Torah, yet engage in wrongful activities that are not expressly prohibited: "[A]nd thus he will become a sordid person within the permissible realm of the Torah."[58] Therefore, Nachmanides explains, "after having listed the matters which [God] prohibited altogether Scripture followed them up by a general command that we [be holy] . . . . And such is the way of the Torah, that after it lists certain specific prohibitions, it includes them all in a general precept."[59]

Thus, similar to later methods of interpreting both ethics codes and the Constitution, Jewish legal theory views broad provisions as a necessary basis

---

and man, but in addition defines in legal categories, applies legal terms, perceives through legal concepts, the relationship between man and God. . . ."); id. at 322 ("The Jew's mode of dress, his diet, dwelling, behavior, relation with men, his family affairs, and his business affairs were all prefixed and premolded, in a national cloak, in a set of laws that was clear, severe, strict, detailed, that accompanied him day by day, from cradle to grave.").

In addition, many of these commandments can be further divided into component parts, resulting in a substantially larger number of enumerated obligations. Finally, there exist other imperatives that, although for methodological reasons are not tallied as commandments, nonetheless present yet additional enumerated obligations. See generally Maimonides, supra.

57 5 Nachmanides, supra note 55, at 88 (explicating Deuteronomy 6:18); see also Yoseph Albo, *Sefer Ha-Ikkarim* 3:23, quoted in Menachem Elon, *Jewish Law: History, Sources, Principles* (Bernard Auerbach & Melvin J. Sykes trans., 1994). Rabbi Albo explained:

It is impossible for the Torah of God to have covered all possible cases that may ever arise, because the new situations that constantly arise in human affairs, in law, and as a result of human enterprise are so manifold that a book cannot encompass them. Therefore, general principles, which the Torah only briefly suggests, were revealed orally to Moses at Sinai, so that the halakhic authorities of every generation would use them to derive new laws.

Id. at 241 (footnotes omitted).

58 3 Nachmanides, supra note 55, at 282 (explicating Leviticus 19:2).
59 Id. at 282-83.

for the derivation of unenumerated principles. In fact, Jewish law may provide a particularly helpful interpretive model for the analysis of ethics codes, because both focus on obligations rather than rights. Robert Cover famously contrasted the American legal system with the Jewish legal system through the observation that "[t]he principal word in Jewish law, which occupies a place equivalent in evocative force to the American legal system's 'rights,' is the word 'mitzvah' which literally means commandment but has a general meaning closer to 'incumbent obligation.'"[60] By its nature, the notion of unenumerated constitutional rights

---

60 Robert M. Cover, *Obligation: A Jewish Jurisprudence of the Social Order*, 5 J.L. & Religion 65, 65 (1987). See also Sol Roth, *Halakha and Politics: The Jewish Idea of the State* 97 (1988) (describing Jewish law's "supreme concern with duties or obligations"); Chapter 10 in this Volume ("Jewish law imposes many duties and obligations on the individual that are inconsistent with Western definitions of 'liberty' and autonomy."); Silberg, supra note 56, at 313-14 (observing that "modern law has no interest in duties; its sole interests are rights" and that "[o]ne cannot strike the words 'to have a right' from the modern legal dictionary, but it is definitely possible to exist without the words 'to be obliged,'" in contrast with "the great value which Jewish law attributes to the duty of fulfilling the legal obligation ... [which] is neither exhausted by nor limited to the possibility of civil realization of the ... right of action, as in other legal systems, but relies on, and to no small extent, the religious-moral duty"). Steven F. Friedell, *Aaron Kirschenbaum on Equity in Jewish Law*, 1993 BYU L. Rev. 909, 913 (book review) ("American law, for example, places a high value on individualism, free enterprise, and privacy. Jewish law, while not always opposed to these goals, has other aspirations that may cause conflict[, including] ... the maintenance of a religious community committed to mutual support through acts of loving kindness.").

　　Despite this general distinction, in some areas, such as the rights of criminal defendants, Jewish law appears to offer greater protections than American constitutional law. See, e.g., Chapter 5 in this Volume (citing the Talmud's description of the "painstaking procedural safeguards that were required to be observed before the death penalty could be carried out" and noting that "[s]uch safeguards were implemented throughout the Jewish criminal justice process, including during the apprehension of the individual, the introduction of evidence at trial, the deliberations, the rendering of a verdict, and post-verdict proceedings[,] ... produc[ing] a criminal justice system in which the death penalty was implemented somewhat infrequently"); Donald L. Beschle, *What's Guilt (or Deterrence) Got to Do with It?: The Death Penalty, Ritual, and Mimetic Violence*, 38 Wm. & Mary L. Rev. 487, 508 (1997) (stating that "[t]he procedural demands necessary to sustain a capital sentence [in ancient Israel] were increased to a level that would [have] put the Warren Court to shame"); Irene Merker Rosenberg & Yale L. Rosenberg, *In the Beginning: The Talmudic Rule Against Self-Incrimination*, 63 N.Y.U. L. Rev. 955, 956 (1988) (contrasting the American privilege against self-incrimination with the rule in Jewish law that, "with few exceptions, effectively precluded the admission of any confession of guilt in both criminal and quasi-criminal cases, whether by defendant or witness, in-court or out-of-court, voluntary or coerced, spontaneous or elicited").

　　Yet even these apparent exceptions may instead lend further support to the depiction of an obligation-based jurisprudence underlying the Jewish legal system, as the rights accorded a criminal defendant were, in part, an extension of the interpersonal obligations of rescuing those who are in peril and protecting the sanctity of human life. See, e.g., Rabbi Hershel

may epitomize Cover's characterization of a rights-based jurisprudence underlying American law. Ethics codes, however, appear to comprise a somewhat unique area of American law, in which obligation—the ethical obligations incumbent upon a lawyer—plays a primary role.[61] Therefore, for the purpose of comparative hermeneutic analysis, American ethics codes seem, in this sense, more similar to Jewish law than to American constitutional law.

PART THREE | DERIVING AND IDENTIFYING UNENUMERATED ETHICAL OBLIGATIONS: AN EXERCISE IN COMPARATIVE HERMENEUTICS

A close look at the interpretive methods that have been applied to ethics codes, the United States Constitution, and the Torah may reveal a common approach to the derivation and identification of unenumerated principles based on a common hermeneutic framework employed in the interpretation of broad provisions. The following analysis, therefore, builds on the work of scholars who have compared constitutional and biblical interpretation.[62]

Specifically, this analysis examines three related, but conceptually distinct, interpretive methodologies, each of which has been used to derive both unenumerated constitutional rights and unenumerated biblical obligations,[63] then

---

Schachter, Eretz Hatzevi 243-48 (1992); Talmud Bavli, Pesachim 12a (explicating Numbers 35:25); Rosh ha-Shana 26a (same); Sanhedrin 69a (same); Chapter 5 in this Volume; Samuel J. Levine, *Capital Punishment and Religious Arguments: An Intermediate Approach*, 9 Wm. & Mary Bill Rts. J. 179, 188-89 (2000).

61 Cf. Susan P. Koniak, *Through the Looking Glass of Ethics and the Wrongs with Rights We Find There*, 9 Geo. J. Legal Ethics 1, 28-29 (1995) (elaborating on Cover's analysis, stating that "[u]nlike tax law, tort law or other sources of legal obligation in our normative world, ethics is not merely a source of obligation but the place where obligation is understood as dignifying and ennobling" and that "[i]n legal and judicial ethics we find the possibility of dignifying obligations that are enforceable as law").

62 See Steven D. Smith, *Believing Like a Lawyer*, 40 B.C. L. Rev. 1041, 1068 (1999) ("[T]he similarities between legal and scriptural interpretation are so imposing that they have been noticed by a number of modern legal scholars."); see, e.g., Chapters 3 and 9 in this Volume; Sanford Levinson, *Constitutional Faith* (1985); Robert M. Cover, "The Supreme Court, 1982 Term—Foreword: *Nomos and Narrative*," 97 Harv. L. Rev. 4 (1983); David R. Dow, *Constitutional Midrash: The Rabbis' Solution to Professor Bickel's Problem*, 29 Houston L. Rev. 543 (1992); Ronald R. Garet, *Comparative Normative Hermeneutics: Scripture, Literature, Constitution*, 58 S. Cal. L. Rev. 35 (1985); Thomas C. Grey, *The Constitution as Scripture*, 37 Stan. L. Rev. 1 (1984); Steven D. Smith, *Idolatry in Constitutional Interpretation*, 79 Va. L. Rev. 583 (1993).

63 Although this analysis borrows briefly from the framework developed in Chapter 9 in this Volume, the present discussion provides both a different emphasis and additional insights, applied in the context of interpreting ethics codes.

posits that these three methodologies may be applied for the derivation of unenumerated ethical obligations as well. The analysis is presented both on a descriptive level, through a sampling of court decisions that have employed these methods to interpret broad ethics provisions, and on a more theoretical level, through an examination of the underlying normative rationale behind the use of these methods in the interpretation of ethics codes, the Constitution, and the Torah.

A. Interpretive Methodologies Employed in the Derivation of Unenumerated Constitutional Rights and Unenumerated Biblical Obligations

The first method of deriving unenumerated rights and obligations involves interpretating a broad term found within a legal provision, based on traditions transmitted largely outside of the interpretive process, to include additional unenumerated applications of the provision.[64] For example, the United States Supreme Court has interpreted the Fourteenth Amendment's broad guarantee of "liberty"[65] to include the freedom "to enjoy those privileges long recognized at common law as essential to the orderly pursuit of happiness by free men."[66] Thus, in *Meyer v. Nebraska*, the Court determined that

---

64 See Chapter 9 in this Volume.

65 U.S. Const. amend. XIV, §1 (stating, in relevant part, "[n]o State shall . . . deprive any person of life, liberty, or property, without due process of law").

66 *Meyer v. Nebraska*, 262 U.S. 390, 399 (1923). For a discussion of subsequent cases relying on a similar understanding of the term "liberty," see Chapter 9 in this Volume. More recently, writing the plurality opinion in *Troxel v. Granville*, 530 U.S. 57 (2000), Justice O'Connor cited *Meyer*, 262 U.S. at 390, and its progeny in support of the proposition that "[t]he liberty interest at issue in this case—the interest of parents in the care, custody, and control of their children—is perhaps the oldest of the fundamental liberty interests recognized by this Court." *Troxel*, 530 U.S. at 65 (O'Connor, J., plurality opinion); see also id. at 66 (O'Connor, J., plurality opinion) (citing and characterizing a number of more recent cases as "extensive precedent" supporting the proposition that "it cannot now be doubted that the Due Process Clause of the Fourteenth Amendment protects the fundamental right of parents to make decisions concerning the care, custody, and control of their children.").

In one such precedential case, the Court observed:

[Under o]ur established method of substantive-due-process analysis . . . we have regularly observed that the Due Process Clause specially protects those fundamental rights and liberties which are, objectively, "deeply rooted in this Nation's history and tradition" and "implicit in the concept of ordered liberty," such that "neither liberty nor justice would exist if they were sacrificed."

Washington v. Glucksberg, 521 U.S. 702, 720-21 (1997) (citations omitted); id. at 721 ("Our Nation's history, legal traditions, and practices . . . provide the crucial 'guideposts for

"[t]he American people have always regarded education and acquisition of knowledge as matters of supreme importance which should be diligently promoted."[67] As a result, the Court struck down a Nebraska state law prohibiting teaching any language other than English prior to high school, concluding that the teacher's "right thus to teach and the right of parents to engage him so to instruct their children . . . are within the liberty of the Amendment."[68]

Similarly, Jewish legal authorities have interpreted the broad command "you shall be holy"[69] to require adherence to unenumerated obligations, identifiable through reference to historical narrative and traditions.[70] For example, Nachmanides notes that the Torah does not enumerate a prohibition against drunkenness.[71] Nevertheless, he finds, the command to be holy prohibits actions that violate the concept of holiness, including drunkenness.[72] An express prohibition is unnecessary, he explains, as the spiritual vices and dangers of drunkenness are included within the narrative tradition in the stories of Noah and Lot, and thus are incorporated in the enumerated command to be holy.[73]

The second method of deriving unenumerated rights and obligations looks to the substance of the rules that are enumerated and applies the broad principles underlying those rules, extending the protections and obligations to unenumerated circumstances as well.[74] In *Griswold v. Connecticut*, the United States Supreme Court explained that "specific guarantees in the Bill of Rights

---

responsible decisionmaking,' that direct and restrain our exposition of the Due Process Clause." (citation omitted)); id. at 727 & n.19 (citing cases identifying "those personal activities and decisions that this Court has identified as so deeply rooted in our history and traditions, or so fundamental to our concept of constitutionally ordered liberty, that they are protected by the Fourteenth Amendment").

67 *Meyer*, 262 U.S. at 400.

68 Id.

69 Leviticus 19:2.

70 See Chapter 9 in this Volume. For a discussion of the relationship between law and narrative in Jewish legal theory, including the normative relevance of narrative and the interplay between legal precepts and narrative, in the Torah and other primary and secondary sources of Jewish law, see Chapter 17 in Volume 2.

71 See 3 Nachmanides, supra note 55, at 282 (explicating Leviticus 19:2).

72 See id. at 283.

73 See id. (citing Genesis 9:21, 19:33); see also Maimonides, *Mishne Torah*, Laws of De'oth 5:3; Laws of Festivals 6:20-21.

For a summary of the debate among legal authorities about whether—and if so, to what extent—the celebration of the holiday of Purim presents an exception to this general prohibition, see Shlomo Yosef Zevin, *Hamoadim B'halacha* 203-8 (1955). For a normative analysis of the position that the prohibition is suspended for the celebration of Purim, and an explanation of the *sui generis* nature of Purim in this regard, see Yitzchak Hutner, *Pachad Yitzchak, Purim* 81-82 (6th ed. 1998).

74 See Chapter 9 in this Volume.

have penumbras, formed by emanations from those guarantees that help give them life and substance."[75] Thus, the Court stated, "[v]arious guarantees create zones of privacy."[76] Applying these principles to a Connecticut statute prohibiting contraceptives, after describing at length various unenumerated constitutional protections that stem from such penumbras, the Court found that the statute similarly "concern[ed] a relationship lying within the zone of privacy created by several fundamental constitutional guarantees."[77] On that basis, the Court struck down the statute as "repulsive to the notions of privacy surrounding the marriage relationship."[78]

Here too, Nachmanides presents a parallel interpretive methodology, in his analysis of the command to "do the just and the good."[79] According to Nachmanides, this broad command serves as another basis for obligations beyond those enumerated in the text of the Torah.[80] The identity of these obligations is derived through an examination of the principles underlying numerous enumerated obligations, such as respecting elders, preventing harm to others, and not seeking revenge.[81] Based on these principles, Nachmanides concludes that the command to adhere to "just and good" behavior extends to varied unenumerated areas of interpersonal conduct, such as according neighbors the right of first refusal on land, dressing and speaking to others in a respectful manner, and behaving in a cooperative manner in litigious settings.[82]

Finally, a third method for deriving unenumerated constitutional rights is based in the application of the Ninth Amendment.[83] In his famous concurrence in *Griswold*, Justice Goldberg argued that the Ninth Amendment provides a source for the unenumerated right of privacy in marriage, including the right to use contraceptives.[84] More generally, he concluded, the history and broad language of the Ninth Amendment demonstrated that "the Framers of the Constitution believed that there are additional fundamental rights, protected from governmental infringement, which exist alongside those

---

75 381 U.S. 479, 484 (1965).
76 Id.
77 Id. at 485.
78 Id. at 486.
79 See 5 Nachmanides, supra note 55, at 87-88 (explicating Deuteronomy 6:18); Chapter 9 in this Volume.
80 See 5 Nachmanides, supra note 55, at 87-88.
81 See id. at 88 (citing Leviticus 19:16, 18, 32).
82 See id. at 88.
83 See Chapter 9 in this Volume.
84 *Griswold v. Connecticut*, 381 U.S. 479, 487 (1965) (Goldberg, J., concurring).

fundamental rights specifically mentioned in the first eight constitutional amendments."[85] Notwithstanding the logic of this position, most Justices, apparently concerned that the amendment is cast in terms that are, in fact, too broad to apply, have generally resisted attempts to rely on the Ninth Amendment to derive and identify unenumerated constitutional rights.[86] Nevertheless, the Ninth Amendment has been embraced by some courts and numerous scholars as a valuable tool in constitutional interpretation.[87]

Once more, Jewish law offers a striking parallel, in the broad command to "love your neighbor as yourself."[88] Throughout Jewish legal history, authorities have universally interpreted the command to require "not only [ ] sentiment, but [ ] action, which is motivated by sentiment."[89] Given the number and range of enumerated laws governing interpersonal relationships, the powerful prescription to love one's neighbor as one's self has been understood as a source of rather extensive unenumerated interpersonal obligations.[90] Similar to the Ninth Amendment, the precise legal contours of this broad rule have been the

---

85 Id. at 488 (Goldberg, J., concurring).

86 See infra notes 162-164 and accompanying text. See also Chapter 11 in this Volume.

87 See infra notes 165-167 and accompanying text. See also Chapter 11 in this Volume.

88 Leviticus 19:18; see Chapter 9 in this Volume.

89 Joseph B. Soloveitchik, *Family Redeemed* 40 (David Schatz & Joel Wolowelsky eds., 2000).

90 Analyzing statements in the Talmud and in the work of Maimonides, Rabbi Soloveitchik identifies and conceptualizes three interpretations of the command:

> The first interpretation, phrased in the negative, says that the I must recognize the existence of the thou, I must see thou as real. This act of acknowledgment contains *ipso facto* a contractual relationship with the basic clause that guards the rights of the other in the same manner as I want my prerogatives to be protected from unjust infringement. The relationship is of a *juridic* nature. There is a solidarity awareness; yet solidarity is not to be equated with community. We must not speak of a union. The autonomy has not been completely eliminated. One considers the thou as the other self who is not to be equated with the I. . . . [N]o existential union has been formed as yet. The thou has not entered the I, nor has the I been admitted into the thou. The second . . . interpretation points toward a higher level of interhuman relationship. The latter is raised from an awareness of neutral facticity to an awareness of ontic solidarity. The third notion proclaims "union of being." Individual existence ceases to be solitary. It becomes a community existence, a fellowship of [acts of kindness], rooted in an awareness of unity.

Id. at 143-46 (citing Talmud Bavli, Shabbath 31a; Maimonides, supra note 73, Laws of Mourning 14:1; Talmud Bavli, Bava Metzia 62a). See also Reuven P. Bulka, *Love Your Neighbor: Halachic Parameters*, 16 J. Halacha & Contemp. Soc'y 44 (1988); Yitzchak Hutner, *Pachad Yitzchak, Pesach* 73-76 (6th ed. 1999).

subject of differing interpretations,[91] though unlike the Ninth Amendment, there is no debate as to the legal force of the rule.

B. Applying the Interpretive Methodologies: Deriving and Identifying Unenumerated Ethical Obligations

Courts interpreting ethics codes have, at times, relied on methods similar to those employed in both constitutional law and Jewish law to derive unenumerated legal principles from principles that are enumerated. In particular, a number of courts have found that broad ethics provisions provide a source for the derivation, identification, and application of ethical obligations beyond those expressly enumerated in the text of ethics codes. Thus, notwithstanding the criticisms of Wolfram and other scholars,[92] rather than rejecting broad ethics provisions, these courts have affirmed the normative and practical utility of such rules as a valuable tool in interpreting ethics codes. The courts' application of these methods is perhaps most apparent and, in light of enduring scholarly criticism, perhaps most striking, in the interpretation of rules that prohibit "conduct that adversely reflects on [the lawyer's] fitness to practice law,"[93] "conduct that is prejudicial to the administration of justice,"[94] and the "appearance of professional impropriety."[95]

1. DR 1-102(A)(6): "Conduct that Adversely Reflects on [the Lawyer's] Fitness to Practice Law"

The first of these provisions has faced the objections of scholars and judges who, in the words of one early critic, lack "confidence in an enlightened

---

91 See supra note 90.

92 See supra notes 33-45 and accompanying text.

93 Model Code of Prof'l Responsibility DR 1-102(A)(6) (1981).

94 Model Code of Prof'l Responsibility DR 1-102(A)(5); Model Rules of Prof'l Conduct R. 8.4(d).

95 Model Code of Prof'l Responsibility Canon 9. For a similar approach to broad rules, applied in a very different context, see Martin Kosla, *Disciplined for "Bringing a Sport into Disrepute"—A Framework for Judicial Review*, 25 Melb. U. L. Rev. 654 (2001). Kosla observes that because "[i]t is not possible for the rules and codes of conduct to expressly provide for all misbehaviour that may have an adverse effect on a sport[,] . . . wide-reaching clauses are employed to catch misconduct that falls outside the scope of specific rules." Id. at 655. He concludes that "[n]otwithstanding its imprecise nature, closer examination of the case law reveals that the disrepute clause does have boundaries and limits." Id. at 666.

application of the . . . clause because [they are] uncertain what conduct will be held to reflect adversely on fitness to practice law."[96] These concerns over the broad, and potentially vague, nature of the rule were echoed by the Court of Appeals of Maryland in rejecting an appeal of a trial court's refusal to find a violation of DR 1-102(A)(6).[97] The bar counsel argued that the trial court should have found that a lawyer's "allowing his position as an attorney to be used to induce persons to invest in a scheme that turned out to be fraudulent amounts to conduct that adversely reflects on his fitness to practice law."[98] The appellate court found that the bar counsel's contention "paints with too broad a brush" and instead concluded that "[t]he specific conduct relied upon to demonstrate a lack of fitness to practice law is properly considered under the specific charges of inadequate preparation and neglect (DR 6-101), but not as a predicate for finding a violation for DR 1-102(A)(6)."[99]

Nevertheless, in practice, "most courts have upheld [broad ethics] provisions against constitutional attacks on the grounds of vagueness and overbreadth."[100] Many courts upholding rules modeled after DR 1-102(A)(6) have relied on the reasoning offered by the United States Supreme Court in upholding rules invoking "conduct unbecoming a member of the bar of the court."[101] In a 1968 concurring opinion in *In re Ruffalo*, Justice White explained that

---

96 Donald T. Weckstein, *Maintaining the Integrity and Competence of the Legal Profession*, 48 Tex. L. Rev. 267, 276 (1970).

97 See *Attorney Grievance Comm'n v. Martin*, 518 A.2d 1050, 1054 (Md. 1987).

98 Id.

99 Id.

100 Gross, supra note 45, at 1455 n.245; see also supra note 47. Furthermore, in *Committee on Professional Ethics v. Durham*, the court stated:

> The respondent is unable to cite any case in which a provision of the Code of Professional Responsibility has been held to be unenforceably vague, nor has our research uncovered any such instance . . . . Other jurisdictions which have approached the question of the constitutionality of standards relating to professional conduct, with language similar to [DR 1-102(a)(6)], have upheld the guidelines in the face of vagueness challenges.

279 N.W.2d 280, 282 (Iowa 1979) (citing an extensive list of cases).

101 The Supreme Court quoted a United States Court of Appeals for the Sixth Circuit rule containing language strikingly similar to DR 1-102(A)(6). *In re Ruffalo*, 390 U.S. 544, 554-55 (1968) (White, J., concurring) (quoting Rule 6(3), United States Court of Appeals for the Sixth Circuit). In *Zauderer v. Office of Disciplinary Counsel*, the Court stated:

> Given the traditions of the legal profession and an attorney's specialized professional training, there is unquestionably some room for enforcement of standards that might be impermissibly vague in other contexts; an attorney in many instances may properly be punished for "conduct which all responsible

[e]ven when a disbarment standard is as unspecific as the one before us, members of a bar can be assumed to know that certain kinds of conduct, generally condemned by responsible men, will be grounds for disbarment . . . includ[ing] conduct which all responsible attorneys would recognize as improper for a member of the profession.[102]

Thus, according to Justice White, similar to the broad concepts of "liberty" in the United States Constitution and "holiness" in Jewish law, broad prohibitions on improper conduct by attorneys are interpreted to extend to unenumerated conduct, incorporated through the understanding of members of the community—here, members of the legal profession.[103]

Seventeen years later, in *In re Snyder*, without citing Justice White's opinion in *Ruffalo*, the Court as a whole adopted and further refined his approach

---

attorneys would recognize as improper for a member of the profession."

471 U.S. 626, 666 (1985) (Brennan, J., concurring in part, concurring in the judgment in part, and dissenting in part) (quoting *In re Ruffalo*, 390 U.S. at 555 (White, J. concurring)).

102 *In re Ruffalo*, 390 U.S. at 555 (White, J. concurring).

103 Id. The emphasis on the role of the interpretive community of lawyers in defining the boundaries of ethical behavior is investigated in Susan G. Kupfer, *Authentic Legal Practices*, 10 Geo. J. Legal Ethics 33 (1996). According to Kupfer, on the individual level, "[t]he lawyer looking to the Model Code or Model Rules to solve practical problems quickly realizes the severe practical limitations: either the matter is explicitly contained in a Disciplinary Rule and his/her conduct is mandated or the lawyer is free to formulate a completely subjective approach to the issue." Id. at 51 (footnotes omitted). She explains, however, that in practice,

> [t]he individual (the moral self) undertakes the task of formulating, shaping, and building her morality through discursive practice with others. In postmodern thought, practices occur and their meaning is created through interpretation by members of a discrete community. Discursive practice, in which human experience is shaped by and through this interaction, reconstructs meaning from these patterns of experience. Norms and standards in ethical practice, for example, evolve from these acts of interpretation, not through reference to general principles contained in universal codes.

Id. at 63-64 (footnotes omitted); see also id. at 64 n.80 (citing Stanley Fish, *Doing What Comes Naturally: Change, Rhetoric, and the Practice of Theory in Literary and Legal Studies* (1989)); Stanley Fish, *Is There a Text in This Class?: The Authority of Interpretive Communities* (1980)); Kupfer, supra, at 94 n.224 (relying on Stanley Fish for the concept of an "'interpretive community,' in which one is contingently and historically situated so that one's very construction of knowledge is a product of one's experience").

Although Kupfer further emphasizes that "individual legal actors need to work from their own integrated beliefs because they will find . . . that the profession's ethical norms are too vague or unresponsive to the individual lawyer or client's needs," ultimately she acknowledges that "[o]n the other hand, the ethical constraints of community are necessary to temper the wildest and, perhaps, unacceptable individual judgments." Id. at 65 n.86.

when interpreting and applying a rule subjecting attorneys to discipline for engaging in "conduct unbecoming a member of the bar of the court."[104] The Court reasoned that "[r]ead in light of the traditional duties imposed on an attorney, it is clear that 'conduct unbecoming a member of the bar' is conduct contrary to professional standards that shows an unfitness to discharge continuing obligations to clients or the courts, or conduct inimical to the administration of justice."[105]

In response to concerns over the application of such a broad provision, the Court continued to focus on historical sources of the traditional obligations of attorneys, concluding that "[m]ore specific guidance is provided by case law, applicable court rules, and 'the lore of the profession' as embodied in codes of professional conduct."[106] The Court thus relied on both legal precepts—articulated in case law and court rules, and ethical traditions—the "lore" of the legal profession, as sources of "guidance" for identifying the unenumerated substance

---

The tension Kupfer describes between an individual lawyer's search for ethical truth and the need to rely on the interpretive constraints of the community is inherent more generally in legal reasoning and legal interpretation. Robert Cover describes this tension:

> It is the problem of the multiplicity of meaning . . . that leads at once to the imperial virtues and the imperial mode of world maintenance. . . . Let loose, unfettered, the worlds created would be unstable and sectarian in their social organization, dissociative and incoherent in their discourse, wary and violent in their interactions. The sober imperial mode of world maintenance holds the mirror of critical objectivity to meaning, [and] imposes the discipline of institutional justice upon norms. . . .

Cover, supra note 62, at 16. See also Owen M. Fiss, *Objectivity and Interpretation*, 34 Stan. L. Rev. 739, 747 (1982) ("[A] hierarchy of authority for resolving disputes that could potentially divide or destroy an interpretive community is one of the distinctive features of legal interpretation.").

As I have developed elsewhere, this tension is perhaps most pronounced when the search for truth is founded on ethics, as in Kupfer's analysis, or in morality, as in Jewish law. See Chapter 3 in this Volume. Nachmanides explained:

> [E]ven if you think in your heart [the judges of the High Court] are mistaken, and the matter is simple in your eyes . . . you must still do as they command you. . . . [F]or the Torah was given to us in written form and it is known that not all opinions concur on newly arising matters. Disagreements would thus increase and the one Torah would become many Torahs. Scripture, therefore, defined the law that we are to obey [the High Court] . . . in whatever they tell us with respect to the interpretation of the Torah. . . .

5 Nachmanides, supra note 55, at 206-7 (explicating Deuteronomy 17:11).

104 *In re Snyder*, 472 U.S. 634, 643-44 (1985) (quoting Fed. R. App. P. 46(b) (1989)).
105 Id. at 645.
106 Id.

of the broad prohibition on conduct unbecoming of an attorney.[107] Like Justice White, the *Snyder* Court acknowledged the role that traditional conceptions of ethical conduct for lawyers plays in the interpretation of broad ethics rules.[108]

---

107 Id.

108 Id. at 644-45; cf. *In re Ruffalo*, 390 U.S. 544, 555 (1968) (White, J., concurring). As one scholar noted:

> Although . . . the Court seemed to equate professional lore with the positive disciplinary codes promulgated by state bar associations, the Court also appeared to concede that the competing demands of zealously advocating one's client's cause and advancing the cause of justice must be resolved "in light of the traditional duties imposed on an attorney," which are not neatly captured in the disciplinary codes.

W. Bradley Wendel, *Nonlegal Regulation of the Legal Profession: Social Norms in Professional Communities*, 54 Vand. L. Rev. 1955, 1963 (2001) (discussing and quoting *In re Snyder*, 472 U.S. 634, 644-45 (1985)).

The recognition of the significance of both legal precepts and communal traditions in legal interpretation was explored by Robert Cover in his groundbreaking article, "*Nomos* and Narrative." See Cover, supra note 62. Cover describes a *nomos* as a "normative universe . . . a world of right and wrong, of lawful and unlawful." Id. at 4. *Nomos* includes a legal tradition comprised of "not only a corpus juris, but also a language and a mythos—narratives in which the corpus juris is located." Id. at 9. Narratives, in turn, include "the community's . . . societal norms, attitudes, and aspirations, which 'bespeak the range of the group's commitments' and 'provide resources for justification, condemnation, and argument by actors within the group, who must struggle to live their law." See Chapter 17 in Volume 2 (quoting Cover, supra note 62, at 45).

Cover's framework of *nomos* and narrative thus presents yet another conceptual setting for examining hermeneutic similarities in constitutional law, Jewish law, and ethics. Cover's analysis focuses on interpretation of the United States Constitution, in particular in the context of antislavery construction of the Constitution and interpretation of the Free Exercise Clause by members of insular religious communities. See generally Cover, supra note 62. As a number of scholars have observed, and as I have developed at length, "Cover's very conception of *nomos* and narrative appears influenced by, if not a direct application of, the parallel notions of *halacha* and *aggada* in Jewish legal thought." See Chapter 17 in Volume 2.

Likewise, scholars have applied Cover's framework to ethics interpretation:

> The idea of community is fundamental to American law. It pervades federal and state constitutions, statutes, and common law doctrines. It also suffuses professional rhetoric and regulation. Most important, it links law to politics, culture, and society. . . . Applicable to both civil and criminal law fields, the literature assembles a wide-ranging collection of community norms and narratives.

Anthony V. Alfieri, *Prosecuting Violence/Reconstructing Community*, 52 Stan. L. Rev. 809, 819 (2000) (footnotes omitted); Koniak, supra note 33, at 1390 n.1 ("This Article uses Robert Cover's rich and original vision of law, which he articulated most fully in ["*Nomos* and Narrative"] . . . as a means of understanding the law governing lawyers."); id. at 1392 ("This Article examines the profession's *nomos*—its law—and how it contrasts, competes and coexists with the state's law governing lawyers."); W. Bradley Wendel, *Professional Roles and Moral Agency*,

In considering challenges to provisions prohibiting "conduct that adversely reflects on [the attorney's] fitness to practice law,"[109] courts have similarly adopted the position that members of the legal profession are expected to possess an understanding of what conduct is improper and unethical, even if such conduct is not specifically enumerated in an ethics code. The New York Court of Appeals, citing Justice White's concurrence in *Ruffalo*,[110] rejected arguments for "an absolute prohibition on broad standards" such as DR 1-102(A)(6).[111]

---

89 Geo. L.J. 667, 685 (2001) (book review) ("An ethical principle does not have meaning in the abstract, but takes its content from the normative understanding—the *nomos* in Robert Cover's term—of the community which adheres to the principle" (footnotes omitted)); W. Bradley Wendel, *Value Pluralism in Legal Ethics*, 78 Wash. U. L.Q. 113, 118 (2000) ("The community's *nomos*—the justificatory narrative that locates, constitutes, and gives meaning to the social institution of lawyering—is itself the criterion for ranking the competing professional values." (footnotes omitted)). See also Kupfer, supra note 103 at 65 n.86 (noting that the ethical constraints of community are needed to guide individual moral judgments); Thomas L. Shaffer, *Legal Ethics and Jurisprudence from Within Religious Congregations*, 76 Notre Dame L. Rev. 961, 963 (2001) (suggesting that lawyers can find answers to ethical dilemmas in the context of moral concepts "better than in 'professional' committees that propound and interpret ethical rules").

   The idea that there exist communal narratives and traditions for lawyers has been explored by some of the most prominent and influential ethics scholars. See, e.g., Monroe H. Freedman, *Understanding Lawyers' Ethics* 75-76 (1990) (describing the actions of Sir Marshall Hall and Lord Erskine as "incidents [that] ha[ve] come down in our professional lore from the tradition of the English barrister" and that have "been cited as representing the ideal of an independent bar"); Thomas L. Shaffer, *Faith and the Professions* (1987); Hazard, supra note 1, at 1243-44 (describing a "narrative of the American legal profession [as] convey[ing] a . . . clear ideal . . . of the fearless advocate who champions a client threatened with loss of life and liberty by government oppression" and describing the process through which this "basic narrative has been sustained over two centuries"); Koniak, supra, at 1447-60 (describing the "central and recurring theme in the profession's narratives portray[ing] the lawyer as champion, defending the client's life and liberty against the government, which is portrayed as oppressor, willing, ready and able to use its power to destroy the individual and the values society holds dear"); id. at 1448, 1450 n.263 (observing that "[t]he story has many versions"); Carrie Menkel-Meadow, *Foreword: Telling Stories in School: Using Case Studies and Stories to Teach Legal Ethics*, 69 Fordham L. Rev. 787 (2000); Thomas L. Shaffer, *The Biblical Prophets As Lawyers for the Poor*, 31 Fordham Urb. L.J. 15, 15-17 (2003) (describing role of tradition and mentors in practice of law and identifying John Adams, Andrew Hamilton, army lawyers who defended General Yamashita, and Thomas More as his own mentors); see also Leslie E. Gerber, *Can Lawyers Be Saved? The Theological Legal Ethics of Thomas Shaffer*, 10 J.L. & Religion 347, 353 (1993-94) (describing Shaffer's pioneering work as "narrative legal ethics").

109 Model Code of Prof'l Responsibility DR 1-102(A)(6).
110 See supra notes 101-103 and accompanying text.
111 *In re Holtzman*, 577 N.E.2d 30, 33 (N.Y. 1991).

   Although the precise wording of then DR 1-102(A)(6) is different from that of the "conduct unbecoming" court rule addressed by Justice White, the New York court apparently found the substance of the rules sufficiently alike for the purposes of both its analysis

Instead, the court adopted the "guiding principle" of "whether a reasonable attorney, familiar with the Code and its ethical strictures, would have notice of what conduct is proscribed."[112]

Applying this principle, an intermediate appellate New York State court rejected an attorney's argument that he should not be sanctioned under the New York code's "fitness to practice law" provision[113] for "violating a standard of conduct that had never before been announced."[114] The court held that discipline was appropriate because, although the case was one of first impression, "a reasonable attorney would have been on notice that revealing sensitive information about client matters to reporters could be held to reflect adversely on his or her fitness as a lawyer."[115] Thus, the court upheld the broad rule and, through an analysis of the ethical understandings of the reasonable attorney, interpreted the rule as a basis for an unenumerated obligation that had not previously been identified by the court.[116]

---

of DR 1-102(A)(6) and its more general endorsement of broad ethics provisions. See *In re Holtzman*, 577 N.E.2d at 33.

    In a similar vein, Wolfram groups his negative depiction of broad ethics provisions together with his criticism of Federal Rule of Appellate Procedure 46(c), the "conduct unbecoming" provision addressed and upheld by the United States Supreme Court in *In re Snyder*, 472 U.S. 634, 643-44 (1985). In fact, following his discussion of what is, in his view, the improperly broad nature of DR 1-102(A)(5) and DR 1-102(A)(6) of the Model Code and Rule 8.4(d) of the Model Rules, Wolfram writes that "[u]ltimate breadth is achieved in [Federal] Rule [of Appellate Procedure] 46(c)." Wolfram, supra note 3, at 88. To the extent that the Court's approach in *In re Snyder* proves convincing, it would seem that a similar approach should likewise satisfy Wolfram's concerns over the application of broad ethics provisions. See supra notes 104-108 and accompanying text.

112 *In re Holtzman*, 577 N.E.2d at 48; see also *State ex rel. Neb. State Bar Ass'n v. Kirshen*, 441 N.W.2d 161, 168 (Neb. 1989) ("A reasonable attorney would understand that this type of conduct is prohibited and adversely reflects on his fitness to practice law."); *Comm. on Prof'l Ethics v. Durham*, 279 N.W.2d 280, 284 (Iowa 1979) (adopting standard of "whether a 'reasonable attorney' would understand certain conduct to be prohibited").

113 New York Code of Prof'l Responsibility DR 1-102(A)(7) (2002).

114 *In re Holley*, 729 N.Y.S.2d 128, 132 (App. Div. 2001).

115 Id.

116 Id. Indeed, under this analysis, if anything, the absence of enumeration and/or case law addressing such conduct may be considered more a function of the lack of necessity of an express articulation than a reflection of the possibility that the conduct is not ethically prohibited. See *Grievance Comm. v. Rottner*, 203 A.2d 82, 85 (Conn. 1964). The *Rottner* Court held:

> The almost complete absence of authority governing the situation where, as in the present case, the lawyer is still representing the client whom he sues

Other courts have offered similar grounds for rejecting challenges to the application of ethics provisions modeled after DR 1-102(A)(6). The Colorado Supreme Court emphasized that ethics rules are written for lawyers, not for the public:

> Since a disciplinary rule is promulgated for the purpose of guiding lawyers in their professional conduct, and is not directed to the public at large, the central consideration in resolving a vagueness challenge should be whether the nature of the proscribed conduct encompassed by the rule is readily understandable to a licensed lawyer.[117]

> clearly indicates to us that the common understanding and the common conscience of the bar is in accord with our holding that such a suit constitutes a reprehensible breach of loyalty and a violation of the preamble to the Canons of Professional Ethics. This determination is sufficient to support the judgment and to render unnecessary a discussion of the specific canons which the court found were violated by the defendants.

Id. at 85. But see *In re Gadbois*, 786 A.2d 393, 400 (Vt. 2001) (quoting Restatement (Third) of the Law Governing Lawyers §5 cmt. c) (adhering to the comment of the Restatement that "a specific lawyer-code provision that states the elements of an offense should not, in effect, be extended beyond its stated terms through supplemental application of a general provision to conduct that is similar to but falls outside of the explicitly stated ground for a violation").

117 *People v. Morley*, 725 P.2d 510, 516 (Colo. 1986) (en banc); cf. *Comm. on Prof'l Ethics v. Durham*, 279 N.W.2d 280, 284 (Iowa 1979) (rejecting a challenge to broad ethics provisions in part because "the Code of Professional Responsibility was written for lawyers by lawyers"); Koniak, supra note 32, at 1393 n.15 (citing Robert W. Gordon, *The Independence of Lawyers*, 68 B.U. L. Rev. 1, 10 (1988) (referring to "scholars of the profession, who understand the importance of the substantial heterogeneity in background, substance of work and work-setting of the modern bar, [but] have also described and accepted the existence of a core of shared normative understandings"); Deborah L. Rhode, *Ethical Perspectives on Legal Practice*, 37 Stan. L. Rev. 589, 595-605 (1985)).

Martha Johnston contrasts the Code of Professional Responsibility with the Military Code, in evaluating whether:

> the legal profession is sufficiently cohesive and differentiated from society by its own history and traditions to give content to seemingly imprecise professional rules and to justify the application of a more lenient standard of vagueness to those rules, along the lines of that applied to the Military Code in *Parker v. Levy*. This rationale has been adopted by some courts, but for several reasons it appears misplaced. . . . [First,] it is less likely in the legal context than in the military context that the interpretations of [the] code[] will be uniform. . . . [Second,] the myriad interpretations of the ABA Code by various state and federal courts cannot carry the same authority as the years of narrowing construction of the Code of Military Justice by the

As to the argument that "DR 1-102(A)(6) does not articulate what constitutes conduct affecting a lawyer's fitness to practice law,"[118] the Connecticut Supreme Court responded that "[l]awyers are chargeable for deviations from the codes governing their conduct, even though the application of the canons to particular circumstances may not be readily apparent."[119]

Perhaps the Vermont Supreme Court's analysis best reflects the approach of courts that have examined the norms and traditions of the legal profession in interpreting broad fitness to practice provisions as a source for the articulation of unenumerated ethical obligations. Although it acknowledged that

---

United States Court of Military Appeals. . . . [Third,] the legal profession is simply not as homogeneous, traditional and specialized in function as the military. . . . [Finally,] the Military Code provision was upheld under a diluted standard of vagueness review because the special responsibilities of servicemen in defense of the country, and the overriding need for discipline and obedience in the armed forces justify more limited constitutional rights for servicemen than for civilians.

Martha E. Johnston, *Comment, ABA Code of Professional Responsibility: Void for Vagueness?*, 57 N.C. L. Rev. 671, 687-88 (1979). See also Damtoft, supra note 48, at 1407-8 (distinguishing *Durham* from *Parker v. Levy*, 417 U.S. 733 (1974), which upheld 10 U.S.C. §933 (1964), a provision of the Uniform Code of Military Justice prohibiting "conduct unbecoming an officer and gentleman"). Damtoft argued that "[t]he law, training, and traditions of ethics in the civilian legal practice . . . are not as clearly developed as the military standards of behavior" and, "[t]herefore, the penumbra of clearly prohibited behavior under a broad standard for attorney conduct is considerably narrower than it is in a military context, and as a result, the Iowa Supreme Court's reliance on collateral interpretations of the provisions for clarification may not be well founded." Id.

Cf. also Painter, supra note 6, at 722 n.286 ("[I]t is possible that standards would be preferable to defined rules, if courts and agencies would build valuable precedent interpreting the standards as they have in contract and corporate law. A number of factors, however, distinguish the law governing lawyers from contract and corporate law."); Zacharias, supra note 4, at 237-38:

[P]rofessional codes must be evaluated differently than ordinary legislation and administrative schemes—even those that include legal "standards" as flexible as the standards in the codes. Flexible legal standards ordinarily rest on a premise that courts or some other lawmaking body will flesh out the standards and enforce more specific guidelines for behavior. . . . In contrast, professional code provisions rarely are fleshed out; clarifying ethics opinions are scarce, ad hoc, and generally inaccessible.

Id.; id. at 241 (citing scholarship in support of the proposition that some code provisions "set guidelines for conduct about which the rulemakers do not share, and do not expect to attain, a consensus"); id. at 276 (asserting that "a highly generalized provision cannot assist the courts in filling gaps in the substantive law").

118 *Statewide Grievance Comm. v. Rozbicki*, 595 A.2d 819, 825 (Conn. 1991).

119 Id. at 825 (quoting *Patterson v. Council on Probate Judicial Conduct*, 577 A.2d 701, 708 (Conn. 1990) (citing *Grievance Comm. v. Rottner*, 203 A.2d 82, 84-85 (Conn. 1964))).

the "generality of the phrase" in the fitness to practice rule "does make the rule susceptible to varying subjective interpretations," the court concluded that "the everyday realities of the profession and its overall code of conduct provide definition for this type of phrase and thus give adequate notice of which behavior constitutes proscribed conduct."[120]

2. DR 1-102(A)(5); Rule 8.4(d): "Conduct that Is Prejudicial to the Administration of Justice"

Not surprisingly, controversy has also surrounded the broad ethics provision, codified in both the Model Code and the Model Rules, prohibiting "conduct that is prejudicial to the administration of justice."[121] This provision has been criticized because of the concern among some scholars that "[a]rbitrary enforcement can be expected if, for example, there is no consensus on what types of conduct are included."[122] Some courts have likewise expressed dissatisfaction with the broad nature of the rule and its application to unenumerated areas of obligation. Typical of this view is the argument of one judge who, on the grounds that the language of the rule "does not give . . . guidance" to "[c]areful lawyers," dissented from the majority's "exten[sion of] the rule for the first time" to a new set of facts.[123]

Nevertheless, similar to the approach of a number of courts toward fitness to practice provisions, "most courts have upheld [prejudicial to the administration of justice] provisions against constitutional attacks on the grounds of vagueness and overbreadth."[124] Thus, a more common view of the rule may be that of the Court of Appeals of Maryland, which rejected an attorney's argument that the rule did not provide him sufficient notice.[125] The court bluntly responded that the attorney "could not be more incorrect."[126] As the

---

120 *In re Illuzzi*, 632 A.2d 346, 349 (Vt. 1993) (quoting *ABA/BNA Lawyer's Manual on Professional Conduct*, 101:1001 (1987)).

121 Model Code of Prof'l Responsibility DR 1-102(A)(5) (1981); Model Rules of Prof'l Responsibility R. 8.4(d) (1983).

122 Johnston, supra note 117, at 685.

123 *In re Masters*, 438 N.E.2d 187, 197 (Ill. 1982) (Simon, J., dissenting). Cf. *In re Discipline of Two Attorneys*, 660 N.E.2d 1093, 1099 (Mass. 1996) (stating that "[t]he better course, where possible, is to deal with alleged professional misconduct under specific rules . . . rather than to invoke the general language of DR 1-102(A)(5)").

124 Gross, supra note 45, at 1455 n.245 (citing sources).

125 *Attorney Grievance Comm'n v. Goldsborough*, 624 A.2d 503, 511 (Md. 1993).

126 Id.

court explained, "[i]t strains credulity to say that, merely because this Court had never previously addressed similar circumstances, an attorney with Goldsborough's experience was not 'on notice' that the conduct alleged by Bar Counsel could violate the Rules of Professional Conduct."[127]

Significantly, again similar to the interpretation of fitness to practice provisions, many courts have emphasized that because ethics codes are written for lawyers, the interpretation of prejudicial to the administration of justice provisions depends, in part, on the understanding of the professional legal community.[128] Indeed, like the constitutional guarantee of liberty and the biblical command to be holy, this prohibition, found in both the Model Code and the Model Rules, is applied to unenumerated situations on the basis of an examination of tradition that lends content and meaning to the broad ethics rule.[129]

---

127 Id.

128 See, e.g., id. at 510 (holding that Rule 8.4(d) "is sufficiently definite to pass constitutional muster [because] [t]he Rule applies only to lawyers, who are professionals and have the benefit of guidance provided by case law, court rules and the 'lore of the profession'" (internal quotations and citations omitted)); *Howell v. State Bar*, 843 F.2d 205, 208 (5th Cir. 1988) (quoting inter alia, *In re Snyder*, 472 U.S. 634, 645 (1985)) (finding that "[t]he traditional test for vagueness in regulatory prohibitions is whether 'they are set out in terms that the ordinary person exercising ordinary common sense can sufficiently understand and comply with, without sacrifice to the public interest'" and that, therefore, "[t]he particular context in which a regulation is promulgated . . . is all important" and noting that DR 1-102(A)(5) "applies only to lawyers, who are professionals and have the benefit of guidance provided by case law, court rules and the 'lore of the profession.'"); *In re Keiler*, 380 A.2d 119, 126 (D.C. 1977) (noting that DR 1-102(A)(5) "was written by and for lawyers" and explaining that "[t]he language of a rule setting guidelines for members of the bar need not meet the precise standards of clarity that might be required of rules of conduct for laymen.").

129 See, e.g., *Howell*, 843 F.2d at 206. The court in *Howell* relied on the tradition of the bench and bar to provide a context for DR 1-205(a)(5) by recognizing that

> [t]here was nothing startlingly innovative in DR 1-102(A)(5)'s contents. Since the early days of English common law, it has been widely recognized that courts possess the inherent power to regulate the conduct of attorneys who practice before them and to discipline or disbar such of those attorneys as are guilty of unprofessional conduct.

Id. (citing, inter alia, *In re Snyder*, 472 U.S. 634, 643 (1985)). Emphasizing the special role attorneys play in the justice system, the court noted that such a position has always incorporated a corresponding obligation:

> Case after case can be cited in support of the general proposition that, as officers of the court, attorneys owe a duty to the court that far exceeds that of lay citizens. . . .
> The Texas cases which both antedated and followed the adoption of DR 1-102(A)(5) demonstrate quite clearly that the State's primary concern

Alternatively, some courts applying prejudicial to the administration of justice provisions have employed an interpretive methodology more closely resembling the interpretation of constitutional conceptions of privacy and the biblical command to do the just and the good.[130] Rather than turning to general notions of communal tradition, these courts have identified unenumerated conduct prejudicial to the administration of justice by looking to the substance of, and extending the contours of, enumerated ethics rules.

Applying this methodology, the Superior Court of Rhode Island concluded that a lawyer is prohibited from appearing before a judge to whom the lawyer has loaned money.[131] The court acknowledged that there was no such express prohibition, despite many enumerated ethics rules that are implicated when an attorney lends money to a judge.[132] Accordingly, the court derived

---

consistently has been with the obligation of lawyers in their quasi-official capacity as "assistants to the court."

Id. at 207; *In re Hinds*, 449 A.2d 483, 497-98 (N.J. 1982) (citing, inter alia, *In re Ruffalo*, 390 U.S. 544 (1968)) (noting that "DR 1-102(A)(5) is framed in broad language and gives the appearance of an aspirational standard, rather than a disciplinary rule [but that] [c]ourts have held that a broad disciplinary rule may acquire constitutional certitude when examined in light of traditions in the profession and established patterns of application"); Keiler, 380 A.2d at 126 ("The language of the rule is clear. It is not a new standard but a restatement of a previously existing one."); *Office of Disciplinary Counsel v. Campbell*, 345 A.2d 616, 621-22 (Pa. 1975). While enforcing broad ethical proscriptions, the Pennsylvania Supreme Court declined to address the outer limits of the proscriptions and noted that the attorney should have known that he was violating them:

> We need not today define with exactitude the boundaries of the conduct proscribed by Disciplinary Rules 1-102(A)(5) and 1-102(A)(6). Certainly respondent's activities were within those bounds and respondent knew or should have known that such was the case. Since respondent had fair notice that his course of conduct was prohibited by the Code of Professional Responsibility, he cannot claim to have been prejudiced by the arguable vagueness of the Disciplinary Rules when applied to other hypothetical situations.

Id. at 622.

130 See supra notes 74-82 and accompanying text.
131 *Hurley v. Fuyat*, C.A. No. 92-5082, 1994 WL 930891, at *7 (R.I. Super. Jan. 5, 1994) (unpublished opinion).
132 See id. (stating that "[b]oth the old and the new rules explicitly prohibit a lawyer from making loans to a judge"). The court cited and described the following:

> DR 7-110 (prohibiting a lawyer from giving or lending anything of value to a judge); Rule 3.5 (prohibiting a lawyer from seeking to influence a judge by means prohibited by law); Rule 8.4(f) (forbidding a lawyer from knowingly assisting a judge in conduct that is a violation of applicable rules of

this prohibition through an interpretive methodology involving an examination of the principles underlying the enumerated rules, in conjunction with the identification of a broader source of unenumerated obligations.[133] Specifically, the court relied on the broad provision against "engag[ing] in conduct that is prejudicial to the administration of justice" to provide a conceptual basis for the unenumerated prohibition.[134] The court found that

> [t]his sweeping edict is not only broad enough to encompass the specific prohibition against lawyers making loans to judges that is encompassed elsewhere in the rules but also implicitly forbids a lawyer from appearing before a judge to whom he or she has loaned money, particularly where the existence of the loan has not been disclosed.[135]

> judicial conduct); Rule 21, Canons of Judicial Ethics (prohibiting a judge from receiving loans from litigants, lawyers or others whose interests are likely to be submitted to the judge for judgment). If a judge wrongfully solicits a loan from a lawyer, the lawyer is obligated to refuse the request and report the judicial misconduct to the appropriate disciplinary authorities. [Additionally,] see . . . DR 1-103 (requiring a lawyer possessing knowledge of another lawyer's conduct that is prejudicial to the administration of justice to report the violative conduct to a tribunal or other authority empowered to investigate or act upon such violation); Rule 8.3(a)(b) (requiring lawyers to report to the appropriate professional authorities the professional misconduct of judges and other lawyers).

Id. (citations omitted).

133 See id.

134 Id. (alteration in original) (quoting DR 1-102(A)(5); R. 8.4(d)).

135 Id.; cf. *In re Rinella*, 677 N.E.2d 909, 914 (Ill. 1997) (finding a violation of DR 1-102(A)(5), "reject[ing] respondent's contention that attorney misconduct is sanctionable only when it is specifically proscribed by a disciplinary rule" and concluding that "we do not believe that respondent, or any other member of the bar, could reasonably have considered the conduct involved here to be acceptable behavior under the rules governing the legal profession"); id. at 916-17 (Freeman, J., concurring in part and dissenting in part) ("No rule need have existed to inform respondent that his conduct, which was so obviously improper, was violative of the rules of professional conduct. . . . Furthermore . . . implicit in the Code is that every attorney, in the exercise of professional judgment, will conduct him or herself in a manner which will not potentially compromise the attorney-client relationship."). The Minnesota Supreme Court likewise upheld on the constitutionality of Disciplinary Rules 1-102(A)(5) and (6):

> Disciplinary Rules 1-102(A)(5) and (6) do no more than reflect the fundamental principle of professional responsibility that an attorney, as an officer of the court, has a duty to deal fairly with the court and the client. This duty embraces all of the ethical strictures of the code of professional responsibility. Read in

3. Canon 9: "Avoid Even the Appearance of Professional Impropriety"

Perhaps the broadest ethics provision serving as a source for unenumerated ethical obligations, and the one arousing the most criticism from scholars and courts, is the command, codified in Canon 9 of the Model Code, to "avoid even the appearance of professional impropriety."[136] Though he may have leveled the sharpest attack on the appearance of impropriety standard,[137] Wolfram is far from its only critic among leading ethics scholars.[138] According

---

conjunction with the other disciplinary rules, we conclude, as have other courts, that these phrases are sufficiently well defined to satisfy due process.

In re N.P., 361 N.W.2d 386, 395 (Minn. 1985).

136 Model Code of Prof'l Responsibility Canon 9 (1981).
137 See supra notes 34-41 and accompanying text.
138 See supra note 41.

It is not clear why a nearly identical provision regulating the conduct of judges has not been subjected to the same criticism as Canon 9. See Code of Judicial Conduct Canon 2 (1990) ("A judge shall avoid impropriety and the appearance of impropriety in all of the judge's activities."); see also id. Canon 3E(1) ("A judge shall disqualify himself or herself in a proceeding in which the judge's impartiality might reasonably be questioned. . . ."); 28 U.S.C. §455(a) (2002) ("Any justice, judge, or magistrate judge of the United States shall disqualify himself in any proceeding in which his impartiality might reasonably be questioned."); Leslie W. Abramson, *Appearance of Impropriety: Deciding When a Judge's Impartiality "Might Reasonably Be Questioned"*, 14 Geo. J. Legal Ethics 55, 55 (2000) ("The Codes of Judicial Conduct refer throughout to the appearance of impropriety."). *See generally Roberta K. Flowers, What You See Is What You Get: Applying the Appearance of Impropriety Standard to Prosecutors*, 63 Mo. L. Rev. 699, 703 (1998) (contrasting the Model Rules of Professional Conduct and the Judicial Code of Conduct).

Professor Gillers, for example, a harsh critic of the appearance of impropriety standard for lawyers, see text infra, notes the "interesting distinction between ethics codes for lawyers and those for judges." Gillers, supra note 41, at 632. Specifically, "[w]hereas lawyer codes have come to disfavor the 'appearance of impropriety' as a standard for evaluating a private lawyer's conduct . . . , judicial codes continue to be sensitive to appearances." Id. (cross-reference omitted). Gillers concludes with a question to the reader: "Why does it make sense, for surely it does, to adhere to an appearance standard for judges but not private lawyers?" Id. at 633. Gillers may have considered the answer to this question sufficiently self-apparent, and/or he may have decided, understandably, that a chapter on judges in a casebook on the law governing lawyers is not the place for a more lengthy discussion of the issue he raised. Yet, it seems that, under closer analysis, the issue does not lend itself to obvious solutions.

One possible answer might lie in a theory that distinguishes between "differing roles played by lawyer and judge." Flowers, supra, at 724. Under such a theory, because the lawyer "is a conduit between the individual and the system . . . the Model Rules regulate the relationship between the attorney and the client. By contrast . . . the judge serves both a functional and symbolic role." Id. at 725. Thus, the theory concludes, the appearance of

to Professor Stephen Gillers, for example, "[j]udicial resort to the 'appearance of impropriety' test bespoke the [Model] Code's inadequacy as a document on which to build a mature jurisprudence of legal ethics."[139] Indeed, Gillers notes that "[e]ven the ABA disowned [the provision]," both by calling it, in an ethics opinion, "'too vague a phrase to be useful'" and by omitting the standard from the Model Rules.[140]

---

impropriety standard "requires judges to consider the effect of both their conduct and their perceived conduct on the public's impression of the system." Id.; cf. Stephen *Gillers, Teacher's Manual, Regulation of Lawyers: Problems of Law and Ethics* 195 (5th ed. 1998) (answering that "judges (unlike most lawyers) wield public power, which requires greater public confidence in what they do and how they do it").

Despite the appeal of this answer, however, questions still remain. First, as Professor Monroe Freedman has argued,

[l]ike judges . . . lawyers are an integral part of the administration of justice, and it is essential that fair-minded people have no reasonable grounds to suspect that the administration of justice is being impaired by the improper conduct of lawyers. The appearance of impropriety is, therefore, an appropriate concern of lawyers' ethics.

Freedman, supra note 108, at 177.

Second, the answer does not explain why the appearance of impropriety standard, as applied to judges, is any less vague than the same standard applied to lawyers. It would seem, rather, that any justification for the validity of interpreting and enforcing such a broad provision in a code of judicial ethics should likewise apply to lawyers' ethics codes.

Indeed, the Commentary to Canon 2 offers a justification nearly identical to that which courts and scholars have offered for broad provisions in lawyers' ethics codes: "Because it is not practicable to list all prohibited acts, the proscription is necessarily cast in general terms that extend to conduct by judges that is harmful although not specifically mentioned in the Code." Code of Judicial Conduct Canon 2(A) cmt. (1990); cf. supra notes 48-50 and accompanying text.

In the context of this article, it is notable that one leading ethics scholar referred to the appearance of impropriety standard for judges as the "basic rule of the Code of Conduct, the one to which all other rules are mere commentary." Andrew L. Kaufman, *Judicial Ethics: The Less-Often Asked Questions*, 64 Wash. L. Rev. 851, 854 (1989). This phraseology evokes Talmudic descriptions of the command "love your neighbor as yourself," Leviticus 19:18, as "a fundamental rule in the Torah," Jerusalem Talmud, Nedarim 9:4, to which "the rest of the Torah is commentary," Talmud Bavli, Shabbath 31a. The comparison between the appearance of impropriety standard and the command to love one's neighbor is significant, as these two broad rules may share a common interpretive methodology. See infra notes 156-175 and accompanying text.

139 Gillers, supra note 41, at 358.

140 Id. (quoting *ABA Comm. on Ethics and Prof'l Responsibility*, Formal Op. 342 (1975)); Model Rules of Prof'l Conduct R. 1.9 cmt. (1983) (stating that "since 'impropriety' is undefined, the term 'appearance of impropriety' is question-begging [and that, therefore,]

In addition to scholarly criticism, like other broad ethics provisions, the prohibition against the appearance of impropriety has faced opposition from courts reluctant to rely on such a broad standard as a source of unenumerated ethical obligations. The United States Court of Appeals for the Second Circuit "caution[ed] . . . that Canon 9, though there are occasions when it should be applied, should not be used promiscuously as a convenient tool for disqualification when the facts simply do not fit within the rubric of other specific ethical and disciplinary rules."[141] Other judges have refused to apply the appearance of impropriety standard because, like Gillers, they have noted its absence from the Model Rules.[142]

Nevertheless, despite the criticism it has sustained, the appearances of impropriety standard stands, alongside DR 1-102(A)(6) and DR 1-102(A)(5)/Model Rule 8.4(d), as yet a third broad ethics provision that

---

the problem of imputed disqualification cannot be properly resolved . . . by the very general concept of appearance of impropriety"). See also Lee E. Hejmanowski, *Note, An Ethical Treatment of Attorneys' Personal Conflicts of Interest*, 66 S. Cal. L. Rev. 881, 897 (1993) (stating that "courts and legal conduct rules renounced that standard on the grounds that, standing alone, it was inherently vague").

141 *Int'l Elecs. Corp. v. Flanzer*, 527 F.2d 1288, 1295 (2d Cir. 1975); see also *Bd. of Educ. v. Nyquist*, 590 F.2d 1241, 1247 (2d Cir. 1979) ("We believe that when there is no claim that the trial will be tainted, appearance of impropriety is simply too slender a reed on which to rest a disqualification order except in the rarest cases."). Cf. Bruce A. Green, *Conflicts of Interest in Legal Representation: Should the Appearance of Impropriety Rule Be Eliminated in New Jersey-or Revived Everywhere Else?*, 28 Seton Hall L. Rev. 315, 320-25 (1997) (discussing the history and evolution of the appearance of impropriety rule in New Jersey). Professor Green argues that

> [a]s presently conceived, the overriding concern of the appearance of impropriety test has evolved from its original focus on confidence in government to the more nebulous concept of confidence in the bar. This has led to the unnecessary reliance upon an ad hoc appearance of impropriety analysis, even in those cases that might be decided by other, more precise, and less restrictive rules.

Id. at 344-45. Professor Kaufman explains:

> I usually tell my students that most of the time the phrase "appearance of impropriety" is a substitute for thought and close analysis. In most cases, what is usually at stake is a lawyer's responsibility to a particular person, and a court ought to be able to supply a more specific reason for disapproving lawyers' conduct than something called the appearance of impropriety.

Kaufman, supra note 138, at 854.

142 See, e.g., *First Am. Carriers, Inc. v. Kroger Co.*, 787 S.W.2d 669, 674 (Ark. 1990) (Bristow, J., dissenting) (observing that "appearance of impropriety . . . is a familiar and oft-quoted phrase but does not actually appear in the language of the Model Rules of Professional Conduct as adopted by this Court").

many courts have applied and interpreted as a source of unenumerated ethical obligations.[143] In fact, of these three rules, the courts' approach to the appearance

---

143 A number of courts have expressed their abiding faith in the continued viability of the appearance of impropriety standard in spite of its omission from the Model Rules. See, e.g., *Lovell v. Winchester*, 941 S.W.2d 466, 468 (Ky. 1997) ("Even though the comment to Rule 1.9 specifically rejects the 'appearance of impropriety' standard . . . the appearance of impropriety is still a useful guide for ethical decisions."); *Cardona v. Gen. Motors Corp.*, 942 F. Supp. 968, 975 (D.N.J. 1996) (describing importance of the "much maligned" appearance of impropriety doctrine); *Heringer v. Haskell*, 536 N.W.2d 362, 366 (N.D. 1995) (acknowledging argument that "the Rules of Professional Conduct have abandoned the 'appearance of impropriety' standard that was the basis for the old Canons and Disciplinary Rules, in favor of a more flexible, fact-based approach," but concluding and citing cases to support the proposition that "[a]lthough the new Rules do not use the language, the 'appearance of impropriety' standard has not been wholly abandoned in spirit"). A Wisconsin Court described the role of the appearance of impropriety test after the adoption of the ABA Model Rules of Professional Responsibility:

> Prior to 1987, the Wisconsin Code of Professional Responsibility provided that attorneys "should avoid even the appearance of professional impropriety." This rule embodied the substance of Canon 9 of the ABA Code of Professional Responsibility. In 1987, Wisconsin adopted the ABA Model Rules of Professional Responsibility, which omit the "appearance of impropriety" language. Instead, the code enumerates specific prohibited conflicts of interest. The change in language was motivated by the fact that the term "impropriety" is not specifically defined.
>
> The obligation to avoid appearances of impropriety is nonetheless implicit in the new Wisconsin Rules of Professional Conduct.

State v. Retzlaff, 490 N.W.2d 750, 752 (Wis. Ct. App. 1992) (citations omitted); *MMR/Wallace Power & Indus. v. Thames Assocs.*, 764 F. Supp. 712, 718 n.9 (D. Conn. 1991) (observing "[t]hat a lawyer is ethically obligated to avoid 'even the appearance of impropriety' is embodied in Canon 9 of the Code of Professional Responsibility," stating that "[a]lthough the Code has not been formally adopted in Connecticut, 'its salutary provisions have consistently been relied upon by the courts . . . in evaluating the ethical conduct of attorneys,'" and noting that "prior to its adoption of the [Connecticut] Rules [of Professional Conduct], this court recognized the Code of Professional Responsibility of the American Bar Association as expressing the standards of professional conduct expected of lawyers" (citations omitted)); *First Am. Carriers*, 787 S.W.2d at 671-72 (noting that "Canon 9 was a part of the ABA Code of Professional Responsibility and the exact language is not in the Model Rules of Professional Conduct adopted by this court," but concluding that "[t]he fact that Canon 9 is not in the Model Rules does not mean that lawyers no longer have to avoid the appearance of impropriety" because, "[w]hile Canon 9 is not expressly adopted by the Model Rules, the principle applies because its meaning pervades the Rules and embodies their spirit"); *Turbin v. Super. Ct.*, 797 P.2d 734, 738 (Ariz. Ct. App. 1990) ("We hold today that the appearance of impropriety . . . still has a definite place in the balancing test the trial court must apply in resolving the question of disqualification."); *Gomez v. Super. Ct.*, 717 P.2d 902, 904 (Ariz. 1986) (finding that "'appearance of impropriety,' however weakened by case law and its omission in the new Rules of Professional Conduct, survives as a part of conflict of interest"); *Pantry Pride, Inc. v. Finley, Kumble, Wagner, Heine, Underberg & Casey*, 697 F.2d 524, 530 (3d Cir. 1982) (citing *Proposed*

of impropriety provision may offer the fullest range of interpretive methodologies parallel to those used to identify unenumerated principles in constitutional law and Jewish law.

Some courts have employed an interpretive methodology for the appearance of impropriety standard similar to that used in interpreting the constitutional guarantee of liberty and the biblical command to be holy.[144] These courts have looked to history and traditional understandings of the role and responsibilities of lawyers as a means for identifying unenumerated ethical obligations based on the appearance of impropriety standard.

For example, applying the standard to a 1996 "side-switching attorney" case, one court rejected the "frequently . . . made" argument that appearance of impropriety "embodies 'an arbitrary and vague standard.'"[145] Instead, the court emphasized the importance of applying and enforcing the appearance of impropriety standard to "engender, protect and preserve the trust and confidence of clients," particularly when an attorney has "chang[ed] sides."[146] "At the heart" of such a scenario, according to the court, "is the suspicion that by changing sides, the attorney has breached a duty of fidelity and loyalty to a former client, a client who had freely shared with the attorney secrets and confidences with the expectation that they would be disclosed to no one else."[147]

Thus, a crucial aspect of the court's analysis relied on what it viewed as traditionally understood—though largely unenumerated—aspects of the attorney's duty of loyalty, corresponding to the expectations of the client.[148] The court demonstrated the extent to which historical traditions support such an

---

Final Draft, ABA Model Rules of Professional Conduct 40 (June 30, 1982) (omitting Canon 9 as overbroad and question-begging)) ("Although the appearance of impropriety standard has been criticized recently, . . . Canon 9 is still the law in this circuit." (citation omitted)); *In re Hinds*, 449 A.2d 483, 498 (N.J. 1982) (referring to "[t]he legal profession's cardinal ethical edict—to avoid even the appearance of impropriety" (internal quotations omitted)).

144 See supra notes 64-73 and accompanying text.

145 *Cardona v. Gen. Motors Corp.*, 942 F. Supp. 968, 974-75 (D.N.J. 1996).

146 Id. at 975.

147 Id.

148 See id.; see also *Heringer v. Haskell*, 536 N.W.2d 362, 366-67 (N.D. 1995) (finding that "[c]ertainly concerns about the public's perception of the legal profession, particularly as it relates to confidentiality of client information, bears some relevance when we examine and interpret the Rules" and deciding that interpreting the appearance of impropriety standard through such factors as "the layperson's view," "public confidence in the legal profession," and "the nature of private law practice in this state" as found in "the common experience in North Dakota law firms" is appropriate). Cf. *First Am. Carriers v. Kroger Co.*, 787 S.W.2d 669, 672 (Ark. 1990) (finding that Canon 9 "is included in . . . 'moral and ethical considerations' that should guide lawyers, who have 'special responsibility for the quality of justice'").

unenumerated obligation, quoting at length a judicial opinion dating back to 1889.[149] The quotation, which eloquently and forcefully details the "obligation" of "fidelity to [the] client," concludes with the insistence that "I cannot tolerate for a moment, neither can the profession, neither can the community, any disloyalty on the part of a lawyer to his client. In all things he must be true to that trust, or, failing it, he must leave the profession."[150]

Other courts have adopted an interpretive methodology for applying the appearance of impropriety standard based on an extension of the principles underlying enumerated ethics rules, thus echoing the interpretation of the constitutional protections of privacy and the biblical requirement to do the just and the good.[151] Under such an approach, one court applying the appearance of impropriety standard found "no doubt that the spirit of the ethical norms adhered to in this district, if not the letter of the Rules of Professional Conduct themselves, precludes an attorney from acquiring, inadvertently or otherwise, confidential or privileged information about his adversary's litigation strategy."[152] The court then cited a number of ethics rules, the letter of which perhaps did not enumerate the precise prohibition articulated by the court, but the spirit of which suggested such an unenumerated prohibition due to an appearance of impropriety.[153] Another court examining the standard, in an effort "to mark its precise contours[,] . . . looked to other provisions of the ABA Model Code for guidance."[154] Thus, the court based its conclusions on a "read[ing]" of both Canon 4 and Canon 5, "together with" Canon 9.[155]

---

149 *Cardona,* 942 F. Supp. at 975 (quoting *United States v. Costen,* 38 F. 24, 24 (C.C.D. Colo. 1889)).

150 Id. (quoting *Costen,* 38 F. at 24).

151 See supra notes 74-82 and accompanying text.

152 *MMR/Wallace Power & Indus. v. Thames Associates,* 764 F. Supp. 712, 718 (D. Conn. 1991).

153 See id. at 718-19 (citing Model Rules of Prof'l Conduct R. 1.6, R. 4.2, R. 8.4); id. at 719-23 (citing and relying on cases that applied appearance of impropriety and similar standards). The court concluded: "That the court has an obligation 'to enforce the lawyer's duty to absolute fidelity and to guard against the danger of inadvertent use of confidential information' pertaining to his adversary's trial preparation and tactics is, upon review of the case law in this area, unmistakably clear." Id. at 719. See also Samuel J. Levine, *The Law and the "Spirit of the Law" in Legal Ethics,* 2015 J. Prof. Law. 1 (2015).

154 *Pantry Pride, Inc. v. Finley, Kumble, Wagner, Heine, Underberg & Casey,* 697 F.2d 524, 530 (3d Cir. 1982).

155 Id. at 530; see Model Code of Prof'l Responsibility Canon 4 (1981) ("A Lawyer Should Preserve the Confidences and Secrets of a Client."); id. Canon 5 ("A Lawyer Should Exercise Independent Professional Judgment on Behalf of a Client.").

At least one court has combined two interpretive methodologies, looking both to the historical function of lawyers and to the implications of other enumerated ethics rules for interpreting and applying the appearance of impropriety standard. See *Arkansas v. Dean*

Finally, more than any other ethics provision, the appearance of impropriety standard seems to articulate a level of generality similar to that of the Ninth Amendment and the biblical command to love one's neighbor, thus suggesting the applicability of a third interpretive methodology, one that provides an independent source for a principle that is otherwise unenumerated elsewhere. In fact, much of the criticism of the appearance of impropriety standard has specifically rejected its use as an independent basis for disqualification or discipline.[156]

It is therefore significant that the United States Court of Appeals for the Ninth Circuit rejected the argument that "the [district] court erred in relying solely on Canon 9 to disqualify the law firms."[157] The court declared that "[s]trong policy reasons support" the conclusion that "Canon 9 alone can be the basis for a disqualification motion."[158] Perhaps the most notable of these considerations, in terms of its broader implications for understanding the nature of ethics codes, posits that "[i]f Canon 9 were not separately enforceable, it would be stripped of its meaning and significance. This suggests that it must be

---

Foods Prods., 605 F.2d 380 (8th Cir. 1979). The court first observed that "[s]ociety has ordained and for centuries honored the privilege against disclosure, to reassure the people that their secrets were safe in the hands of their lawyers." Id. at 385. The court then explored the implications of this traditional function, noting that

> [i]f the reputation and status of the legal profession, and more importantly the freedom and opportunity of the public to obtain adequate legal counseling, are to be preserved, a client must have every reason to expect that disclosures to "his" law firm will not be used against him by any member or associate lawyer in that firm.

Id. at 385-86. Finally, the court concluded that "[i]t is precisely to protect that 'expectation' of safety in disclosure that Canon 9's concern for the appearance of impropriety must be merged with Canon 4's injunction against disclosure of a client's secrets." Id. at 386.

156 See, e.g., *Leber Assocs., LLC v. Entm't Group Fund*, No. 00 Civ. 3759, 2001 WL 1568780, at *7 (S.D.N.Y. Dec. 7, 2001) ("If plaintiff intends to suggest that disqualification is independently justified by [Canon 9], we reject that contention."); *Bd. of Educ. v. Nyquist*, 590 F.2d 1241, 1250 (2d Cir. 1979) (Mansfield, J. concurring) (stating "that an 'appearance of impropriety' is an insufficient ground, by itself, to justify a court's disqualification of an attorney . . . absent a reasonable basis for believing that such an appearance may affect the outcome"); id. at 1247-48 n.1 (Mansfield, J. concurring) (citing a case in which "a combination of an attorney's 'appearance of impropriety' plus his violation of another disciplinary rule might have affected the outcome"); see also Gillers, supra note 41, at 359 (stating that "a few states retain the Code of Professional Responsibility and its Canon 9, "but adding" that doesn't mean that courts in those states will make judgments about conflicts based on the 'appearance' language *alone*").

157 *In re Coordinated Pretrial Proceedings in Petroleum Prods. Antitrust Litig.*, 658 F.2d 1355, 1359-60 (9th Cir. 1981).

158 Id. at 1360.

a sufficient ground for disqualification in itself."[159] Thus, though apparently in the minority,[160] the Ninth Circuit took seriously each of the provisions of the Code of Professional Responsibility, refusing to entertain the possibility that even a provision as broad as the appearance of impropriety standard might be devoid of independent meaning, interpretation, and application.[161]

The comparison to the Ninth Amendment is somewhat striking. Commentators have long noted the virtual "disappearance of the Ninth Amendment from the Supreme Court's constitutional discourse."[162] In fact, as one scholar documented:

---

159 Id.
160 See supra notes 34-41, 137-142, 156 and accompanying text.
161 The Kentucky Supreme Court made a similar observation:

> Although the appearance of impropriety formula is vague and leads to uncertain results, it nonetheless serves the useful function of stressing that disqualification properly may be imposed to protect the reasonable expectations of former and present clients. The impropriety standard also promotes the public's confidence in the integrity of the legal profession. For these reasons, courts still retain the appearance of impropriety standard as an independent basis of assessment.

Lovell v. Winchester, 941 S.W.2d 466, 469 (Ky. 1997); cf. *Sullivan County Reg'l Refuse Disposal Dist. v. Town of Acworth*, 686 A.2d 755, 757 (N.H. 1996) ("The courts of this State are the primary regulators of attorney conduct. It would be inconsistent with this court's supervisory role to relegate the Rules of Professional Conduct to the status of guidelines, to be enforced only when the trial process may be sullied." (citations omitted)). In contrast, the New York high court observed:

> We begin our analysis by noting that what is at issue is a disciplinary rule, not a statute. In interpreting statutes, which are the enactments of a coequal branch of government and an expression of the public policy of this State, we are of course bound to implement the will of the Legislature; statutes are to be applied as they are written or interpreted to effectuate the legislative intention. The disciplinary rules have a different provenance and purpose. Approved by the New York State Bar Association and then enacted by the Appellate Divisions, the Code of Professional Responsibility is essentially the legal profession's document of self-governance, embodying principles of ethical conduct for attorneys as well as rules for professional discipline. While unquestionably important, and respected by the courts, the code does not have the force of law.
>
> That distinction is particularly significant when a disciplinary rule is invoked in litigation, which in addition to matters of professional conduct by attorneys, implicates the interests of nonlawyers. In such instances, we are not constrained to read the rules literally or effectuate the intent of the drafters, but look to the rules as guidelines to be applied with due regard for the broad range of interests at stake.

Niesig v. Team I, 558 N.E.2d 1030, 1032 (N.Y. 1990) (citations omitted).

162 See, e.g., Hon. William Wayne Justice, *Recognizing the Ninth Amendment's Role in Constitutional Interpretation*, 74 Tex. L. Rev. 1241, 1243 (1996).

Although a few Supreme Court justices have mentioned the amendment—usually to provide a kind of indirect thematic support for the assertion of an unenumerated right identified in another provision of the Constitution—no Supreme Court decision, and few federal appellate decisions, have relied on the Ninth Amendment for support. Indeed, federal courts that have discussed the Ninth Amendment have almost exclusively held that it does not confer any substantive rights.[163]

This attitude toward the Ninth Amendment was perhaps most sharply captured in Judge Robert Bork's testimony during his Senate confirmation hearing. Drawing a famous—if not notorious—analogy to an inkblot, Bork declared, "I do not think you can use the Ninth Amendment unless you know something of what it means. For example, if you had an amendment that says 'Congress shall make no' and then there is an inkblot, and you cannot read the rest of it, and that is the only copy you have, I do not think the court can make up what might be under the inkblot."[164]

At the start of an influential article on the Ninth Amendment, Professor Randy Barnett juxtaposes Bork's statement against the United States Supreme Court's landmark decision in *Marbury v. Madison*, declaring: "It cannot be presumed that any clause in the constitution is intended to be without effect; and therefore such a construction is inadmissible, unless the words require

---

163 Mark C. Niles, *Ninth Amendment Adjudication: An Alternative to Substantive Due Process Analysis of Personal Autonomy Rights*, 48 UCLA L. Rev. 85, 89-90 (2000) (footnotes omitted). Another scholar also noted:

> [T]he courts have ignored the Ninth Amendment altogether. They have treated it as though it does not envision judicial protection for unenumerated rights at all, a notion which has gained credence through the inertia of its neglect. Sub silentio, the courts have gradually instilled the idea that there is, in fact, no such thing as Ninth Amendment rights.

Chase J. Sanders, *Ninth Life: An Interpretive Theory of the Ninth Amendment*, 69 Ind. L.J. 759, 761 (1994).

164 *The Bork Disinformers*, Wall St. J., Oct. 5, 1987, at 22, quoted in Barnett, supra note 52, at 1. Professor Mark Niles has depicted the "inkblot interpretation" as "almost certainly the dominant understanding, and consequently the overwhelming treatment, of the amendment by legal practitioner and judges." Niles, supra note 163, at 98; cf. *Troxel v. Granville*, 530 U.S. 57, 91 (2000) (Scalia, J., dissenting) (stating that "the Constitution's refusal to 'deny or disparage' other rights is far removed from affirming any one of them, and even further removed from authorizing judges to identify what they might be, and to enforce the judges' list against laws duly enacted by the people"). See also Chapter 11 in this Volume.

it."[165] Though ethics codes may not demand the same level of attention to textual detail as the Unites States Constitution, the Ninth Circuit's insistence that the appearance of impropriety standard is deserving of independent authority echoes the Supreme Court's approach articulated in *Marbury* and applied by Justice Goldberg[166] and many scholars in the context of the Ninth Amendment.[167]

The application of a similarly general and independent source of unenumerated principles in Jewish law is perhaps most powerfully expressed in the interpretation of the command to "love your neighbor as yourself."[168]

---

165 5 U.S. (1 Cranch) 137, 174 (1803), quoted in Barnett, supra note 52, at 1. See Chapter 11 in this Volume.

166 See *Griswold v. Connecticut*, 381 U.S. 479, 491 (1965) (Goldberg, J., concurring) (stating that "[i]n interpreting the Constitution, 'real effect should be given to all the words it uses,'" and arguing that failure to recognize a constitutional right because it is not enumerated in the first eight amendments to the Constitution "is to ignore the Ninth Amendment and to give it no effect whatsoever").

According to one scholar, Justice Goldberg offered a "rather equivocal reliance on the Ninth Amendment," instead of adopting the position that "the Ninth Amendment constitutes an independent source of rights protected from infringement by either the States or the Federal Government." Thomas B. McAffee, *A Critical Guide to the Ninth Amendment*, 69 Temp. L. Rev. 61, 61-62 n.7 (1996) (quoting *Griswold*, 381 U.S. at 492 (Goldberg, J., concurring)). In any event, the logic of Justice Goldberg's opinion would seem to support such a position. For an attempt to define and explain Justice Goldberg's approach, see McAffee, supra, at 62.

167 In the words of "the very first Ninth Amendment thinker," writing in "the first [article] devoted exclusively to the Ninth Amendment," the amendment "must be more than a mere net to catch fish in supposedly fishless water." Knowlton H. Kelsey, *The Ninth Amendment of the Federal Constitution*, 11 Ind. L.J. 309, 323 & n.7 (1936), quoted in Sanders, supra note 163, at 761-62; see also Charles L. Black, Jr., *Decision According to Law: The 1979 Holmes Lectures* 43 (1981), cited in Justice, supra note 162, at 1243-44 (exhibiting characteristic wit in stating: "I ... move that, having been proposed by the requisite majorities in Congress, and ratified by the requisite number of states, the Ninth Amendment to the Constitution of the United States at long last be adopted"). Professor Massey asserted:

> Construing the [N]inth [A]mendment as a mere declaration of a constitu-tional truism, devoid of enforceable content, renders its substance nugatory and assigns to its framers an intention to engage in a purely moot exercise. This view is at odds with the contextual historical evidence and the specific, articulated concerns of its framers, and violates the premise of *Marbury v. Madison* that the Constitution contains judicially discoverable and enforceable principles.

Calvin R. Massey, *Federalism and Fundamental Rights: The Ninth Amendment*, 38 Hastings L.J. 305, 316-17 (1987); McAffee, supra note 166, at 67 ("To the modern reader, the Ninth Amendment seems quite plainly to recognize rights in addition to those secured by the text of the Constitution and the Bill of Rights.").

168 Leviticus 19:18.

As explicated by Maimonides, the command to love one's neighbor serves as a wide-ranging source of interpersonal obligations, beyond those enumerated in the biblical text, including the general obligation to protect the well-being of another person, to the same degree as one would be concerned about one's own well-being.[169] Specifically, Maimonides delineates a number of actions mandated by rabbinic authorities in connection with the biblical command to love others, including visiting the sick, comforting mourners, and participating in funerals and weddings.[170] In short, Maimonides concludes, one should act toward others in the same manner that one would wish to be treated by others.[171]

This approach to understanding the command to love one's neighbor may offer a final insight into interpretive methodologies that rely on broad rules to derive and identify unenumerated principles in ethics codes, the United States Constitution, and the Torah. Under Jewish legal theory, each verse in the Torah has significance and meaning.[172] Thus, biblical interpretation, like constitutional interpretation, operates under a strong presumption against superfluity, negating the possibility that the phrase "love your neighbor as yourself" is anything other than a legal imperative.[173] Indeed, because this presumption

---

169 Maimonides, supra note 73, Laws of De'oth 6:3; cf. 3 Nachmanides, supra note 55, at 292-94 (explicating Leviticus 19:18) (describing the obligation to hope for the success of others in all of life's realms, including those of wealth, honor, and knowledge). For an analysis of the view of Nachmanides, see Yitzchak Hutner, *Pachad Yitzchak, Shevuoth* 134-38 (5th ed. 1999).

170 Maimonides, supra note 73, Laws of Mourning 14:1.

171 Id.; cf. 3 Nachmanides, supra note 55, at 293 (explicating Leviticus 19:18) (concluding that a person's love for the success of others should be without bounds, as is the hope one has for one's own success).

172 Modern scholars have offered the term "omnisignificance" to describe "the basic assumption . . . that . . . [n]othing in the Bible . . . ought to be explained as the product of chance, or, for that matter, as an emphatic or rhetorical form, or anything similar." James Kugel, *The Idea of Biblical Poetry: Parallelism and Its History* 104 (1981), cited in Yaakov Elman, "*It Is No Empty Thing*": Nahmanides and the Search for Omnisignificance, 4 Torah U'Maddah J. 1 (Jacob J. Schacter ed., 1993). See Chapter 11 in this Volume.

   Professor Elman finds an analogue to this observation in the Talmudic statement that the Torah "[i]s not an empty thing for you, it is your very life, and if [it appears] devoid [of moral or halakhic meaning], it is you [who have not worked out its moral or legal significance]." Elman, supra, at 1-2 (alterations in original) (quoting Jerusalem Talmud, Kethuvoth 8:11 (explicating Deuteronomy 32:47)).

173 In fact, as Professor Elman develops at length, biblical interpretation attributes omnisignificance not only to legal precepts but to biblical narrative as well. See generally Elman, supra note 172; Chapter 17 in Volume 2.

"proceeds directly from the view of Torah as divine revelation,"[174] it precludes application to the Torah of approaches such as Bork's inkblot theory of the Ninth Amendment[175] or those of courts and scholars denying the practical value of the appearance of impropriety standard. Though not divine in origin, if they are to be taken seriously, ethics codes and the Constitution deserve—and demand—a similar respect for their textual integrity, through the interpretation of broad provisions as a source of unenumerated principles.

CONCLUSION

The increasingly legislative form of ethics regulations has produced a statutory structure that, like other legislation, requires careful and close judicial analysis and interpretation. In fact, Professor Monroe Freedman emphasized the "extremely effective means [ethics codes] provide to learn how to draft and analyze statutes."[176] As Professor Freedman observed, "[s]ome of the ethical rules deal with specific, limited issues, like forbidding a lawyer to commingle funds or to engage in *ex parte* communications with a judge."[177] Yet, he noted, "[o]thers are the loosest of canons, forbidding any conduct that gives the 'appearance of impropriety' or that is 'prejudicial to the administration of justice.'"[178] It is the latter category of rules that has prompted many scholars, and some courts, to question the legislative legitimacy of segments of ethics codes, a skepticism that has been expressed in the practical and theoretical rejection, by critics, of the applicability of broad ethics provisions.

Indeed, in the areas of both constitutional law and legal ethics, the practice of deriving unenumerated principles through the interpretation and application of broad provisions has been somewhat precarious. Perhaps by its nature, such a hermeneutic framework is vulnerable to the objection that it is improperly vague, relying on interpretive methodologies that lack the precision generally expected of both legislative schemes and their interpretation.

Nevertheless, to courts and scholars advocating and engaging in such methodologies, the nature of both ethics codes and the United States Constitution, like the nature of the Torah in Jewish legal theory, necessitates the articulation of broad rules to address situations and considerations, beyond

---

174 Elman, supra note 172, at 4.
175 See supra note 164 and accompanying text.
176 Freedman, supra note 108, at 1.
177 Id.
178 Id.

those enumerated, that will inevitably arise in the future. Thus, it is incumbent upon legal authorities, in the context of each of these areas of law, to construct a conceptual framework through which unenumerated principles may be identified and applied.

Though not without encountering occasional criticism and difficulty, legal authorities have relied on a number of interpretive methodologies that have proved largely successful in the pursuit of deriving and identifying unenumerated constitutional rights and unenumerated biblical obligations. Taking the legislative forms of the United States Constitution and the Torah seriously, these authorities have thus demonstrated the utility of a legislative structure consisting of both specifically enumerated rules and broad provisions. If ethics codes are likewise to be taken seriously, scholars and courts should carefully consider adopting similar interpretive frameworks for ethics codes, applying broad ethics provisions as a basis for deriving and identifying unenumerated ethical obligations.

CHAPTER 15

Taking Prosecutorial Ethics Seriously: A Consideration of the Prosecutor's Ethical Obligation to "Seek Justice" in a Comparative Analytical Framework

INTRODUCTION

In many ways, the role of the prosecutor in the American justice system differs significantly from that of other lawyers.[1] The difference may be most evident in the unique ethical duties of the prosecutor, whose professional responsibility

---

1 See, e.g., *Berger v. United States*, 295 U.S. 78, 88-89 (1935) (discussing the standard that governs prosecutorial misconduct).

> The United States Attorney is the representative not of an ordinary party to a controversy, but of a sovereignty whose obligation to govern impartially is as compelling as its obligation to govern at all; and whose interest, therefore, in a criminal prosecution is not that it shall win a case, but that justice shall be done. As such, he is in a peculiar and very definite sense the servant of the law, the twofold aim of which is that guilt shall not escape or innocence suffer. He may prosecute with earnestness and vigor—indeed, he should do so. But, while he may strike hard blows, he is not at liberty to strike foul ones. It is as much his duty to refrain from improper methods calculated to produce a wrongful conviction as it is to use every legitimate means to bring about a just one.

Id. at 88; see also *Imbler v. Pachtman*, 424 U.S. 409, 423 n.20 (1976) ("It is the functional comparability of their judgments to those of the judge that has resulted in . . . prosecutors being referred to as 'quasi-judicial' officers."). See generally Samuel J. Levine, *Judicial Rhetoric and Lawyers' Roles*, 90 Notre Dame L. Rev. 1989 (2015).

includes the obligation to "seek justice."[2] Notwithstanding the aspirational value and general importance of such an obligation, however, the articulation of the prosecutor's duties in the form of a broad directive to seek justice has been a source of criticism among legal scholars.[3] Indeed, more generally, a number of scholars and courts have expressed dissatisfaction with the inclusion of broad ethics provisions in ethics codes.[4] Not surprisingly, those calling for increased specificity view the standard governing prosecutors, arguably one of the broadest of all ethics rules, as unworkably vague for purposes of meaningful interpretation and application.

This chapter responds to such concerns through a comparison to parallel issues of interpretation and application that arise in Jewish law. Specifically, the chapter examines the complex nature of the prosecutor's broad obligation to seek justice, through a consideration of a similarly broad directive in Jewish law: "In all [of] your ways acknowledge [God]."[5] The chapter emphasizes that

---

2 Model Code of Prof'l Responsibility EC 7-13 (1980) [hereinafter Model Code] ("The responsibility of a public prosecutor differs from that of the usual advocate; his duty is to *seek justice*, not merely to convict." (emphasis added)); see also Model Rules of Prof'l Conduct R. 3.8 cmt. 1 (2003) [hereinafter Model Rules] ("A prosecutor has the responsibility of a minister of justice and not simply that of an advocate.").

3 See Fred C. Zacharias, *Specificity in Professional Responsibility Codes: Theory, Practice, and the Paradigm of Prosecutorial Ethics*, 69 Notre Dame L. Rev. 223, 292 (1993) (arguing that the "justice" provisions of Model Rule 3.8 provide minimal guidance for prosecutors). See generally Fred C. Zacharias, *Structuring the Ethics of Prosecutorial Trial Practice: Can Prosecutors Do Justice?*, 44 Vand. L. Rev. 45 (1991) [hereinafter Zacharias, *Can Prosecutors Do Justice?*] (arguing that the noncompetitive "do justice" approach is inadequate because the professional codes do not exempt prosecutors from the requirements of zealous advocacy).

4 See generally Chapter 14 in this Volume (offering a comparative framework for interpreting ethics provisions that have been criticized as vague).

5 Proverbs 3:6; see also 2 The Holy Scriptures 1763 (Jewish Publ. Soc. of Am. 1955) (using the term "acknowledge" in translating this verse). A literal translation of the quoted phrase might read "in all of your ways know Him." I have chosen the term "acknowledge," because, as is often true of translations, this substitution for literalism may, in fact, provide a more accurate and meaningful depiction of the original as expressed in modern English. See generally Aryeh Kaplan, *Translator's Introduction*, in The Living Torah: The Five Books of Moses, at v (Aryeh Kaplan trans., 1981).

Nevertheless, there is clear significance in the use of the biblical term for "knowledge" in the original Hebrew verse, connoting a close form of intimate connection, which is applied here to an individual's relationship with God. See, e.g., Genesis 4:1 (demonstrating use of the term *"yada"*); see also Yitzchak Hutner, *Pachad Yitzchak, Purim* 77-78 (6th ed. 1998); Joseph B. Soloveitchik, *Family Redeemed: Essays on Family Relationships* 94-95, 179 (David Shatz & Joel B. Wolowelsky eds., 2000).

In addition, the final word in the quoted phrase is actually the pronoun "Him," to which the antecedent is clearly "God." In the interest of brevity, the obligation embodied in this verse will hereinafter often be referred to as the obligation to "acknowledge God."

unlike other lawyers, in exercising ethical deliberation and decision-making, the prosecutor must take into account complex implications of the concept of justice. Likewise, Jewish law recognizes and addresses the complexity of ethical and normative decision-making that must be incorporated in the service of acknowledging God. Thus, through this comparative analytical framework, the chapter demonstrates that the prosecutor's broad ethical obligation to seek justice stands as a workable and, indeed, appropriate standard for prosecutorial ethics.

PART ONE | BASIC PRINCIPLES: ILLUSTRATIONS OF THE UNIQUE NATURE OF THE PROSECUTOR'S ETHICAL OBLIGATION TO SEEK JUSTICE

The unique nature of the prosecutor's ethical obligation to seek justice may be demonstrated through examples of the conduct required of prosecutors in carrying out their role in the criminal justice system.[6] Before proceeding to a normative analysis applying this obligation to more ethically complex scenarios, it may be helpful to look at some basic examples that illustrate the prosecutor's ethical duties.

The unique nature of the prosecutor's position is manifest when juxtaposed with that of the private attorney representing a civil client.[7] Yet, the extent to

---

6 See, e.g., Monroe H. Freedman & Abbe Smith, *Understanding Lawyers' Ethics* §§11.01-.16 (2d ed. 2002) (discussing the "special ethical rules" that apply to prosecutors); Charles W. Wolfram, *Modern Legal Ethics* §13.10 (1986) (noting the prosecutor's dual role of bearing responsibility for convicting the guilty and ensuring that the innocent are not convicted).

7 Notably, a number of scholars have delineated theoretical models of legal ethics that would extend the obligation to do justice, to include attorneys representing private clients. Perhaps foremost among several leading scholars advocating such a position is Professor William Simon, who published a series of articles culminating in a book-length "defen[se of] an approach to ethical decisionmaking" adopting the "basic maxim . . . that the lawyer should take such actions as, considering the relevant circumstances of the particular case, seem likely to promote justice." William H. Simon, *The Practice of Justice: A Theory of Lawyers' Ethics* 9 (1998). In fact, Professor Simon expressly compares his model of ethical lawyering for private attorneys with the obligation that ethics codes prescribe for prosecutors. Id. at 10.

Although such suggestions raise important theoretical and philosophical issues, they rely on a self-conscious departure from the law governing the conduct of lawyers. See Samuel J. Levine, *The Law and the "Spirit of the Law" in Legal Ethics*, 2015 J. Prof. Law. 1 (2015) [hereinafter Levine, *The Law and the "Spirit of the Law"*]; Samuel J. Levine, *Taking Ethical Discretion Seriously: Ethical Deliberation as Ethical Obligation*, 37 Ind. L. Rev. 21, 38-40 & 38 n.115 (2003) [hereinafter Levine, *Taking Ethical Discretion Seriously*]; Zacharias, *Can Prosecutors Do Justice?*, supra note 3, at 52 n.26. As a descriptive matter, the ethical obligations

which the prosecutor's conduct stands out, in conformance with the dictates of seeking justice, is perhaps most starkly expressed when contrasted with the role of the opposing lawyer operating in the same arena as the prosecutor—the criminal defense attorney. Although the American adversarial system generally adopts the premise that justice prevails through the exercise of zealous advocacy on the part of opposing sides to a legal dispute, in the context of a criminal case, the prosecutor—and, pointedly, not the defense attorney—has the additional and unilateral obligation to help ensure that justice is done.

A. The Decision to Prosecute

One of the most basic and important decisions for a prosecutor is whether to file charges against a particular defendant. Although this decision may often turn on a number of factors, there are circumstances in which, despite a strong likelihood of obtaining a conviction, a prosecutor remains ethically obligated to refrain from prosecution. Under the Model Rules of Professional Conduct, a prosecutor must not prosecute a charge "that the prosecutor knows is not supported by probable cause."[8] As George Sharswood put it in his groundbreaking 1854 essay on legal ethics, a lawyer should not prosecute a defendant whom the lawyer "knows or believes to be innocent."[9] Although the precise contours of this obligation may be open to interpretation,[10] ethics provisions clearly set forth a standard strikingly different from that of the criminal defense attorney.

---

of a prosecutor reflect the fundamental difference between the prosecutor's role and that of other lawyers in the American legal system. See Levine, supra note 1.

8 Model Rules, supra note 2, R. 3.8(a).

9 George Sharswood, *An Essay on Professional Ethics* 93 (F.B. Rothman & Co. 5th ed. 1993) (1884), quoted in Bruce A. Green, *Why Should Prosecutors "Seek Justice"?*, 26 Fordham Urb. L.J. 607, 612-13 (1999) [hereinafter Green, *Prosecutors*]. The essay was first published as *A Compend of Lectures on the Aims and Duties of the Profession of Law, Delivered Before the Law Class of the University of Pennsylvania* (1854). For a historical discussion of Sharswood's essay, including the history of its first publication in 1854, see generally Russell G. Pearce, *Rediscovering the Republican Origins of the Legal Ethics Codes*, 6 Geo. J. Legal Ethics 241 (1992).

10 According to many scholars, prosecutors "must satisfy themselves of an individual's guilt as a precondition" to prosecution. E.g., Green, *Prosecutors*, supra note 9, at 641; see also John Kaplan, *The Prosecutorial Discretion—A Comment*, 60 Nw. U. L. Rev. 174, 178 (1965) (stating that "regardless of the strength of the case," prosecutors should not file charges unless they "actually believe" that the defendant committed the crime, and that it is "morally wrong" to continue to prosecute unless "personally convinced" of such), cited in Freedman & Smith, supra note 6, at 300. As one scholar has put it, "you never put a defendant to trial unless you [are] personally convinced of [the defendant's] guilt." Bennett L. Gershman, *The Prosecutor's Duty to Truth*, 14 Geo. J. Legal Ethics 309, 309 (2001) [hereinafter Gershman, *The Prosecutor's Duty to Truth*]. In fact, in an earlier article, Professor Gershman argued that

Like other lawyers representing private clients, criminal defense attorneys have an ethical obligation to zealously represent their clients' interests.[11] Yet, criminal defense attorneys are unique in the extent to which ethics regulations permit—and at times require—that they engage in methods of advocacy otherwise considered outside the bounds of ethical lawyering, methods almost diametrically opposed to those comprising the ethical obligations of prosecutors to seek justice. As a threshold matter, unlike a prosecutor, a criminal defense attorney may—indeed, typically does—engage in advocacy even when the facts of the case are contrary to the client's position, including when the attorney knows both that the client committed the crime and that the charge is supported by evidence sufficient for a conviction. Again, in the classic words of Judge Sharswood, when representing a criminal defendant, a lawyer should "exert all his ability, learning, and ingenuity, in such a defense, even if . . . perfectly assured . . . of the actual guilt of the prisoner."[12] Furthermore, alone among attorneys, the criminal defense attorney is exempt from the ethics provision that broadly prohibits "bring[ing] or defend[ing] a proceeding, or assert[ing] or controvert[ing] an issue therein, unless there is a basis in law and fact for doing so."[13] In express contrast to the general prohibition, the Model Rules permit the criminal defense attorney to "so defend the proceeding as to require that every element of the case be established."[14]

---

the proper standard for proceeding with a criminal case should be the prosecutor's "moral certainty" of the defendant's perpetration of the crime. Bennett L. Gershman, *A Moral Standard for the Prosecutor's Exercise of the Charging Discretion*, 20 Fordham Urb. L.J. 513, 530 (1993) [hereinafter Gershman, *A Moral Standard*].

In any event, each of these views appears to endorse a standard different from that mandated under the Model Rules. See Freedman & Smith, supra note 6, §11.05, at 304.

> The ABA standard appears to mean that the prosecutor can ethically go forward . . . regardless of . . . personal[] belie[f] that the accused is [or is not] guilty, and [despite knowing] that there is insufficient evidence against the accused to survive a motion for judgment of acquittal at the close of the government's case.

Id.; see also Bruce A. Green, *Prosecutorial Ethics as Usual*, 2003 U. Ill. L. Rev. 1573, 1588 (finding that Model Rule 3.8(a) "deals with only one aspect of prosecutorial discretion—the core decision whether to prosecute a criminal charge—and incorporates a standard that is both too low and incomplete").

11   See Model Code, supra note 2, Canon 7 ("A lawyer should represent a client zealously within the bounds of the law."); Model Rules, supra note 2, R. 1.3 cmt. 1 ("A lawyer must also act with commitment and dedication to the interests of the client and with zeal in advocacy upon the client's behalf.").

12   Sharswood, supra note 9, at 92, quoted in Green, *Prosecutors*, supra note 9, at 613.

13   Model Rules, supra note 2, R. 3.1.

14   Id. & cmt. 3 ("The lawyer's obligations under this Rule are subordinate to federal or state

B. Disclosure of Exculpatory Evidence and Information

Another "special responsibilit[y] of a prosecutor" delineated by the Model Rules requires "timely disclosure to the defense of all evidence or information known to the prosecutor that tends to negate the guilt of the accused or mitigates the offense."[15] In sharp contrast, consistent with constitutional guarantees and the ethical duty of confidentiality, the criminal defense attorney may—again, typically must—withhold from the prosecution both material and incriminating evidence.[16] As one leading scholar has put it, "[w]hile those protections may not warrant a general prohibition against all prosecution discovery of defense information prior to trial, they do create a mine field of constitutional and other restrictions that must be negotiated before defense disclosure can be required."[17]

C. Candor Toward the Tribunal: Cross-Examination of Truthful Witnesses and Arguing False Inferences

Finally, once a trial has commenced, prosecutors, like all attorneys, are bound by a duty of candor toward the tribunal.[18] Again, however, the prosecutor's ethical obligations differ from those of most lawyers—in particular those of the criminal defense attorney[19]—based on what one scholar has termed the

---

constitutional law that entitles a defendant in a criminal matter to the assistance of counsel in presenting a claim or contention that otherwise would be prohibited by this Rule.").

15 Model Rules, supra note 2, R. 3.8(d).

16 See *People v. Meredith*, 631 P.2d 46, 51-52 (Cal. 1981) (discussing multiple cases involving the applicability of the attorney-client privilege in the criminal context); Model Rules, supra note 2, R 1.6(a) ("A lawyer shall not reveal information relating to the representation of a client. . . .").

17 Wolfram, supra note 6, §13.10.5 n.98, at 767 (citation omitted). The protections referenced above include the protection against self-incrimination, the presumption of innocence, the confidentiality of attorney-client communication, and the protection of attorney work-product. Id.

18 See Model Rules, supra note 2, R. 3.3.

19 Like most other lawyers, prosecutors may not knowingly offer false evidence, including the false testimony of a witness. See id. R. 3.3(a)(3). In contrast, the criminal defense attorney is partially exempt even from such a basic rule of candor. For example, in some jurisdictions, a criminal defense attorney is obligated to accede to the wishes of a client who insists on testifying falsely, and must present the testimony in the form of a "narrative statement." Id. R. 3.3 cmt. 7. In addition, unlike other private attorneys, a criminal defense attorney may not refuse to offer the client's testimony into evidence based on the attorney's reasonable belief that the testimony is false. Id. R. 3.3(a)(3).

The precise extent to which a prosecutor must be satisfied of a witness's veracity before permitting that witness to testify remains a subject of debate among legal scholars.

prosecutor's "duty to truth."[20] For example, a skilled attorney may attempt to discredit a truthful adversarial witness through effective cross-examination.[21] Indeed, as Justice White famously observed, this method of cross-examination comprises "part of the duty imposed on the most honorable defense counsel," despite the fact that such conduct "in many instances has little, if any, relation to the search for truth."[22] Although the propriety of this tactic for

---

For example, Professor Zacharias asserts that "prosecutors need not act as judges of their witness's testimony unless they are sure the witness is falsifying facts." Zacharias, *Can Prosecutors Do Justice?*, supra note 3, at 94. However, Professor Zacharias's position may not represent a categorical view that "it is not the prosecutor's function to make a personal evaluation of the truth." Gershman, *The Prosecutor's Duty to Truth*, supra note 10, at 310 & n.4 (presenting various viewpoints in favor of and against this proposition). Indeed, Professor Zacharias does maintain that "prosecutors should not rely on information they know to be false." Zacharias, *Can Prosecutors Do Justice?*, supra note 3, at 94.

Likewise, in a groundbreaking article on the subject of prosecutorial ethics, Professor Richard Uviller does not appear to permit the prosecutor to forego any and all evaluation of the truth; rather, he prescribes that "when the issue stands in equipoise in [the prosecutor's] own mind, when [the prosecutor] is honestly unable to judge where the truth of the matter lies, [there is] no flaw in the conduct of the prosecutor who fairly lays the matter before the judge or jury." H. Richard Uviller, *The Virtuous Prosecutor in Quest of an Ethical Standard: Guidance from the ABA*, 71 Mich. L. Rev. 1145, 1159 (1973). In an article published many years later, Professor Uviller's position seems to have evolved somewhat, asserting that "the conscientious prosecutor . . . should be assured to a fairly high degree of certainty that he has the right person, the right crime, and a good chance of success with a petit jury." H. Richard Uviller, *The Neutral Prosecutor: The Obligation of Dispassion in a Passionate Pursuit*, 68 Fordham L. Rev. 1695, 1703 (2000); cf. Wolfram, supra note 6, §13.10.4, at 767 ("The prosecutor must take reasonable steps to assess the truth or falsity, and not just the plausibility, of evidence that will be offered."). Refer to note 10 supra and accompanying text.

20 See Gershman, *The Prosecutor's Duty to Truth*, supra note 10, at 314 (identifying sources of the "duty to truth").

21 See Freedman & Smith, supra note 6, §§8.01-.09 (examining the morality of using cross-examination to discredit a witness known to be telling the truth); Wolfram, supra note 6, §12.4.5, at 650-51 (noting the general agreement among commentators that persuading a jury not to believe a truthful witness is permissible).

22 See *United States v. Wade*, 388 U.S. 218, 258 (1967) (White, J., dissenting in part and concurring in part).

> Our interest in not convicting the innocent permits counsel to put the State to its proof, to put the State's case in the worst possible light, regardless of what [counsel] thinks or knows to be the truth. . . . [M]ore often than not, defense counsel will cross-examine . . . and impeach [a prosecution witness] . . . even if [counsel] thinks the witness is telling the truth. . . . In this respect, as part of our modified adversary system and as part of the duty imposed on the most honorable defense counsel, we countenance or require conduct which in many instances has little, if any, relation to the search for truth.

civil attorneys may be open to debate,[23] it is clearly unethical for a prosecutor to engage in a method of cross-examination that would impugn the credibility of a truthful defense witness.[24] Similarly, a criminal defense attorney may rely on truthful evidence to persuade the jury to accept an inference that is favorable to the client, but that the lawyer knows is false.[25] Again, there appears to be some question as to whether civil attorneys may engage in such conduct,[26] but there is general agreement that prosecutors may not argue false inferences to support a conviction.[27]

Each of these scenarios exemplifies a different aspect of the prosecutor's ethical obligations, and taken together, these examples illustrate some of the basic contours of the prosecutor's duty to seek justice. In each case, the prosecutor is required to forego conduct that would increase the likelihood of obtaining a conviction, in favor of conduct that will increase the likelihood of obtaining justice. Indeed, on a normative level, the appropriate prosecutorial

---

Id. at 257-58 (White, J., dissenting in part and concurring in part).

23 Compare Freedman & Smith, supra note 6, §8.06, at 222-23 (stating that in representing either a civil client or a criminal defendant "there is general agreement that a lawyer can properly cross-examine a truthful and accurate witness to make [the witness] appear to be mistaken or lying" and that "the prevailing view is that the lawyer is ethically required to do so unless tactics dictate otherwise"), and Green, *Prosecutors*, supra note 9, at 631-32 (stating that "in all likelihood" this tactic "is acceptable" for lawyers in civil proceedings), with Wolfram, supra note 6, §12.4.5, at 651 (stating that "the justifiability of a system of searching for 'weaknesses' in a witness' testimony with no regard to its accuracy is most supportable, if supportable at all, in the context of the criminal justice system," and that "it seems extremely doubtful that it should be extended to civil cases").

24 See Freedman & Smith, supra note 6, §11.01, at 294-95; Wolfram, supra note 6, §12.4.5, at 651; Green, *Prosecutors*, supra note 9, at 631-32, 632 n.113.

25 See William H. Fortune et al., *Modern Litigation and Professional Responsibility Handbook* §13.5.1, at 426-27 (1996); Green, *Prosecutors*, supra note 9, at 631-32. In fact, at least one court has apparently held that a criminal defense attorney "must argue a false inference that is fairly supported by the evidence," granting a writ of habeas corpus based on counsel's failure to do so. Fortune et al., supra, §13.5.1, at 427 (citing *Johns v. Smyth*, 176 F. Supp. 949 (E.D. Va. 1959)).

26 Compare Fortune et al., supra note 25, §13.5.1, at 428 (stating that "the answer is unclear" but that "leading authorities argue that it is unethical for a civil lawyer to knowingly argue for a false inference"), with Green, *Prosecutors*, supra note 9, at 631-32 (stating that "in all likelihood" this tactic "is acceptable" for lawyers in civil proceedings).

27 See Fortune et al., supra note 25, §13.5.1, at 427-28; Green, *Prosecutors*, supra note 9, at 632 & n.113 (quoting *United States v. Universita*, 298 F.2d 365, 367 (2d Cir. 1962); *United States v. Lusterino*, 450 F.2d 572, 574-75 (2d Cir. 1971)). Moreover, at least one federal court of appeals has held that a prosecutor cannot present an argument based on facts outside the record to rebut defense counsel's argument in support of false inferences. See Fortune et al., supra note 25, at 427-28, 427 n.5 (quoting *United States v. Latimer*, 511 F.2d 498 (10th Cir. 1975)).

response in each of these scenarios appears fairly self-evident. It would seem to conflict with fundamental notions of justice for a criminal defendant to face a conviction when the prosecutor does not believe the evidence supports such an outcome, or on the basis of a jury's inability to consider evidence that would tend to exculpate the defendant, or through a prosecutor's distortion of the implications of a witness's testimony or other truthful evidence.

PART TWO | BEYOND BASIC PRINCIPLES: FURTHER ANALYSIS OF THE NORMATIVE IMPLICATIONS OF THE PROSECUTOR'S ETHICAL OBLIGATION TO SEEK JUSTICE

Beyond the basic—and somewhat intuitive—responsibilities implicit in the duty to seek justice, the prosecutor often faces more complex ethical challenges, extending to situations in which the ethically proper course of action seems considerably less obvious. An analysis of these scenarios may suggest that, consistent with the complex nature of the prosecutor's mode of ethical decision-making, it may be not only helpful but perhaps necessary to consider the prosecutor's ethical duties through guidelines articulated in broad principles such as the provision requiring that the prosecutor seek justice.

A. Nondisclosure of Nonexculpatory Evidence and Information

A well-known New York case presents an intriguing variation on the prosecutor's duty to disclose evidence tending to negate or mitigate the defendant's culpability.[28] Following several months of plea negotiations, unbeknownst to the defendant, the complaining witness died; four days later, the defendant accepted the prosecutor's plea offer.[29] The defense attorney moved to withdraw the plea, arguing that the prosecutor had been obligated to disclose the witness's death, knowledge of which might have affected the defendant's decision regarding the plea offer.[30]

The New York Court of Appeals rejected the defense attorney's argument, emphasizing that the information concerning the death of the witness "would not have constituted exculpatory evidence—i.e., evidence favorable to

---

28   See *People v. Jones*, 375 N.E.2d 41 (N.Y. 1978). The facts of this case have also provided the basis of a hypothetical question posed in countless interviews to candidates for positions in prosecutors' offices.

29   Id. at 42.

30   Id.

an accused where the evidence is material either to guilt or to punishment."[31] Rather, the court found that the information the prosecutor failed to disclose constituted "nonevidentiary information pertinent to the tactical aspects of a defendant's determination not to proceed to trial."[32] As the court further explained, "notwithstanding that the responsibilities of a prosecutor for fairness and open-dealing are of a higher magnitude than those of a private litigant, no prosecutor is obliged to share [an] appraisal of the weaknesses of [the] case (as opposed to specific exculpatory evidence) with defense counsel."[33]

Insofar as it describes the contours of the prosecutor's legal obligation to disclose exculpatory information to the defendant, the court's conclusion stands on firm analytical ground: because the information at issue did not tend to negate or mitigate the defendant's culpability, it was not subject to disclosure requirements.[34] Nevertheless, as a normative matter, it may not appear quite as clear that the prosecutor's conduct in this case complied, in a broader sense, with the unique ethical duty to seek justice. If the prosecutor's professional responsibility is, in fact, seen to extend beyond the goal of conviction, to include the promotion of fair and just criminal proceedings, then the ethical obligation to seek justice might be understood as requiring disclosure to the defendant of information that, albeit not technically exculpatory, may be crucial to the defendant's decision-making process.[35]

B. Decision Not to Prosecute: Perjury Charges Against the Elderly Mother of a Criminal Defendant

In the course of a criminal trial, following the government's presentation of evidence, the defendant may offer evidence to rebut the government's case. For example, the defense attorney may offer the testimony of an alibi witness, who will testify that when the crime transpired, the defendant was with the witness

---

31 Id. at 43.

32 Id.

33 Id. at 43-44.

34 See id. at 44-45. For an apparently contrary approach, see *Virzi v. Grand Trunk Warehouse & Cold Storage Co.*, 571 F. Supp. 507, 512 (E.D. Mich. 1983) (finding that the plaintiff's attorney had an obligation to inform opposing counsel that the plaintiff had died during the course of settlement negotiations).

35 Using Professor Bruce Green's framework, the prosecutor's conduct in this scenario would arguably seem to violate the objective of "affording the accused . . . a lawful, *fair* process." Green, *Prosecutors*, supra note 9, at 634 (emphasis added).

rather than at the scene of the crime. The alibi witness may be a close friend or relative of the defendant—or, at times, poignantly, the defendant's elderly mother. Despite the sympathy that a mother's testimony may evoke in the trier of fact, to the extent that her statement proves to be, in a particular case, flatly contradicted by substantial and highly reliable testimony or physical evidence, it will appear patently fabricated and will have minimal, if any, bearing on the outcome of the case.

Under these facts, the prosecutor is faced with a clear case of perjury by the defendant's mother, providing grounds for criminal charges and a strong possibility of conviction. Yet, the prosecutor in such a scenario will likely choose not to investigate or prosecute the perjury charge. As a descriptive matter, the decision not to prosecute undoubtedly falls within the broad range of prosecutorial discretion.[36] In addition, there may be practical considerations supporting the prosecutor's decision.[37] Nevertheless, on a normative level, the decision not to prosecute an individual who has perjured herself in open court arguably constitutes an abdication of the prosecutor's duty to seek justice, which seemingly requires undertaking an attempt to convict those who have clearly committed crimes.[38]

---

36 See generally, e.g., Richard S. Frase, *The Decision to File Federal Criminal Charges: A Quantitative Study of Prosecutorial Discretion*, 47 U. Chi. L. Rev. 246 (1980) (examining prosecution rates and prosecutors' reasons for declining to prosecute defendants in the federal system); Gershman, *A Moral Standard*, supra note 10 (exploring challenges to the prosecutor's charging power in different hypothetical situations); Kenneth J. Melilli, *Prosecutorial Discretion in an Adversary System*, 1992 BYU L. Rev. 669 (describing the central role of the prosecutor and of prosecutorial discretion in the adversary system); Robert L. Misner, *Recasting Prosecutorial Discretion*, 86 J. Crim. L. & Criminology 717 (1996) (identifying trends that have strengthened prosecutorial power and proposing an outline for tying the exercise of prosecutorial discretion to the availability of prison resources); Ellen S. Podgor, *The Ethics and Professionalism of Prosecutors in Discretionary Decisions*, 68 Fordham L. Rev. 1511 (2000) (analyzing four prosecutorial decisions and focusing on education as a means to help "prosecutors navigate the discretionary decision-making process"); James Vorenberg, *Decent Restraint of Prosecutorial Power*, 94 Harv. L. Rev. 1521 (1981) (examining the nature, scope, and effect of prosecutorial discretion and suggesting that it may be overly broad and in need of reform). See generally Bruce A. Green & Samuel J. Levine, *Disciplinary Regulation of Prosecutors as a Remedy for Abuses of Prosecutorial Discretion: A Descriptive and Normative Analysis*, 14 Ohio St. J. Crim. L. 143 (2016).

37 Refer to note 96 infra and accompanying text (describing inadequate resources as one practical reason not to prosecute).

38 In Professor Green's framework, such prosecutorial conduct might violate the objectives of "enforcing the criminal law by convicting and punishing . . . those who commit crimes" and "treat[ing] lawbreakers with rough equality." Green, *Prosecutors*, supra note 9, at 634. However, Professor Green qualifies the first of the objectives as including punishing only "some (but not all) of those who commit crimes." Id. Therefore, Professor Green's approach may provide a particularly helpful framework for considering whether the defendant's mother's perjury should be prosecuted.

C. Leniency for Cooperators

As numerous scholars have observed, the prevalence of cooperators—criminal offenders who provide the prosecutor with information and/or testimony, in exchange for possible leniency in criminal charges or sentencing[39]—presents prosecutors with various practical and ethical challenges.[40] Nevertheless, the problems that arise in the use of cooperators have not deterred prosecutors from increasingly relying on cooperation as an indispensable tool in the investigation and prosecution of crime.[41]

---

39 This definition borrows from Michael A. Simons, *Retribution for Rats: Cooperation, Punishment, and Atonement,* 56 Vand. L. Rev. 1, 2 (2003).

40 See, e.g., Freedman & Smith, supra note 6, §11.13, at 318-19 (suggesting that the lack of guidance and the incentives for "snitches" to cooperate with prosecutors may not always produce accurate information); John G. Douglass, *Confronting the Reluctant Accomplice,* 101 Colum. L. Rev. 1797 (2001) (questioning the reliability of testimony from one type of cooperator—an accomplice—in the context of the Confrontation Clause of the U.S. Constitution); George C. Harris, *Testimony for Sale: The Law and Ethics of Snitches and Experts,* 28 Pepp. L. Rev. 1 (2000) (addressing the legal and ethical challenges posed by cooperative testimony and describing the offer of leniency or immunity provided in exchange for such testimony as an exception to the rule against paying for witness testimony); Graham Hughes, *Agreements for Cooperation in Criminal Cases,* 45 Vand. L. Rev. 1 (1992) (discussing several potential problems with the use of cooperating witnesses, including the possible validation of criminal activity and the potential for unreliable information); Cynthia K.Y. Lee, *From Gatekeeper to Concierge: Reigning In the Federal Prosecutor's Expanding Power over Substantial Assistance Departures,* 50 Rutgers L. Rev. 199 (1997) (critiquing the extent of the federal prosecutor's power over substantial assistance departures from mandatory sentencing guidelines when negotiating with cooperating witnesses); Cynthia Kwei Yung Lee, *Prosecutorial Discretion, Substantial Assistance, and the Federal Sentencing Guidelines,* 42 UCLA L. Rev. 105 (1994) (recognizing the paradox created by the relationship between knowledge and culpability: the more a cooperating witness knows about a particular crime, the more culpable that witness is likely to be); Ellen Yaroshefsky, *Cooperation with Federal Prosecutors: Experiences of Truth Telling and Embellishment,* 68 Fordham L. Rev. 917 (1999) (using interviews with prosecutors to explore the dilemma posed by prosecutors' frequent reliance on inaccurate cooperator testimony); Ellen Yaroshefsky, *Introduction to Symposium, The Cooperating Witness Conundrum: Is Justice Obtainable?,* 23 Cardozo L. Rev. 747, 749 (2002) [hereinafter Yaroshefsky, *Introduction*] (noting that although the dangers of using cooperating witnesses have been widely accepted, the concern about the use of such witnesses is on the rise).

41 See, e.g., Simons, supra note 39, at 3, 14 (stating that "cooperation has never been more prevalent than it is today" and citing statistics demonstrating increasing cooperation); see also Freedman & Smith, supra note 6, §11.13, at 318 (describing use of cooperators as "an increasingly troublesome area for prosecutors, who regularly obtain information and testimony from people who can incriminate others in exchange for promises of leniency," but noting that "in some cases, because of [a] lack of adequate evidence, it would be difficult, if not impossible, to prosecute without such 'cooperation'"); Steven M. Cohen, *What Is True? Perspectives of a*

Compared with the ethical concerns scholars have raised in exploring the tactics of working with a cooperator, the more fundamental issue, surrounding the ethical propriety of granting leniency in exchange for assistance, has received considerably less attention. Entering into a cooperation agreement may arguably represent instance in which a widely-accepted practice among prosecutors seems to contradict the normative nature of the prosecutor's paramount and fundamental obligation, to seek justice. After all, in light of the crime the cooperator has committed, and the corresponding punishment that should therefore constitute the cooperator's just deserts, it seems to subvert justice for the prosecutor to grant leniency on the basis of the practical utility of the information and assistance the cooperator has provided.[42]

Thus, in each of these scenarios, the laws and provisions regulating prosecutorial ethics give prosecutors the discretion to engage in conduct that appears to undermine the prosecutor's underlying ethical obligation to seek justice. Whether the decision proves detrimental to the defendant—such as a refusal to disclose information that would assist the defense but that falls short of being exculpatory, or ultimately benefits the defendant—such as a decision to offer leniency if the defendant acts as a cooperator or not to prosecute a defendant's mother for perjury, the prosecutor's choice in each case resists simple normative explanation.

Instead, a normative justification for these decisions seems to require a more complex and nuanced consideration of the prosecutor's ethical obligation to seek justice. In an effort to undertake such an analysis, it may be helpful to look to another system of legal and ethical decision-making, specifically, Jewish law's approach to issues of ethical complexity. Perhaps the Jewish legal system offers an analogue that may be useful in constructing a more thoughtful and

---

Former Prosecutor, 23 Cardozo L. Rev. 817, 817 (2002) (observing that "at the core of almost every complex criminal case sits an accomplice (or cooperating) witness"); id. at 819-20 (asserting that "in the federal [criminal justice] system, the notion of salvation through cooperation is pervasive" and that "the almost mystical qualities of cooperation—the prospect of receiving a substantially reduced sentence . . .—is known to every criminal defendant"); Yaroshefsky, *Introduction*, supra note 40, at 749 (describing "an accepted proposition that an effective criminal justice system is dependent upon informants and other cooperators"); id. at 750 (noting that "there exists a theoretical recognition of the dangers associated with cooperating witnesses and, over time, scholars, judges, and lawyers have made numerous proposals to reduce those dangers" but that "most of those have gone unheeded").

42 The prosecutor's conduct may thus violate the objective "to treat lawbreakers with rough equality, that is, similarly situated individuals should generally be treated in roughly the same way." Green, *Prosecutors*, supra note 9, at 634.

thorough understanding and appreciation of the complex nature of the prosecutor's ethical duties and decisions.[43]

PART FOUR | LEGAL AND ETHICAL DECISION-MAKING IN A COMPARATIVE NORMATIVE FRAMEWORK

A. Underlying and Overarching Normative Directives

The underlying and overarching normative directive governing the ethical conduct of the American prosecutor is the broad obligation to seek justice. In Jewish law and philosophy, although a number of broad provisions serve as basic sources of legal and ethical obligation,[44] the underlying and overarching normative directive may be found in the biblical imperative: "In all of your ways acknowledge [God]."[45] In both legal systems, however, the contours of the broad directive are delineated, in part, by various specific obligations. In Jewish law, enumerated obligations provide a means for acknowledging God in every area of human activity.[46] Although not as comprehensive, specific rules,

---

43 Indeed, I have suggested elsewhere that hermeneutic and analytical elements of Jewish law may provide a particularly apt and valuable source for further exploration and understanding of various areas of the American legal system, including: constitutional law, see, e.g., Chapters 3, 4, 9, 10, and 11 of this Volume, and Chapter 17 of Volume 2; criminal law, see, e.g., Chapters 5, 6, 7, and 8 in this Volume, and Chapter 26 in Volume 2; and legal ethics, see, e.g., Chapters 14 and 16 in this Volume and Chapter 18 in Volume 2; Levine, *Taking Ethical Discretion Seriously,* supra note 7; Samuel J. Levine, *The Broad Life of the Jewish Lawyer: Integrating Spirituality, Scholarship and Profession,* 27 Tex. Tech L. Rev. 1199 (1996) [hereinafter Levine, *Broad Life*].

44 See Chapters 9 and 14 in this Volume.

45 Proverbs 3:6; see also Maimonides, *Mishne Torah,* Laws of *De'oth* 3:2-3:3; Maimonides, *Commentary on the Mishna, Introduction to Pirke Avoth,* ch. 5; Moses Hayyim Luzzatto, *Mesillat Yesharim* 336-39 (Shraga Silverstein trans., 1966); Yitzchak Hutner, *Pachad Yitzchak, Pesach* 123-26 (6th ed. 1999); Levine, *Broad Life,* supra note 43, at 1204-6.

46 See, e.g., Aryeh Kaplan, *The Handbook of Jewish Thought* 78 (1979) (stating that the commandments "penetrate every nook and cranny of a person's existence, hallowing even the lowliest acts and elevating them to a service to God" and that "the multitude of laws governing even such mundane acts as eating, drinking, dressing and business, sanctify every facet of life, and constantly remind one of [one's] responsibilities toward God"); see also Chapter 14 in this Volume (citing Maimonides, *Sefer Ha-Mitzvoth* (Soncino 1940); *Sefer Hahinnuch: The Book of Mitzvah Education* (Charles Wengrov trans., 1985); Joseph B. Soloveitchik, *Halakhic Man* 33 (Lawrence Kaplan trans., 1983) (originally published in Hebrew as *Ish ha-halakhah,* in 1 Talpiot 3-4 (1944)); Moshe Silberg, *Law and Morals in Jewish Jurisprudence,* 75 Harv. L. Rev. 306, 309, 322 (1961)). See generally Chapters 12 and 13 in this Volume; Levine, *Broad Life,* supra note 43.

governing a considerable range of the prosecutor's conduct, are designed to be consistent with the fundamental obligation to seek justice.[47] Nevertheless, as is typical of any legal framework, the finite set of delineated rules comprising both Jewish law and the regulation of prosecutorial ethics can address only a limited number of scenarios. Therefore, legal and ethical decision-makers are required to engage in various methods of reasoning and interpretation, in order to apply the rules to the overwhelming number of cases not expressly addressed.

Moreover, beyond the cases that entail interpretive analysis of enumerated rules, other scenarios may be categorized as presenting ethical or legal dilemmas that require appeal to meta-principles of ethical decision-making and legal application. These scenarios include relatively basic cases, in which ambiguity results from uncertainty regarding the applicability of a given rule, as well as more complex cases, which involve a choice among competing and, at times, conflicting values. In such cases, broad provisions and principles, including the directives to seek justice and to acknowledge God, provide methodological guidelines for determining the mode of legal analysis appropriate for resolution of the difficult ethical issues.

B. Basic Cases

1. Clear Obligation

Perhaps the most basic case of ethical decision-making involves a situation in which the ethically proper conduct is delineated through a clearly defined

---

47 See Green, *Prosecutors*, supra note 9, at 634 ("Doing justice comprises various objectives which are, for the most part, implicit in our constitutional and statutory schemes.").

> Most obviously, these include enforcing the criminal law by convicting and punishing some (but not all) of those who commit crimes; avoiding punishment of those who are innocent of criminal wrongdoing (a goal which, as reflected in the "presumption of innocence," is paramount in importance); and affording the accused, and others, a lawful, fair process. Additionally, most would agree, the sovereign has at least two other aims. One is to treat individuals with proportionality; that is, to ensure that individuals are not be[ing] punished more harshly than deserved. The other is to treat lawbreakers with rough equality; that is, similarly situated individuals should generally be treated in roughly the same way.

Id.; see also Steven K. Berenson, *Public Lawyers, Private Values: Can, Should, and Will Government Lawyers Serve the Public Interest?*, 41 B.C. L. Rev. 789, 815 (2000) (characterizing Professor Green as "contend[ing] that the 'do justice' standard in fact comprises a series of more specific objectives").

and applicable obligation. The Jewish legal system, which consists of legal and ethical obligations relating to all areas of life, mandates a particular mode of action in the context of numerous situations specified in the Torah and in later legal texts.[48] For example, the Torah prohibits engaging in *melacha*—sometimes loosely translated as "work"—on the Sabbath.[49] In turn, the Talmud identifies thirty-nine general categories of activity that are included within the biblical prohibition.[50] Although determining the definition and application of each of these categories requires interpretive analysis, the interpretive process will ordinarily yield a clear delineation of the range of activities included within each general category.[51] Thus, refraining from one of these activities on the Sabbath presents a basic case in which an individual acknowledges God through observance of a clear obligation.

The case of a clear obligation in Jewish law may provide an analogue for basic cases in which the prosecutor's obligation to seek justice dictates a clearly identifiable mode of ethically proper conduct, such as the requirements to prosecute only on the basis of probable cause, to disclose exculpatory information, and to engage in candor toward the tribunal.[52] Again, although determination of the precise contours of these requirements may involve an interpretive process, the normative application of the duty to seek justice in these cases is largely unambiguous and therefore not dependent on a complex form of ethical analysis.

2. Indeterminate Applicability of a Clear Obligation

A somewhat more difficult case involves a situation in which, under a specific set of facts, the decision-maker is unable to determine the applicability of an otherwise clearly defined obligation.[53] In such a scenario, the decision-maker has unsuccessfully exhausted the possibility of resolution through the ordinary interpretive process. Instead, it is necessary to resort to an alternative method

---

48 Refer to note 46 supra and accompanying text.

49 See, e.g., Exodus 20:10.

50 See Talmud Bavli, Shabbath 63a.

51 See Chapter 3 in this Volume.

52 Refer to part one supra (discussing prosecutors' duties under the "seek justice" obligation).

53 This discussion accepts the premise that legal arguments are generally susceptible to determinacy, and that there may be one course of action that arguably represents the proper resolution of the scenarios under consideration in the text. Thus, the reference to an "indeterminate application" of a clear rule involves the relatively unusual situation in which the decision-maker lacks some element of basic information necessary for an informed and reasonable interpretive resolution of the basic question of the applicability of the rule.

of resolution, a meta-principle of decision-making regarding the applicability of the rule under consideration.

To return to the example of the prohibition of *melacha* on the Sabbath, in Jewish law, with respect to most issues of legal and religious significance, each day of the week, including the Sabbath, begins at night.[54] However, it is not clear—indeed, it is indeterminate—under Jewish law whether night commences at sundown or at a later stage of darkness.[55] Thus, it is consequently not clear whether *melacha* is permitted during the "twilight" period between these two points in time, both at the beginning of the Sabbath and at the end of the Sabbath. As a result of the absence of a method of interpretation that may be employed to resolve this uncertainty, the proper mode of conduct during the period is instead determined through a more general principle: with respect to the applicability of a biblical obligation in a given scenario, uncertainties are resolved in favor of requiring adherence to the obligation.[56] Therefore, those activities that are prohibited on the Sabbath as forms of the biblical definition of *melacha* are likewise prohibited during the "twilight" period of time.[57]

In the context of legal ethics, similar situations arise, in which neither ethics provisions nor their interpretation yields a resolution to an ethical dilemma. As a result of the indeterminate nature of the applicability of the ethics rules in such circumstances, it seems necessary to look beyond specific interpretive method-ologies and instead to resort to broad principles of ethical decision-making.

---

54 See Levine, *Broad Life*, supra note 43, at 1203 n.13.

55 See, e.g., Maimonides, *Mishne Torah*, Laws of the *Sabbath* 5:4; Hershel Schachter, *Eretz Hatzevi: Be'urei Sugyot* 61-69 (1992) [hereinafter Schachter, *Eretz Hatzevi*]. Conceptually, this indeterminacy may be understood not as a consequence of a factual uncertainty, regarding whether the twilight period is considered day or night, but rather as a reflection of the dual nature of this time period, which retains properties of both day and night. As a result of this duality, the legal characteristics of this time period mirror those applied to the category of actual legal uncertainty. See 1 Aharon Lichtenstein, *Leaves of Faith: The World of Jewish Learning* 214 (2003) (referring to the teachings of Rabbi Joseph B. Soloveitchik and describing "a category of doubt regarding two conflicting matters that issues from the balanced conflict between two certainties, and not from uncertainty itself"); 7 *Mesorah* 44 (Hershel Schachter & Menachem Genack eds., 1992) (citing the teachings of Rabbi Joseph B. Soloveitchik); Hershel Schachter, *MiPninei HaRav* 164 (2001); Joseph B. Soloveitchik, 1 *Shi'urim le-Zekher Abba Mari* 107-29 (2002); Joseph B. Soloveitchik, *The Lonely Man of Faith*, *Tradition: J. Orthodox Jewish Thought*, Vol. 7, No. 2, 1965, at 5.

56 See, e.g., Maimonides, *Mishne Torah*, Laws of the *Sabbath* 5:4. See generally Aryeh Leb Ha-Cohen Heller, *Shev Shemat'ta*; Shimon Shkop, *Sha'arei Yosher* Section 5.

57 See Maimonides, *Mishne Torah*, Laws of the *Sabbath* 5:4. For a discussion of the rules governing the status of rabbinically legislated forms of *melacha* during this period of time, see Schachter, *Eretz Hatzevi*, supra note 55, at 67-68.

Somewhat parallel to the principle in Jewish law that uncertainties are resolved in favor of adherence to biblical obligation, for the attorney representing a private client, cases of ethical uncertainly are often resolved in favor of the best interests of the client.[58] Indeed, ethics codes arguably support such a result, through repeated—express and implied— emphasis on the attorney's duty of zealous representation of the client's interests.[59] Thus, the attorney's general ethical obligation to pursue the interests of the client provides a meta-principle for ethical decision-making in the face of apparently insoluble uncertainty. In light of the availability, in both Jewish law and legal ethics, of relatively mechanical means for resolving these cases of indeterminacy, such scenarios may be categorized as more closely associated with basic cases of ethical decision-making than with instances of genuine ethical complexity.

Notably, the United States Supreme Court has appeared to endorse the application of a similarly mechanical approach in the context of prosecutorial ethics as well. Addressing the scope of the prosecutor's duty to disclose

---

58 See, e.g., David B. Wilkins, *Legal Realism for Lawyers*, 104 Harv. L. Rev. 468, 473 (1990) ("[T]he traditional model strongly implies that doubts about the exact contours of the law should be resolved in the client's favor."). It should be noted that this discussion is limited to an analysis of the prevalent model of client-oriented legal ethics. One of the central areas of contention among contemporary ethics scholars relates to numerous proposals for alternative models that have been offered to supplement or replace the current model. See generally Levine, *Taking Ethical Discretion Seriously*, supra note 7 (describing and providing a critical analysis of alternative models).

59 See Model Code, supra note 2, Canon 7; Model Rules, supra note 2, R. 1.3 cmt. 1; see also Wilkins, supra note 58, at 473 n.17 (stating that "the rules of professional conduct generally support the view that all doubts should be resolved in favor of furthering the best interest of the client" (citing Model Code, supra note 2, DR 7-101 (A)(1), EC 7-4, EC 7-5; Model Rules, supra note 2, R. 3.1 cmt. 1)).

   Professor Zacharias offered a similar observation:

> When the codes authorize lawyers to choose between emphasizing partisanship and important third party or societal interests, lawyers' natural [personal and economic] incentives encourage them to select partisanship. Lawyers who make that choice can readily justify their conduct as mandated by the code by claiming adherence to the code provisions that call for zeal.

Fred C. Zacharias, *Reconciling Professionalism and Client Interests*, 36 Wm. & Mary L. Rev. 1303, 1340 (1995); cf. Heidi Li Feldman, *Codes and Virtues: Can Good Lawyers Be Good Ethical Deliberators?*, 69 S. Cal. L. Rev. 885, 898 (1996) ("The more frequently a black letter ethics code is inconclusive, the more opportunities there are for . . . interpreting the rules simply to permit pursuit of the client's ends, without regard to independent ethical concerns.").

   For a discussion of the ramifications of the prevalence of this approach, see Levine, *Taking Ethical Discretion Seriously*, supra note 7, at 56-58 & nn.151-52.

exculpatory evidence of a material nature, the Court determined, "because we are dealing with an inevitably imprecise standard, and because the significance of an item of evidence can seldom be predicted accurately until the entire record is complete, the prudent prosecutor will resolve doubtful questions in favor of disclosure."[60] According to the Court's reasoning, in the face of a matter of ethical indeterminacy, the prosecutor's mode of ethical decision-making should comply with the broad principle of resolving uncertainties in favor of protecting the constitutional rights of the criminal defendant. Thus, the Court's prescription for the prosecutor parallels the apparent obligation of the private attorney—substituting the rights of the criminal defendant in place of best interests of the private client—as the overarching principle of ethical guidance.

Nevertheless, notwithstanding the utility—and perhaps the normative appeal—of such an approach to resolving ethical dilemmas that arise in the representation of private clients, a close look at the prosecutor's ethical obligations suggests that the approach is inadequate, if not utterly inapposite, in addressing the ethical challenges that scenarios of indeterminacy pose to the prosecutor. The Court's decision was ostensibly premised on the application of a fundamental rule of prosecutorial ethics, portraying the prosecutor as the "'servant of the law, the twofold aim of which is that guilt shall not escape or innocence suffer.'"[61] In short, as the Court explained, "though the attorney for the sovereign must prosecute the accused with earnestness and vigor, [the prosecutor] must always be faithful to the client's overriding interest that 'justice shall be done.'"[62]

Upon further review, however, the Court's solution, instructing the prosecutor to resolve doubts in favor of the criminal defendant, seems consistent with only one aspect of the prosecutor's duty to seek justice: the obligation to guarantee the fair and just protection of the defendant's rights.[63] However, the Court's approach fails to account for the prosecutor's coextensive duty to ensure that criminals are properly prosecuted and, when appropriate, justly convicted. The dual nature of the prosecutor's ethical obligation resists simple prescriptions in the face of uncertainty.[64] To the extent that a uniform solution, such

---

60 *United States v. Agurs*, 427 U.S. 97, 108 (1976).

61 Id. at 111 (quoting *Berger v. United States*, 295 U.S. 78, 88 (1935)).

62 Id. at 110-11.

63 See Model Rules, supra note 2, R. 3.8.

64 Professor Zacharias offered the following description of the attitude expected of private attorneys:

> Private lawyers confronting ethical dilemmas usually find themselves torn between promoting a single client's goals and safeguarding their own

as the one offered by the Court, satisfies only one element of the prosecutor's duty, it entails a corresponding risk of ignoring—or even violating—the full range of obligations included in the ethical obligation to seek justice.

Perhaps a normative analysis of the ethical decision-making of prosecutors should more fully appreciate the distinction between the duties of private attorneys and those of prosecutors, a distinction that is reflected in the differences in the respective natures of their ethical dilemmas. A suitable analytical framework for prosecutorial ethics must incorporate an acknowledgment of the unique tensions and conflicts that require the prosecutor to carefully balance competing interests, rather than simply relying on a uniform principle for choosing among them. Thus, turning again to the Jewish legal system as a comparative analytical model, it may be helpful to explore the approaches in Jewish law for addressing scenarios that involve not mere instances of indeterminacy

---

> professional or moral self-interest. The disciplinary rules resolve these conflicts largely by casting trial lawyers as agents who must champion client interests, subject only to narrow limits on extreme behavior.

Zacharias, *Can Prosecutors Do Justice?*, supra note 3, at 57. In contrast, Professor Zacharias noted that the prosecutor

> has no single client. The prosecutor is simultaneously responsible for the community's protection, victims' desire for vengeance, defendants' entitlement to a fair opportunity for vindication, and the state's need for a criminal justice system that is efficient and appears fair. Described accurately, the prosecutor represents "constituencies"—and several of them at one time.
>
> This multirepresentation is significant for the structure of prosecutorial ethics. . . .
>
> Prosecutors . . . face conflicts among their constituents' interests as well as between constituent and personal interests.

Id. at 57-58 (footnotes omitted).

Similarly, describing the unique challenges inherent in the prosecutor's obligation to seek justice, Professor Green has explained:

> A prosecutor is a representative of, as well as a lawyer for, a government entity that has several different, sometimes seemingly inconsistent, objectives in the criminal context. Of these, convicting and punishing lawbreakers is only one, and it is no more important than others, such as avoiding the punishment of innocent people and ensuring that people are treated fairly. As the government's surrogate, the prosecutor's job is to carry out all these objectives and resolve the tension among them.

Green, *Prosecutors*, supra note 9, at 642. See also Levine supra note 1; Levine *The Law and the "Spirit of the Law"*, supra note 7.

or uncertainty, but outright conflicts that require more complex forms of consideration and resolution.

C. Cases of Ethical Conflict and Complexity

1. Prioritization Among Conflicting Normative Obligations and Values

Partly as a result of the large number and wide range of legal and ethical obligations that comprise the Jewish legal system, an important segment of Jewish law relates to the sometimes inevitable—and often irreconcilable—conflicts that arise in attempting to fulfill different obligations. The conflicts may materialize in a variety of ways, but they all share the need for mechanisms of prioritization among obligations; in addition, each conflict poses its own unique challenges, thereby necessitating a correspondingly particularized method of resolution.

One form of conflict involves contemporaneously applicable and competing positive obligations. In some cases, the issues of priority are limited to determining the appropriate order for undertaking different obligations. In other scenarios, as a result of time constraints, the conflict precludes fulfillment of all of the obligations, thus presenting the more difficult question of which obligations are to be observed and which are to be foregone. In both of these situations, the appropriate resolution of the conflict depends on the application of a number of principles of prioritization that relate to both general and specific qualities of the conflicting obligations.[65]

A more direct form of conflict involves a scenario in which a positive obligation may be fulfilled only through the simultaneous violation of a negative commandment. Though subject to numerous limitations and qualifications, the general principle for resolving such a conflict prescribes fulfilling the positive commandment in spite of the incidental violation of the prohibition.[66]

---

65 See 2 Aryeh Kaplan, *The Handbook of Jewish Thought* 107-10 (Abraham Sutton ed., 1992) [hereinafter Kaplan, *1992 Handbook*] (discussing the principles of prioritization that appear in Jewish law); see also Shlomo Yosef Zevin, *Hamoadim B'Halacha* 194-95 (1955) (same).

66 See Kaplan, *1992 Handbook*, supra note 65, at 109-10; Hershel Schachter, *B'Ikvei Hatzoan* 14-18 (1997) [hereinafter Schachter, *B'Ikvei Hatzoan*]; Elchanan Wasserman, *Kobetz He'aroth* 107-9 (Elazar Wasserman ed., 2003). For a normative and philosophical analysis of the priority in such circumstances of the positive commandment vis-à-vis the negative commandment, see Ramban (Nachmanides), *Commentary on the Torah* 309-10 (Charles B. Chavel trans., 1973) [hereinafter Ramban] (explicating Exodus 20:8); Meir Simcha of Dvinsk, *Meshech Chochma* 522 (explicating Deuteronomy 34:12).

Finally, in addition to complex principles of prioritization that govern situations of unavoidable conflict among obligations, an overarching and generally applicable principle of prioritization prescribes that, in the absence of exceptional circumstances, obligations in the Jewish legal system are suspended when necessary to fulfill the superseding obligation to save a life.[67] Thus, for example, in the face of life-threatening danger, notwithstanding the legal and philosophical significance and centrality of the Sabbath to Jewish thought,[68] any and all activities otherwise prohibited on the Sabbath should be performed—without hesitation or delay.[69] Indeed, virtually any plausible possibility of danger to life, however remote, overrides nearly every competing obligation in Jewish law, not only permitting—but mandating—violation of the dictates of the competing obligation.[70]

Conceptually, methods of resolving cases of competing obligations in Jewish law may present an analytical framework for evaluation of cases of ethical complexity relating to the prosecutor's obligation to seek justice. For example, principles of prioritization in Jewish law may offer insight into the United States Supreme Court's instruction that a prosecutor faced with an uncertainty regarding the obligation to disclose exculpatory information should resolve doubts in favor of protecting the constitutional rights of the criminal defendant.[71]

Through an analogy to parallel cases in Jewish law, the scenario addressed by the Court may be seen as involving contemporaneous positive obligations. Thus, perhaps the Court's resolution, prescribing disclosure as the ethically proper course of action, reflects a mode of analysis that takes into account the dual nature of the prosecutor's ethical duty to seek justice and concludes, on the basis of principles of prioritization, that the obligation to the defen-

---

67 See Talmud Bavli, Yoma 85a-85b; Maimonides, *Mishne Torah*, Laws of *Sabbath*, ch. 2. For discussions of the contours of this principle, see Kaplan, *1992 Handbook*, supra note 65, at 38-49; Schachter, *B'Ikvei Hatzoan*, supra note 66, at 14-18; Soloveitchik, supra note 46, at 34-35. See also Levine, *Taking Ethical Discretion Seriously*, supra note 7, at 57 n.151.

68 See, e.g., Talmud Bavli, Chulin 5a, Commentary of Rashi (highlighting the importance of the Sabbath); Maimonides, *Mishne Torah*, Laws of *Sabbath* 30:15 (same); Ramban, supra note 66, at 312-13 (same).

69 See Maimonides, *Mishne Torah*, Laws of *Sabbath* 2:2-2:3; Soloveitchik, supra note 46, at 34.

70 See Soloveitchik, supra note 46, at 34-35; see also Schachter, *B'Ikvei Hatzoan*, supra note 66, at 228-32; Hershel Schachter, *B'kashruth Dag Ha-tuna Sheb'kufsoath*, 1 Mesorah 66, 71-72 & n.5 (Hershel Schachter & Menachem Genack eds., 1989) (noting the prevailing view that this principle does not extend to an extremely remote possibility of danger to life, such as when there exists a "one-in-a-thousand" chance of danger).

71 *United States v. Agurs*, 427 U.S. 97, 108 (1976). Refer to notes 60-62 supra and accompanying text (discussing *Agurs*).

dant takes priority over other obligations. More likely, however, the case may be understood as presenting directly conflicting obligations. After all, in this scenario, relying on the prosecutor's duty to the defendant entails, to a corresponding degree, rejecting the applicability of the prosecutor's duty to convict a deserving defendant. In such a case, the Court may have concluded, the operative principle of prioritization weighs in favor of the duty of disclosure, despite the resulting detriment to the likelihood of conviction.

As a final alternative, the Court may view the protection of the defendant's constitutional rights as an overarching principle that takes priority, regardless of the nature of the consequences or the competing interests. Indeed, such an approach may be consistent with the general function of a criminal defendant's constitutional protections, which, when violated, supersede the undeniable utility of improperly obtained evidence in securing a conviction.[72]

This conceptual framework may similarly help explain the somewhat contrary—and contrarian—approach of the New York Court of Appeals, which held that a prosecutor was not obligated to disclose to the defendant the fact that the complaining witness had died.[73] The court expressly and extensively acknowledged the dual nature of, and competing values implicit in, the prosecutor's ethical obligation to seek justice.[74] Ultimately, the court concluded, because the death of the witness was not exculpatory, the prosecutor was not required to inform the defendant of its occurrence.[75] The court emphasized that to obligate disclosure in such a scenario would, in effect, improperly place upon the prosecutor the obligation to reveal nonexculpatory weaknesses in the prosecution's case.[76] Arguably less than fully compelling in its logic, and certainly not without its critics,[77] the court's approach might be better

---

72 See, e.g., *Agurs*, 427 U.S. at 103 (noting that "a conviction obtained by the knowing use of perjured testimony" must be set aside if the "testimony could have affected the judgment of the jury").

73 See *People v. Jones*, 375 N.E.2d 41, 42 (N.Y. 1978). Refer to part two, section A supra (discussing *Jones*).

74 See *Jones*, 375 N.E.2d at 43-44 (citing *Berger v. United States*, 295 U.S. 78 (1935); *Brady v. United States*, 397 U.S. 742 (1970); *People v. O'Neill*, 164 N.E.2d 869 (N.Y. 1959)) (describing competing elements of a prosecutor's obligation to seek justice).

75 Id. at 44-45.

76 Id. at 43.

77 The court's decision has been subjected to criticism on a number of grounds, including the apparent license it grants for continuous prosecution in the absence of evidence necessary to obtain a conviction. See, e.g., Michel Proulx & David Layton, *Ethics and Canadian Criminal Law* 661-62 (2001) (finding the holding in *Jones* "not consistent with the Canadian tradition of prosecutorial ethics" and stating that "if the Crown knows that an essential witness is dead, and the case can no longer be proved, the Crown has a duty not only to make disclosure but to go further and to stay the case").

understood through the lens of the comparative conceptual framework of cases in Jewish law involving complex ethical decision-making.

Significantly, the court's depiction of the dual nature of the prosecutor's ethical duties articulates not only competing—but also conflicting—obligations, suggesting that resolution of the issue requires a meta-principle of ethical decision-making. Thus, to the extent that the court's conclusion contradicts the Supreme Court's analysis, perhaps it relies on contrary principles of prioritization. Specifically, the New York court's decision may be premised on an approach that recognizes the importance of protecting the rights of the defendant, but that nevertheless—either as a result of balancing the prosecutor's conflicting obligations, or as a matter of overarching principle—prioritizes the exercise of the prosecutor's duty to convict deserving defendants.[78] Such prioritization should not—and clearly, in the view of the court, does not—relieve the prosecutor of the unique obligation to seek justice for the defendant in the process of pursuing a conviction.[79] At the same time, however, absent compelling and overriding

---

Tellingly, in arriving at its decision, the New York Court of Appeals formulated a variation on the fundamental principle that "'innocence [shall not] suffer,'" e.g., *Agurs*, 427 U.S. at 111 (quoting *Berger*, 295 U.S. at 88), proclaiming—axiomatically and without supporting reference—that "a fundamental concern of the criminal justice system, of course, is that an innocent defendant shall not be convicted; not that a possibly guilty actor shall escape conviction because the People are not able to establish his guilt." *Jones*, 375 N.E.2d at 44. The Canadian view of prosecutorial ethics would apparently reject such a distinction.

78 Alternatively, the court may have conceptualized the issue of disclosure of nonexculpatory information as simply presenting a basic case of clear obligation, rather than a case of ethical conflict and complexity. Refer to part two, section A supra (explaining the complexity of the decision not to disclose). Under this approach, once it is determined that the information at issue is not exculpatory, there is no obligation of disclosure to the defendant. As such, there remains, in this regard, no significant component of the duty to seek justice that conflicts with—or even competes with—the clear obligation to seek the conviction of a deserving defendant.

79 Indeed, the court was careful to reserve a decision regarding a hypothetical variation of the facts of the case before it:

> [I]n the course of plea negotiation a particular defendant staunchly and plausibly maintains . . . innocence but states explicitly and creditably that as a matter of balanced judgment in the light of the apparent strength of the People's proof [the defendant] wishes to interpose a negotiated plea to reduced charges to avoid the risk of a more severe sentence likely to attend conviction after trial; failure of the prosecutor to reveal the death of a critical complaining witness might then call for a vacatur of the plea. Silence in such circumstances might arguably be held to be so subversive of the criminal justice process as to offend due process.

Jones, 375 N.E.2d at 44.

Likewise, several years later, the New York Court of Appeals considered a case in which the prosecutor "deliberately dissembl[ed] and [told] half-truths for the purpose of misleading defense counsel into believing that [the crime victim] was still alive and subject to call

circumstances, the court's approach recognizes—indeed, it mandates—that the prosecutor fulfill the obligation to seek justice through effective prosecution.[80]

So understood, on one level, the process of resolving scenarios of competing and conflicting normative and ethical obligations, in both Jewish law and American prosecutorial ethics, differs considerably from the decision-making process relating to situations involving indeterminacy of obligation. Unlike cases of indeterminacy, which may be settled through fairly mechanical application of general principles of resolution, cases of conflict require more complex resolution, through the application of principles providing for prioritization among competing values and obligations.

Still, on another level, both modes of decision-making share the common characteristic of producing a singular and definitive solution, on the basis of clearly articulated justification and reasoning. Thus, despite the potential uncertainty and difficulty initially posed by these situations, through the process of arriving at a solution to the issue, any contrary values or concerns become not only superseded, but virtually negated.[81]

A more thorough analysis of the prosecutor's ethical obligations might include scenarios of even greater ethical complexity, involving a choice among

---

as a witness when, as [the prosecutor] well knew, [the victim] was dead." *People v. Rice*, 505 N.E.2d 618, 618-19 (N.Y. 1987). The court found that "the acts of the prosecutor constituted a serious violation of his duties as an attorney and as a prosecutor" and that "such conduct is reprehensible and cannot be condoned," though it also held that the conduct did not amount to reversible error. Id. at 619 (citations omitted).

80 Thus, without detracting from the rights of the criminal defendant or the prosecutor's unique ethical duty to protect those rights, the court's analysis recognizes, and in part relies upon, the importance of the prosecutor's ethical obligation to pursue a proper conviction. As Professor Zacharias observed,

> [A] noncompetitive approach to prosecutorial ethics is inconsistent with the professional codes' underlying theory. The codes . . . do not exempt prosecutors from the requirements of zealous advocacy. . . . [T]he codes signal that prosecutors can achieve justice while operating within the adversary system's rules. . . . [A]dvocates are meant to do their best. To the extent prosecutors temper advocacy . . . , they call into question the essential assumptions of the very system the rules codify.

Zacharias, *Can Prosecutors Do Justice?*, supra note 3, at 52 (footnote omitted); see also Green, *Prosecutors*, supra note 9, at 642 (offering a "conception of the duty to seek justice" that "does not imply that [prosecutors] should 'pull their punches' or otherwise act to level the playing field between themselves and the defense"); Bruce A. Green, *The Ethical Prosecutor and the Adversary System*, 24 Crim. L. Bull. 126, 129-30 (1988) ("A prosecutor is not supposed to be neutral and detached. It is not the prosecutor's duty to present both sides of a criminal case. Nor is it the prosecutor's duty to urge the jury to draw inferences in favor of the defendant."). See also Levine supra note 1; Levine, *The Law and the "Spirit of the Law,"* supra note 7.

81 See Schachter, *B'Ikvei Hatzoan*, supra note 66, at 17-18.

conflicting harms, thereby defying simplistic—or even satisfactory—resolution. Rather than presenting indeterminacies or conflicts, which may be resolved through general principles of decision-making or prioritization, the most complex cases demand ethical deliberation of a different order. Resolving such cases would require looking beyond standard modes of ethical consideration, relying instead on an application of the most general and overarching of all principles of prosecutorial ethics: the obligation to seek justice. The conceptual framework necessary for interpreting and applying this principle may find an analogue in an overarching principle in Jewish law: "In all of your ways acknowledge [God]."[82]

2. Choosing Among Conflicting Harms

Beyond principles of interpretation and prioritization, the Jewish legal system recognizes the existence of situations that fall outside the general conventions of legal and ethical decision-making. Because they present a choice between conflicting harms, these situations require considerations beyond the range of ordinary normative ethical analysis. Instead, under such exceptional circumstances, the analysis may entail a careful balancing of the relative degree of benefit and harm resulting from each of the alternatives. Indeed, the resolution of this analysis may prescribe actions that, although generally prohibited, may qualify in rare cases as ethically proper conduct.

For example, returning again to the example of the Sabbath, the act of placing dough in the oven and baking bread on the Sabbath constitutes one of the activities included within the biblical prohibition on *melacha*.[83] In addition, rabbinic legislation[84] prohibits removing bread from the walls of the oven on the Sabbath past a particular stage of the baking process.[85] The Talmud observes that if an individual placed dough in the oven on the Sabbath, it is proper for that individual to remove the dough from the walls of the oven before it bakes—even in violation of rabbinic legislation—in order to prevent the completion of the baking process, which would constitute a violation of the more stringent biblical prohibition against baking bread.[86] In such a case, the benefit of preventing

---

82 Proverbs 3:6.
83 See Talmud Bavli, Shabbath 73a.
84 For a discussion of the premises and parameters of rabbinic legislation, see generally Chapter 4 in this Volume.
85 See Talmud Bavli, Shabbath 117b. See also Lichtenstein, supra note 55, at 48.
86 See Talmud Bavli, Shabbath 3b.

violation of the biblical prohibition outweighs the harm of violating the rabbinic prohibition.[87]

Moreover, the Talmud relates a broader principle that, in rare circumstances, permits violation of a stringent biblical obligation, in the case of overwhelming necessity.[88] In describing such conduct, the Talmud employs the seemingly paradoxical terminology of *aveira lishma*: "a transgression for [sincere] purposes."[89] Not surprisingly, the application of such a principle is greatly limited, subject to extensive qualifications.[90] Specifically, in addition to limitations on the circumstances that qualify as presenting the requisite overwhelming necessity,[91] the individual committing the transgression must have a pure and idealistic motivation, free from any element of personal interest.[92] Under such exceptional conditions, the violation of an otherwise stringent prohibition may qualify as conduct that, in the Talmud's characterization, fulfills the overarching principle of acknowledging God "in all [of] your ways."[93] In such an unusual case, the Talmud explains, "*all* of your ways" extends to include actions that constitute justified transgression of the law.[94]

---

87 See Schachter, *B'Ikvei Hatzoan*, supra note 66, at 16.

88 See id. at 16-18. Cf. Chapter 4 in this Volume (analogizing the principle of rabbinic authority to temporarily suspend a negative biblical commandment to the work of a doctor who may amputate a limb to save a subject's life).

89 See Talmud Bavli, Nazir 23b.

90 Indeed, one leading contemporary scholar of Jewish law and philosophy has written that

> this apparent priority of telos and motivation over formal law has no prescriptive or prospective implications. At most, it means that, after the fact, we can sometimes see that a nominal violation was superior to a licit or even required act; but it gives no license for making the jump.

Aharon Lichtenstein, *Does Jewish Tradition Recognize an Ethic Independent of Halakha?*, in *Contemporary Jewish Ethics* 102, 121 n.25 (Menachem Mark Kellner ed., 1978).

As Rabbi Lichtenstein acknowledges, however, this severe conceptual limitation on what he terms "idealistic transgression," id. at 107, does not represent a universal understanding of this concept. See id. at 121 n.25 (citing Maimonides, *Commentary on the Mishna, Introduction to Pirke Avoth*, ch. 5); see also 2 Lichtenstein, supra note 55, at 330 n.22; Schachter, *B'Ikvei Hatzoan*, supra note 66, at 16-18 (citing various sources).

91 See Schachter, *B'Ikvei Hatzoan*, supra note 66, at 16.

92 See id. at 16-18; Naftali Tzvi Berlin, *Herchev Davar* (explicating Genesis 27:9); 3 Eliyahu Dessler, *Michtav M'Eliyahu* 149-50 (Aryeh Carmell & Chaim Friedlander eds., 1964); Hutner, supra note 45, at 141-44 (citing Avraham Grodzinski, *Torath Avraham* 159 (1978)); Chaim Shmulevitz, *Sichos Mussar* 92-96 (Eliyahu Meir Klugman & A. Scheinman trans., Samson R. Weiss & Bezalel Rappaport eds., 1989).

93 Proverbs 3:6.

94 See Talmud Bavli, Berachoth 63a; see also Maimonides, *Commentary on the Mishna, Introduction to Pirke Avoth*, ch. 5; Rabbenu Bachya ben Asher, *Kad Ha-kemach*, in *Kisvei Rabbenu Bachya* 74 (Chaim Dov Chavel ed., 1995).

The conceptual framework for choosing among conflicting harms in Jewish law may offer a normative analogue for consideration of similar issues, representing some of the most difficult ethical challenges facing the American prosecutor, in the effort to carry out the obligation to seek justice. As in Jewish law, situations arise in the work of the American prosecutor that exceed the bounds of decision-making susceptible to ordinary principles of interpretation or prioritization. Rather than seeking a clearly just result in these cases, the prosecutor may have to accept a certain element of injustice, and thus, instead, seek to identify, evaluate, and balance the relative degree of injustice that may result from alternative ethical decisions.

Such an analytical framework may help justify a conclusion not to prosecute the mother of the criminal defendant, who has undeniably—and unsuccessfully—committed perjury in an attempt to serve as an alibi witness in behalf of her son.[95] On a practical level, the prosecutor's decision not to file perjury charges in this case may be based on a consideration of the best way to allocate limited prosecutorial resources.[96] Conceptually, however, practical impediments to pursuing a particular criminal charge may not provide a satisfactory normative explanation for a decision not to prosecute.

Instead, it may be helpful to evaluate the ethical alternatives available to the prosecutor on the basis of a normative analysis, grounded in the overarching obligation to seek justice. The decision to pursue perjury charges against the defendant's mother may satisfy the letter of the criminal statute, thus satisfying the prosecutor's ethical obligation to prosecute and seek the conviction of those who have broken the law. Nevertheless, such a result may not account for the arguably limited culpability of the offender in this scenario, thus failing to satisfy principles of individualized justice.[97] Conversely, a decision not to file

---

95 Refer to part two, section B supra.

96 See Leslie C. Griffin, *The Prudent Prosecutor*, 14 Geo. J. Legal Ethics 259, 264 (2001).

> [B]ecause of "limitations in available enforcement resources," [p]rosecutors do not have the ability to punish all crimes. Their budgets constrain their capacity to try cases and force administrators to develop policies that allow prosecution of some crimes but not others. Police resources, court schedules, and prison capacity may impose similar constraints.

> Id. (footnote omitted) (quoting Wayne R. LaFave, *The Prosecutor's Discretion in the United States*, 18 Am. J. Comp. Law 532, 533-35 (1970)).

97 Id.

> [T]here is an additional "need [for prosecutors] to individualize justice." ... There are times when a rigid application of the rules may not do justice

charges may seem appropriate in light of the apparent lack of substantial moral culpability on the part of the defendant's mother. At the same time, however, such a decision carries with it a failure to attempt to bring to justice the perpetrator of a crime in open court.

Thus, the prosecutor faces an ethical dilemma, the resolution of which may prove unavoidably unsatisfactory, if not inevitably unjust. At best, the prosecutor can choose to balance competing harms, opting for a method of ethical decision-making that achieves a relative sense of justice, under the circumstances. As in the case of the individual who has already placed dough in the oven on the Sabbath,[98] the prosecutor cannot prevent the wrongful act of perjury. Instead, the prosecutor may determine that the preferable—and just— course of action should mitigate the damage that will result from the perjury. Similar to the circumstances in which an adherent should choose to violate a rabbinic prohibition rather than violating a more stringent biblical prohibition,[99] the prosecutor may choose to forego available perjury charges against the defendant's mother, in order to avoid the further injustice that may result from prosecuting an individual of arguably minimal culpability.

Finally, an extension of these principles may help provide a methodology for considering the ethical challenges and difficulties underlying a prosecutor's reliance on the assistance of a cooperator, in exchange for possible leniency.[100] On a practical level, working with an informant or witness who has committed a crime undoubtedly calls for a substantial measure of ethical caution on the part of the prosecutor, including—but not limited to—cautious assessment of the reliability of the information or testimony provided.[101] Yet, without discounting the serious nature of the issues, these concerns may perhaps be

---

and when "flexibility" and "sensitivity" are necessary to a just outcome. This tension between rigorous enforcement of the general criminal laws and flexible adjustment to individual circumstances is a constant in discussions about the merits of prosecutorial discretion. Legislators and prosecutors are always striving to strike the proper balance.

Id. at 264-65 (second alteration in original) (footnotes omitted) (quoting LaFave, supra note 96, at 534).

98 Refer to notes 83-87 supra and accompanying text.

99 Refer to notes 83-87 supra and accompanying text (explaining how an individual who places dough in an oven on the Sabbath may remove the dough before the completion of the baking process, in violation of rabbinic legislation, to prevent violation of a biblical prohibition).

100 Refer to part two, section C supra (discussing the role of cooperators).

101 Refer to note 40 supra (providing a list of sources that detail the practical and ethical challenges cooperators create).

categorized as procedural or incidental challenges, which likewise arise in the course of most criminal prosecutions. To the extent that these challenges may be amplified in dealing with a cooperator, they may be viewed as representing a difference in degree rather than in kind.

On a normative level, however, cooperation agreements present a direct and central challenge to the prosecutor's ethical obligation to seek justice. Fundamentally, the prosecutor's willingness to grant leniency in exchange for assistance seems to embody a willingness on the part of the prosecutor to place—or at least to permit—limitations on the proper administration of justice.[102] Though a cooperation agreement may serve as an effective means for prosecuting other criminals, it appears—often somewhat proportionately—to undermine the just prosecution of the cooperator. Indeed, prevailing justifications for reliance on cooperators embody an expressly utilitarian model of criminal justice,[103] largely

---

102 Although decisions regarding plea agreements and sentencing reductions, among others, may ultimately be subject to judicial approval, the prosecutor retains considerable discretion, if not ultimate practical authority, over many of these decisions. See generally Green & Levine, supra note 36; Griffin, supra note 96 (commenting on the unreviewable quality of prosecutorial discretion and suggesting the use of internal control mechanisms to limit that discretion); Podgor, supra note 36 (analyzing "four key prosecutorial decisions" that permit "a wide breadth of discretion" and calling for improved education to avoid "varying results").

103 See, e.g., Hughes, supra note 40, at 14-15.

> The Principles of Federal Prosecution set out by the United States Department of Justice recognize in very general terms the propriety of permitting the prosecutor to make a utilitarian calculation. Under these principles a prosecutor has a duty to neutralize the largest number of units possible of culpability and dangerousness expressed in behavior that the criminal code prohibits. As to each potential defendant, the prosecutor must make a difficult calculation to measure the moral weight of the culpability, including the harm done, and the future danger to the public. When she can gather no more evidence without inducements, the prosecutor then decides whether to proceed and prosecute those suspects against whom the already produced evidence makes a case or whether to extend leniency or full immunity to some suspects in order to procure testimony against other, more dangerous suspects against whom existing evidence is flimsy or nonexistent.

Id. Professor Simons has also recognized this utilitarianism in prosecutorial decisions:

> The cost-benefit analysis that underlies the utilitarian model of cooperation is as simple as it is compelling. The "cost" is the leniency given the cooperator; the "benefit" is the additional crime fighting produced by the cooperation. Prosecutors should use cooperators when the benefit outweighs the cost, and judges should reward cooperators with sufficient leniency to ensure that prosecutors can continue to engage in these socially beneficial transactions.
> This utilitarian understanding of cooperation is pervasive....

accepting, as an inevitable byproduct of the agreement, the decision not to seek just retribution for the cooperator.[104]

It may be helpful to consider an alternative model—or at least an alternative understanding of the utilitarian model—that would focus on the ethical dimensions of the prosecutor's role in the cooperation agreement. Perhaps the concept of *aveira lishma* in Jewish law[105] provides a framework that can inform the articulation of such a model. Not unlike the situations that give rise to the possibility of *aveira lishma*, the circumstances surrounding a potential cooperation agreement preclude an entirely satisfactory outcome. On a most basic level, the prosecutor who is considering entering into a cooperation agreement is faced with at least two crimes, only one of which can be appropriately prosecuted. Thus, in place of the ordinary pursuit of justice, which entails often difficult—but broadly normative—ethical decisions, the nature of a cooperation agreement incorporates a recognition that the prosecutor is seeking a different kind of justice—a balancing of relative harms. Therefore, the decision-making process and the accompanying ethical considerations differ not only in degree, but also in kind, from even the most complex ethical challenges that otherwise confront the prosecutor.

Under such circumstances, acknowledging the impossibility of attaining an ideal form of justice may, paradoxically, help delineate the ethical contours

---

> The utilitarian approach also permeates the ways that prosecutors talk about cooperation. . . .
> The prosecutor's utilitarian approach to cooperation has been recognized and implicitly approved by the Supreme Court. . . .
> Perhaps the most fully developed utilitarian model of cooperation [is based on an] explicitly economic analysis [of the] "market" for cooperation.

Simons, supra note 39, at 22-23.

104 At least one commentator has argued that cooperation agreements may be justified on retributive grounds as well. See generally Simons, supra note 39 (discussing the hidden retributive components of cooperation). But see Hughes, supra note 40, at 13 (asserting that "most cooperation agreements would be difficult to fit into any concept of repentance or rehabilitation").

> [P]rosecutors . . . likely would assert that the cooperator, by his conduct, will strike a blow at crime and, in some cases, will effectively terminate the activities of a criminal organization to which [the cooperator] once belonged. This potential is undeniable, and this form of "restitution" may make the bargain a good one for society, but the cooperator's actions are not the same as an unsolicited demonstration of a change of heart by a criminal.

Id. at 13 n.47.

105 Refer to notes 88-94 supra and accompanying text (exploring the Talmudic principle of *aveira lishma*, which allows violation of a stringent obligation in cases of overwhelming necessity).

that guide the prosecutor's determination of whether to enter into a coopera-tion agreement. In this framework, the prosecutor may view the measured res-olution to offer leniency in exchange for assistance as constituting an exercise in ethical decision-making, contributing to the pursuit of justice, rather than merely a concession to utilitarian concerns.

Concomitantly, however, it might be instructive to view the extensive limitations on the applicability of the concept of *aveira lishma* as an indication of the need for increased ethical boundaries regulating prosecutorial reliance on cooperators. In Jewish law, the exceptional license to acknowledge God through violation of the law is contemplated only under conditions of dire necessity, and even then, only when the individual committing such a trans-gression does so with the purest of intentions.[106]

It may not be desirable to impose such severe restrictions on the circum-stances that will permit a prosecutor to use a cooperation agreement; likewise, it may be unrealistic to limit the utilization of cooperators to cases in which the prosecutor can demonstrate purely idealistic motivations. Nevertheless, in taking seriously the ethical obligation to seek justice, it may be advisable for prosecutors to exhibit a more conscious awareness of the ethical and norma-tive challenges presented by increasingly common reliance on cooperators. A greater recognition, among prosecutors, of the inherent—yet, at times, necessary—injustice latent in the decision to grant leniency to a criminal offender who cooperates, may allow for a more complex understanding of the overarching ethical obligation to seek justice.

CONCLUSION

Rabbi Yitzchak Hutner, a leading twentieth century scholar of Jewish law and philosophy, offered an insightful analysis of the role, in the Jewish legal system, of the biblical directive, "in all of your ways acknowledge [God]."[107] As Rabbi Hutner notes, a common perception of the notion of obligation in Jewish law views clear and enumerated obligations as the primary basis for normative and ethical conduct, leaving the broad concept of acknowledging God to play a sec-ondary role.[108] However, Rabbi Hutner explains, a deeper understanding of Jewish law reveals that the directive to acknowledge God is a necessarily broad

---

106 Refer to notes 90-94 supra and accompanying text.
107 Proverbs 3:6.
108 See Hutner, supra note 45, at 123.

expression of the significance and complexity of ethical decision-making and action, in all areas in life, of which clear and enumerated obligations comprise but one category.[109]

Likewise, an analysis of the prosecutor's ethical duty to seek justice should extend beyond cases involving clearly delineated obligations, to include scenarios and issues of ethical and normative complexity. Indeed, the challenges confronting the prosecutor require careful consideration and application of the implications of justice in a variety of situations. Thus, parallel to the comparative analytical framework provided by Jewish law, an accurate conceptualization of prosecutorial ethics should similarly view the directive obligating the prosecutor to seek justice as an appropriately broad articulation of a rule that reflects the ethically complex nature of the prosecutor's decision-making process.

---

109 See id. at 123-26.

CHAPTER 16

Taking Ethical Obligations Seriously: A Look at American Codes of Professional Responsibility through a Perspective of Jewish Law and Ethics

INTRODUCTION

For at least one hundred years, American lawyers and scholars alike have repeatedly criticized various aspects of legal practice, identifying both particular instances of misconduct among lawyers and more general concerns regarding the character of the legal profession.[1] In turn, the organized

---

1 See, e.g., *Enron: Corporate Fiascos and Their Implications*, (Nancy B. Rapoport & Bala G. Dharan eds., 2004) (collecting essays that examine the failure of Enron from "business, financial, legal, and ethical perspectives"); Mary Ann Glendon, *A Nation Under Lawyers* (1994); *The Good Lawyer* (David Luban ed., 1983) (collecting essays that "ask whether the professional ideal is itself morally worthy"); Anthony T. Kronman, *The Lost Lawyer* (1993) (addressing "a crisis in the American legal profession," namely that it "now stands in danger of losing its soul"); Sol M. Linowitz with Martin Mayer, *The Betrayed Profession* (1994) (proposing to offer "suggestions as to how we lawyers might rekindle pride in our profession and restore the practice of law to the respected position it once occupied"); Deborah L. Rhode, *In the Interests of Justice* 1 (2000) (noting that "it appears from the chronic laments by critics" that "[l]awyers belong to a profession permanently in decline"); *The Task Force on Law Schools and the Profession: Narrowing the Gap, Am. Bar Association, Legal Education and Professional Development – An Educational Continuum* 207-21 (1992) (identifying and developing four categories of values that are fundamental to the legal profession); William H. Simon, *The Practice of Justice* 1 (1998) ("No social role encourages such ambitious moral aspirations as the lawyer's, and no social role so consistently disappoints the aspirations it

American bar has engaged in a number of efforts to improve both the ethical conduct and the reputation of lawyers. These efforts range from the adoption of ethics codes, often revisited, reconsidered, and, at times, substantially revised,[2] to seemingly perennial professionalism movements, largely premised

---

encourages."); Roger C. Cramton, *Enron and the Corporate Lawyer: A Primer on Legal and Ethical Issues*, 58 Bus. Law. 143 (2002); Eugene R. Gaetke, Foreword, *Renewed Introspection and the Legal Profession*, 87 Ky. L.J. 903, 903 (1999) (noting that "the legal profession is again immersed in a process of self-assessment, reflection, and reform" partly because "the nation is again enduring turmoil engendered by allegations of indiscretion and misconduct at the highest levels of our national government . . . lawyers are inordinately implicated"); Robert W. Gordon, *A New Role for Lawyers?: The Corporate Counselor After Enron*, 35 Conn. L. Rev. 1185 (2003); Robert W. Gordon, *"The Ideal and the Actual in the Law": Fantasies and Practices of New York City Lawyers, 1870-1910*, in *The New High Priests* 51 (Gerard W. Gawalt ed., 1984); Robert W. Gordon, *The Independence of Lawyers*, 68 B.U. L. Rev. 1, 33 (1988) (discussing the professional autonomy of lawyers and stating that "the norms of independent practice need to be authoritatively declared and promoted, acted upon by powerful lawyers, and institutionalized in elite legal practice" to be effective); Susan P. Koniak, *Corporate Fraud: See, Lawyers*, 26 Harv. J.L. & Pub. Pol'y 195, 195 (2003) (arguing that "without lawyers, few corporate scandals would exist"); Donald C. Langevoort, *Where Were the Lawyers? A Behavioral Inquiry into Lawyers' Responsibility for Clients' Fraud*, 46 Vand. L. Rev. 75, 77 (1993) (asserting that "the apparent incidence of complicity must trouble both the public and the profession" even without actual data on the frequency of complicity or the effects of attorney efforts to deter client misconduct); Samuel J. Levine, *Faith in Legal Professionalism: Believers and Heretics*, 61 Md. L. Rev. 217 (2002) (examining the views of Dean Anthony Kronman, including his "loss of faith in the legal profession"); Samuel J. Levine, *Rediscovering Julius Henry Cohen and the Origins of the Business/Profession Dichotomy: A Study in the Discourse of Early Twentieth Century Legal Professionalism*, 47 Am. J. Legal Hist. 1 (2005); David Luban, *The Adversary System Excuse*, in *The Good Lawyer*, supra, at 83, 85-86 (relating the example of Edward Bennett Wiliams' use of a tactic called "graymailing" in his defense of former CIA director Richard Helms); William H. Simon, *Wrongs of Ignorance and Ambiguity: Lawyer Responsibility for Collective Misconduct*, 22 Yale J. on Reg. 1, 30 (2005) (criticizing the bar for its "visceral clinging to the prerogatives of ignorance and ambiguity" in response to the SEC's implementation of Sarbanes-Oxley); Rayman L. Solomon, *Five Crises or One: The Concept of Legal Professionalism, 1925-1960*, in *Lawyers' Ideals/Lawyers' Practices* 144, 145 (Robert L. Nelson, David M. Trubek & Rayman L. Solomon eds., 1992) (arguing that "professionalism, as conceived by the elite of the bar, is a set of symbolic rhetorical and normative concepts having consistent content"); David B. Wilkins, *Who Should Regulate Lawyers?*, 105 Harv. L. Rev. 799 (1992).

2 See, e.g., Monroe H. Freedman & Abbe Smith, *Understanding Lawyers' Ethics* 2-6 (3d ed. 2004) (reviewing the history and purposes of the ABA ethics codes); Stephen Gillers, *Regulation of Lawyers* 3-6 (7th ed. 2005) (reviewing revision efforts, including those of the Kutak Commission, the Ethics 2000 Commission, and the Task Force on Corporate Responsibility); Charles W. Wolfram, *Modern Legal Ethics* 48-67 (1986) (discussing the development of, rationales for, and implementation and revision of ethics codes); Richard L. Abel, *Why Does the ABA Promulgate Ethical Rules?*, 59 Tex. L. Rev. 639 (1981); Benjamin H. Barton, *The ABA, the Rules, and Professionalism: The Mechanics of Self-Defeat and a Call for*

on the claim that the practice of law has lamentably devolved from the status of a noble profession to become merely another form of business.[3]

---

a Return to the Ethical, Moral, and Practical Approach of the Canons, 83 N.C. L. Rev. 411, 437 (2005) (noting that the ABA Model Code or Professional Responsibility was revised four times in eight years); Reed Elizabeth Loder, *Tighter Rules of Professional Conduct: Saltwater for Thirst?*, 1 Geo. J. Legal Ethics 311, 323-34 (1987) (expressing doubt that any revision of "a given set of black letter rules" could create the consensus required to promote compliance on a voluntary basis); Margaret Colgate Love, *The Revised ABA Model Rules of Professional Conduct: Summary of the Work of Ethics 2000*, 15 Geo. J. Legal Ethics 441, 442-43 (2002) (observing that the Ethics 2000 Commission set out to make minimal substantive changes to the Model Code, but in the end, revised nearly every rule); Nancy J. Moore, *Lawyer Ethics Code Drafting in the Twenty-First Century*, 30 Hofstra L. Rev. 923, 925-32 (2002) (reviewing the ABA's efforts to revise an existing code before undertaking to develop an entirely new one); Thomas Morgan, *The Evolving Concept of Professional Responsibility*, 90 Harv. L. Rev. 702, 704 (1977) (observing that "pressure for revision of several basic concepts of professional responsibility is both sound and inevitable"); Alice Neece Moseley, Fred H. Moody, Jr., & John H. Vernon, III, *An Overview of the Revised North Carolina Rules of Professional Conduct: An Examination of the Interests Promoted and Subordinated*, 32 Wake Forest L. Rev. 939 (1997) (examining North Carolina's revised professional responsibility rules); Richard W. Painter, *Rules Lawyers Play By*, 76 N.Y.U. L. Rev. 665, 668 (2001) (pointing out the trend of successive revisions of ethics codes toward more clearly delineated rules and away from general standards); Russell G. Pearce, *Rediscovering the Republican Origins of the Legal Ethics Codes*, 6 Geo. J. Legal Ethics 241 (1992) (examining "the significant impact that [George] Sharswood's treatise had upon the drafting of the codes," and suggesting that the codes must be read in light of historical context); Deborah L. Rhode, *Ethical Perspectives on Legal Practice*, 37 Stan L. Rev. 589, 589-92 (1985) (discussing conflicts between professional ideals, individual autonomy, and lawyers' public responsibilities); Ronald D. Rotunda, *Teaching Professional Responsibility and Ethics*, 51 St. Louis U. L.J. 1223, 1226 (2007) (noting that court involvement has compelled the bar to change its ethics standards); Ted Schneyer, *Professionalism as Bar Politics: The Making of the Model Rules of Professional Conduct*, 14 Law & Soc. Inquiry 677 (1989) (examining the "internal politics of the bar" through the development of the Model Rules); Symposium, *Ethics 2000 and Beyond: Reform or Professional Responsibility as Usual?*, 2003 U. Ill. L. Rev. 1173 (collecting articles that "thoughtfully analyze and critique specific aspects of Ethics 2000, both with regard to what it did and did not do"); E. Norman Veasey, *Ethics 2000: Thoughts and Comments on Key Issues of Professional Responsibility in the Twenty-First Century*, 5 Del. L. Rev. 1, 3 (2002) (stating that the recent revision of the Model Rules was intended to address the problem of non-uniform state regulation and the impact of technological development on legal services); Fred C. Zacharias, *The Future Structure and Regulation of Law Practice: Confronting Lies, Fictions, and False Paradigms in Legal Ethics Regulation*, 44 Ariz. L. Rev. 829, 830 (2002) (noting the bar's tendency to revise the individual provisions of ethics codes rather than question their underlying premises).

3 See, e.g., *Comm'n on Professionalism, Am. Bar Ass'n, in the Spirit of Public Service: A Blueprint for the Rekindling of Lawyer Professionalism* 3 (1986) (reporting negative perceptions of the public toward lawyers generally); Chapter 18 in Volume 2 (noting that "a voluminous debate over the characterization of legal practice as a business or a profession" has developed

This chapter suggests that the ethics codes themselves, through both their substance and their underlying assumptions, contribute to the problematic nature of American legal ethics. Focusing on the prevailing and most influential source of ethics codes, the American Bar Association's Model Rules of Professional Conduct, this chapter argues that the Model Rules fail to sufficiently mandate ethical obligations. This failure permits lawyers a degree of discretion that relegates many ethics rules to the status of optional guidelines. Moreover, this chapter observes, the permissive nature of many rules renders their enforcement largely untenable, thus further undermining the credibility and authority of these codes as a basis for the ethical conduct of lawyers.

In response to these concerns, this chapter looks to an alternative source of ethical guidance, the Jewish legal system, and suggests that a number of features of Jewish law and ethics might prove helpful in formulating, interpreting, and

---

in recent years); Nancy J. Moore, *Professionalism Reconsidered*, 1987 Am. B. Found. Res. J. 773 (reviewing *Comm'n on Professionalism*, supra); Russell G. Pearce, *Law Day 2050: Post-Professionalism, Moral Leadership, and the Law-as-Business Paradigm*, 27 Fla. St. U. L. Rev. 9 (1999) (envisioning how the organized bar could achieve a higher level of moral leadership were it to approach the profession as a business); Russell G. Pearce, *The Professionalism Paradigm Shift: Why Discarding Professional Ideology Will Improve the Conduct and Reputation of the Bar*, 70 N.Y.U. L. Rev. 1229, 1232 (1995) ("[T]he widespread perception . . . that law practice is a business. . . . has provoked a professional crisis."); see also Rob Atkinson, *A Dissenter's Commentary on the Professionalism Crusade*, 74 Tex. L. Rev. 259, 276-77 (1995) (explaining the development of the "current professionalism crusade" and its focus on "voluntary compliance with aspirational standards"); Robert F. Cochran, Jr., *Professionalism in the Postmodern Age: Its Death, Attempts at Resuscitation, and Alternate Sources of Virtue*, 14 Notre Dame J.L. Ethics & Pub. Pol'y 305, 305-6 (2000) (noting that professionalism movements predictably follow highly publicized scandals involving lawyers); Eugene R. Gaetke, *Expecting Too Much and Too Little of Lawyers*, 67 U. Pitt. L. Rev. 693, 694 (2006) (opining that current ethics codes set standards of lawyer conduct that are inconsistent with public expectations); Anthony T. Kronman, *Legal Professionalism*, 27 Fla. St. U. L. Rev. 1, 1 (1999) ("The legal profession in America is passing through a period of anxiety and self-doubt, an identity crisis of unprecedented proportions."); Russell G. Pearce, *The Legal Profession as a Blue State: Reflections on Public Philosophy, Jurisprudence, and Legal Ethics*, 75 Fordham L. Rev. 1339, 1341 (2006) ("The dominant—although not exclusive—modern conception of the lawyer as a hired gun . . . asserts that the proper functioning of the legal system requires lawyers to remove personal ethical values from their work."); Thomas L. Shaffer, *Inaugural Howard Lichtenstein Lecture in Legal Ethics: Lawyer Professionalism as a Moral Argument*, 26 Gonz. L. Rev. 393, 395 (1990-91) ("The professionalism campaign is a nostalgic appeal to a particular kind of moral leadership. . . ."); Thomas L. Shaffer, *The Lost Lawyer: Failing Ideals of the Legal Profession*, 41 Loy. L. Rev. 387 (1995) (reviewing Kronman, supra note 1); Richard Wasserstrom, *Lawyers as Professionals: Some Moral Issues*, 5 Hum. Rts. 1 (1975) (addressing basic moral criticisms of the lawyer's position with respect to his client and the world at large).

applying more well-considered and effective ethics codes for the practice of law in the United States. In particular, building in part on my work elsewhere,[4] this chapter suggests that American ethics codes might begin to incorporate the notion of obligation that underlies Jewish law, which includes the broad imperative to exercise ethical conduct and deliberation even in the absence of clearly applicable regulations. At the same time, to the extent that enforcement of American ethics codes may often remain elusive, this chapter suggests that the Jewish legal system may provide a model for ethical adherence, relying more upon communal commitment to shared ethical values and principles than on the threat of official discipline and punishment.

PART ONE | ETHICS WITHOUT OBLIGATIONS: A CRITICAL LOOK AT THE MODEL RULES OF PROFESSIONAL CONDUCT

The prevalence, in the Model Rules, of provisions that do not mandate a particular ethical outcome suggests a refusal or inability among the organized bar to take seriously ethical obligations and aspirations.[5] Indeed, the discretionary nature of many of the rules often provides lawyers the opportunity to disregard

---

4 See, e.g., Chapter 14 in this Volume (arguing that "Jewish law may provide a particularly helpful interpretive model for the analysis of ethics codes"); Chapter 15 in this Volume (emphasizing that "the prosecutor must take into account complex implications of the concept of justice," and that "Jewish law recognizes and addresses the complexity of ethical and normative decisionmaking"); Samuel J. Levine, *Taking Ethical Discretion Seriously: Ethical Deliberation as Ethical Obligation*, 37 Ind. L. Rev. 21, 57 nn.151-52 (2003) [hereinafter Levine, *Taking Ethical Discretion Seriously*] (noting that Jewish law acknowledges the ethical complexity of legal decisionmaking).

5 Scholars have documented numerous areas in which the Model Rules leave ethical decisions to the discretion of the lawyer. See, e.g., Gaetke, supra note 3, at 721-22 & nn.124-29 (identifying situations in which "[t]he current rules ... grant considerable discretion to lawyers"); Bruce A. Green & Fred C. Zacharias, *Permissive Rules of Professional Conduct*, 91 Minn. L. Rev. 265, 269-70 & nn.16-22, 276-78 & nn.41-55 (2006) (noting that professional rules generally use the permissive term "may" rather than mandatory terms such as "must" or "shall"); W. Bradley Wendel, *Public Values and Professional Responsibility*, 75 Notre Dame L. Rev. 1, 11-12 & nn.31-33 (1999) (noting that some rules "by their terms leave room for deliberation"); Fred C. Zacharias, *Reconciling Professionalism and Client Interests*, 36 Wm. & Mary L. Rev. 1303, 1335-36 & nn.101-8 (1995) (listing areas open to a lawyer's discretion in the negotiating context and stating that "[i]n practice ... the codes provide authority for virtually any negotiating approach the lawyer chooses to take"); see also Levine, *Taking Ethical Discretion Seriously*, supra note 4, at 49 n.141 (reviewing scholarly documentation of the fact that ethics rules are not exhaustive, thus requiring discretion on the part of lawyers). See generally David B. Wilkins, *Legal Realism for Lawyers*, 104 Harv. L. Rev. 468, 470-78 (1990) (setting forth the traditional model of legal ethics and the legal realist critique of that model).

ethical deliberation, without fear of serious consequences.[6] Moreover, the legislative history of many rules indicates that when considering the possibility of drafting a rule in a manner that would require greater adherence to ethical conduct and principles, the ABA has often chosen a less demanding formulation of the rule.[7]

---

6 See Green & Zacharias, supra note 5:

> Not surprisingly, given lawyers' self-interest and the structure of some of the rules, many practicing lawyers take an extremely lawyer-protective view of permissive rules. They assume that whenever ethics provisions permit lawyers to act in a certain way, the provisions are defining an area in which lawyer conduct is meant to be unconstrained. On this understanding, the choice of conduct belongs entirely to individual lawyers. A lawyer's decision within the area covered by a permissive rule is both unregulated by the disciplinary process and intended to be free from other regulatory oversight.

See also Heidi Li Feldman, *Codes and Virtues: Can Good Lawyers Be Good Ethical Deliberators?*, 69 S. Cal. L. Rev. 885, 898 (1996) (stating that "[t]he more frequently a black letter ethics code is inconclusive," the more frequently opportunities arise for "interpreting the rules simply to permit pursuit of the client's ends, without regard to independent ethical concerns").

Moreover, Professor Zacharias noted that:

> When the codes authorize lawyers to choose between emphasizing partisanship and important third party or societal interests, lawyers' natural [i.e., personal and economic] incentives encourage them to select partisanship. Lawyers who make that choice can readily justify their conduct as mandated by the code by claiming adherence to the code provisions that call for zeal.

Zacharias, supra note 4, at 1340; see Fred C. Zacharias, *Coercing Clients: Can Lawyer Gatekeeper Rules Work?*, 47 B.C. L. Rev. 455, 495 (2006) ("Other rules simply give lawyers discretion to act, which allows them to base their decisions on personal, potentially venal, incentives"); see also Levine, *Taking Ethical Discretion Seriously*, supra note 4, at 56-57 & nn.151-52.

7 See discussion infra Part one, sections A-C. One example can be found in the ABA's resistance to the Security Exchange Commission's (SEC) proposal, pursuant to Sarbanes-Oxley regulations, to mandate that lawyers disclose corporate wrongdoing. See Green & Zacharias, supra note 5, at 271-72; see also Sarbanes-Oxley Act of 2002 § 307, 15 U.S.C. § 7245 (Supp. III 2005) (directing the SEC to issue rules regulating the professional conduct of attorneys); Model Rules of Prof'l Conduct R. 1.6(b)(2)-(3); id. R. 1.13(c); Stephen Gillers & Roy D. Simon, *Regulation of Lawyers* 173-75 (2007) (reviewing the legislative history of amendments made in 2002 and 2003 to Model Rule 1.13 by the ABA House of Delegates, and the recommendations of the ABA Presidential Task Force on Corporate Responsibility).

For further analysis of the organized bar's response to Sarbanes-Oxley regulations, see, for example, Thomas G. Bost, *Corporate Lawyers After the Big Quake: The Conceptual Fault Line in the Professional Duty of Confidentiality*, 19 Geo. J. Legal Ethics 1089 (2006); Roger C. Cramton, George M. Cohen & Susan P. Koniak, *Legal and Ethical Duties of Lawyers After Sarbanes-Oxley*, 49 Vill. L. Rev. 725 (2004); Lawrence J. Fox, *The Fallout from Enron: Media Frenzy and Misguided Notions of Public Relations Are No Reason to Abandon Our Commitment*

A. Model Rule 6.1

One way for lawyers to distinguish themselves as engaging in ethical conduct might be to practice law in the public interest without receiving compensation for such service.[8] Accordingly, addressing pro bono publico service, an early draft of Model Rule 6.1 included the obligation that "[a] lawyer *shall* render unpaid public interest legal services."[9] As adopted in 1983, however, the rule no longer included a mandatory provision, stating instead that "[a] lawyer *should* render public interest legal service."[10] Although the rule was amended substantially in 1993, the revisions merely quantified the optional standard for pro bono work, seemingly resigned to the idealistic declaration that "[a] lawyer *should aspire* to render at least (50) hours of pro bono publico legal services per year."[11]

---

to *Our Clients*, 2003 U. Ill. L. Rev. 1243; Susan P. Koniak, *When the Hurlyburly's Done: The Bar's Struggle with the SEC*, 103 Colum. L. Rev. 1236 (2003); William H. Simon, *After Confidentiality: Rethinking the Professional Responsibilities of the Business Lawyer*, 75 Fordham L. Rev. 1453 (2006).

8 See, e.g., Leslie Boyle, *Meeting the Demands of the Indigent Population: The Choice Between Mandatory and Voluntary Pro Bono Requirements*, 20 Geo. J. Legal Ethics 415, 416-17 (2007); Steven Lubet & Cathryn Stewart, *A "Public Assets" Theory of Lawyers' Pro Bono Obligations*, 145 U. Pa. L. Rev. 1245, 1261-62 (1997); Michael Millemann, *Mandatory Pro Bono in Civil Cases: A Partial Answer to the Right Question*, 49 Md. L. Rev. 18, 59-60 (1990); Deborah L. Rhode, *Cultures of Commitment: Pro Bono for Lawyers and Law Students*, 67 Fordham L. Rev. 2415, 2415 (1999); Chesterfield H. Smith, *A Mandatory Pro Bono Service Standard—Its Time Has Come*, 35 U. Miami L. Rev. 727, 727 (1981); see also *Symposium on Mandatory Pro Bono*, 19 Hofstra L. Rev. 739 (1991). But see Esther F. Lardent, *Mandatory Pro Bono in Civil Cases: The Wrong Answer to the Right Question*, 49 Md. L. Rev. 78, 79 (1990); Jonathan R. Macey, *Mandatory Pro Bono: Comfort for the Poor or Welfare for the Rich?*, 77 Cornell L. Rev. 1115, 1119 (1992).

9 Model Rules of Prof'l Conduct R. 8.1 (Discussion Draft 1980), quoted in Gillers & Simon, supra note 7, at 390 (emphasis added).

10 Model Rules of Prof'l Conduct R. 6.1 (1983), quoted in Gillers & Simon, supra note 7, at 390 (emphasis added).

11 Model Rules of Prof'l Conduct R. 6.1 (2006) (emphasis added); see also Gillers & Simon, supra note 7, at 390-92 (presenting the legislative history of the 1993 amendments). Although at least one commentator perceived the 1993 amendments as indicating a "trend towards mandatory pro bono," B. George Ballman, Jr., Note, *Amended Rule 6.1: Another Move Towards Mandatory Pro Bono? Is That What We Want?*, 7 Geo. J. Legal Ethics 1139, 1139 (1994), the Model Rules have yet to include a provision requiring pro bono service. See generally Tom Lininger, *From Park Place to Community Chest: Rethinking Lawyers' Monopoly*, 101 Nw. U. L. Rev. 1343, 1353 (2007) (reviewing Deborah L. Rhode, *Pro Bono in Principle and in Practice* (2005)) (noting that Rhode's book describes the fifty hour recommendation of Model Rule 6.1 as "toothless"). But see Samuel R. Bagenstos, *Mandatory Pro Bono and Private Attorneys General*, 101 Nw. U. L. Rev. 1459 (2007) (suggesting that a mandatory system of pro bono service may actually result in undermining the service as a whole).

Pursuant to the work of the Ethics 2000 Commission, which represented the ABA's comprehensive attempt to revise its code of ethics to demonstrate greater fidelity to ethical principles,[12] in 2002, an additional sentence was appended to the beginning of Model Rule 6.1: "Every lawyer has a professional responsibility to provide legal services to those unable to pay."[13] Though presumably intended to emphasize the ABA's commitment to the importance of pro bono service, the 2002 addition may instead illustrate shortcomings of Model Rule 6.1 and, more generally, some of the attitudes underlying the Model Rules.

Specifically, the revised version of Model Rule 6.1 now opens with a definitive declaration that pro bono service constitutes an aspect of the lawyer's "professional responsibility," a term presumably signifying an ethical duty included among the most fundamental of the lawyer's obligations.[14] Nevertheless, the remainder of the rule continues to refer to pro bono service in exclusively optional and aspirational terms.[15] Thus, the current version of the rule indicates a resistance, on the part of the ABA, to impose a mandatory ethical obligation, even in fulfillment of a duty that the ABA has identified as a basic component of the lawyer's professional responsibility.

B. Model Rule 1.5

The ABA's continued failure to promulgate a model rule mandating pro bono work thus represents a refusal to impose an obligatory duty in the context of the lawyer's service to the public, and toward those in need of legal representation. Perhaps more disturbing, at times the Model Rules have been drafted in ways that permit a lawyer to avoid ethical conduct vis-à-vis the client, potentially allowing the lawyer to engage in self-interested actions that prove detrimental to the interests of the client. For example, as in many professional relationships, one of the most common issues of contention between a lawyer and a client revolves around money.[16] With the apparent aim of mitigating some of the

---

12 See Love, supra note 2, at 441-42; Moore, supra note 2, at 923; Veasey, supra note 2, at 1.

13 See Model Rules of Prof'l Conduct R. 6.1 (2006).

14 See id.

15 See id.

16 See Gillers, supra note 2, at 136 (observing that attorney "fees are often a basis for client complaints or bitterness"); Wolfram, supra note 2, at 557 ("A typical report of bar committees and researchers is that fee disputes are frequent, and a high proportion of client and public complaints about lawyers involve charges of excessive fee charges."). As the North Carolina State Bar Newsletter has described it,

tensions that might arise, Model Rule 1.5 provides guidelines for various aspects of the lawyer's fees.[17] Here again, however, earlier drafts of the rule incorporated a mandatory ethical obligation for lawyers, only to be replaced by a more permissive version of the rule.[18]

The earliest draft of the rule required that a fee agreement, stating "the nature and extent of the services to be provided[,] ... *shall be* expressed or confirmed in writing."[19] A subsequent draft likewise continued to mandate that the "basis or rate of a lawyer's fee *shall be* communicated to the client in writing."[20] When the Model Rules were adopted in 1983, however, the ABA again relieved lawyers of a mandatory ethical obligation, modifying Model Rule 1.5 to read: "[T]he basis or rate of the fee shall be communicated to the client, *preferably* in writing."[21] On its face, the change seems merely emblematic of a pattern of decisions by the ABA, similar to the decision regarding the nature of pro bono responsibilities, premised on a general approach that limits the degree to which lawyers' ethics should be deemed mandatory.

Upon closer analysis, however, the modification of Model Rule 1.5 may prove more troubling. As an official comment to the rule puts it, "[a] written statement concerning the terms of the engagement reduces the possibility of misunderstanding."[22] Ostensibly, both clients and lawyers alike have an interest

---

> Historically, a problem which has plagued both the Bar and the public has been the number of disputes between lawyers and clients relating to fees. Fee disputes have generated numerous grievances filed with the State Bar against lawyers, but the grievance procedure is neither a proper nor satisfactory forum for effectively dealing with the problem.

Moseley, Moody & Vernon, supra note 2, at 940 n.3 (quoting *Professionalism Report*, N.C. St. B. Newsl. (N.C. State Bar, Raleigh, N.C.), Fall 1992, at 8); see also Alan Scott Rau, *Resolving Disputes Over Attorneys' Fees: The Role of ADR*, 46 SMU L. Rev. 2005, 2006 (1993) (stating that "the suspicion persists that disputes over fees constitute a major and particularly intractable share of all attorney-client conflict"); id. at 2018 ("[I]t appears certain that both the number of litigated cases appearing in the reports and the number of complaints made to the bar's disciplinary agencies give a very inadequate picture of the prevalence of fee disputes between attorney and client." (footnote omitted)).

17 See Model Rules of Prof'l Conduct R. 1.5 (2006).

18 See Gillers & Simon, supra note 7, at 60-61 (providing the legislative history of Model Rule 1.5).

19 See Gillers & Simon, supra note 7, at 60 (quoting Model Rules of Prof'l Conduct (Unofficial Pre-Circulation Draft 1979)) (emphasis added).

20 Model Rules of Prof'l Conduct R. 1.5 (Proposed Final Draft 1981), quoted in Gillers & Simon, supra note 7, at 61 (emphasis added).

21 Model Rules of Prof'l Conduct R. 1.5(b) (1983), quoted in Gillers & Simon, supra note 7, at 61 (emphasis added).

22 See Model Rules of Prof'l Conduct R. 1.5 cmt. [2] (2006).

in avoiding such misunderstanding; thus, both would presumably benefit from mandating that fee agreements be put in writing.[23] More likely, though, the primary function of placing fee agreements in writing would be to protect the client, in the case of an ensuing fee dispute with the lawyer.[24] After all, to the extent that the client remains unable to point to a written statement of the fee arrangement, the lawyer would arguably gain an advantage in interpreting any ambiguity, due to the lawyer's relative experience, power, status, sophistication, and credibility.[25] Thus, the ABA's willingness to allow a lawyer to evade

---

23 See Wolfram, supra note 2, at 503 n.48 ("There are few good reasons not to reduce agreements to writing.").

24 See id. at 503 ("The desirability of a writing is suggested by occasional statistics from fee arbitration agencies showing that a high percentage of disputes involve unwritten fee agreements." (footnote omitted)); see also Gillers, supra note 2, at 136-37 ("Why would a profession—which . . . is supposed to put service and the public interest above the quest for wealth . . .—refuse to require written fee agreements . . . ?"); Lawrence A. Dubin, *Client Beware: The Need For a Mandatory Written Fee Agreement Rule*, 51 Okla. L. Rev. 93, 95 (1998) ("With the widespread recognition that the use of written fee agreements would be beneficial to lawyers and clients in reducing the large number of fee disputes, . . . why is there no such mandatory rule?"); Stephen Gillers, *Caveat Client: How the Proposed Final Draft of the Restatement of the Law Governing Lawyers Fails to Protect Unsophisticated Consumers in Fee Agreements with Lawyers*, 10 Geo. J. Legal Ethics 581, 602 (1997) ("Mandating a written fee agreement of some specificity is probably the single most important step a client-friendly document could take to reduce the imbalance between buyer and seller."); John Leubsdorf, *Ideals, Realities, and Lawyer Fees*, 10 Geo. J. Legal Ethics 619, 621 (1997) ("Professor Gillers is on the mark when he urges that written fee agreements should be required."); Lee A. Watson, Note, *Communication, Honesty, and Contract: Three Buzzwords for Maintaining Ethical Hourly Billing*, 11 Geo. J. Legal Ethics 189, 200-201 (1998):

> The most practical solution to the problem of unethical billing is communication between attorney and client because it levels the playing field and promotes satisfaction of both parties. . . . It is certainly more difficult for an attorney with dishonest urgings to cheat an informed client because the essence of [the] deception lies within [the] ability to withhold information from [the] client. . . . A signed contract that reflects the negotiated fee leaves less to chance than a situation in which the client is uninformed.

Cf. Gabriel J. Chin & Scott C. Wells, *Can a Reasonable Doubt Have an Unreasonable Price? Limitations on Attorneys' Fees in Criminal Cases*, 41 B.C. L. Rev. 1, 68 (1999):

> One malpractice treatise recommends that attorneys engage in detailed fee discussions with prospective clients and that the agreements be reduced to writing. If shrewd attorneys will have this discussion in order to protect themselves from fee disputes and malpractice claims, there is no reason not to expect ethical attorneys to have this discussion for the benefit of their clients.

25 See Gillers, supra note 24, at 605-6. Furthermore, the client is likely to face the question of whether to retain a second lawyer in such a dispute. As Professor Gillers observes,

a mandatory requirement to reduce a fee agreement to writing may represent not only a generally permissive attitude to the promulgation of ethical obligations, but also an outright instance of favoring the interests of the lawyer to the potential detriment of the client.

Indeed, recognizing the unseemliness of condoning a lawyer's failure to provide a client with a written fee schedule, the Ethics 2000 Commission

---

> If . . . the fee dispute does go to court, the embattled but determined client will have to decide whether to hire a lawyer to defend the claim of her former lawyer. The former lawyer may seek a fee far greater than he was willing to accept "in settlement" without a suit. That heightened sum, giving the lawyer negotiating room, also will have an *in terrorem* effect on the client. Who knows what the courts will do? Maybe judges, once lawyers, will accept it. These realities make it risky for the former client to forego new counsel in the fee dispute, but then why not save the expense of having another lawyer and add the savings to the "settlement"? The deck is stacked against the former client. . . .

Id. at 606; Professor Wolfram raised similar concerns about fee disputes:

> Fee suits can be ugly affairs. . . . The lawyer suing for fees often appears pro se, creating an imbalance of expenditures for legal services that might prove particularly galling to a nonlawyer client. The lawyer's access to the client's deepest confidences, and the realization that these can be spread abroad in the fee suit, may appear treacherously near blackmail.

Wolfram, supra note 2, at 554. As Professor Wolfram explained, a client in a fee dispute has at least three additional concerns:

> A client dissatisfied with the size of a fee or unhappy at the extent or quality of legal services rendered after paying a fee in advance is faced with unpleasant prospects. The idea of hiring a second lawyer to pursue the first through the courts is unattractive because it simply adds additional fees to the original problem. It might be difficult to find a lawyer willing to litigate against another. And the delays of litigation may put economic pressure on the client to forego any relief.

Id. at 556.

In an effort to combat some of these concerns, "[c]ourts quite uniformly resolve ambiguities in a fee contract against the lawyer, who has almost invariably drafted it." Id. at 503; see also Wilkins, supra note 1, at 875 n.326 (discussing a proposal to make "lawyers who do not submit written fee agreements bear the burden of proof on all matters in any subsequent dispute with the client") (citing *Comm'n on Evaluation of Disciplinary Enforcement, Am. Bar Ass'n, Report to the House of Delegates* 56 (1991)). Another effort has focused on methods of fee arbitration. See Wolfram, supra note 2, at 556-58; see also Leubsdorf, supra note 24, at 622; Moseley, Moody & Vernon, supra note 2, at 940 n.3 (discussing a repealed North Carolina professional responsibility rule "mak[ing] nonbinding fee arbitration, subject to client consent, a prerequisite to suing a client for a fee"); Rau, supra note 16, at 2020-21 (reviewing proposals made in 1970 and 1974 by two ABA committees).

recommended deleting the word "preferably" from Model Rule 1.5.[26] The aim of the proposal was apparently to provide clients, at long last, the measure of protection contemplated in the early versions of the rule, which mandated putting fee agreements in writing.[27] Nevertheless, the ABA rejected the proposed modification,[28] thus reaffirming the rule's articulation of a mere preference for written fee agreements, and providing an option for a lawyer to make a calculated decision that disregards the effects on the client and instead protects the lawyer's own interests.

C. Model Rule 1.6

The approach of the Model Rules to the lawyer's duty of confidentiality may serve as yet another example of the ABA's apparent unwillingness to require lawyers to engage in mandatory ethical conduct. In particular, Model Rule 1.6 presents a number of scenarios that constitute exceptions to the duty of confidentiality.[29] In the years preceding the adoption of the Model Rules, Model Rule 1.6 evolved through several different stages.[30] The earliest drafts of the rule provided that "[a] lawyer *shall* disclose" information about a client when, and to the extent necessary, to prevent the client from committing an act that would result in death or serious bodily harm to another.[31] In contrast, later drafts no longer included mandatory disclosure, instead stating that "a lawyer *may* reveal" information about a client to prevent the client from committing a crime or fraud likely to cause such results as death, substantial bodily harm, or substantial financial injury.[32] Likewise, as adopted in 1983 and later amended, the rule currently permits—but still does not require—disclosure "to prevent

---

26 See Gillers & Simon, supra note 7, at 61.

27 See id. at 60-61.

28 Id. at 61.

29 See Model Rules of Prof'l Conduct R. 1.6(b)(1)-(6) (2006).

30 See Gillers & Simon, supra note 7, at 79-80.

31 Model Rules of Prof'l Conduct R. 1.7(b) (Discussion Draft 1980), quoted in Gillers & Simon, supra note 7, at 79 (emphasis added); Gillers & Simon, supra note 7, at 79 (quoting Model Rules of Prof'l Conduct (Unofficial Pre-Circulation Draft 1979)) (emphasis added).

32 Model Rules of Prof'l Conduct R. 1.6(b) (Revised Final Draft 1982), quoted in Gillers & Simon, supra note 7, at 80 (emphasis added); Model Rules of Prof'l Conduct R. 1.6(b) (Proposed Final Draft 1981), quoted in Gillers & Simon, supra note 7, at 79-80 (emphasis added).

reasonably certain death or substantial bodily harm," among other circumstances.[33]

On one level, the final version of Model Rule 1.6 may prove less troubling than the revisions to Model Rules 6.1 and 1.5. The failure of the Model Rules to require pro bono service or mandatory written fee agreements seems problematic, in part, because of the apparent absence of any corresponding promotion of the interests of the client or the public. Instead, these rules appear to function primarily as a mechanism for lawyers to avoid increased ethical conduct. In contrast, to the extent that Model Rule 1.6 limits the lawyer's obligation to disclose information about the client, the rule accordingly serves to protect the client's interest in confidentiality. Indeed, although the Model Rules allow for exceptions, the duty of confidentiality stands as one of the central elements of the attorney-client relationship, and one of the most fundamental ethical obligations that a lawyer owes the client.[34] Thus, it might follow, the ABA's decision not to include mandatory disclosure provisions represents a measured determination that the ethical obligation of confidentiality stands paramount, and, therefore, even in exceptional situations, it would be inappropriate to require disclosure of information about the client. In light of the counterbalancing interest of confidentiality, perhaps the absence of mandatory disclosure provisions indicates a thoughtfully crafted compromise position, rather than a permissive attitude toward ethical obligations.

Despite the potential plausibility of such an analysis, a careful look at Model Rule 1.6, in the context of the official comments to the rule, suggests a less satisfying conclusion. In delineating the justification for the rule's exceptions to confidentiality as necessary to prevent death or serious bodily harm, the comment first articulates the general principle that "the public interest is usually best served by a strict rule requiring lawyers to preserve the confidentiality of

---

33 Model Rules of Prof'l Conduct R. 1.6(b)(1) (2006); Model Rules of Prof'l Conduct R. 1.6 (1983), quoted in Gillers & Simon, supra note 7, at 80.

34 See, e.g., Model Rules of Prof'l Conduct R. 1.6 cmt. [2] (2006) ("A fundamental principle in the client-lawyer relationship is that, in the absence of the client's informed consent, the lawyer must not reveal information relating to the representation . . . . This contributes to the trust that is the hallmark of the client-lawyer relationship."); Freedman & Smith, supra note 2, at 129-58 (providing a detailed description and defense of the significance and extent of the lawyer's duty of confidentiality); Lawrence J. Fox, *MDPs Done Gone: The Silver Lining in the Very Black Enron Cloud*, 44 Ariz. L. Rev. 547, 551 (2002) (describing client confidentiality as a "core value for a lawyer"); Susan P. Koniak, *The Law Between the Bar and the State*, 70 N.C. L. Rev. 1389, 1427-47 (1992) (describing "the centrality and power of the norm of confidentiality in the bar's *nomos*").

information relating to the representation."[35] As the comment further explains, however, the exceptions to the rule "recognize [...] the overriding value of life and physical integrity and permit[ ] disclosure reasonably necessary to prevent reasonably certain death or substantial bodily harm."[36] Although the comment thus provides a rationale for these exceptions, the discretionary nature of the rule fails to fully comply with the implications of the asserted rationale. If the premise underlying the exceptions to the rule includes the recognition of an "overriding" value of life and physical integrity, a more appropriate formulation of the rule would require, rather than merely permit, disclosure to prevent death or serious physical injury. Nevertheless, the rule leaves open, at the discretion of the lawyer, the decision whether to disclose information to save a life.[37] Thus, Model Rule 1.6 appears to present yet another example of the ABA's refusal to mandate conduct that would appear more consistent with ethical principles, instead allowing a lawyer the option of acting in a way that best suits the lawyer's own interests.

Indeed, given the discretionary component of the rule, it seems unlikely that a lawyer would choose the option of disclosing information pursuant to the exceptions, even in the face of overriding concerns of death or serious physical harm to another.[38] As another comment to Model Rule 1.6 emphasizes, the nature of discretionary disclosure provisions implies that failure to disclose will not violate the rule.[39] Therefore, a lawyer will not face negative professional or financial consequences as a result of a decision not to disclose information, regardless of any harm caused to others. Conversely, a lawyer who decides to reveal information pursuant to an exception to the rule may, at times, risk the possibility of discipline and/or litigation, in case the lawyer's decision is later reviewed, and it is determined that the circumstances did not actually permit disclosure.[40] Thus, contrary to the outcome that the rule is purported to encourage, the self-interested lawyer will probably choose not to disclose

---

35 Model Rules of Prof'l Conduct R. 1.6 cmt. [6] (2006).

36 Id.

37 See Model Rules of Prof'l Conduct R. 1.6(b)(1) (2006).

38 Cf. David McGowan, *Why Not Try the Carrot? A Modest Proposal to Grant Immunity to Lawyers Who Disclose Client Financial Misconduct*, 92 Cal. L. Rev. 1825, 1828 (2004) (suggesting that because lawyers are reluctant to create costs for themselves, disclosure is unlikely to increase "even in cases where disclosure could stop unlawful conduct or help rectify its consequences").

39 Model Rules of Prof'l Conduct R. 1.6 cmt. [15] (2006).

40 See McGowan, supra note 38, at 1829-30.

information, even to save a life.[41] In fact, the ABA Task Force on Corporate Responsibility, which recommended expanding the circumstances under which disclosure should be permitted—though still not required—seemed to acknowledge that, in practice, state ethics provisions permitting disclosure are rarely employed by lawyers.[42]

The impression that Model Rule 1.6 produces the practical—if not intended—result of favoring the interests of lawyers may be reinforced by the rule's inclusion of yet another exception to the duty of confidentiality, which was absent from the drafts of the rule. Starting with its adoption, and continuing through every revision, Model Rule 1.6 has permitted disclosure "to establish a claim or defense on behalf of the lawyer in a controversy between the lawyer and the client."[43] Thus, notwithstanding the presumed and professed centrality of confidentiality as a basic component of the attorney-client relationship and, therefore, as a fundamental element of the lawyer's ethical responsibilities, the client's interests in confidentiality lose their special status when confronted with the lawyer's conflicting interests against the client.[44] Indeed, the self-interested

---

41 Cf. id. at 1825 (asserting that "the costs disclosure creates for lawyers who blow the whistle" must be addressed if lawyers are to be encouraged to disclose clients' financial misconduct); id. at 1828 (observing that "[b]ecause disclosure is permissive, lawyers choose whether they will create these other costs," and concluding that lawyers are unlikely to incur such costs); David Rosenthal, *The Criminal Defense Attorney, Ethics and Maintaining Client Confidentiality: A Proposal to Amend Rule 1.6 of the Model Rules of Professional Conduct*, 6 St. Thomas L. Rev. 153, 166-68 (1993) (observing that, in addition to the possibility that disclosure may result in discipline, "[f]rom an economic standpoint, a more tangible, often damaging consequence of disclosure exists," particularly for criminal defense attorneys, because "[t]he reputation of criminal defense attorneys travels swiftly through the ranks of criminal defendants and once the attorney is labeled as untrustworthy, that attorney may likely be hard pressed to retain any future clients").

42 See *Task Force on Corporate Responsibility, Am. Bar Ass'n, Report to the House of Delegates* (2003), quoted in Gillers & Simon, supra note 7, at 81-82.

43 Model Rules of Prof'l Conduct R. 1.6(b)(5) (2006).

44 Indeed, in the words of one leading scholar, "[n]o exception to the attorney-client privilege has done as much to draw [the privilege] into question as the exception allowing lawyer self-protection." Wolfram, supra note 2, at 308. As others have put it, permitting lawyers to disclose confidences for the purpose of collecting fees "is sanction for blackmail." Freedman & Smith, supra note 2. at 155. For consideration of possible justifications for these exceptions, see Wolfram, supra note 2, at 308-9.

In fact, when adopted in 1983, Model Rule 1.6 did not allow disclosure to save the life of the "Innocent Convict." See Simon, supra note 1, at 4 (giving the example of lawyer Arthur Powell and innocent convict Leo Frank). In such a scenario, the client admits to a lawyer, in confidence, to having committed a capital crime for which an innocent individual has been convicted. See id. Under the original version of the Rule, the lawyer ostensibly was not permit-

lawyer, involved in a controversy with a client, might be expected to disclose information in spite of—or, in part, because of—the detrimental effect disclosure will have on the interests of the client. Ultimately, then, the discretionary nature of Model Rule 1.6 often seems to operate in a way that establishes as paramount the interests of the lawyer, allowing the lawyer to decide, primarily on the basis of those interests, whether to reveal confidential information about the client.[45]

---

ted to reveal this information because such disclosure would not prevent future harmful conduct by the client. *See* Levine, *Taking Ethical Discretion Seriously,* supra note 4, at 30-33, 37-42. Not surprisingly, the prohibition against disclosing confidences to save the life of the Innocent Convict engendered harsh, though not universal, criticism. See id. at 38-42 & nn.112-18. The prohibition seemed particularly disconcerting when juxtaposed with the provision permitting disclosure for the lawyer to collect a fee. Professors Cramton and Knowles argued that:

> [A] profession that justifiably asks for and receives permission to disclose confidential client information when its own economic interests are at stake (e.g., to collect a fee from a client) cannot plausibly take the position that the threatened death or serious injury of another does not justify an occasional sacrifice of confidentiality.

Roger C. Cramton & Lori P. Knowles, *Professional Secrecy and its Exceptions:* Spaulding v. Zimmerman *Revisited,* 83 Minn. L. Rev. 63, 111-12 (1998) (footnote omitted). Professor Fischel observes that:

> The same lawyer who is prohibited from disclosing information learned while representing a client to exonerate someone falsely accused of a capital crime . . . is perfectly free to disclose confidential information when he or she is the one accused, falsely or not. Nor is there any requirement that the lawyer's liberty be at stake, or even that the lawyer be accused of anything criminal. A simple fee dispute with a client is sufficient grounds to disclose confidential information. The lawyer's interest in collecting a fee is apparently a higher priority than exonerating an innocent defendant about to be convicted of a capital crime. . . . Confidentiality means everything in legal ethics unless lawyers lose money, in which case it means nothing.

Daniel Fischel, *Lawyers and Confidentiality,* 65 U. Chi. L. Rev. 1, 10 (1998).
　More general critiques of the rules of confidentiality abound among scholars as well. See, e.g., Simon, supra note 1, at 56, 222 n.9; Wolfram, supra note 2, at 243-47; Simon, supra note 7, at 1453-54, 1468; Fred C. Zacharias, *Rethinking Confidentiality,* 74 Iowa L. Rev. 351, 376-89 (1989) (analyzing the results of empirical studies testing the justifications for strict confidentiality); Fred C. Zacharias, *Rethinking Confidentiality II: Is Confidentiality Constitutional?,* 75 Iowa L. Rev. 601 (1990) [hereinafter Zacharias, *Rethinking Confidentiality II*] (same).
45　Even a brief survey of ethics regulations over the past few decades reveals many instances in which the organized bar promulgated ethics rules that seemed to promote lawyers' economic self-interest, at times to the detriment of the client. Indeed, the United States Supreme Court has struck down various regulations that appeared designed, at least in part, to protect the economic interests of lawyers. See, e.g., *Supreme Court of Va. v. Friedman,* 487 U.S. 59, 67-70 (1988) (striking

D. Enforcement

Finally, the discretionary nature of so many ethics provisions may have an additional detrimental effect, beyond the contours of specific discretionary rules. On
a broader level, the extent to which the Model Rules allow important aspects of a
lawyer's ethical obligations to remain optional, rather than mandatory, arguably
contributes to a general undermining of the authority and credibility of ethics
codes as a source of the lawyer's professional responsibility. Indeed, although
ethics codes set forth the substantive basis for attorney discipline, even mandatory ethics provisions remain notoriously underenforced.[46] The enactment of

---

down regulations limiting admission "on motion" to state residents as unconstitutional in violation of the Privileges and Immunities Clause); *Zauderer v. Office of Disciplinary Counsel,* 471 U.S.
626, 655-56 (1985) (reversing, on First Amendment grounds, reprimand for using an illustration
in advertising materials); *Supreme Court of N.H. v. Piper,* 470 U.S. 274, 287-88 (1985) (striking
down regulations limiting bar admission to state residents as unconstitutional in violation of the
Privileges and Immunities Clause); *Bates v. State Bar,* 433 U.S. 350, 384 (1977) (striking down,
on First Amendment grounds, restrictions on advertising by lawyers of routine services and their
availability); *Goldfarb v. Va. State Bar,* 421 U.S. 773, 791-93 (1975) (striking down mandatory
minimum fee schedules as a form of price fixing).

    Many scholars have criticized the sometimes self-serving nature of lawyer self-regula-
tion. See, e.g., Wolfram, *supra* note 2, at 21 ("Few persons who are not lawyers would judge
the . . . history of [bar] regulation to be one in which the public interest has regularly been
vindicated."); Green & Zacharias, *supra* note 5, at 312 ("[T]here is little doubt that ethics
codes traditionally have included self-serving propositions.") (citing Zacharias, *Rethinking
Confidentiality II, supra* note 44, at 628 nn.138-39, 629-30 nn.144-45); Geoffrey C. Hazard,
Jr., Russell G. Pearce & Jeffrey W. Stempel, *Why Lawyers Should Be Allowed to Advertise:
A Market Analysis of Legal Services,* 58 N.Y.U. L. Rev. 1084, 1087 (1983) (arguing that "participants in the debate on lawyer advertising have failed to appreciate that legal services
are a market commodity"); Andrew M. Perlman, *Toward a Unified Theory of Professional
Regulation,* 55 Fla. L. Rev. 977, 999 (2003) ("[T]he ABA's structural rules . . . have emphasized self-protection and public image at the expense of more appropriate emphases. . . .
[T]here is ample evidence that ethics codes have, in fact, advanced these goals more clearly
than other identifiable objectives."); Deborah L. Rhode, Keynote, *Law, Lawyers, and the Pursuit
of Justice,* 70 Fordham L. Rev. 1543, 1557 (2002) ("[R]egulation of the legal profession has
been designed primarily by and for the profession, and too often protects its concerns at the
expense of the public."); Schneyer, *supra* note 2, at 724-33 (criticizing the bar's insistence on
designing ethical rules to protect lawyers, its disfavor of regulation by nonlawyer actors and
institutions, and its preference for role-based ethics rules); William H. Simon, *Who Needs the
Bar?: Professionalism Without Monopoly,* 30 Fla. St. U. L. Rev. 639, 640 (2003) (elaborating
"on the widely felt doubts about monopolistic self-regulation").

46 See *Standing Comm. On Prof'l Discipline, Am. Bar Ass'n, Survey on Lawyer Discipline Systems* 1-8
(2001) (listing the number of complaints brought against lawyers and the types and frequen-
cies of sanctions imposed); Wolfram, *supra* note 2, at 80 ("Recurring impressionistic accounts
claim that the state of lawyer discipline demands urgent attention," in part because "there are
ample reasons to believe that discipline is selective, episodic, subject to constraints of fluctuating

discretionary rules—which are, by definition, unenforceable under prevailing disciplinary norms[47]—in areas central to ethical behavior, reinforces the perception that ethics rules are often, at best, aspirational or hortatory. In short, the Model Rules send the message that the self-interested lawyer faces minimal—if any—actual risk in disregarding ethics codes and their underlying principles.[48]

PART TWO | THE JEWISH LEGAL MODEL

In light of the apparent limitations on the effectiveness of the ABA Model Rules of Professional Conduct in improving the reputation and ethical conduct of American lawyers, perhaps American ethics codes should look to an alternative model as a counterexample for the codification and implementation of ethical norms. Specifically, the Jewish legal model offers a different approach to the formulation and interpretation of ethical provisions, grounded in mandatory legal and ethical obligations that require the individual to take seriously both

---

budgets and personal ability, influenced by political instability, and subject to like influences that grossly distort the extent to which lawyer discipline reflects levels of deviance and compliance among lawyers."); Barton, supra note 2, at 424 & n.47 ("[T]he minimum Rules governing lawyers are, in fact, notoriously underenforced."); Lisa G. Lerman, *Lying to Clients*, 138 U. Pa. L. Rev. 659, 747 n.349 (1990) ("The underenforcement of the legal ethics codes is well-documented."); Deborah L. Rhode, *The Profession and the Public Interest*, 54 Stan. L. Rev. 1501, 1512 (2002) ("Disciplinary rules and enforcement processes have not adequately curbed ethical abuses. . . ."); Wilkins, supra note 5, at 493 ("[T]he rules of professional conduct . . . tend to be systematically underenforced."); Fred C. Zacharias, *What Lawyers Do When Nobody's Watching: Legal Advertising as a Case Study of the Impact of Underenforced Professional Rules*, 87 Iowa L. Rev. 971, 973 (2002) (exploring "the ramifications of maintaining unenforced or underenforced rules in the professional codes of lawyer responsibility"). But see Charles W. Wolfram, *Toward a History of the Legalization of American Legal Ethics—I. Origins*, 8 U. Chi. L. Sch. Roundtable 469, 470 (2001) ("While lawyer discipline was once scandalously under enforced and is still criticized by many as lax, there is no doubt that its incidence has increased significantly in the past thirty years."

47 See supra note 6 and accompanying text.

48 See David Luban, *Ethics and Malpractice*, 12 Miss. C. L. Rev. 151, 152 (1991) (making the "routine observation that the codes are drastically underenforced"). According to Professor Luban, given the current state of underenforcement,

> if one were to give realistic advice to aspiring lawyers about how to avoid attorney discipline, it would be this: "If you don't steal your clients' money, neglect their affairs, get convicted of a felony, engage in substance abuse, or get caught lying to a court, you have little to fear from the disciplinary system."

Id. at 152; see also Zacharias, supra note 2, at 861-62 ("[M]any rules simply go unenforced or are patently underenforced . . . . [O]ne could safely hazard the assertion that few rules truly are enforced in a way that makes lawyers fear discipline for violating them.").

the formal delineation of a rule and the underlying ethical principles reflected and incorporated therein. An analysis of this approach may prove helpful in promoting an enhanced and more serious attitude toward ethical obligations in American legal practice.

A. Ethical Obligations: The Mandatory/Optional Dichotomy

A number of scholars have drawn a contrast between the predominance of rights as the guiding value in American law and jurisprudence, and the notion of obligation as the central principle in Jewish law.[49] At its core, the Jewish legal system consists of 613 biblical commandments, as applied and implemented through rabbinic interpretation and legislation.[50] Though dependent on the presence of a variety of circumstances and conditions that trigger their applicability, commandments, by definition, mandate a prescribed course of action in response to a given scenario.

The mandatory nature of ethical obligations in the Jewish legal system extends to areas of conduct, such as giving aid to those in need, that might seem more consistent with voluntary aspirations than with the dictates of legal strictures.[51] In fact, the biblical term *tzedaka*, often translated as "charity," contains the root *tzedek*, the biblical word for "justice."[52] Thus, as a form of implementing social justice, both the individual and the community as a whole must fulfill a legal and ethical obligation to contribute resources to those requiring assistance.[53] The legal status and implications of this obligation parallel those of other financial obligations.[54]

---

49 See, e.g., Chapter 14 in this Volume (citing Sol Roth, *Halakha and Politics: The Jewish Idea of the State* 97 (1988); Robert M. Cover, *Obligation: A Jewish Jurisprudence of the Social Order*, 5 J.L. & Religion 65, 65 (1987); Steven F. Friedell, *Aaron Kirschenbaum on Equity in Jewish Law*, 1993 BYU L. Rev. 909, 913 (book review); Shahar Lifshitz, *Distress Exploitation Contracts in the Shadow of No Duty to Rescue*, 86 N.C. L. Rev. 315, 337-61 (2008); Moshe Silberg, *Law and Morals in Jewish Jurisprudence*, 75 Harv. L. Rev. 306, 313-14 (1961)). See generally Amihai Radzyner, *Between Scholar and Jurist: The Controversy Over the Research of Jewish Law Using Comparative Methods at the Early Time of the Field*, 23 J.L. & Religion 189 (2007-8).

50 See, e.g., 1 Aryeh Kaplan, *The Handbook of Jewish Thought* 59-82, 231-60 (1979).

51 See Meir Tamari, *"With All Your Possessions": Jewish Ethics and Economic Life* 248-61 (1987) (discussing charitable obligations).

52 Id. at 248.

53 See Chapter 25 in Volume 2.

54 See Joseph B. Soloveitchik, *Yemei Zicharon* 43-45 (1996) (citing Talmud Bavli, Bava Bathra 8b; Maimonides, *Guide for the Perplexed* 3:53).

In further contrast to the American legal system, the substance of Jewish law comprises a comprehensive set of obligations, in principle addressing every area of human endeavor. Thus, the Jewish legal system regulates activities both public and private, both interpersonal and ritual, both individual and communal, thereby extending the notion of religious observance and ethical obligation to all realms of life.[55] As Rabbi Joseph Soloveitchik has put it, "[t]he marketplace, the street, the factory, the house, the meeting place, the banquet hall, all constitute the backdrop for the religious life."[56] In this perspective, "[t]he true sanctuary is the sphere of our daily, mundane activities, for it is there that the realization of [religious and ethical obligation] takes place."[57] Applied to commercial activities, the corpus of Jewish law, from the biblical text to modern commentaries, contains a pervasive emphasis on scrupulous adherence to honest and ethical business dealings, and includes detailed prohibitions against taking unfair advantage of those who are vulnerable.[58]

Notwithstanding the inherent authority of Jewish law to prescribe specific obligations in all realms of human activity, in practice, determining the

55 See, e.g., Kaplan, supra note 50, at 78 (stating that the commandments "penetrate every nook and cranny of a person's existence, hallowing even the lowliest acts and elevating them to a service to God. . . . [,] sanctify every facet of life, and constantly remind one of [one's] responsibilities toward God" (footnote omitted)); see also Chapter 12 in this Volume ("[T]he range of *halacha*, Jewish legal and ethical thought, encompasses all facets of the human experience, emphasizing the importance of an ethically unified life and demonstrating that every area of life has moral significance."); Samuel J. Levine, *The Broad Life of the Jewish Lawyer: Integrating Spirituality, Scholarship and Profession*, 27 Tex. Tech L. Rev. 1199, 1204 (1996) [hereinafter Levine, *Broad Life*] (observing that "an individual who views religion as the center of life can incorporate other aspects of life, such as a secular career, to broaden that life," and concomitantly unify all areas of life).

56 Joseph B. Soloveitchik, *Halakhic Man* 94 (Lawrence Kaplan trans., 1983) (originally published in Hebrew as *Ish ha-halakhah*, in 1 *Talpiot* 3-4 (1944)).

57 Id. at 94-95; see also Levine, *Broad Life*, supra note 55, at 1205 ("[A]ccording to Maimonides, through my professional career I could actually serve [God], while Ramchal taught that I could utilize my career as a means towards piety"); id. at 1205 nn.21-22 (citing Moses C. Luzzato, *Mesillat Yesharim* 336-39 (Shraga Silverstein trans., 1966); Maimonides, *Mishne Torah*, Laws of De'oth 3:2-3).

58 See Tamari, supra note 52, at 47 (citing legal interpretations of the biblical prohibition against placing "'a stumbling block in the path of the blind'" as extending to "the giving of unwise business advice to someone, or the provision, through perfectly legal transactions, of goods that are to the buyer's physical or moral detriment" (quoting Leviticus 19:14)). Indeed, Jewish law requires particular protection of those unable to navigate the legal system, see id. at 48; Chapter 13 in this Volume, in apparent contrast to the treatment of the client who fails to obtain a written fee agreement from a lawyer and thereby remains at a disadvantage in an ensuing fee dispute. See discussion supra part one, section B.

appropriate conduct mandated in a particular situation may involve a complex analytical process, which at times depends on balancing various conceptual and practical interests.[59] Nevertheless, once a decision has been reached, the terms of the decision stand not merely as a suggested resolution, but as defining the contours of obligation, thereby requiring strict adherence. For example, in the Jewish legal system, with very limited exceptions, the value of preserving life overrides other legal and ethical obligations.[60] As a result, Jewish law does not merely permit, but requires, violation of virtually any commandment to the extent necessary to respond to a life-threatening situation.[61] In fact, it follows that "it is forbidden to delay such violation of [a commandment] for the sake of a person who is dangerously ill."[62]

The mandatory obligations in Jewish law to assist those in need, to engage in fair business practices, and to act to save a life, stand in stark contrast to discretionary provisions in the Model Rules that, at most, recommend—but do not require—that a lawyer perform pro bono services, place fee agreements in writing, and disclose confidences when reasonably necessary to prevent a death.[63] Arguably, though, the differences between obligations in Jewish law and in American ethics codes merely reflect broader differences in the two legal systems. The notion of mandating a particular mode of action obtains from the basic premises underlying Jewish law, as a religious system grounded in divine wisdom and command. Because American law instead emphasizes rights and personal autonomy, the American legal system is far less likely to impose additional duties.[64] Indeed, American law does not mandate charitable contributions; prohibits fraud but does not prevent shrewd—if seemingly unfair—business dealings; and does not generally require action to save the

---

59 See Chapter 15 in this Volume ("[E]ach conflict poses its own unique challenges, thereby necessitating a correspondingly particularized method of resolution.").

60 See id. at 1359 & n.67 (citing Talmud Bavli, Yoma 85a-85b; Maimonides, *Mishne Torah, Laws of Sabbath*, ch. 2; 2 Aryeh Kaplan, supra note 50, at 38-49; Hershel Schachter, *B'Ikvei Hatzoan* 14-18 (1997); Soloveitchik, supra note 56, at 34-35); see also Levine, *Taking Ethical Discretion Seriously*, supra note 4, at 57 n.151 ("[N]early every obligation in Jewish law is suspended to save a life."); Russell G. Pearce, *To Save a Jewish Life: Why a Rabbi and a Jewish Lawyer Must Disclose a Client Confidence*, 29 Loy. L.A. L. Rev. 1771, 1776 (1996) ("To save a life, one may violate all of Jewish law, except idolatry, incest and adultery, and murder.").

61 See Maimonides, supra note 60, 2:2-3; Soloveitchik, supra note 56, at 34.

62 Soloveitchik, supra note 56, at 34.

63 See discussion supra part one, sections A-C.

64 See supra note 49 and accompanying text.

life of a person in mortal peril. Likewise, it may not seem appropriate for the American legal system to place such obligations on lawyers.[65]

Despite the appeal—and, to some degree, the descriptive accuracy—of such an argument, it may fail in the context of the role and responsibilities of American lawyers. The existence of codes of ethics for lawyers, adopted by courts to have binding legal authority, grows out of an expression of the special role of the lawyer in American society and, in particular, within the American legal system.[66] Even among those who have questioned, at times convincingly, both the value and the validity of referring to lawyers as professionals, there remains an abiding insistence that lawyers maintain high ethical standards.[67] Therefore, the general absence of a given obligation in American law need not preclude the possibility that such an obligation should nevertheless be imposed on lawyers.[68] At the same time, of course, the mere presence of a particular

---

65 See, e.g., David Luban, *Calming the Hearse Horse: A Philosophical Research Program for Legal Ethics*, 40 Md. L. Rev. 451, 472-73 (1991) (citing the argument that "a *pro bono* duty in effect selectively taxes lawyers to provide a public service" and that "if it is in the public interest to make legal services available to all, the expense should fall on the entire public, not just on the lawyers"); Nancy J. Moore, *"In the Interests of Justice": Balancing Client Loyalty and the Public Good in the Twenty-First Century*, 70 Fordham L. Rev. 1775, 1786 (2002) (arguing that lawyers "should not be obligated to perform as agents of the state in situations where private citizens have no similar obligation"); id. at 1786 n.51 (noting that under American criminal law and tort law, "[p]rivate citizens do not have a legal duty to prevent death or substantial bodily harm, even when it is the result of an intended criminal act"); see also David A. Hyman, *Rescue Without Law: An Empirical Perspective on the Duty to Rescue*, 84 Tex. L. Rev. 653, 655 (2006) ("The common law approach to rescue is straightforward. Absent a limited number of specific exceptions, there is no duty to rescue, regardless of the ease of rescue and the consequences of nonrescue."); Saul Levmore, *Waiting for Rescue: An Essay on the Evolution and Incentive Structure of the Law of Affirmative Obligations*, 72 Va. L. Rev. 879, 880 (1986) (noting that "[the American] legal system is seen as one that . . . rarely deters antisocial omissions, and virtually never rewards rescuers"); Ernest J. Weinrib, *The Case for a Duty to Rescue*, 90 Yale L.J. 247, 247 (1980) (observing that "the courts have uniformly refused to enunciate a general duty to rescue, even in the face of repeated criticisms that the absence of such a duty is callous"). See generally Simon, supra note 7 (critiquing a libertarian/formalist vision of legal ethics); William H. Simon, *The Belated Decline of Literalism in Professional Responsibility Doctrine: Soft Deception and the Rule of Law*, 70 Fordham L. Rev. 1881 (2002) (critiquing literalism in legal ethics).

66 See Rhode, supra note 45, at 1545-46.

67 See sources cited supra note 3 (listing works criticizing the use of the word "professional").

68 See, e.g., Rhode, supra note 1, at 50-57 (arguing that "lawyers need to accept moral responsibility for the consequences of their professional actions" by adhering to "more ethically demanding professional codes and institutionalized practices"); Simon, supra note 1, at 138-39 (discussing a lawyer's responsibility to take actions that "seem likely to promote justice"); Rhode, supra note 45, at 1546 (arguing that, unlike other private citizens, "lawyers, as officers of the justice system,

obligation in Jewish law need not suggest that such an obligation would likewise prove appropriate in the context of the work of American lawyers. However, to the extent that the organized bar claims to uphold, as a matter of its professional responsibility, the ethical values of serving those in need, protecting clients in potential litigation against their lawyers, and recognizing the value of human life,[69] changes in the formulation of the Model Rules, to incorporate mandatory forms of ethical obligation, would demonstrate a more fully realized commitment to these underlying ethical principles.

B. Beyond the Mandatory/Optional Dichotomy

The possibility of improving the ethical conduct and reputation of American lawyers through increased mandatory ethics rules may represent the most direct method of enhancing the sense of ethical obligation among the organized bar. However, as demonstrated in the legislative history of various provisions in the Model Rules, the ABA has often remained resistant to articulating ethics rules in expressly mandatory terms.[70] Consequently, to the extent that such resistance is likely to continue, it may prove necessary to instead suggest interpretive methodologies to be applied to the Model Rules—as currently formulated—in a manner that aims to promote closer adherence to ethical principles. Toward that end, approaches to legal and ethical obligations in Jewish law may again provide a helpful model.

1. Unenumerated Ethical Obligations

Although the Jewish legal system applies to all areas of human behavior, as any set of rules intended to regulate a broad range of activities, the scope of specific obligations enumerated in the Torah remains, inevitably, somewhat limited. Indeed, in the words of the medieval scholar Nachmanides, "it [would

---

have a special obligation to pursue justice"). Cf. James E. Fleming, *The Lawyer as Citizen*, 70 Fordham L. Rev. 1699, 1715 (2002) ("Lawyers . . . may attribute only partial authorship of their acts to the law themselves. . . ."); Koniak, supra note 34, at 1438 (noting "the potential for ethics rules to compete and conflict with other law"); Luban, supra note 65, at 473 ("The *pro bono* duty, rather than constituting a tax on lawyers, can be viewed as a fee which they pay the public in return for special privileges granted to the legal profession."); Simon, supra note 7, at 1456-57 ("All lawyers are formalists some of the time . . . . Some lawyers, however, are formalists all the time. . . . [T]hey do not feel constrained by any public interest that is not fully articulated in positive rules. They thus stand ready to exploit 'loopholes' and 'technicalities'. . . .").

69 See discussion supra part one, sections A-C.

70 Id.

be] impossible to mention in the Torah all aspects of [a person's] conduct with . . . neighbors and friends, and all [of a person's] various transactions, and the ordinances of all societies and countries."[71] Therefore, in addition to the commandments addressing particular responsibilities and prohibitions, the Bible prescribes a number of more general principles, to be applied to govern situations not delineated in the Torah.[72]

Scholars of Jewish law have identified several biblical verses that provide a basis for obligations that, although not expressly enumerated, are no less mandatory than enumerated commands. The verse "you shall be holy" has been understood to prohibit various forms of improper behavior that are not otherwise enumerated.[73] Similarly, the command to "do the just and the good" extends the range of interpersonal obligation beyond those actions enumerated as commandments.[74] The general rule to "love your neighbor as yourself" prescribes wide-ranging care for the needs and well-being of others.[75] Perhaps the broadest of biblical admonitions, "in all of your ways acknowledge [God],"[76] captures the centrality of mandatory obligations in Jewish thought, expressly applying the ethical imperative to all of life's endeavors.[77]

Of particular relevance to a consideration of the interpretation of American ethics codes, in addition to identifying biblical sources articulating broad legal and ethical obligations, scholars of Jewish law have formulated interpretive methodologies for the derivation and application of specific unenumerated biblical obligations.[78] Nachmanides relies upon biblical narrative to delineate the substance of the instruction "you shall be holy."[79] For example, through an analysis of the stories of Noah and Lot, Nachmanides concludes that drunkenness, though not otherwise the subject of an express command, is prohibited as a violation of the notion of holiness.[80] Likewise, employing a methodology that explores the nature of biblical obligations, Nachmanides interprets the command to "do the just and the good" as

---

71 See 5 Ramban (Nachmanides), *Commentary on the Torah* 87-88 (Charles B. Chavel trans., 1976) (explicating Deuteronomy 6:18); see also Chapters 9 and 14 in this Volume.

72 See Ramban, supra note 71, at 88; see also Chapters 9 and 14 in this Volume.

73 Leviticus 19:2; see also Chapters 9 and 14 in this Volume.

74 Deuteronomy 6:18; see also Chapters 9 and 14 in this Volume.

75 Leviticus 19:18; see also Chapters 9 and 14 in this Volume.

76 Proverbs 3:6; see also Chapters 12 and 15 in this Volume.

77 See Chapter 15 in this Volume; Levine, *Taking Ethical Discretion Seriously*, supra note 4, at 46 n.137.

78 See Chapters 9 and 14 in this Volume.

79 See Leviticus 19:2.

80 See Chapter 14 in this Volume (citing 3 Ramban (Nachmanides), *Commentary on the Torah* 282 (Charles B. Chavel trans., 1971)); Chapter 9 in this Volume.

mandating interpersonal obligations beyond the scope of those enumerated.[81] Thus, he derives such unenumerated obligations as adopting a respectful and appropriate attitude and manner toward others, even in the context of adversarial situations such as litigation proceedings.[82] On a broader level, both Nachmanides and his illustrious medieval predecessor, Maimonides, understand the imperative to "love your neighbor as yourself"[83] as a basis for requiring an expansive degree of care and consideration for the interests of others,[84] including, for example, visiting the sick and comforting mourners.

Notably, in the context of American codes of legal ethics, both courts and the ABA have similarly acknowledged practical limitations on the range of conduct delineated in enumerated ethics provisions.[85] As the Unites States Supreme Court observed in 1856, "it is difficult, if not impossible, to enumerate and define, with legal precision, every offence [sic] for which an attorney or counsellor [sic] ought to be removed."[86] Likewise, in the Preamble to the 1908 Canons of Professional Ethics, the ABA emphasized that "[n]o code or set of rules can be framed, which will particularize all the duties of the lawyer in the varying phases of litigation or in all the relations of professional life."[87] Moreover, in an explicit endorsement of unenumerated ethical obligations, the Preamble declared that "[t]he following canons of ethics are adopted by the American Bar Association as a general guide, yet the enumeration of particular duties should not be construed as a denial of the existence of others equally imperative, though not specifically mentioned."[88] In addition, a number of courts, including the New York Court of Appeals, have endorsed the enactment of broad ethics provisions as a means of regulating those activities otherwise unaddressed in enumerated rules.[89]

---

81 See Deuteronomy 6:18; Chapter 14 in this Volume (citing 5 Ramban, supra note 80, at 87-88); Chapter 9 in this Volume.

82 See Chapter 14 in this Volume (citing 5 Ramban, supra note 80, at 87-88); Chapter 9 in this Volume.

83 Leviticus 19:18.

84 See Chapter 14 in this Volume (citing sources); Chapter 9 in this Volume.

85 See Chapter 14 in this Volume.

86 *Ex parte* Secombe, 60 U.S. (19 How.) 9, 14 (1856); see also Chapter 14 in this Volume.

87 Canons of Prof'l Ethics Preamble (1908).

88 Id.

89 See *In re Holtzman*, 577 N.E.2d 30, 33 (N.Y. 1991) (per curiam) ("Broad standards governing professional conduct are permissible and indeed often necessary." (citation omitted)); see Chapter 14 in this Volume.

In practice, the presence of broad rules in ethics codes has attracted considerable criticism from courts and scholars, who have found such rules unworkably vague and, thus, too difficult to interpret and apply precisely and consistently.[90] Responding, in part, to these arguments, the ABA omitted from the first version of the Model Rules some of the broad ethics provisions that had been included, fewer than fifteen years earlier, in the Model Code of Professional Responsibility.[91] Nevertheless, a number of broad rules remain, and, perhaps more significantly, broad ethics provisions continue to be enforced by courts as a basis for lawyer discipline and/or disqualification in instances of violations of unenumerated ethical obligations.[92] The interpretive methodologies employed by these courts echo, to some degree, those formulated by scholars of Jewish law for deriving unenumerated biblical obligations. This dynamic suggests the potential for looking more closely at the Jewish legal system as a model for enhancing the degree of obligation in American legal ethics.

For example, both the Model Code and the Model Rules prohibit "conduct that is prejudicial to the administration of justice."[93] In a manner somewhat parallel to the methodology applied to interpret the command to "do the just and the good," courts have expansively analyzed principles underlying these enumerated ethics rules, thereby identifying unenumerated conduct likewise prohibited as prejudicial to the administration of justice.[94] Another broad Model Code provision, omitted from the Model Rules but still retained in a number of jurisdictions, prohibits "conduct that adversely reflects on [the lawyer's] fitness to practice law."[95] In a manner that evokes the reliance on biblical narrative to delineate unenumerated obligations mandated in the imperative "you shall be holy," courts have looked to the nature and narratives of the practice of law, through an examination of "'the everyday realities of the profession and its overall code of conduct,'"[96] to derive unenumerated violations of fitness to practice

---

90   See Chapter 14 in this Volume.
91   Compare Model Rules of Prof'l Conduct (1983), with Model Code of Prof'l Responsibility (1969); see also Chapter 14 in this Volume. .
92   See Chapter 14 in this Volume; see also Model Rules of Prof'l Conduct (2006).
93   Model Rules of Prof'l Conduct R. 8.4(d) (2006); Model Code of Prof'l Responsibility DR 1-102(A)(5) (1983).
94   See Chapter 14 in this Volume. .
95   Model Code of Prof'l Responsibility DR 1-102(A)(6) (1983).
96   *In re Illuzzi*, 632 A.2d 346, 350 (Vt. 1993) (quoting *ABA/BNA Lawyer's Manual on Professional Conduct* 101:1001 (1987)).

provisions.[97] Finally, Canon 9 of the Model Code instructs lawyers to "[a]void [e]ven the [a]ppearance of [p]rofessional [i]mpropriety."[98] Despite its omission from the Model Rules, a number of courts continue to apply the appearance of impropriety standard as a basis for prohibiting a wide range of unethical— yet unenumerated—activities, echoing the broad scope of unenumerated obligations mandated by the command to "love your neighbor as yourself."[99]

To the extent that courts, scholars, and the organized bar take these methods seriously, perhaps they may likewise impact the interpretation and application of ethics rules that facially do not impose mandatory imperatives. To be sure, it would be implausible to interpret existing Model Rules provisions to require universal pro bono service, written fee agreements, or disclosure of confidences to save a life. Indeed, the final version of the Model Rules presumably expresses the ABA's collective view that, on balance, such conduct generally should not be obligatory.[100] Nevertheless, the implementation of broad ethics provisions as a means for the interpretation of these rules might suggest that, at least at times, such conduct should, indeed, be considered mandatory.

For example, although circumstances may often support, as reasonable, a lawyer's decision not to place a fee agreement in writing, in other cases, the failure to provide a written fee agreement may appear to have been designed by the lawyer to gain an unfair advantage over the client.[101] In such a scenario, the lawyer's behavior, though technically consistent with the letter of Model Rule 1.5, may concurrently prove prejudicial to the administration of justice, may reflect poorly on the lawyer's fitness to practice law, and/or may carry the appearance of impropriety.

Similarly, against the backdrop of an ongoing debate about appropriate limitations on the duty of confidentiality, the ABA, through its promulgation of the current form of Model Rule 1.6, adopted an approach that places the importance of confidentiality as paramount, permitting a lawyer to remain silent in the face of resulting danger to others.[102] However, even among scholars who support expansive approaches to the duty of confidentiality, many find

---

97 See Chapter 14 in this Volume.

98 Model Code of Prof'l Responsibility Canon 9 (1983).

99 See Chapter 14 in this Volume.

100 See discussion supra part one. For a thoughtful analysis of possible motivations for and implications of the formulation of ethics rules in a discretionary or permissive manner, see Green & Zacharias, supra note 5, passim.

101 See discussion supra part one, section B.

102 See discussion supra part one, section C.

it unseemly—if not downright immoral—for a lawyer to maintain a confidence in a case such as the "Innocent Convict," in which a client confesses to the crime for which an innocent person is going to be executed.[103] Although Model Rule 1.6 does not require disclosure in such a case, the failure to reveal confidences to save the life of a wrongly convicted individual might arguably be understood to contradict ethical notions of fitness to practice, proper administration of justice, and/or the appearance of appropriate attorney conduct.

Finally, scholars have proposed a variety of arguments to support the proposition that pro bono service should be mandatory.[104] Although virtually all jurisdictions seem to concur with the ABA's general determination, codified in Model Rule 6.1, that pro bono representation should retain aspirational status,[105] a more nuanced approach might take into account the resources and abilities of a particular lawyer. In this context, looking beyond the contours of Model Rule 6.1, a lawyer who is personally and professionally capable of providing pro bono services, but fails to do so, might be held to have acted in a way that is inconsistent with fitness to practice law, promoting the administration of justice, and/or maintaining the appearance of propriety.

2. Obligatory Ethical Deliberation

As noted above, the ABA has often demonstrated a resistance to articulating ethics rules in the form of mandatory obligations, resorting instead to promulgating discretionary—or permissive—rules.[106] Moreover, notwithstanding the conceptual validity, and practical utility, of employing interpretive methods for deriving unenumerated ethical obligations through the application of broad ethics provisions, the dominant attitude among courts, scholars, and the organized bar remains opposed to such efforts.[107] As a result, lawyers are ultimately often presented with discretionary ethical directives that, ostensibly, may be either followed or disregarded, at the will of the lawyer.[108] Therefore, perhaps a more effective alternative for promoting a greater degree of ethical obligation should

---

103 See discussion supra note 44.
104 See sources cited supra note 8.
105 See Gillers & Simon, supra note 7, at 392 ("No state yet requires lawyers to perform pro bono work, and no state is actively considering such a requirement, but a number of states require lawyers to report their pro bono hours, and other states encourage lawyers to do so."); see also Gillers, supra note 2, at 169-70.
106 See discussion supra part one. See generally Green & Zacharias, supra note 5.
107 See Chapter 14 in this Volume.
108 See Green & Zacharias, supra note 5, at 270 & nn.16-22, 276-78 & nn.41-55; Levine, *Taking Ethical Discretion Seriously*, supra note 4, at 24.

address underlying assumptions regarding the nature—and, consequently, the interpretation—of discretionary ethics rules. Once again, sources in Jewish law and ethics may prove valuable in the consideration of such an approach.

Despite the wide range of conduct regulated under Jewish law, through both enumerated biblical commands and extensive unenumerated obligations, many of life's activities appear to fall outside of the scope of these categories.[109] Nevertheless, as a number of scholars of Jewish law have explained, those areas of life do not comprise a category of "optional" activities, in which individuals may choose a particular mode of conduct without reflecting upon the ethical implications.[110] Rather, as instructed in perhaps the broadest of biblical imperatives, "in all your ways acknowledge [God],"[111] every human action is subject to ethical consideration and, therefore, requires careful ethical deliberation.[112] Indeed, in this framework, the extent to which a given activity initially seems beyond the bounds of ethical guidelines may, in fact, indicate the complexity of carrying out the activity in an ethically appropriate manner.[113] In short, as Rabbi Yitzchak Hutner observes, Jewish thought renders virtually nonexistent the category of conduct that would be deemed truly "optional," in the sense of activities that are outside the realm of ethical deliberation.[114]

At first glance, such an approach appears inconsistent with the stated attitude of the Model Rules toward discretionary ethics provisions.[115] The Scope

---

109 See Moshe Sokol, *Personal Autonomy and Religious Authority*, in *Rabbinic Authority and Personal Autonomy* 169, 207 (Moshe Sokol ed., 1992):

> The fact is that most of one's waking hours are spent at work, or with one's family. Certainly these situations call for obedience to appropriate standards of behavior: it is wrong to cheat at work, for example, or hurt a spouse's feelings. Nevertheless, for great stretches of the day each individual must decide for [one's self] how [one] will work, with what commitment, how warm [one] will be toward [one's] children, how much time [one] will spend working for good causes, and so on.

> See also Levine, *Taking Ethical Discretion Seriously*, supra note 4, at 46 n.137 (citing Yitzchak Hutner, *Pachad Yitzchak, Pesach* 123-26 (6th ed. 1999); Rabbenu Bachya Ibn Paquda, *Chovoth Ha Levavoth* (4:4); Aharon Lichtenstein, *Does Jewish Tradition Recognize an Ethic Independent of Halakha?*, in *Contemporary Jewish Ethics* 102, 102-23 (Menachem Marc Kellner ed., 1978); Sokol, supra, at 169-216).

110 See, e.g., sources cited supra note 109.
111 Proverbs 3:6.
112 See supra notes 56-57 and accompanying text.
113 See Chapter 15 in this Volume.
114 See Hutner, supra note 109, at 123-26; see also Yitzchak Hutner, *Pachad Yitzchak, Purim* 51-53 (6th ed. 1998).
115 See infra notes 116-18; see also Green & Zacharias, supra note 5, at 280-87; Levine, *Taking Ethical Discretion Seriously*, supra note 4, at 46; McGowan, supra note 38, at 1825 n.1; Fred

section introducing the Model Rules declares that, in contrast to rules that "are imperatives, cast in the terms 'shall' or 'shall not' . . . [o]thers, generally cast in the term 'may,' are permissive."[116] Because the latter category "define[s] areas under the Rules in which the lawyer has discretion to exercise professional judgment," the Scope section cautions that "[n]o disciplinary action should be taken when the lawyer chooses not to act or acts within the bounds of such discretion."[117] Therefore, it would seem to follow, when an ethics rule leaves a decision to the discretion of the lawyer, the permissive nature of the rule allows the lawyer to proceed without resort to ethical deliberation or justification.[118]

Alternatively, however, the Scope section's reference to the lawyer's "discretion to exercise professional judgment" may be understood to imply that, although a discretionary rule does not mandate a particular mode of action, the rule does instruct the lawyer to engage in a decision-making process that employs the lawyer's professional judgment.[119] Specifically, this process arguably may require ethical deliberation, including consideration of the ethical implications and consequences of the lawyer's choice of conduct.[120] Indeed, a number of ethics scholars have evaluated such a reconceptualization of discretionary ethics rules,[121] suggesting an approach that, in many ways, resembles the complex analysis often necessary in the interpretation and application of the command "in all your ways acknowledge [God]."[122] Imposing an obligation

C. Zacharias & Bruce A. Green, *Reconceptualizing Advocacy Ethics*, 74 Geo. Wash. L. Rev. 1, 46-47 (2005).

116 Model Rules of Prof'l Conduct Scope [14] (2006).

117 Id.

118 See supra note 6.

119 See Levine, *Taking Ethical Discretion Seriously*, supra note 4, at 49 n.140 (arguing that "with discretion comes the responsibility to exercise professional judgment"); see also Green & Zacharias, supra note 5, at 281-82.

120 See Levine, *Taking Ethical Discretion Seriously*, supra note 4, at 46-52.

121 See, e.g., Green & Zacharias, supra note 5, at 281-87; id. at 285 n.81 (citing Mario J. Madden, *The Indiscreet Role of Lawyer Discretion in Confidentiality Rules*, 14 Geo. J. Legal Ethics 603, 604-5 (2001); Limor Zer-Gutman, *Revising the Ethical Rules of Attorney Client Confidentiality: Towards a New Discretionary Rule*, 45 Loy. L. Rev. 669, 705-6 (1999)); Andrew M. Perlman, *Untangling Ethics Theory from Attorney Conduct Rules: The Case of Inadvertent Disclosures*, 13 Geo. Mason L. Rev. 767, 790-91 (2005); Zacharias & Green, supra note 115, at 52-55.

122 Proverbs 3:6; see also Geoffrey C. Hazard, Jr., *Law, Ethics and Mystery*, 82 U. Det. Mercy L. Rev. 509, 514-18 (2005). Such an approach may prove particularly relevant in the context of prosecutorial ethics, given the extent to which prosecutors exercise discretion in ethical decisionmaking. See Chapter 15 in this Volume; see also R. Michael Cassidy, *Character and Context: What Virtue Theory Can Teach Us About a Prosecutor's Ethical Duty to "Seek Justice,"* 82 Notre Dame L. Rev. 635, 653 (2006) (arguing that "a renewed focus on virtue . . . can provide meaningful guidance for conscientious prosecutors striving to do what is right"); Bruce A. Green, *Why Should Prosecutors "Seek Justice"?*, 26 Fordham Urb. L.J. 607, 616

of ethical deliberation may provide yet another method to improve the ethical posture of the Model Rules, in a manner that remains consistent with both the present form of the rules[123] and their ultimate deference to the lawyer's appropriate exercise of discretion.[124]

For example, such an approach may not always require that a lawyer disclose confidential information to protect the life of a third party, but it also would not permit the lawyer to blithely ignore the consequences of maintaining client confidences regardless of ethical implications.[125] Likewise, while acknowledging the value of pro bono representation and the potential importance of placing fee agreements in writing, this approach would nevertheless recognize that such conduct may not always represent the only appropriate course of action. Thus, lawyers would maintain the discretion to forego pro bono service or written fee agreements, subject to the obligation to engage in a careful ethical analysis supporting the reasoned conclusion that, under the circumstances, they found another course of action preferable. In short, a deliberative model of discretionary ethics rules contemplates a variety of acceptable responses to an ethical question, but at the same time, this approach takes ethical

---

(1999) (describing the disciplinary rules governing areas where prosecutors have discretion as "incomplete"); Bruce A. Green & Fred C. Zacharias, *Prosecutorial Neutrality*, 2004 Wis. L. Rev. 837, 842 ("The fact that prosecutorial decisions are discretionary does not imply that they are, or should be, standardless."); Leslie C. Griffin, *The Prudent Prosecutor*, 14 Geo. J. Legal Ethics 259, 262 (2001) (arguing that prosecutorial discretion relies on both substantive moral theory and public moral judgment); Ellen S. Podgor, *The Ethics and Professionalism of Prosecutors in Discretionary Decisions*, 68 Fordham L. Rev. 1511, 1513-14 (2000) (advocating increased education about the discretionary nature of prosecutors' decisionmaking process); Fred C. Zacharias, *Specificity in Professional Responsibility Codes: Theory, Practice, and the Paradigm of Prosecutorial Ethics*, 69 Notre Dame L. Rev. 223, 248 (1993) [hereinafter Zacharias, *Specificity in Professional Responsibility Codes*] ("[M]ost of the unique ethical dilemmas prosecutors face are governed *solely* by the ['justice'] requirement."); Fred C. Zacharias, *Structuring the Ethics of Prosecutorial Trial Practice: Can Prosecutors Do Justice?*, 44 Vand. L. Rev. 45, 104 (1991) (examining the shortcomings of a "well-interpreted, reinforced 'do justice' rule").

123 See Levine, *Taking Ethical Discretion Seriously, supra* note 4, at 59 n.154 (discussing the deliberative model of legal ethics and noting it can be applied to existing ethics rules).

124 Such a framework finds an analogue in the abuse of discretion standard of review applied to certain kinds of discretionary judicial rulings. See id. at 59-63; see also Green & Zacharias, supra note 5, at 282.

125 See Levine, *Taking Ethical Discretion Seriously*, supra note 4, at 51-55. Cf. Maura Strassberg, *Taking Ethics Seriously: Beyond Positivist Jurisprudence in Legal Ethics*, 80 Iowa L. Rev. 901, 949-50 (1995) (discussing the practical effects of viewing law as including something more than positive law).

obligations seriously by insisting that a response be justified on the basis of meaningful ethical deliberation.[126]

C. Enforcement

Finally, it might be instructive to analyze the possible impact an increased degree of ethical obligation could have on the enforcement of ethics rules, as well as other possible ramifications for lawyers' adherence to, and attitudes toward, ethics regulations. In theory, replacing discretionary rules with rules formulated as imperatives[127] sends a message to lawyers that, unlike rules that are inherently unenforceable, because mandatory rules are, indeed, obligatory, violations of these rules will be identifiable and, consequently, potentially subject to enforcement. Interpreting broad ethics provisions to impose unenumerated ethical obligations[128] and reconceptualizing discretionary rules so as to require ethical deliberation[129] may be expected to bring about similar results. These interpretive methods may promote adherence to ethical principles, premised in part on the proposition that ethical obligations extend beyond conduct expressly delineated in mandatory rules.

Perhaps more likely, however, models of increased ethical obligation may have a negative effect on efforts to promote enforcement of ethics rules and adherence to their underlying goals. On one level, notwithstanding the theoretical benefits of these models, they may prove inherently difficult to implement. For example, reliance upon broad ethics provisions to curtail unethical conduct has

---

126 See Levine, *Taking Ethical Discretion Seriously*, supra note 4, at 46-63; see also Feldman, supra note 6, at 887 ("If one believes that good lawyering practically always demands good ethical deliberation, then it follows that the honorable mode of legal analysis should practically always dominate the technocratic one."); Serena Stier, *Legal Ethics: The Integrity Thesis*, 52 Ohio St. L.J. 551, 554 (1991) (outlining the integrity thesis, which makes it possible to "integrat[e] one's cherished personal values with one's obligations as an attorney"); Wendel, supra note 5, at 6 (pointing to the logical necessity of uncovering "the moral principles that are implicated by the practice of lawyering"); W. Bradley Wendel, *Value Pluralism in Legal Ethics*, 78 Wash. U. L.Q. 113, 117 (2000) ("[T]he lawyer seeking to act ethically must take account of different value claims that may not be comparable with one another in an impersonally rational, mathematical, or algorithmic manner."); Zacharias, supra note 5, at 1359 (suggesting that lawyers should be required to discuss certain subjects with clients, so as to aid lawyers in distinguishing partisanship from objective, independent duties).

127 See supra part two, section A.

128 See supra part two, section B.1.

129 See supra part two, section B.2.

been criticized as imprecise and, therefore, unsuited for enforcement.[130] Likewise, evaluating compliance with a requirement of ethical deliberation to support discretionary decisions may prove highly challenging, if not ultimately elusive.[131] Although a variety of methods may be offered to overcome these objections,[132] practical obstacles to enforcement still remain.

More fundamentally, increasing the degree of ethical obligation may exacerbate problems presently associated with underenforcement. As currently adopted and interpreted, many ethics rules remain rarely—if ever—enforced.[133] Although a number of causes may contribute to underenforcement, including the unenforceability of discretionary rules,[134] failure to enforce mandatory rules may have serious consequences, potentially undermining the general credibility of ethics codes as a system of regulation.[135] To the extent that additional ethical

---

130 See Chapter 14 in this Volume (citing criticisms).

131 See Zacharias, supra note 5, at 1367 (observing that "[a] requirement of introspection, by definition, is difficult to enforce," because "[d]iscliplinary authorities cannot know what lawyers 'have thought,'" and that "[u]pon questioning, lawyers can rationalize most conduct after the fact"). Cf. Stephen Gillers, *More About Us: Another Take on the Abusive Use of Legal Ethics Rules*, 11 Geo. J. Legal Ethics 843, 846 (1998) (positing the "near-impossibility of proving the lawyer's 'true' motive").

132 See Levine, *Taking Ethical Discretion Seriously*, supra note 4, at 59-60 n.154. See generally Chapter 14 in this Volume (responding to various scholars' objections to broad ethics provisions).

133 See supra notes 46-48 and accompanying text.

134 See supra note 6.

135 See Loder, supra note 2, at 328 (summarizing David Luban's analysis that "even lawyers who believe in the ethical superiority of a certain course of conduct will engage in substandard behavior if they perceive other lawyers will so behave without sanction" and that "[s]ince lawyers suspect the unrealistically stringent rules will go unenforced, they will act not from a rational assessment of the most ethical behavior, but from fear of professional disadvantage" (citing Luban, supra note 65, at 460 n.24, 461)); Tanina Rostain, *Ethics Lost: Limitations of Current Approaches to Lawyer Regulation*, 71 S. Cal. L. Rev. 1273, 1307-8 (1998) ("In a rational-actor model of legal ethics, enforcement—the detection of wrongdoing, apprehension of the wrongdoer, and conviction—bears the full weight of ensuring compliance with rules. Even with well-drafted rules and appropriate sanctions, a regulatory regime will founder unless the rules are enforced at a sufficient level to deter wrongful conduct."); Zacharias, supra note 2, at 857 ("[U]nderlying most professional regulation is the faulty assumption that professional discipline works to deter lawyer misconduct. This premise is inherently questionable. Many aspects of the codes are not seriously enforced, nor can they be. Moreover, so long as the disciplinary process remains secret, lawyers are unlikely to be deterred. . . ."); Fred C. Zacharias, *The Professional Discipline of Prosecutors*, 79 N.C. L. Rev. 721, 772 (2001) ("[W]hen disciplinary agencies fail to enforce the codes altogether, or fail to enforce them against a segment of the bar, they encourage disrespect for the codes' letter and spirit. This disrespect can take numerous forms. At the simplest level, the affected segment of the bar . . . may simply have less inclination to follow the governing code's mandates.

obligations prove difficult to enforce, they accordingly may have the deleterious effect of reducing even further the perceived authority of ethics codes.

Indeed, Jewish exegetical tradition understands the biblical events of the Garden of Eden as an illustration of the negative consequences that may ensue from perceptions of unenforced mandatory rules.[136] As the Talmud notes, in relating, to the serpent, God's command not to eat from the tree of knowledge,[137] Eve states that God has also instructed not to touch the fruit of the tree.[138] Although the motivation for Eve's expansion of the prohibition remains open to interpretation,[139] in the Talmudic reading of the story, the serpent thereby found an opportunity to entice Eve to eat from the fruit of the tree. The serpent first caused Eve to touch the fruit, thus violating God's command, as she depicted it.[140] Subsequently, when Eve was not punished for her actions, it appeared to her that God was not enforcing the prohibition.[141] Of course, because her conduct did not, in fact, violate God's command, which was limited to not eating from the fruit, Eve was not subject to punishment. Nevertheless, the serpent argued that just as the supposed prohibition against touching the fruit had not been enforced, Eve would likewise not be punished for breaching the prohibition against eating the fruit.[142] The serpent's devious logic succeeded in convincing Eve and Adam to eat from the fruit of the tree, which violated God's command and resulted in punishments that included their banishment from Eden and their ultimate deaths.[143]

The Talmud thus concludes with the broader observation that, at times, the addition of mandatory obligations and prohibitions may prove to have

---

More subtly . . . [their] adversaries may feel a need to counteract the . . . misconduct by engaging in misconduct of their own . . . . [T]his in turn will reduce their own respect for the codes and for the disciplinary authorities in other areas."); Zacharias, supra note 46, at 1006 ("[S]ubstantial underenforcement of the advertising rules breeds disrespect for professional regulation. It seems to tell lawyers that the rules do not mean what they say. In the long run, this may encourage lawyers to violate or bend other professional rules.").

136 See Talmud Bavli, Sanhedrin 29a.

137 Genesis 2:17.

138 Id. at 3:3.

139 See 2 Eliyahu Dessler, *Michtav M'Elyahu* 142 (Aryeh Carmell & Chaim Friedlander eds., 1995); 1 Harav Boruch Haveli Epstein, *The Essential Torah Temimah* 21 (Shraga Silverstein trans., 1989) (explicating Genesis 3:3).

140 See Talmud Bavli, Sanhedrin 29a, Commentary of Rashi.

141 See id.

142 See id.; Rashi, *Commentary on the Torah* (explicating Genesis 3:4), reprinted in 1 *The Metsudah Chumash/Rashi* 31 (Avrohom Davis trans., 4th ed. 1996).

143 See Genesis 3:6-24; see also Samuel J. Levine, *The End of Innocence*, Hamevaser, Dec. 1989, at 8, 10 (exploring rabbinical insights into the nature of the Tree of Knowledge).

negative effects.[144] Specifically, the failure to enforce added obligations may send the message that wrongful conduct will not be subject to punishment, thus providing a license for more widespread violations.[145] Similarly, in the realm of American legal ethics, the addition of ethical obligations that seem difficult to enforce may serve to amplify a more general impression among self-interested lawyers that ethics rules are underenforced and, therefore, do not require adherence. Consequently, lawyers may increasingly fail to take ethics codes seriously as a source of ethical guidance and influence.[146]

Perhaps, though, problems resulting from underenforcement of ethics rules are but symptoms of a more fundamental defect in lawyers' attitudes toward the purpose and function of ethics codes.[147] To the extent that lawyers perceive ethics codes essentially as a disciplinary system regulating the practice of law, underenforcement of code provisions undermines the credibility and value of the rules.[148] Instead, however, lawyers may seek an alternative function for ethics codes, as reflecting ethical norms shared among the community of lawyers, and thereby inherently deserving of respect—independent of the possibility of enforced discipline.[149] Under such a framework, the primary

---

144 See Talmud Bavli, Sanhedrin 29a; see also Rashi, supra note 142, at 31 (explicating Genesis 3:3).

145 See Chaim Shmulevitz, *Sichoth Mussar* 126-28 (1980).

146 See supra note 135.

147 For discussions of various functions of ethics codes, see Gaetke, supra note 3, at 737-41; Rostain, supra note 135, at 1339 & n.282; Zacharias, supra note 135, at 771-72; Zacharias, *Specificity in Professional Responsibility Codes*, supra note 122, at 225-39; Zacharias, supra note 46, at 1003-4.

148 See supra note 135; see also Rostain, supra note 135, at 1303-19.

149 For example, as Professor Gaetke observed:

> An interesting study of why people obey the law . . . criticizes common instrumental views of compliance, which posit that peoples' behavior is "motivated by self-interest" and which lead to a preoccupation with "manipulation of behavior through the control of punishments and incentives." It sees such views as inadequate to explain what really determines citizens' desire to comply with the law. Instead, the study found that people focus on "normative issues," such as "the legitimacy of legal authorities and the morality of the law." The author of the study concludes that "[p]eople are more responsive to normative judgments and appeals than is typically recognized by legal authorities. Their responsiveness leads people to evaluate laws . . . in normative terms, obeying the law if it is legitimate and moral." If this is true for citizens in general, there is reason to believe or at least hope that the same conclusion could be reached about lawyers and the rules that govern them.
>
> What the . . . study suggests . . . is that lawyers will be more likely to obey new rules regarding professional behavior if the rules reflect values that are moral in their content and are legitimate in the sense that they are supported by a consensus within the bar.

motivation for adherence to ethics codes owes more to a common sense of values than to the threat of punishment.[150]

Gaetke, supra note 3, at 729-30 (quoting Tom R. Tyler, *Why People Obey the Law* 165-68, 178 (1990)) (second and third alterations in original). Furthermore, Professor Rostain argues that:

> While rules are undoubtedly important, the focus of legal ethics cannot be limited to debates about their content or the schemes through which they are enforced. For regulation to be effective, it needs to be undergirded by widespread commitments among lawyers to the values reflected in the regulatory enterprise. A central concern of legal ethics scholarship must be to investigate, articulate, and shore-up such collective commitments in the context of law practice.

Rostain, supra note 135, at 1340. Cf. Susan P. Koniak, *Through the Looking Glass of Ethics and the Wrongs with Rights We Find There*, 9 Geo. J. Legal Ethics 1, 28-29 (1995) ("Unlike tax law, tort law or other sources of legal obligation in our normative world, ethics is not merely a source of obligation but the place where obligation is understood as dignifying and ennobling. . . . In legal and judicial ethics we find the possibility of dignifying obligations that are enforceable as law."); Thomas D. Morgan & Robert W. Tuttle, *Legal Representation in a Pluralist Society*, 63 Geo. Wash. L. Rev. 984, 1004-5 (1995) ("The lawyer's moral duty to obey the law rests primarily on the concept of consent. . . . The obligation binds because it is self-imposed, self-chosen. . . . Lawyers *do* stand in a moral relationship with the legal system and *do* possess duties of fidelity to that system."); Simon, supra note 45, at 652-58 (proposing "competitive ethical regimes" to supplement the "low-commitment ethics of the ABA rules").

Building on Professor Robert Cover's work, Professor Koniak demonstrated that the bar's *nomos* includes a commitment to both legal precepts and narratives. See Koniak, supra note 34, at 90 n.1 (citing Robert M. Cover, *Bringing the Messiah Through Law: A Case Study*, in *NOMOS XXX: Religion, Morality and the Law*: 201 (J. Ronald Pennock & John W. Chapman eds., 1988); Robert M. Cover, "The Supreme Court, 1982 Term—Foreword: *Nomos* and Narrative," 97 Harv. L. Rev. 4 (1983); Robert M. Cover, *Violence and the Word*, 95 Yale L.J. 1601 (1986)); id. at 1391-92 (arguing that despite the legal profession's unique dependence on the state, the profession maintains its own normative world that may coexist or compete with the state's). For examples of scholarship exploring narrative traditions of lawyers, see Levine, *Taking Ethics Codes Seriously*, supra note 4, at 553 n.108; see also Chapter 17 in Volume 2.

150 See supra note 149; see also Cassidy, supra note 122, at 692-93 ("Professional norms are hollow without reference to the moral aspirations and sensitivities of individual actors working within their framework. . . . Virtue cannot be taught in law school. . . . It also cannot be commanded by rules. . . . The advantage of virtue theory is that it provides a noncynical response to this failure of codification."); id. at 693 (responding to criticism on the generality of virtue theory by suggesting that "a renewed focus on the virtues might promote a culture of thoughtful decisionmaking in the prosecutorial community, thus providing individual prosecutors with the intestinal fortitude necessary to resist both institutional pressures and the unscrupulous direction of other actors within the system"); Rostain, supra note 135, at 1338 (analyzing "the role of collective professional norms in forming individual commitments" in view of "the importance of participating in shared practices

To conclude this analysis, it may be appropriate to turn once again to the Jewish legal system to provide an analogue for an alternative vision of legal ethics. As Rabbi Soloveitchik has eloquently described, Jewish thought emphasizes fidelity to ethical and religious principles as an expression of a commitment to fulfilling personal and communal obligations, independent of any possibility of human enforcement of those principles.[151] Likewise, perhaps lawyers can begin to take ethical obligations more seriously, embracing—rather than resisting—heightened expectations of ethical behavior, thereby demonstrating a shared commitment to values and principles underlying the practice of law.

CONCLUSION

The following story is told of Rabbi Levi Yitzchak of Berditchev, one of the Chasidic masters around the turn of the nineteenth century:[152]

> Once the Czarist Russian government put a ban on the importation of all Turkish tobacco. Anyone found possessing this contraband would be severely punished. One day during Passover, Rabbi Levi Yitzchak asked his disciples for some Turkish tobacco for his pipe. They scattered through the ghetto and soon came back with several packets of tobacco, enough to fill a large can. Rabbi Levi Yitzchak then told his followers to bring him a piece of bread. They looked at him in astonishment and protested, "But Rabbi, it is Passover and we have no bread!"[153]
>
> The rabbi's face grew more stern. He repeated, "I command you as your Rabbi! Search the entire ghetto and bring me a piece of bread." His followers went all through the ghetto and ransacked every house in the ghetto. Several hours later they returned to Rabbi Levi Yitzchak and told him that they were sorry. They had fine-combed the entire ghetto, and they could not find a single crust of bread.

---

that foster normative commitments to collective values embodied in law and the legal framework," as opposed to undue focus on individual discretion).

151 See Soloveitchik, supra note 54, at 48-50. Indeed, Jewish history repeatedly offers moving testimony to the power of such commitment, even when religious adherence has carried its own risk of punishment and persecution. Cf. John Silber, *Obedience to the Unenforceable* (1995).

152 For descriptions of Rabbi Levi Yitzchak of Berditchev's life and teachings, see Aryeh Kaplan, *The Chasidic Masters and Their Teachings* 69-85 (rev. 2d ed. 1989); Aryeh Kaplan, *The Light Beyond* 16-18 (1981); Elie Wiesel, *Souls on Fire* 89-112 (Marion Wiesel trans., 1972).

153 See Exodus 12:19.

> Then Rabbi Levi Yitzchak raised his eyes and said, "Master of the Universe, see how faithful Your children are. The Czar has hundreds of soldiers, police and agents guarding his borders, watching that no Turkish tobacco enter his land, yet in a short while, I can have all I want. But You, O [God], have but once given Your children a commandment not to have bread in their houses on [Passover],[154] and to this very day, not a scrap is to be found."[155]

This story provides an insightful lesson about the power of commitment, and at the same time, offers a poignant illustration of both the effectiveness and limitations of legal rules. In the face of strict warnings of harsh punishment, the Czar's subjects openly defied the prohibition against importing Turkish tobacco. Their unwillingness to commit themselves to these rules rendered futile the Czar's extensive network of guards enlisted in an attempt to enforce the prohibition. In contrast, the community's commitment to God's command to rid all homes of bread on Passover resulted in careful adherence to religious principles, despite the absence of official human mechanisms of enforcement. In short, shared communal norms and values prevailed, while official legal pronouncements remained rejected and ignored.

For more than a century, American lawyers and scholars have explored various methods for improving the ethical conduct of lawyers and the reputation of the legal profession. Efforts have ranged from broad calls for increased professionalism to the enactment of ethics codes, consisting of rules designed to capture essential components of ethical legal practice. Though not entirely without success, these efforts seem repeatedly to fall short of producing, among lawyers, a genuine sense of dedication to ethical norms. In part, the current state of ethics codes, often leaving ethical decision-making to lawyers' unfettered discretion, contributes to the impression that the organized bar continues to place its own interests above those of both clients and the general public. Therefore, formulating and interpreting various ethics provisions to impose a greater degree of mandatory ethical conduct might demonstrate a resolve among lawyers to take more seriously their ethical obligations. Perhaps more importantly, however, in place of a reluctant adherence to ethics rules, out of a fear of possible enforcement, the community of lawyers must be willing to undertake a sincere commitment to ethical conduct, premised upon a shared sense of ethical values and principles.

---

154 See id.
155 Aryeh Kaplan, *Encounters* 100-101 (1990).

Index